Marriage AND THE Family

Gilbert D. Nass

University of Connecticut

Gerald W. McDonald

Florida State University

Marriage AND THE Family

SECOND EDITION

▲ ADDISON-WESLEY
PUBLISHING COMPANY
Reading, Massachusetts
Menlo Park, California
London · Amsterdam
Don Mills, Ontario · Sydney

Sponsoring Editor: Ronald R. Hill

Development Editor: Kathe G. Rhoades

Production Editor: Barbara H. Pendergast

Designer: Margaret Ong Tsao

Illustrator: William Taylor

Cover Design: Ann S. Rose

Cover Photograph: Bouveret Adagnan, *Wedding Company at a Photographer's Studio.* European Art Color Slides, copyright P. Adelberg, Inc. 120 W. 70th St. New York 10023

Library of Congress Cataloging in Publication Data

Nass, Gilbert D.
   Marriage and the family.

   Bibliography: p.
   Includes index.
   1. Family life education.   2. Family—United States.
I. McDonald, Gerald W.   II. Title.
HQ10.N37   1982   306.8   81-12696
ISBN 0-201-06240-2   AACR2

ISBN 0-201-06240-2
ABCDEFGHIJ-DO-898765432

# Preface

If there is one thing almost everyone would agree on, it is that American society is constantly changing. For many people, the rapidity of change is difficult to accept, and there is a tendency to regard change as synonymous with the erosion of long-standing values. Marriage and family life are particular targets for the pessimists. Many social problems are being blamed on the "decline of family values," and there is a longing in some quarters for a return to a past when, it is assumed, marriage and family life was stable and harmonious.

While there is no doubt that achieving satisfying intimate relationships presents a considerable challenge in our society, we believe that change has always been a part of human experience and that new systems and roles emerge in response to new conditions. Marriage and the family were not necessarily better in the past; indeed, people today have many more choices than previous generations. To a great degree, they can make of their relationships what they want them to be. This book is intended to help students recognize this and to foster a flexibility in their attitudes that will enable them to make the choices that will best suit their own needs.

A major theme of the text is that achieving satisfying interpersonal relationships requires work. During the process of building a relationship conflict is bound to arise. We have tried to convey to the student the realization that adjustment in interpersonal relationships is a continuing process throughout the life cycle. For this reason we make use of the research on marital adjustment in a number of

v

chapters. The need to develop positive, flexible systems of communication is another theme we emphasize. In addition to having a chapter on couple communication, we deal with communication in a variety of contexts; for example, as applied to sexual relationships. While communication is not the single key to happy marriages and families, it is important enough to merit significant coverage.

The book is written from the sociological perspective. However, research findings from other fields, such as social psychology, are incorporated as appropriate. Theoretical material is presented in a clear, straightforward manner. Different points of view are examined, and when issues have not been resolved, we do not hesitate to say so.

Changes in this Edition

This edition of the text has undergone major reorganization to make it a more useful and accessible tool for students. Unit I introduces the student to the concept of marriage and the family as institutions and outlines the major sociological frameworks that the student needs to be familiar with in order to understand fully the ideas and research contained in the rest of the text. The unit has been streamlined from four chapters to two, and a number of topics have been integrated into later chapters where they seemed more pertinent.

Unit II takes a broader focus than in the first edition. Four chapters deal with topics related to the formation of intimate relationships. Special emphasis is given to the changing roles of men and women, the development of couple relationships, physiological aspects of human sexuality, and communication in intimate relationships. These chapters may be regarded as preparatory for understanding the next unit.

Unit III, on marital and family relationships, contains five chapters on marriage and the family across the life cycle. The unit begins with chapters on marital and sexual adjustment and concludes with a chapter on marriage and the family in the middle and later years.

The final unit of three chapters takes up the issues of crisis and change confronting families today. A new chapter on Families in Crisis covers marital violence, child abuse, alcoholism in marriage, and problems facing adolescent family members. This unit also gives prominent attention to marital disso-lution and remarriage and alternatives to traditional marriage.

Since the publication of the first edition in 1978, much valuable new research has been done on marriage and family relationships in the United States. Therefore, we have revised and rewritten every chapter to bring it up to date with current thinking in the field. There is considerably more coverage of sex roles. Chapter 3 examines the biological and social influences on males and females that affect the roles they assume later in life. Chapter 7 contains a section on role behavior in marriage and the role adjustments facing couples in dual-worker marriages. More attention is given in this edition to the male role in family planning, pregnancy and childbirth, and parenting. Sexual jealousy, the personal experience of divorce, single parents, adjustment in remarriage and blended families, and retirement are other topics that receive emphasis.

Special Features

A special feature of the second edition is the inclusion of "Highlights," brief discussions or reprints set off from the text. The topics selected for highlighting are those we felt would be of particular interest to today's students. How do dual-worker couples deal with the problem of child care? What are marital and family therapy? How do children feel when their parents divorce? We think these and the other issues we've chosen will not only be interesting to read, but will stimulate thinking and discussion.

Beginning with Unit II, each chapter also contains a "Case Study" with discussion questions. The purpose of these true-to-life cases is to direct attention to the practical implications of the concepts covered in the chapters. For example, the case in Chapter 13 concerns a mother's decision to give up custody of her two children to her former husband, a phenomenon that is becoming increasingly common.

Study Aids

To increase the effectiveness of the text as a learning resource, we have included a number of study aids. Each chapter is preceded by a brief outline of major headings. New terminology is boldfaced in the text; the page number on which a term first appears is boldfaced in the index for easy reference. Concise summaries appear at the end of each chapter. Review and Discussion questions test knowledge of chapter content and require students to apply concepts to their own experience. A list of annotated suggested readings concludes each chapter. Finally, there are figures and tables within each chapter which illustrate or clarify points made in the text.

Supplements

Two supplements have been designed to accompany the second edition. The Study Guide is intended to help students understand and review the material in the text. Each chapter contains chapter objectives, an outline of major headings and subheadings, a variety of review questions, and brief reprinted excerpts which take up issues in the text. The excerpts are followed by questions that require students to apply what they have learned. The Instructor's Manual and Test Item File contains lecture outlines for the instructor, additional topics for discussion, information on films available for use with the text, and test items. The number of test items has been enlarged significantly over those available with the first edition.

Acknowledgments

I am grateful for the thoughtful criticisms and suggestions of the following reviewers:

Luella K. Alexander, University of South Florida

John B. Benson, Texarkana College

Kathleen M. Campbell, Bowling Green State University

Mary Beth Collins, Central Piedmont Community College

J. Kenneth Davidson, University of Wisconsin, Eau Claire

Verna Guatney, Central Washington University

Ronald E. Hughes, California State University, Fullerton

Marilyn Ihinger-Tallman, Washington State University

Patrick McKenry, Ohio State University

Laurel Richardson, Ohio State University

Rita P. Sakitt, Suffolk County Community College

Robert J. Stout, St. Petersburg Junior College

John C. Touhey, Florida Atlantic University

Nancy Voight Wedemeyer, University of Texas, Austin

Professor Patrick McKenry provided valuable consulting assistance on several chapters; his suggestions for the preparation of Chapter 12 were especially helpful. Professor Dwight Bolling of Tidewater Community College provided useful guidance on Chapters 3 and 4, and Professor Barbara Settles of the University of Delaware helped determine the focus of the financial appendix. Writers Peter Kinder and Libby Kaponen helped shape the text into direct, readable prose. Tom Corneille spent many hours tracking down current research.

The following people provided valuable input on content and substantive decisions:

Jeanette Ames McIntosh

Linda Harris

Sandi Schrader

Laurence H. Lang

Albert S. Dreyer

E. Duwayne Keller

Frederick Humphrey

Pamela Cooper

In addition, I would like to give credit to Jay Nass for his extensive library research work over the period of 1980.

I also want to acknowledge the sizable contribution of the editorial and production staff of Addison-Wesley. Their support was instrumental in seeing the second edition through to completion. Finally I wish to thank my coauthor, Gerry McDonald. His professionalism and grasp of the issues have contributed immeasurably to the quality of this book.

Storrs, Connecticut   G.D.N.
November 1981

Contents

unit I

Marriage and the Family in Perspective

The American Family: Yesterday and Today

a Family Tree by norman rockwell

1

"As far back as our knowledge takes us, human beings have lived in families. We know of no time when this was not so. We know of no people who have succeeded for long in dissolving the family or displacing it. Instead, men have exercised their imagination in the elaboration of different styles of family living and different ways of relating the family to the larger community."

MARGARET MEAD AND
KEN HEYMAN

When the earliest settlers from Europe arrived on the shores of the North American continent, they brought with them a family tradition rooted in antiquity. This tradition, extending back to the ancient Hebrews, Greeks, and Romans, supported the development of the United States as a nation, and for over two hundred years it has continued to influence the political, economic, and social history of the American people.

Throughout the nation's history the accelerating pace of social change has inevitably strained the institutions of marriage and the family. Never has this been more true than in our own time. The present generation has witnessed a soaring divorce rate; a jump in the number of one-parent families; an increasing number of illegitimate pregnancies, particularly among adolescent women; a growing number of unmarried couples cohabiting; a postponement of child-bearing by many women; and, most significantly, the participation of both spouses in the marketplace, with consequent changes in the child-care role.

Newspapers, television, and films reflect the tremendous interest and concern that people feel about these changes. A television news team in Oakland, California, broadcast a story on one of its members who arranged with his wife to trade jobs for a year—he is caring for the house and baby and she is covering the news. He finds the role of homemaker much more time-consuming than he expected, though he enjoys the freedom to schedule his own time. She is challenged and excited by her return to news reporting, yet has misgivings about missing too much of her child's

3

early development. Both husband and wife wonder about what it will be like when the year ends and they resume their original roles.

Another television program dealt with the struggle of one unmarried teenage father to gain custody of his child, a situation that apparently is becoming more common. The film *Kramer vs. Kramer* emphasized the personal growth of a father who learns what is involved in raising a child alone. In a lighter vein, the television series "One Day at a Time" portrays a divorced woman's experiences in establishing a career and a personal life for herself while coping with her teenage daughters' growing independence. Unmarried parents, single parents, step-parents—all are seeking ways to gain personal satisfaction and rear healthy children at the same time.

Does this mean that marriage and the family in America are in serious trouble, or are they merely changing in response to different demands? This question cannot be answered without a careful consideration of what we mean by family. The examples we have presented suggest that marriage and family are not static concepts. Rather, they seem to change with conditions, and they serve a number of major functions for both individuals and societies. The family has always existed in a variety of forms, yet it has remained fairly stable over time. Perhaps the ideas and expectations that Americans of today have regarding marital and family relationships bear little resemblance to the "ideal" family of childhood fantasy. Nevertheless, the present-day structure of marriage and the family may be a reasonably accurate reflection of contemporary ideas about the qualities that make life good and satisfying.

To get a balanced view of marriage and the family as dynamic social institutions, we will first consider their nature and the functions they serve. To gain perspective, we will also briefly trace the roots of the family in Western civilization and consider how the American family is changing.

THE NATURE OF MARRIAGE AND THE FAMILY

So far we have been talking about marriage and the family as if everyone knows what they are—and to some degree everyone does. Since most of us have grown up in families and all of us have observed families, we have picked up a substantial amount of information on the subject. In fact, many people would say that they not only know what a family is, they also know what it should be, who may be regarded as family and who may not, and how these people should behave toward one another.

This knowledge is undeniably useful, but the insight it provides is limited because marriage and family systems vary greatly around the world. In examining the family patterns of a large number of societies, we find that variation is the rule, and we see that each variation might be viewed as a different solution to the same problem—providing for human survival and growth.

Defining Marriage and the Family

Though marriage and the family are often spoken of together, it is important to note that strictly speaking, they are not the same. **Marriage** may be defined as an institutionalized mating arrangement between human males and females (Stephens, 1963). It usually involves a public ceremony of some kind to signal its recognition by society, and the relationship is characterized by economic cooperation and the expectation of permanence. The word **family** generally refers to a social group having specified roles and statuses (e.g., husband, wife, father, mother, son, daughter) with ties of blood, marriage, or adoption who usually share a common residence and cooperate economically. A family is usually based on the marriage of one or more couples living in a socially approved sexual relationship, and it is usually expected to include children for whom the adults accept responsibility. We might distinguish between marriage and the family by saying that marriage is the institutionalized means of legitimizing offspring—it gives children a place in society; whereas the family is the institutionalized means of rearing the children (Stephens, 1963).

While it is true that the traditional family structure in Western society has been a married couple (male and female) and their children, there have always been variations on this pattern. For example, a widowed female and her children have always been considered a family, though there is no longer a marriage involved. Recently variations have appeared in increasing numbers, such as the never-married adult with natural or adopted children and the homosexual couple (two males or two females) with children from previous heterosexual relationships. From these examples we can see that the words family and marriage are not interchangeable and, in fact, may be more appropriately termed "marriages" and "families."

Functions of the Family

As a basic social institution, the family has historically fulfilled certain vital functions in society. In addition, it has functioned to meet the needs of its individual members. We can group these societal and individual functions into seven categories.

REPRODUCTION   The family ensures that the population of a society will be maintained; in other words, it makes certain that a sufficient number of children will be born and properly cared for so that dying members will be replaced. Human young are helpless at birth and for years remain dependent upon adults for care and for instruction in the basic elements of survival. That the human race is not extinct we owe largely to the nurturing practices of human families. Individual family members, particularly females, are assured of help and some degree of protection in the rearing of the young. By institutionalizing the reproductive function, the family also provides its individual members with a sense of " 'immortality,' or . . . continuity, with ongoing society" (Winch, 1971).

SOCIALIZATION   Every child born into a society must be taught the norms and values by which the society maintains itself. Traditionally, the family has been responsible for educating its children to become participating members of their society. This transmittal of culture is called **socialization**; it is a process that becomes more demanding as society becomes more complex. It is largely because of the complexity of the modern world that the function of socialization is now shared with schools, churches, and other institutions outside the family.

ECONOMIC COOPERATION   Historically, the family has been central to the economic organization of most societies, acting both as a unit of production and as a unit of consumption. Prior to the Industrial Revolution, families tended to be self-sufficient economic units, with all members, including small children, contributing to the economic maintenance of the group. But as a consequence of industrialization and urbanization, the family has, for the most part, become a consuming unit, with the result that children are now regarded more as economic liabilities than as assets. It is still true that family members cooperate in meeting economic needs, but the burden now falls of necessity upon the adults. Even when older adolescents are willing and available to contribute to the family's support, the highly specialized nature of the American economy prevents their doing so in any significant way.

PROTECTION   The family protects society's interests by encouraging its members to maintain the **norms** (rules or expectations) upon which the society rests, and it is protected in return by state officials such as the police and the courts. Not only does the family provide a setting within which children may safely be reared, it also serves as a place of refuge for its adult members. When either physical or emotional assaults threaten a family member, there is a place to go and there are other people from whom to derive comfort and help.

ASSIGNMENTS OF SOCIAL ROLES AND STATUS   In any social organization, the members must know what is expected of them and what they can expect of the others. The family defines for people many of the primary roles they will play in their lives and, to some extent, the amount of prestige they will enjoy. Even in contemporary American society, where status is more often achieved than inherited, property, wealth, and power are often acquired through the family. It is through the family that children acquire their legal identity, their identification with racial, ethnic, and religious groups, and their social class.

AFFECTION AND EMOTIONAL SECURITY   Within the family each member may form intimate personal relationships and affectional ties that provide emotional security. The marital bond may provide companionship and moral support in addition to sexual gratification. Bonds between parents and children enable the young to try out various behaviors as they grow toward adulthood in an atmosphere of acceptance and freedom. The family is the arena for our earliest practice in interpersonal relationships.

SENSE OF PURPOSE AND MEANING   Human beings have always felt a need to understand their place within the scheme of things. Traditionally, the family has transmitted religious beliefs and otherwise supported its members in finding a sense of purpose and a satisfactory explanation of the nature of the world in which we live. The family has also served to clarify and maintain the relationships of its members to the rest of society.

Families of Orientation and of Procreation

Most people participate in two families during their lifetime. The family into which one is born is called the **family of orientation**. Orientation, the process of getting acquainted with the existing situation and environment, is part of the function of socialization discussed earlier. The family that is established when one marries and produces offspring is called the **family of procreation**. A dramatic change of roles takes place when one leaves the family of orientation and, through marriage, enters the family of procreation. In addition, the formation of a new unit by two people reared in different families of orientation may require each to assume new role obligations based on the expectations of the other. The success of the new unit depends, among other things, on the ability of the newly married couple to make these adjustments.

Kinship Systems

In all societies, each family is part of a **kinship system,** a set of relationships based on the birth cycle and regulated by social norms (Williams, 1970). The kinship system assigns to each individual a certain position that derives from the biological fact of birth, the sex of the individual, and the person's order of birth within the sibling group. In turn, this position within the kinship system confers certain rights and duties upon the individual. Of course, each person occupies more than one position in a kinship system. For example, a male who is a son may also be a brother, nephew, and cousin. Moreover, he is a son to both his mother and his father, and each of these relationships has its own set of rights and obligations. These rights and obligations may be further differentiated if the male is the eldest son, and they may be entirely different if the person is female.

Williams (1970) comments that

> Americans tend to regard the relatively isolated small conjugal unit of husband, wife, and children—characteristic of our society—as perfectly natural; but it is quite special. In many historical, as well as preliterate societies, the kinship unit has been a larger group, often including several generations and various collateral branches and having much greater family continuity than in our society.

In the past, these kinship units tended to control almost everything about a person's life. Who his or her parents were determined an individual's residence, social position, and occupation. The kinship system controlled mate selection as well as leadership positions, determining who would succeed to specific ranks or offices. In exchange for the control surrendered to the kinship group the individual received certain benefits. The kinship group would provide automatic support in disputes; in health care, security, and sharing of resources; and in the determination of social status.

 FAMILY FORMS

The Nuclear Family

The idealized American family is a self-sufficient social group consisting of a mother, father, and children who reside together. This smallest family unit is called the **nuclear family.** Nuclear families may also consist of any two or more individuals related by blood, adoption, or marriage who share a residence and function as an economic unit. The nuclear family in the United States usually consists of two generations. When the children grow up, they move away to establish their own nuclear families, and with the death of the parents the original unit is dissolved.

The nuclear family is not the most common family form throughout the world, and it never has been. Nuclear units are combined in various ways to form larger familial groups; we will use the term **extended family** to refer to all family groupings more complex than the nuclear family.

Extended Families

In sociological terms, the ties among members of extended families may be formed along marital lines (based on **conjugal** relationships), or they may be formed along blood lines (based on **consanguinal** relationships). The most familiar form of the extended family in our culture is one in which the nuclear family is joined by grandparents or related adults or children, such as aunts, uncles, or cousins. In recent years, however, a variation on the extended family has become increasingly common. This is the blended family, in which one or both spouses has a child or children from a previous marriage. The blended family thus consists of the interweaving of several families through the remarriage of the original spouses. Blended families will be discussed in Chapter 13.

Members of a true extended family are completely interdependent economically; they own economic resources in common and share income as well as goods and services. They are in daily contact though they may not always live together, and thus they are also psychologically interdependent, finding emotional support, protection, and socialization almost completely within the kinship group (Yorburg, 1975). The additional adult members provide other role models for the children and a sense of historical continuity and perspective (Kempler, 1976). Grandparents, aunts, and uncles can be welcome buffers when parent-child conflicts arise, and they also help to relieve the burden of round-the-clock responsibility when parents need time for themselves. The extended family offers a greater range of human resources to contribute to the health and welfare of the family as a whole.

The Ewing family of the popular television series "Dallas" fits the definition of an extended family very well. Every member of the family is supported by the Ewing Oil empire. Although one or another of the family members may leave from time to time, it is expected that they will all live together in the family mansion. Jock and Miss Ellie Ewing, the parents, exert nominal control over their sons, J. R. and Bobby (each of whom has brought a wife into the family home), and over their granddaughter, Lucy. Another son, Gary, has left home but is still bound to the family by an extraordinarily strong feeling of obligation.

The Ewings represent one type of extended family. But there are other varieties as well. In some societies, three or more generations of males may be living with all their wives and children as an extended family. As the sons marry, their wives become new members of the household, and as the daughters marry, they go off to become members of the households of their husbands. The same structure may exist in reverse, with all females of the family remaining in the family home and bringing in their husbands, while all males leave the family upon marriage and move to their new wife's home. However, this arrangement does not occur as frequently.

THE JOINT FAMILY Another type of extended family formed along blood lines is the **joint family.** This family unit consists of a number of married couples, usually brothers and their respective wives and children, living in the same household. The family is joint in the sense that resources are pooled, rooms are shared, and mutual obligations exist between the different nuclear units of the family.

THE STEM FAMILY   The **stem family,** also formed along blood lines, is sometimes called the minimal form of the extended family. In this family system, only one child, usually the eldest son, inherits the family property. His sisters and brothers must find other homes and means of livelihood once they become adults.

The stem family, which is common in rural Ireland, ordinarily passes through several developmental stages over time. If the heir marries and has children before his parents' death, the household is composed of three generations. Young and unmarried brothers and sisters also live in the household. When the parents die and the siblings grow up and leave, the household diminishes in size, so that it resembles the nuclear family. The process of expansion then begins again.

Changes in the size and structure of the unit also occur in the joint family. Such a family may also pass through a nuclear phase if too great an increase in family size forces them to divide the family property and split up into separate groups.

Trend to the Nuclear Family

A trend of major significance observed throughout the world in recent years has been the increasing prevalence of the nuclear family. Not only in Western countries, but also in the developing nations of Africa and the Middle East, the extended family is playing a less important role and the nuclear family a more important one.

Many social scientists attribute this trend to the effects of industrialization and urbanization. An industrial economy by its very nature requires that individuals leave home and settle where jobs are available. This demand for physical mobility has weakened the extended-family structure. Because the status that individuals can achieve outweighs the status ascribed to them at birth, the family has less to offer. Equally important, commercial and civic organizations in urban society have now taken over many of the functions the family once performed (such as protection, education, or the lending of money) thereby lessening the importance of the extended family (Goode, 1964).

The Modified Nuclear/Modified Extended Family

While the importance of the extended family has diminished, particularly in industrialized nations, it has by no means disappeared altogether. Few nuclear families exist in a kinship vacuum, and ties among kin are maintained through visits, letters, and gifts. Particularly in times of crisis, such as illness or unemployment, family members provide services and even financial support for close kin who need it. These ties are generally considered to be voluntary, however, involving few rights or obligations.

In many societies, the choice of a marriage partner is not left up to the eligible young man or woman. In India, for example, parents seek suitable mates for their children.

It appears that the most accurate description of families in the Western world is modified nuclear/modified extended. Thus the family may be isolated geographically or occupationally, but not psychologically or financially. At the same time, family members beyond the nuclear group rarely share a residence or feel that they have the right to make demands upon one another.

Is the Nuclear Family Universal?

Some social scientists have claimed that the nuclear family, the mother-father-child unit, is a universal structure because it performs tasks that are essential to society. They contend that the nuclear family, although it may be embedded in the larger kinship structure, is recognized as a separate and distinct unit by every society in the world (Murdock, 1949).

Other social scientists have questioned this. They argue that not all societies have been fully investigated or adequately described. Moreover, they suggest that before we can determine whether or not a society recognizes the nuclear family as a unit, we have to know what properties characterize the family. For example, do the members of the nuclear unit have to live together to constitute a family? Must there be reciprocal economic obligations between husband and wife? Some social scientists have suggested that whether or not the nuclear family is universal may depend upon how we define that institution (Stephens, 1963).

It is certainly possible to imagine ways of organizing society that would eliminate the need for the nuclear family. The tasks usually performed by the family could be performed by other institutions instead. In fact, such a situation exists to some degree in the kibbutzim of Israel and the communes of the People's Republic of China. Other historical examples of societies in which the nuclear family has not existed to any meaningful extent include the Nayars of India and several American Indian groups (Lee, 1977).

This interest in the universality of the nuclear family is part of a larger question concerning the importance of the family to the existence of societies. The issue of the universality of the family should be addressed in two different ways. First, we are inquiring whether or not every society in history has had a social organization that could be called a family. Second, we want to know whether it is possible for a society to survive without the family. The first question can be answered with a simple yes or no, and it appears from the research that the family institution is "virtually universal" (Lee, 1977). However, simply because this is so, we cannot then conclude that the family is necessary for the existence of the society.

 MARITAL FORMS AND CUSTOMS

Monogamy and Polygamy

The only form of marriage now legal in the United States is **monogamy,** the exclusive mating of one man and one woman. We may think that monogamy is the only "natural" way to mate, but 85 percent of societies around the world permit some form of **plural marriage** or **polygamy.** There are three possible types of plural marriage: (1) **polygyny,** in which a man has two or more wives; (2) **polyandry,** in which a woman has two or more husbands; and (3) **group marriage,** in which two or more men and two or more women are married in common to each other.

The most widespread form of plural marriage is polygyny. Polygyny is common in so-called primitive societies, but in more advanced societies it is usually reserved for the wealthy. Having several wives is often regarded as an indication of high status and prestige. Although people sometimes think of polygyny as an excuse for sexual promiscuity, in reality the rules that make it workable—having sexual intercourse with each wife in regular rotation, for instance—may make sex as much an obligation as a pleasure. Women in polygynous marriages may be pleased by the fact that they are married to a man of importance, and another dividend for the females is that there are more hands to share the work. While jealousy is often a problem, it does not appear to be a universal one (Stephens, 1963). A contributing factor in the

HIGHLIGHT 1.1

The Nuclear Family in the Israeli Kibbutz

The **kibbutz** (plural **kibbutzim**) of Israel provides an example of a form of social organization in which the nuclear family does not in fact perform many of the tasks usually associated with it. The kibbutzim are agricultural collectives in which living arrangements are communal, property is held in common, and children are reared by the group. Although there are several types of kibbutzim, our concern is with the most radical form, which was prevalent among the early settlers of modern-day Israel.

The kibbutz was originally intended as a means of revolutionizing Jewish society. As is the case with many revolutionary movements, the proponents of the new order regarded traditional institutions and customs with suspicion. Since the family was one such holdover from the bourgeois past, both marital and family relationships were deemphasized. There was no marriage ceremony, and a couple, though they were permitted to share a room, were regarded by the commune as separate, independent individuals. They did not function as an economic unit, for each individual was regarded as a contributor to the larger economic unit, the kibbutz. They were discouraged from public demonstrations of affection and from spending their leisure time together. Although they were encouraged to develop a loving relationship with their children, they were not responsible for raising and educating them. These were the tasks of the kibbutz, which housed the children in communal nurseries and dormitories and provided nurses and teachers to educate and socialize them.

For a variety of reasons, the antifamily bias of the early communes has ended. Today the nuclear family has taken its place within the communal structure. Children are still raised communally, but their visits with their parents are more frequent. Some children even sleep in their parents' quarters. Moreover, children's relationships with their parents are regarded as highly important to their psychological development. In contrast to earlier practices, many couples are united in a marriage ceremony and many have possessions regarded as their own. Thus the nuclear family in the kibbutz does seem to perform the important functions of providing emotional security for children and emotional satisfactions for parents and marriage partners. It seems clear that the nuclear family in the kibbutz, though functioning differently than in outside society, continues to thrive.

Children of an Israeli kibbutz.

jealousy of cowives seems to be that the women have less choice than the men in deciding to be part of a polygynous marriage.

Polyandry is extremely rare and seems to go hand in hand with group marriage. Most often the husbands are brothers. A major incentive for polyandry appears to be economic. A man may try to form a polyandrous union in order to get another man to work for him. Where there is a shortage of land, polyandry may help to assure that a man will have enough land to support his family (Stephens, 1963).

Norms Related to Marriage

CHOOSING A MARRIAGE PARTNER   In our society, people are usually free to choose for themselves the person they will marry, and their choice is based on the notion of romantic love. Two people fall in love and decide to marry because they believe that being in love is the best reason for getting married. In many societies, however, love is not a primary basis for mate selection.

In these societies, marriages are arranged by the elders of the family, who select a suitable spouse for their offspring. In the arranged marriage, partners are often chosen as a means of creating alliances between kinship groups. It has been suggested that the exchange of spouses developed from the fact that in primitive societies there was little else to exchange, and the establishment of friendly relations between neighboring groups was of critical importance (Fox, 1967). The marital exchange is usually accompanied by the payment of money, goods, or services by either the bride's or the groom's family to the other family. If the woman brings the payment, it is called a **dowry;** if the man brings the payment, it is called a **bride price.**

There are other, broader rules about who may marry whom, and they exist in all societies. The rule of **endogamy** requires that a mate be chosen from within one's own group; in our society, people generally marry within their own racial, religious, or ethnic group. When they do not, they may risk social disapproval. The rule of **exogamy,** by contrast, requires that a mate be chosen from outside particular groups. In most societies people do not marry their close blood kin.

RESIDENCE AFTER MARRIAGE   When a couple is married, the wife may move to the home of her husband or the husband to the home of his wife. Sometimes they move periodically from one residence to the other, or, as in our society, they may set up an entirely new home. Rules of residence are those customs that determine where a newly married couple will live. These customs fall into three major patterns: (1) **matrilocal,** where the couple lives with or near the wife's family; (2) **patrilocal,** where the couple lives with or near the husband's family; and (3) **neolocal,** where the couple sets up a new household separate from that of either spouse's family.

Rules of residence are important because they determine the alignment of kin and, often, the distribution of authority within the family. Whoever moves, whether husband or wife, is at a disadvantage because that person loses the support of relatives and moves to a place where he or she is an outsider. Thus rules of residence determine not only with whom the person will maintain social relations but also what his or her power within the family will be.

FAMILY AUTHORITY   When the power and authority over the family rest with the males, the family system is described as **patriarchal.** Male dominance has been common throughout the world. The social structures of the ancient Hebrews, Greeks, and Romans were patriarchal, and the pattern continues to the present in most Asian and Latin American countries. Male dominance is often associated with lower status for women and a "double standard" of sexual behavior.

A **matriarchal** system would be one in which the power of the family rested with the women. We have all heard of the legendary Amazons, but they are only a myth and, in fact, there are no known societies that are truly matriarchal. Even in societies where inheritance and residence follow female lines of descent, usually the power within the family still is wielded by males.

Under an **egalitarian** system, marital power would be shared between husband and wife and decisions would be reached by partners who are on an equal footing. This is an emerging system in the United States and some other industrialized countries. However, most sociologists who deal with the issue of family power believe that on balance, men still possess more authority in marriage than women do.

THE INCEST TABOO   Virtually all societies have rules prohibiting sexual contacts between certain closely related kin. These rules, known collectively as the **incest taboo,** are among the strongest prohibitions in every society. Most commonly, the incest taboo prohibits sexual intercourse and marriage between parent and child and between brother and sister.

The reasons for the incest taboo have been debated for years. Some people believe that humans have a natural aversion to incest; others think that the incest taboo arose because of the harmful effects of inbreeding. Still others contend that the reasons for the taboo lie in the fact that incest creates a confusion of relationships within the family and a consequent disruption of expected lines of authority. None of the theories proposed so far has satisfactorily explained the origin, or the persistence, of the incest taboo.

REMARRIAGE   In the United States, the courts are now granting more than one million divorces a year (U.S. Bureau of the Census, 1980), and many people marry two or more times. Sociologists have coined the term **serial monogamy** to describe a series of marriages in which the individual each time expects to be monogamous with the current partner while the marriage lasts. Remarriage is generally accepted in the United States, though sometimes religious beliefs prohibit it. All societies have rules and regulations about remarriage. For example, until about a hundred years ago, Chinese law and custom made no restrictions on remarriage for widowed men, but remarriages of widowed women were viewed with disfavor.

Customs Related to Children

NUMBER OF CHILDREN BORN   In recent years, the availability of various birth-control methods has made family planning somewhat more predictable. The number of children that a couple will produce is often directly related to the needs of their society and of their family. When children are an economic asset, large families are common. When they are an economic liability, family size tends to be smaller. Sometimes a society will encourage people to have more children as a means of gaining strength in dealing with outsiders. At other times, societies will provide incentives for people to limit their families or have no children at all in order to make scarce food or other resources adequate for those already born.

PARENTAL AUTHORITY OVER CHILDREN   All societies recognize parental authority over children until they reach the age of majority (adulthood as defined by the society). In some cultures, parental authority continues in fact, if not legally, because of continuing financial dependence or traditions of residence or inheritance. In the United States, parental authority often extends through the years of higher education because children are still financially dependent upon their parents and have not yet established their own homes. In countries where it is traditional for sons to marry and remain in the home of their parents, authority generally remains with the father, even though the sons are adults.

RULES OF DESCENT AND INHERITANCE   Descent may be defined as **matrilineal,** through the mother's line; **patrilineal,** through the father's line; or **bilineal,** through both the male and female lines. Our society has a modified bilineal descent pattern in that children generally take the name of their father, but inherit through either male or female lines. They may take the religion of either the mother or the father, if there is a difference, and may develop equally close relationships with relatives on either side.

Throughout history and around the world, the rules of inheritance have applied most strictly in the matters of money, land, and the means of production. Inheritance may be patrilineal, where property passes through the males of the family, or matrilineal, where it passes through the females. Even in matrilineal inheritance, however, the property is likely to be controlled by males; for instance, it may pass from a man to his sister's son. Nearly always, the inheritance of major property is through the males, and female rights to property may be very limited or even nonexistent. **Primogeniture** refers to the exclusive right of inheritance belonging to the eldest son.

ROOTS OF THE FAMILY IN WESTERN SOCIETY

The American family today is the product of thousands of years of human experience. From prehistoric times to the present, people's ideas of family life have been shaped by the problems they faced. The demands we make upon the family today range all the way from basic survival to personal fulfillment. By looking at the history of the family in Western culture we can better understand the complexities and contradictions that exist in the contemporary American family as it attempts to meet the many requirements that individuals and society place upon it.

The Ancient Hebrew Family

The roots of the modern American family extend back to the ancient Hebrews. The philosophy and practices of the Hebrews were of major significance in the development of Christian beliefs. The ancient Hebrews were a nomadic people who wandered the deserts of Arabia in search of the best grazing land for their flocks of sheep. In about the twelfth century B.C., they settled in the area called Canaan, where they gradually became farmers and began to cluster in towns.

The early Hebrew family was strongly patriarchal, with males dominating every aspect of life. Men had virtually complete authority over their wives and children. Under Hebrew law a man could divorce his wife simply because he grew tired of her. Children who were persistently disobedient risked being put to death. Fathers arranged the marriages of their children and had the right to sell their daughters as concubines (mistresses) or servants, though they were not permitted to sell them into prostitution: "Do not prostitute thy daughter, to cause her to be a whore" (Leviticus 19:29).

Although the status of women in Hebrew society was low, they were treated with respect so long as they fulfilled their assigned roles and retained their virtue. Their primary duties were to bear a large number of children, preferably male, and to carry out all manner of housewifely tasks. While most Hebrew males had only one wife, high-ranking or wealthy patriarchs were permitted to practice polygyny. It was not uncommon for a man of high rank to take an extra wife as well as a number of concubines.

The early Hebrews regarded sexuality as an accepted part of human nature. Sexual liaisons outside of marriage met strong social disapproval, but within marriage sexual intercourse was considered divinely willed, both for reproductive purposes and for its own sake (Murstein, 1974). Female menstrual functions were considered unclean, however, and this attitude contributed to the low status of women. Their status was further diminished in that the Hebrews practiced a double standard of sexual conduct for men and women. A nonvirginal bride or an adulterous wife could be put to death by her husband's command, but a husband could engage in sexual relations with as many wives and concubines as he could support.

The subject of love was much written about in the Hebrew testaments. There are many accounts of men and women falling in love: "And Jacob loved Rachel; and said, I will serve thee seven years for Rachel thy younger daughter" (Genesis 22:18). But while love was regarded as desirable in the marriage

The absolute authority of the Hebrew patriarch is represented by the biblical account of Abraham, who was instructed by God to sacrifice his son Isaac. In this illustration, Abraham and Isaac ascend Mount Moriah in preparation for the sacrifice.

relationship, it was not the basis for marriage. Rather, marriages were usually contracted as a means of uniting two family groups. At first **betrothal** (engagement) was considered the beginning stage of marriage. Fathers could betroth their children at early ages, but the marriage would be consummated only when the couple reached the minimum age for marriage (thirteen years for boys, twelve years for girls). As time went by, betrothal became distinct from marriage, the usual betrothal period lasting about one year.

Finally, divorce, like most other aspects of Hebrew life, was a privilege reserved for males. It was easy for a man to obtain a divorce on a number of grounds, of which the wife's barrenness was the most common. In some instances, a divorced woman was entitled to have her dowry returned.

The Greek Family

By the fifth century B.C., the Greeks had formed city-states powerful enough to defeat the Persians, and Greek culture reached its peak. During this time, the city-states of Athens and Sparta competed for dominance.

The patriarchal family system was even stronger in Greece than it was among the Hebrews, and Greek women ranked even lower than Hebrew women. Athenian wives were not allowed to leave the house without permission, and even indoors they were confined to their own apartments. They were uneducated and, therefore, were no match for their learned husbands. Their sole purpose was to bear children. The women of Sparta likewise were valued solely as bearers of children.

The double standard of sexual morality was exaggerated under the Greeks. Men were permitted to have sexual relations with female concubines and prostitutes as well as with male lovers. The social ideal for men seemed to be a full expression of sensuality with a minimum of restraints. For women, adultery was not only grounds for divorce, it was a criminal act for which a woman could be put to death (Reiss, 1960). If the husband committed adultery, his wife could obtain a divorce only if she could prove that he had deprived his own family of adequate support.

Fathers had complete control over the lives of their children, even to the extent that they could leave infants (usually deformed or sickly ones) to die of exposure. As was true of Hebrew children, disobedient Greek children could be put to death. Childrearing stressed citizenship and fitness, but the Spartans put more emphasis on selective breeding and militarism than did the Athenians.

The Roman Family

The patriarchal system was strongest of all in Rome. Indeed, before the end of the Punic Wars in 202 B.C., the power of the *paterfamilias*, the oldest male member, extended down through all generations of his descendants. Even his grown, and perhaps politically influential, sons had no control over their property or income because the patriarch had sole ownership of all family wealth and lands (Bardis, 1964).

Unlike Greek women, Roman women were respected as mistresses of their husband's households and were treated as their social and intellectual peers. Even so, they were under the control of their husbands and had no legal status. This situation changed somewhat while the men were off fighting in the Punic Wars. The women then began to attain greater power because they were left to manage the family estates. At the same time they became better educated and more active politically. As a result of these changes, many Roman wives were unwilling to submit to their husband's domination once he returned. The shift in the male-female balance of power made marriage less important to a woman's status, and many women began to avoid marriage unless a husband could bring both emotional satisfaction and economic gain (Bardis, 1964).

Under the Roman system, marriages could be contracted by means of an elaborate religious ceremony attended by priests and witnesses, or by a secular agreement between parents in which the bride was sold to her husband, or even by a declaration that a couple who had lived together for at least a year were to be considered married from that time on. The latter practice is the forerunner of common-law marriage, which is still recognized in some parts of the United States. Though Roman males took concubines and prostitutes (often slaves) for their sexual pleasure, they had only one wife; the Romans had outlawed polygyny (Bardis, 1964).

Divorce was for the most part a private matter in which the state did not interfere. It was possible to be divorced simply by handing a written statement from one spouse to the other in the presence of seven witnesses. This happened with such regularity that it prompted the Latin church father Tertullian (150–230 A.D.) to comment that "the fruit of marriage is divorce."

As was true in the earlier cultures we have described, the Roman patriarch had the power of life and death over his children. At its most extreme, this meant he had the right to abandon offspring to die of exposure and to sell his children into slavery. Abortion was illegal, but it was practiced widely nevertheless. At the same time, childless Roman men (but not women) were permitted to adopt an heir who could be either an independent person or a son purchased from his natural father (Bardis, 1964).

Roman fathers could have their children married or divorced without their consent. The *paterfamilias* continued to exercise authority over his sons throughout his lifetime; his daughters were passed over to the control of their husband's father. Girls were betrothed by their fathers in early adolescence, and they took a dowry into marriage. The new husband controlled the dowry but was required to return it if there was a divorce. If the husband died, the dowry was returned to the wife's family (Bardis, 1964).

The Influence of Christianity
on the Family

With the decline of the Roman Empire in the fourth century A.D., European history became a series of struggles among warring barbarian tribes. The Catholic church, centered in Rome, first challenged the authority of Rome, and then gradually established a position of dominance. During the Middle Ages, a time when Europe became a mosaic of independent farms and manors controlled by secular lords, the Catholic church emerged as the most important influence over family life.

THE CHURCH POSITION ON WOMEN In the early centuries A.D., women were eagerly welcomed into Christian congregations. The congregations wanted to swell their numbers, and women were respected for their good works. The early Christians were influenced by Jesus' teaching that all people were equal in the sight of God because all had divine souls, but they were also influenced by the Greek idea that the spirit and the body were separate and opposing entities. Some Christian men began to fear that their sexual attraction to women interfered with their spirituality, and they soon associated women with the idea of original sin. Christian leaders taught that Adam's fall from grace resulted from the weakness of Eve. By the Middle Ages, the attitude of the Christian clergy toward women had become so negative that in A.D. 585 the Council of Macon seriously debated whether women had souls as men did (Murstein, 1974).

THE CHURCH POSITION ON MARRIAGE AND CELIBACY The early Christian leaders, notably St. Paul, regarded a life without sexual expression as the highest form of virtue. Sex was considered a necessary evil acceptable only within marriage and for the purpose of procreation. The church encouraged its members—and compelled its priests—to remain celibate and pursue a life of service.

Yet even with this emphasis on sexual purity, most Christians still chose to marry. The early Christian church followed the Roman law, the essential requirement of which was that the partners consent to the union with affection. Eventually, however, the Roman Catholic church came to look upon marriage as a sacred union and began to insist that marital vows be exchanged at the church entrance with a priest in attendance. By the thirteenth century, the ceremony had moved inside the church, with the clergy actually performing the marital rites.

THE CHURCH POSITION ON DIVORCE Christian policy regarding divorce was a matter of continuing debate in the early centuries A.D. (Bardis, 1964). In the fifth century, the church officially proclaimed that marriages could not be dissolved, but it wavered in its enforcement of this doctrine for five hundred years, accommodating itself to the view of the Germanic tribes that divorce was a personal privilege and not subject to interference by the clergy. By the tenth century, however, the Christian church was very well established, and it insisted on judging all requests for marital dissolution. Bishops' courts were willing to grant approval only for annulments and separations. An annulment was a public statement that the marriage had been illegal in the first place, perhaps because the bride and groom were too closely related or because they had previously been involved in a secret marriage. Separation—the ending of cohabitation without the privilege of remarriage—was permitted in cases of adultery, cruelty, or religious heresy.

ATTITUDES TOWARD CHILDREN   The early Christians placed a high value on each human life. As a result, they strongly opposed the severe treatment of children that characterized the earlier societies we have described. As the power of the patriarch declined, the status of children rose. Abortion, infanticide, child selling, and sentencing children to death were all condemned. Nonetheless, Christians expected children to obey their parents and to care for them when they became old (Bardis, 1964).

Toward the New World

During the sixteenth century, much of Europe became embroiled in violent disputes over religious and political issues. In an upheaval known as the Protestant Reformation, those who challenged the old ideas broke away from the established Roman Catholic church. Protestantism soon gained a strong foothold, and it became the dominant force in English political life. In the early seventeenth century, some Protestant dissenters, most notably the Puritans, fled to the New World to escape religious persecution. These first English colonists in America carried with them notions of family life not very different from those that prevailed at the end of the Roman era.

 FAMILY LIFE:
THE AMERICAN EXPERIENCE

The Colonial Era

English colonists began settling the American continent at the beginning of the seventeenth century. New England was initially colonized by Puritans who had broken with the Church of England and were seeking religious freedom, and the South was settled by people who had not broken with the Church of England but who hoped to increase their wealth in the New World. Social scientists are cautious in generalizing about family life in colonial times. Variations existed between the North and South, the pace of change was rapid, and it is difficult to weed out inaccurate myths passed down as facts by earlier generations of historians. Nevertheless, it is possible to draw some tentative conclusions.

THE PROTESTANT WORK ETHIC   The newcomers to America had a highly developed concept of "Christian duty." People were expected to respect their elders, to take care of the old and the young, and to work as diligently as was humanly possible. The idea that there was something particularly righteous about hard work became known as the Protestant work ethic, and it still has a compelling influence over the behavior of many Americans. In colonial days, the work ethic contributed greatly to the settlement of the frontier and the establishment of a new nation.

COURTSHIP AND MARRIAGE   Social conditions in early America speeded the trend begun in Europe toward individual, rather than parental, mate selection. Immigrants to America were generally young and physically removed from the patriarchal control of the families they left behind. On the continually expanding frontier, people were separated even more from kinship ties as they moved westward.

During the colonial period the family was called upon to provide for virtually all the needs of its individual members. Food, clothing, shelter, economic support, education, religious training, recreation, and affection all came from the family unit. In addition to promoting the independence of the nuclear family, American frontier life also encouraged a spirit of individualism, and immigrants from all social classes were equalized by the hardships of life in an untamed land. Individuals advanced or failed according to their own talents and effort rather than according to their family's social standing. People tended to choose their mates on the basis of their personal qualities, although financial considerations were not entirely overlooked.

Under primitive early conditions, romance at first had little room to blossom. Because population was sparse and transportation was poor, people usually married neighbors. Courtships were brief and could not even begin until the young woman's parents had agreed to her betrothal. Many Puritans seemed to hope that ease and mutual comfort could be found in marriage (Schnucker, 1975). But while they felt that love should flower within a good marriage, they did not consider romantic love a prerequisite for selecting a partner. As Puritanism declined, however, more and more marriages were based on romantic attraction.

Puritan couples were wed in civil ceremonies. In this, as in other matters, they had broken with the Church of England by declaring that marriage was not a sacrament and should not be performed by the church. Instead, civil authorities established marriage laws. The posting of **banns,** a public announcement of the proposed marriage, was required in order to give persons who might object to the marriage an opportunity to make their objections known. In addition, the couple had to obtain their parents' consent as well as register with the civil authorities before the marriage could take place. Since the Southern colonists had not broken with the Church of England, they were married by clergymen when this could be arranged. But ministers were few and population was sparse between plantations and on the frontier. When there was no one available to marry them, some couples simply began to live together until a circuit-riding clergyman came by to formalize the relationship. By that time, some were so fully accepted as husband and wife that it seemed unnecessary to go through the motions of an official ceremony. Although some of the colonies tried to discourage these "common-law" marriages, most begrudgingly recognized them as valid. Once a common-law wife became pregnant, there seemed to be no advantage to protesting the arrangement.

ATTITUDES TOWARD SEXUALITY Although we now use the word puritanical to mean something like antisexual, Edmund Morgan, in his classic study "The Puritans and Sex" (1973), concluded that the Puritans had a more realistic view of sexuality than is commonly supposed. Like the Old Testament Hebrews, from whom many of their ideas were derived, the Puritans regarded sexual satisfaction as an acknowledged human need—but one that was to be indulged only within marriage, and only when it did not interfere with glorifying God. Sexual intercourse and recreation were forbidden on the Sabbath, which was to be devoted to religious activities.

Unmarried couples who had sexual relations risked fines, whipping, and forced marriage, since they were considered unfit to marry anyone else. Adultery was officially punishable by death, and this sentence appears to have been carried out at least a few times. The death penalty gradually gave way to whipping, imprisonment, or banishment, the stigma of being forced to wear a scarlet *A* on the clothing, or branding on the forehead with an *A*-shaped iron.

In spite of the Puritan's strict disapproval of premarital sex, once the terms of the marriage contract had been spelled out, restrictions were relaxed for the betrothed since they were considered nearly married. Many engaged in the extraordinary colonial practice of **bundling,** spending the evening or even the whole night lying together in bed, fully dressed. Bundling began because warmth and fuel were at a premium. What the bundling couple were supposed to be doing in bed together was keeping warm while they talked. To make sure that nothing else happened, parents sometimes slept in the same room or separated the couple with a low bolster or board placed down the middle of the bed. Mothers occasionally even tied their daughters' ankles together before leaving them to their bundling (Kenkel, 1973).

While the Puritans punished men as severely as women for sexual misconduct, there was a clear double standard in the South, perhaps because the landed aristocracy was at first short of women and later had access to large numbers of black slaves. Upper-class men were permitted great sexual freedom outside of marriage. Taking mistresses was common, and wives actually met with social disapproval if they did not graciously accept this fact.

Laws against racial mixing were ignored when white men sought out black women for sexual liaisons. But a strict black-white double standard was maintained, for if a black man showed even the slightest sexual interest in a white woman, he risked being put to death.

GENDER ROLES   Like the early Christians, the Puritans looked upon the biblical account of creation as evidence of the inferiority of women. Thus it is not surprising that women in colonial society were relegated to a position of subservience. The Puritan woman's place was in the home, where her time was devoted to caring for her children, cooking, spinning, weaving and sewing, and other domestic chores. A wife's earnings and property belonged technically to her husband, and widows ordinarily had no control over their husbands' estates. A woman could not marry without the consent of her father, nor did she have the right to sign contracts or to vote (Gruver, 1981).

For their part, Puritan men were occupied with public activities, including business matters and political participation. Husbands were expected to provide support for their families. Although corporal punishment of wives was permitted, the evidence suggests that American men were generally faithful husbands who treated their wives with tenderness and respect (Gruver, 1981).

While most colonial women stayed in the home, not all did. Thanks to the chronic labor shortage in newly settled areas, women on the frontier could be found in many areas of economic life, working as everything from botanists and lawyers to managers of sawmills and taverns. These women may even have held greater authority at home and enjoyed some emotional closeness and equality with their husbands than did their female descendants (Somerville, 1974).

Life for the small minority of upper-class Southern women contrasted markedly with the conditions of Puritan women. Admired by Southern gentlemen as delicate, sensitive creatures, they were placed on a pedestal, freed by servants from domestic chores, and encouraged to develop social graces.

ATTITUDES TOWARD CHILDREN   During the colonial period, a typical New England household consisted of a husband and wife, their children (often as many as six or seven), at least one grandparent, and often servants or apprentices (Gruver, 1981). Children were a valuable economic asset, for labor was always in short supply. In addition to the economic advantages of having a large number of children, the Puritans heeded the Old Testament admonition to be fruitful and multiply. According to their religious beliefs, children were a blessing from God. Furthermore, every child was a potential new member of the church and added to the population of the colony, both important considerations at the time.

Though Puritan children were loved, they were not indulged. The family stood as a symbol of the larger society; as a result, children were expected to know their place. The disrespectful child could expect to be punished severely. Since Puritan doctrine embraced the idea that humans enter the world in a state of sinfulness, raising children to be good Christians was thought to be a matter of breaking their will and teaching them obedience, humility, and religious faith.

Despite their strict upbringing, older children enjoyed a relative degree of independence due to the conditions of frontier life. The abundance of free land made it possible for many young adult men to leave home to establish their own farms. In order to keep their adult children close by, parents had to relax some of their controls (Gruver, 1981).

DIVORCE   Despite the esteem in which the Puritans held marriage and the family, they made relatively liberal provisions for divorce. This apparent contradiction can be explained as part of their rebellion against the Church of England, which permitted separations but not divorce. And even though the South had not broken with the church, it was unwilling to set up church courts in the New World. Since there was thus no institution to hear requests for separation, some Southern couples simply separated on their own.

Most Puritans, while entitled to divorce, did not take advantage of this provision. There were only twenty-five divorces granted in Massachusetts in the fifty-three years between 1639 and 1692, an average of one every two years, even though men were allowed to divorce their wives for adultery, desertion, or even cruelty. It was harder for women to win a divorce. A wife could not divorce her husband for adultery unless she could prove that he had deserted the family or failed to support them. Despite this double standard, more colonial women than men instigated divorce proceedings, perhaps because marriage was more central to their lives and a bad marriage was therefore less tolerable (Leslie, 1979).

Nineteenth-Century Family
Life in America

During the nineteenth century, the United States was transformed from a rural, farming society into an urban and industrialized one. For awhile there were two separate influences on the evolution of the family: the frontier and the process of urbanization.

THE CHANGING PERCEPTION OF THE FAMILY When they moved westward, pioneer families became separated both from kin and from the land they had owned. The resulting isolation they experienced strengthened the nuclear family, but it weakened the patriarchal system. Grandparents were usually left behind because they wanted to remain settled and also because pioneering required vigorous physical work from every member of the family. Children on the frontier did not have to consider the opinions of their grandparents; consequently, it did not occur to them in later years to try to control their own grandchildren (Leslie, 1979). Moreover, the strengths and skills needed to tame the wilderness were considerable, and individuals had a chance to demonstrate their own worth. The relative equality enjoyed by frontier women is attested to by the fact that the Western states were the first to grant women the vote.

In the Eastern cities, by contrast, increasing industrialization contributed to a more rigid separation of roles. While men went to the offices and factories, women were given over to the tasks of homemaking and children were sent off to the newly instituted public schools. The atmosphere of the business world was so demanding that there developed a tendency to idealize the family as a place of refuge—as historian Christopher Lasch (1977) described it, a "haven in a heartless world."

As the family came to be viewed in a sentimental light, so did the roles of wife and mother. In the popular magazines of the pre–Civil War period, women were portrayed as being intuitive, pious, pure, and domestic. Their major accountability was to provide for the moral welfare of society. For their part, men were expected to possess the qualities of toughness, competitiveness, emotional restraint, and objectivity that were required for success in the business world.

Even though their lives were bound to the home, women did gain additional legal rights as the nineteenth century progressed. Married women eventually won the right to hold property (single women already had this right), to inherit equally with males, to petition for divorce, and to bring other kinds of court action. It became increasingly acceptable for single women to work at certain "respectable" jobs, such as teaching and office work. Middle- and upper-class women gained greater educational opportunities, and some of these women began to take up careers. With other options open to them, some women chose not to marry or to marry later than was customary. And many more marriages were ending in divorce.

ATTITUDES TOWARD SEXUALITY The sexual attitudes of mid–nineteenth-century Americans were much influenced by the code of morality that existed in Victorian England, a code that may be termed antisexual. Even though young people in the United States were becoming more and more independent financially and socially, they were much affected by the Victorian belief in sexual self-restraint. The new sexual restrictiveness was based on Protestant teachings about the sinfulness of physical desires. As in the past, these antisexual attitudes were applied more vigorously in regard to women than to men. Women who engaged in sexual liaisons were ruined socially, while it was expected that men would have sexual relationships with willing women. The nineteenth-century habit of dividing women into two categories—"good" women who were sexually pure and therefore marriageable and "bad" women who were ruined for marriage because of their unchaste behavior—may have led many men to marry women for whom they felt no attraction at all. It is not surprising that many Victorian marriages were based more on duty and respect than on affection and sharing.

ATTITUDES TOWARD CHILDREN   The nineteenth-century perception of children was somewhat contradictory. The idealization of family life was accompanied by a new appreciation among the middle and upper classes of childhood as a distinct stage of personal development with specific physical and emotional needs. Childrearing manuals and children's books made their first appearance during this period. European travelers to America commented on the loving attention that was lavished on American children. Some of them thought the

During the nineteenth century, the home became the domain of women and the outside world the domain of men. Men socialized in restaurants and bars, but women almost always entertained their friends at home.

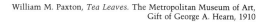

William M. Paxton, *Tea Leaves.* The Metropolitan Museum of Art, Gift of George A. Hearn, 1910

young were spoiled and undisciplined, with a degree of influence over their parents that was considered shocking by European standards. Others thought American children were delightfully spontaneous and independent, as was appropriate for citizens of a democracy.

But life for lower-class children was anything but rosy. As industrialization progressed, the family was transformed from a producing unit into a consuming unit. As a result, children became an economic liability, and the poor had no recourse but to send their children to work in the factories to help support the family. Eventually, middle-class reformers, outraged by the low wages, long hours, and dangerous working conditions endured by children, initiated child-labor legislation.

The Changing American Family

Many people today regard the industrial age, the nineteenth and early twentieth centuries, as the golden age of marriage and the family. They view with alarm supposed deviations from traditional patterns, seeing in them signs of the decline of the family. What we have tried to show, however, is that change is characteristic of all institutions, including marriage and the family. Still, within a particular culture, change is balanced by continuity. In this respect, the postindustrial age, the last third of the twentieth century, is no different from earlier periods.

If there are changes in the nature of the family, they have occurred in response to a much altered environment. In a pluralistic society, the family is taking many forms to meet diverse needs. Yet, as dissimilar as these forms may seem to earlier ones, their roots lie in their predecessors. Current practices can best be described not as breaks but as outgrowths of the past.

NEW GOALS AND EXPECTATIONS According to Burgess et al. (1963), in the traditional patriarchal family of the past, family unity was determined by societal rules and rigidly specified roles. What has been emerging, by contrast, is a type of family unified by mutual affection, companionship, and common interests. The ideal form of the new "democratic" family is one in which the marital union is based on affection; the husband and wife are mutually involved in decision making; major decisions are by consensus; and common interests and activities coexist with a mutually agreed upon division of labor and a recognition of individual interests.

The ideas that decisions in marriage should be made by consensus, that the division of labor within the family should be mutually agreed upon, and that the individuality of each member should be nurtured may be the most significant recent changes in perceptions of marriage and the family. Modern spouses are moving toward what might be termed joint partnership. While strong elements of the traditional division of roles by gender retain a significant hold in many marriages, there is a noticeable movement toward choosing a marital style that is closely tailored to the needs of the particular couple rather than to societal expectations. Roles traditionally reserved for one gender are more open to the other. Increasingly, women are participating in the working world while men are taking on some functions in the home that not long ago were considered the sole province of women.

A few scholars have expressed concern about the impact on the family of this gradual disappearance of the clear gender-role differentiation of the past and the developing state of **androgyny**. Androgyny in this sense refers to the idea that there are no distinct role expectations or behavioral expectations based on sex. They contend that the movement away from traditional role divisions is resulting in an overemphasis on individual self-fulfillment and consequent lack of emphasis on the family unit. But the majority of sociologists argue that the movement toward androgyny can be a positive factor in building marital and family relationships, for it forces couples to define their roles and their relationship to each other in a way that will be mutually beneficial. Instead of making decisions on the basis of one family member's needs (traditionally, the husband's), an androgynous couple is more likely to evaluate issues in terms of their impact on each family member. The world has changed so radically that there seems to be little reason for the perpetuation of roles that may not be suited to current needs.

STRENGTH AND STABILITY   The family has always existed in a variety of forms. Even the brief historical review in this chapter reveals that the family has had to adapt to the social, economic, and political realities of each era. Its strength lies in its ability to absorb change and provide continuity.

The American family survived the hardships of settling a new continent and establishing a nation. It survived the move from farms to cities and the Industrial Revolution. Today it faces the demands of high technology, inflation, changing sexual norms, and increased expectations for personal fulfillment. No doubt the family is under stress; it always has been—only the types of stress are new. Still, there are many positive signs.

If 96 percent of Americans still marry, clearly almost everyone believes that marriage and family life will bring satisfactions not available to those who remain single. Though divorce is common, five out of six divorced men and three out of four divorced women remarry (Furstenberg, 1980). As noted in Fig. 1.1, most people still place a high value on family life. Because at one time or another most people are part of a family breakup or close to someone who is, there is increased openness about personal and family conflict. The necessity to cloak all family problems in secrecy no longer exists, and people are free to explore options for greater satisfaction in their lives. But perhaps the most positive trend is the steadily diminishing pressure to conform to an idealized concept of the American family. Social scientists have provided Americans with a more realistic picture of traditional family life. Books,

Tradition and Change: The Japanese-American Family

The Japanese-American family presents a study in contrasts. Although each succeeding generation has assimilated more of American culture, the Japanese heritage continues to influence family life even among today's highly Americanized younger generation.

The Japanese began immigrating to the United States in significant numbers around 1890. Among first-generation Japanese-Americans (known as *Issei*), the family was patriarchal, with the father and other male members in positions of dominance. High status was given to old people, who provided a link to ancestors and served as models for the younger generation. Extended families were the norm, and even though this pattern did not exist among the earlier immigrants, the extended family has continued to be important to succeeding generations.

In keeping with the hierarchical structure of the family, Japanese wives were subservient to their husbands. Marriage was seen as a duty rather than a means of achieving happiness. An aspect of Japanese culture with important implications for husband-wife and parent-child relations was the tendency to avoid direct confrontation. In contrast to American couples, who tend to express anger openly, *Issei* couples conveyed their feelings indirectly—for example, by making a general remark that the spouse would be expected to take note of. Similarly, instead of telling a child to stop misbehaving, a Japanese mother might say to her husband in front of the child that children seemed to be especially naughty these days. This means of indirect communication has proved both beneficial and damaging for Japanese-Americans today. While this technique helps avoid confrontation, it also makes it difficult for Japanese-Americans to deal with the emphasis American society places on openly expressing one's true feelings.

Another aspect of the Japanese system that has affected family relations is the profound emphasis given to one's membership in and loyalty to an overriding group. In the *Issei* family the focal group was the household, or *ie*. A primary function of the *ie* was the socialization of children to become dependent upon and responsible to the family unit. One means of creating dependency was through sleeping arrangements. Second-generation Japanese-Americans who were asked about their sleeping arrangements reported that as children they slept with their parents until a relatively late age (Kitano and Kikumura, 1976). A sense of group loyalty was achieved by teaching children that they were representatives of the *ie* and as such must not bring shame upon the household. Second-generation Japanese-Americans reported that they had been instilled with the idea that they must not bring shame upon the Japanese community, which in America became an extension of the household (Connor, 1974).

Facing severe racial discrimination and seeking to preserve their culture, the *Issei* acquired few American traits. But their children, born in America during the period from about 1910 to 1940, became significantly more acculturated. Many of these *Nisei*, as they are called, were educated at American universities and succeeded in rising into the middle class. However, they retained many of their parents' values, particularly concerning the importance

(continued)

HIGHLIGHT 1.2   (continued)

of the family, and often remained in Japanese neighborhoods and associated primarily with other Japanese.

It is the third-generation Japanese-Americans (known as *Sansei*) who have become the most "Americanized." These young people, most of whom are in their twenties and thirties, have more friends among non-Japanese than among Japanese. One consequence of this is their rising rate of intermarriage. Whereas only 5 percent of *Issei* and 15 percent of *Nisei* married outside their group, the rate of intermarriage for *Sansei* has reached 50 percent in some areas of California and Hawaii. Young Japanese-Americans are also breaking away from family ties as they grow older, although family anniversaries and holidays remain important now as in the past. In addition, the rigid separation of male and female roles is breaking down. And even though separation and divorce rates among Japanese-Americans are much lower than among non-Japanese, Kitano and Kikumura (1976) believe the rates are rising.

Despite their high degree of Americanization, the *Sansei* still exhibit some distinctly Japanese characteristics. Connor (1974) found that compared with Caucasians of about the same age and educational level, *Sansei* place greater emphasis on identification with the family unit and have a greater need to affiliate with and receive support from others. Membership in the ethnic community still retains a strong hold, as evidenced by the fact that in general Japanese-American students are reluctant to leave the West Coast to attend college in the East or take advantage of the greater opportunities offered by some large Eastern cities. Connor also found that *Sansei* continue to foster dependency in their children through their style of caretaking. This has become a source of conflict in many Japanese-American families, since it goes against the American goal of promoting independence and autonomy in children.

Sources: Connor, J. W. Acculturation and Family Continuities in Three Generations of Japanese Americans. *Journal of Marriage and the Family*, February 1974, pp. 159–165.

Kitano, H. L., and Akemi Kikumura. The Japanese American Family. In C. H. Mindel and R. W. Habenstein (eds.), *Ethnic Families in America*. (New York: Oxford, 1976).

magazines, and television bombard us with information about new family life-styles devised to meet the problems and expectations of Americans today.

In the midst of a complicated world, Americans still find that their greatest emotional support comes from their family. The poet Robert Frost wrote, "Home is the place where—when you have to go there—they have to take you in." We find confirmation of our abilities at work and in the community, but in the family it is what we are, not what we do, that counts (Douvan, 1980). A recent national study shows that Americans recognize that marriage and parenthood are not easy, and they often need outside help or counseling in times of stress. Yet for most, the family is still the center of meaning and joy in their lives. Americans value marriage and parenthood more highly than any other aspects of their lives, and they rate their marriages as happy more often than did people in the 1950s (Douvan, 1980).

Percent

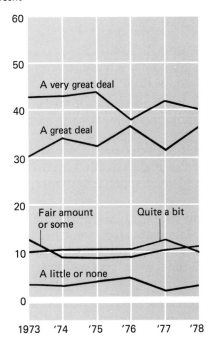

Fig. 1.1

Public attitudes on satisfaction with family life. Most Americans place a high value on family life. Three of every four adults since 1973 say they find "a very great deal" or "a great deal" of satisfaction with family life. (Source: General Social Surveys, National Opinion Research Center, University of Chicago. Reprinted by permission.)

Perhaps more than at any other time Americans today have an opportunity to make of their families what they want them to be. And that is the theme of this chapter: *"The* family, considered as a species, is molded by history and thus lies beyond our power to control. Not so those *particular* families to which we personally belong. The past lives in us always; but what we make of it, individually, is up to ourselves" (Demos, 1975).

SUMMARY

1. The main purposes of this chapter are to introduce and explain the concepts of marriage and the family; to trace the origins of the family and the historical predecessors of the American family; to describe the evolution of the American family; and to show that marriage and the family, like all social institutions, are characterized by change.

2. The family is a social group with specified roles and statuses related by blood, marriage, or adoption that typically shares a residence and cooperates economically. It is commonly based on the marriage of one or more couples living in a socially approved sexual relationship, and it usually involves the expectation of having children for whom the adults of the family accept responsibility. The family is almost always thought of as the basic social unit. As such it performs certain functions: reproduction,

socialization, economic cooperation, protection, assignment of social roles and status, and the bestowing of affection and emotional security as well as a sense of purpose and meaning.

3. Marriage is an institutionalized mating arrangement that serves to legitimize children and give them a recognized place in society. The family is the institutionalized means of rearing the children.

4. The organization of the family varies from culture to culture. The most common type of family organization in the United States is a modified form of the nuclear family. In many other societies the extended family is more common. All societies have rules and customs governing such aspects of family life as mate selection, marriage ceremonies, choice of residence, care of children, divorce, inheritance, and authority over family members.

5. American ideas about the family were strongly influenced by the ancient Hebrews, Greeks, and Romans, all of whom had patriarchal family systems. The early Christians and later the Roman Catholic church modified the ancient views, and they were eventually transmitted by way of the seventeenth-century Protestant dissenters to the New World.

6. In colonial times, the conditions of frontier life led to increased independence of the nuclear family and accelerated the Western European trend toward individual mate selection. For the most part, there was a division of labor by sex. Children were valued as economic assets, and sexuality was regarded as natural and appropriate within the context of marriage.

7. During the nineteenth century, America changed from a rural to an urban-industrial society. As a result, gender roles became more rigidly defined and the family began to be idealized as a "haven in a heartless world."

8. Perhaps the most notable shifts in the function of the family in the postindustrial era are the greater emphasis on consensus and mutual growth and the movement away from rigid roles and toward androgyny.

REVIEW AND DISCUSSION

1. Compare the attitudes toward women and children in one of the following societies with current attitudes in the United States:

       Hebrew   Greek   Roman   Colonial America
              Nineteenth-century America

2. What differences can you find between your own attitudes toward marriage and family life and those of your parents? Your grandparents?

3. What problems and adjustments might you have to face if your mate was chosen for you by your parents for economic and social reasons rather than chosen by you on the basis of love or companionship? Do you think it would be an easier situation or a more difficult one? Why?

4. Describe some examples of how people in the United States are carrying on family customs typical of other parts of the world brought here by themselves or by previous generations.

5. Although many people are worried that marriage and the family in America are in serious trouble, we have taken the position that all social institutions evolve and change in response to changing environment and that the differences from earlier times are not necessarily bad. What is your view on this issue? Offer supporting arguments.

SUGGESTED READINGS

Aries, P. (1965). *Centuries of Childhood: A Social History of Family Life.* New York: Random.

Examines the development of the modern conception of family life and the modern image of the nature of children. Deals primarily with the family, children, and school in pre–nineteenth-century France and England, using paintings, diaries, the history of games and skills, and the development of schools and their curricula.

Degler, C. (1980). *At Odds: Women and the Family in America from the Revolution to the Present.* New York: Oxford.

Traces the evolution of the role of women in the family from the Revolution to the present day. Degler argues that the fact that women have demanded an increasingly greater voice has not weakened the family. Because many family functions are now performed by teachers, doctors, and the like, the family can concentrate on fostering affection between husband and wife and raising children in an atmosphere of love.

Goode, W. J. (1964). *The Family.* Englewood Cliffs, N.J.: Prentice-Hall.

Covers the relationship between family systems and the larger social structure, using a framework of sociological theory and data gathered from societies past and present.

Lasch, C. (1977). *Haven in a Heartless World: The Family Besieged.* New York: Basic.

The thesis of this book is that the state and the "helping professions" have usurped the family's authority. Psychiatrists tell mothers how to care for babies, educators raise and train children, and social workers advise on just about everything else. The result, says Lasch, is that parents are unable to direct their own lives or those of their children.

Seward, R. R. (1978). *The American Family: A Demographic History.* Beverly Hills, Calif.: Sage.

A sociologist looks at U.S. census records and finds the American family a remarkably sturdy institution.

The Study of Marriage and the Family

The Importance of Systematic Research

The Development of Family Study

Studying Marriage and the Family

Theoretical Frameworks and Their Uses

The institutions of marriage and the family are common to virtually all societies. But despite their central roles in human life, it was not until the middle of the nineteenth century that they became the subject of systematic study. Since then, investigation into these areas has become the focus of several academic disciplines and has provided a source of practical information for the general public. This chapter introduces marriage and the family as a field for scientific study. Its purpose is to explain the importance of the scientific perspective, to describe how family study developed, and to introduce the major theoretical frameworks that underlie many of the ideas and themes in the rest of this text. It is important to understand the development of marriage and family theory and research in order to grasp the nature of the questions asked about marriages and families and the ways in which social scientists have attempted to answer these questions objectively.

THE IMPORTANCE OF SYSTEMATIC RESEARCH

It might seem that marriage and the family would be unusual—or unnecessary—subjects to consider from a scientific point of view. We all come from families; and we know, or think we know, something about how they operate. We have observed our parents' marriage, and many of us have experienced our own intimate relationships. It is reasonable, then, to assume that we know a lot about the subject. But can we always be sure that what we have learned from our own experience is correct or generally applicable? In order to answer this question, let us consider an example.

Imagine a physicist walking along the street. He sees a stone fall from a ledge, an apple drop from a tree. Over a period of time, he watches many objects of various sizes and shapes fall from various heights. On the basis of these observations, he concludes that all objects fall at the same speed. He has discovered the law of freely falling bodies. But no one would base a science on these observations. No physicist would suggest that these casual observations were scientifically valid. They may be excellent sources of ideas, but they are not scientific data. The reason is that they have not been collected systematically under controlled conditions that could be repeated. The physicist must measure carefully the speed of falling objects, weigh and measure the objects, and so on. Once this systematic research has been done, we may begin to trust the findings.

This is obvious in physics, which is a highly advanced, precise science with a long tradition of careful research. It is equally true of the social sciences. Just as we should not trust the casual observations of the physicist, we should not trust unsystematic observations of human behavior. Suppose someone traveled to a number of businesses for the purpose of observing the job-turnover rates for women and concluded after a year of observation that women should not be hired for higher-level positions because they are likely to get married and quit or leave the company when they decide to have a family. Before accepting this conclusion, a thoughtful person would ask what types of jobs were observed, whether the observer saw a representative group of men and women, whether the judgments drawn were biased by the observer's attitudes, and so forth. In short, we would expect our observer to study this issue in a systematic way so that we could trust the conclusions of the research. As it happens, research on turnover rates has been done. What has been found is that when occupational level and income are held constant, turnover rates do not vary significantly according to sex (U.S. National Commission for UNESCO, 1977). Thus, a scientific research orientation often allows us to see beyond what our casual observations, or "common sense," might lead us to believe.

Of course, casual observations are not always wrong. But when they are, they can have negative effects on people's lives. The assumption that women are not suitable for higher-level positions has had obvious implications for women in our society. Many other unsupported assumptions—about the roles of men and women in marriage, male and female sexuality, the effect of maternal employment on children, the undesirability of conflict in marriage—have also contributed to the problems of marital and family life.

The methods of gathering and assessing data are, therefore, of the utmost importance because they provide the basis for conclusions about human behavior and for the actions people take based on these conclusions. When data come from systematic research, we know how they were collected; ideally, we could collect the same kind of data again and obtain the same results in subsequent research. We can also perform statistical analyses of the data to see how much confidence we should have in the results. We would then have a more secure basis for our conclusions and our actions.

It is likely that some of our ideas or beliefs about how marriages and families operate are correct, but others may not be accurate. The scientific approach to research allows us to systematically test these assumptions, whether they are based on our limited observations of our own families or families with which we are familiar, or whether they are more rigorously based on theoretical assumptions of the nature of marriage and family relationships. The topics covered in this book, and the discussions therein, utilize such a scientific approach.

THE DEVELOPMENT OF FAMILY STUDY

Throughout history the family has been the subject of folklore, religious thought, philosophical discourse, literature, and everyday observation. The insights of Socrates and Aristotle, the teachings of Jesus, the dramatic works of Shakespeare—in fact, all the great works of literature—have provided humankind with much wisdom about intimate relationships. Yet valid as their observations may be, none of these thinkers sought to organize his work into a systematic body of research. Instead, they were interested in describing how marriage and family relationships *ought* to be, rather than exploring how they *are*. The scientific study of the family did not begin until the mid-nineteenth century, and it was based on first, the development of the **empirical method,** which relied on observation and experience to verify data, and second, the work of Charles Darwin (Christensen, 1964).

A Brief Historical Perspective

In 1859, English naturalist Charles Darwin published *The Origin of Species,* a landmark work which proposed that humans and all other complex life forms had evolved from simple organisms. Through a process of "natural selection," those species best able to adapt to their environments survived; less adaptable species disappeared. This idea was summed up in the phrase "survival of the fittest." Darwin believed that the evolution of living things had not ended; it was an ongoing process.

Some thinkers sought to apply Darwin's theory of biological evolution to society and its institutions. These Social Darwinists, as they became known, focused their attention on tracing the evolution of the various social institutions. The family was a natural place to begin their examination, for it was the most fundamental social relationship they could identify. They tried to discover universal laws governing the development of the family and, using data accumulated from a number of sources, attempted to identify the phases of the family's evolution. By today's standards, their techniques were not very scientific, but their work did much to awaken interest in this field of study. A French Social Darwinist, Fredrick Le Play, lived among working people and used both interviews and first-hand observations to collect data. In doing this, Le Play was among the first to develop a number of the research techniques sociologists use today (Christensen, 1964; Adams, 1980).

Darwin's work had important social consequences. In particular, the theory of the "survival of the fittest" was used to justify exploitative business practices during the period of industrialization. According to this argument, the strong would inevitably prevail in the competition for survival and the weak would be pushed aside. Thus social problems such as poverty were viewed as a consequence of the law of nature.

The response to this philosophy was the social reform movement. Reformers recognized that the doctrine of the "survival of the fittest" prevented society from attacking the problems of poverty, child labor, and other ills and that these problems were in turn undermining the family. Sociologists belonging to the so-called "Chicago school" took the position that much was known about the family and the urban ills that were afflicting it, and that what was needed were solutions to the problems. However, a second academic branch of the reform movement held that the characteristics of the modern family were far from clear and required more investigation. These sociologists placed more emphasis on research than on problem solving (Christensen, 1964; Adams, 1980).

DEVELOPMENTS SINCE 1920   The development of statistical measurement in the early years of the twentieth century dramatically advanced the scientific study of the family. Statistics permitted social scientists to develop systematic means of conducting research and caused them to emphasize scientific investigation rather than social reform. At the same time, the focus of study was shifting from broad examinations of the family in various societies and cultures to particular aspects of family relationships; that is, from the family as a social institution to the family as "a unity of interacting personalities" (Burgess, 1926).

The leading exponent of this view was Ernest Burgess of the University of Chicago. Burgess made the study of marital adjustment a major sociological issue. His research efforts and those of his students shed light on numerous aspects of family life and provided a starting point for later research into such issues as how Americans choose mates, how family members interact, how people are affected by divorce, and how families deal with aged members. The great achievement of Burgess and his contemporaries is that they helped identify a large number of verifiable facts about the family.

Early sociologists concerned with the social ills that accompanied industrialization and urbanization felt that the focus of their discipline should be on understanding the workings of society in order to correct social problems.

Perhaps the most important development in the study of marriage and the family since Burgess's pioneering work has been an effort to develop theories to explain various findings. Instead of simply accumulating data that *describes* how family members interact, sociologists are attempting to *explain* these phenomena. Later in the chapter we will consider the principal theories in use today.

STUDYING MARRIAGE AND THE FAMILY

The practical problems facing a social scientist who wishes to study marriage and the family are quite different from those facing, say, a research chemist. If the chemist wants to study a certain compound, that compound can be separated into its elements in a laboratory. Not so the family. The unique characteristics and the sensitive topics of concern in this area make research especially problematic.

Barriers in Family Study

A major challenge social scientists face is the need to be objective. All of us are involved with issues relating to marriage and the family. Dating, sex, marital conflict, children, divorce—these are universal concerns in American life. Social scientists, like other people, have families and opinions about their own families and the families of others. What makes these men and women different is that they have an obligation when acting as professionals to put aside their personal values and biases. They must attempt to observe the family with as much objectivity as possible, although their ability to be objective usually does not match that of the chemist performing an experiment.

Another obstacle to conducting research on marriage and the family is the participants in the research. Sociologists obviously do not work with elements, compounds, or animals in a laboratory; they work with people. Many of the topics they wish to study are highly sensitive. Some—such as incest, sexual relationships, and family violence—are the subject of societal taboos or inhibitions which prevent people from talking candidly with researchers. Also, many people feel that what happens within the family should remain private. Participants often are those who don't mind sharing personal information and thus are not always representative of society at large. An additional problem is that participants may want to make a favorable impression on the researcher; consequently, they sometimes will say what they think the researcher wants to hear.

Occasionally family research becomes the subject of public debate. A good example is the controversy several years ago over a grant given by the National Science Foundation for research into the question of why people fall in love. Senator William Proxmire called the $83,000 grant "the biggest boondoggle of the year," and added, "I don't want the answer." Proxmire, evidently, cherished the notion of romantic love and its mysteries. However, the recipient of the grant, psychologist Elaine Walster, pointed out, it "is the illusion of romantic love among the young that leads to broken marriages . . . and broken families, which in turn contribute to the disorientation, instability, disunity and even violence of American life." Viewed from this perspective, it would seem that the reasons people fall in love are well worth investigating. But it is not always easy to convince those unfamiliar with the purpose of particular research that it is worth the necessary investment of time and money.

The Sociologist's Tools

The methods used to overcome some of the problems mentioned above include those introduced by Le Play a century ago: direct, systematic observation of subjects in the field and survey research. Observation is the oldest and most natural method of studying behavior. We all watch what is going on around us, observe how people behave, and draw conclusions from our observations. Systematic observations of behavior in context can sometimes help us to see and understand patterns of behavior and interaction. For example, much useful evidence on how parents interact with their newborn children has been gathered through observation. But, in order to investigate attitudes, beliefs, and behaviors systematically and in more detail, it is necessary to use more reliable indicators than observation, no matter how systematic. Thus, survey research has become a major tool of sociologists.

Survey research involves collecting data by asking people questions about their beliefs, attitudes, and behaviors. It is done by having subjects complete questionnaires or by going door-to-door, telephoning, or using face-to-face or other interview techniques. The Gallup, Yankelovich, and Roper polls, for example, have assessed how people feel about a wide variety of family-related issues, such as abortion, the changing role of women, and whether or not boys

"How would you like me to answer that question? As a member of my ethnic group, educational class, income group, or religious category?"

Drawing by D. Fradon; © 1969 The New Yorker Magazine, Inc.

should be raised differently from girls. Surveys are usually intended to assess the opinions of a particular **population,** or group, of people, whether of a whole country, a region, or a much smaller group. For that reason, the **sample** of the population chosen to participate in the survey ideally should be large enough to be representative of the population at large. The sample group should include the same percentage of men and women, young and old, rich and poor, and so on as the total population. However, because of the sensitive nature of many issues related to marriage and the family, researchers in this area of study often have difficulty collecting truly representative samples. Thus, marriage and family research is often characterized by smaller and less heterogeneous samples. We have attempted to characterize the nature of the samples studied throughout the text as we discuss research findings, and the reader should keep such limitations in mind.

The other difficulty confronting the researcher once a sample has been selected is ensuring that the questions to be asked are framed in such a way that they will be most likely to elicit honest answers. Alfred Kinsey, in his pioneering surveys of sexual attitudes and behavior, found that he obtained more accurate information if, rather than asking, "Have you ever masturbated?" he phrased the question, "When was the last time you masturbated?" Similarly, in recent research on family violence, wives identified as victims of abuse were asked, "When was the last time your husband hit you?" rather than "Has your husband ever hit you?" Often, researchers ask several different questions on the same topic in order to minimize the chance of bias being introduced by a single, poorly worded question.

It is important to make a distinction between scientifically designed surveys and those conducted by some newspapers and popular magazines. As we pointed out, a well-designed survey takes care in selecting a sample of the population and makes every effort to obtain honest responses through well-designed questions. In magazine surveys, there are generally no controls over the sample to make sure that it is representative of even the magazine's readership, much less of the country as a whole. Nevertheless, some magazine surveys have been carefully designed, and on some topics they are the best source available. We will refer to several magazine surveys—and point out the possible limitations of their findings—at various points in the text.

Disciplines Involved in Family Study

A number of academic disciplines are involved in investigating questions related to marriage and the family. Four areas deserve particular mention: anthropology, psychology, home economics, and sociology.

Until very recently, anthropologists studied so-called primitive, usually preliterate, societies. Today, however, urban anthropologists examine industrial societies as well. Among the areas they investigate are the forms of social organization and social relationships in the society, the economic system, religion, government, language, legends, customs, and personalities of the inhabitants (Bierstedt, 1974).

If anthropologists are concerned with a broad overview of a society, psychologists are concerned primarily with individuals within society and the relationships between individuals. Recently they also have begun to look at the family as a group. Home economics, a practical science, is directed toward providing services to the family, for example, by helping families learn to make appropriate choices in the management of economic resources.

In this book, we draw on research from anthropology, psychology, and home economics at various points. However, our primary source of information is the field of sociology. Sociology focuses on the relationship between individuals and society. Sociologists who specialize in family studies attempt to investigate and explain the nature of the social order and the interpersonal dynamics of the family as a social group. Among the kinds of questions they investigate are: How do family members interact with one another? How do their relationships change? How does the family relate to other groups and the social system as a whole? How are mates selected? What are the sources of power within a marriage? It is these sociological issues that will occupy most of our attention in this book.

THEORETICAL FRAMEWORKS AND THEIR USES

As we noted earlier, a major emphasis of sociologists today is on developing theories or theoretical frameworks. In the broadest sense, a **theoretical framework** is a systematic viewpoint from which a social scientist analyzes and describes a body of information. The purpose of developing a particular viewpoint from which to approach information is to provide an orderly interpretation of events. Theoretical frameworks help researchers organize and interpret the data they gather. Theoretical frameworks also help sociologists decide what questions to raise and how to carry on their research. In addition, they help in formulating broad concepts from empirical data and analyzing how these concepts are related to one another. Most marriage and family research is guided by a theoretical framework. Consequently, in discussing research studies it is often necessary to refer to theoretical explanations that underlie the researcher's conclusions. To provide a background for better understanding the discussions in this text, this section briefly describes five of the frameworks that sociologists use. They include the structure-functional, conflict, symbolic-interaction, family development, and social exchange frameworks.

Structure-Functional Framework

The **structure-functional** framework examines how a society's structures perform a useful function for that society. Historically, structure-functionalism developed out of the natural sciences. Structure-functional theorists suggest an analogy between society and the natural world. They regard society as a system similar to a biological organism in that it is composed of parts that stand in a particular relationship to one another. One feature of an organism is that it maintains itself; that is, it survives by means of its life-sustaining systems and by adapting to its environment. Similarly, society has subsystems that are crucial for its survival. Prominent among them are the family, the economy, and religious, political, and educational institutions.

THREE CATEGORIES OF FUNCTIONS   The main question asked by structure-functional theorists is, What function does a subsystem serve for the maintenance of the organism? What contribution does it make to the whole? With regard to the family, then, the question is, What does the family provide, contribute, regulate, and so forth, for the society? How is the family related to the larger framework of society, and how does this relationship contribute to the maintenance of the society?

As we have noted, the parts that make up this organism we call society are themselves systems, and the same question of function can be asked about each part. McIntyre (1981) has identified three main categories of function of the family:

1. Functions of the family for society.
2. Functions of the family for the family itself as a subsystem.
3. Functions of the family for the individual family members.

In the first category, the family's most important tasks are to produce new members of society and to provide for their socialization into society. There is a very wide range of family behavior in different cultures, but the functions of procreation and socialization are considered to be universal.

In the second category, the family itself is the system being maintained, and anything contributing to the survival of that system may be termed functional. From a structure-functional perspective, the family's major stabilizing mechanism has been considered by some to be division of labor by sex (McIntyre, 1981). According to Talcott Parsons, Robert Bales, and other structure-functionalists, for any small group to function effectively and survive, tasks must be allocated and role differentiation must occur. Small groups tend spontaneously to develop a structure of interlocking roles; that is, leaders and followers emerge. The family has traditionally generated such a structure by the distribution of power by sex. Men have functioned as breadwinners, performing what is termed the **instrumental** role. Women's role has been to serve the needs of the family members, designated the **expressive** role. Some structure-functionalists have considered this division of labor to be the way by which families have been able to maintain stability of structure and to function effectively in society. However, recent changes in family systems have prompted some family theorists to question this.

Studies of the function of the family for the individual member have focused in large part on how relationships within the family affect the personalities of individual family members. An example of this is studies of the mother-child relationship and its possible connection with emotional disturbances of children.

The relation of structure-functional theory to the family may be summarized as follows:

1. Society has functional requirements that must be satisfied if it is to survive; these are satisfied through subsystems called social institutions. The family is a subsystem which serves, in various ways, the functional requirements of the larger society.
2. At the same time, the family is itself a system with its own functional requirements which are met by the family members.
3. The family is composed of individuals whose needs are met by the family system.

CRITICISMS OF STRUCTURE-FUNCTIONAL THEORY One of the main criticisms of the structure-functional approach is that it is deceptively simple. It is not always possible to determine what is or is not a functional necessity for the maintenance of a social system. For instance, divorce has traditionally been viewed as dysfunctional (having undesirable effects). But seen in another light, divorce may be functional because it provides for the orderly separation of family members and permits people to end potentially destructive relationships.

As noted earlier, critics have also objected to the strong emphasis structure-functional theorists have placed upon defining men's roles as instrumental and women's as expressive. The instrumental designation for men suggests that they are by nature task-oriented and rational, qualities that are suited to providing for the basic survival needs of the family. The expressive designation for women suggests that they are by nature nurturant and suited to contributing primarily to the emotional content of family life. Today most theorists do not believe that family role activity is biologically determined or that it emerges out of some "natural" order.

Perhaps the most serious difficulty with the structure-functional theory lies in the fact that it seems to place a high value on stability and equilibrium.

When equilibrium is a major value, then roles that do not disrupt social harmony are regarded favorably and changes in these roles are seen as threatening. The theory has been used at times to justify social-class differences and poverty by rationalizing that they help to maintain the social structure (McIntyre, 1981). In short, criticism of the structure-functional framework centers on its apparent acceptance of the status quo. Because it focuses on explaining existing systems, it tends to regard change in these systems as dysfunctional. Also, by emphasizing cooperation in society, it places social conflict in a negative light.

Conflict Theory

The second principal framework, **conflict theory**, is, in a sense, directly opposed to the structure-functional approach. Conflict theory regards conflict as a central and inevitable part of human relations. Rather than stressing stability and equilibrium, it stresses change; instead of focusing on eliminating conflict, it focuses on managing it (Turner, 1978). Turner (1978) lists the following sets of assumptions embedded in conflict theory:

1. While social relationships display systemic features, the relationships are rife with conflicting interests.
2. This fact reveals that social systems systematically generate conflict.
3. Conflict is therefore an inevitable and pervasive feature of social systems.
4. Such conflict tends to be manifested in the bipolar opposition of interests.
5. Conflict most frequently occurs over the distribution of scarce resources, most notably power.
6. Conflict is the major source of change in social systems. (p. 127)

CONCERN WITH SOCIAL PROBLEMS   Conflict theorists tend to look at large social units, such as whole societies, and attempt to find conflicting forces which explain the behavior of individuals and families. This focus on social forces in conflict causes them to place greater emphasis on the disruptive aspects of society and on social problems. The sense of estrangement or alienation in urban-industrial society is one such problem. Damage to the quality of life from misuse of the environment is another.

A major difference between functionalists and conflict theorists lies in their attitude toward how sociologists should respond to society's problems. Where functionalists tend to support the status quo, conflict theorists question existing norms and behaviors by asking whom the existing norms and behaviors benefit. The answers, conflict theorists believe, may suggest that society should be actively involved in assisting people with different interests to cooperate in producing a more humane social world (Young, 1976).

GENDER ROLE AS SOURCE OF CONFLICT   Functional theorists believe that the family roles assigned to men and women stem from the functional requirements of the family as a unit in society. Conflict theorists, by contrast, take the view that all social systems are characterized by a relationship between the powerful and the powerless. The dynamics of the system flow from the struggle by one party of the relationship to achieve and maintain dominance over the other party (Chambliss, 1973).

Karl Marx and Friedrich Engels were the major contributors to the early development of conflict theory. They argued that the conflict between men and women was integral to a capitalist society; in fact, they viewed it as the first and most basic example of class antagonism. Women were dominated and exploited by men because of their economic dependence on men through the institution of monogamous marriage. Gender-role differentiation, according to conflict theory, is far from being a stabilizing functional mechanism. Instead, it is the result of outright exploitation and is itself a source of conflict that is bound to produce social change. While the disadvantaged position of women is functional for some elements of the economic system, it fails to utilize the full potential of women to contribute to the society.

Conflict theorists, then, view conflict as part of the human condition and they link conflict to social change. Two people or groups who for any reason are in opposition will come to some sort of resolution of their differences. They may settle their conflict verbally; they may find ways to tolerate each other or to avoid one another completely; they may join together to create a new life based on mutual interests; they may join to meet a threat from the outside; or one may destroy the other. In any of these cases, social conflict will result in change.

CONFLICT WITHIN THE FAMILY   In the study of family relations, conflict theory has been applied to the interpersonal level to study conflict within marriages and families. Until recently, most scholars and counselors had assumed that eliminating conflict was a primary goal. Couples were told that fighting was bad for the marriage and often felt guilty if they did fight. Conflict theory, by contrast, assumes that the differing attitudes, preferences, and goals of various family members make the family inescapably a system in conflict (Sprey, 1979). The conflict theorist does not ask, "How do we eliminate family conflict?" but rather, "How do we manage the existing family differences?"

For that reason, the conflict theorist focuses on how family members make rules of daily operation which allow them to cooperate even though they disagree. The conflict theorist is also interested in the subtle tensions that exist between a person's need for privacy and the obligation to be involved intimately with loved ones. These "separate" versus "togetherness" issues are especially crucial in family relations (Sprey, 1979). It follows, then, that conflict theorists also do not assume that the family can supply all the individual's needs. Rather, there are many different sources of rewarding relationships with other people. Conflict theory suggests that the family need not and probably cannot provide the primary emotional support for everyone (Sprey, 1979).

CRITICISMS OF CONFLICT THEORY   A major challenge to the conflict prespective is the argument that in viewing social systems entirely in terms of power struggles and opportunities for change, conflict theorists work from too limited a perspective. Critics argue, for instance, that all interactions are not dominated by discord and that conflict does not always cause social change, nor is social change always caused by conflict.

Symbolic-Interaction Framework

Where functionalism considers social systems arranged in an organized and fixed structure and conflict theory considers systems in conflict, the **symbolic-interaction** framework focuses on the dynamic, ongoing process of social interaction through which people arrive at shared meanings about social behavior (Babbie, 1980). The symbolic aspect of this perspective refers to the symbols—primarily words, actions, postures, and facial expressions—which people use to communicate and arrive at agreements. Language is seen as one of the major ways in which meaningful symbols are shared in societies. Symbolic interactionists believe that by studying the interactions of two, or of a few, people they can learn something about the values and expectations of the whole society. In their view, society is made up first and foremost of people's interactions with one another. Symbolic interactionism developed out of a social psychological perspective. Because of their interest in interpersonal behavior, interactionists focus on the dynamics of social relations, particularly the socialization process and the development of personality.

In studying marriage and the family, interactionists examine the internal workings of the family. They attempt to analyze both observable behavior and the attitudes and expectations family members have regarding each other. In so doing, they consider symbols used in interpersonal communication, the meanings these symbols have for different family members, and how such shared meanings create, sustain, and change "definitions of situations" for families and individual family members.

The basic assumptions of the symbolic-interaction framework have been outlined by Manis and Meltzer (1978):

1. Distinctively human behavior and interaction are carried on through the medium of symbols and their meanings.
2. The individual becomes humanized through interaction with others.
3. Human society is most usefully conceived as consisting of people in interaction.

4. Human beings are active in shaping their own behavior.
5. Consciousness, or thinking, involves interaction with oneself.
6. Human beings construct their behavior in the course of its execution.
7. An understanding of human conduct requires study of the actors' hidden behavior.

EMPHASIS ON ROLES   One area of special interest to interactionists is that of role and status. Role theorists believe that people fill roles just as actors take parts on the stage. But just as different actors would play the same part somewhat differently, no two people—even though they may perform the

Native Americans protest infringement of their rights before Mt. Rushmore, South Dakota. In the view of conflict theorists, such conflict is integral to social life and essential for bringing about social change.

same role and have the same status—perform in precisely the same way. This is partly due to the differences in the persons with whom they interact. However, there are also different sets of expectations for each person, and these expectations alter the perception of role (Biddle and Thomas, 1966).

CRITICISM OF THE SYMBOLIC-INTERACTION FRAMEWORK   Symbolic interactionism has been criticized for its failure to deal with certain issues that some regard as central in human interaction. For example, some have argued that this approach is not applicable to the study of social organization and that it ignores how power is used in human relationships. Critics contend further that this perspective neglects the emotional aspects of human interaction and fails to consider the unconscious processes at work in human relationships. Finally, some social scientists believe that some of its concepts cannot be researched except to a very limited degree (Manis and Meltzer, 1978).

The Developmental Framework

The developmental approach to the study of the family focuses on families as they move through the different stages of the "family life cycle." The developmental framework often uses census data to describe demographic changes in the family life cycle over time, such as the departure of children from the family. It is a composite theory which has borrowed liberally from several schools of thought in sociology, psychology, and anthropology.

From the structure functionalists, developmentalists incorporated the idea that the family is a social system functioning according to its own internal laws and yet subject to the demands of the larger society of which it is a part. From the interactionists, they have incorporated the view that the family is a "unity of interacting personalities" and have also recognized the significance of social roles in the conduct of family life (Hill, 1974). The developmentalists have added to these concepts a time dimension: the explanation for a family's behavior can be attributed to its developmental stage at any point over the family life cycle (Rowe, 1981).

The major assumptions of the family-development framework, as outlined by Aldous (1978) are as follows:

1. Family behavior is the sum of past experience of family members as incorporated in the present as well as in their goals and expectations for the future.
2. Families develop and change over time in similar and consistent ways.
3. Humans not only initiate actions as they mature and interact with others but also they react to environmental pressures.
4. The family and its members must perform certain time-specific tasks set by themselves and by persons in the broader society.
5. In a social setting, the individual is the basic autonomous unit. (p. 15)

THE LIFE CYCLE OF THE FAMILY Developmentalists describe the family as being similar to the human organism in its process of birth, maturation, and death. They focus on the fact that families have **careers** or **histories,** that is, changing family roles and role clusters over time, from the time the family is formed until its dissolution (Aldous, 1978). They make a distinction between the **lifetime family** and the **lineage family.** The lifetime family history is concerned with the sequential fulfillment of family roles as family members get older. The lineage family history shows the continuities of successive generations of families (Aldous, 1978).

At each stage in a lifetime family's growth, it has certain **developmental tasks** or responsibilities to be accomplished at various stages of the life cycle. These tasks arise partly from individual needs and partly from cultural norms (Rodgers, 1973; Aldous, 1978). Developmental tasks arise at particular points in the career of a family. For example, a young couple may live with one set of parents at the beginning of their marriage, but later, especially with the birth of children, need to establish their own home. Raising the money to start their own household is a developmental task.

The family life career is the series of stages a family will experience: before children arrive; as children are born, mature, and enter school; as they leave home; as the original couple adjusts itself to the "empty-nest" stage; as they enter retirement; until both the partners die. The career is then completed (Rodgers, 1973; Aldous, 1978).

FAMILY RESEARCH BASED ON THE DEVELOPMENTAL APPROACH Using the developmental approach, researchers have tended to study a particular segment of the family life cycle, attempting to establish that present behavior is based on past stages and to predict future behavior. The early marriage period has received some attention, as has the transition from that period to the birth of the first child. In studying the parent-child relationship, developmentalists have found that family crises often arise because parent and child are simultaneously trying to accomplish their respective age-related developmental tasks. The husband-wife relationship has also been studied from the perspective of the time/stage cycle as children are born, reared, and sent on their way.

CRITICISMS OF THE DEVELOPMENTAL FRAMEWORK A major weakness of the developmental approach is that it has been worked out most thoroughly in reference to the contemporary nuclear middle-class family. It remains to be seen how broadly this framework can be applied to variant family forms which may have different life stages and developmental tasks to be accomplished.

Another related difficulty is that having children is an implied value of the developmental approach. The stages of development have been established with the ages of the children in mind, and studies of childless couples have only entered the framework as examples of the early stages of family development or as control groups. Permanently childless couples are largely excluded from study, the implication seemingly being that such couples are not families. This position will become increasingly difficult to defend as more couples in our culture choose not to have children.

A final word should be added concerning the difficulty of testing the developmental framework. Several methods have been proposed, the most promising of which involves investigating a group of families throughout their life histories. This "longitudinal" approach is, of course, costly and time-consuming. Retrospective family histories (what people recall about earlier periods of their lives) have been used as have cross-sectional analyses of families. But, in order to be complete, research findings on all segments of the family life cycle will have to be arranged in a consistent and coherent manner. This has yet to be done with any regularity (Schaie and Gribbin, 1975).

Social Exchange Theory

Social exchange theory is among the newest of the sociological frameworks to be applied to the study of marriage and the family. Its roots are found in economic theory and behavioral psychology, particularly the works of B. F. Skinner. Thibaut and Kelley (1959) systematized it as a social psychological theory. However, its development as a sociological theory is attributed largely to George Homans (1961) and Peter Blau (1964).

The basic premise of this framework can be described as follows: individuals in social interactions attempt to maximize rewards and minimize costs in order to obtain the most profitable outcomes (outcomes = rewards − costs). For example, when a man invites a woman out to dinner, he makes an investment in time and money which he hopes will be repaid by the woman in terms of companionship, pleasure, and perhaps a deepening of the relationship. If he feels that the evening has been a success, that the rewards he has gained equal or exceed the costs—that is, the outcome is profitable—he is likely to seek to continue the relationship. If not, he is likely to break it off. Likewise, if the woman feels that the evening has been more rewarding than costly, she is likely to seek a continuation and, perhaps, a deepening of the relationship.

Social exchange, then, uses the concepts of cost and reward to analyze interactions in relationships. Although costs and rewards may refer to tangible things (e.g., money, property), they also include intangibles (e.g., status, attention, worry, pressure, companionship, love, social approval). The term **resources** is used in this context to refer to those tangible or intangible possessions that individuals have which are considered rewarding by others. Resources, as rewards, "are as broad as the range of things, relationships, and feelings which are *valued* by human beings" (Libby and Carlson, 1973; italics in original).

Libby and Carlson point out that in social interactions people do not always seek immediate rewards. They may engage in behavior that they do not expect to be rewarding in the short term but that they do expect profit from in the long run. Scanzoni and Scanzoni (1976) emphasize that often exchange transactions are not conscious acts. The people involved in them may be only dimly aware or may be unaware that the exchange process is taking place.

What factors must be considered in analyzing the exchanges that occur in marital and family relationships? Simpson (1972) observes that we cannot understand why people behave as they do without knowing what they want from their interaction and what influences direct the exchanges they make. Among the influences that have been identified as important factors in exchange within marriage are the couple's "normative orientations," their "cognitive orientations," their general pattern of exchange relationships, and their perceptions of the permanence of the institution of marriage and of their marital relationship (McDonald, 1981). Let us consider each of these in more detail.

NORMATIVE ORIENTATIONS   The couple's expectations of marriage in general and of the roles of marital partners are termed their **normative orientations.** These expectations are based on their common patterns of socialization and on the similarities in the motivations and values they have acquired (Abramson et al., 1958). In American society, for example, people are socialized into the expectation that couples marry for reasons of love and that their general marital role is to be a loving spouse. They are also socialized to have particular expectations of the roles of husband and wife. These cultural expectations influence the exchanges that occur in marriage. Thus, if the husband and wife have been socialized into traditional views of marriage, with the husband being the breadwinner, or provider, and the wife being the homemaker, the nature of the exchange relationship will largely be governed by these expectations.

However, expectations of marriage differ today from those held even a generation ago. Marriage is less rigidly controlled by societal expectations; the partners negotiate far more of the rules governing their marriage than couples did in the past (Scanzoni and Polonko, 1980). The same is true regarding their expectations of their respective roles within marriage.

Each marriage has a number of different roles and subroles. Within the husband and wife roles are such subroles as provider, housekeeper, sexual partner, responsibility for child care, and others (Nye, 1976). These roles may be shared or they may be "assigned" to one spouse or the other. Such "assignments" may be ascribed by societal norms, or they may be negotiated, and renegotiated over time, by the marital partners themselves. Marital role expectations vary significantly for the husband and the wife with respect to

(1) who performs the role, (2) the availability of resources with which to negotiate, and (3) the general nature of the power-dependence relationship. These variations account for the variety of types of marital relationships evidenced in the United States today.

COGNITIVE ORIENTATION   **Cognitive orientation** refers to a person's beliefs, values, and attitudes. General socialization experiences, particularly the existing "normative orientation," largely determine an individual's cognitive orientation, as well as the personal expectations held regarding marriage and gender roles and the bargaining patterns that person has established in prior interactions. These all contribute to what Murstein, Cerreto, and MacDonald (1977) call "attitudes regarding exchange." These attitudes may differ within family roles. However, they have significant effects on how couples initiate and evaluate social transactions or exchanges and their resulting outcomes. In general, tl.ey contribute to the nature of the exchange relationship and bargaining patterns that characterize marital and family interactions.

EXCHANGE RELATIONSHIP   The **exchange relationship** is defined as the general patterning of social transactions involving the availability and/or exchange of valued resources between spouses, the costs and rewards associated with these transactions, and the expectations that result in each partner's appraisal of the benefits and costs of the relationship. The exchange relationship is dynamic and ongoing in nature. Exchange relationships often change when resources become redistributed. For instance, if the wife goes to work or returns to college in anticipation of a career, the partners may have to bargain in renegotiating their exchange relationship. As the wife begins sharing, or preparing to share, the provider role, she may want the husband to begin sharing the housekeeper and/or child-care roles.

The exchange theorists have been interested in learning the degree to which exchange behavior between husband and wife is cooperative and not competitive. Cooperative relationships are those in which the partners work together to increase their joint profits, whereas competitive relationships are those in which each spouse is trying to maximize his or her individual profits. When a couple engages in cooperative behavior, they are working toward what Scanzoni (1976) calls "maximum joint profit." According to Nye (1976), much of the activity of husbands and wives contributes to the needs of both at the same time, and this is one of the main attractions of marriage. Cooperative exchange relationships tend to be characterized by mutual trust and commitment to the partner, whereas competitive relationships often involve mistrust, a lack of commitment to the relationship, and an overriding concern with individual gain.

MARITAL PERMANENCE   In our society, marriage is generally regarded as a long-term, if not always life-long, relationship. As a result, bargaining in marriage with a particular partner is directly related to time. First, it is related to past experiences with that partner; and second, it is related to the individual's anticipated future with that partner. For that reason, the expectation of marital permanence plays a large role in governing the type of exchange relationship which exists in a marriage, particularly cooperative arrangements, and therefore the very nature of the marriage itself.

APPLICATIONS OF SOCIAL EXCHANGE THEORY   The basic ideas of social exchange theory have been used to explain and predict a wide range of social behavior. In recent years, a number of researchers (Murstein, Cerreto, and MacDonald, 1977; Burns, 1973; Scanzoni, 1979; Scanzoni and Polonko, 1980) have applied the concepts of social exchange to marriage and family relationships. The theory has offered useful explanations of how couples come together—how relationships form—and of how people go about selecting a mate. Exchange theorists believe their ideas have application to many other aspects of marriage as well. For example, in explaining marital breakups, exchange theory views divorce as resulting from "a breakdown in the exchange process and an unjust distribution of rewards" (Scanzoni and Scanzoni, 1976, p. 11). If one spouse feels that he or she is putting much more into the marriage than the other and that the costs in terms of bad feelings, anxiety, and other negative factors far exceed the rewards, that partner may decide to terminate the marriage (Scanzoni and Scanzoni, 1976). To date, social exchange theory has had less influence on studies of parent-child relationships and the operation of exchange networks in extended families.

CRITICISMS OF SOCIAL EXCHANGE THEORY   The two principal criticisms leveled at social exchange theory are that (1) it assumes human beings are rational, calculating, and constantly assessing rewards and costs in social relationships; and (2) the concepts of "rewards," "costs," and "resources" are so broad and individualistic that they cannot be specified with any consistency. Consequently, it poses too simplistic a model for analyzing human interactions (Holman and Burr, 1980). The first criticism involves general assumptions regarding human nature, for which all social theories may be taken to task. In recent years, exchange theorists have been attempting to refute the second charge by focusing on the nature of the exchange relationship per se, rather than the rewards and costs experienced by individuals, while at the same time attempting to identify the resources used in exchange and the factors that are generally costly or rewarding to individuals such as physical violence and social approval.

However valid these criticisms are, social exchange, like the other frameworks we have examined, is a valuable tool for organizing thinking about marriage and the family today. We will use these frameworks at appropriate points throughout the text to explain and clarify changing trends and existing research in the marriage and family field.

SUMMARY

1. The purposes of this chapter are to explain the importance of the scientific perspective, describe how family study developed, and introduce the major theoretical frameworks that underlie many of the ideas in this text.

2. It is important that research be gathered in a systematic way because it enables us to be more sure of the accuracy of reported findings. Systematic research ideally can be duplicated, thus giving us a sounder basis for drawing conclusions and taking action based on these conclusions.

3. The scientific study of marriage and the family began in the mid-nineteenth century and was dramatically advanced by the development of statistical measurement in the early twentieth century. The focus of study has shifted with changing societal trends.

4. In studying marriage and the family, sociologists make use of direct observation and especially of survey research. Among the difficulties of survey research are obtaining a representative sample to study and making certain that the questions asked are not biased.

5. In order to understand why marital and family behavior takes the forms it does and why it is subject to experimentation and change, social scientists use theoretical frameworks. These frameworks are useful because they permit an orderly interpretation of events, enable the social scientist to decide what questions to investigate, and help in formulating broad concepts.

6. A number of frameworks have been proposed to describe and interpret marital and family structures and relationships. Five of the major approaches are structure-functional theory, conflict theory, symbolic-interaction theory, developmental theory, and social exchange theory.

REVIEW AND DISCUSSION

1. Explain briefly how marriage and the family came to be subjects of scientific study.

2. What are some of the practical problems facing social scientists who study marriage and the family?

3. Explain what is meant by survey research. How is it conducted?

4. Can you think of some areas of family life that could best be studied through direct observation?

5. Select one of the theoretical frameworks and describe the major assumptions underlying it. Do you agree with these assumptions? Why or why not?

SUGGESTED READINGS

Burr, W. R., R. Hill, F. I. Nye, and I. L. Reiss, eds. (1979). *Contemporary Theories About the Family*. Two Volumes. New York: The Free Press.

   Critical review of current theories on family and family interactions. Volume I essays cover research-based theories; Volume II integrates these with existing sociological theory.

Duvall, E. M. (1977). *Marriage and Family Development*, 5th ed. Philadelphia: J.B. Lippincott.

   A leading proponent of the family life cycle idea discusses families in the various developmental stages.

Lee, G. R. (1977). *Family Structure and Interaction: A Comparative Analysis*. Philadelphia: J.B. Lippincott.

   Assesses the contributions of various areas of research to an understanding of family structure and interaction.

Nye, I., and F. Berardo (1966). *Conceptual Frameworks for the Study of the Family*. New York: MacMillan.

   Introduces a variety of conceptual frameworks for studying the family, including the structure-functional, interactional, developmental, and others.

Stephens, W. N. (1963). *The Family in Cross-Cultural Perspective*. New York: Holt, Rinehart and Winston.

   Uses the tools of anthropology to explore the family from a cross-cultural perspective.

unit II

Developing Intimate Relationships: Coming Together

The Changing Roles of the Sexes

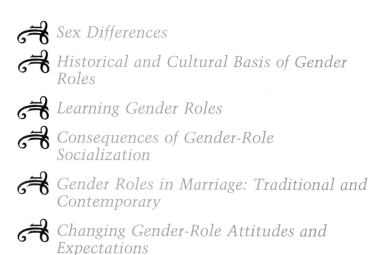
*"And I will show of male and
female that either is but the
equal of the other."*

WALT WHITMAN

Throughout much of American history, **gender roles**—the behavior patterns expected of men and women—have been quite rigidly defined. Certain types of work and ways of behaving were assumed to be natural to each sex, and individuals were expected to perform accordingly. The traditional roles assigned to women have been those of homemaker and mother. The major tasks associated with these roles have included taking care of the house and providing for the physical and emotional needs of the husband and children. These tasks are consistent with expressive behaviors that were assumed to be characteristic of the female such as nurturance, passivity, and emotional warmth. The traditional roles assigned to men have been those of provider and head of the household. The husband's tasks have included providing economic support and social position for the family. The male has been characterized as aggressive, tough, unemotional, and achievement-oriented—traits that are consistent with the instrumental tasks that society assigned to him, as well as consistent with the values most cherished by the society.

What have been the results of such role expectations in American society? How have they affected intimate relationships between men and women? Are the assumptions about masculine and feminine traits really true? It is important to consider these issues for several reasons. First, our identity is closely bound to our perceptions of ourselves as men or women. Moreover, our sense of masculine or feminine identity profoundly influences our behavior and our expectations of our partner's behavior within an intimate

63

relationship. When the role expectations of a man and a woman coincide, their relationship is more likely to run smoothly. But today traditional expectations, particularly those concerning women's roles, are changing (Scanzoni and Fox, 1980). As a result, many marriage partners, and males and females in general, are facing the difficult challenge of reevaluating long-held beliefs to accommodate their changing needs.

In order to understand the role changes taking place today and the stresses these changes are placing on marriage and family relationships, it is useful to consider male and female roles from a number of perspectives. This chapter examines biological, social, and cultural influences on gender identity and explores some consequences of gender expectations in American society. In addition, attention is given to how traditional role attitudes are changing. In Chapter 7 we will consider in more detail the changes that are occurring in role behavior in marriage.

 SEX DIFFERENCES

At birth a child is normally identified and labeled immediately as either a male or a female. This labeling has far-reaching effects on the subsequent socialization and role expectations for the child.

Sex Differentiation

As shown in Fig. 3.1, the genital system begins to develop during the fifth or sixth week of embryonic life. At this stage, the genital tissues (**gonads**) are undifferentiated and the sex of the embryo cannot be determined reliably; however, this does not mean that the embryo's sex is undecided. Whether the tissues will develop into the penis and testicles of a male or the clitoris, ovaries, and vagina of a female is determined at conception by the chromosomal composition of the fertilizing sperm. By the seventh week, male sex hormones begin circulating in the bloodstream of males but not of females. At this point, the genitalia will have differentiated enough so that a developing testis can be recognized. If no testis appears to be forming, it is likely that the gonad is developing into an ovary. By the twelfth week of life, the process of differentiation is complete.

Differences in Physical Vulnerability

Even though the sperm cell contains no more Y than X chromosomes, many more males are conceived than females. In fact, researchers estimate that for every 100 females conceived from 130 to 180 males are conceived (Stoll, 1974).

Since many more males than females are conceived, we might expect to find more men than women in an average population. However, many more male than female fetuses are spontaneously aborted, more males than females are stillborn, and premature male babies are more likely to die. In the United States, 106 male babies are born for every 100 female babies. Thus, at birth the sex ratio of males to females is almost equal (Stoll, 1974).

Fig. 3.1
Prenatal differentiation of external genitalia.

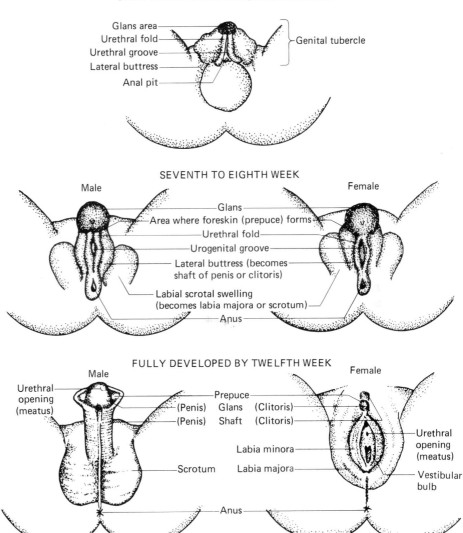

UNDIFFERENTIATED BEFORE SIXTH WEEK

Glans area
Urethral fold
Urethral groove
Lateral buttress
Anal pit
Genital tubercle

SEVENTH TO EIGHTH WEEK

Male   Female

Glans
Area where foreskin (prepuce) forms
Urethral fold
Urogenital groove
Lateral buttress (becomes shaft of penis or clitoris)
Labial scrotal swelling (becomes labia majora or scrotum)
Anus

FULLY DEVELOPED BY TWELFTH WEEK

Male   Female

Urethral opening (meatus)
Prepuce
(Penis) Glans (Clitoris)
(Penis) Shaft (Clitoris)
Labia minora
Labia majora
Scrotum
Urethral opening (meatus)
Vestibular bulb
Anus

This pattern of higher mortality for males continues throughout life. In the United States, one-third more males than females die before their first birthday (Barfield, 1976). And even though life expectancy is increasing for both sexes, between 1900 and 1970 the female death rate was consistently lower than the male death rate (Stockard and Johnson, 1980).

At birth males typically are heavier and longer than females (Bardwick, 1971); however, they have breathing, reflex, or heart problems more often than females do (Singer et al., 1968). Males are also susceptible to some genetic conditions that do not affect females, including color blindness, hemophilia (uncontrollable bleeding), and baldness (Barfield, 1976). Females can be carriers of the chromosome causing these conditions and may pass the trait along to their offspring.

Some problems may occur more often in males because males lag behind females developmentally. For example, stuttering, language disorders, and reading difficulties are more frequently found in males (Barfield, 1976).

The fact that more men than women die from accidents or injuries may be related to the tendency of men to lead more dangerous or highly active lives. However, research on men and women working at similar tasks in similar environments—such as religious orders—has found that women in these situations still outlive the men (Madigan, 1957; Barfield, 1976).

Since males smoke more than females do, it is not surprising that they have a higher death rate from lung cancer. However, as more women smoke their death rate from cancer increases. Men's higher death rate from heart attack has been popularly attributed to occupational stress. But while stress probably plays a role in the higher incidence of heart disease in men, there is evidence that until menopause women's hormonal output somehow protects them from heart ailments (Barfield 1976). Additional evidence that males are more physically at risk than females is offered by the fact that females resist infection better than males do.

Perception and Motor Skills

Male-female differences have been found in the areas of sensory perception and motor skills. Although males typically equal or surpass females in gross motor coordination, females from infancy on have better fine motor coordination than males. Females have more success in putting together toys with small, intricate parts, and their ability to manipulate embroidery needles and surgeon's instruments is better than that of males (Maccoby and Jacklin, 1974; McGuiness and Pribram, 1979).

Females exhibit more sensitivity to certain aspects of their environment than males do, and they tend to be more socially oriented. For example, baby girls stare at faces more often than baby boys do (Bardwick, 1971). From infancy females have greater sensitivity to taste. As adults women are more sensitive to odors (Maccoby and Jacklin, 1974; Barfield, 1976). Additionally, females have better night vision, process information faster, receive subtle visual and verbal messages more accurately, and are less distracted by visual objects while listening (McGuiness and Pribram, 1979).

Males, on the other hand, are more sensitive to extreme cold, less sensitive to extreme heat, and have better daylight vision. Males tend to play with objects more than females do and to use objects in novel ways. They also perform tasks that require depth perception or mechanical abilities better than females do (McGuiness and Pribram, 1979). We cannot assume, however, that the bases of such physical and motor differences are exclusively biological, since the differential socialization of males and females can strongly influence the development of differing physical characteristics and skills.

Intelligence and Achievement

Men and women usually score equally well on intelligence and standardized achievement tests. From grade school through college, however, females as a group earn higher grades than males do (Stockard and Johnson, 1980).

Yet researchers have found that males do better than females on spatial problems. For example, males are able to distinguish a figure from the background more easily than females are. They also do better on quantitative problems and problems that require restructuring. After the age of eleven, males excel in math. Eleven-year-old females, on the other hand, score higher on tests of verbal ability (Hoffman, 1972). Why is this so? According to Hoffman, girls are not encouraged to explore or master their environments; instead, they are taught to seek out help. As a result, then, of being socialized into gender-appropriate behaviors and activities, a young girl may learn to focus her attention on interactions with others—that is, on social skills. This requires that she learn to express herself well verbally. Boys, by contrast, are encouraged to explore and experiment, and therefore they approach objects and problems in their environments more directly.

By adolescence there are distinct differences in the performance of boys and girls in math and science. Some researchers suggest that girls' poorer performance in these subjects is related to their growing awareness that these are "inappropriate" areas of study for girls (Bardwick and Douvan, 1971; Davidson and Gordon, 1979).

Physical Strength and Aggression

An obvious male-female difference is physical strength. Both men and women secrete the sex hormone testosterone, but men secrete much more than women do. While men secrete 30 to 200 micrograms daily, women secrete only 5 to 20 micrograms. As a result of this hormonal influence, males tend to be larger and physically stronger. The greater physical strength of males becomes especially evident in sports. Although well-conditioned, accomplished female athletes could challenge and defeat less well-conditioned men, they are usually at a disadvantage in contesting an equally trained and accomplished man (Douglas and Miller, 1977).

Douglas and Miller indicate, however, that many women athletes, such as the swimmer Diana Nyad, are rapidly approaching and may surpass the achievements of men. Still, the majority of women are not as strong as men of equal height and weight. This is particularly true of untrained men and women, where the differences are especially great. Untrained men are generally stronger than untrained women, and there is a much wider gap between trained female athletes and untrained women than between male athletes and untrained men (Douglas and Miller, 1977). This difference is probably a consequence of the socialization process. During childhood and adolescence, males are more likely than females to be encouraged to participate in physical labor or athletics and are typically provided with a wider range of organizations and facilities in which to do so.

Aggression—combative or destructive behavior—is a sex difference that has been the focus of much study. Bardwick (1971) studied infant males and

The difference in physical strength between men and women can be partially accounted for by the encouragement society gives men to be more physically active than women. Today women athletes like Diana Nyad are gaining rapidly on their male counterparts, especially in world-class swimming and track where the gap in performance records has been closing.

females and found the males to be more aggressive. Singer and associates (1968) found that male toddlers have to be disciplined more often than female toddlers. Maccoby and Jacklin (1974) argue that males may be innately more aggressive, citing as evidence the fact that both subhuman male primates and human males typically express aggression in similar ways, that male aggression is almost universal across cultures, and that levels of aggression are responsive to the level of the sex hormone testosterone.

Nevertheless, it is important to consider the role of cultural influence, as well as biology, on aggressive behavior. Historically, in nearly all societies women have been assigned primarily care-giver roles while men have generally been expected to be providers and to defend their families and villages. Thus, females are trained to nurture while males are trained to fight. In American society, it is males and not females who are encouraged to defend themselves with physical force. This is true from childhood. Aggressive behavior in males is clearly tolerated, encouraged, and often rewarded in our society. Aggression can be seen, then, to have a strong cultural component rather than being entirely a function of biology.

While many researchers believe that males are more aggressive than females, some suggest that although girls may not show as much physical aggression as boys, they may be equally aggressive in a different way. For example, in a study of first graders, girls were more often openly hostile to newcomers than boys were. They would tell the newcomer that he or she was unwelcome, and they would ignore and move away from the new child, refusing the child's invitations to play. Boys, on the other hand, were more likely to invite the new child to play with them (Feshbach and Feshbach, 1973).

Unsupported Sex Differences

Although there are a number of differences between males and females, Maccoby and Jacklin (1974) have concluded that many commonly assumed differences do not, in fact, exist. In American society, males are assumed to be more logical and less emotional than females, and females are assumed to be more passive, submissive, and sympathetic and less adventurous than males. Another common assumption is that women are less achievement-motivated than men. According to Maccoby and Jacklin (1974), there is no research evidence to support the theory that women lack the motivation to achieve. Likewise, females have not been found to be more passive or submissive than males. They are not more sociable or suggestible. Females are not better at rote learning than males and both sexes are equally interested in the visual world around them.

The case is far from closed, however. Lamb et al. (1979) and Block (1976), among others, have challenged Maccoby and Jacklin's conclusion that there are few important differences between males and females. Much is still not known about specific sex differences on a number of important characteristics, and a great deal of research is currently being done.

Sex Irregularities

Some of the most significant findings on the influence of chromosomal sex on role behavior have emerged from studying children who are born with biological irregularities and consequently are assigned to the "wrong" sex at birth. Occasionally, for example, a child with XY chromosomes may be born with imperfectly developed external genitalia that resemble not a penis and scrotum, but a vagina. When this happens the child, who is genetically male, may be raised as a female. If the role behavior characteristically exhibited by boys and girls is biologically determined, it should not be possible to socialize such a child into the "wrong" sex role. However, researchers have found that children raised as members of the "wrong" sex have no more difficulty with their gender than children raised as members of the "appropriate" sex (Green and Money, 1969). A boy raised as a girl feels comfortable wearing girls' clothes and behaving in a feminine way. Similarly, a girl raised as a boy readily displays traits associated with masculinity. At the age of three or four the gender identity becomes firmly established and children understand that they are boys or girls. They are aware that adults expect different behaviors from boys and girls. Therefore, a four-year-old biological girl raised as a boy would strongly resist any attempts to change her socialized gender. The same would be true of a four-year-old biological boy raised as a girl (Money and Ehrhardt, 1972).

HISTORICAL AND CULTURAL BASIS OF GENDER ROLES

If gender roles are largely the result of genetic differences, the behavioral expectations of men and women should be basically the same in all cultures. However, if we discover great variation in the behavior of the sexes from one society to another, then gender roles must not be as "natural" as we sometimes suppose.

Origins of Gender Roles

The process whereby the division of tasks began to be assigned by sex has been the basis of much speculation. According to Gough (1971), role differentiation probably began with a physiological change that occurred during the process of human evolution. Since the human body has an upright stance, the human female is unable to carry her unborn child for as long a time as the less upright female primate. Thus, humans are born earlier and are less developed at birth than are primates. As a result, the human infant is helpless for a longer time and requires longer, more intensive care. Since the human mother was occupied with caring for her helpless infant, she was less able to be involved in other activities.

Biological differences between males and females further encouraged women to take the primary responsibility for child care. Not only was childbearing a function only of women, so was nursing the infants. This meant that women could not easily participate in the long hunting expeditions that were so important to human survival in early hunting and gathering societies (Adams, 1960). Women would have had to interrupt the journey every few hours to nurse their infants. Since hunting also involves periods of absolute stillness, concentration, and quickness, a woman carrying a young, vocal, hungry infant would probably be unsuccessful at providing both meat and child care.

Men, on the other hand, free from childbearing and nursing responsibilities, would have more opportunity to hunt and capture animals. They therefore became the hunters of meat while women gathered plant foods and fished in nearby waters. Since it was the men who provided the more highly valued resource, it was they who controlled its distribution. Because of this and because of their superior physical strength, they assumed the more powerful and dominant position within early human groups (Friedl, 1975). Of course, such explanations must be regarded as theoretical, since we cannot reconstruct the events of early human history.

Cross-Cultural Studies

In order to assess the relative influence of biology and environment on gender roles, researchers have studied cross-cultural differences. They have found that gender roles tend to be similar and persistent across most cultures, but not inevitable.

Examining the evidence from 110 cultures, Barry and his associates (1957) found that 82 percent of these societies socialized females to be passive and nurturant, and males to be dominant and achievement-oriented. Girls were taught to be helpful and comforting and to take care of younger siblings. Boys, on the other hand, were trained to achieve and compete and to rely on their own abilities. These findings seem to suggest that the gender roles that prevail in our own society are dominant in other societies as well. However, these same researchers found that the prevailing gender roles were not universal. In about 15 percent of the societies they studied, boys and girls were not socialized into different behaviors based on sex. In some cultures, males and females were encouraged to accept what American society would regard as nontraditional gender roles.

Even so, "male" dominance and "female" passivity are encouraged in most cultures. In our own culture, a man who is the primary or sole wage earner will most likely determine where his family will live, and his salary will determine how well they will live. To exert dominance in our society, a man does not need physical superiority, but he probably does need to be the primary wage earner. In other societies, dominance and passivity may take quite different forms.

Nowhere is the separation of roles by gender more evident than in the division of labor. An early study of preliterate societies (Murdock, 1937) found that labor was sharply divided according to sex. As was the case in early hunting and gathering societies, men in these societies were usually assigned tasks that required a great deal of physical activity or extended travel away from the home, while women were assigned tasks that required less physical strength but more sustained effort and could be performed near the home. Thus, men were hunters, miners, makers of weapons, and builders of boats. Women gathered, cooked, ground grain, and carried water; they made clothing and baskets. Although many occupations were almost exclusively male, none were exclusively female (Murdock, 1937).

The fact that in most cultures men and women are assigned different roles would appear to support the idea that behaviors usually regarded as masculine and feminine are largely biologically determined. But Margaret Mead's classic study (1935) of three tribes in New Guinea casts doubt on this assumption. Mead studied the behavior of males and females in these societies and made some startling discoveries. In none of these tribes were the males dominant and the females passive. For example, by Western standards, the Arapesh socialized both sexes into the feminine role. Both males and females were passive, gentle, unaggressive, and nurturant toward children. Aggressiveness in any form was strongly discouraged. By contrast, in the Mundugumor tribe, both men and women were extremely aggressive, suspicious, and violent. Women had little maternal orientation; they disliked pregnancy and nursing and were particularly hostile to their daughters. In our society, we would describe the behavior of both male and female members of the Mundugumor tribe as being markedly masculine in its characteristics. The Tchambuli tribe, on the other hand, did encourage different roles for men and women, but the roles were reversed from what we considered traditional. Males were the submissive partners. They produced beautiful carvings and paintings, spent much time talking among themselves, and took care of the children. Females, by contrast, were energetic and domineering. They wore no ornaments, and they managed the family's economic affairs. Mead concluded from her observations that male and female behavior is not determined by biological sex, but is a result of social training and societal expectations, which differ for males and females. This remains the dominant view among social scientists today.

LEARNING GENDER ROLES

As we have seen, culture plays an important role in shaping male and female behavior. Through various agencies, including parents, teachers, peers, toys, books, and others, children learn gender-role conduct deemed appropriate. The process of role socialization is sometimes complicated and subtle, and sometimes straightforward. It begins at birth and continues during the child's school years and even into adulthood.

Parents as Socializers

From the time a child is born, parents make fine distinctions in how they perceive and treat the newborn based on the infant's sex. Thus begins the stereotyping of gender identity. Rubin and his associates (1974) interviewed thirty pairs of first-time parents. Fifteen were parents of sons, and fifteen were parents of daughters. Although the male and female infants were the same length and weight and had similar reflex responses, heart rates, and muscle tone, the parents believed that there were distinct differences between boys and girls. Parents of newborn daughters described their babies as small, beautiful, delicate, and weak, whereas parents of newborn sons described their babies as firmer, stronger, more alert, and better coordinated than the females.

Similarly, Hanson (1980) studied sex stereotyping by medical personnel attending the delivery of newborn babies. Even though the male and female babies were of similar size and weight, the medical team, in speaking to the parents, described the males as being "sturdy, handsome, big, tough." The female babies, by contrast, were described as "dainty, delicate, sweet, charming."

Several researchers (Moss, 1967; Block, 1976; Lamb et al., 1979) suggest that parents respond differently to their children on the basis of sex and that such differential socialization results in different behaviors in boys and girls. These behaviors, in turn, fit into our cultural gender-role stereotypes.

Will, Self, and Datan (1976) found that mothers *believed* they responded in similar ways to both boys and girls, but that in fact they did not. When a group of twelve mothers participating in an experiment individually cared for the same six-month-old baby dressed either as a girl or a boy they did in fact treat the infant differently. When the experimenter left three toys on a table for the mother to choose from—a fish, a doll, and a train all made of a similar material—the mothers handed the train more often to the infant when it was dressed in blue pants and gave the doll to the infant when it was wearing a pink dress. Some mothers said the baby in the pink dress was "sweet," and one mother described the same baby in blue pants as having "a little boy's face."

Other researchers have found that parents play with girl children differently than they play with boy children. Parents with girls are more likely to engage in "sociable play," which involves more talking and social interaction during play. With boys, however, parents engage more often in "active play"; that is, in rougher, more physical play (Tauber, 1979). This same researcher suggests that fathers are more concerned than mothers that males behave like boys and females behave like girls. Although both parents discouraged girls from too much running and jumping, fathers more strongly reprimanded active girls. According to a Yankelovich poll (1977), fathers disapproved more often and more intensely than mothers when boys played with dolls. Fathers, it seems, express more aggression, competition, and physical play with their sons and more affection and gentleness with their daughters. It is not surprising, since they encouraged more emotional, affectionate responses from girls, that ten out of twenty fathers in one study described girls as seeking kisses or as being a "bit of a flirt" (Lidz, 1976).

It would seem that many parents actively socialize their children into gender-role behavior they believe is appropriate to each sex. Behavior that may be rewarded in a boy may be discouraged in a girl and vice versa. For example, a little girl may be hugged and patted when she stays close to her mother, while a little boy may be told he should go off and play. Parents may also be more willing to help their daughter assemble a new toy. However, they may say to their son, who asks for the same assistance, "You can do it

The different socialization of boys and girls begins early in life. Girls are rewarded for pursuing passive, domestic activities, whereas boys are encouraged to be active and adventurous.

yourself." As a result, the son learns that boys are competent and aggressive, and the daughter learns that girls are more helpless and dependent. Yet if some parents teach their children certain roles and behaviors consciously and purposefully, others are probably unaware that they have different expectations of male and female children. They may simply assume that boys and girls are innately different and treat them accordingly.

Hartley (1959) observed that throughout childhood girls are allowed more flexibility in gender-role behavior than boys. In addition, boys learn the rather narrow range of behaviors they are permitted to exhibit through "negative" processes—that is, by being told what *not* to do rather than what to do. It is not until the onset of puberty that girls begin to experience pressure to modify their behavior to that considered appropriate for girls. Unfortunately, there has been little research done to reexamine Hartley's conclusions, although her work was published over twenty years ago.

It does appear that a growing number of parents are less concerned than parents of the past that their children conform to gender-specific behavior. In a national sample of over 1200 families, only 17 percent of parents agreed definitely that boys and girls should be raised in different ways, while 35 percent agreed partially, 42 percent disagreed, and 6 percent said they were uncertain (Yankelovich, 1977). But, as Scanzoni and Fox (1980) point out, many parents continue to make distinctions in how they raise their children based on sex which tend to perpetuate traditional gender expectations.

However, they further comment that children whose parents are better educated experience less exposure to sex stereotypes than children whose parents are less well educated.

GENDER IDENTITY   As a result of early socialization by parents or other primary care givers, children begin to acquire a **gender identity**—an awareness of themselves as male or female. A three-year-old boy has heard his mother and father call him a "big boy" or a "little man." He may not know exactly why he is a "little man," but he does know he is a boy. Although preschool children can identify themselves as a boy or a girl, they may not be able to label the sex of others. When asked to do so, they may use superficial criteria such as clothing, height, or length of hair. For example, when a five-year-old looking at a naked baby was asked if the baby was a boy or a girl, the child replied, "I don't know—it's hard to tell with the clothes off" (Lidz, 1976). Children, then, become aware of the existence of two sexes and learn to refer to themselves as a boy or a girl long before they understand the biological difference between males and females (Katcher, 1955).

It is not until the age of about six that a child understands that he or she will remain a male or a female for life (Kohlberg, 1969). Before that age, a boy may state that he is going to be a mommy when he grows up and a girl may fantasize about becoming a "big man." Once a child grasps the idea that people's sex will not change even if their hair grows long or is cut short, the child makes a greater effort to act as either a boy or a girl (Kohlberg, 1969). Kohlberg contends that gender identity is extremely resistant to change, a claim that has recently been contested (Kagan, 1979; Lamb, 1979).

According to Kohlberg (1969), children begin to form the concept of themselves as boys or girls by observing "boy" or "girl" behavior. For instance, a female child identifying herself as a girl joins a group of girls playing house. Similarly, a male joins a group of boys playing baseball and reinforces his developing image of himself as a boy.

Identification with the parents also contributes importantly to a child's gender identity. One theory suggests that small children of both sexes tend to identify more closely with their mothers than with their fathers because during the preschool years both boys and girls generally spend more time with their mothers. Later, as the male child spends more time with the father and other masculine models, he increasingly acquires masculine sex-role behaviors (Lynn, 1969; Maccoby and Jacklin, 1974).

Recent research with adolescents (McDonald, 1977, 1980) supports what is termed a "social power theory" of parental identification. This theory states that rather than identifying with the same-sex parent, adolescent youngsters tend to identify more with the parent they perceive as having the most power—that is, they identify with the parent they see as having the most expert knowledge and skill, the best guidance and advice, and the most influence and control over their behavior and opinions.

HIGHLIGHT 3.1

What Do You Want to Be When You Grow Up?

Preschoolers' ideas about adult occupations are already ossified stereotypes. I often tell the story of a friend who took a childrearing leave of absence from her job as a newspaper reporter. One day, when her three-year-old, Sarah, expressed interest in a TV story about a crime reporter, my friend decided to explain her own career: "Before you were born, I used to have a job like that," the mother said, building to a simple but exciting description of journalism. "I went to fires or to the police station and the stories I wrote were printed in the newspaper with my name on them."

After listening attentively, Sarah asked, "Mommy, when you had this job before I was born, did you used to be a man?"

Obviously, the child had not yet developed the concept of gender constancy; but what necessitated the magical thinking that turned her mother into a man was Sarah's inability to associate the exciting job of a newspaper reporter with the female sex.

Seventy Wisconsin children, ages three to five, had much the same problem. When asked "What do you want to be when you grow up?" the boys mentioned fourteen occupations: fireman, policeman, father/husband, older person, digger, dentist, astronaut, cowboy, truck-driver, engineer, baseball player, doctor, Superman, and the Six-Million-Dollar Man. Girls named eleven categories: mother/sister, nurse, ballerina, older person, dentist, teacher, baby-sitter, baton-twirler, iceskater, princess, and cowgirl.

Next, the children were polled on their more realistic expectations: "What do you think you really will be?" they were asked. The girls altered their choices toward even more traditional roles—changing from ballerina, nurse, and dentist, to mother—while the boys changed to more active, adventurous futures—for instance, from husband to fireman.

Taking into account the narrow range of occupations familiar to nursery-school children, it still seems pitiful to have had job options closed to you before you are three or four years old.

Pittsburgh children of the same ages were asked "What do you want to be when you grow up?" followed by "If you were a boy (girl), what would you be when you grow up?" For the first question, most chose stereotyped careers: policeman, sports star, cowboy, and one "aspiring spy" for the boys; nursing and the like for the girls. To the second—what they would be if they were the "opposite" sex—the children answered with stereotyped other-sex occupations as well. But their reactions to that second question were striking. The boys were shocked at the very idea of being a girl. Most had never thought of it before, some refused to think about it, and one "put his hands to his head and sighed. 'Oh if I were a girl I'd have to grow up to be nothing.' "

The girls, on the other hand, obviously had thought about the question a great deal. Most had an answer ready. Several girls mentioned that this other-sex occupational ambition was their true ambition, but one that could not be realized because of their sex. More poignantly, the gender barrier had become so formidable that it even blocked out fantasies and dreams. Thus, one blond moppet confided that what she really wanted to do when she grew up was to fly like a bird. "But I'll never do it," she sighed, "because I'm not a boy."

Source: From *Growing Up Free* by Letty Cottin Pogrebin. Copyright © 1980. Used with permission of McGraw-Hill Book Company.

Teachers and Schools as Socializers

Through parents, children first learn what behaviors are expected of males and what behaviors are expected of females. By the time children are old enough to begin school, they identify with either boys or girls. From nursery school on, teachers and school staff further reinforce these stereotypes.

In order to explore how strongly boys and girls in nursery school adhere to their "appropriate" male and female roles, researchers conducted an experiment with "girl" and "boy" toys. An experimenter, who brought the toys as gifts, instructed teachers to encourage children to pick toys intended for the other sex. The teachers, who were well-liked by all the children, tried to persuade boys to accept "girl" toys and vice versa. The girls showed less resistance to accepting "boy" toys. They calmly gave practical reasons for not taking the toys. For example, they explained that their brothers might take the toy or that "it wouldn't be fun." Boys, on the other hand, were quite resistant to picking a girl's toy. They appeared anxious, argued with the experimenter, or tried to discredit the teacher by suggesting that she was ill or overworked. One boy who called himself "Charlie the Cowboy" explained to the experimenter that the teacher must have temporarily lost her memory— why else would she offer him a necklace? Thus, in line with the earlier discussion of Hartley's (1959) thesis, it appears that young boys feel more pressured than young girls do to act in gender-appropriate ways. They appear more afraid of being labeled a "sissy" than girls do of being labeled a "tomboy" (Ross and Ross, 1972).

In what ways do teachers reinforce gender-related behaviors? One study found that nursery-school teachers reward boys for aggression and girls for dependency. Teachers also tended to help nursery-school girls perform particular tasks while giving boys the directions to carry out the assignment on their own, thus reinforcing the perception of boys as capable and independent and of girls as helpless and uncertain (Serbin and O'Leary, 1975).

Another study showed that, in general, nursery-school teachers paid more attention to boys than to girls, giving them more praise, instruction, and affectionate hugging (Sebin et al., 1973). Similarly, although most elementary-school teachers are women in a position of authority, they apparently continue to assume that females are the weaker sex. They frequently encourage boys to dominate girls in the classroom, assuming males to be more powerful than females (Baumrind, 1972).

Even so, elementary-school boys are punished more often, receive a higher proportion of low grades than their numbers on intelligence scores warrant, are less likely to be promoted than girls are, and receive more disapproval from female teachers. Male elementary-school teachers, on the other hand, are more approving of boys and give them more leadership positions (Lee and Wolinsky, 1973). Lee and Wolinsky suggest that since male primary-grade teachers are in the minority, boys are at a disadvantage in female-dominated elementary

BLOOM COUNTY   by Berke Breathed

Reprinted by permission.

schools in that female teachers tend to favor obedience and passivity—qualities that girls are more often socialized to exhibit.

In junior high school and high school, divergent roles for males and females are further strengthened. Some researchers have identified a declining interest among adolescent girls in traditionally male-dominated areas of study and a corresponding increase in their interest in areas that foster social skills (Bardwick and Douvan, 1971; Davidson and Gordon, 1979). The explanation for this seems to be the perception that is encouraged during adolescence that girls should develop skills that contribute to their preparation for marriage. Adolescent girls may feel that if they pursue male-dominated subjects, young men will consider them unsuitable as potential mates (Scanzoni and Fox, 1980). This may help to explain why girls tend to choose different elective courses than boys—home economics, for example, as opposed to carpentry or auto mechanics.

It seems likely, though, that many girls today are less concerned about appearing to have "unfeminine" interests than were girls in the past. In homes where higher education and pursuit of individual goals are valued, girls entering college may even be encouraged to pursue traditionally male-dominated fields of study, since these are largely the areas that promise success, recognition, and advancement.

Other Agents of Socialization

In addition to parents and teachers, there are many other sources from which children learn appropriate gender roles. Among the most powerful socializing agents are toys, books, and television.

TOYS   As with other means of communication, toys communicate to children a particular view of the world. Dolls, games, and other toys are designed to encourage behaviors in children that reflect a particular culture's attitudes and preferences, including its view of male and female roles.

One researcher who surveyed toys available to children found "an astonishing display of sexist characteristics in the most stereotyped forms" (Mitchell, 1973). Toys for girls are designed primarily to encourage them to learn domestic activities. Baby dolls, for example, encourage girls to model the mother role. Other dolls—such as girlfriend/boyfriend dolls or families of dolls—are meant to orient girls toward human interactions. Although some dolls are made for boys, their appearance (usually muscular) tends to reflect the stereotype of males as tough and aggressive.

Boys' toys generally include a great variety of noisy, power-driven vehicles, as well as guns and space gadgetry. Many boys' toys are designed to be taken apart and put back together by the child, a characteristic that is not true of girls' toys. Mitchell believes that such toys encourage boys to manipulate, construct, and destroy and that they appeal to power, whereas girls' toys appeal to passivity.

As noted earlier, researchers have found that parents give more positive reinforcement to boys who play with "boy" toys and to girls who play with "girl" toys. Boys receive more negative responses when they take up a "female-type" activity then girls do when they take up a "male-type" pastime (Fagot and Patterson, 1969). If parents want to discourage a girl from playing with a war game, they are likely to tell her that it is not a toy she would like. On the

Even though more women are moving onto the corporate ladder, there is still a problem of moving them up. Those who rise rapidly may find themselves accused of using their sexual charms to get where they are. Executive Mary Cunningham resigned from the Bendix Corp. in the face of rumors of a romantic liaison with her boss.

other hand, if parents discover their son playing with a doll, they are likely to be more strongly disapproving. Girls face more disapproval if they take their toys apart, while boys commonly engage in this behavior without parental comment (Mitchell, 1973).

Children themselves learn quickly to identify and prefer "appropriate" sex-related toys (Nadelman, 1974; O'Leary, 1977). According to Fein and her associates (1975), children know by the age of two which toys are for girls and which are for boys. Twenty-month-old girls picked bracelets, dolls, and irons more often, while twenty-month-old boys more often picked hammers, trucks, and guns.

BOOKS   In recent years, a number of studies have attempted to determine what kinds of images of male and female roles are presented in childen's books. These studies suggest that children's books tend to reinforce and encourage acceptance of gender-role stereotypes.

When U'Ren (1971) assessed school textbooks, she found that they include far more pictures of males than of females. Only 15 percent of the pictures that included people were of women. Other studies have demonstrated that males are more often the focus of the reader's attention, while females more often play only small, insignificant roles. In an analysis of prize-winning preschool picture books, Weitzman and her colleagues (1972) found that boys were consistently presented as active and adventurous, while girls were presented as helpless, passive, or unproductive. Female roles in these stories included watching or encouraging males in their actions or helping mother in the kitchen. In these books, female characters were outnumbered by male characters eleven to one. In some books, there were no women or girls at all, and animals were seldom presented as female.

In another study of one hundred children's books often found in libraries, researchers found that the same theme emerged. The majority of titles surveyed featured males. Girls were twice as likely as boys to be depicted in subordinate roles and in the home (Stewig and Knipfel, 1975). School books in use today often present this same stereotyped picture of the American family (Stockard and Johnson, 1980). Typically, the husband goes to work; the wife stays home. Girls help their mothers with household chores; boys go off on adventures. Usually this "average" family is portrayed as having two children, an older brother and a younger sister.

TELEVISION   Perhaps more than any other medium, television has a particularly strong effect on children's ideas of the way men and women look and behave. Since 95 percent of the homes in America contain at least one television set, it is the rare child who has not been exposed to television. Between the ages of three and sixteen, the average girl or boy spends more time in front of the television than in school (Gerber and Gross, 1976).

An examination of descriptions of programs in the weekly magazine *TV Guide* offers some clues about how males and females are portrayed. An advertisement for the series "Flo" stated: "Miriam wins a Yellow Rose lottery to accompany Flo on a free trip to Disney World—provided she can wrench herself away from her husband, kids, and chores." In a series entitled "Ladies Man": "Alan's male ego takes a beating when he's mugged by a woman—a detail he's too humiliated to admit to anyone" (*TV Guide*, December 8, 1980). Such programs tend to reinforce stereotypes about males and females. The message in this episode of "Flo," for example, seems to be that when women are given an opportunity to do something entirely for themselves, they experience conflict over "abandoning" their primary responsibilities—those of homemaker and mother.

Research on the portrayal of men and women on television supports this observation. Tedesco (1974) found that women are usually portrayed in one of three ways—in a sexual context, a romantic context, or in family roles. Women portrayed in a sexual context are often shown wearing tight sweaters, bikini bathing suits, or low-cut dresses or acting in a seductive manner. Men, by contrast, are usually depicted as powerful, intelligent, and rational, as illustrated by many detective programs which show resourceful men solving complicated mysteries. Females are pictured as more sociable, warm, attractive, and youthful than males (Tedesco, 1974). Males are portrayed as multi-dimensional, combining both good and evil qualities, whereas females are typically portrayed only as good. Television females are inclined to follow the advice and wishes of males, but male characters seldom defer to the wishes of others (Sternglanz and Serbin, 1974).

TELEVISION AS AN AGENT OF CHANGE   We have seen that television reinforces male and female stereotypes. But could television also be used to change people's attitudes about "appropriate" and "inappropriate" gender-role behavior? As noted earlier, studies have shown that boys are more committed to the masculine stereotype. Because of this, Davidson and her associates (1979) concluded that girls might be more likely to be influenced by nontraditional portrayals of women on television. These researchers conducted an experiment with five- and six-year-old girls to determine if girls' views of female roles could be altered by television portrayals of girls in traditional, neutral, or nontraditional roles. The first group of girls was shown cartoons in which girls, who were slightly older than they were, built a clubhouse and competed successfully in sports with males. A second group saw girls portrayed in traditional ways, behaving more submissively and passively. A third group viewed "neutral" programs where boys and girls were depicted as neither strongly masculine nor strongly feminine. After the programs each group of girls was asked to match pictures to descriptions which included a gender-role related adjective. The girls in the latter two groups picked more sex-stereotyped adjectives to describe females than did the girls in the first group. Thus, it appears that the group of girls in Davidson et al.'s research, when shown females in nontraditional roles, was able to modify their perceptions about female behavior in the direction of less sex stereotyping.

CONSEQUENCES OF GENDER-ROLE SOCIALIZATION

Socialization of individuals into gender roles greatly influences the subsequent attitudes and behavior of males and females. For example, women's self-concepts appear to be different from men's. In addition, socialization into traditionally defined masculine and feminine roles affects men's and women's perceptions of their roles in marriage.

Self-Concept

How does socialization affect our self-concept? Is either sex more self-confident than the other? According to Maccoby and Jacklin (1974), men and women hold equally positive concepts of themselves. Even so, females are more likely to be envious of males. Kindergarten girls were more likely than boys to say that they wanted to be the other sex (Ollison, 1977). Similarly, as adults only between 2.5 and 4 percent of men were able to remember wanting to be females, whereas between 20 and 31 percent of women remembered wanting to be males (Sherman, 1971).

The explanation for this difference seems to be related to the fact that throughout history men have been the more highly regarded sex. They have more often been the explorers and adventurers, the inventors, and the heads of government. Although women today may have more opportunities for freedom and fulfillment than in the past, males still enjoy the more advantageous position.

Research suggests that as adults, men and women value different personal qualities and have different feelings about themselves. In one study conducted during the late 1950s, men and women were asked to select from a list of adjectives those that they believed best described themselves. The results showed that in comparison to the male subjects, the female subjects reported greater empathy, warmth, and unselfishness; greater social morality and honesty; greater personal satisfaction; and more democratic and domestic feelings. On the negative side, they expressed greater personal inadequacy, greater personal fear and weakness, less personal maturity, and less personal conviction. Male subjects, by contrast, reported feeling greater competence, intelligence, and imagination; greater ego-centrism; and greater control over the environment (Bennett and Cohen, 1959). It seems likely that the different concepts the men and women in this study had about themselves were related to their different socialization as well as the different roles males and females tend to assume as adults.

Another study conducted around the same time found that not only college men, but also college women believed that males were superior in more ways than females (McKee and Sheriffs, 1956). Over a decade later, research with female college students revealed that these students held more positive attitudes toward male academics than toward female academics. In this study, two groups of women were given identical scholarly articles. One group was told the article was written by "Joan T. McKay," and the other group was told the author was "John T. McKay." The students were asked to judge the article on its value, persuasiveness, writing style, and general competence. The female students rated the article by "John" much higher than the article by "Joan" (Goldberg, 1968). Thus, in 1968 female college students apparently still accepted the stereotyped notion that males are superior intellectually. It seems likely, however, that this attitude is changing as a result of the women's movement and the growing numbers of women who have proved their competence in the academic world.

Educational Consequences

Although more and more women are attending college and achieving impressive records, men still receive more diplomas and more academic advantages than women. In 1977 women received 44 percent of the bachelor's degrees, 47 percent of the master's degrees, and 24 percent of the doctoral degrees issued. Men and women generally enroll in different graduate programs. Women still concentrate in traditionally female-dominated disciplines such as education, the arts, and the humanities, whereas men dominate such fields as medicine, engineering, and law (U.S. Bureau of the Census, 1979). Only in the last decade have women been accepted to elite, formerly all-male universities such as Yale, Harvard, and Princeton. In the beginning, the newcomers encountered considerable antagonism from some male faculty members opposed to the admission of women. Some of these professors were openly hostile, making the women targets of sarcasm; others ignored them entirely when they attended classes (Clinton, 1980). Although there has been some improvement in the treatment of undergraduate women at the newly converted coeducational universities, women who attempt to advance in the academic world often encounter resistance. Since the early 1970s, very few women have been hired for administrative or faculty positions in colleges and universities (American Association of University Women, 1978). Examining colleges and universities across the country, studies show that only one-fourth of full-time college faculty are women, and that most of these positions are in the lower professional categories, such as lecturer, instructor, or assistant professor.

Even when a woman is able to secure a faculty position, she is more likely than a man to lose it. According to the American Association of University Professors (Clinton, 1980), 70 percent of all male professors are tenured (they cannot be dismissed without just cause), whereas less than half of women professors are granted tenure. Perhaps this can be explained partly by length of service. Many women have not been faculty members long enough to receive tenure. Nevertheless many women academics do not believe this is the only reason, and some are turning to legal action through sex-discrimination suits to improve their standing in the academic world.

Economic Consequences

The differential socialization of men and women has important implications in the world of work. Women may have the same education and work experience as men, but women at all levels of employment earn less than men. For some time, female workers have earned only 59 percent of what male workers earn. Women with a college degree fare little better. The average salary for male college graduates in 1977 was $17,891 as compared to $10,861 for female college graduates (U.S. Bureau of Labor Statistics, 1979).

Not only are men better paid than women, they hold many more high-level positions in the business world. According to *Fortune* magazine, in 1978, fewer than 1 percent of the officers and directors of over two thousand major companies were women. Why? Apparently, employers still believe women are not as competent or as aggressive as men. An article in a major news magazine reveals that male supervisors rarely trust women with difficult assignments. In steel and construction firms, women executives are particularly rare. A recruiter explains women's absence from these positions: "The feeling is that a bunch of hard noses won't take orders from a woman" (*U.S. News and World Report*, December 8, 1980). It appears, then, that differences in salaries and advancements for men and women are based largely on deeply held sex stereotypes.

Another factor that may be related to women's low representation in high-status, traditionally male-dominated positions is one which has been labeled the "fear-of-success" motive (Horner, 1972). According to this explanation, many females deliberately underachieve; that is, they intentionally do not perform as well as they could in occupational activities because they are afraid that success will have negative social consequences. For example, they believe that they may be perceived by males as too assertive or independent to be attractive as marriage partners. Some researchers (Komorovsky, 1976; Scales, 1977) suggest that such fears may, in fact, be justified. Women may suffer negative social repercussions from success in areas not traditionally considered female territory.

GENDER ROLES IN MARRIAGE: TRADITIONAL AND CONTEMPORARY

Thus far we have considered how male and female socialization differentially affects individuals. But what impact does socialization have on couples in intimate relationships? How does a man's and a woman's sense of role identity influence the expectations they bring to a marriage?

Males and females have traditionally been assigned mutually exclusive roles in marriage and family relationships, with husbands performing the "instrumental" role of breadwinner and wives performing the "expressive" role of homemaker (Parsons and Bales, 1955). In many contemporary marriages, however, there is an increasing emphasis on individual preferences or abilities instead of traditional gender-related roles. As we shall explore further in Chapter 7, husbands and wives are more frequently negotiating or bargaining with each other to decide who performs what roles in the family rather than simply "blindly" following traditionally defined family roles based on sex.

The Male as Breadwinner

As we have noted, men are encouraged from an early age to be achievement-oriented. They are expected to attain success in the world of work particularly. Their sense of worth as a man has traditionally been closely tied to their ability to succeed at a job, as measured by their earning power. In marriage, they have typically looked upon their role as being that of provider. According to Lopata (1971), this expectation is shared by wives, who believe it is the duty of their husbands to provide money for the family's needs. A more recent survey confirms that, generally, men and women have the same view of the husband's role. Seventy-four percent of married women in one survey strongly or partially agreed that men should be the family breadwinners (Yankelovich et al., 1977).

Concentration on achievement, while strongly encouraged in American society, may not be all that beneficial to men, however. Indeed, it has been suggested that the emphasis on success may hamper a man's ability to develop other important aspects of his personality and may negatively affect his interpersonal relationships. The Grant Study of Adult Development (Vaillant and McArthur, 1972) supports this view. This study proposed to examine the psychological health of men over several decades. Two hundred sixty-eight Harvard graduates from the classes of 1942 and 1944 were selected for their high level of independence, psychological health, and career success. Almost

CASE STUDY   *Money and Masculinity*

A successful doctor, [Marty B.], divided his time between research, which he found enjoyable but not very rewarding financially, and the practice of internal medicine, which was more lucrative but not so enjoyable. Marty felt it a strain to deal with many diverse people; he was more comfortable with animal research, which also fulfilled his creative talents and led to his writing a number of solid scientific papers. So far, so good. But then Marty's wife, Janet, an actress who had only middling success, became an actors' agent and clicked right away.

Soon, Janet began to earn more money than Marty. At first he joked about it with her and even with close friends, but, as it turned out later, the joking was uneasy and laden with anxiety. Marty decided to increase his patient practice at the expense of his research. He forced himself to make more money—when he actually needed less, thanks to Janet's high income.

They began quarreling about many small things—arguments without resolutions because they had nothing to do with the real issue: that her new money-making powers were a threat to his masculinity.

Marty and Janet came to see me because they were considering separating after eight years of a happy marriage. After a number of sessions, it became clear that Marty felt that Janet's success meant she didn't need him any more; that he had been diminished as "the man of the house." This was not easy for Marty to admit; he had always claimed he was happy to see Janet doing what she wanted to professionally. But this was the first time he had to face her actually succeeding at it. Marty agreed, with some ambivalence, to go into psychoanalytic therapy. As therapy evolved, his problem with "masculinity" emerged even more clearly. He had never felt comfortable competing with men; this was a contributing factor to his going into animal research. He really received very little gratification from his medical practice, but he needed to make a lot of money to feel competent as a man. He resented Janet's success but since he was not aware that his manhood was threatened, he found "other" things to complain and argue about. After three years of therapy and six months of a trial separation, Marty worked through his problems. Their marriage and Janet's success both survived.

Source: Robert Gould, M.D., © Ms. Magazine Corp., 1973. Excerpt reprinted with permission.

FOR CLASS DISCUSSION

1. In this case study Marty began to experience difficulties when Janet began to succeed financially. Do you think this is a common problem for men whose wives become successful? Can you suggest ways—short of the wife's quitting her job—to enable both partners to succeed in careers without harming their marital relationship?

2. What evidence have you seen in your own experience that suggests that American men are socialized to equate earning power and masculinity? Do you believe this is a problem, or does the problem lie more in changing longstanding patterns of masculine behavior?

all had served in World War II, and the great majority were lawyers, doctors, business executives, or college professors. However, their success in the world of work seemed to inhibit their success in marriage and childrearing. They reported that they had little genuine communication with their wives and children, and they were found to be unskilled at self-reflection. Referring to the more gentle, tender side of men's natures, one man complained that "(that) side never got a chance to grow. All we heard was drive, success, work."

The Female as Homemaker

Just as men have traditionally been socialized to be breadwinners, women have been socialized to be homemakers and mothers. How do women feel about the role they are expected to take?

A 1972 Harris poll asked a national sample of American women how often they felt that "having a loving husband who is able to take care of me is much more important to me than making it on my own." Half of the respondents, including those under the age of thirty, said they "frequently" felt that way. When asked how often they felt that raising children is as challenging as holding a top career position, over 60 percent of all respondents answered "frequently" (Blake, 1974). Gallup surveys conducted in 1976 and 1980 on the ideal life-style preferred by American women found that nearly three-quarters of the respondents said they would choose a marriage with children as the most interesting and satisfying life for themselves. There was also evidence that many women would like to combine *part-time* rather than full-time work with marriage and parenthood. In effect, they would prefer a work situation that did not interfere with what they perceive as their primary role.

Other research, however, suggests that there are many women who are not necessarily satisfied with the role of homemaker. Three-quarters of the women in a sample of forty housewives reported being bored with their lives (Oakley, 1974). Women who are solely occupied with preparing meals, washing clothes, grocery shopping, and caring for children may experience little variation in their routines and little adult stimulation. Also, according to Oakley, if we look closely at the homemaker's day, we notice that she is working an average of seventy-seven hours per week. As a result, some homemakers do appear to fit the stereotype of the housewife who has become passive, unimaginative, bored, and exhausted. Such women feel remote from their husband's work problems and their children's activities outside the home (Lopata, 1971; Bernard, 1972). They may be less able to interact with people who have different life-styles, such as single working friends. Their talk, like their lives, tends to revolve around home and child care.

Other homemakers, according to Lopata, interpret their role in a more creative way. For instance, although these women generally supervise household duties themselves, they usually delegate chores to family members. These women develop better interpersonal relations with their husbands and pursue both individual interests and interests they share with their husbands. Although not all homemakers have the same opportunities, a woman who is able to effectively manage a household, develop a fulfilling personal relationship with her husband, and pursue her own interests generally feels an increased sense of competence and satisfaction.

 CHANGING GENDER-ROLE
ATTITUDES AND EXPECTATIONS

It is becoming increasingly evident that in the United States today attitudes toward gender roles are changing, both in and out of marriage. These changes seem to be occurring more rapidly for women than for men. Sexton (1979), for example, reports that men continue to be more traditional than women in their gender-role expectations.

A long-term study conducted by the University of Michigan's Survey Research Center and Population Studies Center (1980) seems to support this view. The study found significant changes over the past two decades in the attitudes of adult American women regarding outside employment, child-bearing, and family roles. The subjects in the study were a random sample of 969 white Detroit-area women who had just married or just given birth to a first, second, or fourth child. These women were interviewed by telephone in 1962, 1963, 1966, 1977, and 1980. As of 1980, 90 percent of the original participants were still with the study.

Among the questions they were asked was whether they agreed or disagreed with the statement: "Most of the important decisions in the life of the family should be made by the man of the house." In 1962, 66 percent of the women agreed with this statement; in 1977, only 33 percent agreed with it; and in 1980, only 23 percent agreed with it. A second question asked the women whether they agreed or disagreed with the statement: "It's perfectly all right for women to be very active in clubs, politics, and other outside activities before the children are grown up." In 1962, only 44 percent of the mothers agreed; in 1977, 60 percent agreed; and in 1980, 64 percent agreed. The study also found that some of the women who had originally planned to remain at home ended up working outside the home after all. In 1962, 54 percent of the women did not plan to work at all, but in 1980, 64 percent were working, 30 percent of them full-time.

Another finding of the study was that the original group of women tended to be less traditional than men in regard to gender-role issues and not substantially different in their thinking from their daughters (most of whom were about eighteen years old). A likely explanation for the change in attitudes expressed by the women over the years of the study is that it resulted from changes they experienced in their own lives. Particularly significant were the experiences of returning to school for more education and combining the roles of wife and mother with jobs outside the home. In this regard, Scanzoni and Fox (1980) observe that the issue of women working is shifting from one of "... an all-or-nothing dilemma between career/job *or* marriage and children ..." to one of "... the *nature* of what the occupational and domestic *combination* will be." They also observe that to facilitate these combinations, growing numbers of young women are planning to marry later and have smaller families.

Another study (Yankelovich, 1980), prepared for the President's Advisory Committee for Women, suggests that since the mid-1970s there has been a dramatic shift in American public opinion regarding the role of women. This study found unqualified acceptance by husbands of the right of their wives to work and overwhelming support for the concept of reproductive freedom and the right of women to participate in public life. At the same time, the study showed that people are realistic about the stresses experienced by women who work outside the home and supportive of the need for programs such as day

This satirical cartoon on the mid-nineteenth-century women's rights movement reflects men's concerns about what would happen if women gained equality. The shift of male opinion toward a more positive view of working wives has been very recent.

HIGHLIGHT 3.2   *Seeking a New Balance in Marriage*

... The winds of change have had their effect. Everyone expects just a little more of marriage, and some expect a lot more. Resistant to change as marriage is, our expectations for it increase with each gain. We now expect to be companions, friends, partners, working and sharing equally in decision making, parenthood, in mundane household tasks, in responsibility, in sex. . . .

But it is a struggle. It is a difficult job to find a balance, and the burden of initiating change often falls on the woman. After all, men didn't ask for all the changes that have happened. They were happy with what they had—or at least thought they were. Since they didn't initiate the changes, they are the reactors, they are often on the defensive. For the most part, men liked their well-defined role as the producers, the bosses and decision makers in our society. Their identity did not depend upon their marriage or their woman. Their job and the outside world gave them an identity, and when the going got rough out there, the wife was waiting at home to soothe the bruises and bolster the ego. . . .

And now look what's happened. The man is expected to participate in full-time parenthood, to become housekeeper, shopper, secretary, baby-sitter, cook. Furthermore, everything he learned early in life about how to defend himself and conquer as a man—to be cool, uninvolved, masterful, and invulnerable—is now being held against him. He is asked to become more emotional, be able to cry, talk about his feelings, communicate more expressively. . . .

Along with learning and adjusting to new roles, men have had to face up to their image as "symbols of oppression." Furthermore, even if they do change and grow in new directions, society still expects them to continue carrying out the responsibilities of their traditional roles. . . .

For the women who want to step out of the old patterns, the push for long-deserved freedom and recognition has brought heartaches and headaches as well as advantages. . . . The woman is expected to be . . . able to juggle motherhood, career, and marriage, remain attractive, jog and exercise, pay her own way, open her own doors, and educate her man sexually and emotionally. . . .

It's a real dilemma that both men and women are facing today. It's new ground for both of them, and both are uneasy, testing, pushing, retreating, and questioning where it will lead them. There *is* new balance in the relationships between men and women today, but we have no magic formulas to show us how to make it work. In theory, marriage is a fifty-fifty deal, and both partners have to put in a hundred percent of themselves. But the way it works out in reality, in the daily sharing of tasks, emotions, and problems is a varying percentage. . . . Much as we may aspire to and work toward equality in marriage, it is never exactly an equal arrangement. Only in time do the inequalites, the humanness of each, balance out.

Even our changing attitude toward sex roles does not mean instant alteration. It isn't that a door has been suddenly flung open; it is more like a stone cast into a pond where the ripples spread gradually in ever-widening circles.

Source: From *The Marriage Premise* by Nena O'Neill. Copyright © 1977 by Nena O'Neill. Reprinted by permission of the publisher, M. Evans & Co., Inc. New York, N.Y. 10017.

care to help working mothers. Most Americans now believe that husbands and wives should share financial decision making and household and parenting chores. These attitudes represent a considerable shift from the thinking of the mid-1970s, when the majority of Americans still regarded housework as women's responsibility, though so far this shift has been more in attitudes than in behaviors (see Chapter 7).

While these studies indicate that Americans are changing their perception of the female role, there is evidence that some young adults still subscribe to traditional role expectations. These young people are likely to be male, to come from lower socioeconomic groups, and to be less successful academically (Bayer, 1975). College students, by and large, tend to endorse women's rights and sexual equality in employment. In a 1973 survey, only 41 percent of male freshmen polled and only 19 percent of female freshmen polled supported traditional women's roles (Bayer, 1975).

The Movement toward Androgyny

In addition to changes in attitudes toward women's roles, there are new perceptions today regarding the qualities that are desirable in men and women. It is becoming increasingly evident, for example, that the strong, silent male and the retiring, submissive female are stereotypes that are difficult for most men and women to live up to. Modern life in America requires that both males and females exhibit qualities of strength and competence as well as interpersonal skills and nurturance. As a result of this realization, men and women have been moving toward what some have termed androgyny—a blending of both masculine and feminine characteristics in the same individual. The androgynous man may be described as one who is assertive, self-confident, and achievement-oriented, but also loving, emotionally sensitive, and communicative. Similarly, the androgynous woman is defined as one who is loving, emotionally supportive, and gentle, but also assertive, independent, and self-confident. According to Spence and Helmreich (1978), this trend toward androgyny is a positive one. These researchers found that androgynous people have better emotional health and better social adjustment than men who have more exclusively "masculine" characteristics and women who have more exclusively "feminine" characteristics. They found that androgynous people are achievement-oriented, have a high level of self-esteem, are socially competent, and have no problem with their gender identity.

Pressures on Modern Men and Women

Although gender roles are changing, it should be emphasized that the changes are by no means easy or painless. Some people believe that American society has come to expect too much of its men and women. Psychiatrist Herb Goldberg writes of the pressure on today's male to "be all things to all people." Goldberg describes this "superman" as ". . . capable provider, the aggressive competitor, and gentle lover, the fearless protector, the cool, controlled one under pressure and the emotionally expressive person at home." He asserts that "too many men are destroyed trying to live up to these impossible tasks" (*U.S. News and World Report*, December 8, 1980). Other observers have made the same point with regard to women—especially those women who are working at full-time jobs and at the same time trying to maintain a loving relationship with their husband, raise healthy children, and care for the home.

SUMMARY

1. The purpose of this chapter is to examine the origins and the cultural and biosocial basis of gender roles, and to explore how male and female roles are changing.

2. There are a number of observable physical and behavioral differences which appear to be biologically based, while others are more influenced by learning. However, the extent to which male-female differences are affected by biology and environment is uncertain.

3. Children are socialized into male and female roles by a number of agencies, including parents, schools, toys, books, peers, and the various communications media. All of these agents of socialization tend to reinforce traditional gender-role stereotypes.

4. Gender-role socialization has implications for people's self-concepts; their economic, educational, and political opportunities; and their intimate relationships. In general, men and women have somewhat different self-concepts and value different personal qualities.

5. Within the marriage relationship, husbands are still expected to concentrate most of their energy on professional and monetary pursuits. Likewise, wives are still primarily responsible for homemaking and child care. Recent public opinion polls indicate that many American women believe that an ideal life-style would be one in which they could combine marriage, parenthood, and part-time employment.

6. Although many individuals are reluctant to give up familiar gender roles, male and female roles are changing. More men and women are expressing both masculine and feminine characteristics, and roles are increasingly being negotiated.

REVIEW AND DISCUSSION

1. Identify five or more physical or behavioral differences between males and females that are present in infancy or childhood.

2. Explain why socialization might play a role in the greater tendency of males to display aggressive behavior.

3. Describe how parents, teachers, and television affect children's socialization into gender roles. Do you think it is possible to raise children in non-sex-stereotyped ways? How might this be accomplished?

4. What advantages for intimate relationships do you see in the movement of Americans toward gender equality? Are there any disadvantages to this trend?

5. What kind of gender-role relationship characterizes your parents' marriage or another adult couple you are familiar with? Do you think you will adopt similar roles in your own marriage? Why or why not?

SUGGESTED READINGS

David, D., and R. Brannon (eds.) (1976). *The Forty-nine Percent Majority: The Male Sex Role*. Reading, Mass.: Addison-Wesley.

A book of readings on the male sex role. Includes articles dealing with the dimensions of the male role, socialization to the role, and challenges to the role.

Maccoby, E. E., and C. N. Jacklin (1973). *The Psychology of Sex Differences*. Stanford, Calif.: Stanford University Press.

Reviews and evaluates research on sex differences. Concerned mainly with developmental, intellectual, achievement, and social-behavior aspects.

Sexton, L. G. (1979). *Between Two Worlds: Young Women in Crisis*. New York: William Morrow and Company.

Informal portraits of fifteen American women born between 1945 and 1955 coming to terms with personal, societal, and career-role choices presented by contemporary society.

Rubin, M. (ed.) (1980). *Men Without Masks: Writings from the Journals of Modern Men*. Reading, Mass.: Addison-Wesley.

Selected excerpts from diaries of more than thirty men of our times, including famous men and others less well known. Deals frankly with their experiences as children and parents, with work and lovers, and with the tasks of middle and old age.

———. (1981) *The Sexes: How They Differ—And Why.* Newsweek (May 18):72–83.

Describes recent research on sex differences, including controversial findings on differences in brain organization of men and women, and probes the debate such findings have provoked.

Developing Intimacy

"The meeting of two personalities is like the contact of two chemical substances; if there is any reaction, both are transformed."

CARL JUNG

The need for intimate relationships is present at birth and continues for a lifetime. Although some people learn to live without the emotional support of relatives, friends, lovers, or spouses, we generally think of people lacking these relationships as being sad and lonely.

Most people still regard marriage as the ultimate intimate relationship, a peak reached through progressive involvements in dating and courtship from adolescence on. This chapter examines the various stages and factors involved in the development of intimate, heterosexual relationships. It explores how dating and courtship patterns and nonmarital sexual activity have changed over time and considers the various cultural, social, and psychological factors—including love—that influence why one person selects another for a mate.

 THE BEGINNINGS OF INTIMACY

When we talk about intimacy, we are not necessarily talking about sex. Many types of intimate relationships—relationships with parents and friends, for example—have no sexual involvement. Rather, intimacy means simply the opposite of isolation and alienation. It involves closeness and sharing instead of distance.

Our first intimate relationships are with our parents. Their love forms the core of our emotional and physical nurturing as children and helps us learn how to love. For many people, sisters and brothers provide another focus for love and caring.

97

Childhood friendships can be an important supplement to intimacy with family members. When youngsters approach adolescence they usually begin actively seeking intimate ties outside the family. For many, it is their friends rather than their parents in whom they confide their joys and problems. These early attempts to recognize and express their feelings—initially to someone of the same sex—are a step toward heterosexual intimacy (Mitchell, 1976).

In time, the desire to confide in a friend of the same sex usually gives way to wanting to share emotional experiences with someone of the opposite sex. But many adolescents have a hard time establishing intimate relationships on any level with contemporaries of the opposite sex. Intimacy requires honesty and openness, and many adolescents are afraid to be open for fear of being rejected. Some are confused about who they are and, therefore, are unable to communicate honestly.

Adolescent couples may experience considerable physical passion and a degree of emotional sharing. Nevertheless, their romances are usually short-lived. Full intimacy cannot spring from insecurity. It requires, instead, openness between relatively mature people who have a sense of who they are and are not afraid of losing their identities through joining a partner (Mitchell, 1976).

 DATING AND COURTSHIP

The ability to form intimate heterosexual relationships is a learned skill. In America, much of this learning occurs through the dating process. Although dating, especially in the early years, may be more for recreation than for courtship, and although dating sometimes takes place in a "games-playing" atmosphere, it offers people the chance to experience intimacy in interpersonal relationships.

Changing Courtship Patterns

Dating, when it results in finding a marital partner, is a part of what sociologists call the courtship pattern. Dating is relatively new in the United States. The generation that grew to maturity in the 1920s was the first to date; before that, when social life centered on small towns and city neighborhoods, couples "kept company" or "walked out together" under supervision. Couples were likely to have known each other for a long time before any romantic interest developed. Often they were neighbors. But the automobile, the telephone, urbanization, higher education and involvement in the workplace for women, and many other factors ended that system. What replaced it—dating—retained some of the formality of the earlier courtship process, but there was a crucial difference: before, the pairing took place after romance had entered the picture. Dating had no such precondition as prior intimacy.

In the 1950s, dating and courtship followed a fairly predictable sequence established over previous decades. LeMasters (1957) identified six stages: group dating, random dating, steady dating, getting "pinned," engagement, and marriage. Each stage represented an increasing commitment, and each stage had its own set of expectations about the exclusivity of the relationship and the level of sexual intimacy that was appropriate, though certainly not all individuals or relationships moved smoothly or sequentially through all these stages.

Behavior—among females, at least—was different in each succeeding phase. According to McDaniel (1969), young women in the random-dating phase were unconcerned about the marriage-oriented reasons for dating, and were more assertive and direct in their relations with men. They took a prominent role in developing the dating relationship. This was, of course, a significant change from previous eras. However, when they reached the going-steady phase, they became less assertive and more "receptive." That is, they began to assume the role of the pursued and were less open in taking initiative in the relationship. By this stage, they were dating for the purpose of mate

"Dating," in which a boy and girl go out together unchaperoned, is a relatively recent phenomenon. Today many young people "get together" rather than date formally.

selection. In the pinned/engaged stage, when the girls were presumably ready for marriage, they were almost entirely receptive. Their dating served as preparation for marriage. McDaniel concluded that the shift for girls from the phase in which they took considerable initiative in the relationship to the phase in which they were purely receptive was not one that the young women readily accepted. Rather, they felt that passivity in the later stage of courtship was what the boys expected of them. They learned to let the male take the lead because of the males' dislike for girls whom they viewed as aggressive. McDaniel speculated that the fact that the girls had not really accepted their passive role was a source of conflict for newlyweds, since the girls were forced to conform to expectations that they did not, in fact, truly share.

McDaniel implies that for women of the 1960s, at least, acceptance of the traditional pattern of receptivity was diminishing. By the early 1970s, many aspects of dating and courtship had changed, but the general outline characteristic of the 1950s remained valid. Especially changed were the correlations between the stages of dating and the degree of sexual involvement, and the addition, for many, of a new stage in the process: cohabitation. The two developments are related. Many young Americans today engage in sexual intercourse in much earlier phases of courtship than before, and many couples become involved in intimate relationships that involve sex but do not lead to marriage. Cohabitation is part of the courtship pattern; it may be a long-term commitment but, as we'll see in Chapter 14, it is seldom permanent. The cohabiting couple may marry, but more likely they will separate and begin the dating process all over again. This freedom to shift back and forth from one stage of the dating and courtship process to another represents another change from the expectations of earlier times.

Dating Patterns Today

The dating patterns of a few decades ago have also changed. The term many now use for "dating" is "getting together." This term reflects both the increasing informality of the process and the role changes that influenced it. The traditional dating script required the male to initiate each step. He asked for the date; he planned what the couple would do; and he paid any expenses. During the 1960s, a new formula began to appear. For many, the established dating ritual was displaced by "getting together," which somewhat removed the burden from the male by allowing the female to initiate and pay for social activities, if she wished. Getting together also involved less formal planning. A group of young people might meet at the movies, and some of them might pair off later. What began to appear, in short, was a more androgynous, less ritualized system of contact between sexes.

Several studies have indicated that among high-school students today, most begin dating (going on planned dates) at age fourteen or fifteen. There is some evidence that the trend is toward being older at the time of the first planned date, but this may be because more teenagers are socializing by "getting together" (Dickinson, 1975; Hansen, 1977). Getting together may also account for the decline in the frequency of dating among high-school students. One researcher reported that the percentage of white students who dated once a week or more dropped from 67 percent in 1964 to 59 percent in 1974, a difference of about 8 percent (Dickinson, 1975). Still, Hansen (1977) found that half of the high-school students in her sample who dated did so at least once a week.

Factors in Heterosexual Attraction

A number of factors have been found to be important in influencing whom we are attracted to as potential candidates for an intimate relationship. Among the characteristics that have been identified consistently are:

1. Desirable personality traits, such as honesty, a sense of humor, and social competence.
2. Proximity, or close physical distance. We tend to be attracted to people who live relatively close to us and with whom we are likely to have frequent contact. The reason for this seems to be that more frequent interaction between people helps to increase their mutual liking for one another.
3. Reciprocal liking. We tend to find people attractive who like us and show a genuine interest in us.
4. Similarity and complementarity. We tend to like others who are similar to us in attitudes, interests, values, and personality. In some instances, however, we find people attractive who, rather than being similar to us, possess characteristics that seem to complement our own. Thus, a woman who holds a traditional view of the roles of men and women may prefer a man who displays traits regarded as traditionally masculine, since these traits complement her sense of femininity.

Although each of the factors we have mentioned plays a role in determining whom we are attracted to, in the early stages of social interaction, and especially in choosing partners to date for the first time, perhaps the major factor influencing whether the couple will seek to continue the development of their relationship is physical attractiveness. Un-American as it may seem, in dating everyone does not start off with an equal chance; those who are considered physically attractive have a better chance than those who are less attractive. Studies show that men and women who are regarded as very attractive are more sought-after as dates than less attractive people, no matter what other personality characteristics they may have (Mathes, 1975).

THE MATCHING HYPOTHESIS   According to the **matching hypothesis,** a theory first advanced during the 1950s, people choose dates and mates who are like themselves in terms of social desirability. Total social value is presumed to be a combination of social skills, intelligence, wealth, prestige, physical attractiveness, and appealing personality traits. A number of experiments testing this theory have indicated that an overwhelming preference for physically attractive people casts doubt on the theory, but that people's realistic assessment of their chances for success in dating tends to restore it to some extent (Berscheid and Walster, 1974).

In one test of the matching hypothesis, a computer dance was set up for first-year college students. The researchers evaluated each subject on four points: personality, intelligence, social skills, and physical attractiveness. Pairs were assigned at random, except that, as a concession to social custom, women were always paired with men taller than themselves. At intermission, subjects were asked to fill out a questionnaire indicating how well they liked their dates and whether they wanted to date that person again. The results: the more physically attractive the date, the better he or she was liked. No other variables seemed to make any difference (Walster et al., 1966).

It seems likely that in computer dances people are not as afraid of rejection as they are in normal dating situations so their dating choices might be different from those in ordinary dating situations. Therefore, another experiment was set up to determine whether people would prefer dates more like themselves in terms of looks if actively required to choose a partner. The researchers found that although highly attractive men and women were still strongly preferred, less attractive people did tend to choose less attractive dates than those chosen by highly attractive people (Berscheid et al., 1971). Men and women who think they are unattractive are more likely to consider going out with less attractive dates and less likely to try for dates with attractive people (Berscheid and Walster, 1974).

ATTRACTIVENESS OF WOMEN   Good looks seem to be more important to a woman's popularity than a man's. While women want a date who is honest, physically attractive, considerate, respectful, and who has a good personality (McGinnis, 1958; Wakil, 1973), men are more likely to choose dates primarily on the basis of physical attractiveness (Berscheid and Walster, 1974).

Women are aware of the high value men place on dating attractive women. In one study, women were asked to list the items that concerned them most about dating. "Making herself as attractive as possible to attract the boy of her choice" headed the list (McDaniel, 1969). For women, their physical attractiveness tends to be positively correlated to their satisfaction with their leadership ability, popularity, and self-consciousness (Berscheid et al., 1971).

Generally, then, even though physical attractiveness is certainly not the only factor influencing whom people date or develop relationships with, it is a major factor initially, influencing the person's chances of involvement. Other factors, such as personality traits and shared values, become more important as the relationship grows more intimate.

Adjustments in Dating

Learning how to act on a date is an important part of adolescent socialization. Whether young people get together in a movie theater, a pizza parlor, or at a

---

HIGHLIGHT 4.1   *Meetings*

As a student she had fallen wildly in love with a married man with the somewhat uncommon name of, let's say, Albert Prince. He was in med school, on the way to becoming a gynecologist. In time the affair broke up, and the two of them went their separate ways.

Years later in another city, when she was working in a hospital, she got a message to call a Dr. Albert Prince in Pediatrics. Delighted, she quickly dialed the number. A strange voice; false starts; confusion. It was a different Dr. Albert Prince. He took her out to coffee.

—Married five years, two children

A very old lady stumbled in a crosswalk on Boylston street in Boston. She sank to the pavement, her ankle twisted under her. Immediately two passersby lifted her up by the arms and helped her to the curb. There, the young man steadied her while the young woman waved down a cab. They put her into it, exchanged names, and drove off. The young man and woman started to talk. They invited the very old lady to the wedding.

—Married four years

A college radical leader, he had written an angry manifesto that was circulated around the campus. One day after a rally, as he was walking away in his uniform of jeans, blue pastic windbreaker and uncombed hair, this girl accosted him.

"Did you write that crap?" she demanded. For twenty minutes they wrangled about politics there on the path while people walked around them. Finally she snapped, "Man, you are a bad trip" and stormed off in her jeans, blue plastic windbreaker and uncombed hair.

The next summer, which he spent with his wealthy parents on Long Island, he was a guest at a flossy wedding. He was milling around, champagne glass in hand, in the big striped tent on the lawn overlooking the Sound. Suddenly he saw a huge picture hat. There was a face under it that he knew from somewhere.

"You! he said.

"You! she said.

—Married three years, one child

"She was coming down the staircase at the old Post building on E street. It's a parking lot now. I thought, 'what lovely eyes.' Then she smiled, and I was a goner."

—Married 38 years

Source: Michael Kernan, *Washington Post,* 1977. Reprinted with permission.

party, they find out which behaviors are appealing to those of the opposite sex and which are not. Since differences of opinion are bound to become apparent as a relationship progresses, they may also begin to learn how to cope with interpersonal conflicts (Collins et al., 1976).

Studies of high-school and college students reveal that many feel inadequate, ill at ease, and self-conscious when they begin dating. Many report that they don't understand people of the opposite sex and have problems establishing relationships with them. While some of these problems may indicate that many young people have not made a smooth adjustment to dating (Herold, 1973), an alternative interpretation might be that the traditional dating system in which young people compete for dating partners and behave in ritualized ways makes the formation of satisfying heterosexual relationships more, rather than less, difficult (Libby, 1977).

It seems, however, that experience with dating makes people more comfortable with its demands. A survey of 430 Midwestern college students found that for both males and females there was a strong correlation between high dating adjustment and four factors in the dating experience: (1) early age at their first date, (2) frequent high-school dating, (3) frequent college dating, and (4) amount of emotional involvement with a dating partner. The last two factors seemed to be particularly important (Herold, 1973).

DIFFERING EXPECTATIONS A common problem in dating is disagreement between partners about how much sexual intimacy is acceptable in the relationship. There is evidence that both males and females expect physical intimacy to grow as the level of affectionate involvement increases. However, there is some disagreement between males and females in younger age groups on the level of sexual intimacy they feel is desirable. Among seventeen-to-nineteen-year-olds in one study (Collins et al., 1976), males expected more sexual intimacy on a date than females. Expectations were more similar in older age groups, with twenty-to-thirty-year-olds in near agreement on the level of sexual intimacy desirable at different levels of relational involvement. The movement toward greater agreement between the sexes seems to occur largely because of changed attitudes on the part of the females. With dating experience, they seem to become more comfortable with higher levels of sexual intimacy.

Another problem frequently encountered in dating is that the partners may have different sets of expectations as to the purpose of the relationship. When this occurs, it can lead to misunderstanding or disappointment. A study of student nurses by Skipper and Nass (1966) illustrates this point. The primary motivation of these young women for dating was courtship—they wanted to find a mate. But the men they had the opportunity to date—college students and students in medical school—were primarily interested in dating as a form of recreation. Both groups of males held a stereotyped view of nurses as sexually permissive. As a result, the women felt that in order to continue dating they had to be more sexually open than they wanted to be. This compromise distressed them, as did the fact that their dates did not share their interest in building a deeper emotional attachment which might lead to marriage. While this situation emphasized the difficulties young women may encounter, it may be true that, just as often, the male in a relationship is seeking a deeper commitment whereas the female is largely interested in dating for recreation.

BREAKING UP   Few people reach adulthood without having had a relationship they cared about come to an end. When this happens, it is usually a painful experience. Some people feel that they have failed or been rejected; others may feel that a heavy burden has been lifted from their shoulders. Yet this weeding out of unsatisfactory relationships is an important part of dating and courtship. Even though breaking up may be difficult, couples who do so before marriage are spared some of the psychic and all of the legal costs of divorce (Hill et al., 1976).

How many dating couples eventually break up? While there is little hard evidence on this question, research on 231 college dating couples revealed that 45 percent (103) had broken up by the end of the two-year study (Hill et al., 1976). Some relationships had lasted a month, some had lasted five years, with a median duration of sixteen months before breakup. When they tried to find a basis for predicting which couples would stay together and which ones would not, Hill and his colleagues found that sexual intimacy and living together were not related to the permanence of the relationship. A factor that did emerge as significant, however, was matching. Couples who were similar in age, education, intelligence, and physical attractiveness were less likely to break up than couples who were not well matched on these characteristics. A questionnaire and interview study of 155 breakups before marriage (Wassenberg, 1980) found six general explanations for ending relationships: differences in the partners' expectations for the relationship, different goals and interests, jealousy, personality differences, changes in location, and inability to deal with conflicts that arose.

Adjusting to a breakup can by very difficult. Many respondents in Wassenberg's study reported feelings of depression, inability to concentrate, insomnia, physical illness, and mood swings. They also were hesitant about getting involved again. Negative feelings were not universal, however. Some respondents said they felt relieved, that they had grown from the experience, and that they were still friends with their ex-partners.

There is evidence that adjusting to breakups is more difficult for men than for women. This may be because women are somewhat more likely than men to initiate the breakup. Even when the woman is the more emotionally involved partner, she may initiate a breakup because she recognizes that her commitment is not returned. Women are also more likely than men to consider alternatives to the relationship (Hill et al., 1976).

CASE STUDY   *Breaking Up Is Hard to Do*

Kathy and Joe had been going together during the school year when she was a sophomore and he was a junior. Both of them agree that Kathy was the one who wanted to break up. She felt they were too tied down to one another, that Joe was too dependent and demanded her exclusive attention—even in groups of friends he would draw her aside. As early as the spring Joe came to feel that Kathy was no longer as much in love as he but it took him a long time to reconcile himself to the notion that things were ending. They gradually saw each other less and less over the summer months, until finally she began to date someone else. The first time that the two were together after the start of the next school year Kathy was in a bad mood, but wouldn't talk to Joe about it. The following morning Joe told Kathy, "I guess things are over with." Later when they were able to talk further, he found out that she was already dating someone else. Kathy's reaction to the breakup was mainly a feeling of release—both from Joe and from the guilt she felt when

she was secretly dating someone else. But Joe had deep regrets about the relationship. For at least some months afterward he regretted that they didn't give the relationship one more chance—he thought they might have been able to make it work. He said that he learned something from the relationship, but hoped he hadn't become disillusioned by it. "If I fall in love again," he said, "it might be with the reservation that I'm going to keep awake this time. I don't know if you can keep an innocent attitude toward relationships and keep watch at the same time, but I hope so." Meanwhile, however, he had not begun to make any new social contacts, and instead seemed focused on working through the old relationship, and since Kathy and he sometimes see each other at school, in learning to be comfortable in her presence.

From *Divorce and Separation: Context, Causes and Consequences* edited by G. Levinger and O. C. Moles. Copyright © 1979 by The Society for the Psychological Study of Social Issues. By permission of Basic Books, Inc. Publishers, N.Y.

FOR CLASS DISCUSSION

1. Do you think there might have been a different ending to this story if Kathy had expressed to Joe much earlier her concern that he was being too possessive?

2. Should Joe have been the one to bring conflicts out into the open when he realized in the spring that Kathy was not so much in love as he?

 NONMARITAL SEX

American standards regarding nonmarital sex have traditionally been quite restrictive. In the past, there were strong prohibitions on sex between young single people. For women, particularly, sex prior to marriage was regarded as morally wrong. Women who did not observe the prevailing standard of chastity risked the loss of their reputation and, of course, unwanted pregnancy. While many young people today continue to adhere to the traditional view that sex is appropriate only within marriage, many others regard sexual intimacy as a natural and acceptable part of a nonmarital relationship.

To what degree have nonmarital sexual standards changed? Are the same standards applied equally to men and women? What effects, if any, does nonmarital sex have on sexual adjustment in marriage? We will consider these questions in this section.

Changing Perceptions of Virginity

One way of assessing the shift in sexual standards is to consider how young people today feel about the importance of virginity. Berger and Wenger (1973) have examined the concept of virginity in terms of its social function and meaning. They contend that placing a high value on chastity is meaningful in a social system in which men are thought to have property rights to women. In a male-dominated system, women have few valuable resources; their control over their sexual behavior is virtually the only control they have over their own destinies. This perspective would seem to have some application to American society where women traditionally have had little economic power and have been dependent on men to provide for them.

Berger and Wenger further suggest that within such a system there are a number of possible *social* as opposed to *physiological* definitions of female virginity and that it is to a woman's advantage to keep the definition rather flexible. Such flexibility enables her to use her sexual power to obtain some measure of sensual gratification outside of marriage while at the same time not lowering her value in the marriage market. As women gain control of other valued resources, however—especially of economic resources—it would be expected that the ideal of female chastity would lose support.

In a study of predominantly young students at two eastern colleges (Berger and Wenger, 1973), 158 male and 154 female students were asked, "Does it make sense to say a woman (man) has lost her (his) virginity?" Fully 41 percent of the male respondents and 47 percent of the female respondents felt that it did not make sense to speak of the loss of female virginity. An even larger proportion—56 percent of the males and 57 percent of the females—felt that the loss of male virginity was an unimportant concept. The higher percentage of both males and females who thought male virginity was an unimportant concept appears to reflect the lesser emphasis on male chastity that has long characterized our society. One explanation for the findings in general may be that these young people believe that virginity as a social value is less important today than in the past. If this interpretation is correct, it would seem to coincide with the movement in our society toward a more equal place for women.

Results of Survey Research

Survey after survey has confirmed a trend toward more liberal attitudes about nonmarital sex, at least among young people. Researchers studied attitudes toward nonmarital sex at two colleges in different regions of the country in 1958 and again in 1968. The results showed a distinct movement at both schools toward the acceptance of nonmarital sexuality, particularly by women (Christensen and Gregg, 1970). In an extensive survey of attitudes toward nonmarital sex, Reiss (1971) polled about 1000 students and a representative sample of adults. He discovered that males were generally more liberal than females; college students were more liberal than older adults; and blacks were more liberal than whites. While the first two findings remain valid, the gap between blacks and whites appears to be closing (Clayton and Bokemeir, 1980).

A study of 395 students at a southern university revealed that the percentage of women who regarded nonmarital sex as immoral dropped from 70 percent in 1965 to 34 percent in 1970 (Robinson et al., 1972). And a nonrandom sampling of students at another southern university found a substantial decrease between 1965 and 1975 in the number of students who believed nonmarital sex to be immoral. In 1965, 33 percent of the males and 70 percent of the females surveyed disapproved of nonmarital sex; by 1975, the percentages had dropped to 19.5 percent of males and 20.7 percent of females (King et al., 1977).

These studies seem to support—at least in part—the idea that there has been a shift from the traditional double standard toward a developing single standard for men and women. Other research suggests that with age and experience comes a greater adherence to a single standard. Two panels of college students (1967 to 1971 and 1970 to 1974) were studied when they were freshmen and seniors to determine whether their attitudes toward nonmarital sex changed over their college career. Both panels demonstrated a clear movement toward a single standard (Ferrell et al., 1977).

Most studies indicate that over the last two decades, the incidence of nonmarital sex, particularly coitus, has increased (especially for females); the number of partners a sexually experienced person can expect to have over time has increased; and the average age at which a person first has intercourse has decreased (Clayton and Bokemeir, 1980).

INCIDENCE   The data on college men and women indicate that nonmarital sex has grown increasingly common and the gap between males and females experiencing it has diminished considerably over the last few decades (Robinson et al., 1972; Vener and Stewart, 1974). A number of studies have found that the increase in nonmarital intercourse has occurred far more rapidly for females than for males and that the decrease in the gap between the sexes is largely a "catching-up" phenomenon for females. Kinsey's studies of nonmarital sexual behavior during the 1940s revealed that among men in his sample,

The incidence of early sexual experience among American teenagers has risen rapidly in recent years. Whereas sex has always been regarded as a badge of manhood for adolescent boys, many girls now regard sexual experience as a sign of entry into womanhood.

98 percent who did not finish grade school, 84 percent who did not go beyond high school, and 42 percent who had graduated from college had experienced nonmarital sex (Kinsey, 1948). Among women, 18 percent who attended college, and between 30 and 38 percent who did not attend college had experienced nonmarital sex under age twenty. By age twenty the incidence, regardless of education, was about 50 percent (Kinsey, 1953). King et al. (1977) studied the nonmarital coital behaviors of students at a large state university in the South at five-year intervals. The number of women reporting nonmarital sexual intercourse rose from 29 percent in 1965, to 37 percent in 1970, to 57 percent in 1975. Over the same period, the incidence for men increased from 65 percent to 74 percent. A later study of 509 male and 476 female college students (DeLamater and MacCorquodale, 1979) reported results similar to King and colleagues' 1975 findings. Among their sample, 75 percent of college males and 60 percent of college females had experienced nonmarital coitus. These data show the increase in incidence for both males and females over time and the reduction in the double standard for nonmarital intercourse.

AGE AT FIRST COITUS   If the increase in the incidence of nonmarital intercourse for females has been startling, the decrease in the age at first intercourse is even more so. Zelnick and Kantner (1977) found, based on two national surveys, that in 1971, about 25 percent of seventeen-year-old women had had intercourse; by 1976, more than 40 percent had. In just five years, the average age at first coitus for women declined by four months.

What factors help to account for this phenomenon? An obvious one is earlier sexual maturity of young people. Many social observers also believe that the availability of reliable contraceptives is another factor, although there is not a great deal of evidence for this view. A factor that does seem to be very significant is gender-role changes. Miller and Simon (1974) believe that three forces are at work. First, instead of the traditional pattern in which adolescent males engaged in intercourse with girls who had a "bad" reputation, boys are finding that their female peers are interested in having sexual relations. Second, the movement toward a single standard of sexual behavior has permitted girls to be somewhat more sexual and boys to be somewhat less sexual. Third, greater affluence and fads related to the youth culture permit young males to attain the esteem of their peers without having to have intercourse with "bad girls" in order to prove their manhood.

Jessor and Jessor (1975) point out the relationship between social age norms and decisions to engage in intercourse at earlier ages. Like drinking, engaging in intercourse is regarded as deviant at early ages but as more normal when an individual is somewhat older. For example, having intercourse is regarded as more deviant in high school but as more normal in college. These researchers found that young people who engaged in coitus at an age when it was still considered deviant tended to possess certain personal characteristics. They were more tolerant of deviance from social norms, more positive about sex, more likely to express social criticism, and less religious than their peers. They placed a higher value on independence and a lower value on achievement. In short, they seemed to be less conventional than their peers who were virgins.

REACTIONS TO FIRST INTERCOURSE   The reactions of young people to their first experience of intercourse depend on the quality of the physical and emotional interaction. First intercourse between people who trust each other and are caring may be a gratifying experience even if it is not technically proficient.

Some 20 percent of males have difficulty the first time. They may be unable to get an erection, or if they do get one, they may be unable to maintain it long enough to penetrate the vagina. Another difficulty is ejaculating before they want to. For females the physical experience may be painful if there is insufficient vaginal lubrication. According to one survey (Hunt, 1974), only four out of ten young unmarried males and two out of ten females described their first experience with coitus as "very pleasurable." Over a third of the males and almost two-thirds of the females experienced feelings of regret and worry afterward. Some were bothered by moral and emotional conflicts, while others were concerned that they had not performed well enough. For many there was the fear of pregnancy or sexually transmitted disease. A later study found that males were more likely to feel relaxed and/or conquering, whereas females were more tense and guilty and feared discovery (Christensen and Johnson, 1978).

NONMARITAL SEX AND MARITAL ADJUSTMENT   Does sexual experience prior to marriage affect marital or sexual adjustment? Early research on this question found that male and female virgins were slightly more likely than nonvirgins to have good marital adjustment (Burgess and Wallin, 1953). However, another study from the 1950s concluded that nonmarital sex had no effect—either positive or negative—on a woman's marital adjustment (Hamblin and Blood, 1956). In addition, a later study by Ard (1974), which investigated couples married twenty years or more, found no support for the notion that nonmarital sexual intercourse has any ill effects on marriage.

There is, however, one factor which may have a negative effect on later marital happiness: the age of the woman at the time of first coitus. According to a survey by *Redbook* magazine, women who were fifteen or younger when they first experienced intercourse were more likely than those who started later to share sex with many partners and use stimulating devices, masturbation, and marijuana in an effort to enhance sexual pleasure. They were the least likely of the women respondents to describe their marriages as good, the least likely to rate marital sex as being good, and the most dissatisfied with the frequency of intercourse in marriage. As a group, they were the most likely to say that they were "mostly unhappy" (Levin and Levin, 1975b). Thus, at least in this study, the quality of these women's subsequent sex lives in marriage seemed to be related to starting intercourse at young ages, although it is difficult to say why. More research on this topic is needed.

LOVE

For most Americans, the essence of intimacy is described by the word love. Love is the primary reason people give for marrying and the major factor they cite as contributing to personal happiness. Each of us has ideas of what love is or should be. For example, a dry cleaner's assistant in Nebraska characterized love as

> . . . a feeling of belonging, of having someone to identify with. To feel overwhelming trust and jealousy at the same time. *Everything* you do and think is shared with the other. When you touch one another, or just hear their voice, there is a desperate feeling of want and need, a feeling inside that actually hurts. (As quoted in Walster and Walster, 1978)

An automobile worker defined love as

> ... wanting the best for another. Love is often expressed by letting the other
> person know you believe in him/her and that you support them in what they are
> doing. You help them to grow as a person. You allow yourself to need the other.
> You support them to the extent of letting them know you share the same fears
> and goals and dreams and hopes. You are willing to be vulnerable. (As quoted in
> Walster and Walster, 1978)

Social scientists, too, have tried to define love. One described it as "... a
strong emotional attachment, a cathexis, between adolescents or adults of
opposite sexes, with at least the components of sex desire and tenderness"
(Goode, 1959). Another wrote:

> Love is an intense feeling of two people for each other which involves bodily,
> emotional, and intellectual identification; which is of such a nature as to cause
> each willingly to forego his personality demands and aspirations in favor of the
> other; which gains satisfaction through creating a personal and social identity in
> those involved. (Koos, 1953)

One of the problems in defining love is that it has so many aspects. When
sociologist John Lee (1973) asked Americans, Canadians, and Britons to talk
about their ideas of love, he found that they meant any of six different things:

1. *Eros:* love of beauty. This is sexual love. Erotic lovers have an intense
   desire for sexual intimacy. They are fascinated by physical aspects of their
   beloved and want to know every detail about them.
2. *Ludis:* playful love. Ludic lovers regard love as a game or pastime. They
   avoid long-range attachments and do not allow their partners to become
   too dependent on them.
3. *Storge:* companionate love. This is "love without fever, tumult, or folly,
   a peaceful and enchanting affection." The attachment of storgic lovers is
   long lasting but not deeply passionate. The feelings are similar to those
   one might have for a brother or sister.
4. *Mania:* obsessive love. Manic lovers are in a perpetual state of anxiety.
   They are consumed by thoughts of the beloved and have an insatiable
   need for attention and affection from the beloved. The manic lover
   alternates between ecstasy when the beloved is present and despair when
   the beloved is absent.
5. *Pragma:* realistic love. Pragmatic lovers take a practical approach to love.
   They seek a match with someone whose personality, background, values,
   interests, and the like will be compatible with their own. Once they find
   such a partner, more intense feelings may develop.

6. *Agape:* altruistic love. This is the classical Christian form of love—love that is patient and kind and demands nothing in return.

The most basic of these typologies are eros, ludis, and storge. Often people's perceptions of love combine attributes of two "pure" forms. Typical combinations are Storgic-Eros, Ludic-Eros, and Storgic-Ludis. Lee believes that the way to have a mutually satisfying love relationship is to understand one's own approach to loving and find a partner who shares that approach. This may not be as easy as it sounds, for individual definitions of love are not necessarily fixed. Moreover, people can experience one kind of love in one relationship and a different kind in another. Yet most people do fall within a basic range in terms of their general perception of what love means to them.

The Wheel Theory of Love

We noted earlier that our first experience of intimacy begins in the family, where as children we begin to form our ideas about loving and being loved. Later on we are influenced by our peers, societal standards, and our own romantic experiences. "Love at first sight," or instant intimacy may well happen in a few cases, but for most people it develops over time. It is a progression to deeper levels of intimacy. Ira Reiss (1960) conceived of this progression as a wheel (see Fig. 4.1).

If love is to develop, easy communication is the first step. When two people meet, they make quick judgments about their *rapport,* or how well they relate to one another. The extent to which a couple can easily develop rapport may depend on factors like social background which provide them a common set of assumptions. Also, the way an individual has been raised to think of people of different backgrounds will have much to do with his or her ability to talk easily with others. Common views of the roles of men and women, which may come from one's upbringing, also aid in developing rapport.

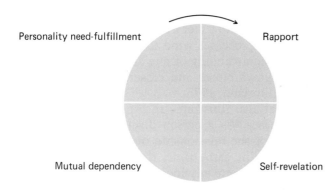

Personality need-fulfillment

Rapport

Mutual dependency

Self-revelation

Fig. 4.1
The wheel theory of the development of love. (Source: Ira L. Reiss, "Toward a Sociology of the Heterosexual Love Relationship," Journal of Marriage and Family Living, *May 1960. Copyrighted 1960 by the National Council on Family Relations. Reprinted by permission.)*

If a person feels rapport with another, that almost guarantees more openness or *self-revelation* in conversation. Here, too, a person's social and cultural background is important since it largely determines what he or she will feel comfortable revealing at a particular stage in a relationship. Sharing intimate thoughts and disclosing personal information deepens the relationship. Each partner becomes the special recipient of personal disclosures and each gains the trust necessary to engage in more self-revelation.

The exchange of self-revelations leads to the creation of *mutual dependency*; in a sense, the couple develops an interdependent habit system. They grow accustomed to doing things that require the cooperation of both. In this stage, if the other person is not available, the individual feels lonely. Again, the social and cultural backgrounds of the partners are important since the types of mutual behaviors they develop grow directly from the type of revelation in the relationship, which in turn depends on their backgrounds.

The final stage in the development of a love relationship is the *fulfillment of personality needs*, including the need for someone to love, someone to confide in, someone to stimulate personal ambition, and other needs of this type. These are crucial emotional needs which relate to family or occupation or both, and they are of great importance to the individual's performance of social roles. To the degree that these personality needs are fulfilled, the couple finds a love relationship developing. In this stage, the other person is felt to be essential for the well-being and existence of the partner.

Reiss chose the wheel to illustrate the development of love because the four processes depend on one another; what happens to one process affects all the others. For example, a reduction in the amount of self-revelation, perhaps because the couple has an argument or because one of them develops an interest in someone else, diminishes dependency and reduces the degree to which personality needs are met, which then affects the couple's rapport. The effects of such a development can be permanent or temporary; the couple may move forward to deeper love, or break off their relationship (thus reversing the wheel), or choose to keep it as it is.

A recent modification of the wheel model was proposed by Borland (1975). (See Fig. 4.2.) Borland suggested that instead of a wheel, the development of a love relationship was more akin to a clock spring with the individual's "real self" at the center. All of the processes wind toward a closer, more intimate relationship and a greater understanding of one another's inner thoughts. As this happens, the couple grows closer and closer, much as a clock spring tightens when it is wound (Borland, 1975).

The clock-spring model also illustrates the spiral progression of a relationship as intimacy increases. As a person discloses more and more, the amount of trust necessary for the relationship increases, and thus the depth of rapport must increase. At the same time, the tighter the clock spring is wound, the more difficult it is to unwind the relationship. If the spring

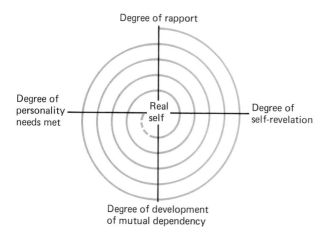

Degree of rapport

Degree of
personality
needs met

Real
self

Degree of
self-revelation

Degree of development
of mutual dependency

Fig. 4.2
*Clockspring modification of the wheel
theory of love. (Source: Ira L. Reiss,
Department of Sociology, Family Study
Center, University of Minnesota,
Minneapolis, Minn. Copyrighted 1960
by the National Council on Family
Relations. Reprinted by permission.)*

becomes overwound, individuals may be so bound up together that they cannot grow, and the relationship becomes threatening because it is "too close." This is particularly true where one individual races ahead of the other in terms of emotional commitment. By short-circuiting the process, by attempting to jump directly to a revelation of one's real self without developing the intervening steps, one can place so much tension on the relationship that it springs loose from its track (Borland, 1975).

Borland's model helps us to see how a relationship winds and unwinds, and then winds itself up again with each new incident. Her metaphor evokes how lovers react to one another and the way their emotions intertwine and move toward greater or lesser intimacy.

Functions of Romantic Love

As we have noted, romantic love is the primary basis for marriage in the United States. In many cultures, the choice of a mate may depend on economic factors or social position, but in America, any reason other than romantic love—whether it is related to economic gain, status, escape from loneliness, or sexual gratification—is regarded as unacceptable or even shameful (Udry, 1974).

Romantic love serves some very definite purposes in our culture. First, it plays a crucial role in supporting the institution of the nuclear family by motivating young couples to leave their families of orientation. This step is obviously fundamental if a new nuclear family is to be established. Love also gives a young couple strength to cope with the difficulties of marital adjustment (Goode, 1959). In addition, in a society such as ours with a very high divorce and remarriage rate, the idea of romantic love motivates people to keep trying to find a partner.

According to Greenfield (1965), romantic love may act as a kind of emotional bait which lures people into marriage. Many societies have prescribed means of getting people to marry. In these cultures, extended kinship systems or matchmakers serve to motivate people toward marriage. In the United States, however, such institutionalized systems do not exist. People have a great deal of latitude in deciding whether to marry. In addition, in our society basic needs—including food, clothing, and even sexual gratification—can be satisfied in the marketplace rather than in the institution of marriage. From a purely materialistic viewpoint, many people would be able to satisfy more of their needs outside marriage, since marriage is economically expensive. Thus Americans have to have an incentive to marry and form the nuclear families that maintain our society. Greenfield contends that romantic love serves as this incentive.

Other sociologists suggest that romantic love is functional in that it provides a sense of well-being (Kanin et al., 1970) and that it is necessary to the extent that it brings people into serious male-female relationships that lead to marriage (Spanier, 1972).

Romantic Love: Gender Differences

Most people take it for granted that women are more romantic than men, but is this really the case? Research on this question has shown that men and women fall in love at different points in a relationship and with different intensity. Men start off with a considerably more romantic view of the male-female relationship (Hobart, 1958), and they also tend to fall in love earlier in the relationship. In one study, 20 percent of the men fell in love before the fourth date as opposed to 15 percent of the women (Kanin et al., 1970). The same study showed that only 30 percent of the men but 43 percent of the women were not sure they were in love after the twentieth date. As noted earlier, men find it harder than women to accept the end of an intimate relationship. They continue to hold out hope long after the relationship is over (Hill et al., 1976), and they find it much more difficult than women to adjust the relationship to one of friendship after a breakup. In fact, breakups are so difficult for men that statistics show that men are three times more likely than women to commit suicide after a relationship dissolves (Walster and Walster, 1978).

There is evidence that women, once they decide they are in love, feel it more intensely than men (Kanin et al., 1970). However, according to Walster and Walster, it is not until the woman is fairly sure of the relationship that she allows her emotions to run unchecked; men are not so restrained. Thus the woman tends to be the last to open emotionally and the first to close (Walster and Walster, 1978).

Romantic Love, Conjugal Love, and
Marital Adjustment

In our discussion of the functions of romantic love, we noted that it benefits society as a whole by promoting the formation and endurance of the nuclear family. Now, on a more personal level, we will consider, in general, the costs and benefits of romantic love to a particular couple. How enduring is romantic love through the length of the relationship? How essential is it for marital adjustment and marital satisfaction?

It is important to make a distinction between *romantic* love and *conjugal* love. Romantic love can be considered as that "emotional bait" described earlier. It is highly idealistic, and it is what people mean when they speak of "love at first sight" or declare that "love conquers all." This kind of love has a mystical quality in which the partners are completely absorbed with each other and are jealous of any "trespasser" or "rival." Knox and Sporakowski (1968) refer to romantic love as "cardiac-respiratory love" with ". . . emphasis upon excited love, thrills and palpitations of the heart" (p. 19).

Conjugal love, by contrast, has a different orientation. It is a more calm, solid, and comforting love relationship than romantic love. Duvall and Hill (1960) question the merits of romantic love as the basis for a permanent well-adjusted marriage. They contend that the myths surrounding romantic love—for example, the notion that a marriage can survive on love alone—create false expectations and cause the marriage to weaken as the couple's emotions change. Instead, they believe the only real basis for an enduring relationship is conjugal love.

> Conjugal love is quite another emotion. It grows as the marriage progresses, thrives on companionship, common experiences, and the number of happy episodes which are scattered throughout a rich marriage. Conjugal love builds on the familiar, the mementos, the souvenirs, and waxes stronger with each additional year of marriage. Unlike romantic love, conjugal love is impossible for newly acquainted young people, since it requires time to form and grows from continuous association. Romantic love is greatest where each party knows least about the other—reality gets in the way of romance. This is the love that is blind. (Duvall and Hill, 1960, p. 340)

Conjugal love, then, can be expected to develop gradually as the relationship becomes increasingly stable and enduring and to replace the idealistic and highly emotional quality of romantic love. Romantic love probably becomes a detriment to high marital adjustment only when couples expect their relationship to endure as romantic love alone and feel that the conjugal-love orientation is somehow boring.

Knox and Sporakowski (1968) demonstrated the gradual shift in orientation among the college students they studied. They found that as college males and females grow older, become more mature, gain greater dating experience, and become increasingly serious in relationships, their orientations shift from being more romantic to being more conjugal, or realistic. By college age, both males and females tend to have more conjugal than romantic attitudes toward love, with females tending to be more conjugal than males. Thus, as Greenfield (1965) suggested, romantic love could be considered as the "emotional bait" which lures people into marriage, and conjugal love could be seen as that subsequent love orientation which contributes to the maintenance and continuance of a stable, long-term relationship.

 MATE SELECTION

Love may be the principal thing people look for in selecting a mate, but it is by no means the only one. Many other factors—societal, cultural, and psychological—influence whom we fall in love with and whether that love will lead to marriage.

Societal Control of Mate Selection

It is a fact that no society, including our own, permits mate selection based on uncontrolled emotional attachments. Love can apparently arise in any society, but if it were allowed free rein, the patterns of social classes and/or kinship on which society operates would be disrupted. Goode (1959) identified five ways in which cultures control the development of love and direct or influence the choice of mates in order to maintain the existing social arrangements of the society.

1. *Child marriage* is the simplest and most widely used means of control. The child is betrothed or married before he or she reaches adolescence and has an opportunity to form any love attachments or resources to resist the marriage. In India, for instance, it was quite common for a child bride to be sent to live with her spouse's family, although the marriage would not be consummated for several years.

2. *Determination of marital partner by kinship rules* is a pattern which is often related to child marriage. In cultures using this device, the elders might arrange for the father's sister's child to marry the mother's brother's child. Some of these schemes can be very complex, but the primary question in any of them is not who will marry whom but when the predetermined marriage will take place.

3. *Social isolation of young people* from any potential mate is an arrangement that is found primarily among the upper classes in Islamic cultures, for example. The purpose of such isolation is to assure that intimate social contact cannot occur. Young girls are physically isolated from boys, and their elders arrange their marriages.

Cultural Differences in
Mate Selection

As noted in the text, all societies exercise some degree of control over the mate-selection process. Dr. David Mace, who with his wife, Vera, wrote about marital practices in Eastern and Western cultures, spoke with a group of young Indian college women about their feelings concerning mate selection.

"Wouldn't you like to be free to choose your own partners, like the young people in the West?"

"Oh, no!" several voices replied in chorus.

"Why not?"

"For one thing," said one of them, "doesn't it put the girl in a very humiliating position?"

"Humiliating? In what way?"

"Well, doesn't it mean that she has to try to look pretty and call attention to herself, and attract a boy, to be sure she'll get married?"

"Well, perhaps so."

"And if she doesn't want to do that, or if she feels it's undignified, wouldn't that mean she mightn't get a husband?"

"Yes, that's possible."

"So a girl who is shy and doesn't push herself forward might not be able to get married. Does that happen?"

"Sometimes it does."

"Well, surely that's humiliating. It makes getting married a sort of competition in which the girls are fighting each other for the boys. And it encourages a girl to pretend she's better than she really is. She can't relax and be herself. She has to make a good impression to get a boy, and then she has to go on making a good impression to get him to marry her."

Before we could think of an answer to this unexpected line of argument, another girl broke in.

"In our system, you see," she explained, "we girls don't have to worry at all. We know we'll get married. When we are old enough, our parents will find a suitable boy, and everything will be arranged. We don't have to enter into competition with each other."

"Besides," said a third girl, "how would we be able to judge the character of a boy we met and got friendly with? We are young and inexperienced. Our parents are older and wiser, and they aren't as easily deceived as we would be. I'd far rather have my parents choose for me. It's so important that the man I marry should be the right one. I could so easily make a mistake if I had to find him for myself."

Another girl had her hand stretched out eagerly.

"But does the girl really have any choice in the West?" she said. "From what I've read, it seems that the boy does all the choosing. All the girl can do is say yes or no. She can't go up to a boy and say 'I like you. Will you marry me?' Can she?"

We admitted that this was not done.

"So," she went on eagerly, "when you talk about men and women being equal in the West, it isn't true. When our parents are looking for a husband for us, they don't have to wait until some boy takes it into his head to ask for us. They just find out what families are looking for wives for their sons, and see whether one of the boys would be suitable. Then, if his family agree that it would be a good match, they arrange it together."

Source: David and Vera Mace, *Marriage East and West* (New York: Doubleday, 1960), pp. 144–145. Reprinted with permission.

4. *Close supervision of marriageable females* is another method of controlling mate selection. As seen in some Latin American countries, this system of chaperonage does not require social segregation; in fact, it permits love relationships to develop—but only between young people who are regarded as suitable according to social class and other criteria.

5. Goode's fifth pattern is one that is *formally free.* Cultures that follow this pattern expect love to play a large role in mate selection, but through a system of indirect controls, they allow for parental influence. Parental socialization makes the young people aware that certain potential mates are ineligible because of race, religion, or other factors. The peer group will then reinforce the parental socialization. This system, which is the one in use in the United States, encourages romantic love, but the parents in essence control the pool of potential mates (Goode, 1959).

INDIRECT CONTROLS IN AMERICAN SOCIETY   A very important form of indirect control of mate selection is the influence of mothers on their marriageable daughters. Bruce (1974) found that mothers who don't work outside the home are more likely than mothers who do to try to assist their daughters' courtship by encouraging potential suitors. It seems that mothers who work outside the home and those who do not view the social placement of their daughters differently. Mothers with outside careers are more likely to expect their daughters to work. The daughter's future therefore will not depend solely on the efforts and status of the husband she chooses. Mothers who don't expect their daughters to have outside careers may try harder to help them marry well because marriage will be the basis of their status in society (Bruce, 1974).

In a later study, Bruce found that 77 percent of daughters and mothers who responded to a questionnaire agreed that mothers should not assist their daughters in the choice of a husband. Even so, there was a significant positive correlation between where the daughter stood in the courtship process (dating around, going steady, or engaged) and the mother's activity to encourage the male and assist the daughter's efforts. The more advanced the stage, the greater the mother's degree of involvement (Bruce, 1976).

Encouragement of possible marriage partners is not the only way in which adults influence mate selection. The general reaction of families and, to a lesser extent, of friends seems to help shape a couple's opinion of their relationship. According to a study of student couples, those who feel the most positive social reactions to their relationship are the most likely to continue it. When family and friends invite the two to social functions as a couple, comment on what a nice pair they make, and include the partner in family activities, it reinforces the couple's feeling that they are well matched. Compared to those who meet with negative social reactions, they are more likely to commit themselves to their relationship, think of themselves as a couple, and act as a unit. But if family and friends reject the partner or avoid

For Prince Charles, finding a suitable queen-to-be was a long and arduous process. Although he was determined to marry for love, he faced a long list of royal restrictions on his choice of a mate: he could not marry a Catholic, a divorcée, a woman who was known to be sexually experienced, or a woman whose lineage was insufficiently aristocratic.

treating the two as an exclusive couple, they may internalize this implied judgment that their relationship is undesirable and come to question it themselves (Lewis, 1973).

Factors in Mate Selection: Narrowing the Field of Eligibles

As might be expected, society does not rely on parents to influence mate selection. In every society, there are both explicit and implicit rules that govern the selection of marriage partners.

EXOGAMY/ENDOGAMY   The most explicit rules governing mate selection are the rules of exogamy and endogamy. **Exogamy** is the social rule or expectation that persons will marry outside their own particular group. For instance, American society is exogamous in the sense that there are taboos against marrying a close blood kin or a person of the same sex. **Endogamy** is the rule or expectation that persons will marry within a particular social group. These societally defined boundaries of exogamy and endogamy define the "field of eligibles" from which individuals are allowed to choose a marital partner.

HETEROGAMY/HOMOGAMY   The field of eligibles is further narrowed by the socially encouraged tendencies toward heterogamy and homogamy. **Heterogamy** refers to our tendency to choose someone with different personal or group characteristics, and **homogamy** refers to our tendency to select someone with similar personal or group characteristics. In both cases, the selection takes place within the field of eligibles. Thus, the rules of endogamy specify the field of eligibles, and then homogamy expectations provide informal societal pressures which operate to restrict further the "field" from which we may choose a mate.

It is hardly surprising, then, that most people tend to choose mates who are similar to themselves in age, intelligence, race, ethnic group, social class, and religion. Certainly, familial and social pressures encourage this. Rubin (1968) reported that virtually all marriages were within the same social class. However, Glenn et al. (1974) discovered a tendency among upper-class American women toward heterogamous marriage. About one-third of them appear to marry men of slightly lower social class than their own. The explanation for this is probably, at least in part, a shortage of eligible upper-class men within their general age group.

INTERRACIAL MARRIAGES   Interracial marriage is a good example of a shift from formal (endogamy) to informal (homogamy) restrictions on the field of eligibles. Historically, marriages between blacks and whites were prohibited by law. With the resurgence of the civil rights movement during the 1950s and 1960s, laws against miscegenation (race mixing) were struck down. Nevertheless, many segments of American society continue to view interracial marriages as outside the range of homogamous expectations. It is not surprising, given these informal pressures, that only 1 percent of American marriages are between people of different races.

During the decade 1960–1970, marriages between blacks and whites increased by 26 percent. Yet even with this rise, such marriages still represent a miniscule proportion of all marriages in the United States (Monahan, 1976). According to Heer (1974), the increase in interracial marriages has been almost entirely in marriages between black men and white women. There has actually been an overall decline in the number of marriages between white men and black women.

Partners in an interracial marriage often encounter problems not common to marriages within the same race. The couple may be rejected by families and friends and may encounter hostility from others. Differences in cultural background may make adjustment difficult, since the family role behavior expected by each spouse may be different. Many sociologists believe that interracial marriages are less stable than marriages between partners of the same race, but the few studies that have addressed this question have yielded contradictory results. For example, a study by Monahan (1970) found that black-white marriages were more stable than black-black marriages and that in marriages in which the husband was black and the wife white the incidence of divorce was lower than in white-white marriages. Heer (1974), by contrast, reported that marriages in which the husband was white and the wife black had a higher divorce rate than marriages between members of the same race. There is consistent evidence, however, that when an interracial marriage occurs between members of equal-status races (as in Hawaii between Asian-American and Caucasian), the likelihood of the marriage failing is not greater than for other marriages (Nye and Berardo, 1973). Thus, it seems that the status of the race is more relevant than differences between cultures.

INTERFAITH MARRIAGES   In a country such as the United States, where there coexist a great number of religious groups, intermarriage is almost inevitable. And, the smaller the religious group, the higher the rate of intermarriage because there are a limited number of marriageable partners. For example, in states where the proportion of Catholics is low, the rate of intermarriage for Catholics is high. Where the proportion of Catholics is high, the rate of intermarriage is low (Nye and Berardo, 1973). Protestants, being the most numerous religious group in the country, have the lowest rate of intermarriage. Despite the fact that the Catholic church has actively opposed intermarriage, about one-quarter of marriages involving a Catholic are to someone outside the faith. Among Jews the rate of intermarriage has traditionally been very small, despite the fact that they comprise only 3 percent of the population. In recent years, however, the rate of intermarriage for Jews has been climbing.

Religious groups oppose intermarriage because of fear that the member will be less dedicated in following the religion than if married to a person of the same faith. They also fear that the children of the couple may not be brought up within the faith. Religious leaders and other critics of intermarriage point to the instability of such marriages as further proof of their inadvisability. If the religious identification of one partner in the marriage is high, this may cause conflict unless the other partner is extremely tolerant. Perhaps even more important as a potential factor in marital instability is the behavior expected by the religious organization. For example, Catholics are instructed by the church to treat the father as the head of the house and the mother as his helpmate. They are expected to send the children to parochial schools, if possible. Birth control—except through "natural" methods—is prohibited.

Lack of agreement between the partners on matters such as these can create serious conflicts.

Theories of Mate Selection

Most theories of mate selection are based on principles of homogamy. These theories emphasize such factors as physical closeness or propinquity, "filtering," and social exchange. One exception, however, is the complementary-needs theory, which stems from the idea that "opposites attract."

COMPLEMENTARY-NEEDS THEORY   Based on personality-need theory, Winch (1958) speculated that people have a tendency to choose a mate whose personality complements theirs, rather than a mate whose personality is very similar to theirs. In short, Winch believed that in the area of personality opposites attract. According to this theory, a person with a dominant, aggressive personality would be attracted to a mate with a submissive, passive personality. An early study by Kerchoff and Davis (1962) suggested that Winch was correct: short-term relationships were more likely to be based on similar values and shared social characteristics, but long-term relationships were more likely to be built on personalities which complemented one another. Several later studies, however, including Levinger et al. (1970), could not replicate these findings. Thus although most of us can cite at least one marital relationship with which we are familiar that tends to support this general notion, overall there seems little evidence to support Winch's ideas (Murstein, 1980).

PROPINQUITY THEORY   The term **propinquity** as used by sociologists refers to the tendency to select mates from among those with whom one has frequent contact. Although this does not necessarily imply homogamy, the assumption seems to be that those living near us have similar social characteristics. However, as Nye and Berardo (1973) observe, the major question is whether people marry those living near them because of the convenience of meeting and interacting with them, or because they share a whole range of social characteristics. In an early study of this tendency to "residential propinquity," Bossard (1932) determined from a sample of 5000 marriage-license applications of couples in Philadelphia that one-sixth of the couples lived within one block of another; another one-third lived within five blocks; and over one-half lived within twenty blocks. Later studies, including a review of research by Katz and Hill (1958), provided support for Bossard's work.

MURSTEIN'S SVR THEORY   Based on general principles of social homogamy which characterize the differing stages through which relationships pass during the mate-selection process, sociologists have formulated a number of so-called "filter theories" (Kerchoff and Davis, 1962; Murstein, 1970). Perhaps the most predominant of these is Murstein's SVR theory. Murstein's (1970, 1980) SVR model is based on two ideas: exchange theory and the concept of a filter. The initials "SVR" stand for the three "filter stages" Murstein identified: stimulus, values, and role (see Fig. 4.3). Each stage acts as a filter to eliminate potential mates from the field of eligibles.

During the *stimulus stage*, initial choices are made from a fairly open field of eligible mates. People are first attracted to each other on the basis of such qualities as physical appearance, verbal and nonverbal communications, and social factors. Physical attractiveness is especially prominent at this stage. A relationship is only established if, through the process of interpersonal exchange, each party arrives at a favorable evaluation of the assets as opposed to the liabilities of the relationship.

Couples who survive this test enter the *value-comparison stage*. Here, the couple shares their attitudes toward marriage, careers, religion, sex, children, and many other values to determine whether they match each other. If these values are compatible, the couple will confirm the initial attraction they felt and experience a feeling of greater intimacy. In a sense, this stage interacts with the stimulus stage, since the attractions that stimulated the relationship initially must combine with value compatibility before the couple can enter the role stage.

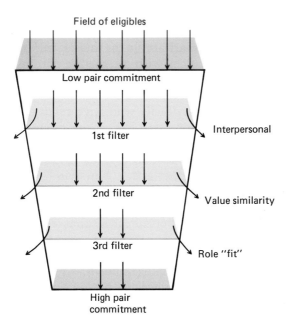

Fig. 4.3
Stimulus-value-role theory of mate selection. (Source: Adapted from Murstein, 1970.)

In the *role stage,* the partners experiment with their compatibility by trying out a variety of roles. They consider whether a long-term commitment is desirable based on the actual and expected behavior of each partner and the extent to which the behavior meets their respective needs. Unless these expectations of performance fit, the couple is likely to break up rather than proceed toward marriage. The important thing at this stage is for the couple to observe a range of behaviors so that they understand what it would be like to be married to each other. Of course, because they are not married, they cannot have a completely representative picture of what a long-term commitment would be like. Again, there is a weighing of assets and liabilities, and again at this stage partners are filtered out. There are notable similarities between Murstein's SVR theory and Reiss's (1960) "wheel theory" of the development of heterosexual love relationships.

SOCIAL-EXCHANGE THEORY AND MATE SELECTION   Employing the concepts of social-exchange theory presented in Chapter 2, several attempts have been made to devise models to explain interpersonal attraction in general (Berscheid and Walster, 1969) and mate selection in particular (Edwards, 1969; Nye and Berardo, 1973). These exchange models, also termed "maximum-profit" models, generally state that in relationships with others, including in mate selection, individuals attempt to maximize their rewards and minimize their costs in order to obtain the most profitable outcome possible. Initially, for instance, a person must decide whether it is more profitable (profit = rewards − costs) to be married than to remain single. Further, he or she must identify, from among the field of eligibles, that potential mate who has the greatest reward/cost ratio, taking into account a range of dimensions including the other's ability to enact the marital role. In this regard, individuals are always comparing the available choices with alternative options in assessing which is to be the most profitable choice or alternative.

This model has certain characteristics that suggest homogamy. Generally, it is assumed that those individuals who have relatively equal resources or assets, whether economic, interpersonal, or personal, would most likely be able to pool their resources and work together for "maximum-joint profit" (Scanzoni, 1979) as well as be able to bargain or negotiate at the same level when decision making or conflict arises. Murstein (1980) has shown support for the notion that individuals tend to match up with someone whose perceived capacity to reward them is approximately equal to their own capacity to give rewards. For instance, it was observed earlier that individuals tend to develop relationships with others who are perceived as having a similar degree of physical attractiveness. Edwards (1969) has stated this perspective in what he terms an "exchange theory of homogamous mating": "(1) Within any collectivity of potential mates, a marriageable person will seek out the individual who is perceived as maximizing his rewards; (2) Individuals with equivalent resources are most likely to maximize each other's rewards; (3) Pairs with equivalent resources are most likely to possess homogamous characteristics; and (4) Mate selection, therefore, will be homogamous with respect to a set of characteristics" (p. 525).

 THE TRANSITION TO MARRIAGE

The transition period between the decision to marry and the perception of the self as a married person usually includes the engagement period, the wedding, the honeymoon, and the first few months of the new marriage. Many people find it a time of some tension as well as a time of joyful anticipation.

Role Transitions of the Engagement Period

Marrying suddenly, without a period of preparation, is likely to make the early months of marriage more difficult. Rapoport (1973) has identified three important developmental tasks of the engagement period to help prepare couples for their new roles.

1. Preparing to be a husband or wife—to live in intimate daily contact with another person, to carry on a joint economic life, and to cope with possible conflicts in the roles of worker and homemaker.
2. Disengaging oneself from other relationships that might compete with the marriage.
3. Preparing to give up the pleasures of single life or accommodating them to the different realities and rewards of married life.

Premarriage Contracts

Some couples go even further in their planning for marriage: they try to spell out the terms of their marital agreement in a personal premarriage contract. These couples negotiate beforehand on such matters as who will make the money and who will decide how it will be spent, who will do the housework, whose work will dictate where they will live, whether extramarital relationships will be permitted and under what conditions, whether there will be children, and how property will be divided in case of divorce. Although the idea of drawing up a premarriage contract is appealing to some, it may not be useful for anything other than focusing discussion. Its legal validity is generally doubtful, and many states prohibit at least some aspects of such contracts. It is difficult for unmarried people to predict what their married life will really be like, what unexpected crises will arise, or how they will react to them.

Nevertheless, working out a premarriage contract may be beneficial insofar as it encourages a couple to discuss the problems they anticipate. This approach may be an antidote to idealization and later disillusionment (Wells, 1976).

The Marriage Contract

A marriage contract is actually an unwritten contract which imposes far greater obligations on the partners than the apparently simple words of the marriage vows suggest. Not only is it unwritten, its penalties are unspecified, and the marital partners are usually unaware of its terms when they enter into it (Weitzman, 1975).

The marriage contract is not static. Over the years, it has changed markedly to reflect changing social conditions, although the changes in society have usually outpaced the changes in the contract. For that reason, society is still dealing with a contract that perpetuates stereotypes of marital relationships which were more applicable some years ago than now.

Weitzman (1975) identified four elements of the traditional marriage contract. First, the husband is recognized as the head of the household. The wife is expected to assume her husband's name, his residence, and his social and economic status. The loss of her name may be regarded as symbolic of the loss of her independent identity even though she may have a professional career. (This is changing in many states, which are allowing women to choose what name they wish to be known by.) Second, the husband is responsible for the support of his family. As a result, in many states he has the power to

Much of the activity surrounding a wedding focuses on the bride, probably because marriage represents a greater change in her status than in that of the groom.

control family income and property. Weitzman contends that the husband's financial authority and advantages reduce the wife's chances to gain experience in financial matters. Third, the wife is responsible for performing domestic services which include housework, child care, affection toward her husband, and sexual and social obligations. This is another area in which there have been some drastic changes; for example, recent court rulings have made it possible under certain circumstances for a wife to bring suit against her

HIGHLIGHT 4.3   *A Marriage Contract: 1855*

The concept of marriage contracts is by no means a new one. In 1855 Lucy Stone and Henry B. Blackwell made the following formal commitment as a protest against conditions which prevailed in many states at that time:

While acknowledging our mutual affection by publicly assuming the relationship of husband and wife, yet in justice to ourselves and a great principle, we deem it a duty to declare that this act on our part implies no sanction of, nor promise of voluntary obedience to such of the present laws of marriage, as refuse to recognize the wife as an independent, rational being, while they confer upon the husband an injurious and unnatural superiority, investing him with legal powers which no honorable man would exercise, and which no man should possess. We protest, especially against the laws which give to the husband:

1. the custody of the wife's person;

2. the exclusive control and guardianship of their children;

3. the sole ownership of her personal property, and use of her real estate, unless previously settled upon her, or placed in the hands of trustees, as in the case of minors, lunatics, and idiots;

4. the absolute right to the product of her industry;

5. also against laws which give to the widower so much larger and more permanent an interest in the property of his deceased wife, than give to the widow in that of the deceased husband;

6. finally, against the whole system by which "the legal existence of the wife is suspended during marriage," so that in most States, she neither has a legal part in the choice of her residence, nor can she make a will, nor sue or be sued in her own name, nor inherit property.

We believe that personal independence and equal human rights can never be forfeited except for crime; that marriage should be an equal and permanent partnership, and so recognized by law; that until it is so recognized, married partners should provide against the radical injustice of present laws by every means in their power.

Source: Bernard, J. *The Future of Marriage* (New York: Bantam Books, 1973). Copyright © 1974 by Jessie Bernard. Excerpts reprinted by permission of Thomas Y. Crowell Co., Inc. and Souvenir Press, Ltd.

Table 4.1 **State Marriage Regulations**

STATE OR OTHER JURISDICTION	AGE AT WHICH MARRIAGE CAN BE CONTRACTED WITHOUT PARENTAL CONSENT		AGE AT WHICH MARRIAGE CAN BE CONTRACTED WITH PARENTAL CONSENT		BLOOD TESTS AND OTHER MEDICAL REQUIREMENTS			
					MAXIMUM PERIOD BETWEEN EXAMINATION AND ISSUANCE OF LICENSE (DAYS)	SCOPE OF MEDICAL INQUIRY	WAITING PERIOD	
	MALE	FEMALE	MALE	FEMALE			BEFORE ISSUANCE OF LICENSE	AFTER ISSUANCE OF LICENSE
Alabama	18	18	17(a)	14(a)	30	(b)	...	...
Alaska	18	18	16(c)	16(c)	30	(b)	3 da.	...
Arizona	18	18	16(c)	16(c)	30	(b)	(d)	...
Arkansas	18	18	17(c)	16(c)	30	(b)	3 da.	...
California	18	18	18(a,c)	16(a,c)	30	(b,e,f,g)	...	...
Colorado	18	18	16(c)	16(c)	30	(b,f,h)	...	...
Connecticut	18	18	16(c)	16(c)	35	(b)	4 da.	...
Delaware	18	18	18(c)	16(c)	30	(b)	...	(i)
Florida	18	18	16(a,c)	16(a,c)	30	(b)	3 da.	...
Georgia	18(j)	18(j)	16(c,j)	16(c,j)	30	(b,e)	3 da.(k)	...
Hawaii	18	18	16	16(c)	30	(b,f)	...	...
Idaho	18	18	16(c)	16(c)	...	(f)	(m)	...
Illinois	18	18	16(c)	16(c)	15	(b,e)	3 da.	...
Indiana	18	18	17(c)	17(c)	30	(b,e)	3 da.	...
Iowa	18	18	16	16	20	(b)	3 da.	...
Kansas	18	18	18(c)	18(c)	30	(b)	3 da.	...
Kentucky	18	18	(a,o)	(a,o)	15	(b,e)	3 da.	...

(a) Parental consent not required if previously married.

(b) Venereal diseases.

(c) Legal procedure for younger persons to obtain license.

(d) Blood test must be on record at least 48 hours before issuance of license.

(e) Sickle-cell anemia.

(f) Rubella immunity.

(g) Tay-Sachs disease.

(h) Rh factor.

(i) Residents, 24 hours; nonresidents, 96 hours.

(j) Parental consent is not needed regardless of age in cases of pregnancy or when couple has a living child born out of wedlock.

(k) Unless parties are 18 years of age or over, or woman is pregnant, or applicants are the parents of a living child born out of wedlock.

(continued)

Table 4.1 **State Marriage Regulations (Continued)**

| State or Other Jurisdiction | Age at which Marriage Can Be Contracted without Parental Consent | | Age at which Marriage Can Be Contracted with Parental Consent | | Blood Tests and Other Medical Requirements | | Waiting Period | |
| | | | | | Maximum Period Between Examination and Issuance of License (Days) | Scope of Medical Inquiry | Before Issuance of License | After Issuance of License |
	Male	Female	Male	Female				
Louisiana	18	18	18(c)	16(c)	10	(b)	...	72 hrs.
Maine	18	18	16(c)	16(c)	60	(b)	5 da.	...
Maryland	18	18	16(c)	16(c)	...	...	48 hrs.	...
Massachusetts	18	18	18(c)	18(c)	30	(b,f)	3 da.	...
Michigan	18	18	(r)	16	33	(b)	3 da.	...
Minnesota	18	18	18	16(q)	...	...	5 da.	...
Mississippi	21	21	17(c)	15(c)	30	(b)	3 da.	...
Missouri	18	18	15(c)	15(c)	15	(b)	3 da.	...
Montana	18	18	18(c)	18(c)	20	(b)	5 da.	3 da.
Nebraska	19	19	17	17	30	(b,f)	2 da.	...
Nevada	18	18	16(a,c)	16(a,c)	...	...	...	...
New Hampshire	18	18	14(q)	13(q)	30(r)	(b)	3 da.	...
New Jersey	18	18	16(c)	16(c)	30	(b)	72 hrs.	...
New Mexico	18	18	16(c)	16(c)	30	(b)	72 hrs.	...
New York	18	18	16	14(s)	30	(b,e)	...	24 da.(t)
North Carolina	18	18	16	16(c)	30	(b,f,u,v)	...	...
North Dakota	18	18	16	16	30	(b,w)	...	...

(l) Generally no, but may be recognized for limited purposes, e.g., legitimacy of children, workers' compensation benefits, etc.

(m) Three days if parties are under 18 years of age.

(n) However, contracting such a marriage is a misdemeanor.

(o) No minimum age.

(p) No provision in the law for parental consent for males.

(q) Permission of judge also required.

(r) Maximum period between blood test and date of intended marriage.

(s) If under 16 years of age, consent of family court judge also required.

(t) However, marriage may not be solemnized within 3 days of date on which specimen for blood test was taken.

(u) Mental competence.

(continued)

Table 4.1 **State Marriage Regulations (Continued)**

STATE OR OTHER JURISDICTION	AGE AT WHICH MARRIAGE CAN BE CONTRACTED WITHOUT PARENTAL CONSENT		AGE AT WHICH MARRIAGE CAN BE CONTRACTED WITH PARENTAL CONSENT		BLOOD TESTS AND OTHER MEDICAL REQUIREMENTS		WAITING PERIOD	
					MAXIMUM PERIOD BETWEEN EXAMINATION AND ISSUANCE OF LICENSE (DAYS)	SCOPE OF MEDICAL INQUIRY	BEFORE ISSUANCE OF LICENSE	AFTER ISSUANCE OF LICENSE
	MALE	FEMALE	MALE	FEMALE				
Ohio	18	18	18(c)	16(c)	30	(b)	5 da.	...
Oklahoma	18	18	16(c)	16(c)	30	(b)	(m)	...
Oregon	18	18	17	17	30	(b)	...	(a,b)
Pennsylvania	18	18	16(c)	16(c)	30	(b,y)	3 da.	...
Rhode Island	18	18	18(c)	16(c)	40	(b,f,v)	...	...
South Carolina	18	18	16(c)	14(c)	...	...	24 hrs.	...
South Dakota	18	18	16(c)	16(c)	20	(b)	...	...
Tennessee	18	18	16(c)	16(c)	30	(b)	3 da.(ab)	...
Texas	18	18	14(c)	14(c)	21	(b)	...	...
Utah	18	18	16(a)	14(a)	30	(b)	...	...
Vermont	18	18	16(c)	16(c)	30	(b)	...	5 da.
Virginia	18	18	16(a,c)	16(a,c)	30	(b)	...	...
Washington	18	18	17(c)	17(c)	...	(b,r,aa)	3da.	...
West Virginia	18	18	(q)	(o)	30	(b)	3 da.	...
Wisconsin	18	18	16	16	20	(b)	5 da.	...
Wyoming	19	19	17(c)	16(c)	30	(b)	...	...
Dist. of Col.	18	18	16(a)	16(a)	30	(b)	3 da.	...
Puerto Rico	21	21	18(c)	16(c)	10(ab)	(b,aa)	...	...

Source: Reprinted from *The Book of the States*, 1980–1981, Vol. 23, page 46, published by the Council of State Governments, Lexington, Kentucky.

(v) Tuberculosis.

(w) Some marriages prohibited if a party is severely retarded.

(x) License valid 3 days after application signed and valid for 30 days thereafter.

(y) Court order needed if party is weakminded, insane, or of unsound mind.

(z) May be waived if certain conditions are met.

(aa) Affidavit of mental competence required. Also, no epilepsy in Puerto Rico.

(ab) Maximum time from blood test to expiration of license.

husband for rape. What has not changed, however, is the fact that the wife who devotes herself to the role of homemaker in order to further her husband's career is likely to be penalized for it if the couple should divorce. It is a difficult job, even for a judge willing to make the attempt, to evaluate the contributions of homemaking tasks to a marital estate. The fourth element of the marriage contract is the wife's obligation to care for the couple's children. The assumption that the woman is best equipped to care for the children is reflected in divorce cases which still usually award custody of children to the mother. Weitzman contends that this assumption places unfair pressure on women who might prefer not to have custody of their children. Such women are made to feel deviant. This stereotype is slowly changing, to the benefit of both sexes and of children.

Weitzman's criticism of the marriage contract has some validity, but as we have noted, its requirements are being adjusted to reflect changing societal needs.

Rituals and Traditions

Marriage represents a transition from one social status to another in the life cycle of the individual. The variety of rituals associated with it is an indication of the importance placed on the formation of new families (Rapoport, 1973).

The wedding itself is a major rite of passage. Like birthdays, graduations, and deaths, it is usually marked by a public ceremony and embellished with special clothes, symbols, pageantry, and gifts which emphasize its significance. Although a few modern weddings are sometimes unorthodox—such as scuba divers getting married underwater—most still follow our society's traditional patterns. Among couples marrying for the first time in 1971, seven out of eight did so in a church or synagogue, seven out of eight brides received an engagement ring, and 85 percent of the brides wore formal wedding gowns (Seligson, 1973). Among the upper class, virtually all weddings are still held in churches (Blumberg and Paul, 1975). Although some couples are now writing their own vows, they still express their commitment in spoken vows of some sort.

The traditions associated with weddings are of ancient origin. The white bridal gown symbolized virginity. The wearing of the bridal veil represented the idea that the woman was no longer to be regarded as available as a potential marriage partner. The showering of rice on the newlyweds symbolized the wish for fertility. Such traditions have been—and continue to be—primarily female-oriented. Often friends of the bride give her a wedding shower to help provide useful items for her new home or lingerie that will make her more attractive to her husband. Her engagement picture is printed in the newspaper. Even the words of the wedding march begin, "Here comes the bride." The reasons these rituals have focused on the female are rooted in the traditional perception that the woman's major role in life is that of wife and mother. Thus the wedding represents a greater change in her status than in that of her husband.

Many modern couples have noted that the traditional wedding ceremony has sexist implications. For example, the idea that the bride is the property, first of her father, and then of her husband is implicit in the segment of the marriage ceremony in which she is "given" by her father in marriage. Because they wish to affirm their equality, some couples today prefer to alter their wedding ceremony to avoid the suggestion of male dominance. Thus, fathers may "present" their daughters rather than "give them away," and couples may omit from their vows such phrases as "love, honor, and obey."

DOONESBURY by Garry Trudeau

Yet even though the traditional meanings of some of the rituals are no longer applicable to most modern couples, traditional wedding ceremonies still serve important functions both for the couple and for the family and friends attending the ceremony. Sociologist Philip Slater (1963) suggests that the marriage helps to integrate the couple back into the social order. During courtship, he points out, couples are permitted to withdraw to some degree from loyalties to family and friends. The marriage, however, serves to bring them back into the social structure by forcing them to focus on obligations outside their own relationship, such as the numerous practical decisions that must be made in preparation for the wedding. Equally important, the wedding serves as a public acknowledgment before family and friends that the couple recognizes that they are entering a new status with new roles, and accompanying privileges and responsibilities. The repetition of the vows in particular helps to confirm the commitment of the new husband and wife to each other and to their new life together.

SUMMARY

1. The purpose of this chapter is to discuss the various stages and factors involved in the development of intimate, heterosexual relationships.

2. Intimacy is usually learned first in the family, later with same-sex friends, and then with persons of the opposite sex. There are different dimensions to intimate relationships in terms of their intellectual, physical, and emotional breadth, openness, and depth.

3. Dating and courtship patterns have changed over time. Today dating often takes the form of "getting together." Cohabitation is a relatively new stage in the courtship process, and many young people shift back and forth from one stage of dating and courtship to another.

4. There is considerable evidence that sexual standards for unmarried young people are in a period of transition. The double standard, which permitted more sexual freedom for males than for females, is gradually giving way to a single standard for both sexes. Surveys indicate that changes in attitudes and behavior have occurred more rapidly among females than among males and that the decreasing gap in sexual experience between the sexes reflects a catching-up phenomenon for females.

5. For most people, romantic love is the only acceptable criterion on which to base a marriage in our culture. Sociologists disagree about whether romantic love is a good foundation for marriage. However, the research suggests that romanticism declines with dating experience and maturity, and there is no evidence that romanticism adversely affects marital adjustment.

6. When a person decides to marry, many factors in addition to love influence the selection of a mate. Both explicit and implicit societal rules act to narrow the field of eligibles, including the rules of exogamy/endogamy and heterogamy/homogamy. Most of the theories of mate selection, including propinquity, filtering, and social exchange, are based on principles of homogamy.

7. Marriage represents a transition from one social status to another. The wedding is regarded as an important rite of passage. The traditions associated with it help bring the courting couple back into the social order by making them focus on obligations outside their own relationship. The vows exchanged by the couple serve as a public acknowledgment of their new roles and responsibilities.

REVIEW AND DISCUSSION

1. How is the idea of physical attractiveness as a basis for selecting a dating partner encouraged by our society?

2. Along with a friend or dating partner, write out a one- or two-paragraph description of your definition of love. Then compare the two descriptions. How similar or different were they?

3. Do you think romantic love is the best basis for marriage in our society? Why or why not?

4. Explain Murstein's SVR theory of mate selection. Do you think this is a satisfactory explanation of the process of mate selection? If not, how would you modify the theory?

5. If you have been to any weddings, describe some of the rituals and traditions they included. What purposes do you think are served by these traditions?

SUGGESTED READINGS

Berscheid, E., and E. H. Walster (1978). *Interpersonal Attraction*, 2d ed. Reading, Mass.: Addison-Wesley.

Centers on interpersonal attraction—from attraction-rejection in a group to attraction-rejection in romantic love. Considers the problem of evaluating others and variables that affect attraction such as similarity and rewards provided by the other person.

Fromm, E. (1956). *The Art of Loving: An Inquiry into the Nature of Love.* New York: Harper.

Discusses the many aspects of love and presents love as an art which requires knowledge and effort rather than as something one "falls into." Makes observations about the barriers that modern society erects between its members and the achievements of love.

——— (1980). "The Games Teenagers Play." *Newsweek*, September 1.

Article exploring current sexual norms among adolescents in the United States. Focuses on the more open sexual climate today and gender-role changes affecting adolescent sexual behavior.

Seligson, M. (1973). *The Eternal Bliss Machine: America's Way of Wedding.* New York: William Morrow.

The author reports and describes modern American marriage preparations and ceremonies, including discussion of ethnic traditions and honeymoons. Written in a lively, humorous style.

Walster, E., and G. W. Walster (1978). *A New Look at Love.* Reading, Mass.: Addison-Wesley.

Two social psychologists present research findings on the most misunderstood of all emotions: love. Among the topics covered are how we choose the people we marry, the problems of frustration, anxiety, and jealousy in a relationship, the dilemma of security vs. excitement, and passionate and companionate love.

Human Sexuality

5

"Sex lies at the root of life, and we can never learn to reverence life until we know how to understand sex."

HAVELOCK ELLIS

Sexuality serves the vital function of reproduction, but people behave sexually for pleasure and emotional release as well as to produce children. Because sexual expression is complex and can have serious consequences, societies have always imposed many rules and regulations on it. Although in America today there is a fair amount of freedom regarding sexual behavior, this is a relatively new thing and much confusion exists about the best way of transmitting knowledge about sex from one generation to the next. The result is that, despite the constant references to sex in movies and on television, many people still understand very little about their sexual functions or about human sexual experience.

Too often sexual relationships occur in an atmosphere of ignorance, misinformation, and inadequate communication. When this is true problems naturally arise, and they typically create friction between the partners and negative feelings about self in each individual. Clearly, it is essential to fulfilling sexual relationships that people have sound information about human sexuality.

In this text we consider human sexuality from a variety of perspectives. This chapter focuses on the basics: sexual anatomy and physiology, sexual response, and common forms of sexual expression. In addition, it considers some common sexual problems and provides information about sexually transmitted diseases. Chapter 8 deals with marital and extramarital sexuality; its particular emphasis is on the sociology of sexual relationships and the role of sexual communication. Chapter 9 provides up-to-date information on family planning, pregnancy, and childbirth.

139

ANATOMY AND PHYSIOLOGY OF SEX

Female Sexual Anatomy

The external female genitalia (Fig. 5.1) are known collectively as the **vulva.** They are normally almost hidden by the hair on the **mons veneris** ("mount of Venus"), the fat-covered area over the pubic bone. At the base of the mons is the **clitoris,** an extremely sensitive organ whose sole function is sexual arousal and orgasm. The clitoris is less than an inch long and is partially covered by the **clitoral hood.** Like the homologous (corresponding) male organ, the penis, the clitoris has a **shaft** and a **glans,** or head. Also like the penis, it is rich in nerve endings and, when stimulated, its hollow areas of erectile tissue engorge with blood, making it stiff.

The clitoris is shielded not only by the pubic hair but by inner and outer "lips" (**labia minora** and **labia majora**). The outer lips are covered with pubic hair; the inner lips contain erectile tissues that become engorged with blood during sexual arousal. On arousal they spread outward, clearing the way to the opening of the vagina, which lies within the inner lips (as does the urinary opening). The **vagina** is an elastic organ normally about three and one-half inches long that can stretch during sexual arousal to accommodate any size penis. Except during sexual arousal and childbirth, its flexible walls fold and relax so that they are touching.

The **hymen,** or "maidenhead," a small membrane which partially obstructs the vaginal opening, seems to serve no physiological function, though perhaps

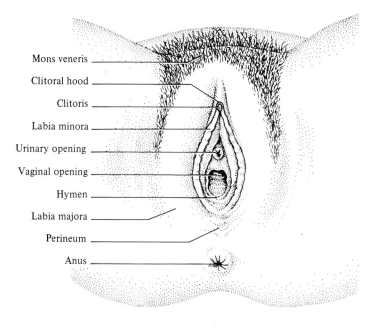

Mons veneris

Clitoral hood

Clitoris

Labia minora

Urinary opening

Vaginal opening

Hymen

Labia majora

Perineum

Anus

Fig. 5.1
External female genitalia

it protects the vaginal tissues early in life. The presence or absence of the hymen has traditionally been assigned great significance, as it usually ruptures the first time a woman has sexual intercourse. In some cultures that place the highest premium on virginity in brides, bedsheets stained by the tiny amount of blood allegedly caused by rupturing the hymen are displayed to the wedding guests as evidence of the bride's purity. Although an intact hymen has been considered positive proof of virginity, it is not a true test. In some women the hymen is flexible enough to stretch during intercourse without breaking; in others it may have been torn before first intercourse, perhaps during athletic activity or by insertion of tampons. In a few women the tissue of the hymen is so thick that it cannot be broken by the insertion of the penis, and a painless surgical incision must be made by a doctor.

Fig. 5.2

Internal view of female pelvis showing the reproductive system and other nearby organs. (Source: Eric T. Pengelley, Sex and Human Life, *Reading, Mass.: Addison-Wesley, 1974.)*

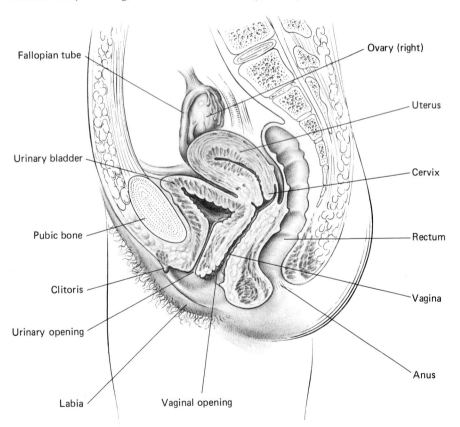

Two small mucus-producing bodies, **Bartholin's glands,** lie at each side of the vaginal opening. Once thought to be the primary source of lubrication for intercourse, they have been found to contribute very little fluid—and that only late in sexual arousal. Most of the fluid that facilitates the entry of the penis into the vagina is secreted through the vaginal walls.

An internal view of the female reproductive system is shown in Fig. 5.2. The vagina leads to the **uterus,** a thick-walled elastic organ the size and shape of a pear. The uterus is capable of considerable expansion to accommodate the growth of a fetus. But, like the vagina, the uterus is usually a potential rather than an actual cavity; ordinarily its sides touch each other. Its narrow neck, the **cervix,** protrudes downward into the upper end of the vagina. The cervical opening (the **os**) is ordinarily no wider than a thin straw, but it is capable of stretching to a circumference of ten centimeters during childbirth.

Two **fallopian tubes** lead from the upper sides of the uterus to the **ovaries,** the almond-sized organs which from the time of birth contain 40,000 to 400,000 **ova** (eggs). The ovaries also produce the female sex hormones, estrogen and progesterone. Rather than connecting directly to the ovaries, the fallopian tubes partially surround them with fingerlike projections that draw the eggs into the tubes, where muscular currents propel them to the uterus.

Male Sexual Anatomy

In the male, the organs corresponding to the ovaries are the **testes,** plum-shaped organs which are usually about two inches long and an inch and a half in diameter. The normal male possesses two testicles, both of which produce sperm cells and the male hormone, testosterone. Normally the testicles move down from the abdominal cavity into the **scrotum** (a sac-like structure below the penis) when the male fetus is seven or eight months old. However, in some cases, one or both of the testicles fail to descend. These undescended testicles may move into place during the first year or two of life, but occasionally this does not occur and the condition is overlooked until adolescence. When this happens, surgery or hormonal treatment may be required. It is important not to ignore undescended testicles because the high internal body temperature prevents the production of viable sperm cells and infertility may result. The exact relationship between heat and sperm production is unknown, but we do know that the insulating scrotum contracts in cold weather and relaxes in hot, to retain or dissipate heat so that the testicles are always about two degrees Fahrenheit cooler than the interior of the body (Guttmacher, 1970).

An estimated 50,000 microscopic sperm cells are produced in the testicles of the average mature male every minute (Gordon, 1974). (See Figs. 5.3 and 5.4.) The sperm then empty into the corresponding **epididymis,** a yards-long tightly coiled canal, where they remain for as long as six weeks to mature (McCary,

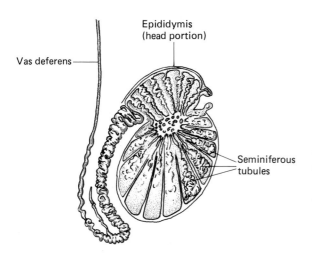

Vas deferens

Epididymis
(head portion)

Seminiferous
tubules

Fig. 5.3
Cross section of a testicle. Sperm are continuously generated in the seminiferous tubules and are stored in the epididymis where they undergo further maturation. During ejaculation, contractions propel the ripe sperm through the vas deferens and on toward the urethra. (Source: Pengelley, 1974.)

1973). Once ripe, they enter the **vas deferens,** a tube which leads to a pouch called the **seminal vesicle.** Sufficient sexual arousal causes **ejaculation,** the forceful exit of the sperm from the body through the **urethra,** a canal running down the center of the penis. There are two epididymides, two vas deferens, and two seminal vesicles in parallel systems, one attached to each testicle.

During ejaculation, a valve at the entrance to the bladder closes, preventing urine from leaving the bladder through the urethra. Instead, the sperm cells mix with fluid from the seminal vesicles and the nearby **prostate gland,** forming the **semen,** or ejaculate. Milky and thick, the ejaculate activates the sperm to help them swim through the vagina. It also provides an alkaline medium that helps to offset the vaginal acidity which would otherwise kill the sperm. To neutralize the acidity of the urethra itself, a few drops of alkaline fluid are excreted into the urethra by the **Cowper's glands** before ejaculation. The average ejaculation releases only about a teaspoonful of semen, but this small volume contains 200 to 500 million or more sperm cells which take up no more space than the head of a pin (Guttmacher, 1970).

Fig. 5.4
Greatly enlarged drawing of a human sperm cell. (Source: Pengelley, 1974.)

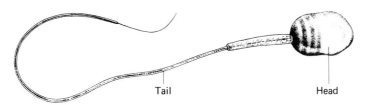

Tail   Head

The **penis** is the organ through which ejaculation of sperm takes place (see Fig. 5.5). Externally, the penis consists of a long **shaft** with a conelike **glans** (head) at the end. At the tip of the glans is the **meatus,** the urethral opening. The glans, particularly the **corona** (the ridge where the glans flares out before joining the shaft) and the **frenum** (the thin tissues where the corona is joined to the shaft on the underside), is extremely sensitive to sexual arousal, for it is laced with abundant nerve endings. The glans is covered by both a thin, sensitive skin and a thicker, retractable foreskin. A cheesy secretion called **smegma** may accumulate under the foreskin. Since this causes a strong odor—and sometimes irritation and infection—the foreskin is often removed. This

Fig. 5.5

Internal view of the male pelvis showing the reproductive system and other nearby organs. (Source: Pengelley, 1974.)

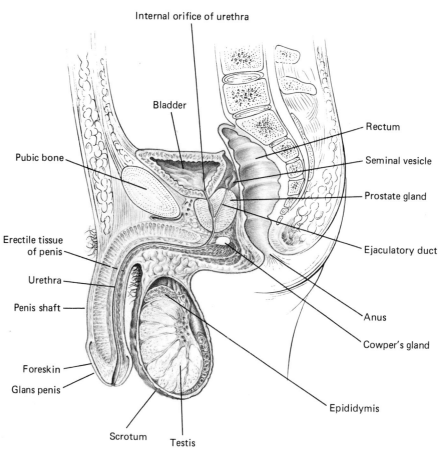

operation, **circumcision,** is very common in American society and is usually performed shortly after birth.

The penis is composed largely of spongy erectile tissue surrounding the urethra. The blood vessels react to sexual stimulation by permitting more blood to flow into this erectile tissue than out of it. This makes the penis enlarge, becoming stiff and erect so that it can enter the vagina. After ejaculation, blood empties from the erectile tissue, and the penis again becomes flaccid (soft).

The average penis is three to four inches long and about one and a quarter inches in diameter. In the erect state, it elongates to six inches or somewhat more and increases about a quarter inch in diameter. There is, however, considerable variation in normal penis size. Despite the fears of an estimated 15 percent of American men that their penis is too small (Berscheid et al., 1973), there is little relationship between the size of the relaxed penis and its size when erect. Small penises commonly double in size with erection; larger penises expand less (Masters and Johnson, 1966). Contrary to popular belief, penis size is unrelated to potency, body build, race, virility, or ability to satisfy or be satisfied by a sexual partner.

The Sexual Response Cycle

In 1966, Drs. William H. Masters and Virginia E. Johnson published the first clinical study of sexual response patterns of humans. This landmark study was based on actual laboratory observation of the physiological changes that occurred during the sexual arousal and orgasm of 382 female and 312 male volunteers. Despite the unromantic atmosphere of the clinic, the volunteers were able to achieve orgasm through various kinds of tactile stimulation: **coitus** (sexual intercourse) in several positions; masturbation; and for the women, breast stimulation alone (which worked for some), and simulated coitus with an artificial penis of clear glass fitted with a special optical system for observation and filming of internal changes.

One of Masters and Johnson's most significant findings was that no matter what the means of stimulation, sexual response always followed the same basic physiological pattern, which was similar for men and women. This response cycle consisted of four phases, which they labeled **excitement, plateau, orgasm,** and **resolution.**

THE EXCITEMENT PHASE Both men and women enter the excitement phase when the body begins to respond physiologically to erotic stimuli. In Masters and Johnson's research this was usually achieved through tactile stimulation of **erogenous zones,** areas of the body which become sexually aroused when stimulated. While the penis and clitoris are the primary erogenous zones in most men and women respectively, other important erogenous zones include the mouth, breasts (in both men and women), **anus,** and **perineum** (the area between the anus and the genitals). The ears, thighs, throat, nape of the neck, eyelids—and, indeed, many other areas of the body—may also be sensitive to erotic stimuli.

The excitement phase for males is indicated by erection of the penis; as it fills with blood it enlarges and lifts away from the body. This change from its relaxed state takes only a few seconds. The scrotum elevates and the skin of the scrotum grows tight and thick. The testes increase in size and elevate.

In females, sexual stimulation causes engorgement of the vaginal area. The lips swell and open outward. The vaginal walls lubricate, a response which usually can be detected ten to thirty seconds after stimulation begins. Lubrication does not, however, mean that a woman is fully prepared for intercourse, because this is only the beginning of her responses. If stimulation is continued after lubrication, the clitoris swells from engorgement. Direct contact with the clitoris may be unnecessary to this reaction and may even inhibit it if stimulation is too rough. The clitoris is so sensitive that indirect friction on the clitoral hood—either through penile thrusting or manual rubbing of the mons—is often sufficient for orgasm. Internally, the uterus begins to expand up to twice its normal size. It rises into the body cavity, pulling the cervix up and lifting the upper end of the vagina. This tenting effect causes the upper two-thirds of the vagina to balloon up and out to perhaps three times its usual diameter, adding about an inch to its length.

In both men and women, response during the excitement phase gradually involves the whole body. The muscles contract, the pulse accelerates, the blood pressure rises, and a rash called the **sex flush** often appears on the abdomen and breasts.

During the excitement phase, engorgement and muscle contraction in women's breasts cause the nipples to enlarge and erect; late in the excitement phase, the whole breast swells. Masters and Johnson also noted some degree of nipple erection in three-fifths of the men they studied.

THE PLATEAU PHASE   There is no clear dividing line between the excitement and plateau phases, but the sensations during the plateau phase are generally more intense.

In men, the penis is already fully erect before the onset of the plateau phase, but the ridge of the corona now grows larger. The testicles continue to swell and rise farther into the scrotum. A few drops of fluid may be secreted from the Cowper's glands; this fluid sometimes contains enough active sperm cells to cause pregnancy. The sex flush spreads and muscular tension throughout the body causes distorting contractions in the face and neck and strong grasping responses in the hands. The abdomen and buttocks tighten, increasing sexual tension, and thrusting pelvic movements that may have started voluntarily become almost involuntary.

In women, the muscular responses of the plateau phase are linked with other changes. The vagina responds to continued sexual stimulation by forming the **orgasmic platform.** Engorgement so swells the lower third of the vagina that its diameter is decreased by up to 50 percent, providing pleasurable friction for both partners during intercourse. While the outer or lower third of the vagina closes in to grip the penis, the upper or inner two-thirds retains its ballooned-out shape. The clitoris temporarily disappears by withdrawing under the clitoral hood, but it is still responsive to stimulation, either from direct rubbing on the mons veneris or from indirect friction on the clitoral hood caused by the penis as its rubs against the inner lips. Finally, the pinkish color of the labia minora deepens, changing to bright red or deep wine.

Late in the plateau phase, the heartbeats of both men and women may rise dramatically to 110–175 beats per minute. Their blood pressure rises, and they may begin to hyperventilate, breathing so rapidly or so deeply that they experience a slight loss of hearing and tingling sensations in the hands and feet.

THE ORGASMIC PHASE When engorgement and muscular tension reach their peak, both men and women experience **orgasm,** the sudden, involuntary release of accumulated muscular tension and pelvic congestion through strong rhythmic contractions. In the woman, contractions in the vagina are joined by deep rhythmic contractions in the uterus. There may be as few as three contractions in a mild orgasm or as many as fifteen or more, gradually decreasing in intensity and occurring farther apart. Before the actual contractions begin, many women feel a momentary sensation of suspension at a point of extreme sensual awareness, and then a single explosive spasm of the orgasmic platform, followed by the rhythmic contractions.

The initial orgasmic contractions in a man occur at exactly the same rate as in a woman—eight-tenths of a second apart. Contractions of the urethra and the muscles at the base of the penis cause forceful ejaculation of the semen, which collects in a bulb in the urethra at the base of the penis just prior to ejaculation. The contractions which have forced sperm cells from the seminal vesicles and prostatic fluid from the prostate gland down to the urethral bulb produce a first-stage sensation of orgasm before ejaculation actually occurs.

Many people wonder whether men and women experience orgasm differently. In a study of written descriptions of orgasm (Proctor et al., 1974), seventy judges were unable to distinguish between the male and female descriptions. Yet there is considerable individual variation in how people describe orgasm, and the same individual may experience orgasm differently at different times:

> I have such different experiences with orgasm. Sometimes it takes energy to hold back. The natural thing when I'm particularly loose is to let go and energy is

released and I can't go to sleep for hours. Other times I'm aroused but it's not a flowing, effortless experience. I need to expend energy. I feel good and then I want to go to sleep. The two experiences contrast with each other. (Boston Women's Health Book Collective, 1979, p. 45)

THE RESOLUTION PHASE   Soon after orgasm, muscular tension begins to subside. The sex flush disappears, the woman's breasts, uterus, and vagina return to their usual size. Pulse rate, blood pressure, and breathing slow down. After ejaculation, the penis gradually returns to its relaxed state; full loss of engorgement may take a few minutes or it may take longer, depending on how long the erection was held and whether sexual stimulation continues after orgasm (Masters and Johnson, 1966).

After ejaculation, men enter a **refractory period** during which sexual stimulation cannot produce another full erection. A variety of factors are involved in the length of the refractory period, including a man's age, frequency of previous sexual activity, and degree of emotional closeness and sexual desire for his partner. Women have no equivalent refractory period, and most are capable of repeated orgasms.

Differences in Male and Female Sexual Response

We have focused on the similarities in sexual response in men and women, but some differences do exist. One of these is the greater variability in female sexual response. Masters and Johnson identified three basic patterns in female sexual response and only one pattern in male response. The male response pattern is shown in Fig. 5.6; the female response pattern is shown in Fig. 5.7. As shown in Fig. 5.7, Pattern A most closely resembles the male pattern, except that it reveals the female potential for additional orgasms without the refractory period necessary for males. In Pattern B the woman reaches the plateau level but does not experience orgasm, and in Pattern C there is a rapid rise to orgasm followed by a quick resolution.

Another important difference is the greater ability of females to experience multiple orgasms, two or more sexual climaxes within a short period. In the past, it was assumed that only a small number of women were capable of multiple orgasms. Kinsey (1953) reported that about 14 percent of his female sample regularly had multiple orgasms. A 1970 survey conducted by *Psychology Today* (Athanasiou et al., 1970) reported a figure of 16 percent. However, Masters and Johnson (1966) demonstrated that multiple orgasms are within the capacity of most women. Over 50 percent of their female subjects were able to experience multiple successive orgasms if stimulation was effectively maintained.

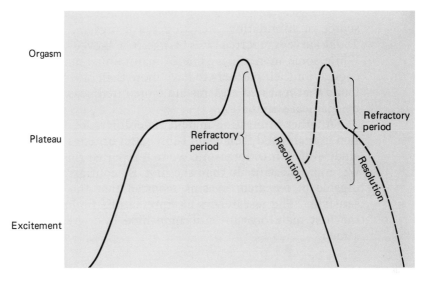

Fig. 5.6
The male sexual response cycle. (Source: William H. Masters and Virginia E. Johnson, Human Sexual Response, *published by Little, Brown and Company, Boston, 1966. Reprinted by permission.)*

Fig. 5.7
The female sexual response cycle. (Source: William H. Masters and Virginia E. Johnson, Human Sexual Response, *published by Little, Brown and Company, Boston, 1966. Reprinted by permission.)*

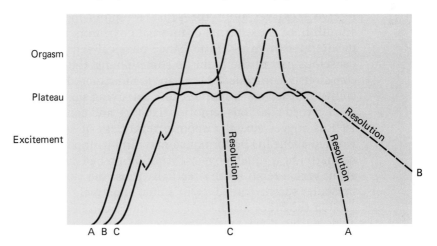

The great discrepancy between capacity and experience may lie in the source of stimulation used to achieve orgasm. The Kinsey and *Psychology Today* surveys reported rates of orgasm achieved by penile-vaginal intercourse. While some men are capable of maintaining an erection and thrusting long enough for their partners to have more than one orgasm, Masters and Johnson found that repeated orgasms are more often possible through manual, oral, or mechanical stimulation.

Another interesting male-female difference involves the subjective reaction of males and females to subsequent orgasms. In the Masters and Johnson study (1966), multiorgasmic women reported that the second or third climax was more pleasurable than the first. By contrast, most of the men who were capable of repeated orgasms reported that the first orgasm was the most satisfying. The researchers interpreted this finding as reflecting the fact that the first male orgasm is accompanied by a greater release of accumulated semen.

 INFLUENCES ON SEXUAL RESPONSE

Sexual reponse is not merely a physiological process. It is inextricably tied to cultural, social, and psychological factors, and it is influenced by hormones, the aging process, and the use of drugs.

Psychological Influences

Orgasm is a relatively uncomplicated physical response coordinated by the part of the spinal cord which lies in the pelvic area. But overall sexual response is subject to a great degree of control by higher parts of the brain, which receive messages from the sense receptors (bodily structures that receive stimuli from the external or internal environment) and decide whether or not to interpret them as erotic. Since physical sensations are projected into the conscious part of the brain, to some extent, the responses that follow can be consciously controlled. Men can, for instance, learn to delay ejaculation, an ability that is very important to a satisfying sexual relationship.

Learned reactions, emotional states, and conscious thought can inhibit as well as trigger sexual response, regardless of sensory input. A man who is worried about his performance may find it impossible to achieve an erection, no matter how much physical stimulation he receives. And a woman's anxiety about sexual relations may actually cause her vagina to tighten in involuntary muscular spasms called vaginismus, effectively preventing intercourse.

On the other hand, sexual responses can be initiated by erotic suggestion alone without any tactile stimulation of the genitals. Despite the overriding importance of the sense of touch to human sexuality, people also respond to certain erotic cues received through the other senses. American men are easily aroused by visual stimuli, such as photographs of nude women. They are particularly excited by the sight of a woman's breasts (Stember, 1975). American women seem to be more diverse in what they find sexually attractive in a man. Music has powerful effects on some people. And there is some

---

HIGHLIGHT 5.1   *What Men Fear Most about Sex*

Even in this era of sexual enlightenment, myths and fears about sex still persist. Wardell B. Pomeroy, coauthor of the Kinsey Report and dean of the Institute for Advanced Study of Human Sexuality, compiled a list of men's most common anxieties about lovemaking. The most prevalent fears, according to Pomeroy, are:

1. "Am I normal?" Men are concerned about whether their sexual behavior resembles that of other males and wonder whether what they do in bed is considered the "normal" way to have sex.

2. Anxiety about impotence. Most men experience sexual difficulty at some time; continuing anxiety about their next performance can become a self-fulfilling prophecy.

3. Anxiety about premature ejaculation. A problem which can afflict men of all ages, premature ejaculation is often brought on by psychological factors and, again, fear of possible repetition can create a self-fulfilling prophecy.

4. Anxiety about general performance. Behind performance anxiety is usually a fear of being rejected.

5. Anxiety over the size of one's penis. Concern that one's penis may be too small is derived from the common but incorrect belief that large and small penises enlarge proportionately upon erection.

6. Anxiety about aging. Some men convince themselves that their sex life will come to an end at some predetermined age.

7. Anxiety about insatiable demands. Threatened by the image of the super lover depicted in novels and movies and by some of the rhetoric of the women's movement, some men are intimidated by their image of the insatiable female.

8. Anxiety about latent homosexuality. Men become concerned that some unforseen event will lead them to discover that they have latent homosexual desires.

9. Anxiety that one's wife will become sexually involved with other men. The "macho" mentality, which encourages feelings of jealousy and possessiveness, may actually hide strong fears of a man's own inadequacy.

Source: Adapted from Wardell B. Pomeroy, "What Men Fear Most About Sex," *Cosmopolitan* (May 1977).

evidence that humans secrete and are subtly influenced by **pheromones,** genital odors which may excite or repel their partners (Kaplan, 1974a).

Cultural Influences

A clear example of the importance of cultural influences on sexual response can be found in studies of the response of men and women to erotic materials. Many studies have concluded that American women are not as oriented toward erotica (sexual materials) as their male counterparts. While early researchers such as Kinsey (1953) attributed this to biological differences, more recent evidence suggests that this is not the case.

Using special devices to measure engorgement of the penis and vagina, Heiman (1975) found that male and female college students exhibited the same degree of sexual arousal when listening to tape-recorded descriptions of sexual behavior. The interesting difference was that the majority of female subjects were unable to recognize the signs of sexual arousal in themselves. Well over half the women said they felt neither vaginal swelling nor lubrication after listening to an erotic tape, although the instruments showed that they exhibited these responses. Heiman theorized that this lack of awareness of the female subjects to their own erotic response was caused by cultural conditioning, which leads women to deny their sexual feelings. In American society, erotic materials have traditionally been aimed at a male audience, for male sexuality has long been socially acknowledged. And even though erotic magazines aimed at women have begun to appear, it is not yet generally acceptable for women to read and derive the same enjoyment from them that men do.

The Influence of Hormones

Hormones are chemical substances produced by endocrine glands that affect the functioning of other organs. Research indicates that hormones play an important role in sexual behavior, but there are differing views about the specific effects.

The hormones most significantly related to sexuality are the **androgens.** They are produced in the testicles of males and in the adrenal glands located above the kidneys in both males and females. In boys, androgen production begins at puberty, causing the development of male secondary sex characteristics such as deep voice, broad chest, and hair growth on the face and chest. In addition to influencing male sexual development, androgen is essential to sexual desire and the ability to experience orgasm. At the time of erotic stimulation, androgen activates certain brain centers to initiate sexual arousal and effect sperm production, erection, and ejaculation. Studies of men suffering from androgen deprivation because of castration (removal of the testicles, usually because of a serious disease such as prostatic cancer) have produced inconsistent findings, ranging from significant loss of sexual interest and activity (Bremer, 1959) to incidences of continued desire and function for as long as thirty years following castration (Ford and Beach, 1951). Thus, while androgen plays an important role in male sexual activity, its role is not absolute, and major variations in the amount of hormone present may not impair sexual functioning.

The female hormones, the **estrogens** produced by the ovaries, produce female secondary sex characteristics and affect the menstrual cycle. However, they have little impact on female sexual desire and activity. Masters and Johnson's research on postmenopausal women (1966) and Kinsey's research on women who have had their ovaries removed (Kinsey et al., 1953) found no significant negative effects on sexual desire. In women, as in men, the important hormones for sexual functioning are the androgens. A study comparing women who had had their ovaries removed to women who had had their adrenal glands removed found that the loss of the ovaries had no effect on sexual activity, whereas loss of the adrenal glands produced decreases in sexual desire and behavior (Waxenberg et al., 1959).

The Effects of Aging

Another influence on sexual response is the aging process. Men respond to aging by requiring longer to achieve erections and ejaculating with less force. Although sperm production ordinarily never ceases altogether, it decreases with aging. The testicles shrivel slightly and become softer, the prostate gland enlarges, and the ejaculate becomes thinner and decreases in volume. Although Kinsey (1953) found that about one man out of four was impotent at the age of seventy, some men retain their sexual potency much longer. Masters and Johnson (1966) found that the sexual capability of a high percentage of men who become impotent after the age of fifty can be restored through training.

When women are between forty-five and fifty-five years old, they begin **menopause,** a time when menstruation permanently ceases. During this "change of life," the ovaries gradually stop producing eggs and secrete a smaller supply of estrogen than before. Among the other physiological changes that take place are thinning of the vaginal walls, narrowing and shortening of the vagina, and shrinking of the outer vaginal lips. During sexual arousal, lubrication is less plentiful and uterine contractions during orgasm become stronger. These changes, which result from diminished production of estrogen, can make intercourse painful. The most common complaint of menopause, however, is "hot flashes"—a sensation of heat caused by dilation of blood vessels, usually in the face. Although most menopausal women do experience some minor discomfort, only about one-quarter feel the need to seek medical help for difficulties related to menopause (Novak et al., 1970).

Medical treatment for menopausal symptoms may include the use of tranquilizers, sleeping pills, or aspirin. A controversial treatment is **estrogen replacement therapy** (ERT) to restore the premenopausal hormonal balance. Although ERT has been shown to relieve some symptoms, recent studies have found that women who received ERT were six times as likely to develop cancer of the endometrium (uterine lining) than women who did not (Antunes et al., 1979). Other research suggests a possible link between ERT and breast cancer (Hoover et al., 1976).

The changes that accompany menopause do not physiologically affect sexual desire and response. Indeed, some women experience increased sexual interest after menopause because they are now free from the fear of pregnancy:

> I feel better and freer since menopause. I threw that diaphragm away. I love being free of possible pregnancy and birth control. It makes my sex life better. (Boston Women's Health Book Collective, 1979, p. 328)

For both men and women, the more sexual activity they engage in during youth and middle age, the more likely they are to be able to continue to enjoy sex in old age. Women over sixty who have had intercourse once or twice a week have longer orgasms and more vaginal lubrication than those whose sex lives have been less active. Our society's assumption that sex is the exclusive privilege of youth is belied by the facts.

The Influence of Drugs

Throughout history, people have tried to enliven sexual experiences or revive waning potency by consuming a variety of foods and drugs. But many **aphrodisiacs** (food or chemicals that are alleged to increase sexual desire and enjoyment), such as bull's testicles and pulverized rhinoceros horn, contain nothing that would enhance sexual performance. The only lift that results from their use is probably derived from the power of suggestion. Certain other substances do seem to affect sexuality, but usually not in the way that people imagine.

Many people believe that alcohol improves sexual enjoyment. In one study of middle-class and upper-middle-class Americans, 60 percent of the respondents reported increased sexual pleasure after drinking (Athanasiou et al., 1970). Alcohol, however, is actually a **depressant**—a substance that reduces the activity of the higher brain centers. It is likely that its reputed pleasure-enhancing ability results from the relaxation of inhibitions which might ordinarily block sexual expression. Whereas a few drinks may remove mental inhibitions, heavy drinking can make erection difficult for men and greatly reduce a woman's capacity for arousal and orgasm.

Marijuana, too, is sometimes used in conjunction with sex. Thirty percent of the women in one survey (Levin and Levin, 1975a), including 63 percent of those under twenty, reported using marijuana during sex. A depressant, marijuana actually decreases sexual performance, but at the same time it loosens inhibitions and produces euphoria and a distorted sense of time which may make people interpret sex as being better. Some users claim that marijuana sharpens their awareness of muscular sensations, especially those associated with orgasm (Kaplan, 1974a). But chronic heavy marijuana use may actually depress desire and impair the ability to experience orgasm (Ellinwood et al., 1975).

Amphetamines are **stimulants** which activate the central nervous system. Since their general effect is to elevate mood and energize behavior, some people believe they enhance sexuality. There is no experimental evidence to support this notion.

Cocaine is also a stimulant which some users claim increases the frequency and intensity of orgasms. However, as with amphetamines, there is no good evidence to substantiate its qualities as an aphrodisiac.

Psychedelic drugs such as LSD (lysergic acid diethylamide), mescaline, and psilocybin produce a warping of perceptions but do not enhance sexual response. Some LSD users feel detached from their own orgasms while those on "bad trips" may lose all interest in sex (Kaplan, 1974a).

L-dopa, a drug used chiefly in the treatment of Parkinson's disease, gained brief notoriety as an aphrodisiac because 2 percent of the male patients treated with it experienced hypersexuality as a side effect. But this effect has not been consistently produced in clinical studies of L-dopa with humans or animals (McCary, 1971).

The legendary aphrodisiac "Spanish fly," an extract of crushed dried beetles, is actually a dangerously corrosive irritant which acts on the urinary tract, causing painful congestion. It may indeed produce an erection, but one which is anything but pleasant. Use of Spanish fly may cause permanent damage to the kidneys and penis, and perhaps even death.

 FORMS OF SEXUAL EXPRESSION

The variety of sexual expression is seemingly infinite, ranging all the way from a sidelong glance to sexual intercourse in its many variations. Sexuality is first expressed by the infant as it strokes its own genitals. Childhood development includes curiosity about the body's sexual functions, attraction (generally temporary) to members of the same sex, and adolescent awakening to sexual desires. Until recently, our cultural heritage imposed many restrictions on sexual behavior, but a relatively wide range of sexual expression is now considered acceptable. Sexual intercourse where the male inserts his penis into the female's vagina is only one of many sexual choices. Indeed, people may favor different forms of sexual behavior under various circumstances or at different times in their lives.

Masturbation

Masturbation refers to erotic self-stimulation. Historical and anthropological records show that it has occurred in human society since ancient times. The extent to which it is practiced and the attitudes toward it vary from culture to culture.

In humans, self-stimulation begins in infancy and is often a continuing form of sexual expression throughout the life cycle. Infants apparently discover self-stimulation of the genitals by accident and then repeat the behavior since it is pleasurable. Children discover the erotic possibilities of rubbing against furniture and toys, and girls in particular engage in self-stimulation by contracting the buttocks. Boys are more likely than girls to learn effective self-stimulation techniques from others.

Before puberty, boys are incapable of ejaculation, but they can have orgasms. The American boy is likely to experience his first ejaculation between the ages of eleven and fifteen with the changes of puberty. For some, ejaculation occurs as a spontaneous nocturnal emission, or "wet dream," because of the pressure of unemptied seminal vesicles; but according to Kinsey's data, two out of three first ejaculations occur as a result of masturbation. Gender has a substantial effect on the practice of masturbation. In one national sample, 66 percent of the males but only 17 percent of the females reported that they had masturbated by the time they were seventeen (Wilson, 1975).

While differences between males and females in incidence of masturbation may depend somewhat on biological differences, they are also the result of differences in socialization of each sex to masculine or feminine identity. Adolescent male peer groups experiment with masturbation and learn to associate sex with drive and achievement. Females have traditionally been encouraged to view sexual activity as service out of love for a husband and for the purpose of procreation. Their initial focus may be on pleasing rather than on self-pleasure. For many females, interest in sexuality for its own sake may not develop until they are in their twenties or even later (Gagnon and Simon, 1974).

Another male-female difference is in the techniques employed in masturbation. Males usually masturbate by manipulating the penis by hand, moving the hand rhythmically over the shaft until orgasm occurs. Females also stroke their genitals, most particularly the clitoral-vulvar area, but there is considerable individual variation in the amount of pressure they apply, the specific area they stroke, the rhythm of stroking, and the direction of stroking (vertical or circular). Despite these differences both men and women reach orgasm in about four minutes, although individuals may choose to take longer so as to prolong the erotic sensations (Masters and Johnson, 1966).

Masturbation is frequently carried over into adult life, especially for use as a sexual outlet when no partners are available. In a survey by the Research Guild (Hunt, 1974), 94 percent of the adult males and 63 percent of the females had masturbated at some point. Despite the wide-spread incidence of self-stimulation, most men and women still feel too ashamed of the practice to admit openly to friends, lovers, or spouses that they sometimes masturbate, even though they readily admit to other kinds of self-pleasure, like eating snacks or sleeping late. This lingering sense of guilt may be the result of parental disapproval when they touched their genitals as children, often too early in life to remember consciously. It is probably also a carryover from long-standing cultural folklore that stamped masturbation as sinful, evil, and likely to result in physical harm to one's body.

Guilt feelings are being erased to some extent by clear evidence that masturbation is a harmless form of sexual expression. According to current psychiatric theory, the tiredness and depression sometimes linked with masturbation are caused not by any debilitating physical effects but by mental conflicts over its use (Roth, 1975). Only a few people appear to use masturbation antisocially or neurotically, as a means of avoiding the problems of adult sexual relationships, as a weapon against a spouse, or as a tool to express hostility toward the opposite sex (Hunt, 1974). Sex therapists encourage masturbation as a simple, quick release for sexual tensions without any pressure to perform. They also recommend self-stimulation to orgasm as a way to become more comfortable with one's own body in heterosexual lovemaking and as a lifelong supplement to other types of sexual behavior (Barbach, 1976; Kline-Graber and Graber, 1976). Masters and Johnson (1966) point out that masturbation at the onset of menstruation helps to free many women from menstrual cramps and backaches.

Despite more liberal attitudes toward self-stimulation, the practice does not necessarily meet people's emotional needs. While masturbation may provide release from sexual tensions, only half of the women in one survey who practice masturbation reported that doing so is always satisfying; 30 percent reported that it is only sometimes satisfying, and 20 percent that it is not satisfying at all (Levin and Levin, 1975a).

Petting and Oral Sex

Like masturbation, heterosexual **petting**—erotic stimulation including kisses, genital caresses, finger insertions, and oral-genital contact—is often an early substitute for copulation. It is a way for young people to experience intense sexual excitement without the actual penetration of the vagina by the penis. It may or may not culminate in orgasm, but for most it is part of the learning process that prepares young people for heterosexual intercourse. Petting behaviors are later carried over into adult sexual relationships as foreplay or simply for sexual variety.

Fig. 5.8
Cross section of the penis inserted in the vagina, with related organs. Arrows indicate the route the sperm take to the site of conception.

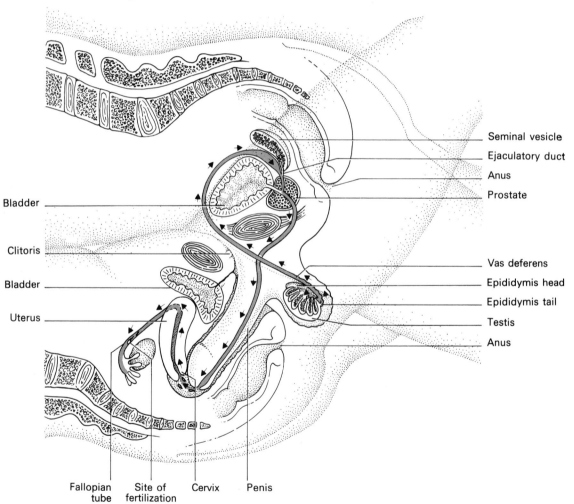

Seminal vesicle

Ejaculatory duct

Anus

Prostate

Vas deferens

Epididymis head

Epididymis tail

Testis

Anus

Bladder

Clitoris

Bladder

Uterus

Fallopian tube

Site of fertilization

Cervix

Penis

Oral-genital contact is used for sexual arousal and often leads to orgasm. Different terms are used to distinguish oral-genital stimulation of women and men: **cunnilingus** is oral stimulation of the vulva, and **fellatio** is oral stimulation of the penis and scrotum.

In American society, oral sex has traditionally been viewed in a negative light. Many people who believe that sex should be reserved for procreation object to oral-genital stimulation on moral grounds. Others consider it unsanitary (it is not, as long as soap-and-water cleansing is used), and some simply feel inhibited about engaging in it. Even so, oral sex is a widespread practice and appears to be gaining more acceptance. Whereas in Kinsey's day oral sex was more common among the better educated, today educational level appears to make little difference. While only 15 percent of high-school-educated married men in Kinsey's sample had engaged in cunnilingus, 56 percent of high-school-educated husbands and 66 percent of college-educated husbands interviewed in 1973 reported doing so (Hunt, 1973). And in 1974, Hunt found that 90 percent of married couples under twenty-five years of age—regardless of educational level—had experienced oral-genital sex. Many female respondents in another survey (Levin and Levin, 1975a) reported that cunnilingus is the chief and sometimes the only way they can reach orgasm.

Anal Stimulation

Like oral-genital stimulation, the practice of anal stimulation and intercourse has incurred objections in our society. Some people consider it a homosexual act, others feel it is unsanitary, and others simply don't like the idea. There is some indication, however, that in recent years this practice has become more acceptable, though not particularly widespread. In the Research Guild survey, over half the couples under age thirty-five reported using manual anal stimulation during foreplay, over a quarter reported engaging in oral stimulation of the anus, and about a quarter had tried anal intercourse (Hunt, 1974).

Anal intercourse carries several dangers. If the man puts his penis or fingers in his partner's vagina after they have been in her rectum, without washing in between, she may get a vaginal infection from anal bacteria. And, because the opening of the anus normally tightens when it is touched, anal intercourse can be painful for the woman or even injure delicate tissue.

Coitus

Coitus refers to penile-vaginal intercourse (see Fig. 5.8). It is usually preceded by **foreplay**—kissing and caressing of the partner's erogenous areas for the purpose of arousal. Once the couple is sufficiently aroused, the penis is guided into the vagina (often the woman is best able to do this). Almost all men experience orgasm with every intercourse, but Hunt (1974) found that only 53 percent of the married women in the Research Guild survey consistently had orgasms with intercourse and 15 percent never did. A survey by *Redbook Magazine* conducted in 1980 reported a somewhat higher rate for its female respondents. Six out of ten said they had an orgasm "every time" or "almost every time" (Sarrel and Sarrel, 1980). Still, this means that some 40 percent of women do not consistently have orgasm with intercourse. We have already pointed out that intercourse alone may not provide sufficient clitoral stimulation for orgasm. Even when it does, there may be differences in timing between partners and needs for different kinds of movement as orgasm approaches. At the point of orgasm, men typically like to penetrate the vagina deeply and then hold this position except for perhaps a few more thrusts. By contrast, women at the point of orgasm typically prefer continued friction with an acceleration of thrusts and pressure on the pubic area (McCary, 1973). If a man is unable to control his ejaculatory reflex, his partner may reach the plateau phase but not reach orgasm because of lack of necessary stimulation. For many women, manual stimulation of the clitoris during intercourse or choosing coital positions which maximize clitoral stimulation are effective means of facilitating climax.

Positions for intercourse are extremely varied, and preference for particular positions differs from culture to culture. The standard position in our society, the so-called "missionary position," was unknown to most cultures of the world until it was introduced by missionaries during the nineteenth century.

 SEXUAL DIFFICULTIES

For many couples, the sexual relationship is not the happy experience it could be. Masters and Johnson (1970) estimated that up to 50 percent of all American marriages are marred by sexual difficulties in one or both partners. Sexual problems are generally the result of a complex interplay of factors: cultural, social, interpersonal, and physiological. They may be manifested in such conditions as premature ejaculation, retarded ejaculation, or erectile inhibition in men, and painful intercourse, lack of arousal, or inability to experience orgasm in women. Until recently, people having sexual difficulties usually kept their problems to themselves, accepted them, or didn't recognize them as problems. Today, however, much more is being said and written about sexual problems, and more people are seeking professional help.

Social and Cultural Factors in Sexual Problems

Perhaps the most important point to make about sexual problems is that the sources of sexual difficulty are far more often social, cultural, and interpersonal than they are physiological.

CASE STUDY   *Psychologically Based Erectile Inhibition*

Bill and Karen attended a party, during the course of which she became quite angry over his lack of attention. As the evening wore on, her anger mounted, ultimately resulting in a rather unpleasant clash with Bill. On the drive home, neither talked. Both felt somewhat responsible, but neither was willing to openly express remorse. Bill was actually feeling some guilt over his actions and was determined to set it right in bed. At the same time, he was still angry about what he perceived to be an excessive response by Karen. With these conflicting feelings dominating his consciousness, he was unable to get an erection. Now Karen really took him to task, suggesting that Bill's present ineptness, together with his earlier indifference at the party, clearly manifested a lack of caring on his part. He feebly assured her that such was not the case, that he was just tired, and that everything would be back to normal the next time. But would it really be fine the next time? This question plagued him as he lay staring into the darkness long after Karen had fallen asleep by his side.

The next day he could think of nothing else. "I have got to make it right tonight—must show her that I still care." However, as the evening approached, his anxiety mounted. By the time he was driving home, the pressure was really intense. He stopped at Joe's Bar for a drink or two to temporarily combat his growing fears. Finally, after an evening spent trying to appear casual and collected on the outside, while inwardly worried and apprehensive, it was time for bed—time for him to function as a lover.

Instead of freely, joyously, and spontaneously getting swept away by the passions of lovemaking, his mind remained focused on his penis, willing it to respond, desperately hoping it would not betray him again. He had now become a spectator of his own performance, cursing his flaccid penis, sick with frustration and concern over Karen's response to his repeated failure. Unexpectedly, but perhaps more damaging, her reaction was not overtly accusatory. Rather she simply withdrew in brooding silence, leaving him alone with his acute misery. At this point, he was firmly on the vicious merry-go-round of the failure-fear-failure syndrome, and, if he didn't get some much-needed help, he was in for a very long ride.

FOR CLASS DISCUSSION

1. What does this case illustrate about the relationship between emotional conflicts and sexual sharing?

2. Do you think that Bill and Karen's expectations of love and intimacy may have contributed to the development of their shared problem?

3. How might this situation have been averted?

4. What do you think they could do to resolve their sexual problem?

Source: R. Crooks and C. Baur (1980). *Our Sexuality*. Menlo Park, Calif.: Benjamin-Cummings, p. 291. Reprinted with permission.

A number of social and cultural factors contribute to sexual difficulties, among them:

1. Negative childhood learning. In American society, children learn early that touching their genitals will be met with disapproval. The resulting lesson is that sexual pleasure from touching the genitals is bad. Many children, especially girls, are given little or no information about their sex organs. And children soon find that asking questions about sex may provoke a negative or embarrassed response.

2. The double standard, which sets up one sexual standard for men and another, frequently opposing standard for women. Two of the primary elements of the double standard are the ideas that men, but not women, are inherently sexual, and that the man is the initiator of any sexual interaction and the expert on how it is to be carried out.

3. The identification of "normal" sex with penile-vaginal intercourse. Viewing coitus as synonymous with sex can create burdensome expectations and exclusive focus on intercourse. This can be a particular problem for women, who are less likely than men to experience orgasm through intercourse alone.

4. Goal orientation. This refers to the tendency in modern American society to focus on bigger, better, and more orgasms as a measure of sexual success. Such an orientation toward the "goal" of orgasm contributes to the perception of sex as a task to be performed. For the man the task is to "give" the woman an orgasm. The woman, in turn, feels she must have an orgasm, for otherwise she has failed the sex-performance test.

5. Self-concept. The feelings and attitudes people have about themselves influence sexual expression. A person who thinks "I'm no good at anything" is likely to have trouble relating well sexually to someone else.

A number of interpersonal factors can also impair sexual functioning, including apathy, ineffective communication between sexual partners, fear of unwanted pregnancy, and sexual orientation (in which a man or woman may be unsatisfied in a heterosexual relationship because of a preference for individuals of the same sex). We will explore interpersonal sources of sexual dissatisfaction further in Chapter 8. Now let us look at how sexual difficulties are most often manifested.

Manifestations of Sexual Problems

PREMATURE EJACULATION **Premature ejaculation** refers to the inability of some men to control their ejaculatory reflexes, with the result that their own or their partner's enjoyment of the sexual experience is significantly lowered.

Masters and Johnson consider it the most widespread sexual problem of American men. The primary factor in premature ejaculation seems to be anxiety. It has been suggested that early secret experimentation conditions males to reach orgasm rapidly before being discovered, and that this pattern of rapid ejaculation is carried over into adult life (McCary, 1973). These factors may cause premature ejaculation by blocking awareness of the sensations which precede orgasm. Just as children cannot learn to control urination until they learn what it feels like to have a full bladder, some men cannot consciously control ejaculation until they can identify what it feels like to be on the verge of orgasm (Kaplan, 1974a; Masters and Johnson, 1970).

RETARDED EJACULATION   **Retarded ejaculation** refers to the inability of a man to ejaculate during coitus. It is a relatively uncommon condition, although some therapists believe that many men have mild forms of the problem.

Retarded ejaculation can usually be traced to psychological causes. A strict religious upbringing, unresolved childhood sexual feelings toward one's parents, suppressed anger, conflicting feelings toward a spouse, and specific traumatic sexual experiences are commonly found to inhibit the ejaculation reflex. Therapeutic programs focus on teaching new sexual behaviors, progressing from self-stimulation to stimulation by the partner to orgasm, and finally ejaculation during intercourse with the partner. In some cases, psychotherapy may help by relieving ejaculation of negative associations (Kaplan, 1974a).

ERECTILE INHIBITION (IMPOTENCE)   Nothing is more devastating to a sexually active man's sense of masculinity than **erectile inhibition** (or **impotence**)—the inability to achieve or maintain an erection. At least half of adult men in the United States have had this experience (Kaplan, 1974b). For most, it is a temporary condition (secondary erectile inhibition), but some men have never during their entire lifetime been able to maintain penetration with a sexual partner (primary erectile inhibition). Only a small percentage of episodes of erectile inhibition stem from physiological causes such as prescription medications, endocrine disorders, or severe diabetes. Far more often, the causes are situational or psychological. Examples of situational causes are fatigue, anger, worry over a career problem, or overindulgence in food or alcohol. Psychological factors may be quite varied. Primary erectile inhibition may stem from a man's having been subjected to restrictive religious teachings or having had a traumatic experience during the first attempt at intercourse. The changing roles of men and women may be a contributing factor to a growing trend for young, educated males to experience erectile difficulties. Many young men seem to be feeling the pressure from sexually experienced young women to perform, as illustrated in the following anecdote (Crooks and Baur, 1980):

Now when I'm with a woman for the first time I can't be sure she is relatively inexperienced or, for that matter, will even think I'm any good. For all I know, she might have been with Harry or Tom last week. The real bummer is that she might think Harry or Tom was a lot better than me in the sack. Also, she can get real demanding. I mean, it was never like this when I was in high school. Then anything you did was just fine. At least they didn't provide you with a critical evaluation. Now they may ask for something I can't deliver. I mean to tell you, it's a real bummer! I wish I was back in high school! (p. 292)

Since the major factor in erection difficulties is anxiety, therapy focuses on creating an atmosphere in which anxiety is reduced by relieving the male of the pressure to perform. Success in overcoming erectile difficulties now seems to be about 60 to 80 percent with therapy (Kaplan, 1974a; Masters and Johnson, 1970).

SEXUAL ANESTHESIA **Sexual anesthesia** refers to the inability of a woman to experience erotic pleasure from sexual contact. To a great degree, this problem seems to be culturally induced, specifically by means of cultural injunctions to female children to suppress their erotic impulses. Despite increasing sexual equality and greater understanding of female sexuality, traces of the double standard that denies female sexual needs still remain, and some women themselves have not yet accepted their rights to equal sexual experience.

Women who have never experienced sexual arousal may view intercourse as a frightening or disgusting ordeal to be endured only for their husband's sake, or they may enjoy its closeness without really feeling anything. Some women labeled "frigid" were aroused by early lovemaking but lost their sexual responsiveness when marital sex became solely a matter of mechanical copulation. Some nonresponsive women accept coitus neutrally; others feel used by their partners and may develop hostility toward them and dislike of sex in general. Some men may accept female passivity as confirmation of what they assume to be the natural state of women; some even find their partner's submissiveness exciting. Many others may feel rejected by a woman's lack of response, complicating the dynamics of their relationship.

Treatment for sexual anesthesia usually requires careful relearning of sexual responsiveness. Therapists encourage these women to communicate openly and without guilt about what they feel and want. In the absence of severe mental disturbances or hostilities between the partners, most nonresponsive women who undergo treatment gradually find that sex is enjoyable; many are eventually orgasmic (Kaplan, 1974b).

FEMALE ORGASMIC DIFFICULTIES   The most extreme form of orgasmic difficulty in women is never reaching orgasm under any circumstances. According to surveys (Kinsey, 1953; Kaplan, 1974a; Hite, 1976), some 10 percent of adult

What Is Sex Therapy?

What is sex therapy? Essentially it is specific, goal-directed, usually behavior-oriented psychotherapy. A sexual problem can be a symptom of an underlying psychiatric disorder; it can be due to a relationship problem; it can be a learned or conditioned phenomenon. For the most part, sex therapy concentrates mainly on alleviating the symptoms, but a competent practitioner should be able to spot and deal with or refer the underlying problems. Development of the skills to handle such problems takes training and supervision. But watch for the converse. Not all psychiatrists and relationship counselors are capable of or interested in dealing with sexual problems. For the purpose of this article, we will assume that the relationship is a good one and that there are no significant psychiatric problems in either partner.

Masters and Johnson gave us the principles of sex therapy. Strict Masters and Johnson therapy is done by a male-female co-therapy team, one of whom must be a physician. The patients spend a period of time, usually two weeks, away from home. Not all sex therapists follow this original design, but most of them do adhere to the basic principles described by Masters and Johnson in their book *Human Sexual Inadequacy*.

Since sexual failure usually leads to fear of failing again, which leads to anxiety, which often leads to sexual failure, the first principle of therapy is to eliminate performance anxiety. This is most easily done by eliminating performance. If a man can't get erections, tell him to stop trying. If a woman has trouble with orgasms, tell her to forget about them for the time being. Tell the couple to stop having intercourse. In fact, tell them they are not even permitted to touch each other's genitals. This allows the couple to relax. There is no longer a race to orgasm, no longer a need to perform. The individuals can look and talk and touch each other without worrying, "If I kiss her she's going to think that I want to have intercourse, and it won't work, and I'll feel bad and she'll cry, and we'll both go to bed depressed."

Prohibiting genital touching also allows the couple to travel back to the stage of their sexual development when sexual tensions were high, sexual response explosive and sexual performance only a dream. This was the time when just touching another person, brushing against a leg or dancing closely approached ecstasy. The amount of sexual energy created by the first real kiss or the first bare hand on bare breast is hard to match. Forbidding intercourse also allows the couple to learn to pet again—not just to get each other ready, but to touch for the sake of touching. The couple is told to pleasure each other, nongenitally, every day, and to talk about what they are feeling. They're instructed to tell each other what feels good and what does not.

This exercise helps to demonstrate another of Masters and Johnson's principles, the concept of sensate focus. Just as it sounds, sensate focus is focusing on sensations. Here is an example. Touch your hand to your wrist and explore. What do you feel? Hair? Skin? Now concentrate on what your wrist is feeling. Skin? Nails? Your wrist is just as capable of feeling as your fingers. Sensate focus allows the pleasurer to enjoy the experience along with the pleasuree. They both become pleasurees. They receive by giving. They give to get. This exercise is almost always pleasant. If not, there is prob-

(continued)

ably an intra- or interpersonal problem. If a couple doesn't like each other, these exercises are likely to fail. If they don't like themselves, they are even more likely to fail.

After a few days the couple should be better able to focus on each other's needs. They also should lose much of their anxiety about performing. They then are ready for the next step, genital pleasuring. It must be stressed that the goal is not erection, lubrication, or orgasm, but giving and receiving pleasure. Once again communication of what feels good and what does not is crucial. During a therapy session the therapist draws out the couple's reactions to the exercises.

When a couple is comfortable with genital pleasuring, they are encouraged to try nondemand intercourse. The penis is permitted into the vagina, and the couple is encouraged to focus on how it feels—no violent thrusting, no writhing, no undulating, just appreciating the feeling of containing or of being contained. Later, slow pelvic movements can be initiated. Finally, when both people are ready, orgasm happens. The partners usually come in with their heads sheepishly hung. "We cheated. We

didn't mean to do it but we accidentally had orgasms." Cured. The pressure was off enough to allow natural sexual response to sneak up and happen.

There are many other tasks that sex therapists assign to couples or individuals. These are individualized to fit the particular clinical situation. If a person is ashamed to be nude in front of a partner, he or she may be told to remove one additional article of clothing each night. If a person is shy about leaving the lights on, a dimmer switch can be installed and the lights can be gradually brightened. If a person is turned off by touching his or her partner's genitals, instructions are given to start at the knee and work up (or at the navel and work down).

"But, doctor, these are artificial, mechanical, unspontaneous, robot-like games."

"Yes, patient, but even Brahms had to practice his scales before he could compose his lullaby."

Source: From Martin Weisberg, M.D., "What Is Sex Therapy?" *The New Physician* (May, 1976), pp. 36–37. Reprinted with permission.

women in the United States have this problem. Less extreme orgasmic difficulties include the ability to reach orgasm only through masturbation but not with a partner, or the ability to reach orgasm through oral or manual manipulation but not through coitus.

While some women resent the current equation of orgasm with satisfaction in lovemaking, insisting that they are contented with the closeness of intercourse and opportunity for giving pleasure, others feel a real need for orgasmic release. In one study (Levin and Levin, 1975a), 29 percent of married women who never had orgasm still rated their sex lives as being good to very good, but 40 percent who were inorgasmic rated the sexual aspect of their marriages as poor to very poor. By contrast, 81 percent of women who are orgasmic all or most of the time described their satisfaction with marital sex as good to very good.

One factor associated with the complete absence of orgasm is the woman's lack of knowledge of her body's responses because she has never masturbated. Another is ineffective sexual techniques of the partner, sometimes because the woman is unable to indicate her needs. More complex sources are usually psychological; fear, anger, hostility, or guilt can inhibit a woman's ability to relax so that she can experience orgasmic release.

Of the women who can reach orgasm under certain circumstances but not others, more are unable to have orgasm during coitus than during oral or manual stimulation. A major reason for difficulties reaching orgasm during coitus is simply that intercourse alone may not provide sufficient clitoral stimulation to produce orgasm. Insufficient duration of coitus may also be a contributing factor, particularly in cases where the male partner is unable to control his ejaculation.

Lack of orgasm through manual or oral stimulation is often rooted in learning. Women who learned as children that self-stimulation is taboo may feel inhibited in engaging in it, even as adults. Those who think of sex entirely in reproductive terms may perceive of clitoral stimulation as necessary for arousal leading to coitus but not leading to orgasm (Hite, 1976).

Regardless of the source of stimulation, orgasmic difficulties may be related to the woman's feelings about the relationship. Some women inhibit their response by trying to rush orgasm to keep from displeasing their partner. For others, fear of pregnancy may block orgasmic release. For still others, anxiety about whether they will have an orgasm may be an inhibiting factor. A sense of security is a significant factor in determining whether or not a woman will be orgasmic; a feeling of privacy and freedom from intrusion as well as a warm, trusting relationship with the sexual partner head the list of conditions indicated by women as important for sexual responsiveness (Fisher, 1973).

Except in cases of severe mental or physical illness or deep animosity toward the partner, all women are capable of sexual responsiveness, including orgasm. Rarely does treatment fail to help women who learn to relax and let themselves enjoy climax. Therapist Helen Kaplan (1974a) suggests that women who are highly sexually responsive and free from psychological problems but who can experience orgasm only through manual or oral stimulation should not consider themselves sexually inadequate, because their pattern seems to fall within the range of normal female sexual functioning. Trying too hard for coital orgasm may make lovemaking a tense and anxious act rather than a form of loving communication.

VAGINISMUS AND DYSPAREUNIA A small number of women are unable to enjoy intercourse because they find it frightening or painful. In some, an involuntary spasm of the muscles in the outer third of the vagina, called **vaginismus,** constricts the opening so severely that penile penetration is impossible. In others, intercourse causes intense pain in the clitoris, vaginal barrel, or soft tissues of the pelvis, a condition called **dyspareunia.**

There are no known physical causes for vaginismus. It appears to be an entirely psychosomatic response to anticipated vaginal penetration. It may be linked to dysfunction of the male partner (out of anxiety or to avoid frustration), a restrictive background, specific traumatic experiences, or attempt at heterosexual intercourse by women who have previously been exclusively homosexual (Masters and Johnson, 1970).

Dyspareunia may stem from unconscious muscular tension associated with traumatic sexual experiences, conscious faking to avoid unwanted intercourse, or any number of actual physical causes for pain, ranging from an unbroken hymen and insufficient vaginal lubrication to rough manipulation of the clitoris and vaginal infections (Masters and Johnson, 1970). A woman suffering from dyspareunia should see a doctor. If there are no indications of physical problems, her condition may respond to behavioral therapy. Masters and Johnson report 100-percent success in curing vaginismus through reeducation as to the facts and acceptability of human sexuality.

SEXUALLY TRANSMITTED DISEASES

Sexually transmitted diseases (STDs) are bacterial or viral infections that attack the genital areas and may cause serious complications elsewhere in the body. Until the 1970s, these infections were called venereal disease (named for Venus, the goddess of love). The phrase sexually transmitted diseases emerged because it was thought to be more to the point and less judgmental. Although most STDs respond readily to treatment, they have nevertheless become epidemic in the United States today. In 1978, for example, over one million cases of gonorrhea were reported, but experts believe another two million cases went unreported (Katchadourian and Lunde, 1980). The majority of cases occur in young people; indeed it is currently estimated that 50 percent of American young people contract either gonorrhea or syphilis—but primarily gonorrhea—by age 25 (Katchadourian and Lunde, 1980).

Aside from practicing abstinence, the best ways to curb sexually transmitted diseases are rapid reporting to doctors by those who think they may be infected and prompt treatment of the carrier and all his or her sexual contacts. Preventive techniques which are fairly effective include "knowing your partner" and the use of hygienic measures before or after intercourse. For men this means using condoms during intercourse and washing the genitals immediately after intercourse; for women, it involves thorough soap-and-water cleansing of the genitals before or after sexual contact.

Gonorrhea

Gonorrhea, often called "clap," is the most common form of STD in the United States. It is caused by a bacteria called *gonococcus* and is transmitted by genital, oral-genital, or genital-anal contact. Contrary to popular myth, it cannot be contracted from toilet seats, drinking cups, or other objects handled by an infected person.

The early symptom of gonorrhea in men is a thin, bad-smelling discharge from the penis. Urination may be compelling and accompanied by a burning sensation. If untreated, the infection can spread, swelling the testicles until they are very sore. Further complications may lead to prostate, bladder, or kidney conditions and even sterility.

Women are often unaware of the early signs of gonorrhea. There is commonly a mild discharge from the vagina, but it may go unnoticed. Because the symptoms are similar to those in common nonvenereal vaginal infections, 80 percent of women who have gonorrhea are unaware of it until more serious complications set in (Sgroi, 1974). If the infection spreads, it may cause sterility or require surgical removal of the pelvic organs.

Gonorrhea can usually be diagnosed through laboratory examination of vaginal or penile discharge samples. Treatment with penicillin or, in cases of allergy to penicillin, tetracycline drugs, usually clears up the symptoms. Recently a new strain of penicillin-resistant gonorrhea has surfaced in the United States. This development has initiated interest in using tetracycline drugs as initial therapy for gonorrhea (*The Harvard Medical School Health Letter*, April, 1981).

Syphilis

Syphilis is far less common than gonorrhea. It is caused by an organism called a *spirochete* and transmitted from open lesions during genital, oral-genital, or genital-anal contact.

The disease develops in four stages. The primary stage is characterized by a painless chancre (sore) which appears at the point where the spirochete entered the body. If the infection goes untreated, the chancre will heal in one to five weeks. After about six weeks, the disease progresses to a secondary stage as a nonitchy rash. If the rash is at all noticeable, most people visit a doctor. Thus it is uncommon for cases of syphilis in the United States to go beyond the secondary stage.

The third stage is a period of latency that may last for several years. During latency there are no symptoms, and after a year of latency, the disease cannot be spread to sexual partners. If still untreated, it eventually manifests itself—as much as forty years later—in serious damage to the central nervous system, cardiovascular system, bones, joints, eyes, and other organs.

Pregnant women with syphilis may pass the disease on to their unborn fetus, sometimes causing mental defects or syphilitic symptoms which appear years later. During the first three stages of syphilis, antibiotic treatment is usually all that is needed. Even in the fourth stage, treatment can be beneficial, although damage already done to the body cannot be repaired (Boston Women's Health Book Collective, 1979).

Herpes

Herpes is caused by a virus known as Herpes simplex, type 2. The type 2 virus is closely related to Herpes simplex, type 1, which causes cold sores or fever blisters. Type 2 herpes, however, affects the genital area and appears to be transmitted mainly by vaginal, oral-genital, or anal sexual intercourse. While the virus is most contagious when open lesions are present, the body may shed active virus cells even when the disease is in its dormant state. Herpes type 2 now rivals gonorrhea as one of the most common sexually transmitted diseases in this country.

Symptoms show up two to six days after contact with an infected person. The most common symptom in both sexes is the outbreak of one or more very painful sores on the genitalia, similar to fever blisters on the lips. There may be other generalized symptoms as well, such as tiredness, swelling of the legs, watery eyes, and painful urination. Although herpes infection apparently causes no major complications in men, women who have contracted genital herpes have a slightly higher risk of developing cervical cancer (Wear and Holmes, 1976). Moreover, a pregnant woman who has an outbreak of herpes at the time of delivery runs a risk of one in four that her newborn child may contract the infection and be seriously crippled or even die (Kaufman and Rawls, 1974).

Treatment of active herpes includes taking hot "sitz baths" (soaking the genital area in hot water) and keeping the area clean and dry. At present there is no known cure for herpes, but a new drug that interferes with the multiplication of the virus cells may hold promise for an effective treatment in the future (Blough and Giuntoli, 1979).

SUMMARY

1. The external genitalia of the female are collectively called the vulva, and include the mons veneris, labia majora, labia minora, clitoris, and vaginal opening. The external genitalia of the male include the penis and the scrotum, which contains two testicles. The focus of sexual stimulation and activity is on the genitals, but many other parts of the body are sexually responsive; they are known as erogenous zones.

2. The sexual responses of both men and women always follow the same physiological pattern. This response cycle consists of four phases, which are labeled excitement, plateau, orgasm, and resolution. There are some differences in male and female experiences of orgasm, but overall the similarities between male and female sexual response far outweigh the differences.

3. Sexual responsiveness is a complex process that goes beyond simple anatomy and physiology. Psychological and cultural influences are extremely important. Other factors that affect sexual response include hormonal changes, aging, and the use of drugs.

4. There are many forms of sexual expression, and a person may favor different forms at different times. Masturbation, once taboo, is now regarded as acceptable and even therapeutic. Petting and oral sex are often engaged in by those who want to defer the decision to engage in penile-vaginal intercourse or those who enjoy sexual variety. Anal stimulation is pleasurable to some people.

5. Coitus (penile-vaginal intercourse) is usually preceded by foreplay, which contributes to both partners' arousal and prepares the female for penetration. Most women require stimulation of the clitoris in order to experience orgasm.

6. Many partners have sexual problems at some time in their relationship. Frequently these problems have complex causes that may be cultural, social, interpersonal, or physiological. Today much information is available about resolving sexual problems and more people are seeking professional help when they need it.

REVIEW AND DISCUSSION

1. Describe the basic components of the male and female reproductive systems and how they function.

2. What are some similarities and differences in the sexual response patterns of males and females?

3. What are some of the popular misconceptions about sexuality mentioned in this chapter?

4. Describe some of the cultural, social, interpersonal, and physiological factors that may contribute to sexual difficulties.

5. Why do you think sexually transmitted diseases have become such a serious health problem in the United States? What steps should be taken to reduce the incidence of these diseases?

SUGGESTED READINGS

Boston Women's Health Book Collective (1979). *Our Bodies, Ourselves: A Book By and For Women.* Revised and expanded edition. New York: Simon and Schuster.

Gives basic and straightforward information on many aspects of women's experience. Covers anatomy and physiology of sexuality and reproduction; sexual relationships; lesbianism; health care; birth control; childbearing; menopause; and self-defense.

Cosaro, M., and C. Korzeniowsky (1980). *STD: A Commonsense Guide.* New York: St. Martins Press.

Describes in easy-to-understand language the symptoms, progression, methods of relief, and, when they exist, cures, for a variety of sexually transmitted diseases. Emphasizes the need for sensitivity to one's own body and social responsibility.

Masters, W. H., and V. E. Johnson (1966). *Human Sexual Response.* Boston: Little, Brown.

Provides scientific data on the physical responses of men and women to sexual stimulation. This is a landmark work in the field of the anatomy and physiology of human sexual response, and it established the basis for current sex therapy and treatment.

Masters, W. H., and V. E. Johnson in association with R. J. Levin (1974). *The Pleasure Bond, A New Look at Sexuality and Commitment.* Boston: Little, Brown.

Discusses ways in which couples can strengthen and intensify their sexual relationship over a period of time. Includes group discussions held by Masters and Johnson with men and women of varied backgrounds about how they seek sexual satisfaction and how they approach marital problems.

Zilbergeld, B. (1978). *Male Sexuality.* Boston: Little, Brown.

Explores the subject of male sexuality, from anatomy and physiology to sexual problems.

Communication in Intimate Relationships

6

"True influence over another comes not from a moment's eloquence nor from any happily chosen word, but from the accumulation of a life time's thoughts stored up in the eyes. And there is one thing greater than curing a malady and that is accepting a malady and sharing its acceptance."

THORTON WILDER

Communication is part of every human interaction. Whenever people are together, they are communicating in some way. Communication may be verbal or nonverbal; it may be used to give information, modify behavior, test reality, or express feelings. But no matter what form it takes, or what purpose it serves, communication is an inevitable and central part of all human relationships, especially intimate ones, and is the ultimate form, perhaps, of "symbolic interaction."

Although no couple can avoid communicating, couples vary enormously in the ways they communicate. How a couple communicates reveals something about the character of their relationship. For example, unhealthy relationships, according to Watzlawick, Beavin, and Jackson (1967), are characterized by communications in which the struggle to define the relationship outweighs the content aspect of the communication; or, to put it another way, conveying information is less important than making comments about each other or controlling the relationship. Healthy couples are less likely to bring the nature of their relationship into every conversation (Watzlawick, Beavin, and Jackson, 1967; Bolte, 1970).

In recent years, there has been much concern about communication in intimate relationships. Some social scientists and couple therapists have tended to attribute all problems between partners to the couple's inability to communicate effectively. Good communication is not the only factor in maintaining a satisfying intimate relationship, but it is certainly an important one. This chapter examines

175

communication between couples in intimate relationships. It focuses on how cultural, social, and personal factors affect couple communication and explores the components of effective communication.

 ## LEVELS OF COMMUNICATION

We communicate both with and without words; our gestures, postures, facial expression, tone of voice, and physical stance all give messages. Most human communication consists of both verbal and nonverbal signals; and these two kinds of signals often provide different kinds of information and serve different purposes. Language, for example, is probably the most effective way to convey specific facts about people, thoughts, things, and events; nonverbal signals may be more effective in conveying feelings. According to the results of one study, the effect of an emotional message on others is conveyed more through the speaker's facial expression and tone of voice than through the words; in fact, the words themselves transmitted only 7 percent of the message's impact (Mehrabian, 1972).

Nonverbal communication may be the most effective way of communicating emotional messages. What feeling do you get about this couple's relationship from the fact that the woman is touching the man's hand as she reads to him?

Language tends to be more consciously controlled than nonverbal behavior, because language is a product of more specialized areas of the central nervous system, while much of our body language (blushing, for example) comes from more basic, involuntary, levels of the nervous system. We can control what we say; we cannot always control what our bodies do. Thus our communications will be more effective if we are aware of the nonverbal signals we are sending and can use them effectively.

Metacommunication

Communications occur on two levels: the content level and the relational level (Montgomery, 1981). The content level refers to the basic communication, the speaker's words. Social scientists have coined the term **metacommunication** to refer to the relational level of communication (Watzlawick, Beavin, and Jackson, 1967; Bateson, 1972). Metacommunication, or "communication about communication," is present in all communications. Its most direct form is a verbal comment upon a communication: "I meant that as a compliment," for example. Usually, though, metacommunication is nonverbal. A smile, a hug, a touch on the arm, a warm tone of voice can all emphasize, underline, or help decode what has just been said, making communication easier and more effective (Montgomery, 1981). Some therapists believe that relationships are more influenced by the kinds of metacommunications the partners exchange than by anything else.

What does the body language of these two people suggest?

Not all metacommunications reinforce what is being said; some contradict, disguise, or distort, the speaker's words. Such contradictions between what is being said and how it is said are called **mixed messages.** If, for example, someone says, "How nice to see you," while continuing to watch television, that person is transmitting a mixed message: saying one thing with words and another with actions.

Sometimes mixed messages can put the listener in an impossible position, one in which any response will be "wrong." Such a contradictory message is called a **double-bind** (Bateson, 1956). For example, during an argument a husband raises his voice and his wife tells him, "Don't get defensive." When he then responds non-defensively or too calmly, she acts hurt and accuses him of mocking her or not caring. In this situation the wife is giving her partner two opposing directives; any response he makes will be rejected or criticized.

Hearing vs. Listening

Even when messages are clear and uncontradictory, they cannot be received unless the partner is listening. According to Watzlawick, Beavin, and Jackson (1967), the message one partner sends is not precisely the message the other receives almost 85 percent of the time. In these miscommunications, people may be hearing—simply perceiving sounds—rather than actively listening—trying to perceive meaning. Really listening to someone else is demanding. A good listener not only concentrates and tries to understand exactly what the partner is saying, but shows the speaker that he or she is interested, concerned, and paying careful attention to what is being said. Sometimes this is done verbally, with questions or comments that reflect understanding. A good listener also uses body language to show attention: eyes are on the speaker, the body is leaning toward the speaker, the listener's facial expression shows the effect of the speaker's words. Someone who is staring out the window or flipping through the newspaper while the partner is talking is not being a responsive listener. Similarly, a speaker who leans against the kitchen counter and talks in a loud monotone, speaking to the other person as though performing upon the lecture platform, is not being a responsive speaker. Such behavior has a tendency to close the mind of the listener.

Being sensitive to the partner's schedule is also an important part of communicating well. When someone is trying to relax at the end of a long workday, or is busy fixing dinner, it is probably not the best time to recount an incident that demands close attention and concentration. Communications made at times like this may be met with what social scientists call "selective attention and selective inattention"—the listener hears what he or she wants to and tunes out the rest (Bowman and Spanier, 1978). This can lead to confusion and complications if the speaker simply assumes that the message has been received.

CULTURAL INFLUENCES ON COMMUNICATION

How men and women communicate in intimate relationships is influenced by early socialization, norms about couple communication, and personal factors. Socialization informs them of how they should act as male or female. Through cultural norms they learn what is expected of them in communicating

---

HIGHLIGHT 6.1   *Open Listening*

Open, clear expression of what we feel is vital to a healthy relationship between marital partners. But it will go for nothing unless it is complemented by open listening. Most husbands and wives seldom really listen to one another at all. They conduct what the philosopher Abraham Kaplan has called a duologue. In a duologue two people dutifully take turns expounding their separate lonely litanies. Everyone knows how such "conversations" go: Susan and Mark discuss the activities of the day, Susan talking about the fact that their son Bobby is going to have to have braces, Mark wondering aloud about the rumors that his company may be involved in a merger. Each is listening to himself rather than to the other. Susan is concerned about the cost of the braces, as well as their nuisance value, and Mark is concerned about what a merger might mean to his position in the company. Since Mark will have to pay for Bobby's braces, and since Susan will also be affected if Mark's job situation changes, they will eventually have to stop their separate soliloquies and start all over again asking one another to repeat what has already been said. We have all been through it a thousand times.

If you really do not want to listen at a given moment, it is possible for you to make that desire known to your mate, and you can expect to have your desire respected. But if your mate is going to continue to respect your desire for such moments of privacy, then you must be prepared really to listen when you indicate a willingness to do so. You must be prepared to enter into a dialogue, as opposed to a duologue. Kaplan describes the true dialogue, in which both partners listen and respond to one another, as communion rather than communication. In a true dialogue, each partner is, certainly, communicating with the other, but because he is also listening, and responding to what he hears, the final result is a form of communion. Good communication, when coupled with open listening, results in communion.

Open listening requires that you become, in effect, transparent, thus letting the other in. You cannot respond properly unless you open yourself completely to what is being said to you. Unless you listen, actively, you cannot hear. Unless you hear you cannot enter into a dialogue. And no true meeting of a husband and wife can occur unless they both enter willingly into such a dialogue.

Source: From *Open Marriage: A New Life Style for Couples* by Nena O'Neill and George O'Neill. Copyright © 1972 by Nena O'Neill and George O'Neill. Reprinted by permission of the publisher, M. Evans and Company, Inc., New York, N.Y. 10017.

in a couple relationship. Their communication patterns are also affected by the concept they have developed of themselves as individuals.

Socialization

As discussed in Chapter 3, many American males have been trained to hide feelings other than anger and pride. Boys often have been socialized to believe that the display of any other emotion is only for girls; boys who acted lovingly, showed fear, or cried were likely to be labeled sissies. Thus, many men have learned to conceal feelings of pain and feelings of affection. Even when bonded with a woman he loves, a man who has been taught to hide his feelings may be unable to express himself or to respond to his partner's expressions of emotion (Gilbert, 1976).

Females, by contrast, have been permitted to express their feelings of affection, nurturance, and empathy, but have been discouraged from expressing anger, aggression, or pride. This, too, can have a negative effect on communication with a partner. Many women may be unable to assert themselves; or, believing that anger is somehow "wrong," may resort to a posture of martyrdom instead.

The extreme effects of this kind of rigid socialization on communication for males was suggested by Balswick and Peek (1971), and termed "inexpressiveness." They described two types of inexpressive males, the cowboy and the playboy. The cowboy, typified by the sort of hero John Wayne usually portrayed, is embarassed and overly polite around women; the playboy, personified by James Bond, treats them as sex objects. The cowboy is too repressed and courteous, the playboy too emotionally detached and manipulative, to communicate effectively with a partner. Try to imagine a John Wayne hero communicating his deepest feelings to the schoolmarms he encounters in his movies, or 007 having a meaningful dialogue with the women he seduces. Genuine intimate communication for such men is virtually impossible.

The cowboy and the playboy, of course, are extremes, and there is evidence that the inexpressive-male stereotype is breaking down. Americans today value companionship in marriage, which in turn requires that both partners be expressive. As Balswick and Peek (1971) point out, however, this is not an easy task. Our society imposes conflicting demands on men: it teaches them to be inexpressive, yet it expects them to be expressive in intimate relationships. This contradiction contributes to the difficulties of intimate communication.

Cultural Norms

In the traditional American marriage of the past, the husband/wife relationship was clearly defined, and each partner knew what was expected. Because roles were clearly delineated by society, there was no need to discuss them. Scanzoni (1979) calls this traditional pattern "spontaneous consensus": the partners have no need to define roles because everything has been defined for them by social norms and customs.

Brickman (1974) uses the term "fully structured" to express basically the same idea: "the behavior of each party is completely specified or prescribed by social norms" (in Scanzoni, 1979). In a fully structured relationship, the interests of the wife were subordinated to those of the husband. Since it was assumed that the husband's interests had priority, the wife simply acquiesced when the interests or needs of the two partners diverged, and there was little discussion of the matter.

The history of the twentieth century shows a movement away from fully structured marriages. Most contemporary middle-class marriages are what Brickman calls "partially structured": some roles are prescribed by social norms, others are not (we shall come back to this topic in the next chapter). This change has profound implications for couple communication, for it means that decisions that once were "spontaneously arrived at" must now be negotiated (Scanzoni, 1979). For example, suppose a woman is engaged to be married and wishes to be a coprovider with her spouse. Since this desire does not follow the traditional assumption that wives stay home while husbands work, this women will have to make her wishes known to her husband-to-be and the couple will have to discuss the implications of such an arrangement. It is easy to see that once couples move away from traditional gender-role patterns, much more communication is required in order to arrive at a satisfactory definition of their relationship.

TRADITIONAL COMMUNICATION PATTERNS Couple communication patterns can also be seen to differ by social class. The closed communication pattern characteristic of traditional marriage relationships is especially apparent in working-class marriages, as evidenced in Komarovsky's (1964) classic study of "blue-collar marriage." The partners in these marriages tend to share few common interests and areas of knowledge. This may be in part the result of less education and limited opportunities. As one husband rather wistfully remarked: "If my wife and I had a little more education maybe we'd have what do you call it—more interests? Maybe we could come together better and life would be more interesting for us" (Komarovsky, 1964).

Whatever the causes, the less education a couple has, the more likely they are to display traditional gender-role norms. Komarovsky (1964) found that men who had not completed high school were least likely to share personal information with their spouses, were least likely to express emotions other than anger openly, were most likely to respond to marital conflicts by withdrawing from them, and were more likely to seek relief from their problems through physical activity rather than by talking about them.

Blue-collar men displayed another traditional trait: they did not talk to their wives about their work. They gave different reasons for their reticence in this area: their jobs were too technical for their wives to understand, talking about their jobs would sound like complaining (something traditionally socialized men are brought up to regard as unmasculine), or their jobs were too boring to talk about. The wives, predictably, believed in talking about their hurts and worries and tried to persuade their husbands to do so; but, in these traditional marriages, the wives did not insist upon communication—they went along with their husbands' desires. As one woman said, "I think the good thing is to talk it (what's bothering you) out and get it out of your system. But I have to leave him alone because if I try to get him to talk he'll get really sore. . . . He is strictly hands off if something hurts him" (Komarovsky, 1964).

More recently Rubin (1976) suggested that working-class couples do not have a language with which to understand each other. Because of their rigid socialization, each partner has been programmed to relate to a particular side of themselves—he to the rational, unemotional side, she to the intuitive, emotional side. When they try to talk, the woman relies on her feelings while the man becomes more and more detached and reasonable. The outcome can be fear, anger, even despair for the woman and isolation for the man:

> I wind up crying and feeling terrible. I get so sad because we can't really talk to each other a lot of times. He looks at me like I'm crazy, like he just doesn't understand a word I'm saying. (Rubin, 1976, p. 118)

It is important to point out that this pattern is not exclusive to working-class couples. In fact, Rubin believes it may be the most common form of couple communication in American marriages regardless of class. Nevertheless, Rubin suggests that middle-class marriages have long placed more importance on companionship, sharing, and exchange of feelings than blue-collar marriages. Thus, middle-class couples have had more practice in developing a language with which to communicate. They also have had more models to emulate, particularly since the couples portrayed in the mass media are largely reflections of middle-class aspirations (Rubin, 1976).

COMMUNICATION AND SELF-CONCEPT

Our self-concept is a product of our relations with other people and our communications with them; to a large extent, we create ourselves from images given to us by others in our interactions with them. The self-concept is a private picture that is painted of who we think we are, what we think we can do, and how well we think we can do it. How we talk and listen, how we think and feel, and how we act and relate to others are based upon what we think of ourselves. Our self-concept is both developed by and expressed in the verbal and nonverbal ways we communicate.

Functions of Role Identities

The self-concept includes a number of different roles. The same man may be a husband, son, lover, political activist, business executive, friend, and community worker. Each of these roles requires somewhat different ways of behaving and communicating and serves to link cultural expectations and individual behaviors. Moreover, each role is modified according to a person's **role identity,** the combination of the role as it is conceived by society and the role as it is conceived by the self.

Role identities prepare people for actual encounters with others and, thus, facilitate communication. For example, knowing how one is supposed to act on an evening out with one's partner—possessing that role identity—makes it much easier to plan one's behavior, including verbal and nonverbal communications. Imagining how the partner will probably react to those communications allows any behavior the partner would find inappropriate to be eliminated.

Positive or negative self-concepts result in large measure from communications with others and the feedback we get from these communications. The more positive feedback this grandmother gives her grandchild, the better the chances the child will feel loved and valued.

Role identities also give people standards for evaluating their behavior in their own terms. Even if behaviors are designed primarily as communications to the partner, they should still satisfy the performer. The identity a person wants to project serves as a built-in censor and prevents the person from doing things or making communications he or she considers embarrassing or inappropriate. A man, for example, may reject the idea of pleading with his partner to do something because he wants to be thought of as forceful and assertive, rather than timid and weak.

Finally, role identities give meaning to intimate relationships. By serving as plans of action and standards for judging how we act and how our partner regards us, they enable us to connect random events and interactions. A man might say to himself, "She seemed to think it was immature of me to say that and other women have thought so, too. I'd better not say it again if I don't want to be considered childish." Role identities help people organize their responses to the situations they encounter in day-to-day living. However, fitting one's role identities to the partner's role identities often requires a process called **identity bargaining.**

Identity Bargaining

When the partners' roles don't fit, communication is likely to be unsuccessful unless they can somehow agree upon who can play what role in the encounter. If, for example, a husband offers to take his wife out to dinner with the idea that they will have a romantic evening and make love when they get home, and she understands this, the evening will probably present no communication problems. But if the wife thinks of the offer as recognition of the fact that she is exhausted from an unusually busy day at the office and doesn't feel up to preparing dinner, their perceptions are different. The wife's perception of the husband's role differs from his perception of that role, and vice versa; the only way the two can accommodate each other is through negotiation or identity bargaining (Blumstein, 1975).

The first step in identity bargaining is establishing oneself in one's role, successfully conveying the desired image. If the performance is a true reflection of what one is like, or if it is not but is, nevertheless, a skillful presentation, the other person will probably accept it. However, in intimate relationships, false self-presentations are difficult to maintain; and even accurate reflections of the self may not always result in getting one's own way. Although the husband may successfully present himself as a romantic figure, the wife may or may not change her own behavior to fit in with his.

The second aspect of identity bargaining is assigning a role to the other person by behaving as though the other really fulfills the role. The husband, in this case, treats his wife as though they are going to make love as soon as they get home. The wife may explain that she is exhausted; or, if her partner is persuasive enough, or the dinner revives her enough, she, too, may take on the role of lover, rather than tired wife.

If, however, she does not fall in with her husband's mood, the two may engage in the third step in identity bargaining: negotiation. The husband explains how he would like his wife to act. She replies by suggesting that he redefine his own role. The result is a working agreement in which each grants the other some of the identities claimed and cast, but perhaps not all of them. The wife might communicate to her husband that she still finds him very attractive, is grateful for the dinner out, but is simply too tired that night; perhaps the following evening would be better. In this process, each partner must strike two bargains—one with the self and one with the other. The husband and wife, for example, might compromise by the wife's agreeing to wear the dress her husband has given her, which she feels is far too young for her, the following evening, if he will agree not to pressure her that night. Identity bargaining thus has both costs and rewards for each partner. Of course, identity bargaining may not always be successful, in which case negotiation turns into conflict. In the example above, if negotiation broke down they would probably go to bed angry at each other.

Communication and Self-Esteem

Perhaps the most significant element of the self-concept that affects communication is self-esteem. **Self-esteem** is an individual's personal judgment of his or her own worthiness or unworthiness. Most research indicates that people with low self-esteem—people who are highly critical of themselves and judge themselves negatively—are more anxious, more insecure, and, possibly, more cynical and depressed than people who accept themselves. Researchers have found a high correlation between poor self-images and vulnerability to criticism, judgment, or rejection by others (Rogers, 1961). People with low self-esteem often can be flattered or pleased by praise because they see themselves as inadequate or inferior. Lacking confidence in their own ideas or abilities, they are likely to accept the verdicts of others uncritically. People with high self-esteem, by contrast, are less likely to be affected as much by either praise or criticism. They believe in their own abilities, perceptions, and feelings. Because they believe in themselves, they are better able to accept other people even when others do not value what they value or agree with what they think.

When people lack a sense of personal value, they tend to be manipulative. Thinking that asking for what they want directly would lead to refusal, they may avoid asking directly and instead, use indirect methods. People with high self-esteem, on the other hand, usually know what they want and simply tell others of their desires. They rarely do what other people expect of them or what they think other people want them to do simply because they want to be liked. Instead, they do what they feel is right according to their own value system. Because they are in touch with themselves and their own feelings, people with high self-esteem are usually able to communicate in a relaxed way with other people. Others feel comfortable around such people, because such people are straightforward.

Enhancing the other's self-esteem has been identified as one of the keys to effective couple communication (Satir, 1972). Responses from someone we love that make us feel valued, secure, and confident enhance our self-esteem. Conversely, responses that consistently attack or devalue our worth as a person lower our self-esteem and make us unconfident and wary. Communication patterns that enhance self-esteem are especially important in intimate couple relationships because it is in these relationships that most of us drop the defenses that serve to protect us in our encounters with nonintimates. This is not to say that partners should not express negative responses; rather, that it is important to be sensitive to the feelings of the other regardless of the content of the communication.

 COMMUNICATION PROBLEMS

Communication Apprehension

Some people experience severe anxiety about communicating with others. Such people have been termed **communication apprehensive.** They are so afraid of communicating with others that they avoid doing so: the fear outweighs the projected gain (Powers and Hutchinson, 1979). Powers and Hutchinson (1979) did a study to see if communication apprehension between spouses was any different from the personality trait of communication apprehension in general. These researchers found that the ramifications of spouse communication apprehension were substantially different from those of communication apprehension in general. Partners who were, in general, very anxious about their communications with each other wanted to assume not less, as expected, but *more* responsibility for communicating well with their spouses and believed that they, in fact, would assume more of this responsibility.

As the researchers had expected, those who were very apprehensive about communication in general displayed significantly lower marital satisfaction than did people who were not apprehensive about communication. The communication-apprehensive respondents thought things between them and their spouses were going well less often; had considered separation more; judged their marriages more negatively; and did not tend to think they would have married the same person if they had their lives to live over again (Powers and Hutchinson, 1979). These findings are particularly significant when one realizes that couples with obvious marital problems would be unlikely to

Communication apprehension—the fear of communicating with others—has been linked with lower levels of marital satisfaction.

participate in a voluntary investigation like this one. The causal connection is unclear, but there does seem to be a direct relationship between anxiety about communication and marital satisfaction.

Ineffective Communication vs. Leveling

Ineffective communication seems to fall into distinct patterns. Virginia Satir (1972), a marriage therapist who has dealt with thousands of couples with communication problems, identified four patterns of faulty communication: distracting, computing, blaming, and placating. All of these behavior patterns get in the way of communication and undermine the partner's self-esteem.

In the **distracting** pattern, when one partner speaks, the other responds with something unrelated to the topic; for example, by ignoring the remark altogether and starting a noisy task, like running the garbage disposal, or by simply walking away. In this way, the "listener" is distracting attention from what the speaker is trying to say. It is impossible to have a real dialogue with someone who is obviously not paying any attention to what you are saying. Distracting tactics effectively end communication on the part of the original speaker—though the distracter's own message may emerge clearly enough.

Another faulty way people communicate is by **computing**: being reasonable, logical, and analytical, but totally devoid of emotions or spontaneity—

both of which are important elements of genuine communications. Emphasizing the facts and rejecting feelings, wishes, opinions, and fantasies keeps communication sterile and one-dimensional. Those who speak or respond this way dismiss both their partner's feelings and their own. Emotions cannot be discussed or even recognized nonverbally when one partner insists on computing.

Blaming the partner by personal attacks or criticisms of character, finding fault with whatever is being said, or interrupting to boss the partner is also extremely effective in blocking communication. Partners who are blamed whenever they try to communicate may quickly learn never to communicate at all; or they may respond by becoming blamers themselves.

The opposite of blaming, **placating,** can be just as fatal to any real understanding between partners, as the placater never risks an argument. Instead, he or she always agrees aloud with whatever has been said by the other (regardless of the placater's real feelings). Constantly trying to please, to soothe, to avoid unpleasantness, the placater succeeds only in avoiding mutual understanding.

In contrast to these ineffective modes of communication, partners who can communicate with each other without blaming, placating, distracting, or computing, who can be open, honest, and direct are what Satir calls levelers. When partners are **leveling** with each other their metacommunications express the same feelings as their words. When a leveler greets his wife with "I'm glad your home," his arms are outstretched, his voice is warm, his eyes loving. Similarly, if her husband has angered her, a wife who can level tells him directly instead of sending a mixed message or adopting an injured air. A leveler, Satir says, "can love deeply and fight fairly and effectively, can be on equal terms with both his tenderness and his toughness" (Satir, 1972).

IMPROVING THE QUALITY OF COMMUNICATION

Communication between the partners is an essential part of maintaining a satisfying intimate relationship. Communication can remain at a low level only so long as no problems arise that require mutual resolution. But real intimacy requires more than simply getting along on the surface. The difficulty of achieving effective couple communication is suggested by a study (see Fig. 6.1) in which marriage and family counselors reported that almost nine out of ten couples who came to them with marital problems had trouble communicating with each other (Beck and Jones, 1973). Couples who are able to communicate well with each other, by contrast, have been found to be more satisfied with their marriages (Rollins and Feldman, 1970).

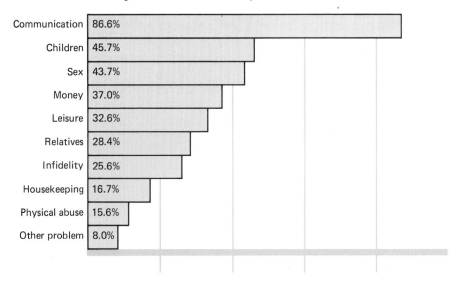

Percentage of all cases with a marital problem

Communication	86.6%
Children	45.7%
Sex	43.7%
Money	37.0%
Leisure	32.6%
Relatives	28.4%
Infidelity	25.6%
Housekeeping	16.7%
Physical abuse	15.6%
Other problem	8.0%

Fig. 6.1
Analysis of the case loads of 266 U.S. family counseling agencies revealed that almost nine out of every ten couples with marital problems were faced with difficulties in communication. Clients would say, "We can't talk to each other"; "I can't reach him"; "She doesn't understand me"; or "Every time we talk to each other, it ends in an argument." (Source: Adapted from Progress on Family Problems, *by Dorothy Fahs Beck and Mary Ann Jones, by permission of the publisher. Copyright 1973 by Family Service Association of America, New York.)*

What, exactly, is effective communication? Satir calls it leveling. Montgomery (1981) defines it as "the interpersonal, transactional, symbolic process by which partners achieve and maintain understanding of each other." By "interpersonal," Montgomery means that the communication is based, not upon cultural norms, but upon unique and specific knowledge of the partner. The partners speak and listen, interpret and react, according to what they know about each other, not according to what society expects of them. For example, the man who refuses to tell his wife about problems at work because doing so violates cultural sanctions ("real men" don't complain) is not communicating interpersonally; the man who discusses the problem with his wife because he knows she wants to hear about it is.

CASE STUDY   *An Ineffective Pattern of Communication*

Sue and Ned had been married about four years when Sue decided, on her way home from work one April evening, that they should try to cut down on their food bills by growing their own vegetables. Their little house had an equally little yard, but there was plenty of sun. When she told Ned of her plans, immediately upon his return from work, he was skeptical of how much money it could save and whether the return for their labor would be worth the effort. However, he went out into the yard with Sue to measure off the plot and agreed to dig it up for her.

As the garden progressed, it became obvious that Sue was putting in twice as much time on it as Ned was, and this became a source of some bickering between them. By June the weeding had become a demanding chore, and

Sue decided on Friday evening that they should both spend all day Saturday working on the garden plot. Ned came home full of plans for an all-day trip to the beach with two other couples with whom they were friendly. The husbands had worked out plans for this together on their lunch hour.

A full-scale quarrel erupted between Sue and Ned, with many angry accusations. By the time dinner was over, both were miserable, but neither was showing any signs of going along with the other's plans. Ned was saying he had opposed the garden from the beginning and they should just forget it. Sue said she had developed the plan to save money and a lot had already been spent for tools, seeds, and fertilizer. To abandon the garden now would mean money wasted instead of money saved.

FOR CLASS DISCUSSION

1. What hints do you find in this case study that Sue and Ned are not doing a very good job of communicating with each other?

2. Do you think it would be a satisfactory solution to this problem for Sue to stay home and work in the garden while Ned goes alone to the beach with their friends?

"Transactional" communicators can receive messages as well as send them. A good communicator possesses listening skills and response styles as well as speaking abilities. As symbolic interaction theory recognizes, effective communication is "symbolic" in that the partners must also agree upon the definitions of the symbols they use: the meaning of words, the meaning of gestures. Partners who communicate well with each other usually have a shared repertoire of symbolic words and behaviors and the meanings they attach to them (Montgomery, 1981). A woman, for example, knows that when her partner, who likes to sleep late, says, "We'll go on Saturday morning," he means around noon.

Effective communication is a process: it develops gradually over time as the result of different interactions between the partners. It may be stable, but it is never static. Effective communication depends upon mutual awareness of the self, the other, and the relationship, and, thus, its form may change as the couple changes. According to Montgomery (1981), four major components are present to some degree in all relationships in which the partners communicate well with each other: self-disclosure, confirmation, transaction management, and situational adaptability.

Self-Disclosure

Self-disclosure refers to revealing personal information to another, expressing what one is and what one feels (Jourard, 1971). Self-disclosure allows a man, for instance, to present himself as he sees himself, to perceive his partner as she perceives herself. People's ways of talking about themselves, of letting themselves be known by their listeners, may vary enormously. Individuals differ in how much they disclose to each other and in how intimate the disclosures are.

Most studies have found gender differences in disclosure. In general, women disclose their feelings more easily than men (Gilbert, 1976). And although men and women have been found to use the same number of words to talk about themselves, women tend to talk about themselves in more intimate terms. Women tend to reveal themselves only to people they like, while men will only reveal themselves to those they trust. Men are more cautious about expressing feelings of weakness or tenderness (Cozby, 1973; Gilbert, 1976).

Social class also influences how much people disclose. Researchers have found that lower-class men tend to disclose less than middle-class men; that middle-class women reveal more about their marriages to friends than do working-class women; and that middle-class mothers tend to speak and respond verbally to their children more than lower-class mothers do (Cozby, 1973; Gilbert, 1976). It seems likely that class variations in self-disclosure result in part from the fact that gender-role norms are somewhat more flexible in middle-class families than in working-class families.

LEVEL OF DISCLOSURE IN MARRIAGE   Intimate disclosures often occur within intimate relationships. But how much should people reveal to their partners? Some therapists and researchers believe that frequent open and totally honest communication between partners leads to greater marital satisfaction, whereas others contend that greater disclosure produces greater satisfaction only up to a certain point: after that point, disclosure may actually decrease satisfaction.

Cozby (1973) found that, while most partners tend to become less polite and restrained with each other after marriage, open expressions of hostilities

HIGHLIGHT 6.2   *Communicating with Children*

In *Between Parent and Child*, Dr. Haim Ginott states:

Children often resist dialogues with parents. They resent being preached to, talked at, and criticized. They feel that parents talk too much. Says eight-year-old David to his mother, "When I ask you a small question, why do you give me such a long answer?" To his friends he confides, "I don't tell Mother anything. If I start in with her, I have no time left to play."

An interested observer who overhears a conversation between a parent and a child will note with surprise how little each listens to the other. The conversation sounds like two monologues, one consisting of criticism and instructions, the other of denials and pleading. The tragedy of such "communication" lies, not in the lack of love, but in the lack of respect; not in the lack of intelligence, but in the lack of skill.

Our everyday language is not adequate for communicating meaningfully with children. To reach children and to reduce parental frustration, we need a new mode of relating to children, including new ways of conversing with them.

The new code of communication with children is based on respect and on skill. It requires (a) that messages preserve the child's as well as the parent's self-respect; (b) that statements of understanding precede statements of advice or instruction.

Eric, age nine, came home full of anger. His class was scheduled to go for a picnic, but it was raining. Mother decided to use a new approach. She refrained from cliches that in the past had only made things worse: "There is no use crying over rained-out picnics." "There

will be other days for fun." "I didn't make it rain, you know, so why are you angry at me?"

To herself she said, "My son has strong feelings about missing the picnic. He is disappointed. He is sharing his disappointment with me by showing me his anger. He is entitled to his emotions. I can best help him by showing understanding and respect for his feelings." To Eric she said:

Mother: You seem very disappointed.

Eric: Yes.

Mother: You wanted very much to go to this picnic.

Eric: I sure did.

Mother: You had everything ready and then the darn rain came.

Eric: Yes, that's exactly right.

There was a moment of silence and then Eric said, "Oh, well, there will be other days."

His anger seemed to have vanished and he was quite cooperative the rest of the afternoon. Usually when Eric came home angry, the whole household would be upset. Sooner or later he provoked every member of the family. Peace would not return until he was finally asleep late in the evening.

What is so special about this approach, and what are its helpful components?

When a child is in the midst of strong emotions, he cannot listen to anyone. He cannot accept advice or consolation or constructive criticism. He wants us to understand him. He wants us to understand what is going on inside himself at that particular moment. Furthermore, he wants to be understood without having to disclose fully what he is experiencing.

(continued)

It is a game in which he reveals only a little of what he feels needing to have us guess the rest.

When a child tells us, "The teacher spanked me," we do not have to ask him for more details. Nor do we need to say, "What did you do to deserve it? If your teacher spanked you, you must have done something. What did you do?" We don't even have to say, "Oh, I am so sorry." We need to show him that we understand his pain and embarrassment and feelings of revenge. How do we know what he feels? We look at him and listen to him, and we also draw on our own emotional experiences. We know what a child must feel when he is shamed in public in the presence of peers. We so phrase our words that the child knows we understand what he has gone through. Any of the following statements would serve well:

"It must have been terribly embarrassing."

"It must have made you furious."

"You must have hated the teacher at that moment."

"It must have hurt your feelings terribly."

"It was a bad day for you."

A child's strong feelings do not disappear when he is told, "It is not nice to feel that way," or when the parent tries to convince him that he "has no reason to feel that way." Strong feelings do not vanish by being banished; they do diminish in intensity and lose their sharp edges when the listener accepts them with sympathy and understanding.

Source: Haim G. Ginott, *Between Parent and Child*. New York: The Macmillan Company, 1965, pp. 24–27. Reprinted with permission.

"We deal with it by talking about it."

Drawing by Koren; © 1975
The New Yorker Magazine, Inc.

at a very high level may become intolerable. Furthermore, affection between partners may lessen if they disclose too much about their intimate feelings and self-doubts. Cozby suggests that spouses are sometimes made anxious or hostile by high levels of intimate disclosure and may want to retreat from such a relationship. This view of the relationship between self-disclosure and marital adjustment has been represented graphically as a curvilinear pattern in which adjustment is shown to be poorer if there is either too much or too little disclosure (see Fig. 6.2). Several studies seem to support this view. A marital-communication inventory developed by Bienvenu (1970) revealed that the item most likely to discriminate between happily and unhappily married couples was: "Does your spouse have a tendency to say things which would be better left unsaid?" Unhappily married persons were far more likely to answer yes to this question then happily married persons. Another study found that couples whose marital satisfaction is high are less likely to disclose their negative feelings toward each other (Dies and Cohen, 1973).

Gilbert (1976), on the other hand, proposes that high levels of self-disclosure may enhance marital satisfaction—provided that a couple is highly committed to the relationship and willing to take risks to achieve greater intimacy. This linear model is represented graphically in Fig. 6.2.

Fig. 6.2

Two interpretations of the relationship between self-disclosure and satisfaction. The diagram on the left suggests a curvilinear relationship between increasing amounts of self-disclosure and satisfaction in a relationship. The diagram on the right suggests that increased self-disclosure produces higher satisfaction— provided a couple is willing to take risks to achieve growth and commitment. (Source: Shirley J. Gilbert, "Self-disclosure, Intimacy and Communication in Families," The Family Coordinator *25:3. Copyrighted 1976 by the National Council on Family Relations. Reprinted by permission.)*

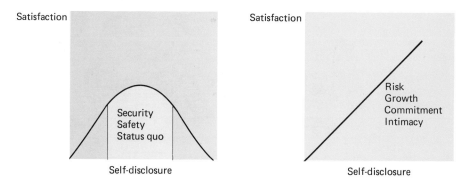

Jorgensen and Gaudy (1980) attempted to determine whether either the linear or the curvilinear models of self-disclosure and marital satisfaction could be verified by empirical evidence. These researchers found from their sample of 120 married couples that there was evidence for only the linear model. In their view, the data suggest, then, that the chances for greater marital satisfaction are enhanced by more frequent self-disclosing types of communication. However, they point out that couples who are not skilled or comfortable in disclosing personal information or are not used to accepting such disclosures from their spouse would need to be educated as to the importance of self-disclosure. In addition, these researchers caution that their findings are tentative and that more work is necessary in this whole area (Jorgensen and Gaudy, 1980).

TYPE OF DISCLOSURE   Self-disclosure may lead to greater intimacy—to a deepening exchange between partners within an atmosphere of trust and commitment to the relationship—or it may actually weaken the bond between the partners. Often the difference lies in the type of disclosure.

Unhappy marriages tend to be high in negative disclosures: threats to alter the relationship, disappointments in the other, and conflicting opinions. But partners may also find the greatest opportunities for intimacy in negative disclosures. Making such risky disclosures without damaging the relationship requires sensitivity to and knowledge of the partner's point of view and a commitment to preserving the other's self-esteem (Gilbert, 1976). A couple whose commitment to each other is very strong may be able to discuss topics which partners who were not as committed—who, perhaps, do not know each other so well, or trust each other so much—might better leave unsaid. For example, in a relationship in which both partners believe strongly in the idea of individual personality growth, the spouses might be able to openly pinpoint weaknesses in each other's character without threatening the relationship. But many less committed relationships could not tolerate mutual exploration of such high-risk disclosures. For these couples disclosures of such an intense nature might undermine the stability of their relationship rather than enhance individual growth.

COMMUNICATION STYLES AND SELF-DISCLOSURE   Self-disclosure among married couples has been analyzed in terms of communication styles; that is, in terms of the process partners use to communicate in situations in which emotions are likely to be aroused.

Hawkins, Weisberg, and Ray (1977; 1980) have defined four styles of communication: conventional, controlling, speculative, and contactful. These might best be defined by using an example. Suppose a husband is upset about something. The **conventional** communicator would avoid the issue by pretending everything was perfectly fine. The **controlling** communicator would show that he was upset but would reject his partner's desire to explore the problem. If she persisted, he would respond defensively, perhaps by attacking her verbally. A **speculative** communicator, without admitting that he was upset, would bring up the subject and start logically explaining his thoughts about it. He would not, however, reveal his feelings about it. The **contactful** communicator would tell his wife he was upset, explain why, and ask for her input on the problem.

The four styles of communication are shown in Table 6.1. Note that both the controlling and contactful styles are highly self-disclosing, in that the speaker expresses feeling forcefully and at length. However, the controlling style minimizes the partner's experience or shows lack of respect for the partner's feelings and thus is a closed communication style. The conventional style is both closed and low in self-disclosure. The partner who is pretending that everything is fine has revealed nothing of his inner state. People who communicate conventionally may also inhibit self-disclosure in their spouses by limiting the level of communication to such surface topics as what needs to be done around the house.

People who communicate speculatively are usually open to exploring all the facets of an issue, but this is done analytically; emotions are not revealed. Thus the communication is low in self-disclosure. However, a speculative communicator is open to the partner's self-disclosures. Both the contactful and the speculative styles display "interest in, respect for, and validation of the internal reality of self and other" (Hawkins, Weisberg, and Ray, 1980), but the contactful style is both open to the needs and feelings of the other and high in self-disclosure.

When husbands and wives were asked to rank the four styles in order of preference, both male and female spouses ranked the contactful and speculative styles first and second, the conventional style third, and the controlling style last (Hawkins, Weisberg, and Ray, 1977; 1980). This finding reflects the value which the couples placed on the modern ideal of intimacy in marital communication.

However, the research also suggested that, despite their belief in intimate communication, there are differences in the communication styles preferred

Table 6.1 Communication Styles by Degree of Openness and Level of Self-disclosure

	CLOSED	OPEN
Low disclosure	Conventional	Speculative
High disclosure	Controlling	Contactful

Source: J. L. Hawkins, C. Weisberg, and D. W. Ray, *Journal of Marriage and the Family,* August 1980. Copyrighted 1980 by the National Council on Family Relations. Reprinted by permission.

HIGHLIGHT 6.3   *Gender Differences in Speech*

Does gender affect a person's use of language? Since American men and women today are moving away from gender stereotypes we might expect the answer to be "no." However, studies by linguists and sociologists show that men and women actually do use language differently. In addition, stereotyped attitudes about men's and women's speech persist. For example, when 466 men and women were asked to describe men's and women's speech they tended to use sex-stereotyped adjectives. Both men and women characterized men's speech as more "forceful," "dominating," "boastful," "authoritarian," "blunt," and "straight to the point," while both sexes described women's speech as "friendlier," "gentler," "faster," more "emotional," and more "enthusiastic" than men's speech. Both men and women believed that women were more likely to talk about "trivial" matters. These adjectives seem to reflect the long-held stereotype of the "instrumental" male and the "expressive" female.

As to actual rather than perceived differences in the way men and women speak, researchers have found that women appear to use more variation in intonation—they change pitch faster and more often than men, whereas men speak in more of a monotone. Furthermore, when asked a question, women are more likely than men to respond with a question. For example, if asked, "What are you reading?" a woman tends to respond, "A newspaper?" One researcher speculates that in answering this way women are indirectly asking, "Why do you want to know?" Women also encourage continued communication by interjecting phrases like "mm hmmm" or directly asking questions when there is a lull in the conversation. Men's talking style, on the other hand, is characterized by brief responses and long silences that appear to discourage conversation.

Other differences in male and female conversational styles have been found. A study conducted at the University of California at Santa Barbara analyzed fifty-two hours of recorded conversations of mixed couples. Women asked far more questions than men and raised about two-thirds of the conversational topics. However, the topics most often discussed were introduced by men. Thus it appears that even though women seem more concerned with continuing conversational contact, men seem to have more power and control in verbal interactions. This idea is supported by the finding that men have a greater tendency to interrupt women during a conversation. In a study in which naturally occurring conversations were recorded, men initiated 96 percent of the interruptions. In a laboratory setting where conversations between strangers were videotaped, men interrupted women 75 percent of the time.

Some researchers believe that the studies that show men as the dominating partner in a conversation reflect the historical and present status of men and women in American society. "Traditionally in our society, women have had neither speaking right nor economic status, and so they have used different linguistic strategies to get their goals," said one researcher. Another stated, "It is not simply an abstraction . . . to talk about dominance, and to say that women have less power than men. You can see how it is actually carried into women's lives, in a minute and personal way, when it's expressed in their conversations."

Source: Adapted from Glenn Collins, "Men's and Women's Speech: How They Differ." The *New York Times*, November 17, 1980.

by husbands and wives and in the styles they believe to be characteristic of each other. The wives tended to perceive their husbands as much more controlling and much less contactful than the husbands believed themselves to be. Moreover, the wives valued the contactful style in their husbands more than the husbands did for themselves. There was also some suggestion that the husbands wanted a bit more speculative behavior from their wives than the wives wanted to give (Hawkins, Weinberg, and Ray, 1980). Thus it appears that while both partners embrace the norm of closeness in marriage, translating this value into communication styles that satisfy the needs of both husbands and wives is still a difficult and evolving process.

A NEW ETHIC OF OPENNESS?   There is some evidence that couples at the dating stage share the desire of married couples to make their communication more open and to disclose more of themselves to each other. A survey of 231 college-student dating couples found that strikingly high proportions of both men and women said they had disclosed their thoughts "fully" to their dates in most areas (Rubin et al., 1980). The researchers had the impression that their data—while difficult to consider historically due to lack of parallel data—reflected a historical shift among student couples toward an ethic of openness. The current generation seemed to believe intimate disclosures should be an integral part of couple relationships. However, many couples' reported behavior corresponded to the traditional gender roles. For example, women had revealed more than men had about certain areas, such as their fears (Rubin et al., 1980). It seems that for dating couples as well as married couples the norms for communication behavior have changed more rapidly than the behavior itself.

Confirmation

During the process of communication, couples give each other **feedback**—information about each other and the relationship. Watzlawick, Beavin, and Jackson (1967) identified three types of feedback response patterns: confirmation, rejection, and disconfirmation. **Confirmation** responses show an acceptance of the partner's self-definition and acceptance of the partner's view of the relationship, as well as an acceptance of what the partner is saying. A confirmation response says, "You are right about yourself and about us." **Rejection** responses show that one partner understands the other's self-definition and view of the relationship but rejects or disagrees with both of them. A rejecting response tells the partner, "You are wrong about yourself and about our relationship." **Disconfirmation** responses refuse even to recognize the partner's self-definition and view of the relationship. A disconfirming response says, in effect, "You do not exist" (Watzlawick, Beavin, and Jackson, 1967).

Among the most important communication skills in intimate relationships are the willingness to share personal information, confirmation of the other as a person of worth, the ability to establish guidelines for interaction, and the flexibility to adapt the communication to the situation.

A survey of 310 marriage therapists showed that confirmation—treating the partner's message and self as worthwhile—was regarded by these professionals as *the* most important component of healthy family functioning (Fisher and Sprenkle, 1978). Other researchers have found that confirmation is significantly linked to marital satisfaction (Clarke, 1973) and to a well-functioning family (Sprenkle and Olson, 1978).

Partners confirm each other by their words, facial expressions, bodily stances, tones of voice, and behaviors. Confirming responses recognize, acknowledge, or endorse the partner (Cissna and Seiburg, 1979); often, such responses show support, sympathy, and affection (Montgomery, 1981).

Most of the communication skills we have described so far confirm the other: levelers, good listeners, and contactful communicators, for example, all treat their partners and their partners' messages as important and worthwhile, whether they agree with them or not. It is the attitude toward the other and toward the relationship and the way that attitude is communicated, rather than simply agreeing with the content of the message, that makes a response confirming.

Transaction Management

Transaction management can be defined as a couple's ability to regulate their communication. It requires two skills: the ability to establish realistic rules for interaction and the self-control to keep the communication flowing toward desired goals (Montgomery, 1981). A couple may, for example, agree to stop name-calling when they are angry; and then, the next time either or both become angry, they attack each other as usual. Such a couple is being controlled by their communication rather than the other way around.

Cultural and social norms provide some guidelines for managing communication. Interrupting, for example, is considered rude; shouting at someone would be inappropriate at a cocktail party. However, in private, the partners must also establish their own rules for communicating. Will screaming be acceptable to both under certain circumstances, or should all discussions be carried on quietly? The answer depends upon the partners' personalities. Some people may have highly unpleasant associations with shouting (memories of painful battles between their own parents, for example), while others may consider it the best way to release tension quickly. If the partners are in disagreement about this, they would, ideally, discuss it and agree upon a mutually satisfying rule: "I know you believe in expressing your feelings directly, and that sometimes you need to shout. But when you shout at me, I get scared. It reminds me of my father yelling at my mother. Do you think maybe you could show your anger in some other way?"

For this to work, of course, the partners would have to arrive together at "some other way," and then the shouting partner would have to stick to the agreement. Making such agreements, or rules, results in more stable, less chaotic, communications and, more importantly, reflects the partners' understanding of and respect for one another. Such rules are the products of the partners' interactions with each other, demonstrations of the fact that the partners are able and willing to respond to one another as worthwhile individuals (Jackson, 1977).

Keeping such rules—controlling the actual interaction—depends upon metacommunication, communication awareness, and communication regulation. The partners would, ideally, use metacommunication, both verbal and nonverbal, to confirm and clarify what they are saying to each other and how they are listening to each other. Serious tones of voice would be used to deliver serious messages; alert, attentive facial expressions would reflect attention to the partner's words (Montgomery, 1981).

Communication awareness means being able to make reliable predictions about future interaction based on an accurate assessment of the present interaction. If, for example, a couple is discussing something, one partner may notice—from the other partner's tone of voice, from the turn the conversation is taking, from knowledge of the partner and of self—that the discussion is likely to turn into an argument. However, the fact that a partner is aware of the incipient argument will not affect whether or not the couple actually has the argument unless one or both of them also possesses the ability to regulate communication. Regulation, here, might consist of simply communicating the fear that an argument is about to begin; if neither partner wants to argue at that moment, both can try to continue the discussion calmly or, if that is impossible, can decide to change the subject. Although learning how to regulate interactions is of great importance to interpersonal communication, there is need for much more research than is presently available on this topic (Montgomery, 1981).

Situational Adaptability

Couples who display **situational adaptability** are able to relate to each other in the manner most appropriate to the situation: they know that what is effective communication in one situation will not necessarily be effective in another. Their behavior is flexible.

Consistent, inflexible patterns of behavior—following rules too rigidly—is detrimental to the quality of relationships (Montgomery, 1981). For example, a couple may agree that they prefer to deal with problems as they come up and that confronting each other immediately is the best way to deal with dissatisfactions and complaints. If, however, a woman comes home from work very upset about the fact that she has not received an expected promotion, and her husband, knowing this, immediately confronts her with the fact that she did not do the dishes that morning even though it was her turn, the couple is not communicating effectively. If such interactions are frequent, the relationship will suffer. A situation-adaptable husband would realize that his complaint about the dishes could wait; his wife's situation and feelings called for sympathy and comfort, not criticism.

Flexibility in self-disclosure has been linked to marital satisfaction (Gilbert, 1976), and general communication flexibility has been associated with competence in communicating (Wiemann, 1977). Situational adaptability is shown in a spouse's ability to assess a number of variables, such as timing, the particular circumstances, and the mood of the partner, and adapt communication behavior accordingly (Montgomery, 1981). Criticism should be given at a time when it will not be likely to undermine the partner's self-esteem. Similarly, when the partner is undergoing a personal crisis, it is appropriate to delay expressing self-doubts until a time when such disclosures can be received empathetically.

The Functions of
Effective Communication

We have said that communication is important to the stability of relationships and that many of the problems between couples have been attributed to communication difficulties. But what contribution does good communication make to an intimate relationship?

A number of researchers have suggested that effective communication helps to validate a person's sense of self (Watzlawick, Beavin, and Jackson, 1967; Cushman and Craig, 1976). Acceptance of the other's self-image is vitally important to each person's well-being. Couples who are able to accept each other's definition of who they are are more realistic in their appraisals and expectations of each other, communicate in a more relaxed fashion, and respond more appropriately to each other (Montgomery, 1981). The four components of effective communication described above give each partner the tools to validate the other's self-image. As one partner discloses him/her self, the other responds with openness instead of with attempts to control. Self-image is further enhanced by the partners' ability to recognize what is going on in a particular communication and to choose the appropriate time and circumstance for their interactions.

Another function of effective communication is to enable the couple to agree on a definition of their relationship (Montgomery, 1981). Sharing information about their feelings and their views of their life together results in what Montgomery calls a "custom-made" definition of the relationship that is unique to the individuals involved. Such a definition will help the partners to work out a way of managing conflict, making decisions, and setting up expectations for behavior and rules for interaction. Self-disclosing, confirming, well-managed, and appropriate communication is essential in formulating such a relationship definition. Self-validation and relationship definition, Montgomery believes, are the most important results of effective communication between partners. All other positive-interaction factors stem from and are secondary to achievement of these two aims.

Effective communication and satisfying relationships interact with and affect each other. As partners apply communication skills to their relationships, the relationship has a chance to become more intimate; as intimacy grows, communication improves. Clearly it is difficult for many people to communicate openly, and no one style of communication is appropriate for all couples. Still, the potential of effective communication is suggested in the following statement:

> ... communication styles that ... foster ... a continued evolution of the relationship offer special hope for the future. ... Couples capable of this can, we believe, engage more competently in meeting the demands and opportunities of an ever more rapidly changing world. (Raush et al., 1974, p. 209)

SUMMARY

1. This chapter examines communication between couples and some of the cultural, social, and personal influences upon that communication. It also focuses on communication problems and the components of effective communication.

2. Communication is used to modify behavior, give information, test reality, and express feelings. It has both verbal and nonverbal components and occurs on both content and relational levels. The term metacommunication has been employed to refer to the relational level of communication, or "communication about communication."

3. There is a difference between hearing—simply perceiving sound—and listening—paying close attention in order to perceive meaning. Good listening skills are essential to effective communication.

4. Men and women are socialized differently, and the way they are socialized as children influences how they will communicate as adults. Traditionally, men have been more hesitant than women to disclose personal information. Today, blue-collar couples are most likely to exhibit traditional communication patterns, in part because companionship and openness have not been as highly valued in working-class marriages as they have in middle-class marriages.

5. Through communication, people form and modify their self-concepts, their sense of who they are. Through identity bargaining, couples negotiate differences in their self-perceptions, perceptions of each other, and expectations about the interaction between them.

6. Faulty ways of communicating seem to fall into identifiable patterns. Four of these patterns are blaming, distracting, computing, and placating. The kind of communication that avoids all these traps is called leveling. Here communication is straightforward and open, with no effort either to evade issues or to control the relationship. Satir (1972) believes that leveling between caring partners helps to enhance self-esteem.

7. Effective communication has four primary components: openness (self-disclosure), confirmation, transaction management, and situational adaptability. Self-disclosure is the revelation of personal information. Confirmation refers to feedback that shows acceptance of the self-definition of the partner and of the partner's view of the relationship. Transaction management relates to the ability to regulate communication by establishing and keeping rules that facilitate reaching desired goals. Situational adaptability is the ability to communicate in a way that is appropriate to the particular situation.

8. Effective communication serves two major functions: it helps to validate each partner's sense of self, and it enables the partners to arrive at a mutually satisfying definition of their relationship.

REVIEW AND DISCUSSION

1. Look around a place such as a cafeteria, where you cannot hear the verbal communications, and describe some of the attitudes and emotions you see being conveyed by nonverbal means.

2. Keeping in mind all your various activities, list all of the roles you played today and the reciprocal roles played by others in your interaction with them. How did you alter your role to suit the person or situation you were dealing with?

3. Why is self-disclosure important in a relationship? How can nondisclosure hurt a relationship? Can too much disclosure threaten a relationship? Give some examples.

4. Describe the communication style (conventional, controlling, speculative, contactful) that you think is closest to your own style. Are you satisfied with this style? Is your partner? If not, how do you think you could change it?

5. What are the components of effective communication? How do they serve to confirm each partner's sense of self?

SUGGESTED READINGS

Bach, G. R., and R. Wyden (1969). *The Intimate Enemy.* New York: William Morrow and Company.

A practical, self-training program for learning how to improve intimate relationships. The authors take the view that true intimacy can thrive in healthy couples only if they fight according to fair, above-the-belt rules.

Miller, S., D. Wackman, E. Nunnally, and C. Saline (1981). *Straight Talk: A New Way to Get Closer to Others by Saying What You Really Mean.* New York: Rawson, Wade.

Aims at building the skills that enable couples to overcome roadblocks to effective communication. Techniques for telling others how we feel without being defensive, asking for what we want without giving orders, resolving conflicts without anger or hostility.

Satir, V. (1972). *Peoplemaking.* Palo Alto, Calif.: Science and Behavior Books.

The author covers aspects of family life and relationships which shape us into the people we are (self-worth, communications, and rules) and shows ways to find how these operate in a family and how to change them to increase the joy of family life. Substantial emphasis on communication.

Scoresby, A. L. (1977). *The Marriage Dialogue*. Reading, Mass.: Addison-Wesley.

Describes marital communication skills which can be learned and applied to improve dialogue between marriage partners. Covers the role of communication in marriage, interpreting marital messages, decision making, and other topics.

Stewart, J. (1982). *Bridges Not Walls*, 3rd Edition. Reading, Mass.: Addison-Wesley.

A collection of articles about aspects of interpersonal communication, including verbal and nonverbal codes, self-perception, and self-disclosure. Concepts are presented in a clear and understandable style.

III

Marriage and Family: Staying Together

Marital Adjustment and Conflict

7

Marital Adjustment

Adjustment over the Family Life Cycle

Resources, Power, and Marital Adjustment

Some Major Areas of Marital Adjustment

Conflict in Marriage

"A successful marriage is an edifice that must be rebuilt every day."

ANDRÉ MAUROIS

For the past forty years, social scientists have been trying to determine why some marriages succeed and others fail. The ability to communicate effectively is, as we have seen, crucial to intimate human relationships, and, not surprisingly, it is one of the major forces in successful marriages. But what is a successful marriage?

When we try to describe the state of a marriage, we use words like happy, satisfying, fulfilling, and loving; social scientists talk about adjustment, stability, and integration. Sometimes these words are used as though they all mean the same thing. All of them, certainly, are qualities couples strive for in marriage, and all of them are difficult to define specifically and precisely.

To clarify discussions of marriage, social scientists make a general distinction between marital quality, a subjective evaluation of a couple's relationship, and marital stability. A stable marriage ends only with the death of one partner; an unstable marriage is terminated by one or both partners via divorce, separation, annulment, or desertion (Lewis and Spanier, 1979). **Marital stability**, then, refers to whether or not the marriage lasts; or, to put it another way, to how it ends.

Marital quality is harder to define. It is obviously linked to marital stability: couples whose marital quality is high are more likely to stay married than couples whose marital quality is low. But this commonsense conclusion is not completely supported by the facts: many marriages of seemingly low quality last until death, while some marriages of seemingly high quality end in divorce (Lewis and Spanier, 1979).

209

Lewis and Spanier (1979) use the term marital quality broadly, to encompass all the components of marital success or failure: for example, satisfaction, happiness, communication, integration, stability, and adjustment. While some of these are individual reactions to the marriage, others are the couple's joint reactions: an individual may feel happy or satisfied, but it takes two to communicate, or to adjust. This interpersonal adjustment, rather than individual or psychological reactions to marriage, will be our main concern in this chapter.

 MARITAL ADJUSTMENT

Marital adjustment is the degree to which couples fit together and satisfy each other's needs, desires, and expectations; or, stated more simply, how well the partners get along with each other (Lewis and Spanier, 1979). No matter how simply it is put, though, getting along with another person for an entire lifetime is a complex process which affects, and is affected by, most aspects of the partners' lives.

Adjustment to Roles

One way of looking at marital adjustment is in terms of the partners' roles. Nye (1976) has found eight different roles in contemporary families. Some of these have traditionally been assigned to the wife, some to the husband, and some to both; however, in recent years, husbands and wives have tended to share more of their roles than they have in the past. The rigid distinctions that once divided roles by sex are breaking down, and today, either the husband or wife or both together fulfill each of the following:

- *the housekeeper role*, which includes the responsibility for buying and preparing food, washing clothes and dishes, cleaning the house, and keeping the household accounts;
- *the provider role*, which focuses on earning the money needed to support the family;
- *the child-care role*, which refers mainly to physical care: feeding, dressing, bathing, and protecting infants and young children;
- *the child-socialization role*, which involves instilling children with certain values and attitudes, and teaching them certain skills and behaviors;
- *the sexual role*, which entails satisfying the spouses' sexual needs;
- *the kinship role*, which requires keeping in touch with relatives and helping them when necessary;

The child-care role as defined by Nye includes seeing to the physical needs of the child. In many modern marriages, the child-care and child-socialization roles are increasingly being shared.

☐ *the recreational role*, which includes organizing and participating in family recreation; and

☐ *the therapeutic role*, which involves listening to, sympathizing with, and reassuring family members and, when appropriate, giving advice or practical help in problem solving (Nye, 1976).

Scanzoni (1979) calls these roles "spheres of interest" and points out that, in the past, the wife had at least two spheres of interest that were hers alone: taking care of the house and taking care of the children (what Nye terms the housekeeper and child-care roles). Power and responsibility in these spheres were relatively straightforward and easy to identify; the wife's power in those spheres was seen (by the husband, at least) as both legitimate and beneficial. Today, however, when spheres of interest often overlap, as they do in many contemporary households in which both spouses work and household duties are expected to be shared, it is much harder to determine who actually has the power and responsibility in each sphere. Often, negotiation is necessary to determine how the power and responsibility should be divided.

Whenever one partner assumes a new role or discards an old one, adjustments must be made in other roles. If, for example, a woman starts working and, thus, sharing the provider role with her husband, the husband will probably be expected to start sharing one or more of her roles: child-care or housekeeper, for example. Changes in the degree of responsibility also require adjustment: if, for example, one partner begins doing all of the vacation planning, the other may be asked to write more letters to relatives or to spend more time with the children on weekends.

Degrees of Marital Adjustment

Dyadic adjustment (the adjustment of two people to each other), of course, is never completed: it is a continuing process throughout the family life cycle. One partner gets a new job, with longer hours, or loses an old job; the couple moves; a widowed mother-in-law joins the household; a baby is born. With each change, new adjustments are required. If, for example, one partner begins working longer hours in order to earn more money, the other may have to be especially sympathetic for awhile; or, as Nye would put it, take on more of the therapeutic role.

For most couples, adjustment does not move solely from good to better or from bad to worse; it does not move steadily in any one direction. A couple adjusts in different degrees at different times. Sometimes the partners may be helping each other adjust to difficult situations; sometimes one partner may be modifying his or her behavior to fit the other partner; sometimes, under the strain of a new, difficult situation, the couple may draw apart for awhile and cease to interact at all, and then, under a new stimulus, begin the process of adjustment again.

A couple's total marital adjustment is made up of a number of different elements. Social scientists have tried to isolate some of these elements to see what makes some marriages succeed and others fail. Spanier (1976) devised a Dyadic Adjustment Scale, which measures those factors found to indicate the quality of a couple's marital adjustment (see Table 7.1). This scale includes self-rating on thirty-two questions. Taken together the answers yield a total adjustment score. The questions fall into four general categories:

1. Dyadic satisfaction—the extent to which the couple is satisfied with their relationship. This is measured by questions like, How often do you and your partner quarrel? Do you confide in your mate? Do you ever regret that you married? Describe the degree of general happiness in your marriage.
2. Dyadic cohesion—the couple's feeling of togetherness. The couple rate themselves on questions like, How often do you have a stimulating exchange of ideas, calmly discuss something, or work together on a project?

Table 7.1 **Dyadic Adjustment Scale**

The following scale was developed to measure adjustment in couple relationships.
Most persons have disagreements in their relationships. Please indicate below the approximate extent of
agreement or disagreement between you and your partner for each item on the following list.

	ALWAYS AGREE	ALMOST ALWAYS AGREE	OCCASION-ALLY DISAGREE	FREQUENTLY DISAGREE	ALMOST ALWAYS DISAGREE	ALWAYS DISAGREE
1. Handling family finances	5	4	3	2	1	0
2. Matters of recreation	5	4	3	2	1	0
3. Religious matters	5	4	3	2	1	0
4. Demonstrations of affection	5	4	3	2	1	0
5. Friends	5	4	3	2	1	0
6. Sex relations	5	4	3	2	1	0
7. Conventionality (correct or proper behavior)	5	4	3	2	1	0
8. Philosophy of life	5	4	3	2	1	0
9. Ways of dealing with parents or in-laws	5	4	3	2	1	0
10. Aims, goals, and things believed important	5	4	3	2	1	0
11. Amount of time spent together	5	4	3	2	1	0
12. Making major decisions	5	4	3	2	1	0
13. Household tasks	5	4	3	2	1	0
14. Leisure time interests and activities	5	4	3	2	1	0
15. Career decisions	5	4	3	2	1	0

	ALL THE TIME	MOST OF THE TIME	MORE OFTEN THAN NOT	OCCASION-ALLY	RARELY	NEVER
16. How often do you discuss or have you considered divorce, separation, or terminating your relationship?	0	1	2	3	4	5
17. How often do you or your mate leave the house after a fight?	0	1	2	3	4	5
18. In general, how often do you think that things between you and your partner are going well?	5	4	3	2	1	0
19. Do you confide in your mate?	5	4	3	2	1	0
20. Do you ever regret that you married (or lived together)?	0	1	2	3	4	5
21. How often do you and your partner quarrel?	0	1	2	3	4	5
22. How often do you and your mate "get on each other's nerves"?	0	1	2	3	4	5

	EVERY DAY	ALMOST EVERY DAY	OCCASION-ALLY	RARELY	NEVER
23. Do you kiss your mate?	4	3	2	1	0

	ALL OF THEM	MOST OF THEM	SOME OF THEM	VERY FEW OF THEM	NONE OF THEM
24. Do you and your mate engage in outside interests together?	4	3	2	1	0

(continued)

Table 7.1 **Dyadic Adjustment Scale—(Continued)**

How often would you say the following events occur between you and your mate?

	NEVER	LESS THAN ONCE A MONTH	ONCE OR TWICE A MONTH	ONCE OR TWICE A WEEK	ONCE A DAY	MORE OFTEN
25. Have a stimulating exchange of ideas	0	1	2	3	4	5
26. Laugh together	0	1	2	3	4	5
27. Calmly discuss something	0	1	2	3	4	5
28. Work together on a project	0	1	2	3	4	5

These are some things about which couples sometimes agree and sometimes disagree. Indicate if either item below caused differences of opinions or were problems in your relationship during the past few weeks (Check yes or no)

Yes   No
29. 0   1   Being too tired for sex.
30. 0   1   Not showing love.
31. The dots on the following line represent different degrees of happiness in your relationship. The middle point, "happy," represents the degree of happiness of most relationships. Please circle the dot which best describes the degree of happiness, all things considered, of your relationship.

0	1	2	3	4	5	6
EXTREMELY UNHAPPY	FAIRLY UNHAPPY	A LITTLE UNHAPPY	HAPPY	VERY HAPPY	EXTREMELY HAPPY	PERFECT

32. Which of the following statements best describes how you feel about the future of your relationship?

  _5_ I want desperately for my relationship to succeed, and would go to almost any length to see that it does.
  _4_ I want very much for my relationship to succeed, and will do all I can to see that it does.
  _3_ I want very much for my relationship to succeed, and will do my fair share to see that it does.
  _2_ It would be nice if my relationship succeeded, but I can't do much more than I am doing now to help it succeed.
  _1_ It would be nice if it succeeded, but I refuse to do any more than I am doing now to keep the relationship going.
  _0_ My relationship can never succeed, and there is no more that I can do to keep the relationship going.

Source: G. B. Spanier, "Measuring Happiness: The Dyadic Adjustment Scale," *Journal of Marriage and the Family*, February 1976. Copyrighted 1976 by the National Council on Family Relations. Reprinted by permission.

3. Dyadic consensus—how often the partners agree. Such questions as, How often do you agree on handling family finances, household tasks, leisure activities, or ways of dealing with parents or in-laws? attempt to measure the degree of consensus.

4. Affectional expression—measures how frequently the partners reveal feelings of love, affection, and concern. This is measured by questions like, How often do you kiss your mate? What is the extent of your

agreement on sexual relations? Has not showing love been a problem? (Spanier, 1976).

It is important to note that scores on self-ratings like this can be misleading. Scales like Spanier's measure only what people say they do, which may or may not be the same as what they actually do. Spanier's scale also assumes that agreement and togetherness are important components of adjustment; however, as we shall see later, a couple can disagree about many things, or be extremely independent, and still be well-adjusted. Every marriage is different.

In devising his scale, Spanier expected to include measures of two other kinds of variables as part of his adjustment score: troublesome dyadic differences, and interpersonal tensions and personal anxiety. But so far these negative elements have been less successful in measuring total dyadic adjustment than the four kinds of variables specified: satisfaction, cohesion, consensus, and affection. This does not mean that differences, tensions, and anxiety do not exist in well-adjusted relationships. Satisfactory adjustment can be achieved despite interpersonal conflict, depending on how people deal with their differences.

Individual Needs
and Marital Adjustment

Although marital adjustment is defined as an interpersonal process, it is dependent upon and affected by the partners' individual needs. Most people need to have intimate relationships with other people and privacy for themselves; that is, they need both closeness and independence. Meeting these two very different needs within a marriage can be difficult at times. The desire for privacy, independence, and freedom can conflict with the demands of the marriage; similarly, the demands of the marriage can conflict with one's life as an individual. Good marital adjustment keeps the need for intimacy with the other and the need for privacy for the self in balance, though this balance takes different forms for different couples.

Askham (1976) found that some couples compromise both intimacy and independence needs. Instead of fully realizing either goal, they settle for a limited amount of each one, perhaps in the process of redefining their goals. In one young marriage, for example, the husband continued to go drinking with his friends several nights a week. His wife retaliated by spending a lot of time at her mother's house or with female friends so she wouldn't be home when her husband returned. Both partners found this pattern of behavior threatening to their marriage and eventually agreed upon a compromise: one night out a week for each of them.

Other couples, Askham found, manage the conflict by satisfying each need alternately. Many couples begin by needing security more than anything else and do everything they can to make sure that the relationship is not threatened by third parties, outside interests, or differing opinions. Often, the emphasis on security and stability begins during the engagement and continues after the wedding as the couple sets up housekeeping together. Once they feel secure as a couple, they often feel able to tolerate more independence in themselves and each other.

Still other couples stress one need at the expense of the other; for some, independence and freedom are so important that marital stability is sacrificed. Then there are other couples who find their relationship with each other so satisfying that independence is dispensed with. "I'm quite content to stay at home," said one married man. "When I go out I'd rather go with the wife" (Askham, 1976).

Finally, some couples meet different needs in different relationships. This is often the case with extra-marital sex, in which the married partner may provide security and the lover excitement; or in friendships, when the friends share interests the spouses do not. For couples who emphasize the independence of each spouse, marriage may, at times, not provide enough security or stability for one partner or the other. The partners may then satisfy their needs for security or stability by seeing their parents regularly.

Whichever strategy a couple adopts, they will need to make some compromises between their needs as individuals and their roles as spouses; and making this compromise is an important part of marital adjustment.

Emotional Maturity and Marital Adjustment

Sociologists and other family researchers have long believed that one of the most significant predictors of marital adjustment is a person's emotional maturity. In attempting to test this hypothesis, Dean (1966) gathered data on couples' perceived emotional maturity from self-ratings and from ratings by the spouse. The results in both cases demonstrated that perceived emotional maturity is positively related to marital adjustment. These findings were later confirmed by Cole, Cole, and Dean (1980). Both studies found that while a husband's perception of himself as emotionally mature, as measured by such adjectives as fair, rational, competent, and relatively easy to get along with, is positively related to both his own and his wife's marital adjustment, a wife's perception of herself as emotionally mature is related to her own marital adjustment, but not to her husband's. A likely explanation for these findings is that a person's self-perception and perception of the spouse as emotionally mature enhance self-confidence and self-esteem, thereby contributing to successful social and marital adjustment.

The causal connection between emotional maturity and marital adjustment is not clear, but Cole and colleagues speculate that a certain level of

CASE STUDY   *Self-Image and Adjustment*

Jessica and Steven grew up in very different family structures. Steven's parents were concert musicians. As a boy, Steven longed for their affection and attention, but they were always preoccupied with their music. A talented junior musician himself, Steven was crushed when he failed to place in a city-wide competition. His mother's critical reaction to this "failure" convinced him that she cared nothing for him as a son. He longed for someone who would love him and recognize him for the sensitive, talented person he was.

Jessica's father had been an authoritarian figure; when he gave orders, everyone jumped to obey. As a young woman, Jessica shared her father's strength and saw herself in his image. She learned early how to take charge of her life and achieve her goals. She pitied those who allowed themselves to be dominated, but couldn't help but take the role of the powerful person in her relationships with men.

When she met Steven, Jessica was working as a secretary and at the same time taking college courses at night hoping to prepare herself for a better career. She wasn't particularly interested in getting involved in a serious relationship, but when she met Steven there was a powerful sexual attraction, and she loved his gentle, caring nature.

Soon after the two fell in love they decided to move into Jessica's apartment. Unfortunately, about that time Jessica was laid off from her job. Steven was very sympathetic and even offered to quit his own job to keep her company. He was confused when Jessica refused the offer. Jessica spent the next six weeks in a disciplined search for a job. She finally landed one at double her previous salary.

Not too long afterward, Steven lost his job.

His own search for employment was far less diligent. His only real interest was in music. He pictured himself not as an ordinary wage earner but as a frustrated musician who was not cut out for the money-oriented culture of today. He was willing to wait indefinitely for the right opportunity to fall from heaven. Eventually, though, he found a job at a gas station and he and Jessica decided to get married. Jessica wanted an elaborate wedding and spent her savings to pay for it. Steven couldn't swing the money for wedding rings, so Jessica bought these as well, even though she found this irritating.

A few weeks after Steven and Jessica were married, the gas station where Steven worked went out of business. After half-heartedly looking for a new job, Steven began to spend more and more time around the house. When Jessica would arrive home from her job the house would be a mess, for Steven couldn't seem to get himself together to keep it clean and instead lay around listening to his stereo to try to keep up with modern trends in music. He planned to compose his own music and, when he felt it was good enough, to sell himself through his tape recordings as a performer.

Jessica grew increasingly frustrated with the situation and spent a lot of time nagging Steven and letting him know that she had lost her respect for him. When she had the time she would cut out descriptions of promising jobs that she saw in the newspaper and urge Steven to apply for them. Her anger had little effect except to make Steven feel more and more worthless.

For his part, Steven began to seek assurances of her love and faith in him. He wanted

(continued)

CASE STUDY   *(continued)*

a family, and promised her that if she became pregnant he would find a job and stick with it. Jessica finally agreed. Three months after Jessica became pregnant, Steven was still unemployed and not looking very hard for a job. Desperate over their increasing unhappiness, the couple finally turned to a marriage counselor.

FOR CLASS DISCUSSION

1. How have Jessica and Steven's self-images contributed to their marital difficulties?

2. One of the suggestions the marriage counselor made to Steven was to seek a position connected in some way with music. Why might this be important to Steven's self-esteem, and how might it help him take a more constructive approach to his problems?

3. What could Jessica and Steven do to help to assure a more equitable power balance in their marriage?

emotional maturity is a prerequisite for satisfactory marital adjustment. The socialization process which begins in childhood helps to prepare an individual for building a life with another adult. When socialization is inadequate, the result may be emotional immaturity, which leaves a person ill-prepared to deal with the normal difficulties of marriage. An alternative view of the dynamics of emotional maturity and marital adjustment is that a good marriage, as measured by satisfactory performance of roles and acceptance of responsibilities, contributes to each partner's emotional well-being and maturity. According to Cole, Cole, and Dean (1980), each of these views has merit, and it may be that they are not mutually exclusive: a certain basic level of emotional maturity is probably essential for successful adjustment, and success in carrying out the tasks of marriage may also contribute to greater maturity.

Youthful Marriages

If emotional maturity is a significant predictor of marital adjustment, it is not surprising that teenage marriages are more subject to marital troubles than marriages between adults. Statistically, those marrying later have a far higher chance of success than those who marry while rather young. Men who marry in their teens are twice as likely to get divorced as men who marry in their twenties; women who marry at ages fourteen to seventeen are twice as likely to get divorced as women who marry at eighteen or nineteen, who themselves are one and a half times as likely to get divorced as women who marry in their early twenties. In youthful marriages, marital satisfaction is usually found to be lower, the risk of disillusionment and failure is higher, and economic, social, and personal problems are greater. Marital adjustment is especially problematic for couples whose primary reason for marrying young is an existing pregnancy. Delissovoy (1973) conducted a longitudinal study of forty-eight young rural couples who married while in high school. The average age of the wives was sixteen, the husbands seventeen. Forty-one of the wives and thirty-five of the husbands dropped out of school, and forty-six of the wives were pregnant at the time of the marriage. Each couple was interviewed five times; the interviews began three months after marriage and ended five years later. The study provides a good example of the kinds of adjustment problems that may contribute to the high rate of subsequent breakup of adolescent marriages, especially those that are complicated by pregnancy.

MONEY After only three months of marriage, money was a problem; and, according to Delissovoy, the main problem was that there wasn't much of it. Some of the couples were on welfare. One-third had already made credit purchases requiring regular payments, and more than half had borrowed money from finance companies, which have very high interest rates. Almost all the couples received help from their parents. Even after three years of marriage, the parents were still providing some goods, money, services, or shelter; and both husbands and wives were more negative in their evaluation of their financial situation. The fact that money problems appeared to be endless seemed to be a major source of tension in these young marriages.

SOCIAL ACTIVITIES The teenage husbands and wives agreed that money was a problem, but disagreed about their social lives: only the wives were dissatisfied with their social activities. For the husbands, social life had not changed with marriage. They continued to go out with their old friends, play basketball after school, and see people at their part-time jobs. The wives tended to be isolated from their schoolgirl friends because of their own childrearing and housekeeping roles; and even when their husbands' friends came to visit, the wives felt left out. Most of the wives wanted to do things with other young couples, but this had happened in only seven of the forty-eight marriages.

The social pattern did not change much with time. After three years, the husbands still saw their old friends and the wives were still isolated. But the wives' attitude had changed: most of them were now resigned to their isolation and said the children didn't leave them much time for socializing anyway.

CHILDREARING The young couples tended to agree about childrearing before they had children and to disagree about it afterward. Most of them had unrealistic expectations about when babies mastered specific developmental tasks. Most, for example, thought that a baby should smile at three weeks, achieve bladder and bowel control at about six months, and begin talking at six to eight months.

By the time their children were two, most of the mothers scored at the low end of a scale designed to test how well they accepted their child. Delissovoy observed that with few exceptions, they seemed to be impatient with and intolerant of their children.

SEX   At the beginning of the marriage, the young husbands rated their general satisfaction with sexual relations slightly below average and their satisfaction with the frequency of sexual relations even lower. The wives expressed higher-than-average satisfaction with their sexual relationship, reporting that the amount of lovemaking was plenty or even a bit too much for them. After three years, the husbands still felt that lovemaking did not occur frequently enough, while the wives felt that too much sex was a problem.

IN-LAW RELATIONSHIPS   Despite their isolation from peers, the young spouses had frequent contact with relatives. Although their parents, who were farmers, manual laborers, and housewives, had generally been shocked to learn that their children would be marrying so young, in most cases, their initial disapproval gave way to resignation and then to active support. Most, for example, helped their children to arrange home or church weddings. As for the young couples, both husbands and wives gave their in-law relationships a slightly better-than-average rating, even those who were forced by economic circumstances to live in their in-laws' homes.

By the three years' interview, Delissovoy found that the husbands' satisfaction with their in-laws had increased slightly, while the wives' rating had dropped a bit. There were indications that the husbands were grateful for their in-laws' help, and that they had begun to feel particularly close to their fathers-in-law. Often the husbands were on a first-name basis with their fathers-in-law and enjoyed doing things with them. But for some wives, the birth of the first child brought resentment of the mothers-in-laws' well-meaning interference in childrearing. Even so, forty-four of the forty-eight couples reported closer relationships with their parents once the first child was born.

RELIGIOUS ACTIVITIES   Even though the young wives in this study seemed isolated from their friends, irritated by their children, displeased about being asked to have sex more than they wanted to, and sometimes annoyed at their in-laws, many reported one source of strength: their church. Church provided social as well as spiritual support. The wives still rated religious activities very highly after three years of marriage, but by then, their husbands' involvement with the church had declined, and some husbands had begun to stay home with the children while the wives attended church.

CONCLUSION Many studies have confirmed the hazards of early marriage, especially when the marriage is complicated by pregnancy and economic hardship. Young people, Delissovoy's findings suggest, tend to romanticize both marriage and childrearing and quickly become disillusioned. They reach a point of marital dissatisfaction at thirty months, which those who marry when they are adults do not usually experience until later. Although most of the young couples Delissovoy studied stayed married during the period of the study, this may have been due in part to the social support given to the relationship by their families and churches. In general, the chances for success in youthful marriages complicated by pregnancy and financial hardship are fairly low.

ADJUSTMENT OVER THE FAMILY LIFE CYCLE

We have said that adjustment is an ongoing process. The research suggests that couple adjustment changes over the years. Studies have been done of couples at various stages of the family life cycle, and almost all have found that, contrary to what one might think, couples in the early years of marriage experience a definite decline in marital satisfaction and adjustment.

Social scientists do not agree about marriages later in the family life cycle. Most studies done in the 1960s found a steady decrease in reported satisfaction throughout the family life cycle (Hicks and Platt, 1970). But more recent research suggests that the pattern may be U-shaped (see Fig 7.1). According to this research, most couples reach their all-time low during their children's teen years, but once the children leave, marital satisfaction and adjustment increase (Rollins and Cannon, 1974). However, the changes in marital satisfaction over the family life cycle are less than clear, and this is an area in need of further research.

Certainly marital satisfaction and adjustment patterns are not the same over the life cycle of all marriages, and how well a couple adjusts to marriage may depend upon how hard they are willing to work at it and how committed they are to keeping their relationship intact. Having a satisfying marriage requires consistent effort at all periods of life (though perhaps some periods are more trying than others) and requires a number of personal and interpersonal skills, such as insight, sensitivity, and flexibility. The amount of time and energy the partners invest in their relationship strongly influence the degree of marital adjustment.

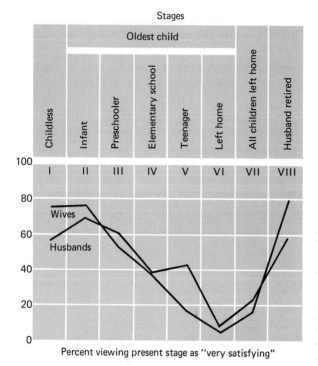

Fig. 7.1

Changes in marital satisfaction over the family life cycle. (Source: Boyd C. Rollins and Harold Feldman, "Marital Satisfaction over the Family Life Cycle," Journal of Marriage and the Family, *February 1970. Copyrighted 1970 by the National Council on Family Relations. Reprinted by permission.)*

The main reason that couples commonly experience declining satisfaction during the early years of marriage seems to be that prior to marriage many couples have a romantic, overly glamorous view of married life. Many people believe the portrayals of marriage they see on television, in the movies, and in popular novels, in which the couple remains on a perpetual honeymoon. The reality of marriage is almost inevitably disillusioning to people who imagine that married life will be dramatic, glamorous, and problem-free. As we discussed in Chapter 4, over time the relationship tends to change from one characterized by romantic love to one characterized by conjugal love. It may be that the more strongly one is romantic-love oriented prior to marriage, the greater the possibility of dissatisfaction and disillusionment as the relationship becomes increasingly stable and routine.

However, in the early years of marriage, even though couples may be experiencing declining satisfaction, positive changes may also be taking place as the conjugal-love relationship strengthens. The partners come to have more and more experiences in common as husband and wife. New values, which they develop together, replace the romantic illusions, and these values are often more firmly grounded in both reality and the partners' personalities. The very fact of having shared experiences, both positive and negative, is a strong bond for many couples. As the partners help each other with real problems, they come to know each other more intimately than they did when they lived in the romantic haze of courtship, and many develop a high level of communication and intimacy. Out of all this grows a sense of trust in each other and a deeper knowledge of the other's character. During the middle and later years of marriage, couples face different adjustment problems. We will consider these in Chapter 11.

Gender Differences in Adjustment

Research has shown that at most stages of the life cycle men tend to be less involved in their marriages than women are. Perhaps this is because traditionally, women have been more dependent upon marriage for their satisfactions and identities than men have been. In a traditional marriage, a man's self-image is bound up in his career, while a woman's is determined by how well she fills her marital and family roles. For this reason, too, wives generally

Humphrey Bogart and Lauren Bacall in a scene from To Have and Have Not. *The early years of marriage may be disillusioning if the couple expects conjugal love to resemble the glamour and romance of courtship as projected in the media.*

make more adjustment to the marriage than their husbands do (Spanier et al., 1975). A wife, particularly one who is dependent upon her husband economically, will probably be more attentive to her husband's needs than he is to hers.

Research has also shown that men are less affected by the different stages of the family life cycle than women are. For example, men's reported satisfaction with their marriages does not change much during the period of childbearing and childrearing, while most women report sharp decreases in marital satisfaction and high levels of negative feelings about their marriages during these years (Spanier et al., 1975). But as more and more women participate in the labor force and husbands assume a greater share of the child-care and child-socialization roles, men may find themselves more affected by the different stages of the family life cycle than they have been in the past. Similarly, as marriages become more egalitarian, husbands may find themselves adjusting to their wives as much as their wives are adjusting to them (Spanier et al., 1975).

Types of Marital Adjustment

Although the adjustments couples face change with the family's changing circumstances as the family progresses through its life cycle, most couples develop specific interactional styles within which adjustment occurs, and these styles tend to remain stable throughout the marriage.

In 1965, Cuber and Haroff studied 211 influential, socially prominent, socially active, economically successful people who described themselves as happily married. Among this upper-middle-class group, the study showed that there were five distinct styles, or types, of marital adjustment which emerged repeatedly, and that these types break down into two major categories: the utilitarian marriage, which is the more common type, and the intrinsic marriage. Since this typology was, in fact, developed from the study of socially prominent "significant Americans," its applicability to marriages in other social classes should be viewed cautiously.

THE UTILITARIAN MARRIAGE **Utilitarian marriages** are workable, rational, and satisfying to those who have them. Some utilitarian marriages are little more than convenient backgrounds for rearing children, working, and living adult lives; and that is the kind of marriage both partners want. They have married "for purposes other than to express an intimate relationship" (Cuber and Haroff, 1965). The following types are subcategories of utilitarian marriages.

In the **conflict-habituated marriage,** tension, though controlled, is the dominant mode of interaction. Both partners seem to enjoy arguing, or, as one conflict-habituated spouse said, "Let me correct that—brawling." The spouses' fights with each other are rarely concealed from their children, though usually

"Let's face it, Ron. The only time we meet each other's needs is when we fight."

both spouses denied this. "Oh, they're at it again—but they always are," said one high-school-age son.

Some psychologists say that the need to do psychological battle with each other is what keeps couples like this together (Cuber and Haroff, 1965). In almost all of these marriages, though, the conflict is channelled, the hostility bridled; the couple has adjusted to the tension and is even happy with it. One doctor who had been married to the same woman for twenty-five years described their marriage as "like a running guerrilla fight with intermediate periods, sometimes quite long, of pretty good fun and some damn good sex. . . . It's hard to know what we fight about most of the time. You name it, and we'll fight about it" (Cuber and Haroff, 1965). The conflict-habituated marriage is far less common than the other two types of utilitarian marriage: the devitalized and passive-congenial styles.

The **devitalized marriage** is one in which the partners, when young, were deeply in love but grew apart as the years passed; this sort of marriage shows the dramatic change that can occur between a couple's early years and their middle age. Most of these couples said that they had been "deeply in love" when they were first married and spent a great deal of time together, enjoyed sex, and identified closely with each other. By the time they were middle-aged, they spent little time together, did not find their sex life satisfying, and shared few interests or activities other than duties. Yet they stayed together.

Couples seem to react in two main ways to this sort of marriage. Cuber and Haroff found that some accepted, somewhat reluctantly, the fact that things had changed. "There's a cycle to life. I'll admit that I do yearn for the old days, but then you get used to it," one wife said. Another reported, "Judging by the way it was when we were first married, things are pretty matter of fact now, even dull. They're dull between us, I mean. The children are a lot of fun, keep us pretty busy, and there are lots of outside things . . . as he said to me the other night, 'You know, you're still a little fun now and then.' "

Others struggle against the change. As one wife said, "I know I'm fighting it. I ought to accept that it has to be like this, but I don't like it, and I'd do almost anything to bring back the exciting way of living we had at first."

Yet, all these spouses assured the researchers that there was "something there." All occasionally shared things, if only memories. Anniversaries were celebrated, "if a little grimly," for what they once commemorated. Many of these people believed that the devitalized mode was the appropriate way for older people to live and be married.

The passive-congenial marriage is like the devitalized marriage except that the marriage has lacked emotional depth from the beginning and neither partner expects excitement or passion in their life together. The couple finds the marriage comfortably adequate; neither ever wanted or hoped for anything else. Marriage is a convenient, and necessary, background for their lives. As one dedicated doctor said of his marriage: "It is convenient, orderly, and solves a lot of problems. But there are other things in life. I spent nearly ten years preparing for the practice of my profession. The biggest thing to me is the practice of that profession."

Those who have passive-congenial marriages have many outside interests, and their creative energies are directed, not into the couple relationship but into other aspects of their lives—careers, children, community activities. The passive-congenial marriage gives them the independence and freedom to pursue those interests. Not surprisingly, passive-congenial partners do not devote much attention or energy to adjusting to the spouse's needs; but as both are presumably in agreement about the limited attention given to the marriage, perhaps they do not need to.

Interestingly, Cuber and Haroff's quotations about the passive-congenial marriage all came from men; their quotations about the devitalized marriage all came from women. One wonders if the sexes are both as satisfied, or in as much agreement, as the researchers think.

THE INTRINSIC MARRIAGE   People who have what Cuber and Haroff call **intrinsic marriages** are bound together emotionally and psychologically. Their relationship with each other is the most important part of life to them both. Sex is very important in these marriages, and sexual problems are uncommon.

Intrinsic marriages are of two types. In **vital marriages**, the couples find their main satisfaction in the life they lead with and through each other. As one man said, "The things we do together aren't fun intrinsically—the ecstacy comes from being together in the doing." The life they have together dominates the couple's thoughts and actions; all other interests are subordinate and secondary. These couples willingly, gladly, give up other things for the marriage: "I cheerfully, and that's putting it mildly, passed up two good promotions because one of them would have required some traveling and the other would have taken evening and weekend time, and that's when Pat and I *live*. The hours with her (after twenty-two years of marriage) are what I live for."

People in vital marriages do, of course, have conflicts at times, but when they disagree, it is about something that is important to both of them, as opposed to the conflict-habituated couple's quarrels over trivial things. And, unlike conflict-habituated couples, people in vital marriages tend to settle their disagreements quickly.

The **total marriage** is like the vital marriage, except that there are more points of meshing; in some cases, all the important aspects of life are shared. Often, these spouses work together. This sort of marriage is rare, but it does exist. In a total marriage, the spouses share all interests and activities enthusiastically; it is as though neither has, or has had, a truly private existence. Interestingly, extramarital sexual relationships, which occur in all the other types (though for different reasons), are almost nonexistent in total marriages.

The typology offered by Cuber and Haroff classifies marriages, not individuals. A vital individual can have a devitalized or passive-congenial marriage. Similarly, a more passive individual can be part of a vital or total marriage. Nor should the five types of marriage be seen as degrees of marital happiness, or stages in marital development. Relationship types tend to persist over long periods; changes from one type to another are rare. They each represent a different kind of adjustment to marriage, a different approach to marriage. In the Cuber and Haroff study, persons in all five categories said they were adjusted to their marriages, and most said they were content, if not happy.

RESOURCES, POWER, AND MARITAL ADJUSTMENT

From a social exchange perspective, marital adjustment can be seen to be strongly influenced by the nature of the power structure and the exchange relationship of the couple in the marriage. All social acts consist of exchanges. Sometimes, the resources exchanged are tangible: people give each other money in exchange for goods. Sometimes, people give something tangible, like money, for something slightly less tangible, like services or information. Resources can also be intangible. Expressions of love, competence at carrying out a role, and providing a sense of security are examples of intangible resources that are exchanged. In short, anything that people can give to or take from one another is a **resource**, and marital adjustment can be viewed as the way spouses share their resources with each other in their exchange relationship to satisfy each others' needs and desires (Foa and Foa, 1980).

As shown in Fig. 7.2, Foa and Foa (1980) divided the resources involved in interpersonal exchange into six categories: love, status, information, money, goods, and services. *Love* as a resource is an expression of affection, warmth, or comfort; *status* is an expression of judgment about prestige, regard, or esteem; *information* includes advice, opinions, instruction, or enlightenment about anything other than love or status; *money* is any coin, currency, or token which has some standard unit of exchange value; *goods* are tangible products, objects, or materials; and *services* are activities performed by one person for another; often, services are labors for someone else.

One way these classes can be ordered is according to how *concrete* or *symbolic* they are (Foa and Foa, 1980). Some behaviors, like giving someone a present, are concrete, tangible, while others, like sighing, are more intangible, or symbolic. Thus, goods and services are placed at the concrete end of the scale, while information and status are placed at the symbolic end. Money and love, which are exchanged in both concrete and symbolic ways, are in the middle.

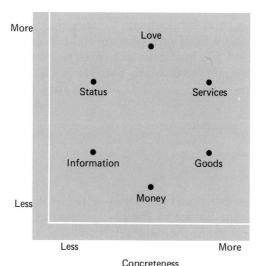

Fig. 7.2
Resources classes plotted according to particularism-universalism and concrete-symbolic dimensions. (Source: "Interpersonal and Economic Resources," Foa, V. G., Science Vol. 171, pp. 345–351, 29 January 1971. Copyright 1971 by the American Association for the Advancement of Science.)

The same classes of resources can also be ordered according to the significance of the person with whom one is exchanging them, which Foa and Foa term *particularism* vs. *universalism*. For example, when cashing a check, the bank teller's identity is relatively unimportant; but the value of a kiss depends entirely upon with whom one is exchanging it. Thus, money is at the universalism end of the scale, while love is at the particularism end. Services and status are less particularistic than love but more particularistic than goods and information. Most social acts involve an exchange of more than one resource, and social relationships such as marriage involve a large number of social acts or interpersonal transactions. In marriage, exchanges or transactions develop particular patterns over time which come to characterize the particular relationship. These exchange patterns are influenced by the distribution of resources between the husband and wife and the subsequent power relationship.

Resources and Power

Traditionally, American society has given men a monopoly over most valued resources, particularly money, education, and social status; and with these resources the power to make many family decisions. If, for example, a husband and wife disagree about buying a house, and the husband, having the only job, is paying for the mortgage, his opinion will probably carry more weight than his wife's. Because he has money and she doesn't, he can void her decision (selecting the house he wants), while she can only try to influence his decision (try to persuade him to buy the house she wants). In this situation, the husband obviously has more power than the wife. Traditionally, society has sanctioned the husband-dominant marriage both directly and indirectly through the resources it has given to men and through social norms which indicate how marriage should be: primarily male-dominant.

However, contemporary marriages tend to be more companionable and egalitarian and less husband-dominated. As noted in Chapter 6, Brickman (1974) has called this a move from a "fully structured relationship," in which social norms dictate each partner's behavior, to a "partially structured relationship," in which some behaviors are dictated by social norms, while others are left up to the partners. Once, for example, the man was the sole financial provider; a wife who worked would have been criticized, and so would her husband. Today, whether or not a wife works is left up to the partners; but social norms would still probably not permit a man to do nothing in support of his family—nor would they approve of a woman who completely ignored her responsibilities toward her children. Marriages today, Brickman contends, are established bargaining relationships in which both partners possess and exchange resources.

Scanzoni (1972) has made an examination of the history of husband-wife relations in the United States since the early nineteenth century. The change in women's status within marriage has come about, he believes, largely through conflict which occurs because of women's efforts to gain a greater share of valued resources. The early feminists, for example, worked to overturn legal restrictions which viewed the wife as her husband's property and thereby prohibited her from owning property herself, signing contracts, and voting. Scanzoni characterized the change in husband-wife relations since the early nineteenth century as a gradual shift in the wife's status from the wife as *property* to the wife as *complement* to the wife as *junior partner*. As women gained more resources outside the home (such as the right to own property and participate in financial matters that pertained to them) they demanded, and received, more resources within marriage, such as the capacity to influence major decisions. However, a wife as complement to her husband has fewer rights and more duties than her husband has. Because the husband is the provider, he has more valuable resources than she does, and thus he has more authority.

When the wife works outside the home, she becomes what Scanzoni calls a junior partner in the marriage. She has fewer required duties, is less obliged to defer to her husband, and has more authority in the family than does the wife who is a complement to her husband; but the junior partner is still subordinate to her husband, because she does not occupy the main provider role in the family. The wife as junior partner often works as hard within the home as the wife who has no outside job. Scanzoni believes that most wives today are in the junior partner position; few achieve the status of *equal partner* in which resources, power, and authority are equally distributed in the marriage. Thus, according to Scanzoni, power is still mainly in the hands of the husband, though the wife is gradually acquiring more power.

A similar view of power relationships within marriage was offered earlier by Blood and Wolfe (1960) and called the "resource theory of marital power." This theory stated basically that the more resources one partner had compared to the other the more relative power to make decisions that partner had.

A major limitation of Blood and Wolfe's analysis was their exclusive focus on tangible economic resources and skills such as money or occupational prestige. Other social scientists have theorized that power in a relationship is determined, not only by economics, but also by emotions. Safilios-Rothschild (1976) has described love as a major resource: those who are equally in love share the power in the marriage. Others (Waller and Hill, 1951; Blau, 1964) have focused on the "principle of least interest," which means that in marriage, whichever partner has the least interest in continuing or preserving the relationship has the most power. If, for example, the husband wants to go to the movies and the wife wants to stay home, whichever partner least desires the company of the other will have the most power. If the husband cares more about going to the movies than being with his wife, he will be able to say, truthfully: "If you don't want to see the film, I'll go by myself." The wife then has the choice of remaining alone or accompanying her husband. If his company is more important to her than getting her own way, she may go with him. Similarly, if the wife says, "Go by yourself, then," and the husband finds his wife's company more important than getting his own way, he may choose to stay home. The partner with the least interest in the relationship can use that lack of interest—and the partner's interest—as a bargaining tool.

Toward Joint Decision Making

As more and more women enter the work force and gain a larger proportion of economic and other resources, egalitarian marriage is becoming increasingly common and husband-dominant marriage less common. In many modern marriages, decision-making is less determined by social norms and cultural expectations and more determined by negotiation, or bargaining. Instead of the husband automatically making decisions in his sphere of interest and the wife making decisions in hers, partners now often make decisions together, each, probably, compromising sometimes: "I'll do the dishes if you'll put the kids to bed." How skilled partners are at negotiating with each other is a major determinant of their level of marital adjustment.

Negotiations are successful in marriage when they result, not in one partner's victory and the other's defeat, but in the maximum possible joint profit (Scanzoni, 1979). For this to happen, the partners must trust each other and be committed to the marriage. If the partners don't trust each other, they can't rely on each other to abide by the agreement; if they don't want the marriage to last, or if they don't think it will last, they will have little incentive to work toward, much less compromise individual desires to achieve, joint goals. The exchanges and negotiations which are undertaken in striving toward these joint goals are major components in interpersonal marital adjustment.

SOME MAJOR AREAS
OF MARITAL ADJUSTMENT

The last few decades have brought enormous social changes to America. Our society in general has become more egalitarian: groups which traditionally have exercised little power are gradually acquiring more influence. Sexual mores have been changing; expectations for sex-appropriate behavior and gender-role differences have become increasingly flexible. As leisure time has increased, values have shifted somewhat from a traditional work ethic toward more acceptance of leisure as a life goal (Orthner, 1975). All of these social changes have naturally had an influence upon marital adjustment.

In Chapter 3, we discussed how gender-role expectations have changed, and we saw that this has been especially true regarding societal attitudes toward working wives. In this section, we will consider the behavior that accompanies those changed attitudes—specifically, the adjustments that take place in dual-worker marriages. We will also consider the kinship and recreational roles, as well as the therapeutic role. Finally, changes in sexual adjustment will be covered in Chapter 8, and financial adjustment will be discussed in the Appendix.

Adjustments in Dual-Worker Marriages

Married women joined the labor force in large numbers during World War II and increasing percentages of them have worked in the female labor force ever since: 15 percent in 1940, 30 percent in 1960, and 40 percent in 1970. By 1979, sixty percent of all female workers were married women, and married women made up approximately 26 percent of the total labor force (U.S. Bureau of the Census, 1980). Also in 1979, 49.4 percent of married women living with their husbands were working.

Women who work tend to be better educated than women who do not work. This could be because better jobs are available to educated women, especially to women with college degrees. The main factor in a wife's employment, however, seems to be whether or not she has small children. The married woman without children is most likely to work; the married woman with preschool children is most likely to be at home taking care of them. Still, 43.2 percent of married women with children under age six and 59.1 percent of married women with children between ages six and seventeen worked outside the home in 1979 (U.S. Bureau of the Census, 1980).

In about half the marriages in the United States today both partners work outside the home. Sometimes, these are called "dual-career" marriages, but a more accurate characterization for most multi-earner couples is "dual-worker" marriages. A **dual-career marriage** is one in which both partners work at jobs that require step-by-step planning to move up the occupational ladder; in addition, the jobs require "a continuous and high degree of commitment" (Rapoport and Rapoport, 1980). These jobs offer personal satisfaction and opportunity for advancement, and they are well-paying. For the most part, a high level of skills and education is a prerequisite. Dual-career marriages constitute a minority of working-couple marriages. The majority of married women who work tend to have nonprofessional jobs, such as salesperson, secretary, cashier, and the like. Most of these jobs cannot properly be called careers, for they do not require the sequential planning or provide the satisfaction which characterizes careers. For the purposes of our discussion, we will refer to **dual-worker marriages.** This is a broader term which can include all marriages in which both partners are employed outside the home.

In the preceding section, we focused on the changing nature of marriage and family in modern society as women have acquired more resources. Those resources have come largely from participation in the labor force. Here we describe more specifically research indicating the impact of wives working outside the home on other areas of adjustment in marriage.

JOB INVOLVEMENT AND JOB SATISFACTION It might seem that people who are highly involved in their work would have little time for enjoying home life and that their marriages would suffer accordingly. It also seems reasonable to assume that people who are bored or dissatisfied with their jobs might be more likely to seek pleasure and satisfaction in their marriages. According to a study by Carl Ridley (1973), there is a relationship between involvement and satisfaction in work and marital interaction in dual-worker families, but it is somewhat different from what might be expected.

Ridley surveyed his subjects on three variables: marital adjustment, job satisfaction, and job involvement. Job involvement was defined as the amount of time devoted to thinking, reading, writing, and talking about the job beyond

Dual-career marriages, such as that between actress Jane Fonda and political activist Tom Hayden, are those in which the spouses' jobs require high commitment and offer personal satisfaction. Most marriages in which both partners hold outside jobs are more appropriately described as "dual worker."

the normal workday. He felt that this kind of extended involvement was most likely to interfere with people's marital roles. He chose professional people as his subjects on the assumption that they would be most likely to be highly involved with their jobs.

Ridley found that for the men in this study, the first two variables, job satisfaction and marital adjustment, were positively related: men who were satisfied with their work reported being satisfied with their marriages; men who were dissatisfied with their work were less satisfied with their marriages. Ridley theorized that because men in our culture are socialized to regard work success as the most important indicator of self-worth, positive feelings about themselves and their jobs carry over into positive feelings about themselves and their marriages.

For women, the relationship between job satisfaction and marital adjustment included another variable: how important the woman considered her job. Among the women who viewed their work as secondary to the marriage, job satisfaction had little effect upon marital interaction. But among the women who considered their job more central, job satisfaction was positively related to marital adjustment. Women who were satisfied with their jobs were more likely to be satisfied with their marriages, if they considered their jobs important (Ridley, 1973).

In general, the couples Ridley interviewed had been more than moderately successful at keeping the third variable, job involvement, from interfering with their marital interaction. But marital adjustment scores were highest for husbands and wives who had low job-involvement scores. The scores were lower when either partner reported high levels of job involvement.

DIFFERENCES IN MARITAL ADJUSTMENT WHEN THE WIFE WORKS   A number of researchers have examined the effects on marital adjustment of the wife working, and although much has been written about this, the issue is complex and present results are inconclusive.

Ronald Burke and Tamara Weir (1976) administered lengthy questionnaires to 189 Canadian couples. All the men studied were professionals; 28 percent of the wives were working outside the home. The researchers found that the working wives were happier and more satisfied with their marriages than the wives who did not work outside the home, but that the working wives' husbands were less satisfied than the housewives' husbands. Husbands with wives who worked, Burke and Weir speculated, might have felt they had lost some of their wives' emotional and physical support. They may have missed the comforts of having their wives wait on them; they may also have felt demeaned by having to perform domestic tasks.

Other research contradicts Burke and Weir's conclusions. Alan Booth (1977) replicated the Burke and Weir study, improving the sampling, mea-

HIGHLIGHT 7.1   *How Couples Divide the Housework*

Three sociologists recently conducted a study of how couples divide up the housework. Richard and Sarah Berk of the University of California at Santa Barbara and Catherine Berheide of Skidmore College in New York asked 748 wives to keep a diary of one full day's household chores. They also asked some 350 husbands to fill out questionnaires on their household tasks. Among the findings:

☐ Wives with full-time jobs still devote almost a quarter of their day to housework.

☐ Only 5 to 10 percent of the nation's husband-and-wife households share housework about evenly. In most families, the woman still does 80 to 90 percent of the housework, even when she takes an outside job.

☐ Couples who share the housework evenly, for the most part, are not the young, college-educated, liberal-minded families. Rather, the most equal sharing occurs among retired couples, because the husband has more free time than he did when he was working and helping to rear children.

☐ Husbands use a variety of dodges to get out of additional housework, such as unfamiliarity with how all-temperature soap powder works, lapses of memory on where things are kept, and procrastination that outlasts the wife's patience—so that she ends up doing the task herself.

For the most part, women in the U.S. are not complaining about housework.

The study found that a full-time homemaker spends eight hours a day on housework, the part-time employed woman seven hours, and the full-time employed woman five hours.

(In comparison, other studies have shown that men spend 10 to 15 hours a week on housework, says Professor Berheide.)

And a close look at what the women do expands the traditional definition of housework. Counted as housework in this study are such duties as child care (including driving the children to events and activities outside the home), gardening and lawn care, planning dinners, grocery shopping, and even fixing the garage roof.

When a woman takes an outside job, it is the children—not the husband—who pitch in the most on housework, the study found.

The husband usually picks up one additional task, such as washing the dishes. And often he makes sure this contribution does not go unnoticed.

Some chores just get done less often when the woman starts working. "There are women who scrub the floors once a day; others do it once a year," says Professor Berheide.

But these findings are not likely to set many working wives trying to renegotiate household chores, Professor Berheide says. Most families cling to their established divisions of labor, finding changes difficult.

Source: Robert M. Press, "A Husband's Housework Is Never Done," August 22, 1980. Reprinted by permission from *The Christian Science Monitor* © 1980 The Christian Science Publishing Society. All rights reserved.

surement, and analysis procedures. Booth concluded that the husbands of employed women were, if anything, more satisfied with their marriages than the husbands of housewives. Booth theorized that even though the adjustment may be difficult and stressful when a wife first starts working, the long-term benefits—particularly the added income and greater personal fulfillment of the wife—outweigh the short-term disadvantages.

A study by Anne Locksley (1980) did not support this conclusion. Locksley analyzed the effects of wives' employment on marital adjustment by comparing marriages of wives employed outside the home with marriages of unemployed wives. Within dual-worker families, she compared the marriages of women who were highly interested in their work with those of women who were working only for the increased income. National survey data were used to measure a representative national sample of 2300 persons on fourteen indicators of marital adjustment.

Locksley found that marital adjustment in dual-worker marriages does not differ significantly from adjustment in single-worker marriages. Both housewives and wives with outside jobs expressed more frustration and dissatisfactions with their marriages than did their husbands, and both felt less adequate as parents, were more upset by marital conflict, and perceived less marital interaction. Nor did the wife's degree of interest in her outside job seem to affect marital adjustment. According to Locksley (1980), conclusions like Burke and Weir's regarding employment are based on "unwarranted assumptions."

DIVISION OF LABOR IN DUAL-WORKER FAMILIES We have suggested that as women assume a greater and greater share of the provider role, men would be expected to assume a greater and greater share of the housekeeper and child-care roles. This theory fits in with the exchange perspective, and it is supported by Nye's analysis of family roles. However, it does not fit the present division of labor in most dual-worker families. Most studies indicate that although expectations and attitudes toward traditional gender roles have changed, actual behavior has not altered significantly.

Araji (1977) found that while a majority of family-role attitudes have become more egalitarian (in theory, men and women agree that women should help perform the provider role and men should help perform the housekeeping role), they are not always accompanied by behavior changes. Although more husbands are helping with child care, and some no longer believe that girls' socialization is primarily the mother's responsibility, women still are responsible for most domestic tasks (Araji, 1977).

Berheide, Berk, and Berk (1976) studied housework patterns among 309 wives, 43 percent of whom worked full-time outside the home. Collection methods consisted of telephone interviews, a self-administered twenty-four-hour diary, and, in some cases, direct observation of the wife at work. The researchers found "very little evidence" of husbands contributing "more than a minimal amount to household work," even among the wives who worked full-time outside the home. These wives did proportionately as much housework as full-time housewives: most of the housework. And even when the women were assisted with household chores, responsibility for housework remained with them. Often, they had to supervise their husbands' household work.

Despite the seeming unfairness of this arrangement, most of the women surveyed accepted the division of labor, for different reasons. Some felt that the specific tasks were boring, tedious, or tiring, but that the larger roles of mother, wife, and homemaker were satisfying. Many of the women, too, had such strong attachments to their families that the housework seemed worth it: "a labor of love may at times not seem like labor at all."

Adjusting to the Kinship Role

One of the first developmental tasks in a marriage is in the kinship role. Although their parents and other relatives have helped to shape their identities and may continue to be frequent visitors, the new couple must put the development of a good working relationship with each other before their loyalties to their families of orientation. Unless the bond between them is stronger than the bonds linking them to the families in which they grew up, the new family may experience difficulties. And anything that a member of either of the original families does that hampers the cohesiveness of the new dyad can be looked on as a potentially divisive in-law problem (Duvall, 1965).

Contrary to what one might expect based on popular stereotypes, however, for most couples, relations with in-laws are not usually a major problem. In Komarovsky's classic study, *Blue-Collar Marriage* (1964), the majority of men reported either a good relationship with the mother-in-law, characterized by affection, positive satisfaction, and minor conflicts, or at least an average one—some favorable comments coupled with minor complaints.

Family background has been found to be influential in adjustment to in-laws. If the two families of orientation are from similar cultures, if the backgrounds of the two families fit together, the couple and their in-laws are more likely to agree about behavior and values, enjoy the same activities, understand each others' concerns, and grant each other the privacy that comes from trust and approval (Kirkpatrick, 1963).

According to most studies, when problems with in-laws do arise, they are more likely to involve the women than the men. The mother-in-law is more often perceived as a problem than the father-in-law; daughters-in-law are more likely to have clashes with their in-laws than are sons-in-law (Kirkpatrick,

1963). But Komarovsky (1964) found that in working-class marriages, husbands are as likely as wives to have difficulty getting along with their in-laws. Even so, only one-third of husbands had strained relationships with their in-laws.

Most in-law problems center around the issue of self-respect. Wives may be sensitive to criticisms of their housekeeping or childrearing; husbands more often feel inadequate when they are less educated than their wives. Sometimes the wife's parents are disappointed that their daughter has married "beneath her"; sometimes the husband is defensive about his lack of education and is thus more sensitive to real or imagined criticism. Of course, less education does not necessarily mean less intelligence or ability, so educationally imbalanced marriages do not always lead to in-law conflict.

Different couples respond differently to criticism by parents. In some marriages, one partner may side with the parents in criticizing the mate, thereby reducing his or her self-respect; in others, the couple may stand together against certain relatives, so that what hurts one affects them both. For example, a taxi-driver reported that he felt it was his duty to protect his wife from her parents: "I try to keep her away from her family as much as I can on account of they do hurt her a lot" (Komarovsky, 1964). In cases like this, in-law problems can demonstrate how well the couple has adjusted to marriage.

Some partners may have been overly dependent upon their parents and may continue to look to them for advice or emotional support on matters that should be decided between husband and wife. This situation can stimulate competition between spouse and parents. A woman who visits her mother too often, or a man who will not make any decisions without consulting his father, is likely to have a spouse who has become jealous of the influence of in-laws.

Adjusting to the Recreational Role

The recreational role is more important to couples today than it was in the past. It is now regarded as an important arena for expressing affection and interdependence and enhancing awareness of each other's interests. Orthner (1975) believes that the importance of recreation to the family has been heightened by three trends: (1) the family is based more on companionship, with its traditional functions having become less important; (2) the amount of leisure time has increased as working hours have been reduced and time-saving devices have become widely available; (3) values have shifted somewhat from the work ethic toward more acceptance of leisure as a life goal.

Orthner (1975) investigated the relationship between the kinds of activities couples engage in during their leisure time and marital satisfaction. He separated leisure activities into three different types based on the extent of interaction required:

1. *Individual activities*, such as reading or gardening, are those that require no interaction with others and may actually discourage it.

2. *Joint activities*, such as playing games, making love, and camping, are those that require a high level of interaction and encourage communication.

3. *Parallel activities*, such as watching television, listening to records, or visiting museums, may be little more than individual activities carried out in a group setting. They require a minimum of interaction.

Each of these types of leisure activities can help reduce marital partners' anxieties, free them to see things in new ways, and act as shock absorbers and stabilizers during times of stress. But Orthner suggests that couples have the greatest chance of improving their relationship when they are engaging in joint activities. Joint leisure activities between partners encourage open communication and role interchange, increasing the possibility for understanding each other and changing behaviors that may be causing problems.

When he surveyed 442 upper-middle-class couples in urban areas of the Southeast, Orthner found that the communication-increasing potential of joint

Participation in "joint" leisure activities—activities that require high levels of interaction and thereby facilitate communication— has been linked to high levels of marital satisfaction.

activities was especially important at two points in the marriage cycle. The first is the early years of marriage, when patterns of husband-wife interaction are being established. A high level of individual activities during the first five years reduced the amount of time left for joint activities and was associated with a low level of marital satisfaction. Conversely, a high level of joint leisure activities during the first five years of the marriage was significantly related to positive marital satisfaction for both partners.

Joint leisure activities become significantly related to marital satisfaction again in mid-life when grown children are leaving the nest and parents are alone together again. If they pursue joint activities they both enjoy, their marital satisfaction is likely to be high, whereas if they engage in individual activities, marital satisfaction is likely to be lower. Parallel activities can also contribute to marital satisfaction in the middle years. It may be that when people have known each other intimately for so long, they do not require such high levels of interaction. Perhaps they are satisfied simply to enjoy the compatibility of doing things like reading books in the same room.

Between these two periods, during the years of childrearing and career building, patterns of leisure activity were found to be only slightly related to marital satisfaction. Orthner suggests that during these years, the relationship between the couple may be given lower priority because couples are concentrating on parental and work goals. Still, even during these years, a preponderance of individual activities by one partner may leave the other feeling rejected. For example, a complaint of wives in some traditional marriages is that the husband spends his leisure time playing golf or going to hockey games and makes little effort to interact with her. If such couples are to achieve satisfactory adjustment to the recreational role, the partner who feels neglected must communicate his or her needs, and the other partner must be willing to make a greater commitment to sharing activities.

Adjusting to the Therapeutic Role

While most couples would agree that one or both spouses should earn the family living, do the housework, care for the children, and fulfill the kinship and recreational roles, some couples do not believe that they should help each other with personal problems—fulfill the therapeutic role. Ironically, the value placed on this role is less than that placed on most other family roles, yet its relationship to satisfaction in marriage is greater than that of most of the other family roles. However, there is evidence that the therapeutic role is beginning to be recognized as an important part of marital adjustment: when husbands and wives were asked if they thought helping the spouse with personal problems was a duty, 60 percent said that it was and 40 percent said that it was desirable (Nye, 1976).

According to Nye, there are four possible positive responses to a spouse's problem. The partner can simply listen to the problem, sympathize, give reassurance and affection, or offer help in solving the problem. Negative responses include criticizing the spouse, disclosing the confidence to a third party, and imposing one's own solutions on the confider. Both husbands and wives disapproved of revealing information about family problems to outsiders, and 85 percent of husbands and wives disapproved of responding to a confidence with criticism.

Women seem to value this role more than men do, and more wives than husbands offer sympathy and support when it is needed (Nye, 1976). In fact, Nye's study showed that wives helped their husbands with personal problems whether the wives considered it a "duty" or simply "desirable." Nye speculates that helping with problems may be a way for wives to obtain information about their husbands' jobs and job-related activities. Enacting the therapeutic role may enable the wife to influence her husband in the provider role. Another, more likely, explanation relates to the different socialization of men and women. Women have been socialized to be more empathetic, loving, and communicative than men. They may be more in the habit of talking about interpersonal matters than men are and therefore may be more comfortable fulfilling this role.

 CONFLICT IN MARRIAGE

No matter how well marital partners fulfill their roles, they will inevitably disagree at times, and, eventually, one will resist the other's claims, negotiations will reach a dead end, and conflict will emerge. One way of looking at conflict is in terms of exchange of resources. From this perspective, conflict is defined as an opposition, a struggle for limited resources or disagreement over incompatible goals (Scanzoni and Scanzoni, 1976).

Although social scientists used to consider conflict destructive and dangerous, something to be avoided at all costs, it is now generally realized that conflict can be constructive. It can strengthen the bonds between partners. When satisfactorily resolved through negotiation, conflict can remove injustice and punishments and increase maximum joint profits. The new bargains that emerge from the conflict can change destructive patterns of behavior and replace them with new, more constructive behavior patterns. During the conflict, both partners suffer and experience pain; but once the conflict has been resolved, each is likely to benefit.

There are two main categories of husband-wife conflict: disagreements about day-to-day matters and major differences of opinion or feeling. The lesser conflicts are highly idiosyncratic and reflect the personalities of the partners;

Constructive Approaches to Conflict

Some couples habitually fall into the trap of dealing with conflict on a win-or-lose basis. They do not seem to realize that this is the least effective, most alienating method they can use. The idea of "winning" a marital conflict is an illusion. In virtually every instance one person's "victory" eventually turns into both spouses' ultimate loss. Winning simply doesn't work.

One husband confided that more than once he had surreptitiously let the air out of a tire or removed the distributor cap from the car to avoid going to a party he didn't want to attend. He said he used to chuckle at his cleverness until it struck him that his wife was always so disappointed that she withdrew into a depressed silence that sometimes lasted several days.

Some husbands or wives will use any handy emotional equivalent of the street-brawler's tactics: gouging a partner's self-esteem, jamming a knee into pride. Strictly speaking, this is not so much a way of winning an argument as it is of having the last word—of recouping one's position after the issue in conflict has already been lost.

Few techniques are so effective at winning marital arguments (or so destructive over the long term) as hoarding old emotional hurts, carefully nurturing them and producing them at a climactic moment.

Some "winners" see any compromise—giving even an inch—as losing. As a result, when they know a compromise is inevitable they deliberately set their demands considerably beyond what they really want. Then they appear to give in—but only to where they wanted to be in the first place. It's the kind of negotiating that goes on in labor contract bargaining, or in political horse-trading. But while it may

be effective there—perhaps because both sides do it and both sides know it is going on—it can be a trap for couples who are trying to learn to reach honest compromises.

Ultimately, the basic reason that "winning" does not work is that it reduces marriage to a power struggle. The alternative to power is love. When couples deal with marital conflict they have a choice. They can opt for power and seek to "win". Or they can opt for love and seek to reach accord.

Consider these constructive approaches to conflict:

☐ Learn what your most frequent or most intense arguments are really about. Do you become involved in conflicts over symbolic issues? If so, cut through the surface disagreements and try to work out the emotional meanings they have for you.

☐ Do not equate "losing" a dispute with a loss of self-esteem. Realize that you are the same person, with the same assets and good qualities, that you were before the issue was joined.

☐ Try to differentiate realistically between your wants and your needs. What one spouse wants at a given time may be irrelevant in terms of the needs of the other, or of the marriage as a unit. There may be moments, too, when your needs are not as important as your partner's.

☐ Keep in mind that marriage is a co-operative enterprise, not a competitive one. The goal is not to settle which of you is right or wrong. The goal is to reach a solution both of you can live with—a compromise that will make life together more pleasant.

Source: M. Lasswell and N. Lobsenz, *No-Fault Marriage* (New York: Doubleday, 1976). Reprinted by permission.

they have been called "tremendous trifles" because, although they pertain to personal habits, preferences, and manners concerning day-to-day living, they can be enormously important to the spouses who are disputing over them (Scanzoni and Scanzoni, 1976). Couples may argue about how high the thermostat should be, whose turn it is to turn the television off, each others' table manners, bedtimes—the list is endless. Trivial as these arguments may seem, people spend a great deal of time and energy trying to resolve them. Typical of these "tremendous trifles" are comments such as, "He has this terrible habit of rolling up his bathrobe and throwing it in the closet" (Steinmetz, 1977).

While few couples have conflicts about the same minor matters, the sources of major conflicts tend to be the same in most marriages: money and disciplining the children, particularly the adolescent children. Thirty-eight percent of the couples Scanzoni and Scanzoni interviewed said money was what they most often disagreed about, 19 percent cited issues connected with children, and about the same number mentioned one of the "tremendous trifles."

Conflict Management

Given the great potential for conflict in any social relationship, but especially an intimate one, it is surprising not that so many marriages break up but that so many endure. Sprey (1979) has theorized that in marriages that last, couples do not settle their differences by resolving conflicts in the sense that the dispute is settled, finally, with one partner winning and the other losing. Instead of completely getting rid of disagreements, the conflict is *managed* through an ongoing give and take. Each partner gives up something, each partner gains something; neither makes a total sacrifice.

The idea that conflicts are managed rather than resolved in relationships that endure does not preclude the possibility that power may be used to influence the outcome of the conflict. Both partners have power in the relationship because of the bond between them; either can threaten to break the bond if the other refuses to give in or change in some way. For example, one might threaten to leave the other if an extramarital relationship doesn't end or excessive drinking doesn't stop. But threats of leaving the relationship, or of other "punishments" such as refusing sexual relations until the conflict is settled, must be used sparingly, for they endanger both partners. If both value the relationship, both would, of course, lose if the threat of separation were carried out. The person making the threat is actually at the mercy of the other, for the other has been given the power to sever the relationship by not complying.

If the demand is not acceded to, the threatener then has to decide whether or not to carry out the threat or to back down. If a threat is made but not carried out—if, for example, the alcoholic husband promises to stop drinking but doesn't—and his wife doesn't leave him as she had threatened to do—the wife's credibility will be undermined. Threatening thus tests the power of both parties. Such behavior should be undertaken cautiously and only when the threatener is really prepared to carry out the threat (Sprey, 1979).

The object of negotiation is not to win out over the spouse and gain the upper hand in the relationship. According to Sprey (1979), solving problems in a marriage is a joint, reciprocal activity which can be seen in terms of cooperation rather than of power. What is needed, Sprey writes, is ways of settling problems which allow people to maintain their differences while finding negotiated solutions both can live with. This is where the communication skills described in the previous chapter can be helpful.

One of the most important of these skills is developing a set of rules that can be used in managing conflicts. Whether couples are able to manage their differences depends upon their ability to use such negotiating tools as bargaining, compromise, accommodation, and even mediation. Separation may occur when negotiation fails, but conflict-management techniques are aimed at avoiding this outcome (Sprey, 1979).

Most people try to avoid separating, despite their differences and conflicts, because of the bond between them. Once a couple has formed an intimate pair relationship, they are tied together not only by their mutual needs, but also by the way the bond has changed them. In a sense, they become to themselves and to others different people. Because they are joined to each other, they have a mutual need to maintain their bond, even though there will always be some tension about doing so.

According to Sprey's theory, the strength and workability of a dyadic relationship cannot be judged so much by the degree of consensus (one of the components of Spanier's Dyadic Adjustment Scale) as by two other variables: the ability to negotiate differences in a spirit of cooperation rather than aggression, and the motivation to continue the relationship. If the bond between a couple is strong, then it is more likely that the partners will make every effort to manage their differences in ways that will satisfy both of them and, thus, prevent the breakdown of the relationship (Sprey, 1979).

SUMMARY

1. Marital adjustment can be defined as the degree to which husbands and wives fulfill each other's needs, desires, and expectations. This chapter focuses on the interpersonal process of adjustment.

2. Marital adjustment can also be viewed as how well the partners fulfill roles. Nye has described a range of family roles, including provider,

housekeeper, child care, child socialization, sexual, kinship, recreational, and therapeutic.

3. Emotional maturity is a significant predictor of marital adjustment. Also, statistically, there is a relationship between age at marriage and marital stability. Teenage marriages are more likely to end in divorce than marriages between adults.

4. Adjustment is an ongoing process which continues throughout the family life cycle. Most social scientists believe that adjustment and satisfaction decline during the early years of marriage but that adjustment and satisfaction rise once the children have left home.

5. Marriages of high quality and stability have interactional styles that remain stable over time. Cuber and Haroff identified five such styles or types of marriage among affluent American couples: conflict-habituated, devitalized, and passive-congenial (the utilitarian marriages), and vital and total (the intrinsic marriages).

6. From a social-exchange perspective, marital adjustment is the ability and willingness to provide resources to the spouse that the spouse needs or wants. A resource is anything valued by the other which is transacted in an interpersonal situation, or any item, concrete or symbolic, that can become the object of exchange.

7. As women have moved into the labor force and taken on more of the traditionally male provider role, it might be expected that men would take on more of the traditionally female roles. However, the evidence indicates that, although there has been considerable attitude change, actual behavior has changed very little: married women who work outside the home tend to do about as much of the housework as full-time housewives.

8. Among other major areas of marital adjustment are the recreational and therapeutic roles. The recreational role is becoming increasingly important to family life. The therapeutic role is now regarded as a duty in many marriages. Men and women differ in how well they perform the therapeutic role.

9. Today most social scientists believe that conflict is not necessarily a negative experience for marriage and that conflicts are best *managed* rather than completely resolved. If couples have bonded—become committed to each other and the relationship not only by mutual needs but by the ways they have changed together—they will probably try to manage their differences. Their ability to do this depends to a great degree on their communication skills.

REVIEW AND DISCUSSION

1. Nye describes eight roles in contemporary marriages. How do you think you and your spouse will assign these roles in your own marriage? Do you think it is possible to share all of these roles? Why or why not?

2. Using Cuber and Haroff's five styles of marriage, characterize the marriage of someone you know and explain why it seems to fit the category you chose. Which style of marriage is most appealing to you? Why? Do you think this typology can be used to characterize all marriages, regardless of social class?

3. Imagine that you are part of a dual-worker marriage that involves children. What kinds of adjustments do you think might be required in this situation?

4. What kinds of recreational activities does your family engage in together? Are they mostly individual, joint, parallel, or a combination of these? How have the kinds of activities your family customarily pursues (or the lack of activities) affected the relationship of family members?

5. Do you think conflict can be constructive in a marriage? In what way? What do you think about the idea that conflicts should be *managed* rather than completely resolved? What might be the advantages of conflict management?

SUGGESTED READINGS

Hall, F. S., and D. T. Hall (1979). *The Two-Career Couple*. Reading, Mass.: Addison-Wesley.

Presents up-to-date look at people trying to juggle two lives, two jobs, and one relationship. Emphasizes coping strategies, from child care and household maintenance to career jealousy and job stress.

Lederer, W. J., and D. D. Jackson (1968). *Mirages of Marriage*. New York: Norton.

Discusses many myths associated with marriage (e.g., "most married people love each other") and aspects of married life such as communication, sex, and destructive elements. Also includes section on how to make a marriage work, and uses examples (dialogues, scenes) to illustrate points.

McGrady M. (1975). *The Kitchen Sink Papers: My Life as a House-husband*. Garden City, N.Y.: Doubleday.

A humorous account of what happened when one man switched roles with his wife—taking care of the house and children while she worked.

A record of his experiences, discoveries, and observations and the effects on their children and their marriage.

Rubin, L. B. (1976). *Worlds of Pain: Life in the Working Class Family*. New York: Basic Books.

An account of the life of American white working-class families today. Considers their childhoods, marriages, work, and leisure, and examines the pressures and strains put on marriages and families by social, psychological, and economic realities.

Wilkes, P. (1975).*Trying Out the Dream: A Year in the Life of an American Family*. Philadelphia: Lippincott.

Wilkes studied an "average American family" (i.e., one that resembles the Census Bureau's statistical picture of the average family). He reports on their lives, problems, successes, and disappointments and finds out how the ordinary family copes with life in America today.

Sexuality in Marriage

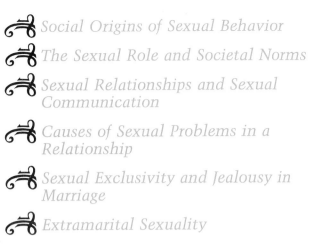
"You mustn't force sex to do the work of love, or love to do the work of sex."

MARY MCCARTHY
DIALOGUE FROM *The Group*

In Chapter 7 we saw that there are a number of different roles within a marriage and that some roles have traditionally been filled by one partner or the other, while others have been shared. This is primarily a result of the different socialization of men and women. For example, men usually enter marriage with the expectation that they will be providers, whereas women traditionally expect to care for the home and children. As these norms are changing, the responsibilities across roles and within roles are changing too.

One of the roles of marriage that has been most strongly affected by societal norms is the "sexual role." The sexual role refers to the responsibility of the marital partners to seek to satisfy their own and each other's sexual needs. Thus it is not to be confused with the term "sex role," which is often used to describe the different behavior patterns expected of men and women. As is true of the other marital roles, the norms for sexual behavior have not remained constant through the years. During the 1960s and 1970s, many commentators thought America experienced a "sexual revolution" of attitudes and behavior. Historically, the primary function of sex was clear—procreation. But those years saw a growing interest in the other functions of sex both within marriage and outside of it. The development of very effective forms of birth control—particularly the contraceptive pill—removed the age-old link between sex and conception. The tremendous expansion of knowledge about sex made available by the pioneering work of such well-known researchers as Kinsey and Masters and Johnson

249

gave people a reliable store of information about both the physiological and the psychological components of sexual behavior. In addition, there were notable contributions to knowledge about the sociology of sexual behavior by such researchers as Reiss. The availability of this information has profoundly influenced American views of male and female sexuality. But while there is no question that attitudes toward some aspects of sex have changed dramatically, attitudes toward other aspects have not. For example, surveys reveal that the attitudes of Americans toward extramarital sex have not changed dramatically since the 1940s.

Changes in sexual attitudes have been accompanied to some degree by changes in the sexual role in marriage. Traditionally sex in marriage was perceived as a wife's duty and a husband's pleasure. As time passed, there was more concern about wives' sexual enjoyment. Today there is an emerging norm of sexual equality in which husband and wife share responsibility for each other's pleasure. This shift is not yet complete; nor has it made sexual adjustment easier. What it has done is put a premium on a couple's ability to communicate with each other. The sexual role today is more often negotiated; society no longer imposes firm prescriptions of the respective duties of husband and wife in the sexual role as well as in other roles.

Even with the new norm of sexual equality in marriage, many couples still experience sexual problems. Sometimes these problems are rooted in recent events or in childhood experiences; sometimes they are related more closely to the marital relationship. Sexual jealousy and extramarital relationships are still prevalent as well.

This chapter deals with a number of topics related to the sexual relationship in marriage. Emphasis is given to the importance of communication, to the relationship between sexual adjustment and overall marital adjustment, and to husbands' and wives' views of the sexual role. In addition, the chapter discusses the problems that can arise in a sexual relationship and examines the issues of sexual jealousy and extramarital involvement.

SOCIAL ORIGINS OF SEXUAL BEHAVIOR

Sexual behavior is not automatic, it is learned. Although each individual is potentially a sexual being, how that sexuality is characteristically expressed results from socialization. The meanings and values people assign to sexual behavior are influenced in childhood by the reactions and teachings of their parents, siblings, peers, and community. In our society parental attitudes about sexual behavior are usually not stated directly and often are negative, stressing the "don'ts" of sexual conduct. Later influences include the values of the adolescent peer group, books, and the mass media, as well as an individual's own sexual experiences.

Sexual Scripts

Although sexual responses are sometimes spontaneous—as when a man has an erection while pressed against a woman he doesn't know on a crowded bus—most sexual behavior is "scripted" (Simon and Gagnon, 1968). That is, it follows certain conventions and norms that tell people how to behave sexually. Gagnon and Simon (1974) explain that a sexual script has two basic components: the external or interpersonal, and the internal. The external defines a sexual opportunity by means of certain interpersonal conventions. For adolescents, going to a drive-in movie might signal interest in petting. For adults, appearing at a singles bar might be a sign of readiness for sexual activity. The internal part of a sexual script specifies the psychic states and motivations necessary for arousal. A woman undergoing a medical examination does not usually respond erotically as the doctor examines her breasts or inserts instruments in her vagina. If her lover did the same type things, the different psychic state she reads into his touches and her own desire for lovemaking might trigger her sexual responsiveness.

According to Gecas and Libby (1976), sexual scripts exist within larger value systems related to institutions such as marriage and the family. These writers have identified four philosophies of sexual behavior present in American society.

The "traditional-religious philosophy" is rooted in the belief that sex outside of marriage is sinful. Unmarried women are expected to remain virgins and marital partners are expected to be sexually faithful to each other. Sexuality is defined in terms of reproduction, though its relationship to affection is acknowledged.

Attitudes toward sexuality are shaped by a variety of socializing agents. Parents, peers, and the mass media are especially influential.

The "romantic philosophy" has helped to moderate the more restrictive traditional-religious code. This philosophy makes love a prerequisite for sexual activity. In the absence of love, intercourse is meaningless; in its presence, intercourse is justified even outside of marriage. In our society, this code is characteristic of the urban middle classes. Women are more likely to have been socialized to this philosophy than men, a fact that often creates problems in heterosexual relations.

The "recreational philosophy" defines sex primarily as fun. This is the code prevalent in men's magazines such as *Playboy* and some women's magazines such as *Cosmopolitan*. The recreational philosophy holds that sexual activity need not be limited to marriage; nor is love a prerequisite. Sex is seen as a way of getting and giving pleasure. It emphasizes enjoyment, playfulness, and abandon.

The "utilitarian-predatory philosophy" defines sex as a means toward some other goal. Sex may not even be pleasurable in itself, but is used to earn money, power, or prestige. A prostitute, for example, exchanges sex for money; an adolescent male may try to "score" to raise his status within his peer group.

Gecas and Libby suggest that the relative influence of each of these philosophies is changing. As a result, new variations are emerging, most particularly "friendly sex." Friendly sex combines sex as recreation and sex as affection. It advocates a single standard of sexual behavior for men and women, accepts sexual intimacies within casual but affectionate relationships, and allows marriage partners to be sexually open to others rather than monogamous.

The scripts described above are not exhaustive, but they suggest the range of meanings associated with sexual activity. Gecas and Libby believe that the awareness people have of their own sexual script and that of their partner has important implications for sexual relationships. If a woman, for example, is acting out of the romantic philosophy while her partner defines sex according to the recreational philosophy, confusion and conflict are likely to occur. Similarly, a person who feels uncertain about which script to follow can experience ambivalence and anxiety. Thus, a woman who has been socialized to follow the traditional-religious script but has been influenced by changing mores toward the philosophy of friendly sex may experience conflict over how to reconcile the two positions.

Motives for Sexual Behavior

Sexual scripts or philosophies are ingrained in each individual and influence a person's overall attitude toward sexual relationships. But this does not mean that people approach each sexual encounter in the same way. An individual's specific motives for sexual relations at a particular time may vary with the situation, the person's state of mind, the needs of each sexual partner, the relationship between the partners, and other factors. Gerhard Neubeck (1972) has described a number of individual and sometimes shifting motives for sexual activity, aside from procreation. Note that a number of the motives he outlines, such as affection, adventure, recreation, and accomplishment, are embedded in the philosophies outlined by Gecas and Libby. Others are more dependent on personality or on physiological and situational factors.

1. Affection—Seeking sexual intimacy out of feelings of love, romance, and a desire for closeness. The physical act may be an expression of a deeper need to be fully united with the other.
2. Animosity—Venting hostility toward the partner through the sexual act, particularly by those who think sex degrading or who use sex as an expression of power. Forcing a partner into sex or capriciously denying sex are expressions of anger and hatred.
3. Anxiety—Using sex as a temporary relief from nonsexual frustrations. The partner becomes a means of avoiding feelings of fear and impotence in other spheres.
4. Boredom—Seeking sex as a momentary break from a dull environment or a boring routine.
5. Duty—Agreeing to sex because it is thought to be expected. The satisfaction comes from having "gotten it over with."
6. Mending wounds—Using sex as a way to make up after an argument or to forget one's troubles.
7. Accomplishments—Keeping up with peers or "scoring," because it seems to be what is expected. The enjoyment of the sexual act is heightened by the knowledge that one is attaining a higher status.
8. Adventure—Seeking sexual variety and excitement, searching for new sensual experiences, giving free rein to one's curiosity and creativity.
9. Recreation—Engaging in sex for the fun of it. Nothing is at stake except the good feelings created.
10. Lust—Engaging in sex to relieve sexual hunger. Every nerve is attuned to the search for sensual sensations.
11. Self-affirmation—Engaging in sex to confirm one's image of oneself. Sex becomes an expression of the kinds of roles one wants to play—"machismo," for example.
12. Altruism—Engaging in sex in order to give another person pleasure or a feeling of being wanted or needed. This is a highly complex motive and if engaged in by both parties may mean some missed communication.
13. Idiosyncratic needs—Acting out unusual desires.
14. Situational influences—Reacting to influences that trigger arousal. These can be almost anything from waking up aroused to having the mood suddenly strike in the middle of an afternoon of studying.

Neubeck's list points to the complexity of motives which can surround sexual behavior. Sex is not simple. It is intimately bound to cultural and social context as well as to personality characteristics. Nor does it become less complicated simply because a couple is married. Although their legal status has changed, the partners remain two individuals who must learn to adjust to each other's needs.

THE SEXUAL ROLE AND SOCIETAL NORMS

As a social institution, marriage provides a means whereby sexuality and reproduction are legitimized. This means that the sexual role in marriage is regulated by societal norms (standards of behavior). What are the norms related to the sexual relationship in marriage? Are they different today than in the past? What expectations do husbands and wives have as to the sexual role of each partner? Do their expectations coincide?

John Carlson (1976) surveyed married couples in an effort to answer these questions. The results of his research show that husbands and wives have somewhat different views of the sexual relationship and that while the cultural norms that surround sexual behavior in marriage are changing, the change appears to be gradual.

Norms for the Sexual Role

The norms for the sexual role in marriage essentially relate to who is responsible for performing the role—specifically, who should initiate sex; whether there is social disapproval of a partner who refuses to engage in sexual activity; and whether the sexual role in marriage is an exclusive one—that is, whether the partners approve of extramarital sex (Carlson, 1976).

Carlson found that husbands and wives had very different ideas about who should initiate sex. Husbands split 45 percent to 44 percent between the views that both partners were equally responsible and that the husband was primarily responsible. Among wives, 44 percent regarded initiation of sexual activity as the husband's responsibility, but only 26 percent saw it as a joint responsibility, and 30 percent saw no responsibility at all. These findings suggest that husbands would prefer to share the responsibility for initiating sex, but that wives tend to view it as the husband's duty.

The second issue, whether or not sanctions are imposed for failing to engage in sex, again reveals a split between husbands and wives. Carlson asked his sample if they approved of a spouse who rarely consented to have intercourse. Among husbands, 81 percent strongly disapproved of husbands who refused. When husbands were asked about wives who refused, the results were about the same. Among wives responding to the same question, 65 percent strongly disapproved of husbands who refused, and slightly more than two-thirds strongly disapproved of wives who refused. Carlson concluded that both sexes feel strongly about the duty to engage in sex, but that husbands feel more strongly about it than wives do.

With regard to the issue of extramarital sex, we might expect to find a significant split between the attitudes of husbands and wives because of the old double standard. However, Carlson found that over 80 percent of husbands and 85 percent of wives disapproved of extramarital sex under any circumstances.

The gender differences in expectations and performance may indicate that wives regard sex as somewhat less important than husbands do. Carlson believes that these differences may also indicate a potential area for trouble in marriage if the partners do not communicate well. Even so, Carlson found that in most instances, people engage in sex when their partner desires to even if they do not; however, husbands are more likely to do so than wives. Twenty-five percent of wives said they never wanted sex unless their husbands did.

Evaluation of the Sexual Role

Carlson found that nearly twice as many men as women (68 to 34 percent) always enjoyed sex, but that over 90 percent of both sexes usually enjoyed it. At the same time, a significantly higher percentage of husbands than wives (85 percent versus 73 percent) rated sex as "extremely important" or "quite important" to them. Only 55 percent of husbands believed that sex was "extremely important" or "quite important" to their wives.

As to the frequency of sex, Carlson found that 37 percent of husbands in the survey desired sex much more frequently than wives, while only 2 percent of wives reported they wanted sex much more often than their husbands. At the same time, more women than men felt they did not fulfill their sexual role. This may be related to the fact that a majority of wives reported that they sometimes did not enjoy sex.

It might be expected that because upper-middle-class husbands are more likely to support gender-role equality, they would also be more likely to want their wives to initiate sex as often as they did. Carlson's data indicates the contrary: these men wish to initiate sexual activity and do in fact initiate intercourse more often than their mates. Another finding was that men who work long hours are actually more, not less, interested in sex. Carlson also found that women who have a college education but have not done graduate work are likely to be more interested in sexual activity than those who have done graduate work.

Religion did not seem to be a very significant factor in how spouses viewed the sexual role. Protestant males were a little more likely to initiate sex, and

Catholic and fundamentalist Protestant wives were more likely to go along with sex when they did not desire it. Wives in these latter groups were also more likely to condemn extramarital intercourse. Carlson reported no significant differences in sexual satisfaction among husbands and wives according to their religious beliefs.

Carlson's study points to the conclusion that ". . . no revolutionary change in marital sexual behavior seems to have occurred among typical American couples during the past few decades." But while the change may not be "revolutionary," there is still evidence that the norms surrounding sex in marriage are changing. This seems particularly true among young couples. In an extensive survey by *Redbook* magazine (Levin and Levin, 1975a), women were asked if they ever initiated sex in marriage. Virtually all the women regardless of age said they did so at least sometimes; 65 percent of the women under twenty-five said they did so half the time or more. Although the respondents in this survey were probably more liberal than American women in general, their responses nevertheless indicate a reduction in the traditional notion that in marital sex the husband should play an active role and the wife a passive one (Bell, 1979).

Sexual Adjustment and Marital Adjustment

Research has shown that sexual adjustment and marital adjustment are closely interrelated (Lewis and Spanier, 1979). A number of studies have found that couples who say they have satisfying marriages also say they have satisfying sexual relations and that couples who say their marriages are unsatisfying say their sexual relationship is also unsatisfying (Hunt, 1974; Levin and Levin, 1957a; Tavris and Sadd, 1977). But whether sexual adjustment leads to good marital adjustment or whether the reverse is true is more difficult to determine.

Reiss, Anderson, and Sponaugle (1980) suggest that overall marital adjustment influences sexual adjustment rather than the reverse. According to this view, in a good marriage a problem with the sexual relationship is unlikely to become so overwhelming as to cause a breakdown in the marriage. What is more likely is that the symptoms of a troubled marriage will show up in sexual difficulties.

Other research has shown that the relationship between sexual satisfaction and marital satisfaction is different for husbands and wives (Udry, 1968). The effect of sexual dissatisfaction on the husband's overall perception of his marriage is greater than on his wife's. But the wife's sexual responsiveness depends considerably more on her satisfaction with the marriage as a whole. The reason for this difference seems to be related to the different expectations of men and women regarding sexuality and marriage. Men are more likely to expect a good deal from sex per se, whereas women are more likely to associate

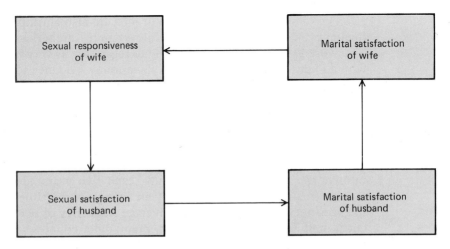

(The arrows indicate the direction of major effect.)

Fig. 8.1
Gender differences in sexual satisfaction and marital satisfaction.
(Source: Reprinted from "Sex and Family Life" by J. Richard Udry
in volume no. 376 of THE ANNALS of The American Academy of
Political and Social Science.

the sexual relationship with the emotional level of the overall relationship. When the emotional quality of the marriage is perceived as unsatisfactory, women are less likely to be sexually responsive (Udry, 1968). Figure 8.1 illustrates this gender difference.

Frequency of Sexual Activity

While the frequency of sexual activity in marriage is not the most important aspect of a healthy sexual relationship, frequency is a useful indicator of the factors that may influence a couple's sexual relationship over the life cycle. Researchers have found, for example, that most married couples engage in sex more often early in the marriage than later. A number of variables contribute to this declining frequency including the presence or absence of children, the partners' careers or jobs, the aging process, and the couple's adjustment to each other.

Couples with no children report the highest rates of sexual intercourse. Having children seems to decrease the frequency of intercourse. For parents of infants or young children this may be because lovemaking has to compete with night feedings, weariness after caring for children, images of each other as parents rather than lovers, and the inhibitions to spontaneity caused by having children in the house (James, 1974).

The marriage partners' careers or jobs are also an important factor in the frequency of sexual intercourse. While some researchers have found that men who work long hours are more likely to regard sex as very important than men who do not (Carlson, 1976), others have found evidence to the contrary (Bell, 1979). Carlson speculates that greater involvement in a job may foster greater need for the emotional and physical outlet of sex. Bell, on the other hand, contends that men whose main source of identity comes from their job are less likely to place as much emphasis on an emotional relationship.

Rates of sexual intercourse generally decline with age, especially the man's age, suggesting that it is the man who determines the frequency of intercourse. According to one study, each five years added to a man's age reduces frequency of intercourse by an average of ten times per year. Between the ages of twenty and forty, the average frequency of sex for married men is cut in half (James, 1974). However, many older couples continue to enjoy an active sex life, despite the decrease in the overall rate of sexual activity.

Other factors that may result in the decline in the frequency of sexual relations include loss of interest in the spouse, loss of reproductive capacity, and boredom. Still, for all the factors that reduce the frequency of sex, it remains a significant marital role throughout life.

SEXUAL RELATIONSHIPS AND SEXUAL COMMUNICATION

What trends characterize marital sexual relationships today? While it is always difficult to determine accurately how people behave in private areas of their lives, one of the best tools for investigating sexual attitudes and behavior has been survey research. Since the 1940s, when Alfred Kinsey did his pioneering studies of American sexual behavior and attitudes, there have been a number of useful surveys of this type.

The *Redbook* Survey

One of the most revealing recent surveys of marital sexual behavior was conducted by *Redbook* magazine (1980). The participants in this survey responded to a questionnaire printed in the magazine. As is true of respondents to sex surveys generally, including Kinsey's, they were not a representative sample of the American population. They were somewhat younger, better educated, and more financially secure than the population as a whole. Thirty-four percent of the women and 23 percent of the men were under twenty-five. Over half the women and slightly less than half the men described themselves as moderates politically, while 29 percent of men and women described themselves as liberals. Nearly half came from families with incomes between

$20,000 and $40,000. All of the respondents had finished high school, and a significantly higher percentage of the men than the women had finished college or had an advanced degree. Thus, the sample tends to reflect the views of better educated, middle-class Americans and to underrepresent the poor, the nonwhite, and the elderly (Sarrel and Sarrel, 1980).

Even so, the 6,000 men and 20,000 women who participated do represent a wide segment of the population in terms of age, education, religious affiliation, and political attitudes. One other factor that contributes to the usefulness of the survey in terms of its findings about marital sexuality is that 80 percent of the respondents were either married, remarried, or cohabiting.

Sarrel and Sarrel (1980), in analyzing the *Redbook* questionnaire data, were especially interested in what was revealed about marital relationships. The question they were asking implicitly was what factors in the sexual relationship are also central to a successful marital relationship. The following

HIGHLIGHT 8.1   *A Survey on Sex and Working Wives*

Has there been a significant change in the sex lives of married couples since increasing numbers of women have joined the work force?

More than half of 400 psychiatrists polled on their clinical experiences say that sexual satisfaction in marriages of working wives is about the same as when wives remained home. But about a fifth of the respondents think that sexual satisfaction has declined. The main reason they cited was the woman's reduced dependence on the husband. The second reason was fatigue.

Another fifth of the psychiatrists believe sexual satisfaction has improved mostly because of the wife's greater self-esteem and personal happiness. Cited also, but to a lesser extent, were, "more shared interest between spouses," "eased financial tensions" and "husband's enhanced respect for wife."

The nationwide survey, conducted by the publication *Human Sexuality*, was tabulated on the basis of the first 400 replies received.

A slight majority (53 percent) agreed that most husbands have sex-related fears about their wives working outside the home.

Some justification for these fears is found in the belief of a large majority (71 percent) of the psychiatrists that extramarital sexual temptation is a greater likelihood for working wives than for those who stay at home. A smaller but still substantial majority of 57 percent (not all answered the question) reported that extramarital sexual involvement is in fact more common.

There was a near-even (52–47 percent) division on the question of whether disputes over household tasks cause greater disharmony in the sexual relationship. However, 60 percent of the psychiatrists found disruption in the relationship when the wife earned more money than the husband.

Source: © *Chicago Sun-Times, 1980. Article by Arthur Snider. Reprinted with permission.*

discussion is based on their analysis of the results. Figure 8.2 summarizes some factors found to characterize the best and worst sexual relationships.

FREQUENCY OF INTERCOURSE AND ORGASM   One of the indicators most surveys use to assess the quality of a sexual relationship is the frequency of intercourse and orgasm. Of *Redbook*'s respondents, 57 percent said they had intercourse one to three times per week; 28 percent said they had intercourse four or more times a week, while 15 percent said they engaged in sex once or twice a month or less.

Sarrel and Sarrel noted a correlation between higher frequency of intercourse and a good sex life, although they also noted that "frequency . . . can be looked at both as a cause and an effect of a good sexual relationship." However, another supposed indicator of a happy sex life—frequency of orgasm— did not prove to be so accurate a barometer. Of the male respondents, 95 percent had an orgasm every time or almost every time they had intercourse, regardless of how they rated their sex lives overall. Since the experience of orgasm is so consistent for men, this was to be expected. What was unexpected

Fig. 8.2

Who has the best (and worst) sex? (Source: Lorna and Philip Sarrel, Redbook, *October 1980. Reprinted by permission.)*

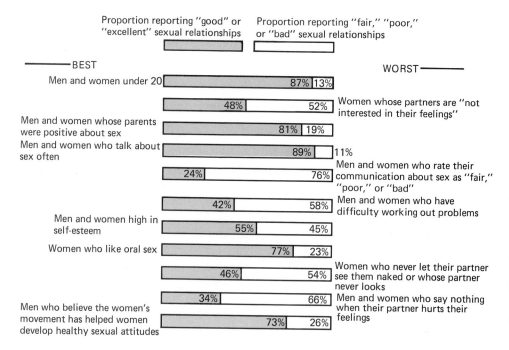

was that of the 60 percent of the women responding who reported they had an orgasm every time or almost every time they had intercourse, almost a quarter did not rate their sex lives as good or excellent.

The lack of a direct relationship between orgasm and a satisfactory sex life does not mean there is no correlation. What it does suggest is that how the sexual partners react to a sexual experience may be a more important factor in sexual happiness than whether they both have an orgasm. When asked how they felt if they did not have an orgasm, almost 70 percent of the female respondents said that not having an orgasm was "no big thing" or that they were only "slightly frustrated." However, 42 percent said their partners felt "guilty," "upset," or "inadequate" if they did not have an orgasm. When their partners felt "okay" when they did not have an orgasm, 80 percent of the women said they were satisfied with their sex lives. But when their partners felt "upset" or "inadequate," only 60 percent felt satisfied with their sex lives—a figure that was lower than the average for the sample. Thus, the more upset the male partner's reaction, the more likely the women were to rate their sex lives unsatisfactory. Sarrel and Sarrel suggest that women whose partners react very strongly when they don't have an orgasm feel they have to try harder to have an orgasm the next time or the partner will be unhappy. When orgasm becomes the major goal of sex, the result is often anxiety and less chance of experiencing orgasm.

COMMUNICATION AND QUALITY The ability to communicate with one's partner about sex was the "single factor most highly correlated with a good sexual relationship." Of the women and men who rated their sex lives "good" or "excellent," 80 percent also rated their communication with their partners about sex as "excellent." Only 20 percent of those who rated their sex lives as "bad" thought their communication was "excellent." The majority of the respondents found that discussing sexual problems with someone besides their partner was not particularly helpful.

Being a good communicator was found to have a number of benefits. Good communicators had sexual relations more often and were pleased about it. Women in this category were more likely to reach orgasm than those who had difficulty talking with their partners. Among men who were poor communicators, the number who experienced premature ejaculation was nearly twice as high as those who were good communicators.

The *Redbook* survey also asked its respondents how well they communicated their feelings generally—as distinguished from relating feelings about sex. Again, there was a direct correlation between good communication and a sex life rated "excellent" or "good." Of those who categorized their ability to communicate their feelings as "good" or "excellent," only one in ten rated their sex lives as "fair," "poor," or "bad." On the other hand, six out of ten respondents who rated themselves bad communicators considered their sex lives unsatisfying.

A 1980 sex survey by Redbook *found that the strongest indicator of a good sexual relationship was the ability to communicate about sex. In addition to talking about sexual needs and desires, partners can be sensitive to nonverbal signals.*

NEGOTIATION AND ASSERTION The *Redbook* survey also showed that assertiveness and the ability to negotiate related directly to the quality of a couple's sex life. According to Sarrel and Sarrel, communicating well about sex is not just a matter of expressing feelings; it also requires asserting one's needs. When the needs of partners conflict, the best way to resolve the situation is to negotiate.

Those men and women who felt it was easy to assert themselves in a disagreement with their partners gave their sex lives generally good ratings. For example, of women who said they found it "very easy" or "easy" to assert their rights in an argument, 58 percent were satisfied with their sex lives, while of those who found it "somewhat difficult" or "difficult" to assert themselves, only 16 percent reported they were satisfied with their sex lives.

Sarrel and Sarrel suggest that what this means, among other things, is that a person must be able to say "no" and mean it, and not cause the partner to have hurt feelings. Still, quite often successful couples compromise their feelings and agree to sex when one partner is not in the mood. Twenty percent of both male and female respondents indicated that they accepted sex 75 percent of the time or more when they did not really want to. The explanation for this was that more than half the people who started out being reluctant "end up enjoying it." However, among the men and women reporting the best sex lives, the rate of accommodation was 25 percent or less.

The *Redbook* survey confirms what we have already seen: "the sexual aspects of a relationship are intimately bound to the quality, the give-and-take, of a relationship as a whole" (Sarrel and Sarrel, 1980).

Sexual Communication: Research Contributions

We have suggested that marital and sexual satisfaction are closely tied to the ability to communicate. Of course, without accurate information about sexuality, even the most sincere efforts to communicate are likely to be ineffective. Until the late 1940s many people had little understanding of their sexual nature. But with the publication of the Kinsey surveys in 1948 and 1953, this knowledge gap began to close. Kinsey provided the first and still the most comprehensive description of American sexual behavior both in and out of marriage. The Kinsey studies provided benchmarks for all that came after. More recently, Masters and Johnson's (1966, 1970) exhaustive research on the physiological and psychological dynamics of sexuality has been a major contribution. They have had a profound effect on the availability of accurate information about sex to both couples and professionals counseling people with sexual problems.

HIGHLIGHT 8.2   *Do Professors Make Good Lovers?*

In analyzing the *Redbook* data the researchers were surprised to discover that for men, higher education has a negative correlation with their reports of the quality of their sexual relationships. Proportionately more men whose schooling stopped with their graduation from high school report good or excellent sexual relationships than men who went on to college or graduate school. Among men with a high-school education, the proportion with the better sexual relationships is 84 percent. For the men who went to college, it is 80 percent; with graduate school it drops to 76 percent. There is no comparable trend in women's responses.

Does this effect show up elsewhere in the data? Here is what was found. In ranking how well they could communicate about sexual matters, once again the high-school-educated men showed up somewhat better. Good or excellent sexual communication with their partners was reported by 76 percent. For both the college and the graduate-school men, the proportion was 71 percent. The pattern also appeared in the men's ability to talk about feelings. Though the men in all categories found it easier to talk about sex than about emotions, the proportion rating "good" or "excellent" at talking about feelings was again highest (64 percent) among the men with high-school educations, slightly lower for those with college (60 percent) or graduate school (61 percent).

Higher education does not affect a man's ability to talk of other things, however. For general communication, 76.4 percent of the men with graduate study claimed good or excellent skills; 72 percent of the college-educated men did so; as did 70.5 percent of the men with high-school educations.

MYTHS DISPELLED   Masters and Johnson disposed of several myths about sexuality which had been accepted for decades. Two of the most prevalent were that (1) there are two types of female orgasm, and (2) simultaneous orgasm represents the pinnacle of a satisfactory sex life.

Most professionals had accepted the views of Sigmund Freud, who speculated that women had separate vaginal and clitoral orgasms. The vaginal orgasm was supposedly characteristic of the psychologically mature woman, while the clitoral orgasm indicated psychological immaturity. Masters and Johnson proved conclusively that there are not two types of orgasm. Regardless of what area is stimulated, whether the clitoris, the mons, the breasts, or another erogenous area, orgasmic contractions take place in the vagina and the uterus (Belliveau and Richter, 1970). This insight has done much to improve the sexual self-image of many women who had felt they were inadequate because they could not experience orgasm through vaginal penetration alone.

The second major sexual myth was that the height of sexual achievement was simultaneous orgasm. Marriage manuals and pornography alike established this impossible goal for generations of Americans. Worse, this myth may have destroyed the pleasure of sex for many. Masters and Johnson demonstrated that orgasms in both the male and female are involuntary responses to stimulation. They pointed out that making the effort to coordinate these responses causes partners to observe themselves mentally, as if they were critiquing a performance instead of being totally involved in their lovemaking. This "assuming (of) a spectator's role" can lead to erectile difficulties in the male and an inability to experience orgasm in the female (Belliveau and Richter, 1970).

MASTERS AND JOHNSON'S GOALS   Masters and Johnson had a very practical reason for their research: they treated people with sexual difficulties like erectile inhibition and inability to experience orgasm. One of their most significant insights was their awareness that they had no standard by which to judge what sexual *function* was. To establish that, they had to bring subjects into the laboratory and observe their responses. The information they developed about the physiology of sex they then applied to its practice (Belliveau and Richter, 1970).

Masters and Johnson recognized that therapists cannot deal with sexual problems in a vacuum and that often one of the roots of sexual problems is a lack of communication between partners. Because sexual response represents "interaction between people," it is necessary to treat both sexual partners. Most sex therapists today subscribe to this view (Masters and Johnson, 1970).

Masters and Johnson's goals have often been misunderstood—as well as misstated. They believe that once people know how sexual response works, they can stop worrying about their behavior and start responding. In addition, their treatment methods are aimed not only at partners who have a specific sexual difficulty but also at partners who are dissatisfied with their sexual adjustment. The estimates of the numbers of such couples range from 30 percent among young liberal middle-class couples to 54 percent among lower-class couples (LoPiccolo and LoPiccolo, 1978).

CAUSES OF SEXUAL PROBLEMS IN A RELATIONSHIP

The problems that can arise in a sexual relationship are not all of the same type or origin. One classification of sexual problems is that provided by sex therapist Helen Kaplan (1974a). Kaplan divides the causes of sexual dissatisfaction or dysfunction into two general categories: immediate and remote.

Immediate and Remote Causes

The immediate causes of sexual dysfunction tend to grow out of the recent past of the individual; an example is that of a man who loses the ability to have an erection because of his reaction to his recent divorce. The immediate causes are those that sex therapists attempt to address. Remote causes are those that psychiatrists have traditionally treated. Remote causes are dysfunctions which grow out of distant relationships and experiences such as the events of childhood (Kaplan, 1974a).

It should be kept in mind that while the focus of the sex therapist and that of the psychiatrist are somewhat different, each can be helpful to the person experiencing sexual difficulties, and the two are not in competition. In this section we will consider some of the more common immediate and remote causes of sexual problems in a relationship.

INABILITY TO COMMUNICATE Many adults retain childhood prohibitions against talking openly about sexual responses and desires. It is hard to unlearn the notion that people we care for will disapprove if we try to put such intimate thoughts into words. But this secrecy puts a great burden on sexual partners. As we have seen already, they have to guess at what kinds of loveplay the partner likes, what turns the other off, and what new things the other would like to try.

Lack of a comfortable vocabulary for body parts and sexual behavior often inhibits communication. Four-letter street words sometimes seem too crude and clinical terms too cold. Some couples speak in euphemisms to sidestep the problem; a few creative lovers invent their own private words. But sexual communication need not always be verbal. Partners often guide each other with their hands to indicate what pleases them. Lovemaking itself can be the ultimate way of communicating the strength of the bonds between two people, but if the couple have nothing to say to each other aside from routine matters, if they have not established emotional intimacy, they can hardly expect to communicate closeness when their bodies touch.

FEAR OF REJECTION   To enjoy sex, partners must relax and abandon themselves to erotic responsiveness. But learned behavior patterns and the dynamics of the relationship frequently cause people to hold back from full sexual involvement. Fearing they will be rejected and criticized rather than reassured, understood, and protected, they never allow themselves the total vulnerability of sexual abandon.

LOW SELF-ESTEEM   Letting go requires more than trust in a loving partner; it is also dependent on self-esteem. Some people are unable to accept sexual pleasure freely because they feel unworthy of it—though they may enjoy giving pleasure. They are not free to explore their own needs without discomfort and even less free to ask a partner to help satisfy these needs. Only people with a good opinion of themselves can say they would like to try something new in lovemaking or ask for specific kinds of help. Burchell, Laury, and Sochet (1975) point out, "High esteem provides a foundation for risk-taking and growth that is nurturing to any relationship" (p. 74).

NEGATIVE BODY IMAGE   People whose self-esteem includes feeling physically unattractive often feel unlovable. Surprisingly, feelings about sex appeal do not seem to center on the areas emphasized in erotic literature. According to a survey of over 62,000 readers of *Psychology Today*, people are more likely to be concerned with whether their torsos bulge and how their faces look than with how big their breasts or penises are (Berscheid, Walster, and Bohrnstedt, 1973). Partners can help by assuring each other of their physical attractiveness.

Excessive concern with one's body image can be a barrier to sexual adjustment.

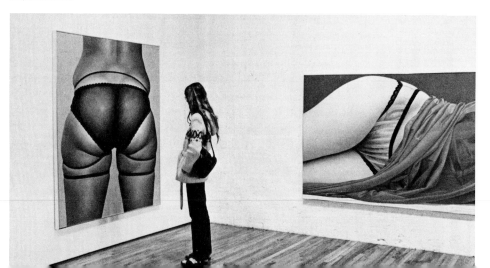

FEAR OF FAILURE Anyone who has ever tried to have an orgasm and failed is susceptible to worries about failure the next time. That worry is often self-fulfilling. Fear of failure is the greatest immediate cause of erectile difficulty in men and is also significant in women's inability to be orgasmic (Kaplan, 1974a).

Men frequently lose their erections during extended lovemaking. Many accept this as natural, continue with foreplay, and eventually regain their erection. But if they start worrying about whether they will become erect again, what would have been only a temporary problem may become a total inability to carry intercourse to completion. If a man has been using sexual activity to bolster his self-esteem, or if his partner is demanding, performance failure may be especially disturbing.

SPECTATORING Orgasmic inability, as we mentioned earlier in another context, is frequently linked to what Masters and Johnson (1974) call "spectatoring." People who feel they are inadequate often follow the progress of their own responses as onlookers rather than becoming deeply involved with the partner. Spectatoring is not unusual; even people who are secure in their sexuality do it sometimes. But they do not let it interfere with full enjoyment of sexual relations.

REPRESSION Many adults have difficulty expressing their sexuality because they were forced to suppress it as children, treating it as something secret. Even though marriage grants cultural approval to sexual expression, they may be unable to allow themselves to enter into comfortable sexual behavior. This is particularly a problem for men who associate their wives with their mothers, with whom, of course, sexual intercourse is forbidden. The same is true for women who have repressed sexual feelings for their fathers and later identify their husbands with their fathers. As a defense against guilt and anxiety, they may deny their sexual feelings, thereby effectively inhibiting their sexual response.

UNREALISTIC EXPECTATIONS Some marriage therapists feel that most sex problems involve unrealistic expectations. Although all healthy humans are capable of sexual responses, good sexual functioning with a partner does not happen automatically. Individuals differ in the strength and character of their sexual responses, and anyone may experience a decrease in sex drive from time to time. It is unrealistic to expect that sexual response can always be delivered on demand or that one partner can be completely responsible for the other's pleasure.

If people have appropriate expectations of their lovemaking they usually get more out of it. There is no reason to assume that all loveplay should entail penile-vaginal intercourse and end in orgasm. To insist on this goal every time creates performance pressures which may make the sexual experience more like work than pleasure; in addition, it may rob sex of excitement and spontaneity.

RESISTANCE TO CHANGE   A sexual relationship must grow and change as the partners do. As we've noted, biologically a man's responses inevitably slow down, while the woman's may become stronger as she reaches her thirties. In a healthy relationship, this shift can be accommodated without anxiety. The older a man gets, the longer he can delay his ejaculation since it gradually loses its urgency. This means a greater opportunity for foreplay and prolonged coitus, making it easier for the woman to be orgasmic. If he is secure in his self-esteem, he will find her increased responsiveness rewarding. But if he is haunted by comparisons with the peak of responsiveness he reached as a young man, he may find it hard to accept his diminished capacity for erection and may see her greater sexual interest as a threat. She, on the other hand, may be increasingly interested in her own orgasms and subtly blame him for any failures to have them.

Relational Causes of Sexual Difficulties

In addition to immediate and remote causes of sexual difficulties, Kaplan (1974a) identifies causes stemming from the couple's relationship.

PARTNER REJECTION   When persons dislike each other or one partner finds the other undesirable, they will rarely be satisfactory sexual partners. The sex therapist can do little for such couples (Kaplan, 1974a).

MARITAL CONFLICT   Couples experiencing marital conflict often carry their problems into their sexual relationship. Some of the causes of marital discord that can affect sexual relations include the transference of problems with parents or other relations to the sexual partner, the inability to trust the partner, the need for control over the relationship, and what Kaplan terms "sexual sabotage."

SEXUAL SABOTAGE   People can make sexual relations unsatisfactory through a variety of sabotaging maneuvers. Not all saboteurs intend to hurt their partners; some may be trying to build defenses against their own fears. Rather than encouraging each other's sexuality, they unconsciously find subtle ways of undermining it. There are four common sabotaging behaviors.

1. Tension creation. Rather than trying to create feelings of relaxation and enhance self-esteem, some people habitually point out faults or raise anxiety-laden issues, like financial difficulties, as a prelude to lovemaking. They may do so innocently, but nonetheless effectively: "I don't know

where we're going to find the money to repair the chimney." Specific sexual demands or criticisms are especially likely to inhibit sexual response.

2. Bad timing. While many lovers are able to perceive accurately when both are in the mood, some people repeatedly make sexual demands when their partners are not interested or refuse advances when they are. Dr. Kaplan described one patient who, when he found his wife lying in bed, freshly washed, perfumed, and ready, took off on a suddenly urgent hour-long errand to the hardware store. Another example would be a woman who habitually complains of being too tired for sex at night except when the male partner is exhausted. Then, she wants to make love.

3. Physical repulsion. Rather than trying to make themselves attractive to their lovers, spouses may unconsciously make themselves unappealing. They may gain weight, neglect personal hygiene, speak crudely or move clumsily, usually without recognizing that these may be defenses against sexual involvement. But as Kaplan remarks, it is no surprise if one partner is uninterested in sex when the other gets into bed needing a bath.

4. Frustrating tactics. A partner who enjoys sex learns what the partner likes and does it. A sabotaging spouse does just the opposite. If the husband is excited by his wife's movements, she keeps still. If she likes to move, he lies on top of her. If she dislikes TV, he leaves it on during intercourse. If he likes to fondle her breasts, she says they hurt. The result: both end up frustrated.

Sexual Problems and Gender Role

Many difficulties in marriage can be traced to conflicting ideas about the appropriate roles of men and women. This is as true in the sexual sphere as in any other.

In nineteenth-century America, lovemaking was something a man did as a release for his sexual needs. The woman was thought not to have any sexual needs and was expected to submit out of a sense of duty. As more information became available about women's sexuality, a new sexual norm evolved which required the man to make sex pleasurable for his partner as well as himself. As noted previously, surveys suggest that younger women, especially, are more aware of their sexual potential and more open about wanting to enjoy it. Expecting equality in the bedroom as well as in the job market, many wives are abandoning their traditionally passive sexual role in favor of a more assertive one.

Marriage therapists are divided on the effect of female assertiveness on sexual adjustment in marriage. Some professionals say male erectile difficulties are on the increase and blame it on the inability of men to function when women place performance demands on them. Greenson (1970) suggests that

The popularity of male erotic dancers with female patrons of nightclubs is evidence of the growing tendency of women to be open about their interest in sex.

in our society as women are becoming more assertive, men are experiencing more sexual problems. "Before World War II," he writes, "the term 'frigidity' was used exclusively in regard to women. Today I find far more men who display sexual coldness or disinterest." Some recent best-selling books have encouraged women to return to earlier standards in the interest of happier marriages. Authors Helen Andelin (*Fascinating Womanhood*) and Marabel Morgan (*The Total Woman*) assert that wives can sustain or reintroduce romance and passion through playful, dependent, childlike behavior and such aids to sexual excitement as suggestive costumes. Some wives who have followed this advice claim that it has saved their marriages, delighting their husbands and enhancing their own sense of femininity (Emerson, 1975).

Critics of this point of view maintain that sex and marriage are best when men and women are equally and mutually involved in making them work. Masters and Johnson (1974) hold that liberation of the woman from her traditionally passive sexual role can also liberate the man from expectations that he always play the part of sexual expert and initiator. Her willingness to take some of the responsibility for lovemaking can help him feel more secure and confident as a sexual partner.

 SEXUAL EXCLUSIVITY
AND JEALOUSY IN MARRIAGE

In one wedding ceremony, the celebrant asks the groom, "Will you have this woman to be your wife; to live together in the covenant of marriage? Will you love her, comfort her, honor and keep her, in sickness and in health; and, forsaking all others, be faithful to her as long as you both shall live?" (*Book of Common Prayer*, 1979). This last clause states the normative expectation of marriage: that of sexual exclusivity or monogamy. Religious and legal norms assert that marriage partners are expected to engage in sexual activity only with their spouse. Often this expectation is not met in practice. In fact, extramarital relationships are fairly common, but surveys indicate that societal disapproval remains very high. When one partner engages in extramarital sex, the other partner is likely to be hurt, and often jealous. But jealousy may also arise even when the other mate is faithful, because jealousy can have either a foundation in fact or no reasonable cause whatsoever.

Although we are talking about sexual jealousy, it is important to note that there are many other types of jealousy which have no relation to sex at all. These forms, such as jealousy over careers, can be as destructive to a marriage as sexual jealousy.

Jealousy and Sexual Property

Kingsley Davis (1936) was the first to consider sexual jealousy from a sociological point of view. He proposed that the marital relationship could be regarded as a property relationship. Thus he defined sexual jealousy as a reaction of "fear or rage to a threatened appropriation of one's property or of what one wants" (p. 395). According to Davis, an analysis of conflicts over property must take into account the perspectives of (1) the owner, (2) the object, (3) the public, and (4) the rival or trespasser. Viewed in this light, jealousy is not the proverbial "love triangle" but actually is a quadrangle. People often forget that society has norms or expectations for jealous behavior as it does for any other interpersonal behavior. Sometimes sexual jealousy is viewed by society as arising from legitimate competition for property and sometimes it is seen as arising from illegitimate competition.

For example, competition with a rival for the affection of someone who is unmarried is considered acceptable to society, since the person being competed for is free to make the best deal possible. However, sexual jealousy in marriage arises in reaction to the threat of illegitimate loss of property to a "trespasser" (a trespasser by definition is someone who comes onto another's property without permission). A spouse is considered property which the marital partner has won fairly through the competitive mate-selection process. Any attempt to interfere with this relationship is viewed as wrong and therefore appropriate grounds for jealousy.

The dynamics of jealousy are the same whether one is confronted by a legitimate rival or a trespasser. In either case, jealousy develops when one thinks there is competition. The competition, itself, is viewed as limiting the rewards and increasing the cost of the relationship. The competition affects one—and possibly both—partner's analysis of alternatives to the relationship.

Marital Sexual Jealousy Defined

Sexual jealousy in marriage arises when a person already possesses the desired property—the spouse—and feels a threat of possibly losing it and the valued resources it provides. The spouse's resources are both tangible, like income, and intangible, like affection. For that reason, a part of the trespasser's threat comes from the spouse's independent access to resources which the jealous partner normally provides. In other words, a particular experience of jealousy stems from either a feeling of being excluded or a fear of loss (Clanton and Smith, 1977).

Sexual jealousy, therefore, refers to two perceived threats: first, that of having less access to the spouse's resources, and second, that of devaluation of the jealous partner's resources by the spouse. The important word here is "perceived." Jealousy is an emotion; at its onset, it does not matter whether it is founded in fact or not because the feeling is governed by the jealous partner's perception of the trespasser. But whether the public positively or negatively sanctions jealousy depends on whether or not society judges the threat to be real.

Changing Marital Dynamics and Jealousy

Early discussions of sexual jealousy tended to focus on male jealousy. Because the wife was traditionally defined as the property of the husband, it was assumed that he had a right to be jealous if threatened with a rival (Davis, 1936). Bernard (1977) argues that because sexual exclusivity was given to men

Sexual jealousy has always been a popular subject for books and films.

but not to women, there was no need for female sexual jealousy to enforce it; another interpretation is that wives experienced sexual jealousy but were simply powerless to enforce it. In traditional marriages, the wife would seem to have more "right" to be jealous. There are usually more threats to her property, both tangible and intangible, for she is far more dependent on her husband than he on her. Thus, she has more reason to fear the loss of resources (McDonald and Osmond, 1980).

While some marriages today are characterized by an imbalanced power/dependence relationship, many are becoming more balanced. As noted in Chapter 7, working wives have risen to the level of a "junior partner." As more wives gain resources independently of husbands, the power that goes with resources will increase their power, and as a result, the experience of jealousy should become more similar for males and females. In addition, marital partners will probably expressly negotiate their own rules regarding standards of conduct to avoid feelings of jealousy and to resolve conflicts when jealousy arises (Cook, 1975).

A crucial aspect of the power/dependence shift is the move toward a balance of resources between the partners. What this means is that the stability of marriages may become governed less by the lack of available alternatives and more by the voluntary commitment of the partners to each other and to the relationship. Voluntary commitment may replace reliance upon the resources of the other spouse. Consistent, committed behavior toward the spouse should increase the level of trust in the marital partner (McDonald and Osmond, 1980).

From the exchange perspective, commitment is the consistent willingness to share one's valued resources with another. As such, commitment is a function of power; that is, the power to supply the resources in a predictable manner. Trust, then, becomes the degree to which one can rely on the spouse's resources being provided in the future. Similarly, Mazur (1977) characterized possessive jealousy as commitment without trust; but possessive jealousy could also include dependency without trust. For that reason, lack of trust is a necessary condition for the arousal of jealousy in a marriage (McDonald and Osmond, 1980).

Is Sexual Jealousy Declining? The new shape of marital relationships has had an apparent effect on monogamy. As marital partners begin to negotiate their relationships instead of following traditional norms, differing expectations—and perhaps norms—of sexual exclusivity seem to be emerging among some couples.

Some researchers now distinguish between extramarital sex, in which the behavior is concealed from the spouse or causes the spouse distress if discovered, and "comarital sex." In **comarital sex** both marital partners permit sexual relationships outside the marriage as a basic right they grant each other.

For some couples, these relationships are not thought to compete with the marriage; they may have no effect on it or they may even improve it (Libby and Whitehurst, 1973).

If comarital sex is negotiated between the partners, is it a guarantee that sexual jealousy will not occur? Bernard (1977) argues that sexual jealousy is declining in our society because the norm of sexual exclusivity is not as strong as it once was. However, it is equally possible that jealousy is not diminishing but is taking different forms as norms are redefined. While this is still an open question, the experience of "swingers" does not support the view that sexual jealousy is declining. The fact is that many swingers give up the practice after a short time because of the problems that one or both spouses encounter in managing feelings of jealousy. Swinging in marriage will be covered in Chapter 14.

EXTRAMARITAL SEXUALITY

Extramarital sex refers to a sexual relationship with someone other than a mate which has not been negotiated with the mate in advance—either generally or in the specific instance.

There is some evidence that people involved in extramarital sex may be more sexually inhibited with their extramarital partner than with their marital partner. Whereas only 7 percent of the women in one survey never had orgasm in conjugal sex, 35 percent never reached orgasm in extramarital sex. Compared with the 67 percent of men and 55 percent of women who found marital sex very pleasurable, only 47 percent of the men and 37 percent of the women found extramarital sex very pleasurable (Hunt, 1974). These data raise an important question: if sex outside of marriage provides less sexual satisfaction than within marriage, why do so many people become involved with extramarital sex?

Prevalence and Characteristics

Surveys conducted by Kinsey during the 1940s found that 50 percent of the men and 26 percent of the women reported having engaged in extramarital sex by the age of forty. Data collected during the 1970s show a small increase in extramarital sexual activity among men since the earlier studies, but a fairly dramatic increase among young women and working women (Hunt, 1974; Levin and Levin, 1975b). According to Levin and Levin, a quarter of married women aged twenty to twenty-five reported that they had had extramarital coitus; in the age group from thirty-five to forty, the incidence jumped to 38 percent. For married working women in this age group, the incidence was 48 percent. These data suggest that married women who work outside the home are catching up to married men in their rate of extramarital sexual activity. No doubt the movement toward gender equality and the increase in the number of the women in the work force are important contributing factors. Working women have more of an opportunity to develop close relationships with men other than their husbands and some of these relationships would be likely to involve sexual relations.

Motivation and First Involvement

It is difficult to generalize about the reasons for people's behavior in intimate areas of their lives, but researchers have found some clues that help explain the motives for extramarital involvement. Cuber (1969) surveyed a group of 437 upper-middle-class married couples and uncovered three main reasons why some of them became involved in extramarital sex: (1) to compensate for problems within their marriage; (2) to meet their needs for intimacy during periods of separation because the husband was away at war or because of career; (3) to enjoy sexual freedom on an equal basis.

The results of a 1975 survey on nonmarital and extramarital sex appear to support the first reason cited by Cuber. This survey found that many wives who had had extramarital sexual experience were more dissatisfied with their marriages or their sex lives than wives who did not. And a large majority of those with poor marriages who never engaged in extramarital sex admitted to a fairly strong desire for it. Even so, about half of the wives who had extramarital sexual experience claimed to be happily married and reported marital sex to be good to very good (Levin and Levin, 1975b).

As to the second reason noted by Cuber, a recent study found that geographical separation in itself does not necessarily lead to extramarital sex. Gersel (1979) interviewed spouses in "commuter" marriages—marriages in which the spouses live separately, often because of career demands. Her research showed that spouses who had not engaged in extramarital relationships in the past were no more likely to become involved with others outside the marriage than if they did not live separately. It is likely that for these couples marital sex meant an exclusive commitment which was more overriding than geographical separation.

How do people first become involved in an extramarital relationship? Edwards (1973) has suggested a theory of how opportunity leads to extramarital sexual involvement. Frequency of contact and maintaining a high level of involvement with someone of the opposite sex—perhaps at work—may cause that person to be seen as an alternative to one's mate. The more attractive these alternatives seem, the more likely one is to feel dissatisfied with the existing marriage. The combination of attractive alternatives, opportunity for involvement, and dissatisfaction with marriage increases the chances that extramarital sexual relationships will develop.

CASE STUDY   *Extramarital Sex in a Youthful*
                  Marriage

Tony and Laurie married just out of high school and in a short time had two children. Because she felt they needed additional income, Laurie went back to work for the telephone company, even though Tony objected that he could support the family adequately. She made arrangements for a babysitter to come when she went to work at 3 P.M. Then Tony was supposed to take care of the children when he returned from his job at 5:30.

Since before they were married Tony had been in the habit of stopping with friends after work for a few beers before going home. He continued this pattern after the marriage and was often late picking up the children. On other occasions he would arrive home, feed the children, then take them to his mother's house for the evening while he joined his friends at a bar.

Laurie could never be sure when she arrived home where the children would be or where Tony would be. This disturbed her and she nagged at Tony about being more responsible

and complained often that he was spending money on drinks and socializing while she was struggling to increase their limited income. Tony countered by saying, "You're never at home, and even when you are we never have any fun because you're always at me about money."

One day a friend mentioned to Laurie that she had seen Tony hanging around with a group of men and women who seemed to have nothing on their minds but having a good time. When Laurie confronted Tony about this, Tony acknowledged it readily and bragged about what a good time they were having. A little drunk, he told Laurie he was having a sexual relationship with one of the women. Laurie was deeply hurt. She had always been a responsive sexual partner and couldn't understand why Tony would turn to another woman. "I have fun with her," Tony said. "You always make me feel like nothing and you've never given me a chance to show you that I can support you and the kids. Why shouldn't I see someone else?"

FOR CLASS DISCUSSION

1. What clues are offered in this case study that Tony may not be fully prepared to accept the responsibilities of a husband and parent?

2. What might be some advantages to Tony and Laurie discussing their marital problems with a professional counselor? Given the pattern they've established, do you think they could work out their problems themselves?

Atwater (1979) interviewed forty women about their extramarital involvement and learned that initial involvement proceeded by stages. The first stage was awareness of the opportunity. Men usually initiated the idea, but the women were also influenced by talking to friends who had already had extramarital relationships. The second stage involved thinking seriously about extramarital involvement—its possible advantages and drawbacks. This stage lasted from as short a time as several weeks to as long as several years. Finally, Atwater found that the situation was more influential than the person. Once a woman had made the decision to have an extramarital relationship and the opportunity arose, she became involved.

Characteristics Contributing to Extramarital Permissiveness

Recent research has indicated that there are identifiable characteristics of people who engage in extramarital sex. Reiss, Anderson, and Sponaugle (1980) attempted to develop a model based on a series of scientifically conducted surveys to understand what personal factors might be related to extramarital sexual permissiveness. These researchers concluded that there are two major sources of influence on extramarital permissiveness: "(1) quality of the marital relationship; and (2) general sexual permissiveness in other areas." Other variables, in their view, may influence extramarital sex—sometimes even directly—but they are of relatively minor importance compared to these.

MARITAL QUALITY   People unhappy in their marriages are more likely to have extramarital relationships than those with happy marriages. However, the data clearly indicate that many who have unhappy marriages never engage in extramarital activity, while many with happy marriages do. Johnson (1970) found that there is a stronger relationship between dissatisfaction with marriage and extramarital involvement for males than for females. Men who find their marriages unsatisfactory are more likely to seek outside sexual involvement than unhappily married women.

Based on the questionnaire responses of over 2,000 married women, Bell, Turner, and Rosen (1975) found that while 55 percent who rated their marriages fair to very poor reported some extramarital involvement, 20 percent of those who rated their marriages good or very good reported involvements as well. For women, whether they have liberal or conservative sexual views seems to be an important factor, along with how they feel about their marriage. Those who have unhappy marriages combined with liberal attitudes toward masturbation, cunnilingus, fellatio, and anal intercourse are more likely to have extramarital affairs than those who are unhappy but sexually conservative. Being happily married is not always a barrier to extramarital involvement for women if their sexual attitudes are liberal; however, conservative sexual attitudes are a barrier to sex outside of marriage for unhappily married women.

SEXUAL PERMISSIVENESS   Reiss, Anderson, and Sponaugle (1980) found a high correlation between sexually permissive attitudes generally and extramarital activity specifically. Positive attitudes toward nonmarital and extramarital permissiveness when combined with a strong endorsement of gender equality and moderate to low religious commitment were strong indicators of a favorable attitude toward extramarital activity.

GENDER EQUALITY Reiss, Anderson, and Sponaugle (1980) found gender equality to be an important indicator of a favorable attitude toward sexual activity outside marriage. Gender equality in this context refers to attitudes toward the division of roles according to sex. A positive attitude toward gender equality would be indicated by agreeing that a working mother can have as close a relationship with her children as a mother who doesn't work outside the home, and by not agreeing that a woman's place is only in the home.

These researchers hypothesized that a commitment to gender equality carried with it a less restrictive attitude toward extramarital activity. This they believed was reflected in the increasing divorce rates for the upper and middle classes—the social classes that tend to be in the forefront of support for the concept of gender equality. They reasoned that the greater role uncertainty caused by gender equality was positively correlated with an increase in unhappy marriages and therefore with extramarital sexual activity.

SEX As noted earlier, more men engage in extramarital activity than women. However, Reiss, Anderson, and Sponaugle (1980) and a number of other investigators have reported that while the percentage of men involved in extramarital activity has not increased, the percentage of women has. This increase may be a result of the increasing commitment to gender equality. Yet even though the gap has narrowed, the sex differences are still very prevalent.

SEXUAL SATISFACTION IN MARRIAGE If sexual satisfaction is considered separately from general marital satisfaction, it seems to have a significant bearing on extramarital behavior. Edwards and Booth (1976) and Johnson (1970), for example, indicate that for both men and women, those who are satisfied with the frequency of sexual relations within marriage are less likely to seek sexual satisfaction outside. Sexual and marital satisfaction are interrelated, however. Marital conflicts may lower the frequency of sex. And serious strains in the relationship—marked by threats to leave and the like—lower the frequency of lovemaking still more and increase the likelihood that partners will seek outside sexual involvement.

Effects on Marriage

What is the effect of extramarital sex on marriage? At present the signals are mixed. According to a number of studies, there is a high correlation between extramarital activity and divorce. But it is difficult to determine whether the outside relationship contributed to the breakup of the marriage or whether it occurred because the marriage was breaking up.

Spanier and Casto (1979) found in a study of thirty divorced persons that while twenty-one of them had had extramarital relations, not one went on to marry the person with whom he or she had been involved. While it is not clear that participating in an outside relationship inclines someone toward divorce, it may; however, given the high rate of extramarital activity, this seems less likely than it once might have. Also, it may be that extramarital activity does not affect some couples' marital adjustment at all.

For other couples, extramarital activity by one or both partners may seriously damage the relationship. No matter how broad-minded they are about sexual freedom, couples are found to experience difficulty if more affection is felt for the extramarital partner than for the spouse. In such cases, it is the emotional rather than the sexual involvement that poses problems within the marriage. And if income is limited, the uninvolved spouse may also resent the other spending money on the extramarital relationship when the money is needed at home (Libby and Whitehurst, 1973).

How Important is Sexual Exclusivity? Cross-cultural data indicate that a sexual custom is accepted within a society only to the extent that it is thought to support marriage and the family as institutions. As we have seen, our society still regards extramarital relations as a detriment to these institutions. However, Libby and Whitehurst (1973) contend that it is unrealistic to expect people to "forsake all others" when they marry. These sociologists believe that attractions to others outside the marriage should be examined realistically by the marital partners to see what degree of outside involvement, if any, their union can tolerate and under what circumstances it might be allowed. Insisting that two people cannot possibly meet all of each other's needs, Libby and Whitehurst advocate a more flexible view of marriage and the sexual relationship within marriage. Perhaps in the future, sex outside of marriage may be seen as improving marital relationships, or at least not interfering with them. If that occurs, extramarital relationships may become more acceptable than they are now. Today, however, most couples still believe that there are compelling reasons for sexual exclusivity in marriage and this norm remains strongly embedded in American culture. The stability offered by a monogamous relationship, the freedom from jealousy it helps to ensure, and the attention it focuses on the marriage are regarded as significant benefits not to be taken lightly.

SUMMARY

1. The purposes of this chapter are to consider the social origins of sexual behavior, the relationship between sexual adjustment and marital adjustment, the role of communication in a sexual relationship, and the problems that various kinds of sexual behavior can cause in a relationship.

2. Sexual behavior is learned. Sexual scripts are part of this learning process and define what constitutes an erotic situation, who the actors must be, and what their behavior must be. Five basic sexual philosophies predominate in the United States: traditional-religious, romantic, recreational, friendly, and utilitarian-predatory. Motivations for sex are varied and depend on a variety of factors.

3. The single most important factor in maintaining a good sexual relationship in marriage is communication between partners. The 1980 *Redbook* survey shows a direct correlation between the ability of the partners to communicate and the quality of their sex life and their marriage. But it is not the sexual relationship that determines the quality of the marriage; rather, the quality of the marriage seems to determine how satisfactory the sexual relationship is.

4. Spouses may bring personal problems to sexual encounters which prevent them and their partners from enjoying sex. Ignorance of effective sexual behavior, inability to communicate, and fear of rejection or failure are some typical problems. To resolve them, both partners have to learn what their own needs are, express them openly, and then work out individual differences in a mutually agreeable way. Sometimes help from professional therapists may be needed.

5. Jealousy seems to grow out of the expectation of sexual exclusivity in marriage. Jealousy arises from the view of the spouse as an item of property which is vulnerable to inroads by a "trespasser." Society sanctions jealousy if the jealous partner is correct in his or her apprehension of a trespasser. It seems likely that sexual jealousy will persist unless people are socialized away from the view that sexual relations should be monogamous.

6. Extramarital sex is more common among men than women, but the number of women engaging in it is growing. Sex outside marriage is strongly disapproved of in American society, yet it is still common. The major factors that appear to influence extramarital permissiveness are marital quality and general sexual permissiveness in other areas. Although it is difficult to assess the effect of extramarital sex on marriage, several studies have found a high correlation between extramarital activity and divorce.

REVIEW AND DISCUSSION

1. Identify the five philosophies of sexual behavior in American society suggested by Gecas and Libby (1976). Which of these views is closest to your own philosophy of sexual behavior? What factors do you think influenced you to adopt this philosophy?

2. What is the relationship between sexual adjustment and marital adjustment? Why do you think researchers have found that the relationship between the two is different for men and women?

3. Explain why communication and assertiveness play such a central role in sexual adjustment.

4. How does the exchange framework account for sexual jealousy? Do you think sexual jealousy will decline in the future? Why or why not?

5. What is your view of extramarital sex? Are there circumstances under which it would be acceptable to you? Would you be willing to be part of a marriage that included comarital sex? Why or why not?

SUGGESTED READINGS

Comfort, A. (1972). *The Joy of Sex*. New York: Crown.

Comprehensive guided tour of human heterosexual response and behavior, arranged alphabetically and accompanied by many illustrations. Emphasizes learning how to enhance each partner's sexual enjoyment.

Gagnon, J. H., and W. Simon (1974). *Sexual Conduct: The Social Sources of Human Sexuality*. London: Hutchison & Co., Ltd.

Discusses the sources and development of human sexuality. Includes coverage of social origins, pedagogy of sex, male and female homosexuality, pornography, and social change and sexual conduct.

Hite, S. (1976). *The Hite Report: A Nationwide Study of Female Sexuality*. New York: Dell.

Presents the results of questionnaire survey that asked women how they feel, what they like, and what they think of sex. The first part of the book discusses orgasm; the second part is a new cultural interpretation of female sexuality.

Sarrel, P., and L. Sarrel (1980). *The Redbook Report on Sexual Relationships*. New York: Redbook Publishing Co., pp. 73-80.

A recent report on sexual relationships based on the responses of 6,000 men and 20,000 women, 60 percent of whom were in first marriages. Focuses on the meanings and uses of communication in sexual relationships.

Smith, J. R., and L. G. Smith, eds. (1974). *Beyond Monogamy, Recent Studies of Sexual Alternatives in Marriage*. Baltimore: Johns Hopkins University Press.

A collection of sixteen essays on various experimental forms of sexual activity, such as swinging, group marriage, and comarital sex.

Family Planning, Pregnancy, and Childbirth

9

🎋 Family Planning: Conception Control
🎋 Pregnancy
🎋 The Pregnancy Experience
🎋 Childbirth
🎋 Advances in Childbirth and Fertility

"It is not only inevitable, but it is also right that we learn to control the size of our family, for by this control and adjustment we can raise the standards of the human race. . . . Contraception . . . involves not only a greater forethought for others, but finally a higher sanction for the value of life itself."

MARGARET SANGER

If the average woman began having intercourse at the age of seventeen and never made any attempt to prevent pregnancy, she would eventually give birth to thirteen children (Guttmacher, 1973). When the United States was a farming society with a small population and much available land, large families were an economic asset. But times have changed, and with them attitudes about unrestricted human reproduction. In urban industrial societies like the United States children have become an economic liability with each new addition to the family creating greater financial demands. On a global scale, overpopulation is seriously straining already limited resources. In some of the less-developed areas of the world, food production lags far behind the need and people are starving.

To ease the problem of famine as well as the environmental problems caused by overcrowding, advocates of zero population growth (ZPG) now urge that couples voluntarily limit their families to two children. The Chinese government has gone further. In 1980 it issued a series of edicts designed to reduce its birthrate to zero by the year 2000. One law raises the minimum ages for marriage to twenty for a woman, twenty-two for a man; another cuts off the monthly allowance for one child if another is born; still another gives preference to first children in entering nurseries, hospitals, and schools.

In this country, there is strong sentiment favoring people's right to choose freely how many children they will have. At the same time, couples want to be able to plan their families based on their personal preferences, economic

283

situation, and career demands. When they do have children, many men and women are taking a more active role in managing both the pregnancy and the childbirth experience. If a couple wishes to have a child and conception does not occur, they expect medical expertise to resolve their problem successfully. In general, Americans are demanding and enjoying greater control over their reproductive functions than was possible at any other time in history.

FAMILY PLANNING: CONCEPTION CONTROL

Whatever their intention, couples cannot limit the size of their familes unless they have access to effective means of birth control. Fortunately, there have been great strides in contraceptive technology as well as in attitudes toward birth control over the past few decades. Information on birth control is much more widely available today than it was in the past. Organizations such as Planned Parenthood/World Population (PPWP) operate on the principle that no one who seeks contraceptive advice should be denied it, regardless of age or marital status (Guttmacher, 1973). The aim of PPWP—"each child wanted joyfully by responsible parents"—eloquently expresses the views of a great many modern Americans.

Methods in Current Use

The methods of birth control currently in use fall into several basic categories depending on how they work to prevent conception: some introduce hormones into the body, some act as a barrier to sperm, and some have sperm-killing properties. In addition, there are several "natural" methods based on the menstrual cycle. Finally, sterilization and abortion have become so widespread that they must also be considered forms of contraception.

The effectiveness of various contraceptive methods is described in terms of **failure rate.** This figure, which is expressed as a percentage, refers to the likelihood of pregnancy's occurring during one year in one hundred sexually active women using a particular method of contraception. We will refer to failure rates throughout the following discussion. Table 9.1 offers a comparative summary of contraceptive methods, their effectiveness and side effects.

THE PILL   Oral contraceptives, known collectively as the **pill,** are believed to prevent pregnancy by introducing into the system synthetic hormones resembling progesterone and estrogen that trick the ovaries into not ovulating. There is some evidence that these synthetic hormones also cause changes in the ovaries which prevent the ova from maturing. When used correctly, the pill is virtually 100 percent effective in preventing pregnancy. According to Planned

Table 9.1 **Comparative Summary of Contraceptive Methods**

METHOD	IDEAL FAILURE[a] RATE	ACTUAL FAILURE[a] RATE	ADVANTAGES	DISADVANTAGES/ SIDE EFFECTS
Birth-control pills	0.34%	4–10%	Easy to use; permits spontaneity of intercourse	Side effects (e.g., change in pigmentation of the face, increased risk of blood clotting). Should not be used by women over 35.
IUD	1–3%	5%	May be left in place for long period of time; permits spontaneity of intercourse	Side effects (irregular bleeding, cramping, increased risk of pelvic infection, possible spontaneous expulsion).
Diaphragm with cream or jelly	3%	17%	No side effects	Not as spontaneous as pill or IUD
Vaginal foam	3%	22%	No prescription required; easy to use	Not as spontaneous as pill or IUD; may irritate vaginal tissue
Condom	3%	10%	Easy to use; helps prevent venereal disease and vaginal infection	Interruption of sexual activity
Withdrawal	9%	20–25%	No cost or preparation	Depends on self-control; interference with sexual pleasure
Rhythm	13%	21%	No cost; sanctioned by Roman Catholic church	Complex; requires high degree of commitment and long periods of abstinence; difficult to use for women with irregular cycles
Ovulation	?	15–25%[b]	No cost; can help a couple plan a pregnancy	Requires firm commitment, practice, careful record-keeping; difficult for women with irregular cycles or those who do not have easily discernable mucus patterns
Douching	?	40%		Disrupts enjoyment of intercourse; may facilitate rather than hinder passage of sperm; possible irritation of vaginal tissue.
Tubal ligation	0.04%	0.04%	Permanent means of birth control; does not affect reproductive system except for tubes	Small chance of surgical complications; possible psychological effects
Vasectomy	0.15%	0.15%	Permanent means of birth control; does not affect sexual functioning	Small chance of surgical complications; possible psychological effects

[a] Hatcher et al., 1980. [b] Wade et al., 1979.

Parenthood, it is the preferred method of birth control for nearly 10 million women in the United States.

Contraceptive pills come in two basic types. **Combination pills** contain a mixture of synthetic progesterone and estrogen, in varying amounts and ratios. The new **mini-pill,** which has been available since 1973, contains progestin (a synthetic progesterone) only. It is less effective than the combination pill and is more often associated with irregular menstrual cycles and spotting between periods (Connell, 1975).

Oral contraceptives may cause one or more of a large number of side effects. Among the most common are changes in the pigmentation of the face, swelling and tenderness of the breasts, fluid retention, nausea, headaches, and vaginal discharge. Sometimes these problems may be alleviated by changing to a different pill (Connell, 1975; Montreal Health Press, 1974). The effect of the pill on sexual motivation is not yet completely certain. While Hatcher et al. (1980) indicate that women taking the pill usually experience heightened sexual desire, Seaman and Seaman (1977) argue that precisely the opposite can occur. They attribute this decreased sexual drive to both biochemical and psychological factors. The Seamans also report that the pill causes depressive symptoms in 30 percent of users which often disappear when they stop using it.

There is a good deal of evidence that birth-control pills can cause more serious side effects, especially in women who smoke and in women over thirty-five. The Food and Drug Administration has accepted research findings that show women who use the pill to be at greater risk of developing blood clots, stroke, and heart attack than women who do not use it. Pill users who smoke are particularly vulnerable. Planned Parenthood advises women not to use the pill if they have had other serious health problems, such as blood clots or inflammation of the veins, liver disease, cancer of the breast or reproductive system, hypertension, heart disease, or unexplained vaginal bleeding. The pill has been linked to liver tumors, high blood pressure, and chemical diabetes. Two other points are worth noting: women who have a history of irregular menstruation may not begin ovulating again after going off the pill, and a small amount of hormone from the pill has been found in the breast milk of nursing mothers who took birth-control pills. The effects of the hormone on their infants, and indeed, the potential danger of the hormones in birth-control pills to unborn fetuses deserve further study (Seaman and Seaman, 1977).

Several long-term studies completed in 1980 reached more optimistic conclusions about the pill. Combined research by eight major medical centers involving nearly 5000 women confirmed earlier findings that the combination form of the pill cut by 50 percent the risk of cancer of the uterine lining during the period in which the women were taking it (Kaufman et al., 1980). Another study of 16,000 young, white, middle-income women concluded that for this group of women at least the risks from taking birth-control pills appear to be negligible. However, this ten-year study did find that increased risk of heart disease, hypertension, and blood-clot formation resulted from combining pill use with smoking; nonsmokers taking the pill faced no such hazard. Additional evidence suggested that the pill protects women against noncancerous breast cysts (Walnut Creek Drug Study, 1980).

While the final word on the safety of the pill has not been written, it seems clear that its use should be approached with caution. For young, nonsmoking women with a good health record, this form of contraception is probably relatively safe, and it is certainly highly effective in preventing pregnancy and permitting complete spontaneity during intercourse.

"MORNING-AFTER" PILL   The **morning-after pill** is actually a series of pills containing a massive dose of a synthetic estrogen known as DES (diethylstilbestrol). Patients are given ten 25-milligram tablets of DES over a five-day period. This high dosage apparently prevents implantation of a fertilized ovum. Treatment must begin within seventy-two hours of unprotected intercourse and preferably within twenty-four hours.

The morning-after pill may have very unpleasant side effects. About 16 percent of women on this treatment experience severe nausea and vomiting (Kuchera, 1972). Furthermore, DES is considered a probable cause of cancer. Between 1940 and 1970, the drug was prescribed for millions of women who had a history of miscarriage, bleeding, or long periods of infertility. It has since come to light that a significant number of the daughters of these women have developed cancer of the cervix or vagina. Because of the very serious risks involved in taking such a large and concentrated dosage of DES, morning-after treatment is approved for use only in emergency situations such as rape or incest.

IUD   The **intrauterine device (IUD)** is a small, flexible plastic object that is inserted into the uterus through the vagina by a doctor. It may be left in place for months or even for several years (depending on the type of IUD), as long as the woman or her partner checks periodically to make sure that it is still in place. The IUD permits intercourse to be completely spontaneous and neither partner has to remember to do anything, since the device works on its own. IUDs are highly effective, with a theoretical failure rate of about 5 percent (Hatcher et al., 1980). They are used by about 6 percent of married women in the United States.

The principle of the intrauterine device has long been known and applied in animals. For example, since ancient times camel drivers have inserted a round stone into the uterus of camels to prevent them from becoming pregnant during long desert treks. Although various metal devices were developed for use in humans during the nineteenth century, they fell out of favor during the early twentieth century. IUDs have been widely available only since 1964.

It is uncertain how the IUD prevents pregnancy in humans. The most widely accepted theory is that cellular and biochemical changes occur in the uterus which lead to the destruction of the fertilized egg and sperm by the body's defense mechanisms. The device also seems to inflame the lining of the uterus so that it becomes unreceptive to the implantation of a fertilized ovum (Mishell, 1975).

IUDs come in a variety of designs (see Fig. 9.1). As shown in Fig. 9.2, all styles have nylon threads that hang down into the vagina so that the wearer can check to ensure that the device is in place. One of the most popular of the newer plastic types is the double-*S*-shaped Lippes loop. The Copper 7 contains a small amount of copper that dissolves slowly. The copper seems to increase the concentration of sperm-destroying cells in the uterus. The Copper 7 must be replaced every three years. Another recent development is an IUD which continually releases tiny amounts of progesterone, making the uterine lining hostile to implantation. The progesterone-containing devices, such as the Progesterone T, must be replaced each year.

There are side effects associated with IUDs. Ten to twenty percent of women using IUDs experience irregular bleeding and pelvic pain. However,

Fig. 9.1
IUDs

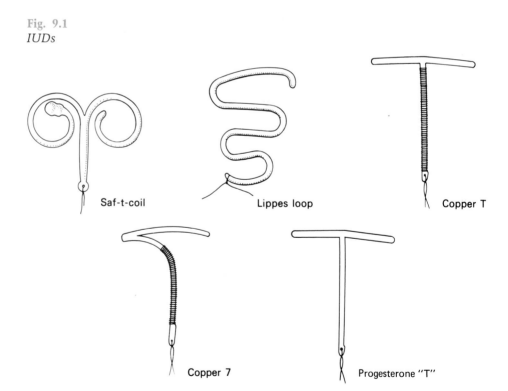

Saf-t-coil   Lippes loop   Copper T

Copper 7   Progesterone "T"

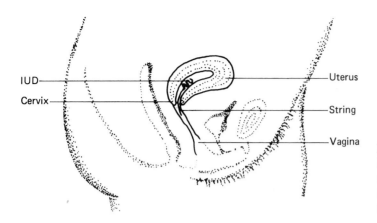

IUD —
Cervix —
— Uterus
— String
— Vagina

Fig. 9.2
Intrauterine device in the uterus. The IUD is inserted into the uterus and the string hangs out of the cervical os.

these problems may disappear after several months of use. Heavy menstrual periods, spotting between periods, and uterine cramps are other side effects. Spontaneous expulsion of the IUD may also occur, especially in younger women and those who have never given birth (Hatcher et al., 1980).

More serious problems associated with IUDs include perforation of the uterus, ectopic pregnancy (in which gestation occurs elsewhere than in the uterus), and increased risk of pelvic infection. An untreated pelvic infection can result in infertility and, in rare cases, even death. As with spontaneous expulsion, women who have not had children appear to be at greater risk of pelvic infection. Many doctors will prescribe an IUD only for women who have previously given birth, and many will not prescribe the device for a woman who has had even one pelvic infection.

DIAPHRAGM   The **diaphragm** is a dome of thin rubber stretched over a flexible, rubber-covered metal ring. It is inserted in the vagina so that it covers the cervix and prevents sperm from passing through to the uterus (see Fig. 9.3). To be effective, it must be covered with a spermicidal jelly or cream. Used properly the diaphragm with spermicide has an ideal failure rate of 3 percent. A study conducted in 1976 at the Sanger Bureau reported an actual-use failure rate of 2 percent. Most of the participants were unmarried women under thirty. Their high rate of success was probably due to proper fitting and careful, conscientious use of the device (Seaman and Seaman, 1977). Much higher actual-use failure rates—as high as 17 percent—have been reported, but it is likely that at least part of the reason for this is improper or inconsistent use.

A major advantage of the diaphragm is that it is free of potentially dangerous side effects such as those associated with the pill or IUD. This has been an important factor in its recent return to popularity. Since a properly fitted diaphragm fits snugly over the cervix, it cannot be felt by the wearer or her partner during intercourse and does not diminish sexual pleasure.

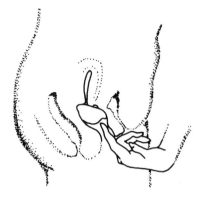

Fig. 9.3
Diaphragm in place over the cervix

The diaphragm does not permit the same spontaneity as the pill and the IUD. The user must insert the device covered with the contraceptive jelly or cream no more than six hours before intercourse in order for the spermicide to be effective. Some experts believe that insertion no more than two hours before coitus is preferable. It may also be inserted just prior to intercourse. An additional application of jelly or cream must be made every time intercourse is repeated before the diaphragm is to be removed. The diaphragm must remain in place at least six hours after the *last* act of intercourse. Rarely, a diaphragm may slip out of place, particularly when intercourse is very vigorous, when the penis is withdrawn and reinserted, or when the woman is on top (Montreal Health Press, 1974).

Properly cared for, a diaphragm should last several years. This includes careful washing, drying, and storage and checking regularly for tiny holes. Diaphragms must be fitted by a physician, and refittings are necessary after a pregnancy, a weight loss or gain of ten pounds or more, and any other condition that might have changed the size of the vaginal canal. A few women cannot wear a diaphragm because of pelvic structure problems such as loss of vaginal muscle tone which can occur after pregnancy.

CERVICAL CAP   The **cervical cap**, a thimble-shaped flexible rubber cup that fits over the cervix, works on the same principle as the diaphragm, providing a physical barrier to block the passage of sperm. However, the cervical cap is smaller, deeper, and more rigid than the diaphragm and fits more securely due to a suction seal created by the rim of the cap hugging the walls of the cervix. The cervical cap has no known side effects and apparently is at least as effective as the diaphragm (Seaman and Seaman, 1977). It provides an effective block against sperm even without using a spermicidal jelly. However, if left in place more than twenty-four hours, its effectiveness is improved by applying spermicide before each coitus. The device may be worn by women whose pelvic structure prevents them from using a diaphragm.

The major drawback of the cervical cap is its lack of wide availability. Although the device was used in the United States before the advent of the pill and IUD, it fell into disfavor and only recently has been "rediscovered." It is widely used in England and other European countries and is manufactured only by Lamberts (Dalston) Limited in Britain. Its only other disadvantage is that it requires that a woman be familiar with her reproductive anatomy so that she can learn proper self-insertion.

In the face of growing concern over the side effects of the pill and IUD, there is new enthusiasm for the cervical cap. Barbara and Gideon Seaman devote an entire chapter to the cervical cap in their book *Women and the Crisis in Sex Hormones* (1977). It seems likely that as more American women become aware of this device and express interest to their medical practitioners, it will come into greater use.

CONDOM   The **condom**, sometimes called a rubber, safe, prophylactic, or skin, is currently the only mechanical method of birth control available for men. The condom (shown in Fig. 9.4) consists of a seven and one-half inch disposable sheath of rubber, latex, or animal membrane with a ring of thick rubber at the open end. During ejaculation semen is caught and held within the sheath and thus prevented from entering the vagina.

Condoms are relatively inexpensive, easy to use, and available without prescriptions from drugstores, family planning clinics, by mail order, and, in some areas, from vending machines in restrooms. Used properly, they provide a very effective form of contraception. They have a theoretical failure rate of 3 percent. Although the actual-use failure rate is usually cited at 10 percent (Hatcher et al., 1980), three British studies which were able to separate out failures due to nonuse and misuse found a failure rate of only 1 percent (*Consumer Reports*, October 1979). Occasionally leakage of semen may occur, but this may be prevented by taking several precautions. These include withdrawing the penis soon after ejaculation (before the penis becomes flaccid) and grasping the ring at the base of the condom during withdrawal. Condoms can break, but they rarely do. They have no side effects and have the additional benefit of providing good protection against the spread of venereal disease and vaginal infections.

Consumer Reports magazine surveyed 1874 readers (1071 men and 803 women) about their personal experiences with condoms. The major disadvan-

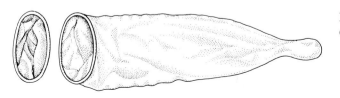

Fig. 9.4
Condom

tage, cited by 76 percent of men and 75 percent of women, was that the condom interrupts lovemaking. Sixty-three percent of the men and 33 percent of the women said that condoms reduced sensation. But 38 percent of the men cited less stimulation as an advantage, since this helped prolong intercourse. It is also worth noting that 19 percent of both men and women considered placing the condom on the penis an arousing experience. Other advantages reported by over half the respondents of both sexes were convenience, ease of use, and peace of mind. For the women, the fact that condoms have no side effects seemed very important; 75 percent of the women respondents mentioned this advantage (*Consumer Reports*, October 1979).

SPERMICIDES   **Spermicides**, substances that kill sperm on contact, are available in a variety of forms, including the creams and jellies used with diaphragms, plus foams, suppositories, and vaginal tablets. The best of these are aerosol foams, which provide good distribution of the spermicide in the vagina and over the cervix. Used with a condom and inserted as soon before intercourse as possible (but no longer than fifteen minutes before), they provide a very effective method of contraception. Hatcher et al. (1980) report an actual-use failure rate of 5 percent for foam and condom. Seaman and Seaman (1977) reported an actual-use failure rate of foam alone of 3 percent, while Hatcher et al. (1980) reported failure rates as high as 22 percent. It seems likely that the high success reported by the Seamans was due to very conscientious use of the foam. Vaginal foam and other spermicides are available in pharmacies without prescription. They may also provide some protection against vaginal infections and venereal disease.

Creams and jellies are considerably less effective than foams and should only be used with a diaphragm. Suppositories and vaginal tablets are the least effective of the spermicides, largely because their distribution in the vagina may be uneven. Foam tablets also frequently irritate the tissues of the vagina.

THE RHYTHM METHOD   The birth-control methods we have described thus far all require the use of chemicals or mechanical devices. **Rhythm**, the only method of birth control officially approved at this time by the Roman Catholic church, is based on avoidance of intercourse during the woman's fertile period. The problem is to figure out just when that is. Ovulation usually occurs in the middle of the menstrual cycle, about twelve to sixteen days before menstruation begins. As a Planned Parenthood manual points out, knowing when that will be is like saying to a passenger on a bus who asks for directions, "Watch me and get off one stop before I do" (Planned Parenthood of New York City, 1973).

The time of ovulation can be estimated by keeping track of the dates when menstruation starts and stops over many months. If menstrual periods are always regular, the time of ovulation may be predictable. However, even women who usually have very regular cycles may experience variations in time of ovulation and menstruation due to illness, fatigue, or emotional factors.

Temperature-taking with a special thermometer that measures **basal body temperature** (body temperature at the resting stage upon waking in the morning) may help make the rhythm method more effective. Immediately prior to ovulation there is a slight drop in body temperature and after ovulation a rise to two-tenths to one-half a degree F above normal. This temperature change indicates when ovulation has occurred. However, it is not helpful before ovulation. Because sperm can remain viable for up to seventy-two hours in the fallopian tubes, and the egg may be receptive to fertilization for twenty-four hours after it leaves the ovary, intercourse is unsafe not only during the five days when ovulation might take place, but also for an additional three to four days before this possible ovulation period and at least one day after it.

The rhythm method is complex and requires a high degree of motivation and commitment. It demands abstinence from intercourse for a large part of the cycle, and it is difficult to use for women who have irregular cycles. The actual-use failure rate for rhythm is about 21 percent (Hatcher et al., 1980).

THE OVULATION METHOD The **ovulation method**, developed by Australian researchers John and Evelyn Billings, is a refinement of the rhythm method. This technique requires that a woman learn to monitor and record the changes in her cervical mucus that indicate periods of fertility.

Following menstruation, many women have a few "dry days" during which there is no vaginal discharge. These days are assumed to be safe for intercourse. Soon after a yellow or white discharge begins, and the fertile period is assumed to have begun. Ovulatory mucus, which is similar in consistency to egg white, appears after several days. Unprotected intercourse is not considered safe from the beginning of the fertile period until four days after the ovulatory mucus begins and the cloudy discharge resumes (a total of nine to fifteen days out of the cycle).

The ovulation method has several drawbacks. Although research on its effectiveness is limited, the failure rate appears to be between 15 and 25 percent (Hatcher et al., 1980). The method requires practice, firm commitment, and careful record-keeping. It is difficult to use for women who have irregular menstrual cycles and for women who do not have easily recognizable mucus patterns (about 30 percent of women). It does have the advantage of being free of side effects and financial cost, and it can help a couple plan a pregnancy as well as prevent it.

WITHDRAWAL In one of the oldest known methods of preventing pregnancy, the man withdraws from the vagina before he ejaculates. Although **withdrawal** (*coitus interruptus*, "being careful," or "pulling out") is medically safe for both partners and requires no equipment, it is entirely dependent on the man's self-control at a time of emotional and physical release, and even then it is not reliable. If any semen touches even the lips of the vagina, the sperm may be capable of making their way up the fallopian tubes. Furthermore, the drops of fluid which leak from the erect penis before ejaculation may contain enough sperm to cause pregnancy. The failure rate for this method is 20 to 25 percent (Hatcher et al., 1980). Despite its popularity elsewhere in the world, in the United States withdrawal is used as a primary method of birth control by only one couple in fifty (Westoff, 1976). Among American teenagers, however, the withdrawal method is very widespread.

DOUCHING   If withdrawal is disruptive to enjoyment of intercourse, so is **douching.** This method requires that, immediately after her partner ejaculates, the woman try to flush all of the semen out of her vagina with a special solution squirted from a syringe or douche bag.

Since sperm can reach the cervical canal as quickly as ninety seconds after ejaculation (Pengelley, 1974), douching is extremely ineffective. Indeed, it is believed that douching may facilitate the passage of the sperm to the cervical opening, since the douche is squirted into the vagina under pressure. In addition, frequent douching may irritate the tissues of the vagina.

Sterilization

Sterilization refers to alteration of some part of the reproductive organs in either males or females so as to make conception impossible. Over a million surgical sterilizations are performed in the United States each year. Sterilization is now the most popular method of contraception for couples over thirty-five, with nearly half reporting that one spouse or the other had been sterilized (Westoff and McCarthy, 1979). Although advances are being made in improving the rate of reversibility of sterilization, it is best regarded as a permanent form of birth control. For this reason, the decision to be sterilized requires careful consideration.

FEMALE STERILIZATION   The most common procedure for sterilization of women is **tubal ligation** (see Fig. 9.5), cutting or tying the fallopian tubes to prevent eggs from reaching the uterus and sperm from reaching the eggs in the tubes. This may be accomplished by a variety of techniques, the most common being **laparoscopy.** The laparoscopic procedure can be performed in an out-patient clinic. The patient is anesthetized (often with only a local anesthetic), her abdomen is inflated with carbon dioxide, and a slender viewing instrument called a laparoscope is inserted through a small abdominal incision, often in the naval to prevent scarring. The tubes are then electrically seared or clipped and separated with special forceps inserted through the same or another small incision. These incisions are so small that they require no stitches and leave

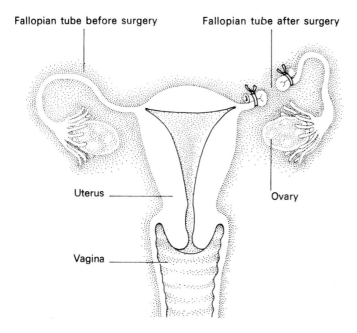

Fallopian tube before surgery   Fallopian tube after surgery

Uterus

Ovary

Vagina

Fig. 9.5
*Tubal ligation. This is a
relatively safe surgical procedure
which is generally irreversible. In
sterilization, the procedure is
performed on both tubes.*

a very small scar. As a result, the procedure has come to be called "bandaid" surgery. In another procedure, called **culdoscopy,** the incision is made through the back of the vaginal wall.

When performed by a skilled physician, tubal ligation is a safe procedure, with the chance of complications only 1 or 2 percent (Porter and Hulka, 1974). Except for blocking the fallopian tubes, the operation does not affect the female reproductive system or negatively alter a woman's sexual response. In fact, women commonly experience enhanced sexual interest because they are no longer anxious about possible pregnancy (Thompson and Baird, 1972).

About 1 percent of the estimated 600,000 women who have a tubal ligation each year in the United States seek reversal. Reversal is quite difficult because the structures involved are so small and difficult to realign. However, the introduction of microsurgery—surgery performed under a microscope with delicate instruments—has improved its rate of success. A recent estimate placed the pregnancy rate for women who have had their tubal ligation reversed with microsurgery at between 50 and 80 percent, depending on such factors as the patient's age, her partner's sperm count, and how much of the fallopian tube was originally destroyed (Matchan, 1981).

Many women have been sterilized by **hysterectomy,** surgical removal of the uterus, or by **ovarectomy,** removal of the ovaries. The use of hysterectomy solely for the purpose of sterilization involves high and unnecessary risk and

HIGHLIGHT 9.1   *Contraceptive Methods—Past and Future*

Throughout recorded history, people have tried to prevent unwanted pregnancies. The book of Genesis and the ancient Hebrew Talmud make mention of *coitus interruptus* (withdrawal). Ancient Egyptian documents and Greek and Roman writings also refer to contraceptive techniques. For the most part, the desire to prevent pregnancy was an individual one. Only a few primitive societies had a specific policy designed to check population growth. The Netsilik eskimos, for example, resorted to selective infanticide to assure that the population did not outstrip the available food supply.

The range of contraceptive methods tried by women in the past is diverse, to say the least. In their efforts to prevent pregnancy, women have worn magic charms, sneezed or jumped up and down after intercourse, and nursed their children for years in the hope of preventing ovulation. They have coated or plugged their vaginas with a variety of substances, including animal ear wax, elephant or crocodile dung, whitewash, grass, feathers, rags, pepper, and balls of lint soaked with acid liquids. They have stoically drunk such concoctions as infusion of gunpowder, froth from a camel's mouth, honey laced with dead bees, and water left from the washing of dead bodies. Occasionally, it was the man who was given the responsibility for preventing conception by such methods as rubbing his penis with onion juice, tar, or rock salt (Havemann, 1967; Rugh and Shettles, 1971).

Contraception—the prevention of pregnancy—is now much less rigorous and far more effective than these ancient methods, thanks to our understanding of the biological processes involved. But as we have seen, none of the birth-control methods in use today is totally satisfactory. What advances can we expect in the future? Will these new techniques help to equalize the burden of responsibility for contraception, which today is still being borne largely by women?

FEMALE CONTRACEPTIVE RESEARCH
Much current research on contraceptive methods for women centers around introducing hormones into the body. These hormonal methods will no doubt be more convenient than the contraceptive pill as we know it today. However, they have the potential side effects of the pill. One method that has already been developed is a progesterone-containing drug that suppresses ovulation for three months. Its side effects include irregular menstrual bleeding and a delay in return of fertility. Although this drug is already being used in some areas of the world, it has not been approved in the United States because it has been linked to precancerous breast tumors in dogs.

Another hormonal technique for preventing ovulation is a progestin-coated vaginal ring that fits like the rim of a diaphragm but is slightly smaller and easier to insert. The ring remains in the vagina for twenty-one days and then is removed to permit the onset of menstruation. Vaginal rings are very effective and appear to have few side effects.

Research is also being done to develop antibodies to HCG, the hormone that signals to the body that a pregnancy has begun and triggers the hormonal process that occurs during pregnancy. A woman would receive a vac-

(continued)

cination against HCG and as a result would menstruate whether or not her ovum had been fertilized.

A new barrier method under development consists of a very absorbent sponge made of collagen (a natural protein) which would be inserted into the vagina to block the cervix. The sponge is treated with zinc additives and acidically buffered to help destroy sperm.

MALE CONTRACEPTIVE RESEARCH

The contraceptive methods currently available to men are limited to condoms, withdrawal, and vasectomy. Although research efforts are under way to expand male contraceptive choices, it is uncertain when effective new methods will be available. Estimates vary from a few years to over twenty years. A major reason for this uncertainty is the difficulty of reducing the male sperm count without producing dangerous side effects. The introduction of hormones, for example, carries a risk of side effects such as are associated with the female contraceptive pill. Furthermore, there is concern that hormonal methods might cause genetic mutations.

Even so, research is proceeding to develop a contraceptive pill for men using a combination of synthetic testosterone and progesterone. The effect of these substances is to suppress pituitary function and thereby reduce the sperm count. Thus far, this method appears to hold promise.

Another approach being investigated is using ultrasonic waves to produce temporary sterility. There are several theories regarding how this works. One is that the sound waves raise the temperature of the testicles and thereby inhibit sperm production. Another explanation is that ultrasound causes molecular changes in the cells of the testicles and interferes with sperm formation. Ultrasound has been used successfully to induce temporary, reversible sterility in experimental animals, but there is no evidence as yet regarding its safety and effectiveness for humans.

Among other ideas under consideration are developing antibodies against a man's own sperm and working with a microorganism called T-mycoplasmas which has been found in infertile men. This microorganism is known to inhibit the speed at which sperm are able to travel.

Even if reliable new contraceptives for men become a reality in the near future, there is an important social consideration that must be addressed. Will women be willing to take a man's word for it that he has been injected with an antisperm vaccine or that he is taking a contraceptive pill? Certainly this would be a greater problem in short-term than in long-term relationships. Nevertheless, it seems doubtful that until social changes create an atmosphere in which men and women feel they have an equal responsibility for birth control, many women will prefer to keep conception control in their own hands.

cost. Death rates from the operation range as high as 300 to 500 per 100,000 hysterectomies (Porter and Hulka, 1974). Hysterectomy is a major medical procedure which should be undertaken only when there is a serious health problem such as ovarian tumor.

MALE STERILIZATION: VASECTOMY   More than a half million men are now being voluntarily sterilized each year in the United States under a procedure which is simpler and even less subject to complications than laparoscopy for women. This minor operation, **vasectomy,** can be performed in a doctor's office under local anesthesia. As shown in Fig. 9.6, the doctor makes a small incision in each side of the scrotum to reveal the two vas deferens, which lie near the surface and are responsible for carrying sperm from the testicles to the prostate gland. The doctor then cuts out a small piece of each tube, ties the ends, sews up the incision with a few stitches, and applies a dressing. The whole procedure takes only about fifteen minutes, and the man can immediately resume all his normal activities except for heavy lifting. Because sperm may be present in the first ten to twenty postoperative ejaculations, alternative methods of birth control must be used until testing determines that all sperm cells have left the genital tract.

Vasectomy does not affect a man's sexual functioning. His testicles continue to produce sex hormones, he continues to have orgasms, and his ejaculations contain almost as much semen as before because seminal fluid from the testes contributes only about 10 percent of the total volume.

The reports from physicians on success rates of reversing a vasectomy have been quite varied, ranging from as low as 18 percent to as high as almost 80 percent (Silber and Cohen, 1978). Microsurgery has been employed to surgically reunite the severed ends of the vas. While the initial results from this technique have been promising, it has been found that many men who have had a vasectomy develop antibodies to their own sperm. These antibodies may contribute to permanent sterility even in men who have undergone reconnective surgery.

Fig. 9.6

Vasectomy. These drawings show the incision in the testicles and the removal of a small portion of the vas deferens on each side.

Vasectomy

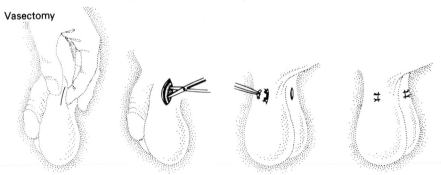

CASE STUDY   *Deciding to Have a Vasectomy*

Chuck and Diane were in their early thirties, had been married for ten years, and had two bright and healthy children. While having a third child would pinch them financially, they felt they could probably afford it. However, the prospect of having another child did not fill them with the joy and anticipation they had felt when they awaited the birth of their first two children. They wondered if it would be right for them to bring another child into the world simply because they could afford it.

Diane had been on the pill since the beginning of the marriage with time out for her two pregnancies. Like many women who accept the risks of chemical methods of birth control, she had grown increasingly concerned about the long-term impact of the drug upon her health. Chuck, too, had been concerned and had agreed that now that Diane was approaching her mid-thirties, when the risks begin to increase, they should try other contraceptive methods. But after the ease and reliability of the pill they found the other options far less compatible with their lovemaking.

At this point, they began to discuss and research permanent means of contraception. Tubal ligation was rejected as a more risky alternative than vasectomy with a greater chance of complications. In addition to concern for Diane's physical safety, both partners felt she had been the one who had carried the burden of contraception throughout their marriage. Now it was Chuck's turn to take responsibility.

The decision was not an easy one. Vasectomies weren't entirely risk-free. There was the small possibility of infection or of failure of the operation. Chuck's doctor mentioned that sometimes there were psychological complications, especially among men who consider their ability to father children an important part of their masculinity. Chuck wasn't very concerned about this problem in his own case, for he felt secure about himself as a person. He and Diane considered other, more serious questions, though. What if they were divorced and Chuck remarried? What if the children were killed in a car wreck?

They agonized over these issues for some time and postponed the decision more than once. Finally, however, they decided to go ahead. They knew their marriage was strong and likely to endure. If one or both of the children were killed, they felt they could never really replace them and believed they would probably be in no condition to try for some time. Ultimately they decided there was little point in living in anticipation of disaster.

Chuck was quite nervous when he went in for the procedure, but the operation was completed successfully and he was back at work the following day. He and Diane felt a great sense of relief that soon they would no longer have to worry about birth control, its side effects, or unwanted pregnancies. They were eager to get on with the rest of their lives.

Source: Adapted from *The Boston Globe*, June 5, 1981.

FOR CLASS DISCUSSION

1. Why do you think vasectomies have grown more popular among American men in recent years? What social factors might help to account for this?

2. Should the length of a couple's marriage be an important factor in their decision to seek sterilization? Why or why not?

Abortion

Abortion, the termination of a pregnancy by the removal of a fetus, has been practiced in many cultures for thousands of years. In ancient China and Europe, for example, abortion early in pregnancy was legal. In the United States before the Civil War abortion was fairly common and newspapers even carried advertisements for abortionists and for drugs that claimed to induce abortion.

During the Civil War era, abortion was declared illegal except in cases in which the mother's life was in danger. The reasons for this are varied. A high mortality rate due to crude, unsafe procedures and a scarcity of antiseptic drugs prompted humanitarian reformers to try to protect women. Economic factors, too, played a role, particularly the belief that population growth was essential to fill the growing demand for labor. Religious groups who held that sex was acceptable only within marriage and for the purpose of procreation also advocated the ban on abortion.

The fact that abortion was illegal did not prevent women from trying to end unwanted pregnancies. Obtaining a relatively safe abortion depended largely on a woman's social class. Upper- and middle-class women could afford to find a cooperative doctor, whereas poor women had to resort to illegal abortionists, often of dubious skill, or to trying to end their pregnancy themselves. Both alternatives took a terrible toll in sterility, injury, and even death.

Even though abortion was legalized in 1973, it remains a highly emotional and divisive social issue. The outcome of the political fight over abortion will have profound implications for many women, especially the poor.

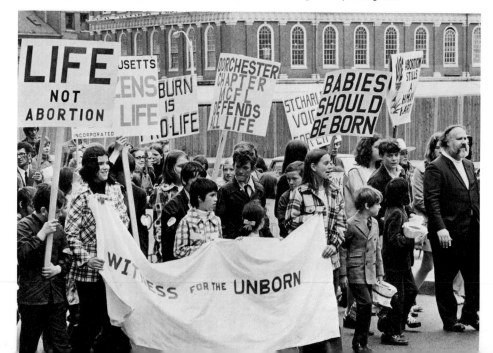

The reemergence of the women's movement during the 1960s saw the beginning of a concerted drive to rescind the ban on abortion. This effort was realized in January 1973, when the United States Supreme Court overturned all restrictive state statutes on abortion. According to the Court, control of her own body is a woman's constitutional right. As Chief Justice Burger put it, "Elaborate argument is hardly necessary to demonstrate that childbirth may deprive a woman of her preferred lifestyle and force upon her a radically different and undesired future" (Wecht, 1975). The Court therefore legalized abortion by request of the mother during the first three months of pregnancy (called the first **trimester**), permitted second-trimester abortions subject to state regulations to safeguard maternal health, and permitted states to restrict abortion after six months (the twenty-fourth week) to cases in which pregnancy endangers the mother's life and health. It is estimated that at least 745,400 legal abortions were performed in 1973, at a rate of 239 abortions for every 1000 live births, while deaths from abortion dropped by over 40 percent (Weinstock et al., 1975). By the late 1970s, almost three out of every ten pregnancies were terminated by abortion (Alan Guttmacher Institute, 1979).

Even though abortion has been legalized, it remains a controversial and emotion-laden issue. Since the Supreme Court decision, highly vocal and well-financed antiabortion groups have brought intense pressure on legislators to make abortion illegal. These "right-to-life" advocates argue that a fetus is a person from the moment of conception and that abortion is murder. Their ultimate goal is the passage of a constitutional amendment prohibiting abortion, and they have been fighting for legislation that will end the use of federal funds for abortion.

The antiabortion groups do not appear to speak for the majority of Americans. A 1979 Gallup survey found that 80 percent of Americans favor permitting therapeutic abortion during at least the first trimester of pregnancy. Only 17 percent opposed abortion under all circumstances. But the antiabortion minority has pressed unceasingly for its point of view and has attracted support from increasingly influential conservative legislators. In June 1977, the Supreme Court provided that states could deny Medicaid payments for abortions and that states could refuse to perform abortions in publicly owned hospitals. The effect of these rulings has been to undermine the ability of many women—especially poor women—to obtain safe abortions. "Pro-choice" advocates, those who believe it is the right of a woman to choose whether or not to have an abortion, contend that right-to-life groups have little concern for the health or welfare of women facing unwanted pregnancies:

> Abortion clinics around the country have been burned, their employees and clients attacked, harassed, and physically endangered. (Boston Women's Health Book Collective, 1979, p. 220)

They argue that much of the money that is now being spent on lobbying and court cases might better be used to improve abortion services (Boston Women's Health Book Collective, 1979).

Whatever an individual's views on the issue, it is clear that abortion has become an important, though not a primary, method of birth control. Though not risk-free, it is relatively safe, particularly when performed during the first trimester. The death rate for legal abortions performed during the first trimester is 1.7 deaths per 100,000 abortions. This is considerably lower than the death rate due to childbirth complications, 11.2 deaths per 100,000.

METHODS USED DURING THE FIRST TRIMESTER **Menstrual aspiration** (also known as menstrual regulation, vacuum aspiration, or endometrial aspiration) has become a common procedure for very early abortion (prior to the eighth week of pregnancy). The doctor simply inserts a slender tube through the cervical opening into the uterus and extracts the monthly menstrual lining by means of a suction pump. No local anesthesia is required as it is not necessary to dilate the cervix. The procedure takes only about two minutes, can be conducted on an outpatient basis, and can be done before pregnancy can be confirmed, making it a less traumatic experience for some women. The patient may briefly have some painful cramping.

The most widely used abortion technique after the seventh week and through the twelfth week is **vacuum curettage**. It is very similar to menstrual aspiration except that the cervical opening is dilated until the tip (vacurette) of a tube can be passed through into the uterus. The fetal tissue is pulled from the uterine wall out of the body by means of a suction pump. The procedure takes about ten minutes. Although complications such as hemorrhage or perforation of the uterus may occur, this happens rarely with a skilled physician.

METHODS USED DURING THE SECOND TRIMESTER   Abortion during the second trimester is more complex, carries more risk of complications than earlier abortion, and is a more difficult physical and emotional experience for the woman. After twelve weeks, the fetus is too large to be aborted by aspiration or curettage, and labor must be induced. Once sixteen weeks have passed, a saline (salt) solution may be injected through the wall of the abdomen into the amniotic fluid. This causes uterine contractions, and the fetus is expelled through the vagina within six to forty-eight hours (Montreal Health Press, 1974). Another method is to inject **prostaglandins** (hormonelike substances that are present naturally in a woman's body at the time of labor and delivery) into the uterus, where they stimulate strong contractions. The fetus is expelled within five to seventy-two hours (Kagan, 1975). If either of these methods fails, a **hysterotomy** (removal of the fetus through an incision) may be attempted.

Having covered the methods of preventing conception or postponing it, we now turn to the subject of pregnancy. For most Americans, it is still true that at some time in their lives they want to experience bringing a child into the world.

 PREGNANCY

While sexual intercourse is a means of expressing deep affection and of gratifying physical needs, it also serves a basic biological function of providing new members for the human race. The creation of a new human life is an extraordinary responsibility, but it can also be a deeply rewarding experience that adds a new dimension to the loving relationship between a man and a woman.

Conception

Human babies are the product of the union of an egg cell from a woman and a sperm cell from a man. These cells are so small that a shoebox could hold all the eggs that produced the earth's current population, and a thimble all the sperm. But, when united, they "know" how to develop into trillions of cells differentiated into the complex systems of the human body (Rugh and Shettles, 1971). The point at which the egg is fertilized by the sperm and they begin this process is called **conception**.

THE FEMALE MENSTRUAL CYCLE   Every month a woman's body prepares itself for the possibility of conception. From an initial supply of perhaps 400,000 immature eggs at birth, only about 400 will eventually mature (Rugh and Shettles, 1971). Every twenty-eight days on the average—though the length of the cycle may vary from twenty-four to thirty-five days—one of the two ovaries is stimulated by hormonal cues to release an egg cell. As the egg is released, it is drawn into the nearer of the two fallopian tubes by the waving, hairlike projections which surround the opening of the tube. For several hours, it remains at the top of the tube where fertilization might take place, then travels down the tube toward the uterus. There hormonal secretions, first of estrogen and then progesterone, have stimulated the uterine lining to thicken, increase its blood supply, and secrete nourishing substances for the development of a fertilized egg. If no sperm fertilizes the egg within eighteen to twenty-four hours, it quickly degenerates, the bloody lining is shed in the process called **menstruation,** and the cycle begins again. For counting purposes, the onset of menstruation is regarded as the beginning of the menstrual cycle. **Ovulation,** the release of an egg from one of the ovaries, occurs ten to eighteen days after the beginning of the cycle.

FERTILIZATION   When a man has an orgasm during penile-vaginal intercourse, hundreds of millions of his sperm cells are forcefully ejaculated through his urethra into the upper part of the woman's vagina. As the microscopic cells swim about in every direction, some die because of the acidity of the vagina, some become tangled in the mucus of the cervix, some do not survive the long swim through the uterus, and some head down the wrong fallopian tube. Those that do enter the tube containing that month's egg must swim against the currents that propel the egg toward the uterus. Many of the remaining sperm cells become trapped in crevices in the body tissue, where they are destroyed as alien matter by the woman's white blood cells.

Sperm cells that reach the upper fallopian tubes can live for two to three days there, and fertilization may take place during that time if an egg arrives. When a live sperm cell manages to collide with a viable egg during the period of twelve to twenty-four hours that a woman is fertile in each cycle, it makes its way through the outer layers of the egg, which then seals itself off to penetration by any other sperm. The collective effect of enormous numbers of sperm cells in the vicinity of the egg is apparently necessary to its penetration by a single cell; they seem to secrete an enzyme which dissolves the covering of the egg (Tortora and Anaguostakos, 1975).

The genetic material from the male, carried as twenty-three chromosomes in the nucleus of the sperm, joins the twenty-three chromosomes of the egg. The 30,000 genes carried on the twenty-three pairs of chromosomes of the fertilized egg serve as a blueprint for the development of a new and unique human being. These chomosomal instructions will become part of every cell in the body and will determine a broad range of traits. One chromosome from each parent is a sex chromosome. The sex chromosomes in the ova are all alike and are called X chromosomes, while the chromosomes found in sperm may be either X or Y. When the male partner contributes an X, the baby will be a girl (XX), and when he contributes a Y, the baby will be a boy (XY).

From Zygote to Embryo

Once fertilization has occurred, the egg, now called a **zygote**, begins to produce more cells through a complex series of divisions. As it does, it is moving down the fallopian tube to the uterus, a journey of about four inches. Approximately seven days after conception, it implants itself in the uterine wall and draws nourishment from it until a saclike organ called the **placenta** can be formed. The placenta acts as an intermediary between the mother and fetus to draw nutrients and oxygen from the mother's bloodstream and excrete wastes into it. The mother's blood never mixes with that of the fetus, for the exchanges take place by diffusion across membranes. So efficient is the transfer that nourishment just digested by the mother can reach the fetus within an hour (Rugh and Shettles, 1971).

The term **embryo** is used in referring to the developing human organism in its first eight weeks of existence. One month after it is conceived, the embryo, which began life as a one-celled structure the size of a pin point, has already developed a head, a curved trunk, and a tail-like structure (the end of a developing spinal column which has temporarily outgrown the rest of the body). A drawing of the embryo is shown in Fig. 9.7. Though only a quarter of an inch long, the embryo has a primitive digestive system in the form of a food tube, a tiny heart, forty pairs of miniature muscle blocks, a primitive brain, a kidney similar to that of a frog which helps with excretion but will later be replaced, and gill slits which become the eustachian tubes of the ears. Its arms appear as buds, which develop hand plates and then definite finger ridges by the time it is six weeks old. At seven weeks, its primitive reproductive organs have differentiated into either ovaries or testicles. By the end of two

Fig. 9.7

The developing embryo at about three weeks. The chorionic villi invade the uterine lining and together with the attached lining form the placenta.

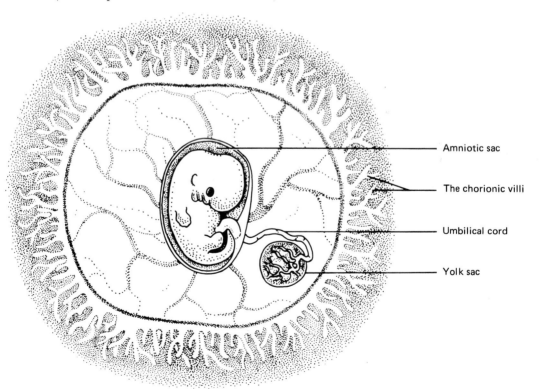

Amniotic sac

The chorionic villi

Umbilical cord

Yolk sac

months, the embryo, about an inch long, has developed rudimentary arms and legs, as well as the beginning of recognizable eyes, fingers, and toes. From this time until birth it is called a **fetus** (Rugh and Shettles, 1971).

Pregnancy Tests

By the time the embryo is a month old, the mother's menstrual period is about two weeks overdue. She may experience some or all of the following symptoms: increased tenderness and enlargement of the breasts, darkening of the area around the nipples, nausea or "morning sickness" (which for some women occurs in the evening rather than the morning), sleepiness, fatigue, and the need to urinate frequently.

Pregnancy should be medically confirmed, for a woman unaware of her pregnancy might continue to use drugs that could be dangerous to the embryo in its critical early development. Tests for pregnancy are generally done in a doctor's office or a medical laboratory. Early pregnancy is usually determined by means of urine-sample tests for the presence of the hormone **human chorionic gonadotropin (HCG)** which is secreted by the developing embryo. When used for women whose periods are at least two weeks overdue, these tests are about 97 percent accurate (McCary, 1971). The fastest test of this type requires only about two minutes. All the woman has to do is provide her first morning specimen of urine.

A blood test is also available for determining the presence of HCG, but is is expensive and is used less commonly. It does have the advantage of detecting pregnancy very early—about five days before the first missed period. A recent innovation is relatively inexpensive **early pregnancy tests (EPTs)** that can be purchased without prescription for home use. These tests are supposed to detect the presence of HCG as early as nine days after a missed period. In recent studies only 3 percent of home tests indicated pregnancy when the woman was not pregnant, but 20 percent failed to detect pregnancy when the woman was pregnant (McQuarrie and Flanagan, 1979). Thus it is advisable to have the testing done by a doctor or medical laboratory.

Fetal Development

During the third month of its development, the fetus is about three inches long. The features of the face take on a more distinct shape, the fingers and toes are well developed, and the eyelids are formed (although they are fused shut). The kidneys, liver, intestines, and lungs begin rudimentary functioning.

By the fourth month, the sex of the fetus can be visually distinguished and such external structures as the fingernails, eyebrows, and eyelashes are present. The weight increases to about four ounces and the length to about six inches. Fine, downy hair covers the skin.

Diagnosing Fetal Abnormality

About 5 out of 100 babies born in the United States have a serious birth defect or will develop mental retardation. Twenty percent of birth defects are hereditary—passed on through genetic inheritance; the remaining 80 percent are congenital—acquired during development in the uterus. Examples of causes of congenital defects are use of drugs and exposure to diseases or X-rays during pregnancy. The age of the mother has also been linked to fetal abnormalities. Babies born to women over the age of thirty-five are more prone to birth defects, and after forty the incidence rises dramatically. Down's syndrome (formerly called mongolism), for example, is found in only 1 out of 2000 babies born to mothers twenty-five years of age, but in 1 out of 50 babies born to mothers over age forty-five (Rugh and Shettles, 1971).

In recent years, a new technique has been developed for detecting a number of severe hereditary or chromosomal disorders. This procedure, called **amniocentesis,** is simple, reliable, and carries relatively little risk to mother and fetus. It is performed between the fourteenth and sixteenth weeks of pregnancy. First, a photographic scan of the position of the fetus in the uterus is made by means of sound waves (ultra sound). Then a hollow needle is inserted through the abdominal wall into the uterus and a sample of the amniotic fluid is extracted. Analysis of the amniotic fluid can reveal a range of chromosomal abnormalities including Down's syndrome, Tay-Sachs disease (a fatal

(continued)

Uterine wall

Placenta

Amniotic cavity

Cervix

Cell culture: Biochemical and chromosomal analyses

Amniocentesis

genetic disease found primarily among Jews), cystic fibrosis, and Rh incompatibility (in which Rh-negative antibodies from the mother destroy Rh-positive blood cells of the fetus).

Fetal abnormalities have been found in 4 percent of fetuses of women undergoing amniocentesis. These women may choose to have an abortion. However, the results of the chromosome analysis may not be complete until the twentieth to twenty-fourth week of pregnancy. As noted in the text, late abortion is more dangerous than abortion performed during early pregnancy and is more emotionally and physically taxing for the pregnant woman, since it requires that the woman go through labor to expel the fetus.

An interesting aspect of amniocentesis is that it can accurately determine the sex of the fetus. But this is an additional piece of information and not the primary purpose of the procedure. Amniocentesis is now recommended for pregnant women who are thirty-five years of age or older. It is not routinely performed on women under thirty-five.

At the end of the fifth month, the fetus has all its essential structures. From this point on, development consists of further refinements and gains in length and weight.

Studies of infants born prematurely at seven months show that reflexes which may be of survival value are already well developed. If held erect, they will try to walk. They will turn toward a touch on the cheek and suck when their lips are stroked. Some fetuses are so skillful in this respect that they suck their thumbs (Rugh and Shettles, 1971). If startled, seven-month-old "preemies" will throw their arms and legs out and cry, as though trying to find something to cling to. Their fingers and toes curl around any object placed across them, another adaptation that probably served our hairier ancestors well.

Despite the sophistication of their motor reflexes, seven-month-old fetuses have only a fairly good chance of survival if they are born prematurely. They weigh only two or three pounds and, due to the immaturity of their central nervous systems, they are unable to regulate their own body temperature. Both their breathing and their temperature maintenance must be aided by special equipment. By eight months, however, the chances of survival increase dramatically.

By the time the fetus reaches full term, it weighs an average of seven pounds. It so fills the uterus that there is very little room for movement. It has lost the downy hair covering its body, and its skin, which was red and wrinkled before, is smoother. From four to two weeks before delivery, the baby's head moves into position in the pelvis, a process known as **lightening** or **engagement**.

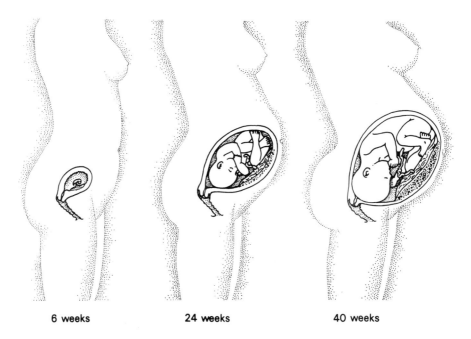

6 weeks   24 weeks   40 weeks

Fig. 9.8
*Development of the fetus at 6 weeks, 24 weeks, and term. The
relationship between changes in the fetus and changes in the
mother is shown.*

It will remain this way until it is born. The development of the fetus is shown
in Fig. 9.8.

 THE PREGNANCY EXPERIENCE

The Pregnant Woman

Pregnancy is a time of a great many physical and emotional changes. How a
woman reacts to the experience will vary according to such factors as her self-
image, her feelings and those of her partner about having children, her
relationship with her partner, the smoothness or difficulty of the pregnancy
itself, her knowledge of childbearing, and her confidence or lack of it regarding
her potential as a parent. She may feel joyful and expectant, or depressed and
fearful. She may feel that pregnancy has robbed her of her sexual appeal or,
conversely, she may feel unusually attractive. Probably she will experience all
these emotions and others at different times during the pregnancy.

During the first trimester (the first twelve weeks), the pregnant woman may have some of the physical symptoms mentioned earlier. In addition, she may have some bowel irregularity because of the increased pressure in her lower abdomen, and her vaginal secretions may increase. Many women, however, are pleased to find that they feel relatively little discomfort:

> Early pregnancy surprised me. I was expecting to feel very different, and instead was feeling things I'd felt before. It was like premenstrual tension. I was a little nauseous. But it's amazing, once I realized I was pregnant the symptoms were tolerable because they are not signs of sickness, but life-producing. (Boston Women's Health Book Collective, 1979, p. 258)

In the second trimester (the thirteenth to twenty-sixth week), the pregnancy becomes more obvious to the outside world. The waistline thickens and the woman begins to gain weight. By the fifth month, the fetal movement can be felt as a light fluttering (this occurs earlier in subsequent pregnancies). Before long the mother will feel solid kicks. The breasts, stimulated by hormones, have enlarged and are preparing for nursing. Fatigue and nausea experienced during the first trimester are usually gone now, and many women feel especially healthy and happy.

The uterus and abdomen enlarge considerably during the third trimester (twenty-seventh to thirty-eighth or fortieth week). The resulting pressure on the stomach as it is pushed upward in the abdominal cavity often causes indigestion, and pressure on the bladder causes frequent urination. The fetal movements are very strong now, and the pregnant woman and her partner may be amazed to feel and even see the outline of an elbow or foot kicking against the abdomen. Painless contractions of the uterus occur in preparation for labor. As the time of delivery approaches, most women feel a sense of impatience and eagerness for the baby to be born.

The Male Partner's Reaction

In the past few years, there have been major changes in the involvement of the father during pregnancy and childbirth. Much of this has been due to the prepared-childbirth movement and changes in the male role that include greater responsibility for childrearing. Whereas in the past pregnancy was seen as something only women could experience, today more expectant fathers want to be informed about the pregnancy and to participate in every possible way. Some enlightened obstetricians ask the father to be present at the woman's prenatal examinations, and husbands frequently attend pregnancy and childbirth classes. Some employers are even beginning to grant paternity leaves after the baby is born.

Like the pregnant woman herself, her partner may experience conflicting emotions. He may feel exuberant, but he may also feel anxiety about the responsibility of helping to support and rear a child. Many husbands are especially solicitous of their wives during this time. The male partner may be fascinated, perplexed, or just amused by his mate's changing shape. Some men feel left out, as the following anecdote shows:

> I wanted to be a part of the process, so when Diana made her first visit to the doctor's I went along. As I started to go down the hall with her to the examining room the nurse told me, "We'll be right with you, Mr. W." So I ended up sitting in the waiting room. . . . When at last the nurse motioned me in, it was to discuss insurance, hospital payment plans and the doctor's billing policy. (Boston Women's Health Book Collective, 1979, p. 37)

Intercourse during Pregnancy

During pregnancy couples often find that their pattern of sexual relations changes. Several studies have found that frequency and/or enjoyment of intercourse tend to drop as the pregnancy progresses (Morris, 1975; Tolor and DiGrazia, 1976). A couple's own feelings about making love during this time are an important determinant of how long to continue intercourse. Some women may feel their body is being invaded; both partners may worry about harming the baby. Other couples, however, may experience enhanced pleasure in their sexual relationship. Masters and Johnson (1966) found that many women have heightened orgasmic potential during the second trimester.

MEDICAL CONCERNS For many years, doctors routinely discouraged intercourse for six weeks before and six weeks after the birth of a baby. But in recent years, medical attitudes have shifted toward support for continuing intercourse throughout pregnancy, since it was felt that the risks to the fetus were slight. Even so, the evidence does not entirely rule out intercourse as a cause of some miscarriages and premature deliveries.

A study which examined records from nearly 27,000 pregnancies found that infections of the amniotic fluid surrounding the fetus were more common among women who had intercourse during the pregnancy. Amniotic infections appeared to be linked to premature birth, infant respiratory difficulties, jaundice, and sometimes death (Naeye, 1979). Although this research is not conclusive, it suggests that caution is called for, especially by women who have had previous miscarriages or premature deliveries. Other warning signals—such as abdominal pain, uterine bleeding, expectation of miscarriage, or rupturing of the amniotic sac—make it imperative to avoid intercourse or genital stimulation of the woman to orgasm.

Prenatal Influences and Nutrition

Despite widespread mythology, most women are not in a delicate condition when they are pregnant. Exercise is healthful in preventing backache and improving muscle tone for labor, although the amount of exercise that is appropriate during pregnancy depends upon the amount the woman exercises prior to her pregnancy. Since the fetus is well cushioned by the amniotic fluid, it will rarely be harmed by jarring even if the expectant mother falls. An extreme example of this is the Welsh woman who delivered a normal baby six months after she was struck by lightning (Tanner and Taylor, 1968)!

Even so, the uterus cannot protect the fetus from all dangerous prenatal influences. In addition to nutrients, many chemicals, viruses, and bacteria pass from the pregnant woman's bloodstream through the placenta to the fetus. Thus any drug ingested by the woman or any disease she contracts may potentially harm her baby. German measles in the expectant mother can cause severe fetal abnormalities and even death. Chicken pox, pneumonia, scarlet fever, and syphilis may so damage the fetus that it is spontaneously aborted or else stillborn at full term. If fetuses do not die from untreated syphilis in the expectant mother, they may be born with misshapen and shortened limbs, distortions in the face and teeth, severe brain damage, or blindness. Unlike syphilis, gonorrhea cannot cross the placenta to harm the fetus. Instead, it reaches the fetus as it is born, causing eye infections which may lead to blindness. Gonorrhea is so widespread that every state in this country requires that the eyes of all newborns be treated with medication immediately after birth (Grover, 1971).

So many drugs can have adverse effects on the fetus that women of childbearing age—even those who do not know that they are pregnant—are cautioned against taking any medication without the advice of a doctor. It is not yet widely known that even aspirin may cause fetal abnormalities. Antihistamines may cause miscarriages or deformities, tranquilizers and antidepressants may cause abnormal development of the arms and legs, and diuretics may cause fetal kidney problems. LSD users may have deformed babies with chromosomal abnormalities. Use of heroin may cause convulsions and sometimes death of the fetus, and morphine addicts may give birth to addicted babies with respiratory problems.

Materials in cigarette smoke pass through the placenta, impairing the circulation of blood in the fetus and lowering its oxygen content. Women who smoke two packs of cigarettes a day may stunt the growth of the fetus by 10 percent, endangering its survival. Smokers are more prone to having miscarriages, premature births, and babies with low birth weight or convulsions than women who do not smoke (Rugh and Shettles, 1971). More infants born to smokers die than infants born to nonsmokers (Meyer and Tonascia, 1977).

Alcohol, too, is dangerous to a developing fetus. Women who drink heavily during pregnancy (three ounces of alcohol a day) give birth more frequently to babies with facial, limb, and heart defects than women who do not drink (Katchadourian and Lunde, 1980). Caffeine, which is present in coffee, tea, and cola drinks, has also been implicated in birth defects.

It is extremely important that the pregnant woman eat enough of the right foods to build fetal health. Her diet should be high in protein, vitamin-

and mineral-rich vegetables, fruits, and whole grains. Protein deficiency in the expectant mother has been linked to low IQ in the child. Other nutritional inadequacies may be responsible for low birth weight, prematurity, infection, and brain damage in the infant, and anemia and other complications in the mother during pregnancy or delivery (Boston Women's Health Book Collective, 1979).

Although until recently doctors insisted that pregnant women restrict their weight gain, the Committee on Maternal Nutrition of the National Academy of Sciences of the National Research Council now urges that pregnant women gain about twenty-five pounds. Most of this weight will be lost when the baby is born or soon after; the rest will be quickly used up in milk production if the mother chooses to nurse her baby. Many studies have shown that if the pregnant woman is permitted to gain weight normally, labor, delivery, and nursing are likely to be easy for her. Her baby is likely to be healthier, smarter, and easier to take care of than the smaller babies born to women who gained less than twenty pounds with their pregnancies (Davis, 1972).

CHILDBIRTH

Despite the possibilities that something might go wrong, most fetuses carried full term in this country are born alive. As they leave the protection of their mothers' bodies, most babies successfully take over their own life-support functions. How the woman views her pregnancy, her physical and emotional readiness for childbirth, support or lack of it from the expectant father, hospital or home delivery arrangements, and physical factors in the course of delivering the baby will make a difference in whether the birth of a child is a joyous occasion or a time of anxiety.

Stages of Childbirth

The process of giving birth is summarized in Fig. 9.9.

FIRST STAGE The process of giving birth is divided into three stages. First-stage labor is signaled by regular contractions of the uterus. Although many women experience mild early contractions at intervals of fifteen to twenty minutes, many others have initial contractions farther apart or as close together as four or five minutes. A frequent indication of the onset of labor is the **bloody show** (the discharge from the cervix of the mucous plug that has protected the uterus from infection during the pregnancy). The rupture of the amniotic sac (popularly called "breaking the bag of waters") may or may not occur at this time.

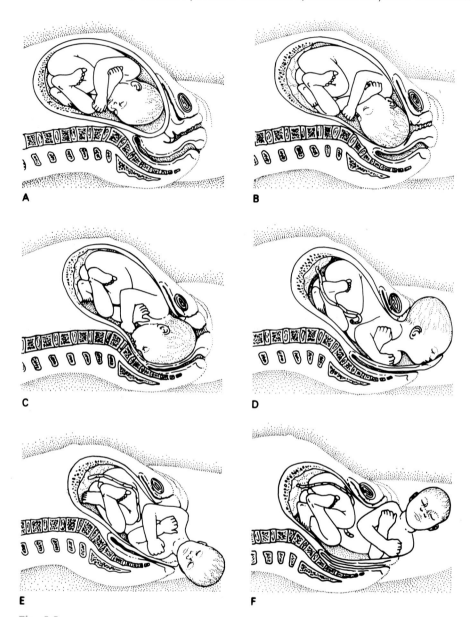

Fig. 9.9

The process of birth. (A) The baby floats in the amniotic fluid before labor begins. (B) Rhythmic contractions force the baby's head against the cervix. (C) Descent through the birth canal begins, with the head gradually rotating and extending. (D) The head crowns and the baby begins to emerge from the birth canal. (E) and (F) Again the baby rotates as first one shoulder and then the other is delivered.

The uterine contractions of first-stage labor are accompanied by dilation of the cervix to permit the passage of the baby's head. The first stage is further subdivided by the extent of dilation: early phase—up to five centimeters; late phase—five to eight centimeters; transition—eight to ten centimeters. The transition phase is the shortest and most difficult part of labor. Contractions come very close together and are very intense.

SECOND STAGE   Once the cervix has dilated to ten centimeters, second-stage labor begins. This stage involves pushing to expel the baby from the body and usually lasts from one-half to two hours. Doctors frequently offer anesthesia. However, as this is a time during which a woman can use her strength to help her baby be born, many who have prepared themselves for childbirth prefer not to have anesthesia. When the baby's head begins to appear (called "crowning"), the attending doctor may perform an **episiotomy,** a small incision to enlarge the vaginal opening and prevent tearing during delivery. Although this is done routinely, it is usually not necessary if hot compresses have been applied and the perineal area massaged with oil throughout second-stage labor to make it more elastic. As the fetus emerges fully, the doctor usually extracts mucus from its mouth and nose with a syringe. Under normal circumstances, the baby will gasp or cry as its lungs suddenly fill with air and it begins to breathe.

When the umbilical cord stops pulsating, it is clamped near the baby's abdomen and clamped again about four inches away. If the father has been participating in the delivery, he may be permitted to cut the cord.

THIRD STAGE   The third stage of labor is the delivery of the placenta. This occurs within two to twenty minutes after delivery of the baby. The placenta is checked for abnormalities and to assure that all of it has been expelled. If some of the placenta is retained in the mother's body, hemorrhaging may result.

One minute, and then five minutes, after the baby is born it is given an **Apgar score** evaluating its heart rate, respiration, muscle tone, reflex response, and color. An Apgar score of 4 or lower indicates that the baby is in distress and needs immediate attention. Most babies have an Apgar score of 7 or higher. Shortly after delivery the baby's eyes are treated for possible gonorrheal infection.

Caesarean Deliveries

The birth process does not always proceed smoothly. A number of complications may arise which call for evaluation by a doctor or midwife to determine whether to continue with a vaginal delivery. In high-risk pregnancies, in premature births, or in instances in which there is a sudden adverse change in the condition of the mother or baby, a **caesarean section** may be called for.

Childbirth: One Father's Observations

More and more fathers are being allowed into the delivery room to watch their children being born. What's it like being there when it happens rather than outside pacing in the waiting room? Here's one father's story of what he felt when he saw his first child's birth.

I watched my baby being born.

I looked into the delivery room's overhead mirror. His head was sliding out, like a turtle peeling out of its shell.

He was absolutely still and almost blue-gray in color.

Then, as if the finger of God touched him, his mouth opened and he started to cry.

As the doctor pulled him out, he turned a shade of purple, then red.

"Adeline, we have a child. It's a boy. It's unbelievable. Look at our beautiful son. Adeline, I love you, you're fantastic."

My wife was under a minimum of anesthesia. She looked at the quivering, howling boy. She smiled, and her eyes shone.

I never knew I could feel the sort of love I felt then. I didn't know human beings had the capacity.

I started crying myself.

I felt a soaring sense that life is a miracle, that this child, his face furious with the shock of entering the world, was precious and unique.

It began at 4:30 A.M. with a nudge in the ribs and "Let's go to the hospital."

Adeline calmly packed her overnight bag.

She was in labor for almost eight hours. The contractions were mild at first. Then they came in stabbing waves. She breathed in rhythm with them.

At one point she gave up. Her body was on a trip her mind didn't want to know anything about. She tried to ignore the next contraction.

In the darkened labor room she grabbed my arm and squeezed.

"Breathe, darling, breathe!" I shouted.

She caught the rhythm again. She relaxed her grip. She groaned. I felt foolish.

The doctor came in.

"Well, we'll have a baby in about ten minutes," he said matter of factly.

Something inside me popped like a soap bubble. For hours I had only been thinking of Adeline and the pain. I had actually forgotten about the end result.

A nurse escorted me like a helpless kitten to the "fathers's dressing room."

I scrubbed hands and arms, donned a surgical gown, paper boots, and a mask. I put my foot right through one of the boots.

The delivery room scene belonged to Adeline. I believe I made it easier for her in some ways by my presence and encouragement. But as close as I was, the arena for the act of birth was her body, and I knew I could never fully share it.

My eyes soaked in everything. The placenta, the umbilical cord, the way it pulsed, almost like a link between a submarine and its mother ship.

I was there. Nobody had to come out and say: "Congratulations, Mr. Brewer, you're a father, your wife just gave birth to a beautiful boy."

I knew it now. I had a son. My son.

Source: John Brewer, Associated Press, January 21, 1976.

This procedure involves making an incision through the abdominal wall and into the uterus. The baby is then removed by the doctor and the incision is stitched.

During the 1970s, the number of babies delivered by caesarean section tripled (from 6 percent to 18 percent). During the same period, caesarean deliveries in **breech presentations** (when the baby is facing feet or buttocks down rather than head down) rose from 11 percent to 60 percent. These figures created enough concern that a National Institutes of Health task force was created to consider the issue. The panel found that several major factors account for the dramatic rise in caesarean deliveries: (1) improvement in the safety of the procedure; (2) the extensive use of electronic fetal monitoring devices during labor; (3) the attitude of surgeons that once a woman has given birth by caesarean section she must have a caesarean in all subsequent deliveries (the reason given is that the uterus might be ruptured through the scar left by the previous operation); (4) the use of caesarean sections in **dystocia,** or difficult labor, which can mean anything from weak contractions to a baby that is too big to be delivered vaginally (*Newsweek*, October 6, 1980, p. 105).

The task force study concluded that the number of caesarean births could be reduced. The procedure has not improved maternal and infant death rates to a degree that warrants such a large increase in its use. For example, while caesarean section is safer than before, maternal deaths related to caesarean deliveries are still two to four times higher than for vaginal deliveries. Moreover, since a new surgical incision has for the most part replaced the

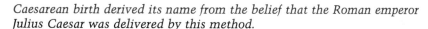

Caesarean birth derived its name from the belief that the Roman emperor Julius Caesar was delivered by this method.

larger incision used in the past, there seems to be less basis for the argument that a woman who has had one caesarean birth must have all subsequent babies by caesarean. As for difficult labor, the task force suggested that doctors should use methods to encourage labor (for example, having the woman walk around) rather than resort to caesarean delivery. Finally, breech babies can be delivered vaginally if a doctor is skilled in the use of forceps (*Newsweek*, October 6, 1980).

Pain Relievers: Some Cautions

Labor may be experienced as painful. For those who find it very difficult, a variety of drugs may be used to ease the childbearing process. **Analgesics** decrease the sensation of pain; **amnesics** erase the memory of pain; and **anesthetics** block all sensation, either by producing unconsciousness or by cutting off the transmission of pain sensations to the brain. Anesthetics may be general, rendering the mother unconscious, or local, in which case they are injected at the base of the spine to numb sensation in the lower body.

Despite their benefits so far as the woman's comfort is concerned, drugs can prolong labor by weakening the uterine contractions. They can also cross the placenta and endanger the fetus. Administered in dosages considered safe for the woman's body weight, analgesics and anesthetics may act as depressants on the fetus's respiratory system. This makes it difficult for newborn babies to begin breathing after birth and may cause mild brain damage from a critical loss of oxygen at the moment of birth. Artificial respiration may sometimes have to be used to get the baby's breathing started.

There is increasing evidence that the depressant effect of pain-relieving drugs given to the woman persists in the baby long after birth. The development of such behaviors as smiling, cuddliness, motor maturity, self-defensive movements, and habituation to neutral stimuli like the sound of a bell may be significantly impaired for varying periods of up to one month after birth, and perhaps much longer. Behavior patterns such as trembling and fearfulness seem to be linked to the long-term effects of certain tranquilizers (Aleksandrowicz and Aleksandrowicz, 1974).

ADVANCES IN CHILDBIRTH AND FERTILITY

The Prepared-Childbirth Movement

Even before evidence on the effects of pain relievers on the newborn began to accumulate, some women questioned the need to be drugged rather than actively participate in delivering their babies. Aided by the pioneering efforts of Dr. Grantly Dick Read and Dr. Fernand Lamaze, more and more women have returned to the age-old practice of childbearing without medication. On the premise that pain is a result of muscular tension, which in turn comes from fear of the unknown, these women and their partners attend special prepared-childbirth classes which teach them what to expect during labor. The woman is taught how to relax with each contraction, often through using special breathing exercises, and to take an active part in pushing during the second stage of labor. Often the father takes the role of labor coach, helping the woman to relax and encouraging her as she uses her breathing exercises. Awake in the delivery room, the mother can watch the birth of her baby in a mirror and she can hold and nurse her infant immediately. For many couples prepared childbirth is a supremely rewarding emotional experience.

Family-Centered Childbirth

Hospital arrangements for labor, delivery, and the postpartum housing of mother and child are no longer as impersonal as they used to be. The current trend is to approximate the natural family setting without sacrificing the safety of the mother and baby. Recent research has confirmed what mothers have long suspected—that something is wrong with the hospital tradition of separating anxious fathers and lonely mothers during labor and delivery and isolating their babies afterward. Under these circumstances, the woman's labor may be prolonged by the fear and stress of unfamiliar surroundings, and the forming of crucial ties between mother, father, and baby may be delayed until the mother's release from the hospital four or more days after she gives birth. Breast-feeding and cuddling, special forms of early closeness between mother and child, are inhibited by such routines.

There is evidence that the hours—perhaps the first day—after birth constitute an important bonding period for mother and child. Maximum early contact with the baby is especially important in stimulating maternal feelings in women who have not been well mothered themselves, who are young or unmarried, do not want their babies, or do not have a good family situation at home. It seems that the more contact the mother has with the baby after birth, the faster she recovers physically and emotionally from childbearing (McCleary, 1974).

Many hospitals now permit the father to be with the mother in labor and sometimes even in the delivery room. A recent study by Case Western Reserve University (Sosa et al., 1980) found that women whose husbands are permitted to be with them during childbirth have shorter deliveries and fewer complications. The women who gave birth with only nurses and doctors present had two to three times more problems during labor that required intervention, spent more than twice as long in labor, were less awake after the delivery, and were less interested in the baby. As mentioned previously, some men act as labor coaches for their wives, helping them to breathe through the contractions according to their training in prepared-childbirth classes. Some hospitals also allow the father to handle the baby. This situation facilitates his attachment to his child far more than if he is only permitted to view it through the windows of a nursery.

Birthing Rooms

Another recent innovation is the birthing room. This is a special room that is usually located in or adjoining a conventional hospital and is furnished in a homelike way. The pregnant woman can have her family, friends, and a birth attendant present as well as her doctor. She labors and gives birth in the same room rather than laboring in one room and giving birth in another. Birthing rooms are becoming a popular choice for women who prefer a more homelike setting, who wish to undergo prepared childbirth without medication, and who have experienced no complications during pregnancy but still want the reassurance of immediate backup equipment in case of emergency.

Rooming-in

Rooming-in arrangements are now offered as an additional option by some hospitals. Instead of the traditional separation of mother and baby, broken by brief periods during which the baby is brought in for breast or bottle feeding (in the latter case the mother is given hormones to dry up her milk supply), rooming-in enables the baby to stay with the mother in a bassinet next to her bed for most of the day. She can look at and cuddle the infant, nurse it, and receive instructions in its care.

A study comparing fifty mothers rooming-in with their firstborns to fifty first-time mothers who did not have rooming-in found that those with rooming-in felt more competent and confident in themselves as mothers when they left the hospital. They felt that they could understand what was wrong when their babies were crying and did not anticipate needing as much help when they got home as mothers who had less experience with their babies. Rooming-in mothers were also quicker to develop a strong attachment to their babies (Greenberg, Rosenberg, and Lind, 1973).

The Leboyer Method

While rooming-in undeniably provides a baby with more loving attention than a nursery does, one crusader is calling for more sympathetic treatment of the baby as a feeling person from the moment of birth. In his book *Birth Without Violence*, French obstetrician Frederick Leboyer argues that emergence from the hours of compression in the birth canal into a brightly lit, noisy room is a terrible shock to the newborn. When Leboyer delivers babies, he dims the lights, asks for silence, and refuses to jar the baby into breathing by holding it upside down and spanking it. Instead, he lays the infant on its mother's belly and allows it to begin breathing gradually before severing the umbilical cord. To further ease the transition, he then immerses the newborn in a bath warmed to body temperature. According to his account, in this approximation of its former weightless floating the infant relaxes, opens it eyes, looks about in awe and curiosity, moves its limbs tentatively at first and then almost playfully, and sometimes even breaks into a blissful smile. Leboyer's methods are attracting considerable attention in this country, but many doctors worry that babies handled so gently will not begin breathing properly. Others contend that the Leboyer method has no special advantages.

Home Birth

In recent years, there has been a renewal of interest in giving birth at home, as most American women did prior to the 1930s. Home birth offers a number

Home birth is becoming increasingly popular among couples who believe their own home is the most desirable setting for this very special experience in their lives.

of advantages, including the familiar surroundings, the presence and often the active participation of family and friends, the ability to make decisions about delivery with a doctor who is sympathetic to the couple's particular needs, the reduced expense, and the assurance that the couple will not be separated from their newborn for any length of time. The major drawback is the lack of immediate emergency equipment should complications arise.

Home birth requires careful planning. Couples are screened for possible risks, they generally attend classes designed especially for those planning home births, and they often employ the services of a midwife who monitors the course of the pregnancy and is present at the birth along with a doctor. Women who are under twenty or over thirty and are giving birth for the first time are considered at higher risk and are usually discouraged from home birth. And women who experience problems during a first pregnancy or have a history of pregnancy-related problems are advised to give birth in a hospital.

Although home birth is common in Europe, in this country it is a controversial issue among medical practitioners. Some states prohibit mid-wives from practicing, and some hospitals make it difficult for doctors who do home births to have hospital privileges. As more women give birth successfully at home and as more research becomes available on the safety of home birth, perhaps this situation will change.

Infertility and Its Treatment

Infertility is generally defined as the inability to conceive after a year or more of sexual relations without contraception. An estimated 10 to 15 percent of couples in the United States who want to be parents are infertile. While many people believe that infertility is always traced to the woman, in fact about 35 percent of cases are caused by male factors, 35 percent by female factors, and the remaining 30 percent by a combination of both.

Infertility in men may be caused by an insufficient production of sperm, low motility (ability of the sperm to swim), inability to deposit sperm in the vagina near the cervix, blockage of the passageways carrying the sperm from the testicles to the urethra, or emotional factors. In women infertility may result from various kinds of pelvic infection, endometriosis (growth of endo-metrial tissue somewhere other than in the lining of the uterus), blockage of the fallopian tubes, failure to ovulate, cervical infection, or emotional factors.

Initial diagnosis of infertility usually includes physical examination of both partners, semen analysis for the man, and a pelvic examination of the woman. In addition, the woman is asked to keep a basal temperature chart every day over two menstrual cycles to determine ovulation patterns. Because male infertility is easier to diagnose (due to the male anatomy), testing often begins with the man. If there are fewer than 20 million sperm cells in the ejaculate, chances for conception are slim (Rugh and Shettles, 1971).

When further testing of the woman is indicated, the couple may have a postcoital test. This requires having intercourse just prior to ovulation and within several hours seeing the doctor for examination of the cervical mucus containing the sperm. Another test that may be combined with this one involves forcing carbon dioxide through the fallopian tubes to determine if there is blockage. If no blockage or other problems are found, the doctor may perform a culdoscopy or laparoscopy in order to view the reproductive system directly.

To date treatment of male infertility has not been very successful. Female problems respond better—particularly problems of ovulation and implantation or cervical conditions. An estimated 50 to 70 percent of all childless couples are eventually able to have a baby (Kaufman, 1978); an estimated 5 percent are eventually able to conceive without medical treatment (Boston Women's Health Book Collective, 1979).

Testing for infertility may be long and arduous. It can rob a couple's sexual expression of spontaneity and privacy, and it can contribute to tensions in a marriage, as the following anecdote shows:

> My husband's sperm count was very low; we were both crushed. I don't think my husband believed it was actually happening. In fact he often talked in the third person, not truly accepting the results. . . . I couldn't say the typical "Oh, it's all right" because we both knew it really wasn't all right. (Boston Women's Health Book Collective, 1979, p. 320)

Couples who learn they are infertile may experience profound grief at the loss of a potential child. They may also feel that they are less manly or womanly.

Once they have accepted the situation, some infertile couples consider adopting a child. However, the popularity of birth control and the legalization of abortion have made it more difficult to find the right child for the right parents. In some cases there is another alternative: **artificial insemination,** whereby sperm obtained by masturbation are introduced into the woman's vagina with a syringe. When the husband is fertile, his sperm is used. But if the husband's sperm production is inadequate, the sperm may come from an anonymous donor. This is called **AID—artificial insemination with donor** sperm. AID is a controversial issue, with important moral, legal, and emotional ramifications. Even so, it is estimated that over 14,000 American babies are conceived annually by this method (Boston Women's Health Book Collective, 1979).

"TEST-TUBE" CONCEPTION   A very recent advance in solving problems of fertility has been popularly labeled "test-tube" conception, because fertilization

Mike Peters © 1978 Dayton Daily News

of the ovum occurs outside the mother's body. This procedure, properly called **in vitro fertilization**, was developed to help women who have blocked fallopian tubes. The mature egg is removed from the ovary and mixed with the husband's sperm. Once the fertilized egg has divided into eight or sixteen cells, it is implanted through the cervix into the uterus. If the procedure is successful, a normal pregnancy continues. Although the success rate for this technique is low so far, the first successful birth occurred in 1978 and since then several other "test-tube" babies have been born.

SURROGATE MOTHERS   Another controversial solution to fertility problems is the use of surrogate mothers who conceive by means of artificial insemination with sperm from an infertile woman's husband. The host mother carries the fetus to term and then surrenders it to the couple who had been unable to conceive. In 1980, a married woman with children of her own was the first reported to give birth as a paid surrogate mother. Although this method is sure to raise a host of complex legal and moral questions (including that of whether it is right to pay surrogate mothers for their services and what happens if a defective child is born), it does suggest how desperately many childless couples want to become parents.

SUMMARY

1. The rapid increase in world population, the rising cost of supporting a child from infancy to adulthood, and people's greater expectations for controlling the course of their lives have led to today's emphasis on family planning and birth control.

2. The methods of birth control now in use are of three general types: some introduce hormonal substances that alter body chemistry; some take advantage of the natural rhythms of the human reproductive cycle; and some are essentially mechanical, acting as a barrier to sperm. The effectiveness of these methods is assessed by their established failure rates. Recently surgical sterilization and abortion have come to be regarded as methods of birth control.

3. Contraceptives that work chemically include the pill, the IUD, and spermicides. Spermicidal creams and jellies are used in combination with a device, such as a diaphragm or cervical cap, that acts as a physical barrier to conception. Foams are often used in combination with condoms. Condoms are currently the only reliable contraceptive available to men.

4. Female sterilization is usually accomplished through laparoscopy, where instruments are inserted into the abdomen through tiny incisions and used to cut the fallopian tubes. Male sterilization is done by vasectomy, a simple procedure involving tiny incisions in the scrotum through which the vas deferens are severed. Abortion is not as safe as preventing conception in the first place, and there is much controversy over its legal and moral aspects.

5. When conception has occurred, an extremely complex process begins that leads from the fertilized egg (zygote) through the embryonic stage (first eight weeks) and the fetal period (third to ninth month) to the birth of a child.

6. Pregnant women experience both physical and emotional changes that may be exciting at some times and anxiety producing at others. Nowadays there is a greater effort to include the father in the pregnancy experience. Pregnant women have special nutritional needs and are advised to avoid all drugs except those prescribed by a doctor who has been examining the woman during the pregnancy.

7. Childbirth (labor and delivery) consists of three stages. The first stage of labor dilates the cervix to allow passage of the baby. The second stage

involves contractions that push the baby from the mother's body. The third stage is the expulsion of the placenta.

8. Recently there have been efforts toward involving the father (and sometimes other family members and friends) in the birth process and making homelike settings available. Home births have also been "rediscovered." New technology is making it possible to correct some problems of infertility, although some procedures are raising difficult moral and legal questions.

REVIEW AND DISCUSSION

1. As a future mother or father, what circumstances for delivery of your baby do you think you would prefer? Hospital? Birthing room? Home birth? Why?

2. What are some of the legal and moral problems posed by such new developments in fertility as *in vitro* ("test-tube") fertilization and the use of surrogates?

3. What factors do you think should be taken into consideration in selecting a method of birth control?

4. List the major advantages and disadvantages of oral contraceptives, IUDs, barrier methods, and natural methods of birth control.

5. In what ways has the male role in pregnancy and childbirth changed in recent years?

SUGGESTED READINGS

Fabe, M., and N. Wikler (1979). *Up Against the Clock.* New York: Random House.

Interviews with ten career women who have made their choices on the pros and cons of having children and a career outside the home.

Family Planning Perspectives.

A periodical which appears bi-monthly and presents current research and discussion of issues related to family planning, pregnancy, and birth.

Kaufman, S. A. (1978). *You Can Have a Baby.* Nashville, Tenn.: Thomas Nelson.

A guide for involuntarily childless couples to current medical information on conception alternatives.

Leboyer, F. (1975). *Birth Without Violence.* New York: Knopf.

Describes Leboyer's unique system of birthing, whereby the infant is delivered in a dimly lit room, handled gently, and immersed in a warm bath to simulate the experience in the mother's womb. Many photographs.

Seaman, B., and G. Seaman (1977). *Women and the Crisis in Sex Hormones.* New York: Rawson.

Points out many serious problems with hormonal forms of birth control (pill, IUD), citing evidence from a large number of studies. Also provides information on nonhormonal forms of birth control.

Parents and Children

10

"Children sweeten labors, but they make misfortunes more bitter; they increase the cares of life, but they mitigate the remembrance of death."

FRANCIS BACON

Becoming a parent is one of the major turning points in an individual's life. While the experience of parenthood can bring great rewards, it also brings to a couple new challenges and new adjustments. Many people approach becoming parents with feelings of joy and expectation, only to be severely disappointed by the day-to-day realities of raising a child.

Perhaps part of the reason for the gap between expectation and reality is that our society has long perpetuated certain myths of parenthood. Many Americans seem to have a certain mystique about motherhood, regarding it as woman's most fulfilling and most natural role. This attitude is frequently accompanied by the notions that children are adorable and that childrearing is fun (LeMasters, 1977).

The fact is that the mystique of motherhood is largely a myth. Of course, the birth of a human being seems miraculous every time it happens, but being a parent—for the mother, as well as for the father—is learned, not natural or instinctive. Similarly, whatever romantic ideas are held about childrearing dissolve in the face of the hard work involved in raising a child. Sometimes children are adorable and fun to be with. But to observe only this, one must have watched only a family picnic (on an exceptionally good day), not a mealtime scene or an angry exchange between siblings. Parents, when asked, may call their work interesting or challenging, but rarely do they call it fun (LeMasters, 1977). The problem with romantic notions of parenthood is that they lead many couples to have children when they are

329

unprepared for parenthood or even unsuited to the task. When this happens, the parents, children, and ultimately society may suffer.

In order to gain a more realistic perspective on parenthood and the interactions between parents and children, it is useful to consider the existing research. We will look at some recent information about the costs and benefits of having children and describe the challenges faced by new parents. Among other topics that seem especially important today are the changing roles of mothers and fathers, the growing number of single-parent families, and child-free marriages. Because of their relevance, we are giving these topics a prominent place in this chapter.

Today more than at any time in the past it is no longer taken for granted that married couples will have children. More couples are choosing not to have children, and those who do have children are limiting the number they have, having them later than couples used to, and spacing them farther apart. Figure 10.1 summarizes how these expectations have changed.

Fig. 10.1

Lifetime births expected by wives 18 to 34 years old, for selected years: 1967–1978. The proportion of wives aged 18 to 34 who expected to have three or more children steadily decreased to less than one-half as many in a little over a decade. Six percent now expect to have no children. One in six wives expect to remain childless or to have only one child. (Source: U.S. Bureau of the Census, 1980.)

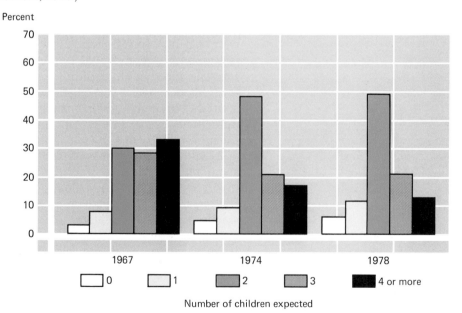

In light of these changes, it may seem surprising to learn that the **birthrate** in the United States (the number of births per 1000 population) has recently been increasing. In 1979, the birthrate increased by 3 percent over the previous year—from 15.3 live births per 1000 population in 1978 to 15.8 in 1979. Similarly, the **fertility rate** (the number of births per year per 1000 women aged 15–44) showed an increase over the rates for the years 1975 through 1978. The rise in the birthrate can be explained by an increase in the number of women of childbearing age (15–44) as well as by an increase in the rate of childbearing. Women in the age groups 30–34 and 35–39 accounted for the greatest increases in the number of women of childbearing age. For the next few years (through 1985) it appears that the continuing increase in the number of women of childbearing age will ensure a continuing rise in the number of births (USDHHS, 1980, 81-1120, 28:13).

 THE VALUE AND COST OF CHILDREN

Economic and Emotional Costs

As noted in Chapter 1, from the colonial period through the early nineteenth century in America, children were an important economic asset. Because the country was a rural, agrarian society in which the family represented the basic unit of production, each new child was an important addition to a scarce labor force. In addition, parents could usually rely on their children to help support and care for them in old age. Today, however, the situation is much different. It is now widely believed that in highly industrialized societies, children provide little or no economic benefit; indeed, they involve substantial economic costs (Espenshade, 1977).

In measuring the costs of children, most economists use two categories: direct costs and opportunity costs. **Direct costs** are out-of-pocket expenses for such articles as food, clothing, and education. **Opportunity costs** refer to the income that a woman (primarily) forgoes when she decides to stay home to care for her children (Espenshade, 1977). The total economic cost of children may be calculated by adding the direct costs to the opportunity costs.

The past decade has seen a dramatic rise in the economic costs of raising a child in the United States. In 1969, the direct cost of raising a child to age eighteen for a moderate-income family (a family with a disposable income of $16,500–20,000 in 1977 dollars) was $35,830. In 1977, the direct cost had risen to $53,605, and by 1980, it was more than double the 1969 figure, reaching $72,894. If we add to these the costs of sending a child to a public university for four years, the total direct cost in each of these three years was $39,924, $64,215, and $83,163 respectively. Finally, when opportunity costs are figured in, the total economic cost of raising a child roughly doubles. Thus in 1977, the total economic cost of raising a first child in a moderate-income family was approximately $107,000; in 1980, the figure was approximately $138,000 (Espenshade, 1977; 1980).

It would be reasonable to infer from these figures that financial costs are the greatest disadvantage in having children. However, when parents were asked about the disadvantages of having children they mentioned emotional costs (such as worry) and restrictions on their freedom more often than financial costs (Espenshade, 1977; Walters and Walters, 1980). Nevertheless, it is true that economic costs are a factor in a couple's decision to limit the size of their family (Hoffman, 1975).

Perceived Values of Children

If the economic and emotional costs of children are so great, why do so many people continue to want children? The answer seems to be that children fulfill important social, interpersonal, and psychological needs for their parents. Their value to parents in meeting these needs outweighs the economic costs of raising them. A recent national study of American married men and women, both parents and nonparents, identified seven major values people associate with having children (Hoffman and Manis, 1979). Since the respondents in this study constituted a representative sample of the American population, the results can be considered applicable to Americans in general. We will describe the seven values ranked in order of importance. This discussion is based on the analysis provided by Hoffman and Manis.

PRIMARY GROUP TIES AND AFFECTION   This refers to a child's role in providing love and companionship and acting as a buffer against loneliness. Even though this value ranked first for both men and women, it appears to be more important to women, a finding that is consistent with the woman's traditional nurturing role. Parents more often than nonparents mentioned primary ties and affection, perhaps because they had experienced this advantage through their own children.

STIMULATION AND FUN   Children are seen as bringing stimulation, activity, and joy to life. In citing this value, respondents made statements such as "They bring happiness and joy" and "Just watching them grow—it's like a built-in change so that each year is different from the one before." As with primary group ties and affection, stimulation was mentioned more often by parents than nonparents and more often by women than men.

EXPANSION OF THE SELF   Children are perceived as fulfilling the human needs to find meaning and purpose in life and to attain a sense of immortality by having a part of the self live on after death. Among the mothers responding,

Jewish women mentioned this value far more often than Protestants and Catholics. The emphasis in the Jewish faith on children as a means of attaining immortality seems to account for this difference.

ADULT STATUS AND SOCIAL IDENTITY   Americans believe that parenthood is a sign of maturity and acceptance into adulthood. This seems to be especially true for less educated and unemployed women and women who have a traditional view of gender roles. These women tend to define motherhood as their primary role in life and therefore see it as the role that gives them acceptance and status.

ACHIEVEMENT, COMPETENCE, AND CREATIVITY   Producing a child can give parents a feeling of creativity, and watching the child grow and develop contributes to a sense of parents' competence. Parents who have a strong need to achieve but have not done so in other spheres may receive vicarious satisfaction from the achievements of their children.

ECONOMIC UTILITY; SECURITY IN OLD AGE   Children are valued for the economic contribution they can make to the family and the security they can offer parents in old age. Not surprisingly, this is not a major value for Americans, probably because, as we have already observed, in this country children are an economic liability rather than an asset. Black parents, however, see more of a role for their children in providing security for them in old age than do white parents. A major reason seems to be that blacks are less likely to feel confident that governmental measures such as social security will benefit them in their later years. They may believe their children will be a more reliable source of care.

MORALITY   Some people feel the experience of raising children helps them become a better—that is, less selfish—person. Although Americans do not rank this value highly, some parents responding did feel that having children had helped them become less selfish.

It is important to note that the values Americans associate with having children are not necessarily synonymous with the motivations individual couples have for becoming parents, although they may be. Some couples start families in response to pressure from parents who want grandchildren or friends who have already started families. Some simply assume that having children is an expected part of marriage. Some may hope to save a troubled marriage, and others may believe that children will fulfill the dreams they have been unable to realize in their own lives. While many couples make good parents regardless of their initial motivation, it is probably safe to say that those who examine their reasons for wanting children and have a realistic view of the potential difficulties involved will be better equipped for the task.

HIGHLIGHT 10.1   *Choosing to Have Children*

My husband and I live comfortably, one might say extremely so, and enjoy our home, our friends, and our city to an enormous degree. More importantly, we enjoy each other and sincerely wondered whether we could ever love another human being, an unknown one at that, as much as we loved each other. We were used to acting spontaneously, going out constantly, thought nothing of skipping meals or working late, or spending Sunday in bed with each other and the *New York Times.* We both love our work and have careers that we bring home with us. We both had flexibility, but with that flexibility went a cyclical income and erratic hours.

But we took the leap. It was a conscious, thought-out, and planned leap.

I was absolutely enchanted by the constant presence of a very powerful little person inside of me who poked, rolled, and hiccuped, and had, from the very beginning, very much of a mind of his own. It is impossible to explain to another person, one who has never had a child, the sheer magic of conceiving, growing, and giving birth. It is even more awesome and I think, much more exciting, if one knows a good deal about the process and so can enjoy it at a number of levels.

This last point encapsulates our unambivalent enthusiasm about our son. As I watch him develop new skills from one hour to the next—as I watch him take apart a toy, throw the pieces into the air after carefully licking each one, and then look at me as if to share his delight—I am able to react both to the excitement of a little person who is clearly fascinated by the plethora of sounds, colors, and textures which we take for granted but also to the ability he has today of taking something apart using all the fingers of both hands; something he couldn't do yesterday. No one had ever told us how much fun it is to watch your own child—or how much more aware you become of the rug under your table or the handle of a spoon, or how funny it is when your son picks up a glass with both hands and pours the contents on his head.

Of course, it's changed our lives. We do go out, but our excursions are more selective. Instead of going to a movie with ten minutes' notice, we get tickets to a ballet or play and make plans accordingly. No, we don't go out to dinner three times a week, but when we do go out we think about what we're really in the mood for and the meal seems to take on a memorable quality.

Without a doubt, having a child has changed our relationship. There is another human being in the house who makes demands, gives affection, and occasionally breaks something we care about. It means there is an entirely new dimension to our lives—both in terms of our individual relationships with our son, and with each other. We find that we articulate our feelings to one another more, both our annoyances and our affection. When I feel rejected because my husband objects that I'm letting our son crawl on a cold floor I say so, and when the baby looks adoringly at my husband and nestles himself in his beard, I enjoy my husband in a way that I never did before. We still travel—but we think about it a bit more and reorganize our itinerary as we learn what seems to be the easiest on ourselves as a family. We still lie in bed on weekends but we often have a very small boy burrowing under the covers with us.

Source: Diana Barrett.

HIGHLIGHT 10.2   *Choosing to be Childless*

To remain childfree was a no-contest choice for us right from the very beginning. Freedom and economics were two major factors in our decision. My husband, Paul, and I found that we could not begin to feel really free until we had put behind us all the preambles and preludes of life: college, graduate school, apprenticeships, the hunt and search of courtship, finding the right mate, the right career, the right city, and finally the general struggle to achieve financial independence.

Now that we have successfully lived through and survived these necessary restrictions of young life, we want to relax and enjoy the fruits of our labors.

There are many kinds of degrees of freedom. Some of us require more freedom than others.

Furthermore, freedom and pleasure of a certain brand can only coexist with spontaneity. One fine summer day, we decided to go to Europe at 2 P.M. and we were on the plane at 8. When we travel, we take our toothbrushes. When our friends with children travel, they take a chock-full Winnebago. Vacation with children is a contradiction in terms. Paul and I each read five books a week. Our friends with children tell us they no longer read books. We have friends, however, who claim that they can have their cake and eat it, too. Dennis and Sarah, both in their early 30s, state publicly and as often as possible that they have both a child and a spontaneous, carefree active life. They live in a semi-posh townhouse, have a three-year-old son, and do, in fact, live exceedingly active, full lives.

Both work full time, socialize, and travel nearly every weekend. They miss very few parties, plays, or lectures. They give much time

to political and social causes. Their social conscience is commendable, their social life is enviable. But their kid, what about him? Dennis, Jr., is literally being raised by a series of babysitters. The babysitters work in shifts—the 9–5 shift, 5–midnight shift, and on weekends there's an extra overnight shift. Dennis, Jr., barely recognizes his mother when he sees her and when he does see her, it is a brief encounter indeed.

Those who derive their satisfaction and fulfillment from freedom, spontaneity, and varied experiences instead of from childbearing will inevitably be called selfish as if there were something intrinsically wrong with trying to enjoy one's life.

But just who is selfish? Reasons for wanting children can be more selfish than reasons for not wanting them. Insecure men often feel that fathering a child is the easiest and most direct way of establishing their masculinity and dismissing any questions of their potency. Insecure women see having a child as the ultimate proof of their femininity.

Having a child is one of the few irreversible acts in life. Almost any other decision can be reversed. An unfortunate marriage can be terminated, an unwanted house can be sold, a car that turns out to be a lemon can be disposed of, but children are not returnable or disposable. There is nothing wrong with not wanting children. The only "wrong" is when we, feeling as we do, have children as a result of societal pressures. Then we become unhappy parents producing unhappy children.

Source: Patricia Lankin.

THE TRANSITION TO PARENTHOOD

Some researchers have defined the transition to parenthood as a crisis that may be disruptive, at least temporarily, to the couple. According to this view, the married couple is an integrated social system of roles and statuses, and adding or removing members forces a major reorganization of the system. With the shift from a dyad (a two-person relationship) to a triad (a three-person relationship), as occurs with the arrival of the first child, there is a disruption of patterns of affection and intimacy (Russell, 1974).

Researchers who take a developmental approach believe that it is more accurate to regard new parenthood as a developmental stage in the family life cycle, with the transition to parenthood being the "developmental task" (Hobbs and Cole, 1976). Looked at this way, beginning parenthood becomes an adjustment task that is accompanied by some difficulty rather than a so-called crisis. For most, new parenthood is a time of learning to cope with change and new demands rather than a time of crisis. There is no doubt, however, that the arrival of a first child creates stress. Though the initial changes in assuming the parental role are among the most major to be experienced by couples, parenthood is perhaps best characterized as a dynamic process with parents making continual adjustments to their child's changing capabilities and needs, as well as to the arrival of an additional child or children.

Initial Adjustments Faced by New Parents

Inevitably, because she has borne the child and will probably provide most of its care during the early months, the mother will find her life greatly altered. One of the major problems many new mothers face is developing a sense of competence about mothering. If she has not had much contact with children before having her own, she may feel inadequate to the task. Often having the help of a caring relative or close friend during the early weeks is of great benefit. With the relative assigned to the house-hold tasks, the mother has the opportunity to rest, regain her strength, learn to care for her child, and develop feelings of confidence about her abilities as a mother.

Fathers, too, face new adjustments when a baby is born. Since most fathers spend less time with the infant, they may feel even less confident about caring for it than the mother does. One way to help the father become more self-assured about his new role is to involve him in the child's care and feeding. Even if a mother is breast-feeding, as more and more women are doing today, the father can share in dressing, diapering, comforting, and playing with the baby. These tasks, too, contribute to feelings of involvement and competence.

The arrival of a baby brings new adjustments for the couple itself. If a mother becomes fully absorbed with the child, the father may feel excluded. The couple may also experience some initial conflict over their sex life. Some women find that in the early months after a child is born they are simply too tired or otherwise uninterested in resuming sexual activity. This, too, can cause strain on the relationship. While the father may feel an increased economic burden, the mother may feel isolated from him and the outside world, especially if she does not take the time to get away from her baby on occasion. Recent awareness of the difficulties faced by new parents has resulted in the formation of parent support groups where new parents can meet to share problems and ideas. Many parents are much relieved to find that the anxieties they are experiencing are not unique but are shared by other parents as well.

Changes Experienced Differently by Husbands and Wives

It is generally agreed that mothers experience more bothersome changes related to the arrival of the first child than fathers do. Russell's research (1974) with 271 married couples aged sixteen to forty-seven shows that the five changes most frequently expressed as bothersome by wives cluster around the emotional and physical self:

1. Physical tiredness and fatigue.
2. Feeling edgy or emotionally upset.
3. Interruptions of sleep and rest caused by the baby.
4. Worry about personal appearance.
5. Worry about "loss of figure."

Russell found that a physically healthy mother experiences less stress, and that the longer the mother had been married the less likely she is to experience parenthood as a crisis.

The husbands' concerns reflected a broader range, including problems external to the physical or emotional self. The five problems experienced most frequently by the 271 fathers in Russell's sample were:

1. Interruptions of sleep or rest.
2. Suggestions from in-laws about the baby.
3. Increased financial problems.
4. Necessity to change some plans because of the baby.
5. Additional amount of work required.

Older men in Russell's sample seemed to experience less stress upon becoming fathers. This is confirmed by data from Nydegger (1974) who found that men who became fathers later in life made a better adjustment to the role than did younger fathers. Nydegger feels that older fathers may have a better sense of their place in the world and what they have to offer a child.

Factors that Provide for a Smoother Transition

Russell found that couples with high levels of marital adjustment were less likely to experience parenthood as a crisis and also reported more positive feelings of gratification in the role of parent. The timing of the birth also seems important. Ryder (1973) determined that wives who have a child in the first year or two of marriage are more likely to feel that their husbands do not pay enough attention to them. Russell notes that there should be sufficient time between marriage and having a child for the couple to develop effective communication patterns. She also points out that the more adequately the couple has handled prior tasks, the better they will be able to handle a current transition, such as the arrival of the first child (Russell, 1974).

 THE CHANGING PARENTAL ROLE

In contemporary American society, there is much confusion surrounding the parental role. This confusion exists at both the societal and the family levels. While parents have retained final responsibility for their children, formal institutions now help fulfill many formerly parental functions. This division of labor has both diminished parental authority and blurred the nature of many tasks (LeMasters, 1977). For example, schools are responsible for a child's education, but parents are held responsible for the child's morality. Can education and morality be divided? What happens if the teacher's rules of conduct conflict with those of the parents—whose views prevail?

At the family level, shifts have occurred in the roles of male and female parents over the past decades. Early psychological theories, especially the ideas advanced by Freud, depicted the mother as the all-important influence in determining the child's personality. Recent research has challenged this notion, and more studies are looking at the contribution of the father and at how the child affects the parents. The distinction between the roles of mother and father is no longer as clear-cut as in the past. Indeed, many new parents in our society are negotiating for themselves how the parenting function in their family is to be performed and by whom.

Mothering

The role of the mother in America has changed dramatically in the past few decades. Smaller families, the need or wish to work outside the home, and changing ideologies have so altered the nature of her tasks that the "traditional" mother rarely exists anymore.

One of the problems faced by the contemporary mother may be overcommitment. In his analysis of the mother's role in our society, LeMasters (1977) suggests that in recent years each of her commitments has expanded. As a wife, she is expected to be an equal partner to her husband, as friend, companion, and lover. The standards of mothering have risen, and she is expected to be informed about what is best for her children, in terms of health, schooling, and emotional well-being. The mother has retained the responsibility of managing the home, with the added chore of overseeing the budget, and she has expanded her role in the community. Finally, the majority of American mothers work outside the home, in addition to performing their family duties.

The variety of options and the lack of guidelines to determine which options she should take can result in a sense of confusion for the mother of a first child. A young child's demands are enormous, and if the mother expects to meet these and other demands simultaneously, she may become distracted, overworked, and exhausted. The more clearly a woman has defined her overall life goals before she has children, the easier it will be for her to decide what emphasis she wishes to place on her children, husband, an outside job or career, and other activities.

Fathering

The role of father in the United States has traditionally been of secondary importance to the role of mother. Perhaps because society has so strongly emphasized the man's role as provider, many people have assumed that men are either incapable or unwilling to function as primary caretaker for their children.

There is increasing recognition, however, that men are more nurturant and more interested in raising children than people have thought. Some evidence for this exists in the growing numbers of single-parent families that are headed by men. Courts are more favorably disposed than in the past to awarding custody of children to fathers in divorce cases. During the past decade, a number of studies have shed new light on the role of the American father, men's attitudes toward caring for young children, and men's interactions with children.

Although the father's interest in the development of older children has been widely acknowledged, many people have assumed that fathers are not very interested in caring for infants. A study of college students at the University of Connecticut indicates that, among this group at least, young men were much more interested in early child-raising than the women students thought they would be. Sixty-two percent of the male students disagreed with the statement "Most males don't think about their eventual role as father until their first child is born." Regarding the statement "A wife has a right to expect her husband to help feed and diaper-change the baby," 78 percent of the men agreed, but only 36 percent of the women thought the men would agree (McIntire, Nass, and Battistone, 1974).

Parke and Sawin (1976), along with other researchers, have found that fathers are much more skillful and nurturant in caring for newborn infants than was previously thought. Observations in the hospital room, between six and forty-eight hours after delivery of a couple's first child, showed that fathers were just as involved as mothers in holding and rocking the baby, touching, looking at, vocalizing to, and kissing their newborn offspring. The babies consumed a similar amount of milk when they were bottle-fed by fathers compared to mothers, and fathers were equally responsive to signs of distress from the infant such as a cough, a spit-up, or a sneeze (Parke and Sawin, 1976).

Research has shown that mothers and fathers have different styles of interaction with their children. Fathers tend to engage in physically stimulating activities, whereas mothers more often engage in intellectually stimulating activities.

Another study of nineteen couples and their infants found that fathers may interact with their newborns even *more* than mothers. When both parents were with the baby, fathers tended to touch and talk to the infant more than mothers did (Parke and O'Leary, 1975). However, because these researchers observed such a small group of people, their finding should be approached with caution. More recently, fathers who were asked about the ways they viewed the role of fatherhood emphasized the importance of participating in infant care and especially relating to the emotional needs of the child (Cordell, Parke, and Sawin, 1980).

Regarding the relationship between adult males and children, Mackey and Day (1979) found that American men interact with children at the same level of intensity as American women and that they interact similarly—in terms of touching, standing close, and making visual contact—with boys and girls. However, fathers and mothers do have different styles of interaction with their children. Fathers tend to offer more physical stimulation and rough-and-tumble play, while mothers are more likely to take an intellectual approach in playing with their children (Clarke-Stewart, 1978). Clark-Stewart found that young children prefer their father's more physical style of play. However, whereas fathers tend to spend time in special activities with their children, such as playing or reading bedtime stories, mothers often continue to bear the routine chores of feeding, bathing, and the like.

Innovations in Parenting

Traditional concepts of parental roles appear to be major factors contributing to the difficulties of contemporary parents. In the traditional view, the father is assigned the instrumental role in the family: he is responsible for earning the family income and accomplishing other specific task-oriented goals. The mother is assigned the expressive role: she is considered the "affective" or emotional center of the family. The limitations of these role designations are increasingly obvious (Walters and Walters, 1980).

In her analysis of parenthood, Rossi (1968) suggested that this traditional division is inappropriate for present-day family and social systems. The demands made upon a woman in her role as mother are in fact largely instrumental. Such tasks as household management require the rationality and efficiency characteristic of the instrumental role. By contrast, success in the contemporary workplace often requires that people make use of affective skills in interpersonal relationships. For example, people who have selling or supervisory positions must be psychologically attuned to others.

Rossi suggests that it is the extremely passive and dependent woman who would experience difficulty in her role as a mother today and the man who failed to integrate affective skills with instrumental skills who would have difficulty as a father. In her opinion, it is more useful and accurate to view both types of skills as necessary to both the mother and father roles.

Today the peformance of family roles is increasingly being shared by husband and wife. As in other areas of the marital relationship, this often involves a process of negotiation, whereby one partner agrees to take on particular tasks in exchange for other tasks to be performed by the other partner. In this way, the couple settles upon "spheres of interest" suitable to their particular situation. For example, in a family in which both the husband and wife work, the husband may agree to do the vacuuming and grocery shopping; the wife, in return agrees to assume the primary child-care role. The couple may also decide to share some tasks, such as preparing the meals or washing the dishes.

Although the practice has not become widespread, there are some couples who have totally reversed the traditional roles. Perhaps the most publicized example is the late John Lennon and his wife, Yoko Ono. After the birth of their son, Lennon became a self-styled "househusband" for five years, caring for the child and the household while Yoko managed their business affairs. Their experience suggests how more flexible role definitions offer parents the opportunity to tailor family roles to their personal abilities and needs.

Goals of Parenting

One of the major challenges of childrearing is determining how best to develop the qualities in children that will enable them to relate successfully to others

CASE STUDY   *Sharing Child Care*

Whenever we talked about having the baby we talked about sharing in the responsibility. We never imagined that there would be obstacles in doing that. But when she came, Carrie left to come to Boston to be with her doctor. I stayed in Toronto because of important work I wanted to finish. After that, the gap got bigger—the first months of the baby's life coincided with the first months in a new house, a new city, and a new job for me. Also, Carrie was nursing. She and Lila spent hours together locked into a pair very close to one another. By the time the pressures had let up on me Carrie was almost drowning in Lila—Lila nursed continuously, it seemed, and cried and crawled after Carrie every time she left the room. I wanted to enter in but I was less knowing and Lila treated me as a threatening stranger. I wanted to relieve Carrie and be with Lila. I wanted to break in and I had to do it soon. So every night when I came home I would catch her up in my arms and then no matter how she pushed and bent backwards out of my arms, I would walk around the house, talking to her about all the things we could see and touch. Slowly she would wind down. And I would take her with me—just the two of us alone— even to get gas. Just to put us in situations where she had to ask me if she wanted to be

lifted or had to talk to me if she wanted to share.

It was hard because I didn't really know how to do anything else but whisk her away from Carrie. And Carrie had spent all that infant time learning how to just be with Lila. I was O.K. while I was intruding myself, but once Lila at least accepted me it was hard to know what next. One thing we did was to begin spending time, all together, the three of us— tumbling on the bed, going for a walk around the reservoir. A kind of strain went out of my relationship with Lila as I became someone who was around, who loved her, who was available to her. The real proof of that is just now coming. I redid the attic over our apartment as a playroom for her. I partitioned a part of it off to be my office. In the playroom I can be totally relaxed with her—there is nothing that can hurt her or that she can hurt. When she plays there and I can be in the study, in a way I feel like I have an equivalent to nursing, a very important way of being side by side with her.

FOR CLASS DISCUSSION

1. How could Carrie have taken a more assertive role in encouraging a closer relationship between her husband and child?

2. One gets the impression that each of the parents in this case study handled the situation rather independently of each other. How might they have worked more effectively as a team in solving their problems?

The process of building self-esteem in children begins with showing them that they are loved and valued.

and face the challenges of life. Baumrind and Black (1967) define eight personality characteristics as aspects of competence in preschool children. Successful preschool children exhibit self-reliance, self-control, and the ability to relate easily to others. They are realistic, contented, buoyant, and able to bounce back after a disappointment.

These researchers attempted to determine what parental practices lead to developing these qualities in preschool children. They found that parents of competent children balanced highly nurturant behavior with high control of their children. These parents made firm demands and were clear in communicating them to the child. Firmness was accompanied by warmth and support.

Other researchers have studied childrearing practices and the development of high self-esteem in grade-school children. Why should high self-esteem be a major goal of childrearing? Coopersmith (1967) and others assert that the individual with low self-esteem feels helpless, vulnerable, and inadequate, while individuals with high self-esteem feel capable of coping with adversity and competent to achieve success. It is these latter characteristics that most people desire for their children.

Coopersmith found that parents who have definite values and clear ideas of appropriate behavior and who enforce their beliefs are more likely to rear children who value themselves highly. Self-confidence on the part of parents also seems to build self-esteem in children. In a study of fifth- and sixth-grade boys and their mothers, Coopersmith found three specific conditions that lead to high self-esteem: parental acceptance of the child, discipline, and respect for the child.

In an article on adolescents, Rollins and Thomas (1975) argued that parental nurturance—accepting and loving behavior—is the key factor related to adolescent self-esteem, conformance to appropriate authority, and acceptance of parental religious values and practices. This view is consistent with the findings of Baumrind and Black and of Coopersmith, who have reported on the importance of parental norms and the explanation of rules as important in the socialization process.

Parental power (the way parents purposefully influence the development of their children) is also significant in the development of self-esteem. Baumrind (1971) reported that parents who have established a set of rules for their children to follow, who have explained these rules clearly, and who enforce them consistently are most successful at helping their children develop positive self-regard. These rules should be general enough to allow much room for the child to experiment with decision making and gradually acquire many important social skills. Baumrind also found that families with either too many or too few rules are less successful in helping their children develop that sense of autonomy that is necessary for comfortable adult interaction.

FACTORS INFLUENCING RELATIONSHIPS OF PARENTS AND CHILDREN

Parent-Infant Socialization

Until very recently, most of the research on parent-child relationships emphasized the crucial role of parents in the personality development and socialization of children. Today, however, there is a growing body of evidence that from birth on children help to determine their parents' behavior (Walters and Walters, 1980). This mutual process of socialization is termed "reciprocal interaction."

In examining the individual differences of infants at birth, Korner (1971) found that about 80 percent of interactions between mothers and newborns are initiated by the newborn. Mothers are affected by a number of characteristics of infants, such as crying, visual alertness, and level of arousal. The child's sex also influences parental response (see Chapter 3), although it is not clear whether this is due to behavioral differences in male and female babies or to the parents' expectations.

© George Dole

"... and that's all I know about sex, so far."

Physiological and Societal Influences

Other research during the 1970s has suggested that a variety of physiological and societal influences play a role in parent-child relationships (Walters and Walters, 1980).

Among the physiological factors that have been linked to parent-child relationships is low birth weight and behaviors related to it (Bell and Harper, 1977). Premature infants in particular are more likely to be abused by their parents (see Chapter 12). Hyperactive behavior in boys and withdrawal behavior in girls are sometimes associated with physiological factors (Victor and Halverson, 1976). These behaviors are apt to be disturbing to parents and may affect parents' perception of and behavior toward a child who exhibits them.

Economic factors inevitably play a role in parent-child relationships. Poor families tend to be families under stress. In such circumstances, it is not unusual to find that children's respect for parents and parents' expectations of children may be low. Scheck and Emerick (1976) asked a group of adolescent males about their perceptions of their parents, and found that the lower the socioeconomic status, the less likely the adolescents were to perceive their parents as being supportive, controlling, and consistent in their discipline.

Yet if poverty causes certain difficulties in parent-child relationships, higher income seems to alter rather than eliminate stress. Indeed, some social scientists believe that tension between parents and children is greater in middle-class families where parents often impose on children ambitions to better their social and economic standing (LeMasters, 1977).

Another influence on parent-child relationships is level of formal education. Scheck and Emerick (1976) believe that level of education is highly related to development of such personal characteristics as intellectual flexibility, breadth of perspective, and tolerance of nonconformity. They conclude that parents who have these characteristics are likely to be more supportive of their children, helping them to develop a positive self-image. Better educated parents would therefore tend to be more democratic in their control and show greater consistency in discipline, so that the children would experience less confusion in knowing how they are expected to behave.

Maternal Employment and Parent-Child Relationships

In Chapter 7, we discussed the impact on marital adjustment when both husband and wife work outside the home. A topic of equal concern to many people today is the effect of full-time outside maternal employment on children. This issue is particularly prominent in view of the marked increase in the participation of mothers in the labor force in recent years.

In families headed by single mothers—those separated, divorced, or widowed—53.1 percent of children under age six and 64.2 percent of children between the ages of six and seventeen have mothers who were in the labor force in 1979. This represents an increase since 1970 of 12.7 percent in the first category and 7 percent in the second category. In families with two parents, 40.9 percent of children under age six and 54.5 percent of children between the ages of six and seventeen have mothers who were in the labor force in 1979. These figures represent increases since 1970 of 13.3 percent and 12.4 percent respectively. Thus, as shown in Fig. 10.2, a majority of children of school age as well as a substantial proportion of children under age six have mothers who are working outside the home (U.S. Department of Labor, 1980).

EFFECTS ON CHILDREN A review of research on the effects of maternal employment on children concluded that maternal employment in and of itself has very little influence on the behavior of children (Etaugh, 1974). According to Etaugh's analysis, young children are not adversely affected by maternal employment in terms of their attachment to the working parent or their cognitive (intellectual) development, provided there is frequent parent-child interaction during nonworking hours and stable, stimulating substitute care. The adjustment of elementary-school children to maternal employment seems to be directly related to the mother's attitudes toward working and home-making. The mother who remains at home even though she feels discontented in the homemaking role may create more problems for her children than the one who provides good substitute care and works outside the home. It has been found consistently that "satisfied mothers—working outside the home or not—have the best adjusted children" (Etaugh, 1974).

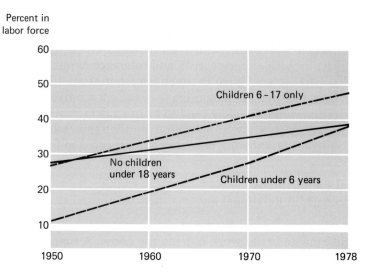

Fig. 10.2
*Married women in the labor force, by age of children. Since 1950,
the labor force participation rate has tripled for married mothers of
preschoolers and doubled for those with school-age children.
Working women account for almost 40 percent of the yearly
income of families where both husband and wife hold full-time
jobs. (Source: "American Families and Living Arrangements," U.S.
Bureau of the Census, 1980.)*

In regard to school work, research suggests that maternal employment
may adversely affect boys' performance and have either a positive influence
or no effect at all on girls' performance. The reasons for this are unclear. In
schoolwork, as in psychological adjustment, children of satisfied mothers
functioned better than children of dissatisfied mothers, whether working or
at home (Etaugh, 1974).

Maternal employment seems to have little effect on the leisure activities
of children, but some influence on perceptions, attitudes, and life goals. In
general, children of working mothers, especially girls, have higher educational
goals and career expectations than children of nonworking mothers. They have
a broader concept of the female role and perceive less difference between men's
and women's roles. Maternal employment has also been found to have
beneficial effects on girls' independence, social adjustment, self-esteem, and
attitude toward women (Hoffman, 1979).

An undesirable consequence of maternal employment in working-class
homes appears to be that sons of working mothers tend to have less admiration

HIGHLIGHT 10.3   *Child Care: How Americans Cope*

The United States is one of the few industrialized nations that does not have a national system of child care. While there are a number of possible reasons for this, a major one is clearly economic. Since World War II, the European countries have been experiencing a declining birthrate and labor shortages. As a result, these countries have instituted policies aimed at encouraging women to have babies and at the same time to join the work force. The United States, however, with its high rate of unemployment and a population that has grown 8.3 percent from 1970 to 1979, has no critical need for more babies or more people in the work force. Yet increasing numbers of

(continued)

Percent of children in child care. The figures are from 1980, or the most recent available for each country. Types of care include day-care centers, preschool, and family day-care providers. (Source: Sheila B. Kamerman and Alfred J. Kahn, Child Care, Family Benefits and Working Mothers, *New York: Columbia University Press, 1981. Reprinted by permission.)*

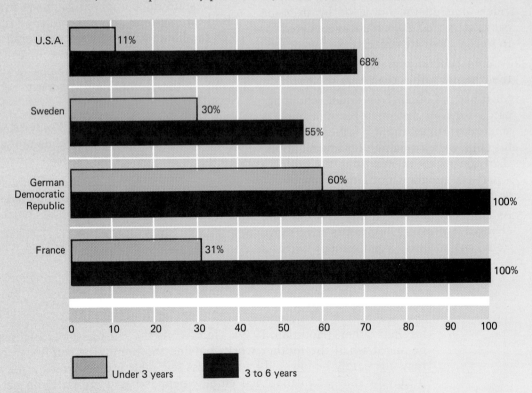

HIGHLIGHT 10.3   *(continued)*

American women, including mothers of small children, are working, most of them out of economic necessity.

How are these working parents coping with the problem of child care? The picture that emerges from recent research suggests that daytime child care in the United States is a complicated and often frustrating system. Here are some of the findings:

☐ Not surprisingly, many parents prefer having their children cared for by relatives. Of the 6.9 million American children of working mothers in 1978, 60 percent were cared for by relatives, including older siblings; 30 percent were cared for by day-care providers outside the home or by in-home babysitters; and 10 percent were cared for in formal day-care centers.

☐ Parents generally prefer child care near their homes rather than near their work.

☐ Most parents of children under school age patch together several types of care in a single day. For example, a father may leave his child with a neighbor for several hours, then someone else may take the child to a part-day program until the close of the working day.

☐ As children get older, the type of day care changes. For example, parents may move from an informal arrangement with a neighbor to a formal program such as a nursery school or day-care center.

☐ The problem of adequate day care does not end when a child enters school. Between 1 and 2 million of the 29.8 million American children aged five to thirteen have no formal care between the time school closes and the time parents return from work.

☐ Day-care providers are badly underpaid. According to one study, nationally, 60 percent of teachers in day-care centers are paid at below the federal poverty level, and family day-care providers are paid even less.

Despite the complexities of the American child-care system, there is evidence that outside-the-home child care is not having a negative impact on family values. According to researchers Sheila B. Kamerman and Alfred J. Kahn of the Columbia University School of Social Work:

> It has yet to be shown that family values have been eroded anywhere by child-care arrangements, whether in nursery schools, centers, or in family-day-care homes.*

* Kamerman, S., and A. J. Kahn. The Day-Care Debate: A Wider View. *The Public Interest* (Winter 1979), p. 81.

Source: Kamerman, S., and A. J. Kahn. *Child Care, Family Benefits and Working Mothers* (New York: Columbia University Press, 1981).

for their fathers (Hoffman, 1979). Thus, while the self-image of daughters may be raised when the mother works outside the home, the self-image of sons may ultimately be lowered by their less favorable attitude toward the father. It may be that when maternal employment is based primarily on need, the father is viewed by sons as failing to provide an adequate income. As sharing of the provider role becomes a more widely accepted cultural norm, this perception may change.

SPECIAL FORMS OF PARENTHOOD

Though the great majority of children in the United States spend their childhood in the company and custody of their two biological parents, a growing number are living in homes with a single parent, a stepparent, adoptive parents, or under the temporary care of foster parents. We will deal with stepparenting in Chapter 13; here our focus will be on single parenting, adoption, and foster care.

Single-Parent Families

In recent years, the single-parent family has increased more rapidly than any other family form. In 1970, the proportion of children under age eighteen living with one parent was 11 percent; by 1979, the proportion had increased to 19 percent, almost one of every five families with children in the home. The makeup of one-parent families also changed somewhat between 1970 and 1979. In 1979, 17 percent of all families with children were maintained by the mother alone and 2 percent by the father alone. This compares to 10 percent headed by women and 1 percent by men in 1970 (U.S. Department of Commerce, 1980).

While these figures represent a great many children in the United States living in single-parent families, it is well to remember that this is not usually a permanent arrangement. Many single parents remarry within a few years, and only a minority of children under age eighteen spend most of their childhood in a one-parent family. Yet these years do represent a significant period in a child's life. Figure 10.3 provides additional statistical data on intact and single-parent families with children, showing changes between 1970 and 1978.

MOTHER-ONLY FAMILIES The emergence of large numbers of households headed by women constituted one of the major changes in American life-styles during the 1970s. The number of female-headed households rose by 51 percent during the decade, from 5.6 million to 8.5 million (U.S. Bureau of the Census, 1980). According to the Census Bureau, the major factors contributing to the rapid growth of woman-headed families are divorce, widowhood, separation, and the tendency of women today to maintain independent households rather than to live with parents or relatives, as they might have in the past. Another factor is the growing number of out-of-wedlock births, particularly to adolescent women. (We consider the difficulties related to teenage pregnancy in Chapter 12.)

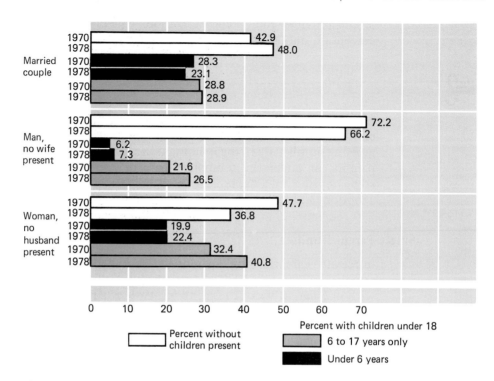

Fig. 10.3

*Types of families, by presence of children under 18 and 6 years:
1970 and 1978. One-half of married-couple families have no young
children in the home, primarily because of postponement of
childbearing and especially the lengthening period of married life
after the children leave home. Men rarely have custody of children
under 6, but one-fourth of the mothers who have sole custody of
the children have one or more preschoolers to care for. (Source:
U.S. Bureau of the Census, 1980.)*

Regardless of how a woman becomes a single parent, she is likely to
experience financial difficulties. About 50 percent of all children living in
families maintained by mothers with no husband present live below the
poverty line (U.S. Bureau of the Census, 1980). The median income for woman-
headed households in 1978 was $8,540 as compared to $17,640, the median
income of all families (U.S. Bureau of the Census, 1980). Of the women who
were granted child-support payments in cases of divorce or separation in 1978,
fewer than three-quarters actually received any payments, and for those who
did, the mean child-support payment was $1,799—not a very substantial sum
(U.S. Bureau of the Census, 1980). There is some evidence that economic

hardship can affect a single mother's perception of her children. A recent study (Desimone-Luis, O'Mahoney, and Hunt 1979) found that in female-headed homes where there has been a substantial drop in income, mothers are more likely to feel that their children are difficult to cope with than when their income remains stable.

The financial difficulties suffered by woman-headed families are not due solely to the lack of a male earner in the family. Other compelling causes are the economic discrimination still prevalent against women workers in the United States and the lack of societal support systems. Women are still employed primarily in lower level jobs and on average earn only 59 percent of what men earn. For single mothers with young children, the problem of finding a job that pays enough to support a family is compounded by the difficulty of finding good child-care arrangements at a reasonable price. Women with little education are especially disadvantaged in finding employment. Recently, however, programs have been established in a few cities to train single mothers currently on welfare for skilled jobs (usually in trades) that will enable them to support their families without government assistance.

Woman-headed families face a variety of other difficulties as well. In practical terms, single mothers carry a double burden in trying to be bread-winners as well as carry out homemaking and child-socialization functions. A single mother may succeed admirably in providing the love and discipline

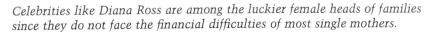

Celebrities like Diana Ross are among the luckier female heads of families since they do not face the financial difficulties of most single mothers.

her children require, but she herself may suffer from the lack of adult sources of love and companionship she needs as an individual.

Little research has been done on the effects of living in a single-parent family on children. There is no doubt that a parent alone has a difficult time fulfilling the functions usually provided by two parents, but the presence of two parents does not necessarily ensure that the children will be happy and well adjusted. Brandwein, Brown, and Fox (1974) examined the divorced woman and her family from this perspective and concluded that the problems of woman-headed families may stem more from societal attitudes than from the absence of the father. They also found that boys raised in mother-only families do not have more problems establishing a masculine identity than other boys.

TYPES OF FEMALE-HEADED FAMILIES The problems of female-headed families differ to some degree depending on the way in which the family came to lack a male parent.

1. The widowed mother has the support and sympathy of the community. Of course, she and her children have suffered a severe emotional blow in the loss of the husband-father. The problems of finances and role that the widow is likely to have are similar to those of other woman-headed families, but she probably receives more support from her kin and friendship network.

2. The never-married mother is more likely than other single mothers to be receiving welfare payments, and she is more likely to belong to a racial minority. In 1978, 233,600 out-of-wedlock births were recorded for whites, and 310,200 were recorded for blacks. In percentage terms, out-of-wedlock births among whites accounted for 8.7 percent of all white births, and out-of-wedlock births among blacks accounted for 47.5 percent of all black births (U.S. Bureau of the Census, Statistical Abstract of the United States, 1980). Thus the single-parent family with a never-married mother as head is a common family unit among black Americans. Furthermore, the likelihood of a successful marriage for never-married mothers is smaller than that of other single parents (LeMasters, 1977).

3. The deserted mother is likely to suffer the same financial problems as the never-married mother, since the father is unavailable and presumably unwilling to offer financial help, and since a major reason for deserting may have been to escape family financial responsibilities. A woman who has been deserted is not legally free to remarry. Deserted mothers may suffer more from feelings of rejection than divorced mothers since in the case of divorced women, the marital dissolution was planned. A deserted mother may find herself thrust into her new role with little warning.

4. The separated mother is in a position similar to that of the deserted mother in that she is not legally free of her husband. However, he is more likely to provide financial support, and if the separation is a legal one decided by the court (see Chapter 13), he has probably been directed by the court to provide some financial support as part of the separation agreement.

5. The divorced mother has the advantage of a clear and legal split with her husband, with custody and financial obligations spelled out. One of her main problems, however, is that court orders to support children often are not lived up to by former husbands. In a study done during the late sixties, it was found that within one year of the divorce decree only 38 percent of former husbands were in full compliance with the court order to support their families. Forty-two percent contributed no support at all after one year, and 67 percent were contributing nothing within four years (Brandwein, Brown, and Fox, 1974). In 1978, only 59 percent of women with children under age twenty-one were awarded child support, and of these 28 percent never received any payments (U.S. Bureau of the Census, 1980).

FATHER-ONLY FAMILIES   Aside from an occasional newspaper feature describing a father trying to raise children in a one-parent household, little has been written about single-parent fathers. Even less sociological research has been done. Census estimates indicate that about 2 percent of all families with children are headed by fathers alone.

Most single-parent fathers do not remain single parents long. The majority of them remarry rather quickly. As single parents, men may suffer from economic difficulties, although seldom as much as women, and, like women, they find little community support for their one-parent situation. Men, too, suffer from the role conflicts of job responsibility, social life, and parental demands. Fathers in one-parent families, particularly if they are divorced, suffer from the same problems of loneliness and role overload as women in one-parent families. Many single-parent fathers resolve these conflicts by remarrying and transferring most of the child care to their new spouses.

Parent-Child Relationships
after Divorce

As noted earlier, single-parent families are formed in a variety of ways. Among Americans, divorce accounts for the highest number of single-parent families with children under age eighteen—42 percent in 1979 (U.S. Bureau of the Census, 1980). Both the widowed parent and the divorced parent with custody face many of the same kinds of problems. In both circumstances, children are undeniably affected. When a father or mother dies, a child is left with a sense of loss that is greater and more absolute than the loss of a parent by divorce. Often in the latter case the noncustodial parent still plays a role in the child's life. Even so, divorce is clearly difficult for most children and creates disruptions in parent-child relationships. However, the age and development level of the child or children are important to take into account in considering the effects of divorce on the children and the parent-child relationship.

Researchers who have investigated the effects of divorce on the behavior of young children have found that the first year following divorce is the most difficult and that boys and girls are affected differently. Boys, for example, seem to be affected for a longer period of time. Whereas girls' behavior was normal two years after a divorce, boys still tended to be more disruptive than boys the same age in two-parent families (Hetherington, Cox, and Cox, 1978). However, the negative effect of divorce on male children is substantially reduced if a divorced mother with custody is able to make a good adjustment to her new role as head of the household (Biller, 1971; Biller and Bahm, 1971).

The children's relationship with the parent who has custody is an important factor in their adjustment to divorce. Children who have a good relationship with the custodial parent seem better able to deal with the divorce. A good relationship with the noncustodial parent, on the other hand, does not seem to help, perhaps because that parent (usually the father) is no longer as influential (Hetherington, Cox, and Cox, 1978).

Divorce, of course, has substantial impact on the parents as individuals as well as on the relationship between parents and children. For the custodial parent, the sense of loss experienced in divorce may be lessened somewhat by the ongoing parental role which has now been enlarged. It is this parent who is likely to exert the major influence on the children since the parent who has custody is in the desirable position, from the children's point of view, of not having seemed to have deserted them.

The noncustodial parent has fewer overt problems than the parent with custody and probably has more time and freedom than he or she has had for years. Yet because this independence is the result of the disruption of close relationships, it may be experienced more as a loss than as a gain. For example, anxiety about the effects of the divorce on the lives of the children is a major problem in divorces where children are involved, and the parent who does not have custody may feel keenly the loss of opportunity to influence the upbringing of the children.

No matter how hard the noncustodial parent tries to maintain closeness with the children, loss of daily contact creates a distance which is hard to counteract. This may be intensified by the children's resentment that this parent has "deserted" them. The noncustodial parent may be called upon to help make major decisions, but is left out of the minor decisions that form the bulk of the parent's role. The role of the noncustodial parent varies, of course, with visiting agreements, geographical distance, the relationship between the former spouses, remarriage, and, most important, the parent's own attitude. Determination to maintain a relationship with one's children can overcome at least some of the difficulties. And, in fact, the joint sharing of custody of children has increased considerably in popularity in the last few years. Shared joint custody allows the opportunity for both parents to be more actively involved in the lives of their children.

Adoption

Adoption refers to voluntarily assuming legal custody of a child who is not biologically one's own. Adoption occurs in a variety of situations. A relative may adopt a child of deceased parents; a new spouse may adopt the children of the partner's former marriage; a couple, with or without children of their own, may adopt an unrelated child. The particular type of adoption obviously influences how the parent-child relationship will develop and what problems parents and child will face.

It has been estimated that about 2 percent of children in the United States are adopted, including adoptions by both relatives and nonrelatives. Adoptions by relatives account for nearly two-thirds of the total, and most of these are adoptions by a stepparent (Bonham, 1977). Although there is a shortage of healthy, Caucasian babies available for adoption (primarily because of the large numbers of unwed mothers who are choosing to keep their babies), there is in fact a surplus of "hard-to-place" children—those from minority or mixed racial background, those with physical, mental, or emotional handicaps, and those over the age of three (Johnson, 1975).

That these children are hard to place is not solely the result of a shortage of couples willing to assume the responsibility of children with special needs. State laws, social attitudes, and particularly the practices of adoption agencies have also contributed to the problem. It has been suggested that because adoption agencies are generally run by people with middle-class attitudes, the emphasis they have placed on income, social status, education, and home ownership has effectively screened out many worthy couples, especially blacks (Aldridge, 1974). Recently, greater efforts have been made to place special children by publicizing the issue and eliminating some unreasonable requirements.

In the past, adopted children usually knew little or nothing about their biological parents. This was due largely to legal restrictions which attempted to protect the parents who had given up their child. Today, however, such restrictions have been loosened and a growing number of adopted children have been seeking their biological parents. Betty Jean Lifton, herself an adoptee, describes the need to learn about one's origins as a prerequisite for establishing a sense of identity. She points out that adoptive parents must try to be sensitive to this need and not interpret it as a rejection of themselves (Lifton,

Although many couples would prefer to adopt children of their own race, a growing number have willingly adopted children from backgrounds different from their own.

1976). This issue is a complex one, for it involves not only adopted children's rights to learn their origins and the possible effect on their adoptive parents, but also the right of the biological parents to retain their anonymity if they so desire.

The attention given to this phenomenon in the media perhaps obscures a more important issue in adoption: how well do adoptive parents and their children get along? Studies have shown that in a majority of adoptions both parents and child feel that the relationship is a good one (Jaffee and Fanshel, 1970; Jaffee, 1974). This is true in adoptions both of babies and of older children.

Foster Parenting

Like parents who adopt, foster parents fulfill an urgent social need. In 1977 nearly 350,000 children under the age of eighteen were removed at least temporarily from parental custody because of abuse, neglect, or other factors, and placed in foster care, whether in family homes, group homes, or child-welfare institutions (Shyne and Schroeder, 1978). Yet because of the laws relating to foster parenting, as well as certain problems inherent in the arrangement itself, foster parents face an extremely difficult situation.

The foster home is viewed by everyone involved as temporary. Parental responsibility for the child is given not to the foster parents but to the social agency involved. The agency's policies are usually related to the foster parents through a caseworker. Under these conditions, it is difficult for foster parents to define their role. Foster parents may be inhibited from developing a close relationship with the child, since they feel the arrangement is temporary and they may soon be parted. Questions of policy relating to the child are decided by the social agency, and the caseworker's decisions override those of the foster parents should a conflict arise. Monetary support for the child is provided by the state. Deprived of most of the functions of parenting, it is not surprising that many foster parents have trouble fulfilling their role or that foster children often experience difficulty in adjusting to the home.

In practice, foster care is not usually a temporary arrangement. Most children, once they are placed in foster care, never return to their own homes (Mnookin, 1973). It has been suggested that agencies should recognize this and focus on finding permanent homes for these children, preferably with the possibility of adoption. At present, however, adoption is not always the best solution, since it usually requires people to give up government subsidies for foster care. The provision of subsidies for adoptive parents could help to remedy this situation.

PARENTHOOD AS A CHOICE

Because parenthood is such a dominant value in American society, there are many pressures upon married couples who choose voluntarily to remain childless. Often they are regarded as selfish, and frequently they encounter pressure from family and friends who warn them that they are missing the most meaningful experience in life (Movius, 1976). Even so, a small but growing group of couples are remaining childless by choice, and there is a growing feeling among many Americans that parenthood should not be an automatic choice for every couple. According to the Census Bureau, in 1978, 6 percent of wives aged eighteen to thirty-four expected to remain childless, and one in six wives expected to remain childless or to have only one child (U.S. Bureau of the Census, 1980).

Who are the women who are deciding not to become parents? In reviewing studies of voluntarily childless women, Houseknecht (1979) found that a disporportionate number of them were highly educated, working at careers, and not identified with formal religion. When married women who planned to have children were compared to those who did not, it was found that the childless women tended to believe that children would disrupt their marriages and life-styles or that these women were awed by the responsibility of motherhood. In interviews with eighty-nine voluntarily childless career women, Fabe and Wilker (1979) found that many of the women felt that their own mothers "were cheated out of their lives" and were "burdened and oppressed in their roles as mothers." As a result, the daughters of these women were afraid of having children of their own.

A study of fifty-two childless wives (Veevers, 1973) reported a consistent pattern in the way the decision to remain childless was reached. Whereas only one-third of the women interviewed reported that they had decided before their marriage that they would remain childless, the remaining two-thirds reported that remaining childless was the result of continuous postponement of the decision.

Another study of twenty-two couples who chose not to have children found a different pattern. Rather than drifting in postponement, these couples spent considerable effort in discussing and evaluating the pros and cons of parenthood vs. a life without children (Cooper, Cumber, and Hartner, 1978).

Both of these studies addressed the issue of outside pressure and how it was handled. In Veevers's study, all the wives reported that they did experience this pressure, both by negative attitudes toward childless women and by explicit promotherhood comments. They further reported that after the first year of marriage the pressure from friends and relatives increased, reached a peak in the third and fourth years, and leveled off after about the fifth or sixth years. Most of the wives said they had considered adopting a child. Veevers viewed this response as symbolically important rather than as evidence of a serious desire for children. The women could use this theme of adoption to convince others that they were "normal" and liked children; furthermore, it eased the anxiety of making an irreversible decision. Veevers also found that the decision to remain childless was a personal one. While some of the wives expressed interest in or support for feminism or concern over population problems, none indicated that these movements contributed to her decision.

Cooper, Cumber, and Hartner (1978) found that the couples in their study also experienced outside pressure which they resisted in several ways. First, they emphasized the positive features of their marriages and the freedom their life-style gave them to put their energy into personal goals. They also tended to devalue the parenthood role by suggesting that many people become parents without giving it any thought and then are unhappy and incompetent once they become parents. Finally, these couples tended to form friendships with others who were not child-oriented.

The need of voluntarily childless couples for support systems has prompted the formation of the National Alliance for Optional Parenthood. The major purpose of this organization is to promote the idea that parenthood is an option, not a duty for every couple. The group seeks to reassure married couples that it is acceptable, even beneficial, to choose nonparenthood. While it seems unlikely that nonparenthood will be the choice of a majority of Americans, this issue does help to point up the fact that parenthood is difficult as well as rewarding and that the happiest children are likely to be those whose parents truly want them and have thought about the costs and rewards of having them.

SUMMARY

1. The purpose of this chapter is to outline the adjustments required when a couple has children, to describe changing perceptions of motherhood and fatherhood, to identify significant factors that influence the relationships between parents and children, and to explore some special forms of parenthood.

2. The economic costs of having children are extremely high. Even so, most couples regard noneconomic factors such as emotional costs as greater disadvantages than financial costs. The psychological needs that children fill and the emotional rewards they offer seem to outweigh the economic burden.

3. The transition to parenthood affects the new mother and the new father somewhat differently. Level of marital adjustment is a significant factor in determining how well the couple will adjust to being a triad.

4. Parental roles are not as clearly defined today as they were in the past, and many couples are negotiating and sharing parental responsibilities. Studies of American men indicate that they are more nurturant and more interested in childrearing than has been assumed.

5. A basic goal of childrearing is to develop competence and self-esteem in children. To achieve this requires a balance between acceptance and love of the child and limit setting.

6. Recent research has shown that not only do parents influence the socialization of their children, the children help determine the parents' behavior. Among the factors that influence the relationship between parents and children are physiological causes (such as prematurity), economic status, education, and maternal employment.

7. Although most children live with both their parents, there is a growing trend toward single-parent families created by divorce, widowhood, separation, and out-of-wedlock births. Single parents face a number of difficulties, including economic problems, role overload, and lack of societal supports.

8. Parent-child relationships are undeniably disturbed by divorce. Researchers have found that the first year following divorce is the most difficult and that boys seem to be affected for a longer time than girls.

9. Some other special forms of parenthood include stepparents, adoptive parents, and foster parents. Adoptive parents of infants probably face the same kinds of adjustments as biological parents; the adoption of special-needs children or older children often requires greater adjustment. Foster parents are handicapped by lack of clear definition of their role.

10. The changing social climate is enabling more couples to choose to be childless without social stigma. Yet couples who are childless by choice continue to encounter pressure from others who are proparenthood.

REVIEW AND DISCUSSION

1. Describe some realistic and unrealistic portrayals of parenting in the popular media (television, books, movies). Why do you think they are realistic or unrealistic?

2. At what point in their relationship should a couple discuss their approach to childrearing—before or after marriage? Why?

3. Did your mother work at an outside job while you were growing up? What benefits or disadvantages did the situation have for you and other members of your family?

4. Do you know anyone who was brought up by adoptive parents, a stepparent, or in foster care? Do you think such a person has problems, adjustments, and rewards different from those of children raised by two biological parents?

5. What is your view of the role that mothers and fathers should fill in childrearing? Should their roles be distinctly different, interchangeable, or should they share some responsibilities and not others?

SUGGESTED READINGS

Berman, C. (1974). *We Take This Child: A Candid Look at Modern Adoption.* Garden City, N.Y.: Doubleday.

Explores the experiences of parents adopting all varieties of children, including black, white, multiracial, and handicapped. The views of parents, social workers, lawyers, and others are combined to give a picture of the adoption process and what it is like to raise an adopted child. Includes a bibliography of books and articles on adoption and a list of organizations concerned with adoption.

diGiulio, R. (1980). *Effective Parenting.* New York: Follett.

> A commonsense approach to being a parent. Identifies seven styles of parenting—the childish parent, doctor, talker, diplomat, martyr, autocrat— as well as the hypothetical ideal, a flexible, loving parent who "gives the child a chance to be good."

Brazelton, B. (1972). *Infants and Mothers.* New York: Dell (paper).

> An excellent book for new parents. It traces the first year of life for three general types of babies—the quiet baby, the average baby, and the active baby—in a case-study format. Describes how the parents and their babies interact and provides commentary by the author throughout.

Ginott, H. G. (1965). *Between Parent and Child.* New York: Macmillan.

> Focuses on teaching parents the skills to communicate effectively with their children. Gives examples of how to interpret the underlying meaning of the child's statements and demonstrates how to comment on the child's *behavior* rather than making judgmental statements that damage the child's self-esteem.

Lamb, M. E. (1977). The Role of the Father: An Overview. pp. 1–63 in M. E. Lamb (ed.), *The Role of the Father in Child Development.* New York: John Wiley and Sons.

> An introductory essay which provides a general overview of the research on the father-child relationship. The essay precedes an anthology of technical, research-based reports examining the role of the father in child development.

Marriage and Family: The Middle and Later Years

"The love of the young for the young, that is the beginning of life. But the love of the old for the old, that is the beginning . . . of things longer."

JEROME K. JEROME

Until recently, there was comparatively little research available on marital and family relationships in the middle and later years. Much of the focus was on the earlier years of marriage, when young children were living at home. Now, however, this is changing rapidly. An important impetus for studying the latter part of the family life cycle has come from the fact that the number and percentage of older people in the United States are growing rapidly. The increase in the aging population has come about largely as a consequence of a declining birthrate coupled with an increase in life expectancy. Since most of us will spend more years as aged persons than previous generations did, we need to know more about intimate relationships during this period of life.

People in their middle and later years face developmental tasks and role adjustments that are different from those they encountered in their earlier years. As their children leave home, their role as parents changes. In time, they may take on the new role of grandparents. Increasingly, middle-aged couples are finding themselves assuming the responsibility of ensuring that their own aging parents are cared for. Retirement from the work force requires additional adjustments, and inevitably the passage of time brings changes in the relations between the marital partners themselves. The couple's sexual relationship may change, health may become a more prominent concern, and the prospect of eventual widowhood must be faced. But while the tasks of the later adult years may be challenging, many couples find this to be a satisfying time of life; a time to renew their relationship to each other, to seek new avenues through which to express their interests, and to enjoy their children and grandchildren in a new way.

The increased attention to middle and older age couples has had the beneficial effect of helping to dispel many popular myths and stereotypes. For example, sociologists have found that rather than becoming isolated, most older parents retain close ties to their adult children and other kin. Similarly, there is evidence that the "empty-nest syndrome"—the depression that middle-aged mothers are reputed to experience when their children leave home—may not be a crisis at all. This chapter will shed light on a number of similar myths as we examine the tasks and adjustments of couples in the middle and later years.

 STAGES IN THE AGING PROCESS

While most of us are aware that individuals pass through a number of developmental stages from infancy to adulthood, quite often we forget that persons in middle age and old age go through a series of stages, too. There are dramatic differences among people aged 45, 55, 65, and 75. In order to set the framework for this chapter, we will look again at the family life cycle and then describe what demographic research has shown about life patterns during the latter part of the cycle.

The Family Life Cycle

Some sociologists trace patterns of behavior which distinguish groups of older people by where they are in the family life cycle. Vital events which constitute the ebb and flow of family life, rather than work and retirement, are used as benchmarks. For instance, one cycle might be:

1. Marriage
2. Birth of first child
3. Birth of last child
4. Launching of last child
5. Death of one spouse

Some researchers add more stages, like where the children are in school. In the divisions given here, the median age in the first four stages is controlled to some degree by the couple themselves and their children; the timing of the last stage is beyond their control.

Sociologists sometimes group people into these life-cycle stages by **cohorts**—all those who are born in a certain period. The people in a particular cohort experience the same public events at about the same time in their lives. For example, all women born in 1928 were about eighteen years old at the end of World War II. Many of them married in the peak marriage year of 1946 and became mothers in the "baby boom" which lasted from 1946 to 1957. Their behavior to some extent may be explained by the year in which they were born.

In order to draw a general picture of the timing of marriage, childbearing, child launching, and widowhood, studies of the family life cycle are based on assumptions about the typical family: (1) it consists of a man and a woman who remain married until one of them (usually the husband) dies; (2) the wife gives birth to the average number of children born to her cohort; and (3) she marries and has children according to the median time schedule for all mothers in her cohort who were ever married (Norton, 1974). Even though these assumptions do not always fit particular families, they provide a standard for statistical analysis of the life patterns within a cohort and reveal differences between cohorts.

Social Characteristics of Older People

Some sociologists and the Bureau of the Census classify older people in terms of the traditional retirement age of 65, largely because this is useful for studying work and retirement patterns. This system, which we will use with the family life cycle, divides the middle and later years into four decades by age. Using these categories, researchers can make some generalizations about what happens at each age level.

By *late maturity* (45–54), 90 percent of Americans have been married at least once, and the great majority live in their own homes with a spouse. Almost half still have a child under eighteen living at home, but this is the time of "launching" offspring from the parental nest. The parents' developmental tasks are to disengage themselves from their children and renew their bonds with each other.

During *preretirement* (55–64), most couples still live in their own homes, but some, especially women, are widowed in this period. Relationships with their children change from full responsibility for them to a recognition of their independence. (Only about 8 percent of families in this group have children under eighteen.) During these years, health is usually good enough to permit couples to enjoy their leisure; many begin to plan for retirement. They also begin to face the idea that one of them will be left alone when the other dies.

In the family of *early retirement* (65–74), the gap between the number of surviving men and women increases. Those couples still together, enthusiastic about life, and with ingenuity, plus enough money, may enjoy a new freedom; for others, retirement may be an unhappy struggle with boredom, loss of self-respect, and poverty.

By *late retirement* (over 75), only 69 percent of older men and 22 percent of older women are married (Harris, 1978). For many, this is a time of deteriorating health and increasing dependence on others for residence, financial support, and emotional attachments. Those who do have their health and exhibit an active interest in life still have to accept some of the limitations of old age, but are more likely to retain their independence (Neugarten, 1975).

Although age categories are helpful in predicting survival of a spouse and other aspects of life for different segments of the older population, studies have shown that age is a relatively poor guide to the differences between people. Sixty-five was chosen as the time for retirement during the Great Depression of the 1930s, when unemployment was high and social planners thought it better to pension off the older generation so more jobs would be available for the younger. Economic and labor considerations of the thirties determined the choice rather than any conviction that people changed dramatically at 65. Some people obviously retain their vigor far beyond 65, while others begin to withdraw from life long before then (Neugarten, 1975).

Demographic Profile of Aging

In 1900, only 4.1 percent of the population were 65 or older. But in 1978, 11 percent of Americans fell into this bracket: 24.1 million people in a population of 218.5 million. Just since 1970, this group has grown by 4 million (U.S. Bureau of the Census, Statistical Abstract of the United States, 1980). When people born during the baby boom reach 55 around the turn of the century, the proportion of older people may rise to almost 13 percent (Rosenberg, 1970).

LIFE EXPECTANCY   In 1920, the average life expectancy at birth for Americans was 54.1 years; by 1979, it was 73.3—an increase of over nineteen years (U.S. Bureau of the Census, Statistical Abstract of the United States, 1980). Along with this dramatic increase in longevity, the survival gap between men and women has widened. Women in 1978 had a life expectancy of 77.2 years, compared to 69.5 years for men. The Bureau of Census projects that in 2000, the average life span for females will be 78.3 years and for males 70 years. The gap would then be over eight years. Scientists speculate that genetic differences by sex, together with differences in the way they live their lives, produce the survival gap. Both men and women average longer lives through increased control over fatal childhood diseases, but male mortality exceeds female mortality by 100 percent or more for seven major causes of death: coronary heart disease, lung cancer, emphysema, motor vehicle and other accidents, cirrhosis of the liver, and suicide (Waldron and Johnston, 1976).

WIDOWHOOD AND REMARRIAGE   Since women, on average, tend to marry men a few years older than themselves, they face the prospect of ten or more years of widowhood at the end of their lives. Over half of the women over 65 in this country (51 percent of white women, 59 percent of black women) are widowed, compared with 13 percent of white men and 23 percent of black men (U.S. Bureau of the Census, 1979, Current Population Reports, P-23:85).

One reason widows are less likely to remarry than widowers is that there are fewer partners available to the women. While in 1910, there were 101.2 men over 65 to every 100 women in that age group, the imbalanced sex ratio has swung so far in the opposite direction that by 1978 there were only 68.9 men over 65 per 100 females of that age (U.S. Bureau of the Census, 1979, Current Population Reports, P-23:85). Widows who would like to remarry are restricted both by the scarcity of long-lived men and by the cultural double standard regarding remarriage. It is considered quite acceptable for older widowers to marry younger women, but not for older widows to marry younger men. After 55, men are five times as likely to remarry as women. The loss of a marital relationship thus is more likely to be permanent for women than for men.

INCOME   One of the most serious problems faced by the aged is financial hardship. Depending on the criteria used, from one-quarter to two-thirds of the elderly in the United States are "poor." In 1978, the median income of those over 65 was $7,660, a figure less than half that for the 55–64 age group. An estimated 3.2 million people over 65 were living on incomes below the poverty level. The precarious financial situation of the aged affects women particularly. Of over 2 million single or no-longer-married aged persons living below the poverty level, women outnumber men by more than four to one (U.S. Bureau of the Census, 1979).

Among the factors that contribute to the economic problems of the elderly are low Social Security and Supplemental Security Income payments, high levels of unemployment, low-paying jobs, and savings and pension plans that have lost their buying power because of inflation. Financial help from relatives does not add substantially to the income of the aged.

Various social and physical problems are linked to financial hardship among the elderly. Compared to the aged who are not experiencing financial difficulty, those who are poor are less healthy, less active, and more isolated from friends and family. Analysis of data on life satisfaction among older people reveals important links between life satisfaction and health, economic resources, and independence in later life (Watson and Kivett, 1976). As a general rule, morale and satisfaction with life decline among the elderly with declining income level (Hutchinson, 1975).

The economic situation of the old has shown some improvement over the last several decades. In 1960, over 35 percent of those 65 and older fell below that year's poverty level, compared to 14 percent below poverty level in 1977 (U.S. Bureau of the Census, Statistical Abstract of the United States, 1979).

Social Security payments are largely responsible for the increased income level of the aged. In 1950, there were 1,771,000 Americans over 65 receiving retirement benefits. In 1978, 18,358,000 retired workers were receiving Social Security benefits (U.S. Bureau of the Census, Statistical Abstract of the United States, 1980).

LIVING ARRANGEMENTS   Over 14 million households are headed by persons 65 years old or older. The trend in the last two decades has been for older citizens to head their own households, whether as head of a family or as an individual living alone. Females living alone represent 36 percent of the households headed by persons over 65; males living alone represent 10 percent. Husband-wife households total 45 percent, and the other 9 percent are households of two or more persons, such as brother-sister households or households including nonrelatives.

About 6 percent of the aged are institutionalized. Of more than a million persons over 65 living in public and private institutions, 96 percent are in nursing homes and the remainder are in residential treatment centers, mental hospitals, or are hospitalized for physical reasons (U.S. Bureau of the Census, 1979, Current Population Reports, P-23:85). Although at first glance, 6 percent does not appear to be a very large figure, the research indicates that well over 20 percent of the aged spend at least some time in a nursing home and a large percentage die in nursing homes.

KINSHIP NETWORKS BETWEEN GENERATIONS

Much of the sociological research done on the family of later life has focused on kinship networks, specifically on the interactions between family members of different generations. Several decades ago, family theorists such as Burgess suggested that there was a trend toward the "isolated nuclear family" consisting of husband, wife, and children who had few ties with the couple's aging parents. If this were true, it would mean that older parents would have only each other; if one partner died, the other would have no family at all (Troll, 1971).

More recent studies conducted during the 1960s and 1970s have not supported this view. After reviewing the research of the 1960s, Troll (1971) concluded that members of different generations in families do interact significantly with each other. Instead of the isolated nuclear family, Troll found that the prevalent family form could be characterized as a **modified extended family** in which married offspring and their older parents kept kinship ties through living close to one another, visits, and mutual aid. Troll suggested that the strength of kinship ties in the later years can be measured in terms of numbers of available kin, residential proximity, the extent of aid between kin, and indicators of emotional closeness. The literature of the 1970s tends to support Troll's basic conclusion as well as shedding new light on family relationships during this phase of the life span.

Number of Kin

Only 3 percent of people over age 65 who are not living in institutions have no living relatives. Although older family members and friends die off more rapidly as one enters old age, few older people are left with no kin at all. Even when kin their own age may be gone, some older people nonetheless enjoy being at the top of a pyramid of descendants. Many older women in one study (Shanas et al., 1968) kept a large supply of birthday and anniversary cards ready for the constant progression of family events involving their children, grandchildren, and great-grandchildren.

The number of kin available to an older person may be less important than the relationship with them. For example, a widow whose only child visits her once a week may be richer in emotional support from kinship ties than one whose five children live nearby but rarely even telephone (Troll, 1971).

Residential Closeness

According to most surveys, older Americans prefer to live close by but in separate households from their adult children. Like younger people, older people wish to be independent if they can. It is usually when they cannot afford to live alone, are in poor health, or have lost a spouse that older people move in with their children. About 30 percent of elderly Americans who have living children choose this alternative (Johnson and Bursk, 1977). Generally, a widowed woman in poor health is the most likely to live with her adult children. These joint households are not true three-generation families because they usually consist of postparental couples and an aged parent. The grandchildren have usually grown up and moved away before the grandparents (most often a grandmother) finds it necessary to move in. Only 8 percent of the families in America can be regarded as truly three-generational, with parents, children, and grandparents residing in one house.

Even though they prefer not to live in the same household with their children, older Americans do tend to live near them. This is especially true of working-class families. According to Shanas et al. (1968), 84 percent of working-class parents over 65 in three industrial societies—the United States, England, and Denmark—lived within an hour's traveling time of one of their children. There are indications, however, that in middle-class families, when parents are middle-aged and their children are just starting families of their own, the generations are likely to maintain greater geographic distance from each other. One of the major reasons for this appears to be the fact that middle-class couples are more likely to move in order to further their careers. But after middle-class parents have retired, they tend to move near one or more of their children (Troll, 1971).

Frequency of Interaction

No matter how far from each other family members may live, they tend to contact each other often. Even middle-class families in which parents live too far from their children for weekly visits nonetheless keep in touch through letters, phone calls, and occasional extended visits. Eighty-four percent of older Americans in the Shanas study (1968) had seen at least one of their children within the week, and 90 percent within the month. In a cross-cultural study of family kin networks, Shanas (1973) found that about 80 percent of elderly respondents from five countries visited their children frequently and received valuable social and psychological support from them. In Farber's (1981) study of kinship patterns, he found that about 90 percent of the respondents either see or want to see their parents and siblings frequently.

Older middle-class Bostonians in another survey contacted one-third of all their available relatives at least once a month. And despite the fact that middle-aged, middle-class parents tend to live some distance from their children, there is more visiting between middle-aged parents and their children than between any other age groups. Seventy percent of middle-aged parents in one study saw their married children weekly, 40 percent saw their own parents weekly, but only 10 percent of married young adults saw their grandparents weekly (Troll, 1971).

Schulman (1975) studied young, white, single people and married couples and concluded that kin interaction during the middle years is limited by the responsibilities of childrearing and work. In this survey, married couples with children to care for saw less of kin than either young singles or older married couples who were less involved with work and were no longer raising children.

It should be noted that frequency of interaction is not in itself a reliable indicator of family closeness. Children may feel obliged to visit aging parents without ever communicating with them on an intimate level. Although one-third of the sons in one study who felt close to their parents visited them often, a third of those who felt distant visited often as well (Troll, 1971).

Kinship Strength

Because kinship ties are so subjective, it is very difficult to measure directly just how strong they are. One indirect method of measuring the strength of family ties is to compare ties to relatives with attachments to friends.

KIN TIES AND FRIENDSHIP TIES   The research suggests that people generally feel that family ties are more important than ties to friends (Hochschild, 1973). The long-term relationships between close kin are characterized by intimacy, concern, and feelings of obligation; consequently, they are more durable (Bahr and Nye, 1974; Troll and Smith, 1976). Friendships, on the other hand, may be held together by mutual values and interests and may not survive over long periods of time or geographical distance. Friends, as equals, sometimes seem to take the place of siblings who have died, but they are less likely to be able to compensate for the loss of a child.

PARENT-CHILD BONDS   Despite the notion that there is a traditional conflict in values between middle-aged parents and their adolescent children, family members are more likely to hold the same opinions than people of the same age who are not related (Troll, 1971). In this regard, Bengtson (1971) found that people believe there is a greater generation gap in society than in their particular family. Johnson and Bursk (1977) in a study of fifty-four pairs of older parents and their children in Boston found that the relationship between this group of parents and their children was affected by parental health, financial situation, living environment, and attitude toward aging. When all these factors were positive, parents had better relationships with their children.

DIFFERENCES IN FAMILY BONDS   Differences in the strength of family bonds have been found to be strongly related to sex. In adults, kinship ties seem to be strongest between women. Wives, for example, are expected to maintain correspondence with kinfolk. They are perceived as the communicators (Bahr and Nye, 1974). Couples are more likely to live near the wife's parents and to get together with the wife's relatives: mutual aid and affection seem to be strongest between the women. Widows are more likely to move in with one of their children—usually a daughter—than are widowers. And even if women do not share the same values as their parents, they are more likely than men to feel close and visit often.

ECONOMIC INTERDEPENDENCE   Many sociologists use the amount of economic interdependence as a measure of kinship strength. Johnson and Bursk (1977) found that mutual aid between generations existed in 93 percent of the aged they studied who had adult children. Such exchange may take the form of money, gifts, services (such as babysitting, housework, and shopping), or advice. Usually there is a flow of aid from the old to the young, but parents in the middle years give both to their children and to their own aging parents. In general, parents keep giving aid to their children as long as they can, until health or financial problems make this impossible. The middle-class elderly are more likely than other groups to give money, gifts, and advice on business or job-related matters. For most of the other forms of help and advice listed in Table 11.1, different income groups are very similar (Harris and Associates, 1975).

The research also suggests that some 70 percent of the aged receive help from their adult children. Often the adult children help their parents financially, in a reversal of the role patterns of earlier years. This usually occurs because of the increased income of the working adult children and the corresponding reduced income of their retired parents (Johnson and Bursk, 1977). Other forms of assistance from adult children to their parents include housework, transportation, meal preparation, help with decisions about housing, medical, and financial matters, and information about how to use community and governmental resources available to the elderly.

But even though adult children are providing important aid to their parents, Treas (1977) believes that demographic and social factors may alter this pattern in the near future. Among the reasons she gives are:

1. Today's aged in their mid-sixties had smaller families than previous generations. Thus many of these people may not have an adult child to call upon for help.

2. Because more younger women are marrying than in the past there will be fewer "maiden daughters" to care for aged parents.

Table 11.1 Ways in which Public 65 and over Who Have Children and Grandchildren Help Them

	TOTAL PUBLIC 65 AND OVER	PUBLIC 65–69	PUBLIC 70–79	PUBLIC 80 AND OVER
	%	%	%	%
Give gifts	90	93	89	86
Help out when someone is ill	68	78	65	57
Take care of grandchildren	54	65	53	34
Help out with money	45	50	44	38
Give general advice on how to deal with some of life's problems	39	45	37	32
Shop or run errands	34	46	29	23
Fix things around their house or keep house for them	26	31	25	20
Give advice on bringing up children	23	25	22	20
Give advice on running a home	21	24	21	17
Give advice on jobs or business matters	20	24	17	19
Take grandchildren, nieces or nephews into your home to live with you	16	20	16	11

Source: Reprinted from *The Myth and Reality of Aging in America,* a study prepared by Louis Harris and Associates, Inc. for The National Council on the Aging, Inc., Washington, D.C., © 1975, p. 75.

3. The influx of women into the work force will affect the pattern of giving help. It is usually women who provide the care-taking tasks for aging parents. Women who have children and hold a job outside the home will have difficulty finding the time to help their aged parents.

Some research since 1970 has investigated the attitudes of young people regarding economic interdependence between generations. Wake and Sporakowski (1972) found that students were more likely than their parents to believe the family should take in or economically support an aged grandparent. A study of blue-collar young adults (Robertson, 1976) found that these young people had no economic expectations of their grandparents but two-thirds of them felt they should help support their grandparents.

MARITAL SATISFACTION AND ADJUSTMENT IN THE MIDDLE AND LATER YEARS

Once it was generally thought that satisfaction in marriage is greatest as newlyweds and gradually declines to a low point in the later years. More recent studies indicate that marital satisfaction follows a U-shaped curve. It is high at the newlywed stage, declines throughout the parenting years, then begins to rise again when the children are launched, and reaches a new peak during the postparental years (Rollins and Cannon, 1974).

Rollins and Cannon (1974) found that the bottoming out of marital satisfaction was due to the pressure of careers and parenting, not to growing older. Among those over 60, marital satisfaction is directly related to their satisfaction with life. The effect of marital satisfaction on one's outlook tends to be greater among women than men (Lee, 1978). This is generally the case at all stages of the family life cycle and most likely results from the fact that women tend to have more "invested" in marriage than men. Even wives who work outside the home generally view the wife/mother role as their most important role with the occupational role being secondary. Men, by contrast, tend to view the occupational role as their primary social role.

Another study (Campbell, 1975) reported that couples in their early postparental years were among the happiest groups in America. This finding supports earlier research by Feldman (1964). He found couples in the process of launching their children to be second only to honeymooners and the elderly in marital satisfaction. Their relationship tended to be marked less by emotion than by a calm, objective attitude. When all children are launched and the wife is over 65, Feldman found that marital interaction is low, but that the couple's relationship is marked by peacefulness and an absence of stress. Couples in this group have a level of marital satisfaction almost as high as the newly married, possibly because of their long experience with marriage.

Atchley (1977) has found that happily married elderly couples feel increasingly comfortable with one another. He also reported that there was more equality in the marriages with less separation of gender and family roles.

In a study of 408 older husbands and wives (aged 60–89), Stinnett, Carter, and Montgomery (1972) found that 95 percent of their respondents rated their marriages happy or very happy. Over half (53 percent) felt that their marriages had grown better over time. Forty-one percent said they had stayed about the same. Only 4 percent felt their marriages were worse. Other studies have shown that older people who are still married are happier, better adjusted, and less lonely than people their age who are unmarried, divorced, or widowed (Stinnett, Collins, and Montgomery, 1970).

This picture contradicts the stereotype that elderly husbands and wives merely exist together. The high level of satisfaction probably is related to the increased time older people have to spend enjoying each other's companionship. While many poor marriages may have broken up before this period, those that last may be based on years of growing understanding, acceptance, and communication, and increasing dependence on each other, rather than on their children or their work roles, for the satisfaction of emotional needs (Stinnett, Carter, and Montgomery, 1972).

However, generalizing about marriage styles in the middle and later years is risky. One researcher has found that marital styles in the later years are exceeded in variety only by those of the early years of marriage (Darnley, 1975).

Sexual Adjustment

In Chapter 5, we noted the effects of aging on human sexuality. During the middle years, women experience the physiological changes of menopause; men require longer to achieve erections and ejaculate with less force. But these physical changes seem to be far less important than a person's attitude toward his or her sexuality. According to one group of researchers (Pearlman, Cohen, and Coburn, 1981), the middle years can be a time of sexual panic for both sexes, with women worrying about their sexual attractiveness and men worrying about losing their sexual potency. But with understanding of the changes they are experiencing and good communication, couples can achieve high levels of sexual satisfaction.

Pearlman and her colleagues surveyed 800 women on a number of topics related to mid-life changes. These women, who ranged in age from their mid-thirties to their mid-sixties, reported that their sexual desire was as great or greater than it ever was. Fully two-thirds of the sample said they enjoyed sex more now than they ever had before. The primary reason given by most women for their increased enjoyment was a good feeling about their bodies. They had found that the old stereotype of the middle-aged woman as past her prime was simply wrong. They felt they were more desirable sexually now than when they were younger (Pearlman, Cohen, and Coburn, 1981). This study also confirmed what earlier research (Neugarten et al., 1963) had suggested: the supposed sexual watershed for middle-aged women—menopause—was regarded by most as of no great concern.

Sexuality in old age is more problematic. While some older individuals continue sexual activity during their later years, others who are still healthy and capable of enjoying an active sex life fail to do so because of societal attitudes about sex in old age. They may feel that they are not supposed to have sexual feelings and that to continue sexual activity is abnormal or shameful. These attitudes arise long before the individuals reach old age; often the people who in their youth believe that sexual behavior is inappropriate in old age are likely to apply their earlier attitudes to themselves.

FREQUENCY AND FORMS OF EXPRESSION　Studies of sexual expression among the aged should be approached cautiously. Whereas some studies use representative samples of older people, others survey only those individuals who are continuing to engage in sexual behavior and base their conclusions on these samples. Also the term "sexual behavior" may mean different things to different researchers. It can refer to coitus, to masturbation, or to other forms of sexual expression or outlet.

A study of people whose mean age was 68 years (Pfeiffer, 1974) found that among this group 80 percent were interested in sexual expression and 70 percent were sexually active. By age 78, one-quarter of the sample were still sexually active. Another study of aged, healthy married couples found similarly

Young people often see the elderly as docile, intellectually deficient, and sexually inactive. Today, however, many older people are challenging these notions, as suggested by this man's T-shirt.

high rates of sexual activity. In this sample, 70 percent of the elderly married couples reported that they were still sexually active (Sviland, 1975). The research indicates that people who enjoy an active and enjoyable sexual life when younger are more likely to continue having sexual relations in their later years. This finding coincides with research on sexuality noted in Chapter 5 that shows that when people continue sexual activity their desire and performance are usually enhanced.

An important factor related to the frequency of sexual expression in old age is one's sex. Studies indicate that men, whether married or single, have similar rates of sexual activity. However, there are substantial differences in the rates for married and unmarried women. In fact, very few aged unmarried women report any sexual activity (Kent, 1975). The reasons for this are largely cultural. First, aged unmarried women are likely to be sexually conservative because they were raised during a period of conservative sexual standards. Second, there are few culturally acceptable partners for aged women. As discussed earlier, women live longer than men, and older men are much more likely to be married than older women. The scarcity of eligible older men, combined with the societal disapproval of older women seeking out younger men, contribute to the lack of sexual opportunity of unmarried older women.

There are a number of reasons why older people decide to discontinue sexual activity. Among the most prominent are poor health, the lack of a partner, the inability to perform, and the belief that sexual behavior is inappropriate for old people. A study of sexuality in nursing homes (Wasow and Loeb, 1978), summarized in Table 11.2, found that the reason given most often for discontinuing sexual activity was lack of a partner. More females than males reported that they had lost interest in engaging in sex, and more males than females reported performance difficulties.

Table 11.2 **Reasons for Discontinuation of Sexual Activity**

REASON	PERCENTAGE OF MALES	PERCENTAGE OF FEMALES
Poor health	16.7	16.3
Lost interest	10.0	27.9
Sex not appropriate	6.7	7.0
No partner	30.0	39.5
Inability to perform	16.7	10.0
Celibate	6.7	2.3
No answer	13.3	2.3

Source: M. Wasow and M. B. Loeb, "Sexuality in nursing homes," in Robert L. Solnick (ed.), *Sexuality and Aging* (revised). Andrus Gerontology Center, University of Southern California, 1978.

In addition to coitus, the most frequent form of sexual expression among the aged is masturbation. Masturbation may be a helpful sexual outlet for widowed individuals, individuals whose spouse is in poor health, and the unmarried. About 25 percent of older men who have regular sexual intercourse also masturbate regularly. Similarly, about a quarter of women over 65 masturbate regularly (McCary, 1973).

Health and Adjustment

Few things have so great an impact on adjustment in the middle and later years as health. In fact, the major factor in determining an elderly person's satisfaction with life is health (Mancini, 1978). As people grow older they become concerned with the physical aging process, alterations in physical appearance, and the increasing chance of a serious illness. The rate at which one ages varies according to a number of factors, including sex, diet, and exercise.

But the importance of the health of an older person is not limited to that individual alone; it has a direct impact on the family. Poor health can cause changes in where the family lives; not only where the older person lives, but other family members as well. It can also affect the way family members interact, and the types and degrees of economic support they can expect. When an older family member's health deteriorates, other members of the family may have to become involved either financially or by just helping out. This is especially true if the older person is single; married couples are better able to cope with ill health without family involvement (Streib and Beck, 1980).

One of the ironies of illness in elderly people is that it leads to an increase in family interaction. Most American families prefer to care for their elderly sick themselves. A study of persons over 65 who were not in institutions revealed that while nearly 5 percent of those over 65 are institutionalized, 10 percent of the elderly were confined to their house or bed at home. For these, the main source of help is the family. Family members cared for the ill and infirm as well as doing the necessary everyday chores (Shanas, 1979). One study reported that family or friends supplied about 70 percent of the services required by severely infirm elderly (Maddox and Dellinger, 1978). At present there is little research on what adjustments the elderly have to make to the increased involvement of their family in their lives.

Styles of Adjustment to Aging

Older people's satisfaction with life and with marriage depends not only on how well they manage to readjust to each other after the various changes in the life cycle but also on how well they cope with the changes as individuals. According to a study of people 70–79 years old in the Midwest, people's

Drawing by Weber; © 1976
The New Yorker Magazine, Inc.

"We haven't much time left, Jake. What do you say
we take a stab at la dolce vita?"

personality differences are more significant to their happiness than the specific ways they have of coping. For instance, some people are happy when they maintain active involvement with family and community during later life; but some people who are relatively inactive are also happy (Neugarten, 1971).

Neugarten defines happiness as taking pleasure in daily activities, seeing one's life as meaningful, accepting the past, feeling that one's life goals have been achieved, holding a positive self-image, and being optimistic. She found that both active and inactive people were capable of meeting these requirements. Seventy percent of those studied had well-integrated, happy personalities which were of one of three distinct types. "Reorganizers" were competently handling a wide variety of activities which they had substituted for their earlier roles. "Focused" individuals were more selective in their activities, doing only a few things they truly enjoyed. A third group, called "disengaged," had withdrawn from role commitments to enjoy a calm, relaxed life.

There were two other kinds of people, however, who also experienced medium to high life satisfaction through defensive striving and tight control over their lives. Those with "holding-on" patterns coped by keeping too busy to feel any losses in their lives. "Constricted" people had limited their social activities, closed themselves to new involvements, and become preoccupied with defending themselves against the effects of aging.

Even people whose response to age is passive dependency—leaning on one or more other people for support—were found to be capable of deriving at least medium satisfaction from life. The only two personality types that had not been able to cope with aging in ways that brought them happiness were those who were apathetic and those with severe psychological problems (Neugarten, 1971).

Failure to adjust to aging can lead to depression, which is so common among the elderly that older people have the highest rate of suicide for any age group in the country. Twenty-five percent of all suicides are people over 65, with the suicide rate reaching its peak among men over 85 (Smith, 1973).

DEVELOPMENTAL TASKS OF THE MIDDLE AND LATER YEARS

Moving out of the Parenting Role

Until the 1960s, some sociologists and psychotherapists believed that when their children left home, it was a traumatic time for the parents, particularly for mothers, who were believed to sink into depressions. This was called the **empty-nest syndrome,** and it was thought to lead to a number of maladaptive behaviors, including adultery, alcoholism, and use of tranquilizers or stimulants. Increasingly, however, the departure of the last child is not seen as a crisis or anything approaching one. Studies have shown that most women regard the empty nest with emotions ranging from relief to joy. Some fathers, however—particularly if the marriage is not good—do suffer from something like the empty-nest syndrome. But if the marriage is sound, the postparental period, as we noted earlier, can be one of greater satisfaction than any period since the honeymoon (Lowenthal and Chiriboga, 1972).

Irwin Deutscher (1962) was puzzled when he discovered that the empty nest was not troublesome to mothers, so he tried to determine why it wasn't. Deutscher's subjects should have felt all the stress associated with the syndrome, had it existed. Not only were their own children gone, but they were of the generations whose own mothers would not have survived, or long survived, the immediate postparental period. Thus, his subjects lacked role models in their own mothers for this role. Still all his subjects reported little or no difficulty.

Deutscher's explanation was that other events in the parent-child relationship prepared the mother for the empty nest—a phenomenon that has been termed "anticipatory socialization." The child's high-school experience, college, and military service in the case of males, gave the parents a foretaste of the child's eventual independence and an opportunity to adapt to it. However, today women face a different problem. To put it in Deutscher's terminology, Does anticipatory socialization prepare a woman to assume another family burden in the place of the one she has just discarded? Is she prepared to assume responsibility for elderly family members who cannot take care of themselves?

This is one of the great ironies of increasing longevity: American women who should be entering one of the richest periods of their lives are now faced

HIGHLIGHT 11.1

Older Parents on Their Grownup Children

The need for approval is profound, and it goes both ways! My children want me to see and validate how they're "making it." But I also yearn to be told that I'm still good, still valued. Our grown children do a lot of scrutinizing of us when they come home—reshaping their opinions of the past and what it did or didn't do to them. This can be a painful but exhilarating exercise.

I see my son and his family once or twice a year. I could see them much more. They keep saying, "Why don't you come up and see us, why don't you come up and see us?" I don't because I feel embarrassed, bored, and more interested in what I am doing. I feel embarrassed at their respect and warmth. If I could be around and invisible and see what they're doing, that would give me a great deal of satisfaction. I don't want them to do things for me, wait on me. I'm interested in what I'm doing here. I don't want to take the weekend off to go— maybe feel in the way with their friends. They're having a good time. I'm having a good time, why can't we just go on separately and talk over the phone, and see each other at Christmas?

I had been on a business trip in the area where my twenty-two-year-old was working, and we had arranged to meet for lunch. Well, by some miracle of perfect planning I found myself walking toward our meeting place just on time. It was a clear, sunlit day, and there on the corner stood this fine human being, bright and funny and attractive and interesting. I couldn't wait to hear what we would talk about and I felt really lucky to be having lunch with him. How great it was to recognize that this wonderful person was my son!

My husband and I decided to live in separate places two years after our youngest child left home. When we told our four adult children about this, all four did unexpected things. Two, who had not felt ready for marriage or in need of it before, telephoned me on the same day from opposite ends of the country and unknown to each other, to say that they were getting married. For me this was an important reinforcement and support because, although they didn't say so in so many words, they seemed to be saying, Don't be disheartened. Marriage is good. Yours was too, even if it isn't working anymore. It's given us something which we value and want to try and live by. The other two did something else: they temporarily moved closer to home after living far away for several years. They didn't say it in words, either, but they seemed to be saying, Don't worry. We can still give each other comfort and reassurance—in times of stress we are still available to each other.

Source: From *Ourselves and Our Children: A Book by and for Parents*, by The Boston Women's Health Book Collective. Copyright © 1978 by The Boston Women's Health Book Collective, Inc. Reprinted by permission of Random House, Inc.

with assuming a second family, with quite different problems from those of the families they have just launched. As we noted earlier, most families with an ill or infirm elderly member prefer to care for him or her at home. They regard institutionalization as a last resort, and often endure severe emotional stress before making the decision to place the relative in an institution. But the primary burden of caring for the old at home falls on the women whose nests have just emptied (Brody, 1978). By its very nature, this new role for the postparental woman may place a great strain on the marriage and on family relationships. This problem will require careful study in the future.

Grandparents and Grandchildren

A combination of factors have caused the role of grandparent to begin in the middle years rather than only in old age. Marriage, childbearing, and child launching have all come earlier in life for the past couple of generations, so the arrival of grandchildren has also come earlier (Troll, 1971; Brody, 1978). These factors, coupled with increasing longevity, mean that the popular image of grandparents is probably more appropriate for great-grandparents, who may be in their seventies and eighties.

The fact that grandparents today are more youthful affects the perception of their role. Many have thought that when Americans have children they raise them according to the most "modern" methods without the interference of grandparents. Grandparents were thought to have a bad influence because of their capacity to disrupt the new family and to interfere with the development of the children. In reality, the relationships between grandparents and grandchildren are quite varied.

Neugarten and Weinstein (1964) identified five styles of grandparent interaction with grandchildren. *Formal grandparents* tended to be older and followed carefully prescribed patterns of interaction. While they were generally solicitous toward both of the younger generations, they were careful not to interfere, offering services and advice only when asked. The second group, the *fun-seeking grandparents*, were generally younger than the formal grandparents. These grandparents tended to take a more active role in their relationships with the younger generations. They viewed their grandchildren as sources of enjoyment and fulfillment and were less inhibited about taking charge of grandchildren and advising the new parents on child care. Some grandparents actually served as *surrogate parents*, taking care of children for mothers who worked outside the home. This role was more often filled by grandmothers. *Reservoirs of family wisdom* were usually grandfathers who sought to dominate their extended families. Finally, there were the *distant figures*. These were grandparents who were not much in evidence—physically or otherwise— except for events like birthdays.

Most grandparents, Neugarten and Weinstein found, were happy with their role. They savored the feelings of continuity and felt valued as a resource for the youngest generation. Some grandparents gain a sense of purpose from the relationship. One recent study of grandmothers reported that 80 percent enjoyed their role and nearly a third found it more enjoyable than raising their own children (Robertson, 1977).

However, grandparents vary considerably in terms of how they feel toward their grandchildren. Some seem to be "glad to see them come and glad to see them go" (Cumming and Henry, 1961); some enjoy a close and loving relationship with their grandchildren; and some see their grandchildren as allies against the parental generation in between.

The middle generation may feel a sense of rivalry with the grandparents for the affections of the children. Since some grandparents are less concerned than parents with what the parents consider a proper unbringing for their children and more concerned with winning love for themselves, they may be more permissive and liberal with gifts than the parents. Family contacts between older people and the younger generations may not be as frequent and as close as the older people would like. But the general picture is that there is a mutual dependency between the generations, and that family relationships serve to give personal meaning to the lives of most Americans (Bahr and Nye, 1974).

Most grandchildren appear to have strong affection for their grandparents. When Robertson (1976) asked young adult grandchildren why they visited their grandparents, more than half of the sample said they did so out of love and because they enjoyed being with them. Twenty percent reported that they

For a variety of reasons, the time when most grandparents played a large role in the lives of their grandchildren seems to be ending. Many people feel this represents the loss of a vital connection between these generations.

did so because their parents did, and only 11 percent said they visited their grandparents because it was expected. Among the characteristics they valued most in a grandparent were love, gentleness, understanding, a sense of humor, and the ability to communicate. They were put off by grandparents who tried to be a pal or teacher or who were too dependent or acted childish.

The relationship between grandparents and grandchildren changes over time. Grandparents tend to enjoy their grandchildren more when they are younger because as children grow up they have less interest in their grandparents (Clark, 1969). Aldous (1978) found that preschool and school-age children liked to do things with their grandparents, but that teenagers were too absorbed in other activities to spend much time with them. However, like Clark, Aldous found that the decline in interest was mutual. Grandparents found it harder to deal with older grandchildren. Still, the role grandparents play in a family depends on a multitude of factors besides the age of the grandchildren. And with grandparents being younger today, it is quite possible that new roles are developing.

Retirement

For the last half century, retirement at the age of 65 has been the goal of most working Americans. In recent prosperous times, people who are financially solvent have welcomed the option of retiring even earlier, at 55 or 60. Nevertheless, the pressure of economic and social trends, such as the crisis in the Social Security system, is changing this pattern. Government authorities and experts in various fields involving aging believe that within a few years people will be delaying retirement until the age of 70 and in some cases will be working part-time after that.

Although people may have less choice in the future about when to retire and under what circumstances, at present the decision to retire is usually voluntary. In the past, poor health was the primary reason for involuntary retirement, but health does not seem to be as important a factor today. This may be because working conditions are safer now than in the past. Another reason may be that people have been retiring at younger ages, before they encounter major health problems.

The primary reason for voluntary retirement is having an adequate retirement income. Pollman (1971), in a study of factors contributing to retirement, found that 47 percent of respondents said that financial solvency was the main factor in their decision to retire. Twenty-five percent cited poor health, and 19 percent said they wanted more free time.

ADJUSTING TO RETIREMENT Early studies of retirement usually concluded that retirement was a traumatic event. This "crisis" perspective of retirement held that the occupational role provides a central source of identity and that the loss of this role is accompanied by feelings of inadequacy. This sense of inadequacy cannot be compensated for by the leisure role the retired person takes on because society traditionally has not accepted leisure as a valid source of identity. According to this view, the breakdown in the retired person's self-esteem and sense of identity can lead to decreased satisfaction with life, poor health, and disengagement (withdrawal) from society (Miller, 1965).

More recent examinations of the impact of retirement indicate that, while the crisis view of retirement may be accurate for some individuals, it is by no means typical. Atchley (1971, 1976) found that although the occupational role is an important one, for many people it is not the major source of identity. Many retired people, rather than becoming disengaged, continue their involvement in a number of other satisfying roles such as community and church activities. Moreover, as mentioned in Chapter 7, our society has become more accepting of leisure as a goal and as a legitimate source of identity (Orthner, 1975).

Other evidence also tends to contradict the view of retirement as a crisis. For example, the fact that many people have chosen to retire before the mandatory retirement age would suggest that these people look forward to their retirement years. One researcher found that 86 percent of the elderly he interviewed were satisfied with their retirement and that those who retired early were more satisfied with their decision than those who retired at the mandatory age (Patton, 1977). Of course, it should be pointed out that those who take voluntary early retirement have an adequate financial base or they would be less likely to choose this option. These people can be expected to view retirement in a more positive light.

There is evidence that in retirement, as in virtually all major life changes, there is an initial period of adjustment. Chatfield (1977), in studying factors influencing life satisfaction among retired persons, found that recently retired individuals had significantly lower life-satisfaction scores than those who were not retired. However, there were no differences in life-satisfaction scores of those retired for a year or more and those who were still working. Part of the reason for the lower scores among newly retired people resulted from the drop in income that usually occurs at retirement. It may be that within a year or so after retirement, many of the newly retired people in this study had found ways to supplement their income.

One implication of our discussion of retirement to this point is that an individual's financial situation is an extremely important factor in adjustment to retirement. How well a person adjusts to retirement may also be related to family factors, particularly the reaction of the retired person's spouse. Often it is the husband who is changing his living patterns and adjusting to unfamiliar roles. Adjustments in the marriage may be difficult at this point, because if his mate is a full-time housewife, she continues to have a well-established role. To suddenly have her husband at home all day, perhaps trying to make himself useful by offering suggestions about how she could do her work more efficiently, makes some women resentful (Fengler, 1975).

CASE STUDY   *Retirement and Role Loss*

Judith Grade was 63 and had never worked a day in her life. Yet two months after her husband Herbert retired, she went out and found a job as a saleswoman in a lower East Side women's clothing store. And six months after that, Herbert Grade left her to settle in Phoenix.

"His company had a policy on age that forced Herb to retire," says Mrs. Grade. "He always loved working. On vacations he'd begin to fidget after the third day. That's how it was after he retired, only magnified a dozen times. He followed me around from kitchen to basement to supermarket, questioning everything I did and issuing orders on how to do it better. I went to work in order to keep my sanity."

In his tiny furnished apartment in Phoenix, Herbert Grade explains why he gave up on a 45-year marriage. "I realized I had an adjustment to make, so I tried getting as close to Judith as possible. But she rebuffed me. As the guy who used to bring home two or three hundred dollars every Friday, I'd been made to feel welcome. But when that was replaced by a little pension check, it seemed I'd been replaced, too. All of a sudden she made me feel expendable."

Judith Grade lamented that her sex life, a source of excitement and warmth over the years, had ended completely with Herbert's retirement. "I might as well have been a stranger, except that a stranger might have had some effect on Herb," says Mrs. Grade.

"Nothing went right. Before he came home to stay, Herb was a foreman in a handbag factory. He was considered an efficiency expert there, I guess. The first morning he sat in that chair and watched me vacuum the carpet. When I was half done, he grabbed the vacuum cleaner from me and began running with it, back and forth, like a football player. 'See how it's done? This way takes half the time,' he told me."

Grade lumbers into the kitchen. He returns with a can of beer to his easy chair, which is covered with a thin greasy blanket. "I was used to keeping active from morning to night, being with people who were getting things done. To have to stop all of a sudden just because I've reached a certain birthday . . . it didn't make sense. I had nowhere to go between 9 and 5. I couldn't sit in the house all day and do nothing. So I tried to give Judith a hand."

Herbert Grade has not yet found anything to replace his work role. But his wife, who divorced him on grounds of desertion, has begun a new life. "I'm the best salesman on the staff," she says proudly. "I sell more garments than any other man or woman in the store. When it comes to leather goods, my boss doesn't order anything without consulting me. I love the business and may even open a leather shop of my own some day."

Source: Adapted from "December Song" by Leon Freilich. Copyright 1975 New York News Inc. Reprinted by permission.

FOR CLASS DISCUSSION

1. Do you think that Herbert Grade was hasty in deciding to leave his wife and move to Phoenix? What could he have done to facilitate his own adjustment to retirement? Could Judith have helped him?

2. What might be some reasons why Judith was able at 63 to begin a new life on her own with relative ease?

The same situation may arise when it is the husband who has taken on the homemaking role after retirement. One 75-year-old husband retired ten years before his younger wife. When she quit her waitress job, he confided, "You can't imagine how uneasy I feel having Sally around the house all day. . . . She doesn't mean to, of course, but she keeps touching everything and destroying the order I arranged. My castle's been invaded and I'm not a bit reconciled to it. I don't know how we're going to work it out" (Freilich, 1975, p. 21).

RETIREMENT OF WOMEN   While most studies of retirement have focused on men, researchers are beginning to deal with the retirement of women. Jaslow (1976) examined the morale of different categories of women and found that employed women had the highest morale, followed by retired women; women who had never worked had the lowest morale. One reason for these findings seemed to be that the working women were younger, healthier, and in a better financial position than the others. Retired women were better off financially than those who had never worked. The women who had never worked were the oldest group and had the lowest levels of income and the poorest health.

Working women evidently experience the same initial lowering of life satisfaction as men do upon retirement. However, after the transition phase, they seem to have a more positive outlook than women who have never worked (Fox, 1977).

THEORIES APPLIED TO RETIREMENT ADJUSTMENT   Crawford (1972) examined two prevalent theories related to aging that have application for adjustment to retirement. According to **role-flexibility theory** (Havighurst, 1954), successful adjustment to retirement would depend on an individual's ability to take up new roles as older ones are dropped. Thus, when a man gives up the role of worker, he would take on a new role such as grandparent to replace it. He would then have as many roles as before, even though they would be different ones. According to **disengagement theory** (Cumming and Henry, 1961), successful adjustment to retirement would depend on the ability of an individual to withdraw (disengage) from the role of worker when society required it. He or she would then have fewer roles but might become more involved in them.

In a study of fifty-three English retired couples, Crawford gathered data on changes in the roles of parent, relative, friend, and organization member that the couples experienced when they retired. She found that greater or lesser involvement in these roles was not related to adjustment to retirement. Thus there was no evidence that either taking on new roles or disengaging from old ones was more conducive to adjustment in retirement (Crawford, 1972).

Even so, programs designed to help the elderly retired remain actively engaged in life do seem to be of some help in the adjustment process. For example, a Tax Aide program sponsored by the American Association of Retired Persons has placed thousands of capable retired volunteers specially trained by the Internal Revenue Service in communities around the country to provide free income-tax assistance to elderly people. Self-help courses in "Senior Survival," covering such topics as adequate nutrition on a low income, and the ins and outs of applying for Social Security benefits, are offered to older people through some colleges (*Modern Maturity*, 1976). In addition, the Foster Grandparents program has rejuvenated many lower-income elderly by involving them in programs to help institutionalized, emotionally deprived, or retarded children. The foster grandparents are paid for their time, but more important, they and their foster grandchildren often develop new interests in life.

Widowhood

Widowhood is primarily a transition faced by women. Of the 12 million widows and widowers in this country in 1975, 11 million were widows. Seventy-five percent of wives will probably be widowed at some time in their lives. Although 60 percent of all currently widowed women are over 65, the median age at which this event occurs is now 56 years. For many women widowhood may be a long-term status, since the life expectancy of women is now well into the seventies and since the probability of remarriage for women is low and rapidly diminishes as women get older (Lewis and Berns, 1975).

For many older people, loss of a spouse is more difficult to cope with than any other life change. Death of a spouse is always a crisis because it is final. It is especially difficult because people usually have little experience dealing with it. The first year after the mate dies is especially difficult. This is a period of high death rates for the surviving spouse and of increased susceptibility to suicide. Death evokes a maze of emotions, including guilt, anger, relief, anxiety, helplessness, hostility, and fear, along with the feeling of loss—all normal reactions. The surviving spouse must—after a period of mourning—relinquish the dead mate and accept the reality of assuming or reassigning the dead spouse's roles.

Different women react differently to the death of their husband. The reaction usually depends on how they felt about him when he was alive. For some, the husband's death means the loss of a unique, deeply loved person, and they are likely to feel a crushing sense of personal loneliness and find their lives seriously disrupted. For others, widowhood simply means a change in status, the loss of social position and a couples-oriented life-style. These patterns are more likely to occur in middle- and upper-class widows. Widows of lower-class husbands may feel more ambivalent. The communication problems of working-class people may lead to greater emotional distance in these marriages. Many working-class women never shift their focus to the

HIGHLIGHT 11.2   *Remarriage after 55*

In recent years, gerontology—the study of aging—has become a burgeoning field for research. Here is a summary of some new findings about marriage among widows and widowers.

- ☐ The happier the first marriage, the quicker and easier it seems to be for people to replace their losses with a new spouse. Those who idealize a dead spouse are usually those who were ambivalent during the marriage and who hide behind their memories to avoid getting involved again.

- ☐ Widows tend to have close relationships with friends and children which help assuage loneliness. Men who have lost both spouse and a work life through retirement seem to have fewer intimate friends, and are thus strongly motivated to seek a new wife, especially if she will take on housekeeping and caretaking duties.

- ☐ Men are definitely the pursuers the second time around, partly because the odds are in their favor, but mostly, it appears, because they need the closeness of marriage more.

- ☐ If a woman has cared for her first husband while he lingered through a long illness, the prospect of that kind of caretaking again makes marriage somewhat less appealing for women.

- ☐ Remarriages contracted by the elderly tend to be successful if they are based on affection, are financially secure, and have the approval of the couple's respective children.

- ☐ Remarriages among the aged are also generally successful if they are based on companionship, the personal character of the spouse, a deep emotional attachment, or a desire for care from the spouse. They are more likely to fail if they are contracted primarily because of financial need.

- ☐ Happily for many older couples, Social Security laws have finally been changed so that, in most cases, neither pensioner loses if two older people marry. However, SSI (Supplementary Security Income) payments are still subject to reduction in many cases when two older people marry.

Source: Reprinted courtesy of the The Boston Globe.

Reasons for remarriage. (Source: Ruth Harriet Jacobs and Barbara H. Vinick, Re-engagement in Later Life, Stamford, Conn.: Greylock Publishers, 1981. Reprinted by permission.)

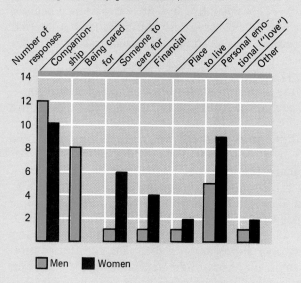

role of wife after their children leave home, and their husbands are less likely to be intimate companions. Almost invariably, however, death causes distress, regardless of the quality of the marriage (Weiss, 1976).

MOURNING AND GRIEF   Balkwell (1981) has summarized the stages of what she calls the healing process of grief. The first stage is shock and bewilderment at the loss. This stage, which may last from a day to two months, is usually marked by numbness alternated with purposeless activity. The second stage is marked by an acute sense of loss, a longing for the dead spouse, and sometimes feelings of guilt. Usually this occurs between the first and twelfth months of widowhood. The widowed spouse may react strongly toward family or friends and withdraw from social contacts. In the third stage, the widowed person begins to try out new roles. It is a difficult time since even the most resolute person can become vulnerable to despair as a result of the inevitable false steps in this process. Until a new role or set of roles is accepted, the widowed person may try to rely excessively on others. In the last stage of the process of grief, the wounds will have started to heal and the widow or widower will have begun to reenter social life.

The period of grieving is full of difficulties for the newly widowed. He or she must face the loss of a significant role in life—that of spouse—financial problems caused by a reduction in income, and health problems which can arise out of mourning.

HEALTH IN WIDOWHOOD   We have all heard stories—fact or fiction—about widows or widowers who die shortly after the death of their spouse. The fact of the matter is that the widowed do have significantly higher death rates than the married in their age and sex groups (Berardo, 1968). Not surprisingly, the period where the gap is greatest between married and widowed is in the first six months of widowhood (Parkes, Benjamin, and Fitzgerald, 1969). The stress accompanying the loss of the spouse seems to precipitate illnesses that can lead to death.

Among the maladies to which the widowed are particularly vulnerable are coronary or arterial diseases. Widows are more likely to have chronic, disabling physical ailments than widowers (Verbrugge, 1979), but widowers exhibit higher rates of mental illness (Gove, 1972a). Perhaps the most publicized health hazard of widowhood is suicide. As noted earlier, suicide rates for the elderly are extremely high; research has also shown that the widowed elderly have higher rates of suicide than their married counterparts (Gove, 1972b).

THE ECONOMICS OF WIDOWHOOD   Economic problems are among the most critical ones to face most widows or widowers. In one study, the median income for the widowed was reported to be half what it was for the married. At the same time, the income for a widow was 75 percent of the income for a widower. We have already seen that many of the elderly live with an income below the poverty line. This is particularly true for widows (Lopata, 1978). According to Lewis and Berns (1975), six out of ten widows had their income reduced to a level where they could not maintain their standard of living. Those surveyed saw their incomes drop an average of 44 percent during the first two years of widowhood.

This financial situation requires most healthy widows to find work. For many women, this is difficult because the skills they may once have had have grown rusty with disuse. Many others may never have had basic work skills to begin with because they never expected to have to work. This may be less of a problem in the future since cohorts entering the later years are more likely to have worked for at least a period of their lives.

Lack of work experience has another serious consequence for a widow; she may be unable to deal with financial matters such as real estate, stocks, and contracts, any of which can have serious consequences for her financial situation (Berardo, 1968). Nevertheless, being forced to assume the roles her husband may have performed may well assist the widow in her transition.

PREDICTORS OF SUCCESSFUL ADJUSTMENT TO WIDOWHOOD For some time, researchers have tried to establish criteria for successful adjustment to widowhood. In her review of the literature, Balkwell (1981) examined three of these criteria.

The first involves differences by sex. Currently the research on whether men or women have an easier time adjusting to widowhood has not yielded consistent results. Those who contend that widowhood is more difficult for women point to the fact that widows generally have more financial difficulties than widowers and that they have fewer chances to remarry. Those who believe the adjustment is more difficult for men cite the fact that widowed men have a much higher suicide rate than widowed women (Gove, 1972b). In addition, many experts on aging believe that widowhood is more traumatic for men because it may involve a number of role losses that occur almost simultaneously. For example, a man may lose his job, his income, his spouse, and his health within a short period of time. He may not know how to carry out the domestic roles his wife filled during the marriage. He is also more likely to become cut off from family and friends because it was his wife who carried out the kinship role (Bock and Webber, 1972). A woman, on the other hand, has usually established roles independent of her wife role in mid-life when her children left home. The loss of her husband is difficult, but the other roles she has assumed remain intact and help provide continuity.

The second factor Balkwell cites is age. There does appear to be a relationship between an older age at widowhood and successful adjustment (Morgan, 1976; Ball, 1977; Carey, 1977). Those widowed under age 45 and who have dependent children have the most difficulty dealing with widowhood

(Maddison, 1968). The reason for this is suggested by Balkwell's third predictor, forewarning of a spouse's death. The greater likelihood of being widowed at a later stage of life may prepare people for the inevitable. At younger ages, it is simply not expected.

The studies indicate that sudden death of a spouse—after an illness of two weeks or less—causes a far more severe and protracted grief than that associated with deaths following longer illnesses. However, this result may have been affected by the fact that the studies focused on individuals under 45 (Glick, Weiss, and Parkes, 1974; Parkes, 1975; Sheskin and Wallace, 1976–1977). Other studies using broader age groups as samples did not support this apparent relationship (Bornstein et al., 1973; Clayton et al., 1973). Further research using somewhat different criteria seemed to reaffirm the earlier conclusions as to persons widowed suddenly while young. It also indicated that the next-most-affected group was middle-aged widows whose husbands' final illnesses took longer than six days (Ball, 1977). Elderly persons whose spouses died of protracted illnesses had a worse record of health problems than those whose spouses died of shorter illnesses (Gerber et al., 1975).

DEVELOPMENTAL TASKS OF WIDOWHOOD   As we have noted, widowhood either changes or curtails a number of roles. For example, the role of sexual partner or companion—integral aspects of the role of spouse—have been eliminated, at least temporarily. The research suggests that the widowed who have fewer roles to replace or who quickly reestablish former roles (for example, by entering a new relationship) are less likely to experience difficulty adjusting than those who are less able to adapt (Shulman, 1975).

Anticipatory socialization can be of value here. Specifically, marital partners can discuss the facts of death and widowhood. Thorough review of

Widowhood is most difficult to cope with for those widowed prior to middle age, probably because the death of a young spouse is usually unexpected.

financial affairs is a good idea. Another task should be to discuss funeral arrangements and purchase of a burial plot, if this is desired, rather than leaving these decisions to a moment of crisis.

Of the widows in Chicago interviewed by Lopata (1973), half reported that loneliness was the greatest problem in widowhood. All said that they were subtly stigmatized by their single status. They were usually excluded from gatherings of couples because they made an "odd" person. Widowed women often find they have no one to escort them to social events, a lack felt most strongly by those widowed young, since most of their friends are still married. Married women often regard them with some suspicion, as though they might try to steal their husbands. Often the only people they can find for friends are other widows.

It would appear then that the widowed person's adjustment to loneliness may well be the most formidable developmental task faced in the later years. It is not so great a problem in the early stages of grieving when there is institutionalized support available, but it becomes a serious difficulty as that support lessens. This is particularly true for widows who have assumed more traditional roles as wives (Lopata, 1975). Many rightly assume that family contacts are extremely important at this stage, but one researcher has discovered that family contacts have no bearing on loneliness. Contacts with neighbors and friends were considerably more important to the widow's morale (Arling, 1976a, 1976b). In other words, it is isolation from one's peer group that seems to be the greatest factor in loneliness during widowhood.

ALTERNATIVE LIVING ARRANGEMENTS FOR THE ELDERLY

The problem of loneliness among the widowed also applies to the aged generally. In the face of retirement, separation from children, and widowhood, older people increasingly turn to each other for companionship and mutual support. Many unrelated older people now live together in communities for older citizens which range from housing projects to trailer parks to leisure communities for the wealthy.

Communities of the Elderly

Many older couples have migrated to the warm climates of Florida and California for retirement since the 1920s. But in 1960, when developers began building Sun City, Arizona, a new town specifically for people over 50 with no live-in children, many people were skeptical. As one journalist put it, "people would resent being cordoned off into what amounted to a staging area in which to play shuffleboard and canasta while waiting for death" (Meehan,

1973, p. 18). The skeptics were wrong, however. Today there are hundreds of retirement communities in the United States. Some are in colder parts of the country, for surveys indicate that some older people would rather retire to areas near their former homes than to sunnier climates. Although they like to maintain continuity with their former lives, they are glad to sell houses that are too big and too expensive to maintain once their children are gone and move into smaller dwellings in communities where maintenance and security are provided along with companionship, social activities, and hobbies.

What do people do in these retirement communities? At Heritage Village, a wealthy retirement community in the hills of rural Connecticut, people keep busy with over seventy possible activities, from drama groups to courses like "Creative Survival," from woodworking to paddle-tennis. Although some do volunteer community work, most engage solely in leisure activities. Many apparently feel that they have "paid their dues" and are interested primarily in relaxing and enjoying their later years.

Life for those in lower-income elderly communities can also be satisfying. Hochschild (1973a; 1973b) studied one such community, Merrill Court, in San

Elderly people, like younger people, tend to seek companionship and intimacy among those close to them in age. This may help to account for the popularity of retirement communities.

Francisco. The thirty-seven female residents and six male residents of this low-income apartment building were 60- to 80-year-olds from small towns in the Southwest and Midwest. Social patterns there centered on what went on "downstairs" in the recreation room, but they spread outward through a network of informal friendships in the apartments upstairs. Downstairs, formal community organization took the form of a service club. Most of the residents and a few nonresidents belonged to it, and in its welter of committees and leadership roles, all but four club members had the chance to chair some activity during a three-year period. At any one time, perhaps a third of the members were in charge of something.

An informal system of visits and sharing met residents' needs for friendship and also served some other functions. Since upstairs gossip found its way downstairs, it served as a means of social control. In judging each other they set moral boundaries for themselves as well. Neighboring also served as a means for making certain that others were all right. If any residents had not opened their curtains by midmorning, the others checked to see if they were sick. Those who were healthy often adopted the few who were not, performing services like shopping, picking up mail, and writing letters for them. Residents, who had once fed large families, still cooked in such large quantities that they had plenty of food to share. Since most of the women distributed food in this way, it could be seen as an informal division of labor. Some Merrill Court residents did perform services, for example, sewing, for a small fee, but even then the exchange was made as noncommercial as possible.

Although most of the residents of Merrill Court were of lower-class background, some held higher status than others, according to what Hochschild called a "poor-dear" hierarchy. The residents saw the differences among themselves as matters of "luck," and granted most status to those with the most luck. Those with the luck to have good health won honor, as did those who had lost the fewest relatives and those whose children were still close to them. Others were referred to as "poor dears."

In this complex series of status levels, most people could find themselves superior to at least some "poor dear." Those active in politics and recreation referred to those who spent their time playing cards or reading newspapers as "poor dears." People in nursing homes were regarded as "poor dears."

Despite the "poor-dear" hierarchy, the residents of Merrill Court related to each other almost like siblings. They exchanged food, cuttings to start potted plants, and kitchen utensils. The things they wanted—such as Mother's Day cards—and the things they could give each other—such as home-canned goods—were much the same from one person to the next. In their sharing of labor, they showed little specialization; they were likely to make and exchange the same things. This kind of bond does not always form in groups of older people. Those who are institutionalized and dependent on nursing staff are unlikely to form mature "sibling bonds" because they do not live as independent adults.

Studies have shown that social ties often diminish with poverty, and ties to the economy diminish with retirement, isolating the old. Against this background, the community which arose among people with modest means at Merrill Court was an adjustment to a bad situation. Feeling that they no longer had responsibilities to younger age groups, these men and women took on responsibilities toward each other. Together they worked out solutions to problems they had not had to face before. When strong family ties are absent, communities of the old may give people a sense that they are part of an "us," not just a "me" (Hochschild, 1973a; 1973b).

Other Alternatives

The usual alternatives for the elderly include remaining in their own home, moving to a retirement community, housing for the elderly, living with family, and institutionalization. There are, however, some other living arrangements that are being proposed and, to a limited degree, implemented. One proposal is that polygyny be legalized for the elderly so that the sexual imbalance in the elderly population will not affect opportunities for family life. Less extreme ideas are day-care facilities for the elderly who live with their working children as well as a variety of suggestions for restructuring the family for the elderly. The latter probably hold more promise than polygyny, but it is notable that they all have in common the re-creation of the family environment.

One suggestion is for the sharing of homes among unrelated elderly (Streib, 1978; Streib and Hilker, 1980). The purpose of the share-a-home concept is to provide the aged with an alternative family environment. Share-a-home participants would pool or share money, labor, and knowledge, thus enabling them to enjoy greater autonomy and a higher standard of living than they could if they lived independently. This family-type arrangement would also help to foster the formation of intimate relationships. Share-a-home has already been tried in Florida, and more communal arrangements of this type are being planned. Another plan would establish an "affiliated family" in which a younger family takes in an unrelated elder who is integrated into the family unit (Clavan and Vatter, 1972). Researchers have also suggested initiating the "expanded family" and the "new extended family." These forms seek to create ties between relatives by previous marriages and the elderly, and to establish new ties with the community (Macklin, 1980).

SUMMARY

1. The purpose of this chapter is to consider the changes that accompany the middle and later years of family life including special problems and opportunities and some ways in which people prepare for and adjust to changes in family situations.

2. Using statistics, researchers can make some generalizations about what happens to people as they age. Some researchers observe the social characteristics of people's lives at various age levels (late maturity, pre-, early, and late retirement) as a measure of change. Others discuss the changing patterns of behavior in older people according to where they are in the family life cycle.

3. It was formerly believed that people became isolated from kin as they aged, but recent studies have indicated that married offspring and their older parents keep in touch through living near each other and patterns of mutual aid. The strength of kinship ties can be measured in terms of the number of kin, frequency of interaction, extent of aid (monetary or services), emotional closeness, and quality of the family relationship.

4. The major events of the middle and later years—departure of children from the home, reduced income, retirement, widowhood, and increasing health problems—result in a loss or a major adjustment of social roles. Anticipatory socialization can help people prepare for new roles and for the mental and emotional adjustments that accompany them.

5. When there are no pressing financial or health problems and the couple is still together, the postparental years may be the happiest and most satisfying of a couple's life.

6. Loss of a spouse is a major change for people in the middle and later years. To adjust to the loss, the surviving spouse must allow a period of mourning, eventually relinquish the deceased, and accept the reality of taking over or reassigning the dead person's roles. Widows usually face more financial pressures than widowers and have fewer opportunities to remarry. Widowers suffer greater role changes than widows, which may contribute to their adjustment difficulties. The social and personal adjustments of widowhood may be facilitated if individuals make an effort to prepare themselves for this eventuality.

7. Increasingly, older people are turning to each other for companionship and mutual support in public-housing projects or leisure communities. If the elderly are adaptable, and if their economic and health problems are not severe, they can continue to live meaningful and satisfying lives.

REVIEW AND DISCUSSION

1. Outline your family's kinship structure in relation to one of your parents and then to one of your grandparents. Take into account the number of kin, residential closeness, frequency of interaction, family bonds, and economic aid. What differences do you find between family members at these two stages of life?

2. Marital satisfaction has been described in terms of a U-shaped curve: a high degree of happiness as newlyweds, a low point when children are growing up, and a rise after the children leave home. How might this curve differ for married couples who have remained childless, such as those described in Chapter 10?

3. Describe the major developmental tasks of the middle and later years. How might "anticipatory socialization" help older people to adjust to retirement and widowhood?

4. Look again at the five styles of grandparent interaction identified by Neugarten and Weinstein. Which style characterizes your own grandparents? Which style do you think you might follow as a grandparent?

5. Do you think you would enjoy living in a community of elderly persons when you are old? Why or why not? Can you imagine some living arrangements that you think you would prefer, assuming you are unable to maintain your own residence

SUGGESTED READINGS

Caine, L. (1974). *Widow*. New York: Morrow.

> This personal account of the author's experiences as a widow explores several aspects of widowhood: coping with grief, the sense of loss, and the roles of a single woman, single parent, and single provider.

Hallberg, E. C. (1978). *The Gray Itch: The Male Metapause Syndrome*. New York: Stein and Day.

> What's behind the 45-year-old man who suddenly feels out of sorts with life? He's tired of his job, his children are leaving home, his wife is taking night classes—and he wonders what he's doing with his life. This is the Gray Itch, and the author tells how to recognize and deal with the symptoms.

Kornhaber, A., and K. L. Woodward (1981). *Grandparents/Grandchildren, The Vital Connection*. New York: Doubleday.

> The authors take the position that both children and their grandparents are better off when they spend large amounts of time together. The book argues that in recent years the vital bond between grandparents and grandchildren has been virtually ignored and that it should be restored.

Kubler-Ross, E. (1969). *On Death and Dying*. New York: Macmillan.

> A landmark work in the area of gerontology. Identifies five phases of the process of death. The book is an attempt to help both dying persons and their families cope with death.

Pearlman, J., J. Cohen, and K. Coburn (1981). *Hitting Our Stride.* New York: Delacorte Press.

Tells how middle-aged women cope with changes confronting them, from aging parents and children leaving home to re-entering the job market, menopause, and changing sexual needs.

Families in Crisis

"Seldom, or perhaps never, does a marriage develop into an individual relationship smoothly and without crisis; there is no coming to consciousness without pain."

CARL JUNG

All families face problems and changes. When these are stressful enough, they may culminate in a **crisis,** or state of disorganization during which family members experience profound disruption of their life pattern or methods of coping with stress (Brammer, 1979). One social scientist calls crises "points of no return," because after a crisis a family is never quite the same (Rapaport, 1963). If a family copes well with crisis, the family will continue to experience positive growth; if a family is unable to cope well with crisis, the family's problems are likely to grow.

There are two main kinds of crisis: developmental and situational (Brammer, 1979). **Developmental crises** are normal and predictable: they can happen to any family during the course of the family life cycle, and when they are coped with successfully, they move the family on to the next stage in its development. These crises, which tend to occur when a family is faced with a major developmental task, are usually temporary. **Situational,** or **event crises** occur only in some families and are almost always regarded as serious problems: alcohol, violence between spouses, and teenage pregnancy, for example. These nonnormative crises can be long lasting, and families often need help from therapists or other professionals to resolve them. If they are not resolved, they can cause the family to disintegrate.

In this chapter, our major focus will be on situational crisis, although we describe examples of developmental crisis as well. In recent years, there has been increasing attention to such event crises as child abuse and teenage pregnancy. Our goal is to explore the family factors and

403

family dynamics that have been identified as contributing to these and other situational crises.

 ## A MODEL OF FAMILY CRISIS

A convenient way of examining both developmental and situational crises was devised by sociologist Reuben Hill in 1958 and has been a major model utilized since then. According to Hill, three factors are involved in determining whether or not a family will be crisis prone: a stressful event (A), the family's resources (B), and the family's definition of the event (C). The interaction of these factors produces the crisis (X). The process through which a family deals with a crisis consists of four distinct stages. At first, the family tends to be numbed by the event that produced the crisis. This *crisis* phase is followed by a period of *disorganization*, during which resentments and conflicts grow and roles are played with less enthusiasm. However, new routines are arrived at eventually and the family begins the *recovery* period, which ends with *reorganization* at a new level.

The Event (A)

A crisis-producing event is a situation for which the family has little or no previous preparation or experience. These events differ in their sources and their effects upon the family. If the event occurs outside the family (wars, political persecutions, or natural disasters, for example), it will often solidify the family. Events that occur within the family (suicide, alcoholism, mental illness, for example), by contrast, are usually quite disorganizing to the family. Loss of a family member, addition of a new family member, disagreement among family members about roles, and sudden changes in the family's status are also stress-producing events, and they may or may not be successfully resolved.

The Resources (B)

One of the most influential factors which determine a family's reaction to a crisis is its resources. Resources include both a family's financial situation and more subjective elements including the family's integration and adaptability. While economic resources play a role, some sociologists believe that family adaptability and integration may be more important than economic factors in determining how a family reacts to crisis. **Family integration** is defined as having common interests, affection, and a sense of economic interdependence that binds its members together. **Family adaptability** is defined as being able to change to meet new circumstances. Families that are

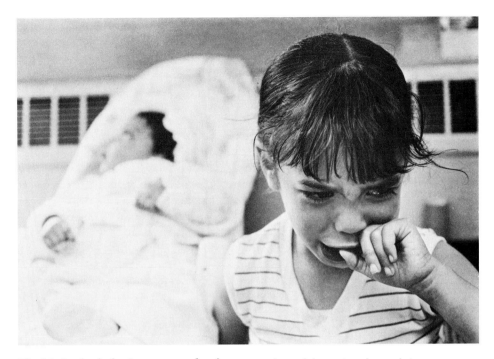

The birth of a baby is an example of a normative crisis, or turning point. Sometimes siblings feel particularly anxious about the changes precipitated by the new arrival.

well integrated and adaptable may be characterized as **organized families.** In organized families, the spouses tend to have good marital adjustment and companionable relations with their children. **Disorganized families** have less of such resources—they are neither well adapted nor well integrated, and they are often headed by couples with low marital adjustment and a relationship with their children that is characterized by conflict. Disorganized families are often socially isolated; that is, they have no kin, friends, or neighbors to turn to in times of stress. It is these families that are most likely to be crisis prone.

The Definition (C)

The crisis-precipitating event can be defined objectively, by an impartial observer; culturally, by the community; or subjectively, by the family. The family's definition of an event as a crisis or simply a challenge depends largely upon its value system. Suppose, for example, that a teenage boy announces that he is going to drop out of school and go to work. Some parents might regard this as a serious threat and become extremely upset, perhaps arguing with their child, lecturing him, or insisting that he continue his education—reactions that might precipitate a crisis. Other parents might find the idea of leaving school to go to work an acceptable alternative and therefore would not be as likely to react in such a way as to cause the situation to escalate into a crisis.

The Crisis (X)

The stressful event, the family's resources, and the family's own definition of the event interact to determine whether or not a crisis occurs. Hill suggests that crisis-prone families may be more vulnerable to stressful events and more likely to define them as crises because they have fewer resources with which to meet crises and have not learned how to deal with stress in the past. Thus, in looking for an explanation of why some families are crisis prone and others are not, sociologists examine closely the B and C factors in Hill's model.

DEVELOPMENTAL CRISES

Although developmental crises are predictable and occur in most families, some aspects of them are new to the family going through them and are apt to be disrupting, at least temporarily. Most families experience a series of normative crises at each stage of the life cycle. The very act of getting married may precipitate a crisis, for it requires changes and adjustments by both partners. New parenthood, a child entering school, an older child leaving home, retirement, a move to a new location, the death of a spouse—each of these is a stress-producing event. Divorce may make this a looped, rather than linear sequence: at any point, a person may become single, then marry, have more children, or blend families.

Each time a person enters the family, or leaves it—totally, as in the case of divorce, or partially, as in the case of a child first going to school or a mother entering the work force for the first time—everyone in the family must adapt to the change. During this period of adaptation, family boundaries (who is in the family and who is not—and when) are often ambiguous, and the family must resolve the ambiguity before it can reorganize. Reorganizing usually means changing who performs what tasks and fulfills what roles, and accepting the new member or changing one's perceptions of the absent member (Boss, 1980).

Families vary enormously in how well and how quickly they adapt to such changes. A couple who has discussed the change in advance and reached an agreement about it may adjust very quickly. Another couple may argue for weeks before they understand the boundary change and find comfortable new roles and tasks, while other couples may try one solution after another until—

months later—they evolve a new family organization that works for them. Whatever the changes a family is experiencing, the more successfully its members have handled prior crises, the better they will be able to cope with new ones. Other factors that have been found to be conducive to good adjustment to crises are family adaptability and integration, affectionate relationships among family members, good marital adjustment of the husband and wife, companionable relationships between parents and their children, and family decision making that permits airing of views rather than an authoritarian approach (Hill, 1958).

The following section considers several examples of developmental tasks that occur in most families. Adjustment to some other normative tasks, such as the birth of a first child, retirement, and widowhood has been discussed in previous chapters. Table 12.1 provides a more complete outline of the major stages of the family life cycle and the emotional processes required for families to deal successfully with various events.

Beginning Marriage

When a man and woman marry, each takes on new roles, as a couple and as individuals. In their own eyes and in the eyes of society, they now have new identities: husband and wife. Making the transition from being single to being married, changing from being self-oriented to being couple-centered, is the first task a couple encounters.

The married pair must first find a place to live, determine how the household tasks are to be divided, and establish relations, as a couple and as married individuals, with the outside world. Each partner needs to disengage him or herself from relationships that interfere with the marriage, or make those relationships fit in with the married state. Research has shown that ignoring this issue often leads to conflict later on (Rapaport, 1963).

The couple's jobs, whether in or out of the home, must meet their financial needs and enhance each individual's self-image. If, for example, the wife is to remain at home tending to household duties, it is important that the couple is able to afford this and that the wife finds the role of homemaker appealing and worthwhile.

Perhaps the most important task is for the two people to learn to find an appropriate "fit" (Rapaport, 1963). This does not mean that the wife and husband must become like each other, or that they must be opposites. Two people with similar personalities may enjoy sharing interests, or they may compete in negative ways. Two people whose personalities are basically different may argue a great deal, or they may complement each other. The essential thing is for the needs and values—whether they were alike or different at the start of the relationship—to fit together in mutually satisfying ways. How successfully a couple is able to do this and make the transition to

Table 12.1 **The Stages of the Family Life Cycle**

FAMILY LIFE-CYCLE STAGE	EMOTIONAL PROCESS OF TRANSITION: KEY PRINCIPLES	SECOND-ORDER CHANGES IN FAMILY STATUS REQUIRED TO PROCEED DEVELOPMENTALLY
1. Between families: the unattached young adult	Accepting parent-offspring separation	a. Differentiation of self in relation to family of origin b. Development of intimate peer relationships c. Establishment of self in work
2. The joining of families through marriage: the newly married couple	Commitment to new system	a. Formation of marital system b. Realignment of relationships with extended families and friends to include spouse
3. The family with young children	Accepting new members into the system	a. Adjusting marital system to make space for child(ren) b. Taking on parenting roles c. Realignment of relationships with extended family to include parenting and grandparenting roles
4. The family with adolescents	Increasing flexibility of family boundaries to include children's independence	a. Shifting of parent-child relationships to permit adolescent to move in and out of system b. Refocus on mid-life marital and career issues c. Beginning shift toward concerns for older generation
5. Launching children and moving on	Accepting a multitude of exits from and entries into the family system	a. Renegotiation of marital system as a dyad b. Development of adult to adult relationships between grown children and their parents c. Realignment of relationships to include in-laws and grandchildren d. Dealing with disabilities and death of parents (grandparents)
6. The family in later life	Accepting the shifting of generational roles	a. Maintaining own and/or couple functioning and interests in face of physiological decline, exploration of new familial and social role options b. Support for a more central role for middle generation c. Making room in the system for the wisdom and experience of the elderly; supporting the older generation without overfunctioning for them d. Dealing with loss of spouse, siblings and other peers and preparation for own death. Life review and integration

Source: E. A. Carter and M. McGoldrick (eds), *The Family Life Cycle: A Framework for Family Therapy* (New York: Gardner, 1980). Reprinted by permission.

marriage depends upon the personal and social resources each has, the families from which they come, and the couple's own expectations and perceptions of their new roles (Rapaport, 1963). Today, many people's upbringing has prepared them for specific roles in marriage, but social change has created somewhat different expectations. A woman may, for example, have been socialized to become a homemaker and mother but she may want to combine marriage and motherhood with an outside career. If her expectations of her own roles within marriage do not mesh with the expectations of her spouse, the couple may have difficulty achieving a satisfactory role fit.

Children Starting School

When children enter school, they become deeply involved in relationships outside the family for the first time. This requires changes in role patterns within the family system for both the child and the parents. School is the first of many separations between parent and child—and this may cause intense feelings of stress, anxiety, and sadness in the parents. Some parents feel that they are losing control of the child. For others, the child's entry into school may mean only that they need to rearrange their schedules. Mothers who left the work force during their child's early years may have to consider whether or not they will return to work (Hock et al., 1980).

For some children, too, the separation from parents creates considerable anxiety. The task for such children is to shift total dependency on parents to shared dependency on parents and classmates and learn to accept people other than the parents (in this case, teachers) as authority figures (Anderson, 1976). How well children are able to do this will depend largely upon how secure and trusting they are and upon how certain their parents are about supporting the child's school entry.

According to Hock and colleagues (1980), whether or not the child's entry into school is stressful for parents depends largely upon their confidence in the educational system and their emotional relationship with the child. Parents of lower socioeconomic status are more likely than are middle- or upper-class parents to feel that they are losing their child to a hostile, alien institution. They are more apt to see the school as a place where they and their children will be powerless.

The transition to school will be less stressful for the entire family if parents recognize that part of the anxiety is theirs and that their anxiety is highly contagious. Once parents have separated their own anxiety from the child's, it is easier for them to face the fact that certain tasks must be performed at certain ages and that going to school is simply the child's "job." Parents can present going to school as part of the normal course of events and allow their children to acknowledge any feelings they have about going to school, positive or negative. However, parents should not give their child the

CASE STUDY *A Family in Trouble*

Joe Caruso is known around Burbank, California, as a hardworking insurance man, active in local politics and a supporter of the Little Theater. Joe used to be an actor himself but now, at age fifty-three, he feels like an extra in his own anguished domestic drama. He would like to hold warm family discussions, but the television set dominates the living room, his youngest teenage daughter is rarely home when he is, and his two eldest daughters have their own apartment. Joe goes to church every Sunday but his children don't. He says grace at every meal, but only reluctantly do they whisper "Amen."

"A father can't always direct the family in his own image," Joe philosophizes. If he could, Joe would recreate the warm experiences he remembers from his own childhood in the Italian section of New York City's Lower East Side: the big Sunday dinners with relatives, family picnics at the beach and neighborhood street festivals. But Joe has moved to California, where he has no relatives and friends are not intimate. "We're spared the buying of gifts and the going to weddings, showers, and banquets," he says sardonically. "But we feel blessed that we have a choice of living styles here."

Two years ago, Joe's younger daughters started experimenting with their life-style. Gina, then sixteen, started popping pills and ran away from home. Joe found her and brought her back. Eight months ago, Christina, fifteen, took off and was arrested as an accomplice in an armed robbery. A condition of her probation was that Joe and his wife, Bonnie, attend classes in effective parenting. They went, but Joe didn't like the idea of strangers meddling in his life. It's not like the old days, when a father could rely on his own kind.

FOR CLASS DISCUSSION

1. In leaving New York for California, Joe Caruso in effect left his ethnic kinship and friendship system behind. How do you think this contributed to his difficulties with his children?

2. If Joe had been more willing to try to learn something in the parenting classes, do you think this would have helped improve the family's communication? Would another approach have been more promising?

Source: *Newsweek*, September 22, 1975. Copyright 1975 by Newsweek, Inc. All rights reserved. Reprinted by permission.

impression that there is any *choice* about whether or not the child goes to school (Anderson, 1976).

This method of dealing with a child's starting school is a good example of a well-handled crisis. The parents acknowledge their own feelings and allow the child to be open as well; they face facts realistically, without exaggerating or minimizing the event; and they communicate effectively. They are concerned about their child, but not overprotective. As a result, the parents and child learn to cope with a new situation and to feel more secure about dealing with other stresses that arise.

NONNORMATIVE FAMILY CRISIS

We have said that families that are able to handle stressful events successfully have a number of things in their favor. They tend to have warm, affectionate relationships with each other; they make decisions together; they learn from experience; they are able to adapt to changing circumstances; and they are well integrated. Families tend to become disorganized and crisis prone when these kinds of supports are lacking. In some cases, the stresses can become very severe and culminate in ever more intense conflict, as when a married couple begins a pattern of abusive behavior. The remainder of the chapter examines some nonnormative family crises and attempts to shed light on features of families under severe forms of stress.

FAMILY VIOLENCE

In recent years, there has been increasing attention to the problem of family violence in our society. No one knows exactly how widespread family violence is, but there are reliable figures on its most extreme form, murder. The F.B.I. estimates that in one-quarter of all murders in the United States the murderer and the victim are related (Steinmetz, 1978). Other forms of violence within the family may also be widespread. Gelles and Straus (1979) found that physical violence of some type was characteristic of 55 percent of the families they studied.

What do we mean by the term **violence**? Social scientists differ in the way they classify behavior as violent. Some have distinguished between legitimate and illegitimate uses of physical force but as Gelles (1973) has pointed out, this distinction may be unsatisfactory because the legitimacy of force depends upon one's point of view. If policemen club students who are taunting them, for example, the act is regarded as legitimate from the point of view of the police. It may also be seen as legitimate by people who believe the police should be treated with respect. However, the students being clubbed and others who might take the students' side would not agree that the use of force was justified.

A useful definition of violence, provided by Gelles and Straus (1979), is "an act carried out with the intention of, or perceived as having the intention of, physically hurting another person." According to this definition, if a woman

Marital violence is not simply verbal abuse such as is shown here; it involves physical abuse as well.

tries to leave the dinner table during an argument with her husband, and the husband pushes her back into her seat, the act is violent if he meant to hurt her (even if he did not); or if she *thinks* he meant to hurt her (whether he did or didn't); or if, to the surprise of them both, the chair tips over and she sprains her back.

Although violence is related to both conflict and aggression, these terms are not synonymous. Violence involves physical injury—perceived, intended, or actual. Aggression refers to any behavior that is intended to harm another, either physically or psychologically. Aggression may be verbal, whereas violence is always physical. Conflict occurs when there is a clash of interests. For example, when everyone in a group wants to watch a different television program and all are trying to get their own way, conflict exists in that group. When conflict escalates into name-calling, verbal aggression occurs, and if a physical attack ensues, conflict becomes violence.

History of Family Violence

Family violence is not a new phenomenon. "Honor thy father and mother," said the Bible, and in medieval Europe, a man had the right to beat and kill the child who did not. Puritan America extended that right to the community:

a 1646 law stated that any child over sixteen who willfully cursed, hit, or disobeyed his parents could be put to death (Steinmetz, 1978).

In colonial America, a law was enacted charging spouses to live together peacefully, and judging from court and parish records, there were many who broke it. Wives and children were not the only victims; one colonial wife was charged with "beating and reviling her husband and egging her children to help her, bidding them to knock him in the head and wishing his victuals might choke him" (Steinmetz, 1978).

In 1874, the case of a nine-year-old girl who had been beaten by her parents came before the Society for the Prevention of Cruelty to Animals. The story drew the attention of the public, ultimately resulting in the founding of the Society for the Protection of Children. A decade later, a North Carolina court declared that although a husband had "no right" to beat his wife, "if no permanent injury has been inflicted, nor malice, cruelty, nor dangerous violence shown by the husband, it is better to draw the curtain, shut out the public gaze, and leave the parties to forgive and forget" (Steinmetz, 1978). The curtain remained drawn for nearly a century.

Until recently, the most prevalent view of family violence was that it was highly abnormal—a pathological aberration. This opinion was shared by all those in a position to study or prevent violence: the courts, the hospitals, the police, the schools. The public did not want to know about family violence, and victims of violence rarely admitted to having been abused.

Today, in large measure because of the efforts of feminists concerned with the plight of battered wives and abused children, family violence is an acknowledged social problem. Even so, there are many who seem to feel that violence among family members is sometimes justified. In one study (Gelles, 1974), wives explained that their husbands hit them because they "deserved" it, and husbands related that they sometimes had to slap their wives to "knock them to their senses." In another study, one out of four men and one out of six women reported that they approved of husbands hitting their wives under certain circumstances. However, wives were slightly more in favor of hitting their husbands than of their husbands hitting them. Additionally, 92 percent of parents surveyed reported that they believe in spanking their children. Whereas some researchers regard these figures as evidence that family violence is "rare," others believe the statistics prove that it is extremely widespread (Steinmetz, 1978).

Family violence has certainly come out into the open. One need only read the newspapers or turn on the television to see the problem portrayed and examined. But it is important to realize that while violence is discussed more frequently, the rate of family violence is probably not increasing. The change may be in its greater visibility and in the public perception of it as a serious concern.

Marital Violence

How widespread is violence between marriage partners? While no one knows exactly, police reports provide a reliable clue: the majority of calls for help received by the police are from spouses involved in domestic disputes, and more police are killed investigating these calls than any other kind. Gelles and Straus (1979) contend that violence is a major feature of American family life and that "the marriage license is unconsciously approved as a hitting license." Research indicates that an estimated 3.3 million wives and .75 million husbands were severely beaten in one year, and 1.7 million spouses drew guns or knives on their partners (Steinmetz, 1978).

Many studies have found that there is not much difference between husbands' and wives' forms of violent behavior. Wives were just as likely as their husbands to throw things, slap, and attack with objects, though husbands more often push and grab. While it seems reasonable to assume that in nonlethal battles, husbands can do more damage than can wives, Gelles and Straus (1979) speculate that the low ratio of reported husband-beating could also be due to husbands' unwillingness to admit that their wives had beaten them.

FACTORS IN SPOUSE ABUSE   Spouse-beating used to be regarded as the evidence of a disturbed personality. Today, however, most sociologists agree that spouse abusers may be exemplary citizens in other aspects of their lives.

How, then, can marital violence be explained? One widespread notion is that the stress produced by poverty is an important factor. But while violence may be more common among lower-class than middle-class families, this is not altogether certain. More violence is reported among lower-class husbands and wives and studies conclude that there is more, but this could be because middle-class families have more privacy. While a lower-class victim of violence has no recourse but public support systems, middle-class victims can afford private agencies that do not disclose their records to caseworkers (Gelles and Straus, 1979). Another explanation for the apparently lower incidence of violence in middle-class families is that middle-class families have more resources for coping with and relieving stress than lower-class families: better housing, higher income, easier access to birth control and abortion, and skills that enable them to change jobs. Others have speculated that middle-class spouses are socialized to talk out their problems rather than resort to violence. Since the inability to communicate effectively is highly related to marital violence, this explanation appears to have merit.

Even so, there is no doubt that marital violence does exist in the middle and upper classes. Many calls to hot-lines for battered wives are from middle-class women. Recent studies show that well-educated, upper-class men, including doctors, lawyers, and executives, do abuse their wives. Indeed, this abuse may be far more widespread than anyone has suspected (Steinmetz, 1978).

A stressful situation that is directly tied to wife-beating is unwanted pregnancy. Gelles (1973) reported that many wives said that although they had been beaten before and after their child's birth, the beatings they received during pregnancy were the most brutal. Many had been punched in the stomach. One explanation for this is that unplanned or unwanted pregnancy is often accompanied by tremendous financial and emotional stresses.

There is also a direct relationship between alcohol use and spouse abuse. Abuse often follows when both spouses have been drinking. Gelles and Straus argue that men who beat their spouses while drunk may get drunk as an excuse to behave violently (Gelles and Straus, 1979).

Employment problems are another factor in marital violence. Men who are unemployed or unhappy with their employment are likely to feel incompetent and inadequate, and these men are proportionately more likely to beat their wives. Job dissatisfaction can and does exist in all social classes, but at the lower end of the socioeconomic scale, a man who sees his role as head of the household but has little education, prestige, or income to enforce this role may resort to violence as a means of maintaining dominance. Family members who are consistently ignored or undervalued may use violence as a way of getting attention: for example, a wife who is neglected by her husband may throw a dish at him (Gelles and Straus, 1979).

Families isolated from friends and relatives are particularly likely to engage in violent behavior. There are two possible reasons for this: one is that being without friends means that a family lacks a support network; in times of crisis, such a family has nowhere to turn and thus experiences more stress. Another theory is that isolated families are more violent because they are not likely to be influenced by other people (Gelles and Straus, 1979). Societal disapproval is less likely to deter them from beating their spouses or children.

Child Abuse

Each year thousands of children are brutally beaten, tortured, sexually assaulted, and sometimes killed by their parents. The extent of the problem of child abuse is difficult to determine because so many cases go unreported and because reporting practices vary so much from state to state. Gelles and Straus (1979) believe that a conservative estimate of abused children would place the figure at between 200,000 and 500,000 children per year.

The incidence of child abuse appears to vary with the sex and age of the child. Data from a nationwide survey indicate that under the age of twelve, boys are more often abused than girls. After puberty, however, girls far outnumber boys as the targets of physical abuse. Conflicts between parent and child concerning the heterosexual relationships of the adolescent girl may contribute to this, as may the increasing physical strength of boys. Physical abuse is not limited to young children, however: nearly one-fifth of the cases in the national survey were teenagers (Gil, 1970).

Child abuse is usually defined as deliberate mistreatment of children resulting in physical injury. Since approximately nine out of ten parents use physical punishment at some time in their children's lives (Steinmetz, 1977), it is sometimes difficult to determine the dividing line between corporal punishment and the kind of abuse that threatens the physical well-being of the child. Perhaps we can say that child abuse results in lasting physical and psychological injury, while the effects of physical discipline, used sparingly, are transient. In recent years, some sociologists have included occasional slaps and spankings in their statistics on family violence. From this perspective, one might conclude that nearly all American families are scenes of violence! However, our concern is with forms of abuse that are potentially life-threatening.

FACTORS IN CHILD ABUSE   Child abuse, like spouse abuse, used to be blamed on the failings of the individual: people who abused their children were "sick." Recent research has concluded that the causes of child abuse are more complex.

A survey of the research on social class indicates a relationship between social class and child abuse. The levels of education, occupation, and income of child abusers are reported to be lower than that of the population at large. One reason child abuse may be more common among lower-class families is that they have fewer resources—financial and social—with which to cope with stress. For a lower-class family that is already living up to and perhaps beyond its income, losing a job will be perceived as a financial crisis of severe proportion, whereas a middle-class family in a similar situation would probably have reserves on which it could draw. When parents have few coping strategies, children may become easy targets on which to vent frustration over stresses such as unemployment or an unhappy work situation. One study found that nearly half the fathers of abused children in the sample were unemployed during the year that preceded the abuse (Gelles, 1973). Another reported that fathers who were dissatisfied with their jobs were more likely to use severe corporal punishment than fathers who were satisfied with their jobs (Steinmetz, 1977).

Abused children are often the products of unwanted pregnancies. They are usually young (under three years of age) and the youngest or only child. Some researchers have found that one-third of the abused children they studied were born prematurely. One explanation for this is that premature babies tend to be more difficult to take care of and thus create more stress for the parents. Another possibility (one that is receiving considerable attention) is that because premature babies often require special hospital care they are separated from their mothers at a time when bonding would otherwise occur (Steinmetz,

1977). Premature or not, an unwanted newborn may be regarded as a burden and as such, deeply resented. Families without stress-reducing resources may respond to the resented child with brutal behavior (Gelles, 1973).

Mental retardation has also been related to child abuse. Some researchers have found evidence that the retardation precipitates the abuse; others contend that the abuse results in the retardation. Steinmetz (1977) concludes that while severe abuse can lead to brain damage, children who *seem* abnormal to their parents in any way—whether or not the children actually are abnormal—are likely candidates for abuse.

The factors we have considered exemplify the general proposition that a family with little money, prestige, and power suffers greater frustrations than a family with adequate income and higher status, and this—in times of particular stress—may lead to abuse. Of course, not all parents who experience severe stress resort to child abuse. The parents who cause physical injury to their children seem to be people who have been raised without love and tolerance. Many abusing parents were themselves abused as children and act toward their own children according to the example that was set for them. Steinmetz (1977) has referred to "the cycle of violence" to characterize the predominance of violence in families from one generation to the next. Abusing parents also seem to lack knowledge of what a child's ability may be at a certain age and how to go about getting the child to behave in the way they desire. They seem not to realize that the child is not merely being stubborn or willful, but really does not understand or cannot perform in the way the parent wants (Spinetta and Rigler, 1972).

Abusing parents seem to suffer from deep feelings of inadequacy, especially a sense that they are failing to fulfill the role expected of parents. This may be reflected in the child's misbehavior or failure to progress as expected. It may also be reflected in failure to meet the cultural definition of a successful family. A home in which the father is unemployed and the mother has been forced to take over financial responsibility is considered a breeding ground for abuse (Spinetta and Rigler, 1972).

Other Forms of Family Violence and Abuse

Recently it has come to light that elderly parents, especially those who are dependent upon their children to care for them, are often physically assaulted and psychologically abused by their children and grandchildren. Various explanations have been advanced: the children are seeking revenge for childhood beatings; or, the children, frustrated by trying to care for elderly, bedridden parents while simultaneously trying to rear their own children, simply can't cope and reach a breaking point. Family researchers are exploring this newly discovered area of family violence.

Some violence between siblings is considered normal by nearly everyone; but statistics suggest that society tolerates levels of violence between siblings that would result in criminal charges if similar acts occurred between strangers, husbands and wives, or parents and children. Gelles and Straus (1980) reported that four out of five children committed at least one violent act against a sibling during a typical year. Of course, it is important to approach this finding cautiously. Nearly every child at one time or another hits a sibling, but we cannot therefore conclude that every child is perpetually violent. Sibling abuse appears to be widespread among adults as well. In one year 138,000 people attacked a sibling with a gun or knife, and 3 percent of all homicides in Philadelphia from 1972 to 1976 were between siblings (Steinmetz, 1977).

The factors involved in violence between siblings vary with age. Young children tend to fight over possesions, eight-to-twelve-year-olds over personal space boundaries, and teenagers over responsibilities and social obligations (Steinmetz, 1977).

SEXUAL ABUSE Sexual abuse of children by family members is a serious problem that is only beginning to attract widespread attention. About 10 percent of girls have a sexual encounter with a male relative; at least 1 percent become involved in father-daughter incest. Sexual abuse of boys occurs less often within their families; about 10 percent have a sexual encounter with an adult male who is usually an acquaintance rather than a relative (*The Harvard Medical School Health Letter*, March 1981).

Father-daughter incest is the most frequently reported form of sexual abuse within the family and is potentially extremely harmful to the child. The sexual contact usually begins when the child is between six and twelve. Fondling and masturbation may continue for years and may proceed to intercourse (*The Harvard Medical School Health Letter*, March 1981).

Incest occurs in all social classes, ethnic, and racial groups. Often father-daughter incest occurs in families where there is an extreme imbalance of power; that is, the fathers are usually domineering and the mothers are very passive. Studies have found that the mothers frequently suffer from medical or psychological conditions that interfere with their traditional mothering responsibilities. In such cases, the oldest daughter usually takes on the mother's tasks, and it is she who is most likely to experience sexual abuse (*The Harvard Medical School Health Letter*, March 1981).

Prevention and Intervention

In the past, efforts to prevent or intervene in cases of family violence were hampered by the widespread belief that the family should solve its own problems. This was true even in cases of child abuse. Many courts would have agreed with the judge who counseled "drawing the curtain" and leaving the family to "forgive and forget." Now that family violence has been acknowledged as a serious social problem, most people believe that society has some

HIGHLIGHT 12.1 | *Marital and Family Therapy*

When the response to stress is disorganization, or when an earlier mode of coping is no longer effective, a family may need professional help to resolve the resulting crisis. Many troubled couples and families do not seek therapy because they do not know where to turn. One useful resource is the American Association for Marriage and Family Therapy, 924 W. 9th St., Upland, CA 91786, a national association concerned exclusively with marital and family therapy. Its members include physicians, ministers, social workers, sociologists, educators, and psychologists. The AAMFT has a toll-free number: (800) 854-9876. In addition, most cities have information and referral services which can help a family determine the kind of help they need and the kind of counselor who might be able to help them.

Relationship therapy (treatment for either marriage or family problems) is based on the principle that change does not occur in any member of a group without it affecting the working arrangement of that system. As a result, therapy focuses on the ways in which the family has adapted to the present life-style and what the consequences of changing that style will be.

When therapy involves a married couple without children, it is assumed that in many cases faulty interpersonal relations are at the heart of the individual's problems within the marriage. For this reason, the focus of therapy is not on a single individual but on the relationship. Couples usually attend therapy sessions together, and the therapy centers on helping them resolve conflicts and improve their interactions. It has been shown that treating only one partner is less helpful in resolving marital problems.

Two areas that are closely linked to relationship problems are communication and role expectations. Unhappy couples tend to communicate less or to communicate less effectively then happy couples, and unhappy couples show less sensitivity to each other's needs. Marital adjustment also suffers when one partner (or both) has certain expectations about the role the other partner should play but never openly expresses those expectations.

A variety of approaches are employed to improve couple communication, depending on the background of the therapist and the needs of the couple. An increasingly popular innovation in marital therapy involves videotaping therapy sessions and then showing the tape to the couple. Viewing their interactions enables the partners to analyze their individual behavior and their patterns of communicating with each other more objectively.

Family therapy, like marital therapy, assumes that an individual family member's problems do not exist in a vacuum. For example, a child's drug problem is perceived as reflecting the more general problems of the family system of which the child is a member. Consequently most family therapists believe that the entire family should participate in therapy if the family member with the specific difficulty is to receive lasting help.

Family therapy is sometimes carried out in a group setting, with the spouses and children and a therapist present. As in marital therapy, considerable emphasis is placed on improving patterns of communication, enabling family members to express their feelings, and learning more positive ways of interacting and solving family problems. Once the family dynamics are understood, the therapist becomes a catalyst for change, acting at different times as an interpreter, an intermediary, a referee, or a negotiator.

responsibility for preventing it from occurring and intervening when it has occurred.

Considerable progress is being made in helping battered wives. In the past, a major obstacle for abused women was that if they wanted to leave their husbands they had no place to go. Today treatment programs, shelters, crisis hot lines, and police units trained in family-crisis intervention have been set up in many communities with considerable success. For example, although family homicides increased overall in 1976, there were none among the 962 families in one city serviced by a trained family-crisis intervention unit (Steinmetz, 1978).

A variety of efforts also are being made to reduce the incidence of child abuse. They include: community education programs, such as television and newspaper advertisements to increase public awareness of the problem; the formation of child-protection teams by state and county welfare departments to investigate reported cases of abuse; evaluation and treatment of abused children and their parents in community mental-health centers; the formation of parent-support groups, often composed of former child abusers, to teach abusing parents more positive ways of dealing with their children. Many communities also are making it a legal requirement for physicians and mental-health workers to report cases of child abuse that they encounter.

ALCOHOLISM AND THE FAMILY

Unlike family violence, alcoholism has always been regarded as a widespread problem in the United States. During the nineteenth century, the clergy of several American churches denounced drunkenness as contributing to poverty, crime, and mental illness. The temperance movement, which resulted in the prohibition of the sale of alcoholic beverages from 1919 to 1933 (a law that was widely disobeyed), was an outgrowth of this attitude.

While most people today would agree that alcoholism can and often does lead to a variety of serious problems, including unemployment, desertion, and illness, these problems and alcoholism itself are perceived as reactions to stress rather than signs of moral decay.

One of the many problems in studying alcoholism is the difficulty of defining the term. **Alcoholism** is characterized as a psychobiological disease, but it is a rather unique disease in that its symptoms are hard to describe accurately. Researchers have tried to identify specific criteria that would separate alcoholism from social drinking, but so far, they have had only limited success. One widely accepted criterion is physiological addiction; that is, physical dependence on alcohol. Another, more ambiguous criterion is self-diagnosis (Steinglass, 1979). The problem with self-diagnosis is that many alcoholics do not believe they have a problem.

Whatever the definition, conservative estimates place the number of alcoholics in America at 9 million. And, contrary to popular belief, only 3 to

5 percent of alcoholics are down and out; the vast majority live at home with their families and perform both family and occupational roles (Steinglass, 1979).

Family Influences upon Alcoholism

Research has shown that there is a relationship between family background and alcoholism. El-Guebaly and Offord (1977) reviewed the literature and reported three well-documented findings that supported this theory. (1) When comparing a group of alcoholics to a control group, researchers found that a high percentage of alcoholics had lost their mothers early in life. (2) A follow-up study on children who had been referred to a clinic for antisocial behavior showed that when these children grew up, their antisocial behavior and alcoholism patterns were very similar to those of their parents. (3) In two other studies of alcoholics, researchers discovered that less than half the alcoholics studied had reached the age of fifteen with both parents living continuously at home. In general, alcoholics' fathers were described as punishing, disinterested, and rejecting; the mothers as overindulgent. Fewer alcoholics than those in the control group were raised by affectionate mothers (El-Guebaly and Offord, 1977).

When Steinglass reviewed the literature in 1979, he found one study which reported that adopted sons of alcoholics had a rate of alcoholism four times higher than that of a control group of adoptees with nonalcoholic parents. Another study compared adopted and biological sons of alcoholics, and found a similar incidence of alcoholism in each group. While it is too early to say whether or not heredity plays a definitive role in alcoholism, many social scientists think heredity and family experiences in childhood predispose people to be alcoholic.

Alcoholism and Marital Interaction

Alcoholism is often associated with a peculiarly rigid style of interaction in marriage. Stephen Gorad (1971) studied twenty couples in which the husband was an alcoholic and twenty couples in which the husband was not. Using an experimental game-playing situation, he found that there were significant differences between the two groups in the way the husbands and wives interacted with each other. Instead of cooperating for their mutual benefit, alcoholic husbands and their wives seemed to be locked in a continuous power struggle. Gorad suggests that they refuse to relinquish their competitive behavior because neither believes that the other is capable of changing.

Gorad also found certain personality characteristics among alcoholic husbands and their wives. Alcoholic husbands tended to display responsibility-avoiding behavior in communicating with their wives even when they were sober. The wives, by contrast, tended to be more direct, open, and willing to accept responsibility than their husbands. Another study of alcoholic husbands and their wives administered personality tests and found that the alcoholic husbands saw themselves as being more feminine and dependent, while their wives saw themselves as being more masculine and independent (Orford et al., 1975).

In considering these studies, it is important to note that they do not explain whether the interactions and personality traits of alcoholic husbands and their wives are contributing factors to the alcoholism, whether they are a result of the alcoholism, or whether the alcoholism might be caused by a third factor, such as low self-esteem and depression (Steinglass, 1979).

Impact of Alcoholism on the Family

When someone in a family becomes an alcoholic, everyone in the family suffers. An alcoholic spouse may lose his or her job, disappear periodically, behave abusively, or have extramarital relationships. The stresses on the family are related not only to the drinking itself, but to these other problems, which are caused by the drinking. Alcoholism affects all aspects of a family's life (Steinglass, 1979).

Like some forms of mental illness, alcoholism is chronic; that is, it lasts for a long time, or recurs frequently, and resists efforts at cure. While a family may require only a few weeks or months to adjust to the birth of a baby, and then settle in to new behavior patterns, it may take years to adjust to the stress of alcoholism, and the alcoholic's ultimate effect upon the family may not be apparent for decades.

But even though the response to the crisis of alcoholism is usually prolonged, families that have an alcoholic member experience stages similar

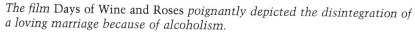

The film Days of Wine and Roses *poignantly depicted the disintegration of a loving marriage because of alcoholism.*

to those that Hill (1958) ascribes to families in other stressful situations: crisis, disorganization, recovery, and reorganization. Jackson (1956) interviewed hundreds of wives of men who were members of Alcoholics Anonymous in order to discover how families adjust to alcoholism. She found that the adjustment process involved seven distinct stages and that a family can proceed through all seven stages or can fail to progress beyond a certain stage. Jackson cautions that her research applies only to the families of alcoholics who are actively seeking help. Also, her model is directed toward families with an alcoholic husband, though it might be assumed to apply generally to families with alcoholic wives. Finally, it should be noted that the model applies to families in which role responsibilities are divided traditionally.

STAGE 1: ATTEMPTS TO DENY THE PROBLEM At some point in the marriage, the husband begins drinking too much—sporadically, at first. After each episode, although family role responsibilities shift and all problems not related to the drinking are minimized, both husband and wife try to explain the drinking away and pretend that it is perfectly normal. As the drinking continues or becomes more frequent, the wife comes to recognize that her husband is an alcoholic, but tries to hide this fact from others, including their children.

STAGE 2: ATTEMPTS TO ELIMINATE THE PROBLEM The family becomes socially isolated, drinking comes to symbolize all conflicts, and both husband and wife try harder to hide the problem from others. The husband and wife draw apart. Each resents the other, both feel tense, and both try to maintain the illusion that there has been no change in their roles. The wife makes trial-and-error attempts to control her husband's drinking, but her efforts seem to fail.

STAGE 3: DISORGANIZATION The wife gives up trying to control her husband's drinking and begins thinking of it as a permanent problem. She stops trying to understand her husband or hide his alcoholism from their children. The myth that the husband is fulfilling his role as father, husband, and provider is abandoned as his drinking bouts and absences from home and job become more frequent. The wife may even begin to doubt her own sanity.

STAGE 4: ATTEMPTS TO REORGANIZE IN SPITE OF THE PROBLEM This stage usually begins when some related crisis occurs. When, for example, the husband beats her or the children, the wife decides that some decisive action is required if the family is to survive. At this point, some wives leave their husbands. Others respond by taking over the husband's roles, and the rest of the family either ignores the husband or treats him like a wayward child. As he sees the ranks of the family closing against him, the husband may try to regain his status as husband and father.

The wife's reorganizing actions (assuming her husband's roles, explaining the problem frankly to the children and telling them that their father's actions are not their fault) usually have a stabilizing effect on the children, because their environment is more predictable. The wife, too, begins to regain her sense of self-worth.

However, even though the family as a unit is more stable, the secondary crises multiply during this stage. If, for example, the husband once saw other women secretly, he may now bring them home. The most disruptive occurrence during this stage is that the husband may try to stop drinking; in this case, as the family regains hope, it reinstates the husband in his former roles, only to be disappointed and become disorganized when he begins drinking again.

STAGE 5: EFFORTS TO ESCAPE THE PROBLEM   The wife may seek legal separation or divorce. If she opts for divorce, she cannot always count on receiving any money that the settlement might direct her husband to provide since he will continue to have difficulty fulfilling his roles responsibly.

STAGE 6: REORGANIZATION OF THE FAMILY   If a separation or divorce does occur, roles are reshuffled. Earlier stages of the crisis (the mother taking on the father's roles, for example) have prepared the alcoholic's family for these changes, and adjustment to divorce may be easier than it is for nonalcoholic families. However, if the alcoholic persists in attempting reconciliation (making phone calls to his wife at work, visiting the family while she is absent and either frightening the children by drunkenness or raising false hopes by sobriety) or tries to seek revenge (behaving violently toward babysitters, for example), reorganization is made more difficult.

STAGE 7: REORGANIZATION OF THE WHOLE FAMILY   If the husband manages to stop drinking, this, too, requires substantial adjustment. A husband and wife who have separated may reconcile, but since they have been in conflict for years, they are likely to have highly unrealistic ideas about what constitutes a good relationship. The reorganized marriage is almost inevitably disillusioning. Once again new role adjustments are required. The wife may have to relinquish her control of the family, and the children must once again adjust their perceptions of their parents and their roles.

Although Jackson's study was prepared some years ago, more recent research in England (Orford et al., 1975) reported styles of coping behavior in wives of alcoholics similar to those found by Jackson. These included such strategies as safeguarding the family interests, withdrawing from the marriage, attacking the alcoholic (physically and verbally), and protecting the alcoholic. Orford and colleagues (1975) also found that the wife's method of coping was related to the husband's drinking outcome. When the wife withdrew from her husband—for example, by refusing to talk to him, avoiding him, not having sexual relations with him, seeking help from outsiders, or considering divorce—

a year later he was apt to be drinking as much if not more than before. However, when the wife was actively involved with her husband—even if that involvement took the form of nagging, pleading, or arguing with him about his drinking, getting drunk herself, trying to make him jealous or look ridiculous, or hiding his liquor—a year later his drinking had *not* increased and sometimes had decreased. In other words, passive withdrawal of the wife was linked to poor results while active involvement was not.

As the authors point out, the explanations for these findings are not clear. They have speculated, however, that the degree of the wife's involvement may be an important indication of the family's degree of organization and the alcoholic's potential for change. Less research is available on families in which the wife is an alcoholic, but even though some of the family dynamics could certainly be expected to be different, the general family response and coping strategies could be expected to be similar.

 PROBLEMS OF YOUTH

An individual's self-image is formed early in life. Children first learn to communicate and to form bonds with others through their experiences in the home. However, some children learn things at home that create serious problems for them later. The children of alcoholics, for example, "often learn that communication is a complicated network of lies and deceit" (Barnes, 1977). The things a child fails to learn can cause problems too. A child who is unwanted or unloved will have a difficult time learning to trust and love others.

Many people believe that rapidly changing American institutions, including the family, have led to the loss of a role for young people. "When, in recent memory, has it been less a privilege to be young in America?" asks writer Scott Spencer (1979). It is Spencer's contention that today's youth "may be the most disturbed and demoralized in this century." He cites the sharp increase in the incidence of teenage and child alcoholism, prostitution, sexually transmitted disease, pregnancy, criminal behavior, and suicide. These problems, he asserts, appear to be related to changes in the family and in society, including a decline in parental involvement with children and a decline in the child orientation of families.

Perhaps because they feel there is no place for them in society, increasing numbers of young people are experiencing **alienation**—a sense of withdrawal or separation from the values of the society. Whereas alienation was once regarded as a phase that middle-class college students went through, it is now viewed as a serious problem that affects high-school students and even young children both in affluent suburbs and in city slums (Lambert et al., 1972).

Lambert et al. (1972) describe alienated young people as connected neither to family nor society, as feeling detached from their own feelings as well as from the people around them. Alienated youngsters tend to live in the present and to be uncommitted and irresponsible; they are uninterested in both their own personal pasts and their country's history. They are often unable to communicate with their parents or other adults. They believe life is meaningless, and they often have promiscuous but unsatisfying sexual relations.

The family situation is a major factor in a youngster's feelings of alienation. Often the father is absent from home and the mother is overprotective, overindulgent, or too involved with the other children. Both parents tend to be permissive and inconsistent in setting limits on their children's behavior (Lambert et al., 1972).

Runaways

An important manifestation of adolescent alienation is the high incidence of teenage runaways. In the past, runaways were not considered a social problem. In fact, they were often regarded as romantic adventurers, like Huckleberry Finn, who were capable of making satisfying lives for themselves. But in our highly technical modern economy, education is a necessary component of career success, and adolescents who leave their family and drop out of school have little chance of succeeding in life. Furthermore, today's young runaways often become the victims of unscrupulous adults, such as pimps and drug dealers.

Just as alcoholics were once blamed for moral weakness, the blame for leaving home was once placed on the runaways themselves. More recently, case workers have pointed out that running away is often a reaction to family stress (Gullotta, 1979). Running away is one of the strongest ways an adolescent can show parents that something is wrong (Lerner and Spanier, 1980).

In legal terms, a runaway is a child under eighteen years of age who leaves home without his or her parents' consent. An estimated million or more children run away from home each year. The predominant age for runaways is fifteen, but an increasing number are in the eleven-to-fourteen age bracket. Adolescent males and females leave home in about equal numbers; and social and economic factors have not been found to be influential. Runaways leave with friends about as often as they leave alone (Lerner and Spanier, 1980).

FAMILY FACTORS LINKED TO RUNAWAYS Obviously, not everyone who runs away does so for the same reasons. The reasons for leaving most often given by runaways themselves included problems at home, family discipline, and difficulties at school (Lerner and Spanier, 1980). In one study, seventy-five percent of the parents of runaways reported prevalent conflict in the family. Half of all runaways are oldest or only children. It may be that firstborns experience greater pressure than younger siblings because parents expect more of them. Runaways are likely to come from divorced families or from homes in which one parent has remarried. Contrary to what many people might think, runaways are not more likely to have mothers employed outside the home than are other adolescents, which indicates that maternal employment is not a contributing factor in a child's running away (Lerner and Spanier, 1980).

Perhaps the most significant family characteristic leading to running away is lack of communication between parents and children. When runaways did communicate with their parents, the children claimed the parents didn't listen and the parents said the children were disobedient, apathetic, and insensitive (Gullotta, 1979).

When communication is the main problem, a family can often be helped by outside agencies, such as family therapists. But little can be done for the adolescents whom social scientists have termed **throwaways**—teenagers who are expelled from the house by their parents. Often, throwaways are adolescents who are caught in the middle of the stress created by a divorce or remarriage. In some instances, single parents and new stepparents do not want to take on the responsibility and problems of raising an adolescent. Economics may also be a factor, causing poor parents to encourage their older children to leave (Gullotta, 1979; Lerner and Spanier, 1980). Reviewing the literature, Lerner and Spanier (1980) speculate that whether the child is a runaway or a throwaway, the departure is caused by a problematic parent-child relationship that was constructed by all parties.

Adolescent Pregnancy

A stressful event faced increasingly by young American women is adolescent pregnancy. Although birthrates in the overall population have been declining, adolescent sexual activity and pregnancy have increased dramatically. According to research by Zelnick, Young, and Kantner (1979), nearly two-thirds of America's unmarried young women aged ninteen have had sexual intercourse. Sexual activity is also starting at younger ages. In 1974, 17 percent of fourteen-year-olds had had sexual intercourse, compared to 10 percent a few years earlier, and it is this younger group that is becoming pregnant and giving birth more frequently (Alan Guttmacher Institute, 1976). One out of every ten women in the United States now becomes pregnant by age seventeen (Zelnick, Young, and Kantner, 1979).

Adolescent women who become pregnant face difficult options. They can have an abortion or they can have the baby. If they decide to have the baby, they can either marry (not many do), put the baby up for adoption, or keep the baby without marrying. Adolescents who decide to keep their babies—and they are increasing in number—face both medical and social risks. Young mothers are more likely to die in childbirth. The maternal death rate is 60 percent higher for teenagers than for women in their twenties. Babies of young teenagers are two to three times more likely to die before they reach their first birthday than babies born to mothers in their early twenties; they are twice

HIGHLIGHT 12.2   *Teenagers on Sex*

It's not like I'm really promiscuous," she says. The tremble in her voice is scarcely noticeable. "It just sounds that way. I only sleep with one person."

The gynecologist, a specialist in adolescent sexuality, nods.

"When you're doing it, it just seems so right and natural. But I'm scared. I never thought I'd be doing this. I feel so guilty. We both do."

"Have you been using any contraceptive?" She pushes back her long hair.

"I don't know if I'd feel right taking those things. You shouldn't use them if you're not married."

The doctor writes. He has heard it all before, thousands of times.

"You've been very lucky," he says mildly. She nods.

"The way I see it, if I use birth control, that makes me a bad girl. If I don't use anything, even if I get pregnant, I'm a good girl who got caught."

Although she's not pregnant this time, she's terrified that she will be and is seeking advice. She's in love for the first time, and having regular sex. Since both she and her partner believe that birth control is "for when you're married," she has already lived through at least two late periods, the special hell reserved for those young girls who, whether from ignorance or confusion, have not been using contraception.

"If only we were older. Then we'd get married. But we're still both so young. Besides,

I couldn't be treasurer of my high-school sorority if I was married."

Another girl now sits facing the gynecologist.

"How many different people have you had intercourse with?" he asks.

It takes her a while to count up.

"Six in the past ten months. You think I'm weird, I bet."

The doctor shakes his head. Nothing surprises him.

"Ever had oral intercourse?"

She nods, twisting a strand of hair. The small room is quiet as the doctor writes.

The silence weighs on the girl. She shifts in her chair, pushing up her sleeves. She is conventionally pretty, dressed in the uniform of her generation: the ubiquitous jeans, clodhopper shoes, too-large shirt.

"I feel really mixed up," she says, and now there is less bravado in her voice. "I almost feel like sex is expected of me. My attitude toward sex has become really warped. Sometimes the way I act scares me."

The doctor continues to write.

"What I really want is somebody who loves me so much that he doesn't want anyone else. I really want to get married and have babies."

She is seventeen and has venereal disease. She had an abortion two years ago and has been sexually active and on pills ever since.

Source: From the book *Not My Daughter* by Katherine B. Oettinger. © 1979 by Katherine B. Oettinger. Published by Prentice-Hall, Inc., Englewood Cliffs, N.J. 07631.

Teenage Parents Always Have Homework!

as likely to be premature or of low birth weight. Teenage mothers often have to drop out of school, and those who do rarely go back to acquire the skills that would enable them to find good jobs. Teenage mothers are thus more likely to have to depend on welfare to support themselves and their children. A survey of women in New York City who had their first babies between the ages of fifteen and seventeen showed that 91 percent had no jobs, and 72 percent were on welfare (Alan Guttmacher Institute, 1979). Even if the mothers marry, they are far more likely to be poor and remain poor than women who have their first babies when they are older.

An equally serious concern is what will happen to the children. Studies indicate that the babies of teenage mothers are likely to encounter a variety of problems ranging from malnutrition, which can and often does cause brain damage, to abandonment and child abuse (McKenry, Walters, and Johnson, 1979).

FACTORS RELATED TO TEENAGE PREGNANCY The causes of teenage pregnancy are complicated, and no single factor can be isolated with certainty beyond the obvious one of failure to use birth control. Despite the availability of information about reproduction, many teenagers do not seem to understand how conception takes place and believe that they are somehow immune to pregnancy. Some researchers have attributed adolescent pregnancy to the individual's self perception, suggesting that low self-esteem is a factor, or to social causes including family problems and poverty. There is evidence that many teenage girls who have sexual relations do not use contraceptives because to do so would suggest that they were "planning" to have sex. By avoiding contraceptives they can avoid seeing themselves as coldly calculating about sexual behavior. Sexual experiences then become something that happens spontaneously, and the young woman can feel that she has been carried away by her passion. The risk of pregnancy seems preferable to confronting the reality that they are sexually active and therefore "bad girls."

Of all the possible factors related to adolescent pregnancy the most important seems to be the young person's level of mental maturity. Adolescents may become pregnant even when contraceptives are available to them because they lack the judgment necessary to deal with their sexuality. Being able to exercise self-control, foresee the consequences of behavior, and understand that sexual behavior can lead to pregnancy requires a degree of mature thinking that most teenagers have "only on their best days," according to one group of researchers (McKenry, Walters, and Johnson, 1979).

Adolescent Drug Use and the Family

Drugs, by definition, change the way people function. Although many teenagers experiment with drugs with no negative consequences, some experience adverse effects upon their health, their ability to perform well in school, and their family relationships. In families that oppose the use of drugs, even brief experimentation by the young person may be enough to precipitate a family crisis. In other families, parents may feel that some experimentation is inevitable and may not become alarmed by it unless they see that it is affecting the child in negative ways.

Despite the attention that has been paid in the media to such problems as heroin use among teenagers, most teenagers are far more likely to use alcohol and tobacco than they are to use heroin. Virtually all teenagers experiment with alcohol at some point and about three-quarters try cigarettes. Marijuana use is also prevalent, although initial use of alcohol, marijuana, or cigarettes is often part of experimentation with one's peer group. A report by the National Institute on Drug Abuse found that among some 17,000 high-school students in the class of 1977, 56 percent had used marijuana at some point and about 34 percent had used it in the past month. The use of other types of drugs, such as LSD, cocaine, and amphetamines—either experimentally or more regularly—was much less prevalent (see Fig. 12.1) (Johnson, Bachman, and O'Malley, 1977).

The choice of drugs a young person will use seems to be sex-linked. Males tend to choose alcohol more frequently, whereas females choose amphetamines more frequently. Females also tend to use a greater variety of drugs than males (Lerner and Spanier, 1980).

FAMILY FACTORS IN TEENAGE DRUG ABUSE The family's reaction to teenage drug use can be influential in determining whether or not a young person will develop a problem with drugs. Some parents become excessively alarmed when they discover for the first time that their child has been drinking or smoking marijuana. Instead of realizing that the use may be experimental, these parents overreact and label the child "bad" or a "dope addict," thus generating a crisis unnecessarily. By using these negative labels they increase the chances of alienating the child from the family and increase the possibility that the child may actually become a drug abuser.

Even though relatively healthy families can contribute to the creation of a drug problem by handling the discovery of drug use badly, serious drug

Fig. 12.1

Lifetime, annual, and 30-day prevalence of use (and recency of use) for eleven types of drugs, class of 1977 (N = 17,087). (Source: L. D. Johnson, J. G. Bachman, and P. M. O'Malley, *Drug Use Among American High School Students,* 1975–1977, U.S. Department of Health, Education, and Welfare, National Institute on Drug Abuse, 1977, p. 24.)

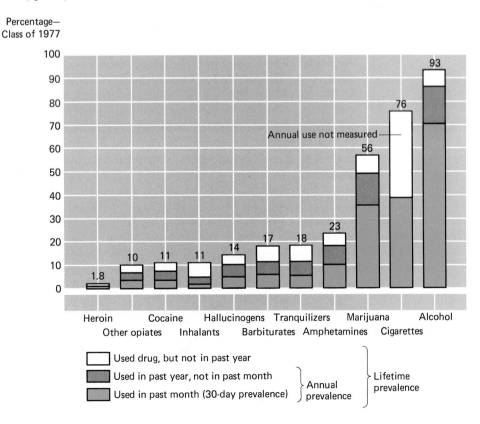

abuse is often linked to pathology within the family. For example, it has been found that the mothers of male narcotics addicts were overly indulgent, overprotective, and overpermissive; fathers were often absent, weak, detached, or uninvolved. Many of the addicts' fathers were alcoholics. Female addicts were often indulged by inept or alcoholic fathers and were competitive with their mothers (Lerner and Spanier, 1980).

Stanton, reviewing the literature, found that adolescents who used many different drugs were those who received little emotional support from their parents and who had lower self-esteem than nonusers. Often, the families of drug users were unable to adapt to the adolescent's growing independence and used the chronic drug use as a way of clinging to their child (Stanton, 1979).

These studies and others support the general conclusion that the family is the main contributing factor to youthful drug abuse. If the family relationships are positive, peers have much less influence upon a young person's decision to use drugs (Stanton, 1979). The one exception appears to be marijuana. According to an examination of 1112 triads composed of a high-school student, his or her best friend, and one parent, marijuana users were more likely to be influenced by peers than by parents. The students whose best friends and parents were regular marijuana users were those most likely to use the drug (Yancy, Nader, and Burnham, 1972).

Adolescent Suicide

Although the nation's overall suicide rate has not changed much in the past fifty years, the incidence of adolescent suicide rose 10 percent during the 1970s. In 1977 alone almost 5000 adolescents committed suicide (McKenry and Tishler, 1979). These figures include only reported suicides. Many more suicides may go unreported due to social stigma or because actual suicide may appear accidental. According to reported figures, about twice as many young males as females kill themselves, though females attempt suicide more frequently.

Adolescent suicide is related to a variety of family factors. The parents of suicidal youngsters tend to have highly unstable marriages. The adolescents themselves often have grown up under economic stress and have moved far more frequently than their peers. Many have a long and bitter history of conflict with their parents. These factors tend to make the young person feel rejected, unloved, and unworthy. Many adolescent suicides have recently experienced the death or suicide of a close relative or friend (McKenry and Tishler, 1979).

Teicher and Jacobs (1966) examined adolescent suicide as a conscious decision that death is the only solution to life's problems. They found that in most cases the suicide attempt is considered in advance and that it is considered only after other alternatives have failed. In their analysis, the "precipitating causes" that some social scientists attribute to adolescent suicide are important only as the final stage in the adolescent's troubled history. The adolescent suicide, Teicher and Jacobs believe, has a long history of problems, and these multiply during the five years preceding suicide. During the last year or two, conflicts with parents escalate to unbearably high levels, and the parents and their child usually perceive the child's behavior very differently. Communication deteriorates, and the adolescent enters what Teicher and Jacobs call the "final stage." As problems with parents multiply and communication with them worsens, the adolescent's ability to handle normal teenage problems decreases. And as these problems become more intense, the adolescent responds with withdrawal, rebellion, or aggression. When nothing helps, the adolescent becomes extremely depressed and completely stops communicating with parents and friends. This isolation, a problem in itself, keeps the adolescent from finding any way out other than suicide (Teicher and Jacobs, 1966).

Many depressed or suicidal adolescents can be helped. Teachers can be trained to recognize such danger signals as the inability to concentrate, decline in performance, or depression, and when necessary can refer their troubled students to appropriate professionals. Hotlines and suicide-intervention centers are useful tools, but often they are staffed by amateurs who must be willing to turn difficult problems over to trained professionals. Family therapy has also proved useful. When a suicidal or depressed adolescent enters therapy, therapists usually find it necessary to consider, and, if possible, treat the entire family—especially the parents. It is generally believed that the young person's problems cannot be treated independently of the problems of the family.

SUMMARY

1. There are two kinds of family crisis: normative or developmental crises, which occur in any family in the course of the family life cycle, and more severe crises such as alcoholism and family violence. These more severe crises can be chronic; developmental crises are usually temporary.

2. According to the model proposed by Hill (1958), whether or not a family experiences stressful events as crises depends upon the interaction of the stress-producing event, the family's resources, and how the family defines the event.

3. Family violence is a widespread, but not new, social problem. Its causes are complicated, but stress, dissatisfaction with one's job, unemployment, poverty, drinking, and a childhood characterized by violence all play a part.

4. Abused children are usually unwanted and unplanned. The stress of caring for them, emotionally, physically, and financially, leads to resentment and brutality. Child abuse is linked to poverty—perhaps because poor families have fewer stress-reducing resources than middle-class families.

5. Alcoholism is a chronic crisis which causes a host of other problems and affects every member of the family. Jackson (1956) found consistent coping patterns reported by wives of alcoholics, and she identified seven stages that the family with an alcoholic father passes through.

6. Most severe adolescent problems, including drug abuse, running away, and suicide, are related to family stress. Parents' lack of love, attention, and consistent discipline are linked to adolescent problems, as are parents' own chronic problems. The parents of problem adolescents may themselves be unable to cope with normal stresses such as their child's leaving home.

7. Adolescent pregnancy, while not usually caused by family stress, creates it: the babies of teenage mothers are more likely to encounter a variety of problems. These range from brain damage caused by malnutrition to abandonment and abuse. Teenage mothers are apt to remain poor, thus contributing to the stresses they already have in raising a child.

REVIEW AND DISCUSSION

1. Describe several crises, either developmental or situational, that your own family has experienced. How were these crises handled? Would you have dealt with them the same way?

2. What are some of the factors that have been linked to marital violence? Which of these do you think may be the most influential? Why?

3. What family factors are related to alcoholism? runaways? drug abuse? Do you think parents are blamed too often for the problems of young people?

4. What suggestions can you offer for countering the high rate of adolescent pregnancy? What could be done to help adolescent mothers avoid falling into a pattern of poverty and possible child abuse?

5. What factors in American society do you think have contributed to young people's feelings of alienation? As a potential future parent, what would you do to help your child achieve a sense of purpose and belonging?

SUGGESTED READINGS

Burgess, R. L., and R. D. Conger (1978). "Family Interaction in Abusive, Neglectful, and Normal Families." *Child Development* **49**:4:1163–1173.

Summary of 1977 study of forty-three low-income families. Examines patterns of interaction pertinent to parental neglect or abuse of children.

Kenisten, K. (1977). *All Our Children: The American Family Under Pressure.* New York: Harcourt.

Surveys the troubles that undercut some contemporary American families: poverty, drinking problems, unemployment, and the like.

Koch, J., and L. Koch (1976). "A Consumer's Guide to Therapy for Couples." *Psychology Today* **9**:10:33–40.

The authors point out some things to beware of in the marriage-therapy market and offer ideas of what to expect from therapy and how to find a marriage counselor.

Oettinger, K. B. (1979). *"Not My Daughter": Facing Up to Adolescent Pregnancy*. Englewood Cliffs, N.J.: Prentice-Hall.

A comprehensive book on the subject of teenage pregnancy. Discusses the incidence of adolescent pregnancy, factors related to it, parent-child interaction, and what parents can do to prevent the problem or cope with it when it occurs.

Straus, M., and R. J. Gelles (1980). *Behind Closed Doors: Violence in the American Family*. New York: Doubleday.

Presents findings of an eight-year study of violence in the American family, examining over 2000 families in an attempt to understand the extent, dynamics, causes, and effects of family violence. Written for the general public, with technical data in appendices.

Marital Termination and Remarriage

13

"To marry a second time represents the triumph of hope over experience."

SAMUEL JOHNSON

"Til death do us part"—those were the last words of the wedding vows of many Americans. They accurately symbolize most couples' hopes for their marriages. Until recently, most marriages ended only with the death of one partner, but increasingly marital partners are ending their marriages voluntarily. In fact, within the last few years, it appears that the proportion of marriages ending voluntarily may have exceeded those ending involuntarily.

Not many years ago, it was uncommon for a family to experience voluntary marital dissolution. Today, hardly a family exists which has not been touched in some way by divorce. This phenomenon may be put into perspective by asking how many individuals will participate during their lifetimes in a reconstituted or blended family—that is, one made up of parts of families formed by previous marital relationships. The answer is startling. According to one researcher, if the current divorce rate does not decline, the odds are one in two that an individual will be a member of a blended family either as a child or as an adult (Furstenberg, 1980). For that reason, this chapter focuses not only on marital dissolution but on adjustments to remarriage and reconstituted families.

 HOW MARRIAGES END

As discussed in Chapter 7, stable marriages are those that end only with the death of one of the partners; unstable marriages are those that are ended willfully by one or both spouses, most commonly by divorce (Lewis and Spanier, 1979). Table 13.1 classifies the types of marital stability. In our discussion, marital stability refers not to the internal dynamics of a particular marriage but to an outcome, that is, to whether the marriage ends in the death of one partner or is ended intentionally.

Death of a Spouse

Until the 1970s, most first marriages ended only with the death of one partner. For the century prior to 1970, the rate of marital dissolutions per 1000 married persons remained relatively stable because the decline in number of marriages ending in a spouse's death was only slightly exceeded by the increase in divorces. Between 1973 and 1974, however, the number of marriages ending in divorce actually exceeded the number ending in death and the gap between the two began to grow. In 1978, it was estimated that there were 1,170,000 divorces and 917,000 deaths of married individuals. Deaths represented only 45 percent of all marital dissolutions in 1978 (Glick, 1980).

What these statistics suggest is that it is increasingly likely that an individual will experience more than one marital dissolution and that these dissolutions may take different forms. This is particularly true for women because of their greater longevity and because they tend to marry earlier in life than men. Divorce is by far the most common means of ending marriages of short duration, but the longer a marriage endures, the more likely it is to end with death, not divorce.

Desertion

Desertion is an informal means of ending a marriage. It involves the sudden withdrawal of one spouse from the family without the agreement of the other

Table 13.1 **Classification of Types of Marital Stability**

	INTACT (STABLE)	NONINTACT (UNSTABLE)
Formal	Legally married	Legal separation Divorce Legal annulment
Informal	Common-law marriage	Separation by informal agreement Desertion

Source: *Contemporary Theories about the Family: Research-Based Theories*, Volume 1, ed. by Wesley R. Burr, Reuben Hill, F. Ivan Nye, and Ira L. Reiss. (Copyright © 1979 by The Free Press, a Division of Macmillan Publishing Co., Inc.)

provision for financial support (Price-Bonham and Balswick,
e marriage is still intact although desertion constitutes
e in almost all states. The number of desertions each year
sess because figures are not usually reported except when
s grounds for divorce.

, desertion was considered a phenomenon of the lower
lusively. Some have even called it "the poor man's divorce,"
ase in the sense that it was primarily lower-income males
wever, desertion certainly has never been undertaken by
me only. Although desertion is still more common among
edominant in lower classes, it is increasing among women.
ment has been the phenomenon of the "runaway wife,"
iddle- or upper-middle-class woman who deserts her family
rice-Bonham and Balswick, 1980).

nen and women desert are somewhat different. The research
nen usually desert because they feel stifled in the relationship,
:onomous. Men, however, appear to desert to avoid the
supporting the family. Whichever spouse deserts, the action
iated with feelings of inadequacy in marital and family roles
d Balswick, 1980).

LIES For the wife of a husband who has disappeared, the
ration may be a part of a continuing cycle of desertion and
ting for many years. In such a situation, the wife is uncertain
ration is permanent or whether her husband will reappear to
in the family. That insecurity, coupled with the financial
may follow, can create a tremendous psychological burden
n to this are added the feelings of rejection she is likely to
sions of her adjustment problem are plain. Little has been
ffects on a deserted husband, but it is likely that his feelings
d be as severe as those of a deserted wife.

tle has been written about the effects of desertion on children.
on them may be worse than in the case of divorce. Because
e not free to remarry, the effects may persist for years. In
ghtfully than the child of divorced parents, the deserted child

who deserts, the principal effect would appear to be an
s sense of inadequacy—which may have led him to abandon
first place. He may feel guilty, homesick, and afraid of being
ied (Skarsten, 1974). The woman who deserts may feel relieved
self as asserting a new freedom and independence which she
in the marriage. Nevertheless, one study found that deserting
ty about leaving their children (Todres, 1978).

EFFECTS ON SOCIETY   According to Snyder (1979), much of the blame for the problem of desertion, particularly among lower-class males, belongs to society. In 1978, there were twenty-two states which had laws prohibiting state aid to families with fathers present in the home. Restrictions such as these actually encourage the father to desert if he is out of work. He has the choice of deserting his family or allowing them to endure hardship.

"The deserting, nonsupporting father," in Snyder's view, is "the scapegoat of family nonpolicy." If he is caught and prosecuted for nonsupport—and every deserted wife applying for welfare must file a complaint for nonsupport—he can be sent to jail. Snyder's study of domestic-relations offenders showed that serving time in prison did not help the man in finding work or, if he had previously had a job, in getting it back. The data showed no improvement in either the amount or the regularity of support payments following a jail term. And serving time did nothing to strengthen family ties. The men Snyder studied were in the lowest earnings groups when they entered jail; their earnings did not increase appreciably after their release.

Those states whose welfare policies encourage a husband to desert are in effect punishing him and his family for his inability to earn a living wage—assuming he is willing and able to work. Some states have recognized this fact and not only grant aid to families that remain intact but also give the husband priority for job training programs (Snyder, 1979).

Annulment

An **annulment** is a legal termination of an invalid marriage. When a condition existed *before* the marriage which made the marriage invalid, a court can issue a decree which returns the marital partners to their prior statuses. Typically, annulment is sought for marriages of very short duration. Only 4 percent of all marital dissolutions are annulments (U.S. National Center for Health Statistics, 1979).

The most frequently cited ground for granting an annulment is fraud, or misrepresentation to the state and/or spouse prior to or at the time of the marriage. According to Rheinstein (1972), the standard for fraud is not clear. Misrepresentations of a sexual nature, such as not admitting to having a venereal disease or refusing to have sexual relations, have been considered to be fraud, but misrepresentations of character, reputation, or wealth have less frequently been accepted as grounds for annulment. Bigamy, however, is grounds, and it accounts for 35 percent of all annulments (Landis and Landis, 1977).

The concept of annulment originated with the Roman Catholic church, which has held that marriages can only be ended by the death of one of the partners. According to the church, a marriage that was valid in the first place cannot be terminated by divorce except under some very limited conditions.

Proving that a marriage was invalid in the first place has often been easier to do and facilitates getting church recognition of the dissolution as well. Today, however, only a very small number of marriages end in annulment because of the relative ease of obtaining a divorce and the greater acceptance of divorce by the Catholic church.

Separation

The difference between **separation** and desertion is that when a couple separates, it is done with the knowledge of both partners and neither partner tries to avoid obligations. Separations fall into two categories: informal and formal, or legal. An informal separation is usually worked out between the parties without the intervention of lawyers and usually occurs when a couple is having marital difficulties and is contemplating divorce. Legal separations are sanctioned by law and are usually accomplished by either a formal agreement or a court decree.

Informal separations can create serious problems if a couple decides eventually to divorce rather than to reconcile. Conflicts over property, support payments, and child custody may arise because these issues were not formally settled earlier. Informal separation may only prolong the adjustment to the marital breakdown. In fact, a major function of legal separation has been to assure the economic protection of the wife and support of any children from the marriage.

A legal separation does not end a valid marriage; it formally ends certain marital rights (such as sexual intercourse) but it does not affect such basic obligations as financial support. It is not a popular remedy for a marital breakdown because neither partner is free to remarry. People usually seek a legal separation when religious or moral reasons prevent their getting a divorce. Each year the courts grant approximately as many legal separations as annulments; legal separations thus account for 4 percent of all marital dissolutions (U.S. National Center for Health Statistics, 1979).

According to Pilpel and Zavin (1964), the provisions of a legal separation agreement usually are: (1) the husband and wife live separately; (2) the right to have sexual relations with each other ends; (3) the economic responsibilities of each spouse are defined and limited (typically, the husband is required to make certain provisions for child support); and (4) responsibility for the children, if any, is assigned and the partner not having custody is granted specified visiting rights. It is not uncommon for a division of property to be made at this stage as well. The purpose of these agreements is often to provide economic security for the wife, but it can also serve as a prelude to a final divorce decree. In some states, the mere fact of a legal separation that has lasted more than a year is grounds for divorce.

DIVORCE

Divorce is by far the most common way marriages end voluntarily. **Divorce** is defined as the dissolution of a socially and legally recognized marital relationship. It is marked by a formal court proceeding (with or without an actual appearance by the couple) ending in a decree of divorce. It is usually accompanied by formal arrangements for the division of property and custody and support of children, if any. The property arrangements may also include a provision requiring alimony to be paid by one former partner to the other, although alimony is less frequently granted today.

Trends in Divorce

In recent years, it has become common for people to point to high divorce rates as an indicator of the decline of the family. We hear various reports that from one in five, to one in three, to one in two, to well over half of all first marriages are currently ending in divorce. However, the determination of specific divorce rates is more difficult than one might think. There are a number of difficulties with comparing divorce data across decades. For one thing, there were and still are regional differences in the way statistics are compiled. Many states lump all divorces together in one category rather than distinguishing between first and subsequent divorces. Some include annulments and divorces in the same category. Legal separations are often not recorded in divorce data. In addition, reasonably accurate estimates of the prevalence of desertion simply do not exist either for the present or, more important, for the past. Thus, it is very difficult to make an accurate comparison of statistics on divorce either over time or nationwide. This situation is compounded by the frequent failure to clarify the statistics by defining the circumstances required for marital dissolution in the reference period used in the comparison (Crosby, 1980).

Keeping all these cautions in mind, it is still fair to say that the divorce rate is much higher today than in previous decades (see Fig. 13.1). Before World War II, there were about 2 divorces per 1000 population. By 1946, that rate had increased to 4.3 per 1000, then an all-time high. Throughout the 1950s, the divorce rate dropped continually until it reached 2.2 per 1000 in 1960, and then it began to climb again. By 1978, it had reached a new high of 5.1 per 1000, and in that year the number of divorces was almost half the number of marriages (2.2. million). The Census Bureau projects that if these rates continue, the proportion of marriages entered into by the current generation of eligibles that will end in divorce over a lifetime will reach 40 percent (Glick and Norton, 1979).

Between 1960 and 1970, the rate of increase in divorce was greatest among men in upper status groups and women in lower status groups, although the

Rate per 1,000

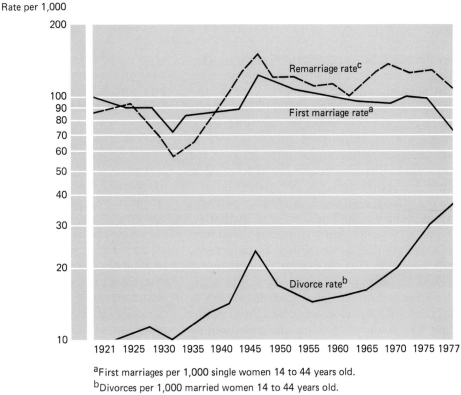

^aFirst marriages per 1,000 single women 14 to 44 years old.
^bDivorces per 1,000 married women 14 to 44 years old.
^cRemarriages per 1,000 widowed and divorced women 14 to 54 years old.

Fig. 13.1
Rates of first marriage, divorce, and remarriage for U.S. women:
1921–1977. (Source: Glick and Norton, 1977.)

rate of divorce increased in all socioeconomic categories. The rate of divorce
also was uniformly higher for blacks: 25 percent of black men and women
between thirty-five and forty-four who were ever married had been divorced.
For whites in the same age group, the rates were 19 percent for men and 21
percent for women. One other significant trend is the number of children
involved in divorce: their number tripled in two decades, from 261,000 in
1956 to an all-time high of 1,123,000 in 1975 (Glick and Norton, 1979).

Norton and Glick (1979) speculate that the increasing rate of divorce has
occurred in part because of the changes in divorce laws which accelerate the
timing, but not the fact, of marital dissolution. Also these researchers believe
that the divorce rate will level off if not decline. From another point of view,
it can be argued that the increasing prevalence of divorce was a social fact that

HIGHLIGHT 13.1   *Divorce Mediation*

Over the past few years, a relatively new process called divorce mediation has become increasingly popular with about-to-be-divorced couples who are trying to reorganize their lives. It is not a concept that works for everyone; some couples are too caught up in their roles as adversaries, and others may have an extreme imbalance of financial or emotional power that makes mediation difficult. Nevertheless, in a growing number of cases, divorcing partners have discovered that professional mediation can not only save them a considerable sum in divorce-related legal fees, but may help them retain a more lasting respect for each other and for their divorce agreement.

The actual process of mediation resembles a mixture of marital therapy and legal counseling. Trained mediators may be appointed by the court, typically in cases where couples have been unable to reach agreement in the courtroom. Divorcing couples may also seek private mediation from lawyers or from social workers who sometimes work in conjunction with legal and financial specialists. In one form of mediation, a husband and wife may confer with two mediators during the same session—typically a male/female, lawyer/therapist team—to work out a settlement so thorough that the couple could, if they chose, represent themselves in court.

The goal of mediation is not reconciliation or ongoing marital therapy. Instead, couples are assisted in separating their negative emotions, such as anger over one partner's extramarital relationship, from the need to reach an equitable agreement that will benefit all parties. In fact, while mediators can counsel a couple in settling financial and property issues, it is in the sensitive area of agreeing on living arrange-

ments and financial support for children that mediation seems to be most effective. As a first step, the mediator may encourage each partner to express painful feelings—anger, frustration, anxiety, guilt over the failure of the marriage. Once the couple has diffused these emotions in the relative safety of the mediator's office, it is more likely that they will be able to reach agreement relatively quickly on issues such as financial support, property division, and child custody.

Whereas, in the past, some lawyers were reluctant to be involved in mediation because of what they perceived as a possible conflict of interest, current legal thinking regards mediation as entirely ethical. Lawyer mediators are careful to point out to couples that they do not represent either party but are there to help draw up a legal agreement that each partner will subsequently take to his or her own counsel.

Experts claim that between 65 and 85 percent of couples who participate in mediation reach a settlement without a court battle. One study of 800 couples conducted by Professor Howard Irving of the University of Toronto found that 80 percent of those couples who had chosen mediation were still holding to their agreement a year later as compared to only 50 percent who had taken the traditional adversary method in court.

Mediation services are spreading throughout the country, and the Association of Family Conciliation Courts, a group of judges, lawyers, and mental health professionals, expects to have available a national directory of more than 200 mediation services in the near future. Mediation services are already available in forty

(continued)

states, with California the only state to have mandated free divorce mediation in all contested custody cases. Couples seem grateful for a process that can not only expedite the resolution of financial and custody issues, but can provide them with a place to talk out their differences and come to a better understanding of the pain and stress that each partner is experiencing.

demanded the liberalization of divorce laws. And whether the divorce rate will level off, decline, or continue to increase is very difficult to determine, since it depends on a variety of social changes.

A Theoretical Model of Divorce

Why do marital relationships dissolve? While this is clearly a complex issue, Levinger (1979) has proposed a model to explain the forces that act to keep a marriage together or cause it to break up. According to Levinger's model, which is closely related to social exchange theory, **marital cohesiveness** can be defined as all the forces that act on the partners to remain in the marriage. The incentives to stay include the attractiveness of the marriage and the barriers against leaving it. What encourages a person to leave the marriage is the attractiveness of other alternatives.

In examining Levinger's model, it is important to clarify three key terms. (1) **Attractions** refer to forces that push people toward a relationship. These attractions are generally positive—for example, feelings of love or admiration for the spouse. (2) **Barriers** refer to the "restraining forces" that keep a relationship intact. They affect behavior only when someone wants to leave the relationship. Barriers keep partners in a marriage by playing on their sense of obligation under the marriage contract or on their fear of social repercussions from a divorce. Barriers can be important in stabilizing long-term relationships by reducing the effects of temporary stresses, but if barriers are all that is keeping a marriage together, the relationship is probably an empty one. (3) **Alternative attractions** refer to persons, relationships, or outside commitments that compete with the marital relationship. An example would be an extramarital sexual relationship. The more energy one invests in exploring alternative relationships, the more likely one is to find someone who promises more than the present relationship offers. In the past, and to a certain extent even today, the male had more opportunities to sample alternative relationships because he spent more time away from home.

Levinger's formula is essentially this: marital cohesiveness equals the net sum of the attractions and barriers inside a relationship minus the net sum of the attractions to and barriers around the most important alternative. There are two qualifications to this formula. (1) The marital partners' feelings toward their relationship may be quite different. One may be so attracted that the existence of barriers lacks any meaning; the other may be continuing the marriage only because of the barriers. In either case, even the partners themselves may not be aware of their true feelings. (2) Low marital cohesiveness does not necessarily mean that a divorce will occur. Divorce often requires mutual consent; one or both partners must have an alternative to their marriage that is preferred and available (Levinger, 1979).

Table 13.2 outlines the factors which research has shown to be related to marital cohesiveness. The sections that follow discuss these factors in more detail.

MATERIAL REWARDS AND COSTS   Perhaps the most important material factors in marital cohesiveness are income and home ownership. Levinger indicates that there is a direct relationship between the income levels of partners and their likelihood to divorce. The higher the husband's income, the less likely he is to divorce; but the higher the wife's income, the more likely she is to divorce. Wives who have an income independent from that of their husband are less likely to be tied to their marriage.

Couples who own homes have been found to have proportionately fewer divorces than those who do not. This may be because of their higher income,

Table 13.2 **Factors Differentiating High and Low Cohesive Marriages**

ATTRACTIONS	BARRIERS	ALTERNATIVE ATTRACTIONS
MATERIAL REWARDS	MATERIAL COSTS	MATERIAL REWARDS
Family income Home ownership	Financial expenses of termination	Wife's independent social and economic status
SYMBOLIC REWARDS	SYMBOLIC COSTS	SYMBOLIC REWARDS
Educational status Occupational status Social similarity	Obligation toward marital bond Religious constraints Pressures from primary groups Pressure from the community	Independence and self-actualization
AFFECTIONAL REWARDS	AFFECTIONAL COSTS	AFFECTIONAL REWARDS
Companionship and esteem Sexual enjoyment	Feelings toward dependent children	Preferred alternate sex partner Disjunctive kin affiliations

From: *Divorce and Separation: Context, Causes, and Consequences* by George Levinger and Oliver C. Moles (eds.) © 1979 by The Society for the Psychological Study of Social Issues. Published by Basic Books, Inc., New York. Reprinted by permission.

but it may also be because owning a home together represents a major commitment and thus acts as a barrier to breakup (Levinger, 1979).

The material costs of marital dissolution consist primarily of the financial costs of divorce. These costs act as significant barriers to divorce when the partners have substantial assets which they hold in common. Still, a wife in a high-income marriage who feels unhappy in the marriage may regard the independence she can obtain as a single person as worth the material sacrifices of divorce.

Although adequate income has been identified as contributing to marital cohesiveness, when Booth and White (1980) asked over 1300 married Nebraskans whether they had *thought* about divorce within the preceding two years, these researchers found that neither the perception of income nor the actual amount was strongly associated with considering divorce. Scanzoni (1975), on the other hand, suggests that a woman who did not feel that her husband was making a fair contribution to the family income might have an incentive to divorce if she felt she could do better alone. Women who work outside the home are more likely to consider divorce than those who don't, and Booth and White (1980) suggest that the mere fact of employment is virtually a prerequisite for women considering divorce.

SYMBOLIC REWARDS AND COSTS Among the possible symbolic rewards that have been found to influence marital cohesiveness are educational and occupational status and social similarity of the couple.

Research suggests that for men a higher level of education is positively related to marital stability (Levinger, 1965, 1979). This may be because a high educational level encourages better marital communication and more companionship in marriage (Blood and Wolfe, 1960; Komarovsky, 1964). However, Cutright (1971) believes that more education generally leads to higher income and that it is the couple's higher standard of living that helps account for the stability of the relationship.

In the case of women, research has shown education and marital stability to be negatively correlated. This finding does not hold firm, however, when factors such as age at marriage, race, and religion are taken into account (Sweet and Bumpass, 1974; Thornton, 1978). Nevertheless, very well-educated women—those who hold a degree beyond the bachelor level—are more likely to divorce (Houseknecht and Spanier, 1976). It may be that highly educated women are more likely to be career-oriented and therefore not as tied to marriage as a major source of identity. Also, because they are more capable of supporting themselves in a well-paying job, they are less dependent on marriage for their financial well-being.

Higher occupational status has also been found to be related to marital stability, but Cutright's (1971) research indicates that, as with education, higher occupational status is important primarily in its relationship to higher income. Higher occupational status may not reduce a couple's likeliness to divorce unless the couple also has a higher income.

Social similarity between the partners in such areas as education, social and economic background, religion, and, to a lesser extent, age is positively related to marital stability. As we noted in Chapter 4, homogamous marriages have been found to be more stable than heterogamous marriages.

Religion is often cited as a factor in the dissolution of heterogamous marriages. For example, marriages between Protestants and Catholics and between Jews and gentiles are less stable than religiously homogamous marriages (Bumpass and Sweet, 1972; Moller, 1975). Religious heterogamy has been linked to a liberal attitude toward divorce (Jorgensen and Johnson, 1980), a finding which might be expected from the partners' willingness to resist the influence of their religious background in mate selection. Strong religious beliefs have been shown to be negatively associated with consideration of divorce (Booth and White, 1980). Levinger (1979) speculates that differences in religious affiliation may affect the couple's relationships with both the nuclear family and their parental kin, and may lead to marital breakdown. The consequence of a heterogamous marriage may well be the loss of an identifiable place in the social and kin network.

Among the traditional symbolic barriers to divorce are various social constraints, such as religious, community, and family pressure. Today, however, social pressures seem to be less effective barriers than they were in the past. One explanation for this is that modern marriage is regarded as a relationship that is expected to be personally satisfying to both partners rather than as an obligation to be carried out regardless of one's emotional commitment. This perception of marriage permits couples to regard divorce as an acceptable solution to marital difficulty (Udry, 1974).

A more important symbolic barrier to divorce is the couple's commitment to the institution of marriage as well as the specific commitment to the partner. Long courtships have been found to be associated with marital stability, whereas previous divorce or divorce between the parents of either spouse has been associated with marital instability (Glick and Norton, 1971; Cherlin, 1978; Levinger, 1979). A commitment to a religion or to a family philosophy which does not regard divorce as an acceptable solution to difficulties increases the symbolic costs of marital dissolution. However, a spouse may not consider these barriers when deciding to end a marriage.

The symbolic rewards of alternative attractions and thus of divorce are assumed to be the greater independence and autonomy possible for the individual who leaves a marriage, particularly for a woman who felt subordinated in the marriage (Levinger, 1979). However, it has yet to be demonstrated that divorce has, in fact, provided women with such substantial emotional rewards.

AFFECTIONAL REWARDS AND COSTS Enjoyment of one's spouse is clearly one of the principal affectional rewards of marriage. Satisfaction with the companionship and esteem offered by a mate, as well as mutual sexual pleasure are, as we have pointed out before, key elements of successful marriages.

Feelings toward dependent children appear to be a primary affectional cost of terminating a marriage (Levinger, 1979). As Bumpass and Sweet (1972) point out, women who do not have children have a substantially higher rate of marital dissolution than do women with children. Kanoy and Miller (1980) recognized the affectional influence of very young, dependent children, but found that otherwise the presence or absence of children neither prevented nor contributed to divorce. Yet, as pointed out earlier in this text, children can contribute to the stress in a marriage, particularly if there are serious problems, such as retardation, physical or developmental handicaps, or value conflicts with the parents.

Even so, in contemplating divorce, couples with children undoubtedly consider the emotional cost, and this cost may be a significant barrier to breaking up the marriage. Jorgensen and Johnson (1980) have shown that wives with children are significantly less liberal in their attitudes toward divorce than are wives who do not have children, and the more children a woman has, the less liberal her views become. However, the presence of children seems to have little effect on husbands' attitudes toward divorce.

The affectional rewards offered by an alternative relationship may include a sex partner who is preferred to the current mate. People who married young or after a very short courtship appear to be particularly vulnerable to seeking alternatives (Carter and Glick, 1976; Booth and White, 1980). Part of the reason for this may be that younger partners do not understand the depth of commitment required in marriage. Also people who marry young may simply have more years during which to be exposed to alternative relationships than people who marry somewhat later (Levinger, 1979).

Another alternative attraction may be the readjusting of kin relationships disrupted by a heterogamous marriage. When people marry someone of a different religion, social class, or race, it sometimes creates a break in their relationship with their families of origin, which may place stress on the couple. However, it is difficult to determine how important a factor kin relationships may be because there is some evidence that parental opposition to a marriage tends to strengthen rather than weaken a couple's relationship, particularly if the couple does not live in the same town as the parents (Levinger, 1979).

Levinger's model provides a useful general framework for evaluating the "pushes and pulls" of marriage and divorce. Perhaps the most important conclusion to be drawn from his analysis is that the factors contributing to marital cohesiveness or marital instability are extremely complex and multifaceted. This is equally true of the experience of divorce, which we will consider next.

 THE EXPERIENCE OF DIVORCE

Even when divorce seems to be the only solution to an unworkable marriage, most people are unprepared for the experience. Although the loneliness of separation may cause grief equal to what people feel when a spouse dies, there is no socially prescribed way to mourn a divorce. Self-esteem suffers because it is painful to be rejected or to admit "failing." Although friends and relatives do help during a divorce, the divorced person is likely to feel very much alone. Paul Bohannon (1971) suggests that divorce is so difficult to cope with because it involves six different overlapping experiences for which people are unprepared. We will organize our discussion of the experience of divorce around his six processes.

The Emotional Divorce

The failure of a marriage is often signaled by the "emotional divorce." This occurs when one or both marital partners begin to withhold emotion from their relationship in order to avoid revealing the hostility or ambiguity of their feelings. Although they may still appear in public as a couple, they are no longer bound by love and trust.

Conflicts occur over the course of every marriage. For couples with healthy marriages, disagreements can lead to a clearer understanding of their differences, negotiated compromises, and an extension of their awareness of each other's needs. But in marriages that are not working, fighting over problems increases the distance between partners. Their lives increasingly move into areas that do not include the other until their relationship occupies only a marginal, dissatisfying place in their lives.

The realization that there is not much feeling left in the marriage may bring acute grief. Just as one mourns the death of people one loves, one grieves over the loss of a mate by divorce (Bohannon, 1971). In an effort to postpone the trauma of separation, people often seem to put off divorce as long as they can. According to various surveys, the decision to seek a divorce may be contemplated for as long as two or three or even ten or twelve years before it is carried out (Rose and Price-Bonham, 1973).

THE PERIOD OF SEPARATION   During the separation process, the marital partners experience a wide range of emotions. According to Hunt and Hunt (1977), they may think about reconciliation, alternate between feelings of love for and hostility toward their mate, and feel hatred and anger more often than any positive emotion. The entire period is one of intense stress—perhaps the greatest stress of the entire divorce process (Weiss, 1975; Hunt and Hunt, 1977). According to Price-Bonham and Balswick (1980), the reason this period is so stressful is that most of the adjustment to the dissolution of the marriage takes place then. This emotional upheaval may be made worse by the combination of any of a number of problems ranging from financial to legal to occupational.

Men and women apparently react to this period in different ways. Studies have found that both sexes are more depressed than their married or divorced peers (Pearlin and Johnson, 1977), but men have a lower overall sense of well-being than women, while women experience greater emotional upheaval than men (Chiriboga and Cutler, 1978).

PERSISTENCE OF THE MARITAL BOND People facing separation have reported that even though their marriages were unhappy, the idea of ending them makes them feel anxious, even terrified. No matter how unhappy the relationship, marriage seems to provide a feeling of security which people are reluctant to give up.

Once a marriage has been disrupted, most partners continue to be drawn to each other even if they no longer feel love or respect. Their shared experiences and interwoven habits have forged an attachment that is not easily broken. It doesn't seem to make any difference whether a person has been rejected or has done the rejecting—both are likely to feel the same anxiety at no longer being accessible to each other. Instead of being relieved by their escape from a burdensome relationship, they may feel lonely, guilty over having caused the separation, obsessed with thoughts of the ex-partner, and overcome with the desire to be reunited (Weiss, 1976).

AMBIVALENCE The relationship of separated spouses is highly ambiguous. They may try to hide their attachment, hide their anger, or express them alternately. Sometimes they express different feelings in different settings. They may be angry adversaries in court, but friends and even lovers outside. Their ambivalence complicates the course of the divorce—they want it because they are angry and disappointed with each other, but they don't want it because they are still drawn to each other. This ambivalence stands in the way of reconciliation, too. When they are in a loving mood, they may try living together again, but soon the conflicts may reappear (Weiss, 1976). Sometimes they engage in sexual relations again. This was true of six out of forty-eight couples in one study (Hetherington, Cox, and Cox, 1976). This behavior, however, often is motivated by a number of factors, and the partner who interprets it as a sign of reconciliation may often be making a mistake (Weiss, 1975).

During the period immediately following the actual divorce, the interaction between ex-spouses is typically characterized by conflict. Hetherington, Cox, and Cox (1976) found that two months after divorce couples argued about finances and support, visitation and childrearing, and sexual relations with others. Although the level of conflict decreased over time, the divorced women felt angry and resentful toward their ex-spouses longer than did the divorced men. Weiss (1975) found that while many ex-spouses feel hostile toward each other for a long time, others are able to get along amiably. In either case, the research shows that divorce does not always end the spouses' relationship; rather, it usually changes it.

The Legal Divorce

A husband and wife must go to court if they want to sever their legal bond. But the legal process only establishes the right of each partner to marry someone else; the actual separation has already taken place.

Until the late 1960s and early 1970s, a person seeking a divorce in the United States had to prove the other partner at fault for the dissolution of the marriage. Today, in most states, the "fault" system has given way to a "no-fault" system. In this section, we will look at the effects of each of these systems on divorce adjustment.

THE PENNSYLVANIA SYSTEM   Spanier and Anderson (1979) examined the Pennsylvania divorce system in 1977 to see how it affected adjustment to marital breakdown. The Pennsylvania system was based on the long-standing concept of fault. To obtain a divorce, the spouse filing the complaint had to establish one of the following grounds: impotence, bigamy, adultery, desertion, cruel and barbarous treatment, indignities, fraud, a two-year (or longer) jail sentence, or consanguinity (close blood relationship between the spouses). This list of grounds omitted a major reason why many people sought a divorce: they simply felt that they could not make their marriage work. But because fault had to be established, a process grew up which encouraged perjury (lying under oath) and the deliberate aggravation of relations between the spouses. This process—although often misrepresenting the true reason for seeking the divorce—virtually always resulted in a divorce decree.

Despite the fact that the Pennsylvania system encouraged the spouses to be adversaries, at least in the court room, Spanier and Anderson (1979) did not find that the system affected the couple's adjustment after the separation. This may confirm the finding noted above that much of the adjustment to marital breakup takes place during the emotional divorce, which typically occurs many months before the legal divorce. However, these researchers did find that the Pennsylvania system encouraged disrespect for the legal system and caused unnecessary emotional distress for persons who had already suffered a great deal.

THE CALIFORNIA SYSTEM   In 1969, California became the first state to eliminate fault as the basis for granting a divorce. In its place, California adopted a single

Divorce Chinese Style

Yao Yitian looked helplessly up at the dais, pleading with the three judges. "In my deepest pain," he told them, "I had the most pessimistic view of life. I even thought of suicide.

"I must tell you, I feel pain every time I hear my wife's voice."

It was the most poignant moment in a sad, rather nasty divorce case. It followed three solid hours of conflicting testimony about exactly who beat whom most viciously, who was guilty of the most callous abuse.

But the shirt-sleeved audience packed into the Peking intermediate people's court had an odd reaction to Yao's plea: They laughed out loud. It began as a titter at the back, grew into a wave, and drowned the next few moments of testimony.

The triumvirate of judges, intent on restoring marital harmony, didn't even glance up.

This cavalier, almost carefree mood was demonstrated often during the hearing—opened to foreign reporters who have been pestering authorities for a firsthand look at Chinese justice. And the repeated guffaws caught the outsiders off guard.

The People's Republic has many virtues, but a gay, carnival atmosphere is seldom among them. This is a country where cheering fans at football matches are instructed over loudspeakers to quiet down. So reporters hardly went to the gray, forbidding intermediate court looking for live theater.

But that's often what we found.

Things got off to a slow start when Mr. Yao, an editor seeking divorce from his wife of eighteen years, recited a long litany of her offenses. The crowd was titillated when he accused her of throwing boiling water on him, but they merely oohed and ahed a little. And

the allegation that she had pulled a knife on him left the spectators unmoved.

But things changed immediately when it came time for Chen Zhengyu to defend herself.

Contesting the divorce vehemently, she began gunning down her husband with a machine-gun barrage of accusations, all delivered in a high-pitched, shrewish whine.

She had been talking for only a few moments when the gallery began nudging each other appreciatively. And within two minutes or so she had brought on the first explosion of laughter.

"He said he wanted to beat me," she shouted. "He said he had the right to beat me. But since it is a socialist country, how can he say that?"

It says a good deal about real attitudes in this communist country that everyone in the room immediately broke up at that line. But there was more to come.

Minutes later, her husband quoted Mrs. Chen as saying, "I just want to make trouble for you. With 800 million people, how can we make progress if we don't struggle?"

This is a bizarre usage of an axiom often repeated by Mao Tse-tung, and it simply brought down the house. Surprisingly, however, the trio of judges waited patiently for things to quiet down without any admonition to the audience, and even seemed rather to enjoy the irony.

But the trial did have its serious side, quite apart from the devastated marriage under examination.

For one thing, it did much to reveal why China's divorce rate is so astonishingly low, a mere 2 percent of all marriages. Even to get to

(continued)

HIGHLIGHT 13.2   *(continued)*

this stage, it was revealed, the husband had to repeatedly petition his unit to look into the case and endure round after round of what seems to have been a kind of enforced reconciliation.

Eventually, the couple was brought before the district court in their neighborhood in eastern Peking. That court seems also to have recommended a reconciliation, but the determined husband managed to force the higher session—a very serious step under the Chinese legal system.

Yet even the damaging evidence heard then (including separate living quarters in a one-

room dwelling, accomplished by partitioning it in half) is no assurance the divorce will be granted.

The tribunal, which included two women and a male chairman, suggested the two try to "compromise" and "correct your thinking." The judges decided they would "investigate further" before reaching any decision. It was at this point the exasperated husband remarked that his wife's voice caused him pain. Many in the audience nodded in agreement.

Source: The Globe and Mail, Toronto, 1980. Reprinted by permission.

standard: "irreconcilable differences leading to the irremediable breakdown of the marriage." Only one spouse had to assert irreconcilable differences and granting of the divorce was virtually automatic. California had adopted this system in order to remedy the ills of a system typified by that of Pennsylvania. The reform had four objectives:

> (a) to slow the "ever-rising tide" of divorce by encouraging marital counseling toward the end of reconciliation; but if reconciliation failed, to facilitate social and psychological adjustment to the divorce itself; (b) to eliminate the hypocrisy of the former system . . . ; (c) to reduce the . . . bitterness surrounding the divorce proceeding and lessen the personal stigma attached to divorce; and (d) to create more equitable settlements of property division and spousal support. (Dixon and Weitzman, 1980)

Dixon and Weitzman found that the results after ten years of experience with the new system were a mixture of the expected and the unexpected. "No-fault divorce" had no discernible effect on the divorce rate. The mandatory-counseling feature of the system did not bring about many reconciliations, and the rate of divorce continued to rise. The law was successful in removing the hypocrisy of the old system, however. It also seems to have somewhat reduced the bitterness that usually accompanied a divorce secured on the basis of establishing fault. The number of hearings on orders to be issued before a final decree of divorce—where many of the bitterest battles in a divorce were fought—declined markedly (Dixon and Weitzman, 1980). One thing the reforms did not do was speed up the divorce process. This was due not to the pace of the legal system but rather to the pace of the divorcing spouses. Contrary to what some people anticipated, the researchers found that no-fault divorce does not encourage couples to divorce more quickly (Dixon and Weitzman, 1980).

Property settlements and spousal and child support appeared to be fairer under the very specific guidelines of the new law. But, according to Weitzman and Dixon, the very rationality and fairness of the new law eliminated one of the benefits of the old system for those who actually did have a valid grievance against their spouse: the punitive element. Particularly for women, it removed a bargaining advantage in negotiating property arrangements and alimony.

The Economic Divorce

Economic divorce takes place because in legal terms marital partners are regarded as an economic unit. Just like a corporation that goes out of business, the assets of the marital partnership must be distributed between the spouses who invested in it (Bohannon, 1971). We discussed child support in Chapter 10, so we will focus here primarily on the division of property between the spouses.

The systems of property distribution followed in the various states have the same goals, although they differ in such details as the way property is calculated and divided. The goals are to make an equitable division of the marital property, provide adequate support for dependent children, and, if

The institution of "no-fault" divorce has helped to lessen the bitterness fostered under the fault concept which required that the filing spouse establish blame for the breakdown of the marriage.

necessary, provide support temporarily for a spouse while he or (more often) she prepares to enter (or re-enter) the work force. About forty-five states and the District of Columbia attempt to divide property either equitably (that is, fairly) or equally, without regard to fault or other similar factors. The settlement depends either on a formula established by state law or on the individual circumstances of the parties. In either case, factors that are often considered include the length of the marriage, each spouse's economic contribution (including in some states the value of a wife's homemaking and hostessing functions if she does not have outside employment), the spouses' relative wealth and employability, and child-custody arrangements.

One of the crucial elements in the calculation of both the property settlement and alimony is the lost career potential of the wife (usually) who gives up the possibility of a career to manage the home. The older a wife in this category is and the more difficult it would be for her—because of age or health—to enter the work force, the better the chance that she will get alimony. Still, unless she is virtually disabled, her chances for permanent alimony are slim.

The first effect most women notice with marital dissolution is drastic downward mobility (Albrecht, 1980). Men may also experience this downward mobility, but usually not as severely as women. In one study of 2400 women between 1968 and 1974, the real incomes of couples who stayed married throughout the period increased 21.7 percent while the income of divorced women declined 29.3 percent and that of divorced men declined 19.2 percent (Espenshade, 1979). This difference also reflects the facts that "children usually remain with the wife after divorce or separation and that alimony and child support fail to compensate fully for the costs of child care" (Hoffman, 1977). Another study of the same sample that Espenshade examined showed that of children in divorced families, 80 percent lived with their mothers, only 6 percent with their fathers, and the rest with other relatives (Bumpass and Rindfuss, 1978). As would be expected, the need to provide for their children spurs divorced women to work for pay if they have not done so before.

The economic problems of divorced women are clearly greater than those of their ex-husbands. But divorced men, too, have to make do with less in terms of assets, and if alimony and child support are involved, husbands may discover that if two can't live as cheaply as one together, they certainly can't live cheaply apart.

The Coparental Divorce

Parents seeking divorce must also deal with the issue of custody of their children and visitation rights for the parent who does not get custody.

Divorce is complicated enough without the physical separation of one parent from the children, coupled with the working out of arrangements to continue the couple's joint responsibilities to the children. When a divorce is

CASE STUDY   *A Mother Gives Up Custody*

After more than a decade of raising five children, Ellen decided to allow her two children—a girl twelve and a boy eleven—to live with their father and his second wife. She had divorced not long after they were born and raised them at first as a single parent and later as a remarried working woman who was also responsible for three teen-age stepchildren.

Though she and her first husband had both remarried, Ellen had been deeply affected by a comment he had made. "He told me," she recalls, "that there he was helping his second wife raise her children, that I was raising our children with my second husband, but that he felt like he had no children himself. Part of me just wanted to give another human being, whom I had once loved, a chance to get to know his own children the only way you can get to know children, by living with them."

And part of her was simply exhausted from the day-to-day strains of motherhood. Though her stepchildren had grown increasingly independent, her own preteenagers still needed her to make sure they had new sneakers and jeans without holes in them, to provide rides to after-school events, and to take care of the thousand other details of on-the-spot parenthood.

Adding to the burden of work and parenthood, for most of the last four years she had been in nearly constant pain from a medical condition. She wound up in the hospital and heeded the advice of several doctors to examine the pressures in her life that were contributing to her difficulties.

"I felt especially for my son," she says, "that maybe I was the wrong person to be raising him at this point in his life. I was trying to be like (televison's) Mrs. Brady. It had been a decade of a merry-go-round life. It had been overwhelming."

An important factor in deciding to allow her first husband custody of the children was that she believed his second wife, her children's stepmother-to-be, was a "dynamite woman."

Ellen's decision seems to be working well for all concerned: both sets of parents, her children, and her ex-husband's stepchildren. The difficult part has been society's judgment of her.

"I lost a lot of close friends," she says, "women who felt threatened by my decision." This society would like people to believe that the only way to be a mother is to live with your children. But it's not true—it's certainly not true when you have grown children. "What my ex-husband and I really have now is serial custody—children have two parents, maybe they need to live with both their parents, but at different points in their lives."

Source: Adapted from *The Boston Globe*, May 10, 1981. Reprinted courtesy of The Boston Globe.

FOR CLASS DISCUSSION

1. What is your reaction to Ellen's decision? Do you agree that a boy entering adolescence might be better off living with his father? Should Ellen have retained custody of her daughter? Why or why not?

2. In this situation Ellen, her ex-husband, and his wife all were compatible. Do you think Ellen's decision would have been possible if this had not been the case?

in the offing, parents may be too involved with their own distress to pay much attention to their children (Hetherington, Cox and Cox, 1976, 1978), but the children may be suffering emotional upheavals of their own and need the parents' emotional support.

The emotional difficulties of children in divorce are intensified by the problem of divided loyalties. Parents with custody sometimes put strong pressure on children to reject the other parent. Torn between their attachments to both parents, young children may feel guilty about this, and try to hide from each parent the strength of their attachment to the other (Kelly and Wallerstein 1976).

Although divorce causes temporary distress, there is no evidence that children whose parents are divorced suffer more emotional problems in later life than children from intact homes. Many parents report that after some initial anxiety, their children adjust to the new situation faster than the parents themselves. This is especially true when the parents, despite their own problems, make an effort to show that they are capable of managing their postmarital situation, of being good parents, and of keeping family life relatively free of stress (Weiss, 1975).

CUSTODY AND SUPPORT   Perhaps the most disturbing thing about divorce for a child is the fact that one of the parents must leave the family circle. Traditionally, custody was granted to the mother since she was assumed to be the more nurturant parent. Today, however, some men are obtaining custody of their children after divorce. The parent with custody normally has almost full-time charge of the children, with the other retaining visitation rights. In an effort to share both the burdens and the rewards of childrearing, some divorced couples have agreed to joint custody of their children. Some take the children on different days of the week, some for different years, or some for different seasons. Some arrangements are mechanically awkward and take the children away from their friends, while others seem more workable. As yet, little is known of what effect these shifts have on the children (Bohannon, 1971; Weiss, 1975).

Which parent has custody and what arrangements are made for financial support are so important to the well-being of the child that some observers have recommended that children be represented by their own lawyers during divorce proceedings. Wheeler (1974), notes that the child's best interests are beginning to take precedence over considerations of parental moral fitness in determining custody. (As an example of this sort of "moral" consideration, mothers were sometimes denied custody if they had been "guilty" parties in the divorce action.) Children should not be overinvolved in the legal aspects of divorce, however, as it could be traumatic for them.

Sometimes parents prolong court battles long after an initial settlement is reached. The noncustodial parent may try to win custody by proving the other has been a destructive influence on the children. The parent with custody may have to obtain court approval before deciding, for whatever reason, to move the children out of state, since doing so will make it hard for the other parent to see them. Complaints about visitation privileges are also brought to court, including stories of children being taken to bars or kept up late, ill-fed, or coming home sick or emotionally upset.

Continuing struggles over custody and support are detrimental to children. A study of records from divorce courts and child-guidance clinics revealed that children from single-parent homes showed emotional stress if their parents' relationship continued to be stormy or if visits with the noncustodial parent were forbidden. By contrast, no children of divorced parents whose agreements on support and custody were mutually reached and subsequently kept had needed help with emotional problems (Brandwein, Brown, and Fox, 1974).

CHILDREN'S RESPONSES TO DIVORCE Kelly and Wallerstein have researched the impact of divorce on psychologically normal California children whose parents were divorcing (Kelly and Wallerstein, 1976; Wallerstein and Kelly, 1975, 1976). Most children were very distressed at being separated from the parent who did not have custody—usually the father. Children of all ages seemed to feel a strong need for the father to continue playing a role in their lives. Most of the children wished their parents would get back together. Strong wishes for reconciliation might take the form of active attempts to bring their parents back together, or fantasies with the child pretending that the absent parent is still present. Preschool children often felt they were to blame for their parents' separation. They explained that the father went away because they were too noisy or too naughty—and refused to believe otherwise. Older children were less likely to feel personally responsible for the divorce. Anxiety about their own future was another common reaction among young children. They saw the disruption of their family as a threat to their whole world. They feared the family structure was no longer a refuge and that they, too, might be rejected (Kelly and Wallerstein, 1976).

Despite these initial symptoms of psychological disorganization, the children gradually adjusted to the fact of the divorce. When Kelly and Wallerstein checked on their subjects a year after their parents had separated, they found that over half of them had returned to a normal developmental pattern. They were as lively and self-confident as they had been before the divorce, and their psychological problems had eased. One-fourth of the children had been having trouble at school or at home before their parents separated, and a year later their condition was about the same. The final fourth of the sample became progressively more troubled after their parents' separation; their sadness lingered, their self-esteem dropped, and their relationships with other people were shallow and unrewarding (Kelly and Wallerstein, 1976).

Some research indicates that children of divorced parents may actually be better adjusted than children in intact families in which there is ongoing conflict and tension (Hetherington, Cox, and Cox, 1978). Hetherington and her colleagues found that some children of divorce are more independent than children from intact families, more empathetic, and display more helping behavior. However, these same researchers point out that how children and parents react to divorce depends upon personality factors, their particular

HIGHLIGHT 13.3 *Children on Divorce*

I remember it was near my birthday when I was going to be six that Dad said at lunch he was leaving. I tried to say, "No, Dad, don't do it," but I couldn't get my voice out. I was too much shocked. All the fun things we had done flashed right out of my head and all the bad things came in, like when he had to go to the hospital with his bad back and when he got mad at me. The bad thoughts just struck there. My life sort of changed at that moment. Like I used to be always happy and suddenly I was sad.

—*An eight-year-old girl*

In a way, I thought I'd made it happen. I thought maybe I acted mean to my mother and my sister and I was being punished by God. So I tried to be really good by not waking Mom before schooltime and getting my own breakfast and maybe God would change his mind. But it's been three years now, and I'm used to it all. Sometimes, when I make a wish with an eyelash, though, I still wish for Dad to come home.

—*A nine-year-old girl*

You never feel permanent anymore. I feel like an animal with a mind. You have to spend so much time with each person. You go from place to place. And I don't feel at home at Dad's. I feel very strange when his girlfriend is around. I think of it as being her fault.

—*A fifteen-year-old girl*

Each man my mother went out with I considered my next stepfather. And with every one I'd try to be that much more caring so that he'd like me and we'd get off to a good start. I finally realized she was just having fun and didn't want to get married again right now. So I bagged the whole thing. I was exhausted trying to be a son to each one. Her boyfriends became just people.

—*A fifteen-year-old boy*

No matter how hard I try to erase the idea, I really want to get married. Even with my parents and all my grandparents divorced, I believe in commitment. In fact, I want a huge wedding with bridesmaids, a partner for my whole life and a family. It's a challenge and the optimism I have is funny to me. But if I'm lucky, I'll have that sense of continuity.

—*A twenty-three-year-old woman*

Source: *Newsweek*, February 11, 1980. Reprinted by permission.

experience, and the kinds of supports they receive. Thus there are many individual variations in adjustment to the coparental divorce.

The Community Divorce

Everyone going through a divorce finds that relationships with friends and kin are altered. No longer part of a couple, former spouses are left out of certain social activities and may even encounter active social disapproval. Thus, in a sense, they find themselves separated from their community.

REACTIONS OF KIN   Once the decision to divorce has been reached, the families will usually be informed. Most families immediately offer help and moral support. In one study of separated and divorced individuals, 84 percent reported that their families had offered sympathy and support since their marriages had broken up (Spanier and Casto, 1979a, 1979b). A study of divorced mothers showed that their principal source of support was their family of origin. Nearly 75 percent received some sort of help from their families (Colletta, 1979). Another study showed that 71.4 percent of divorced female respondents, but only 14.5 percent of divorced male respondents, received aid from their parents (Spicer and Hampe, 1975). This appears to reflect the greater economic needs of women after divorce. The level of interaction between parents and divorcing children also usually increases following marital disruption, but this is truer of women than men and also relates to the fact that women are more often in need of financial support (Espenshade, 1979; Albrecht, 1980).

While there is no doubt that divorce is very difficult for the children involved, there are many individual variations in their adjustment to the situation.

One way that some families try to be helpful is by inviting the divorced offspring to return home. Moving in with parents is primarily a low-income phenomenon. Twenty-five percent of low-income divorced mothers and 4 percent of moderate-income divorced mothers in one sample were living with their parents. It is an unsatisfactory arrangement in most instances (Colletta, 1979). Often it means some loss of independence. Clashes over childrearing and other matters are likely to arise. Men who move in with their parents after divorce don't seem to experience the same difficulties as women. But for men, returning home means a loss of status—from head of household to boarder in their parent's home. Thus, for both men and women, returning home to live with parents is usually a matter of temporary expedience (Weiss, 1975).

The fact that most divorcing couples receive their family's support does not mean that the situation is not upsetting to the family. Divorce is still regarded by some parents as a family disgrace. Siblings may worry that marital instability is contagious and that their own marriages may be affected. Weiss (1975) found that once the families know about the separation, the divorcing couple may find their status subtly lowered.

CHANGES IN KINSHIP PATTERNS   According to a number of studies, divorce brings changes in the kin that people see and can call on for aid. Whereas interaction with one's own blood relatives may often increase, interaction with the ex-partner's family is likely to decrease. This pattern is especially pronounced among divorced men. Some 38 percent of the males in one study never saw their wife's parents again after the divorce, compared to 9.5 percent of women who never saw their husband's parents again (Spicer and Hampe, 1975). This difference in kinship contact reflects our general cultural pattern, in which contact with kin usually takes place through the wife. It also reflects the greater likelihood that the husband's parents will continue to offer financial aid to his ex-wife, rather than the other way around (Spicer and Hampe, 1975; Anspach, 1976).

Unlike the divorced couple, the children have blood ties with both sets of relatives and might be expected to continue to provide a link between them. But interviews with 128 married, divorced, and remarried women with children indicated that this is not necessarily the case. Some children seem to lose the grandparents on the noncustodial father's side when there is a divorce. Whether they will continue to have close relationships with the father's relatives depends on whether they have contact with the father himself. Ninety percent of the children who had no contact with their fathers saw more of their mother's family than of his; but over half of those who were in contact with their fathers saw as much of his family as of their mother's relatives (Anspach, 1976).

RELATIONS WITH FRIENDS   It is difficult for the divorcing couple to know how to break the news to their friends. To say merely, "We've decided to get a divorce," is to leave them wondering what happened. To give too many personal details may expose more of the couple's private lives than they would like. This is especially true among work associates. However, keeping the separation a secret can become awkward also.

According to Weiss (1975), friendships are affected by divorce in three phase. In the first phase, friends generally "rally round" to support the couple in the stressful separation period. This phase gives way to a period in which the friends readjust and begin to respond in particular ways, such as with envy, or condemnation, or even with sexual advances. Gradually, divorced persons stop associating with the couple's friends because of a lack of common interests and move into a stage of "mutual withdrawal" as they find new acquaintances with whom they have more in common. In many cases, the new friends will also be divorced persons rather than never-married singles or married people (Epstein, 1974; Hetherington, Cox, and Cox, 1976).

The Psychic Divorce

This last of Bohannan's six processes of divorce is the most difficult to negotiate successfully. It may not be as stressful as the emotional divorce is. But, whereas the passage of time reduces much of the hurt of the emotional divorce, the psychic divorce requires divorced persons to recreate themselves as autonomous individuals—whole and complete—without a partner to lean on.

The difficulty of this task is increased by the fact that many people marry to avoid becoming autonomous. This is one factor in why so many youthful marriages—made before the partners have established a clear sense of themselves as individuals—fail. It is also why quick remarriage following a divorce often becomes problematic; there is a necessary period of reconstruction before one is ready to try again. Divorced persons who recognize the necessity of becoming autonomous and strive to achieve it are better prepared to try again (Bohannan, 1971).

As we noted earlier, the six stages of divorce are not discrete or sequential; they overlap and affect each other. This is particularly true of the psychic divorce, which proceeds throughout the dissolution process. The difficulties of the psychic divorce were suggested by Hetherington, Cox, and Cox (1976), who noted that the divorced fathers in their study had problems adjusting to everyday life, encountered difficulty in forming relationships with other people—particularly intimate relationships—and experienced changes in self-concept and identity. A major part of the problem of adjusting to the psychic divorce for men is that they tend to deny that they need help or support; women are less likely to deny this need (Price-Bonham and Balswick, 1980).

DATING AND FORMING RELATIONSHIPS Many divorced persons fail to recognize the difference between autonomy and independence. Autonomy means being able to operate as a single unit, but it includes the acknowledgment that relationships with other people are necessary to be a complete person (Bohannan, 1971).

Even if a divorced person accepts the need to form new relationships, there may be real barriers to achieving this goal. In most studies, the biggest social problem cited by divorced persons—especially women—is meeting other unmarried people (Spanier and Casto, 1979b; Kohen, Brown, and Feldberg, 1979). Hunt (1966) found that most people begin dating in the first year after divorce; by the second year, 90 percent were dating. In one study, men consistently had more social activity than women up to three years after divorce (Raschke, 1977). Men also liked their new sexual freedom after divorce, but women did not express this view (Hetherington, Cox, and Cox, 1976).

Dating a number of partners appears to be a pattern for both sexes during the first year after divorce. However, according to several studies, by the end of a year most divorced persons seem to become dissatisfied with casual sexual encounters and want a more exclusive intimate relationship (Hetherington, Cox, and Cox, 1976; Kohen, Brown, and Feldberg, 1979). Hetherington and her colleagues found that the ability to develop one deeper relationship helped divorced persons increase their feelings of self-esteem. Self-esteem, in turn, has been found to be extremely important in facilitating the overall adjustment to divorce.

A "SUCCESSFUL" DIVORCE As our discussion has suggested, divorce is a difficult process. However, it can also be viewed as an opportunity for significant personal growth. As Bohannan (1971) points out:

> A "successful" divorce begins with the realization by two people that they do not have any constructive future together. That decision itself is a recognition of the emotional divorce. It proceeds through the legal channels of undoing the wedding, through the economic division of property and arrangement for . . . support. The successful divorce involves determining ways in which children can be informed, educated in their new roles, loved and provided for. It involves finding a new community. Finally, it involves finding your own autonomy as a person and as a personality.

 REMARRIAGE

Remarriage is not a new concept developed for an age of high divorce rates. It has always been an important part of the American social fabric. When premature deaths were more common than they are now, remarriage served the necessary function of restoring the nuclear family unit. But the modern concept of remarriage is not simply a variation on the past. In earlier times when a parent remarried after the death of a spouse, the dead spouse was replaced. Not so today; typically, the original spouse remains in evidence through child custodial arrangements, so the new spouse serves more as a supplementary parent. Still, we have no rules for, or even effective language to describe, the position of remarried parents (Furstenberg, 1980). The fact that there is no accepted term for a supplementary parent—"Dad II," "Mom II," or "coparent" seem as unsatisfactory as "stepfather" or "stepmother"— is a telling statement about our society's preparedness for this situation (Kompara, 1980).

Recent Trends in Remarriage

Marriage as an institution is far from extinct. Even people whose marriages have failed seem eager to try again. Men are somewhat more likely to do so than women, but the remarriage rates are high for both sexes: five-sixths of the divorced men and three-fourths of the divorced women in this country remarry (Furstenberg, 1980).

Drawing by Koren; © 1978
The New Yorker Magazine, Inc.

Demographically, perhaps the most significant features of remarriage for women during the five years immediately following divorce are: (1) remarriage rates are higher for white than for black women; (2) the younger a woman's age at divorce, the greater her probability of remarriage; (3) women with fewer rather than more children are more likely to remarry; and (4) women with less than a high-school education are more likely to remarry than women with one or more years of college (Price-Bonham and Balswick, 1980; Spanier and Glick, 1980).

In 1970, only 30 percent of all marriages involved a person who had been married before; by 1977, the incidence had reached 41 percent (Glick, 1980). An examination of marriages by age group and previous marital status is revealing. In 1977, 92 percent of grooms and 95 percent of brides under twenty-five were starting their first marriages, but among those aged twenty-five to forty-four, 47 percent of grooms and 55 percent of brides were remarrying following divorce. Among those forty-five or over, 56 percent of grooms and 46 percent of brides were remarrying after divorce. By contrast, in 1970, 40 percent of grooms and 51 percent of brides remarried after being *widowed*. These findings indicate that at each age range more remarriages are entered into by divorced persons than by widowed persons (Glick, 1980). The average interval between divorce and remarriage is about three years—a little less than half the seven-year interval between first marriage and divorce. However, these intervals vary considerably by age groups, with the intervals of both types being shorter in younger cohorts (Glick, 1980).

Glick points out that couples marrying for the first time are closer in age than those engaging in remarriage and tend to be more sensitive about age

Remarriage has become a common pattern in our society. Research suggests that there are some differences between the marital adjustment of first-married and remarried couples.

differences than people marrying for the second time. The wider age gap in remarriages occurs primarily because of the tendency among men to marry much younger women and for women to marry somewhat older men who are established financially. This tendency seems to contribute to the instability of remarriages; the data show that when the gap between the spouses' ages is relatively great, the duration of the marriage is relatively short (Glick, 1980).

Falling in love again rejuvenates people who have experienced the pain of divorce. Many look at their first marriage as a learning experience which prepared them to make a better marriage the next time. Even so, second marriages end in divorce even more often than first ones. The chances for success in a second marriage are only slightly better than 50-50. A 1975 Census Bureau study estimated that 38 percent of women in their thirties in 1980 had already ended their first marriage or could be expected to do so at some point in their lives. Of those who divorce and remarry, 44 percent will divorce again (Glick, 1980). One reason for this may be that second marriages involve stresses that were unknown in the first—interference by ex-partners, the complications of stepparenthood, reluctance of friends to accept the new partner, financial strain (usually on the man), of helping to support two families—combined with the usual marital adjustments. The fact that the partners have demonstrated their willingess to use divorce as a solution to marital problems is also thought to be a factor in the high rate of divorce in remarriages (Weiss, 1975).

There are certain patterns among the remarried relating to education and employment. For both men and women, remarriage is more likely for the less educated than for the better educated. This appears to be particularly true for women with little education who appear to rush back into marriage because they are less employable and hence less self-reliant. Divorced women generally are more likely to remarry if they are not part of the labor force, particularly if they have custody of children who are not yet in school. According to the 1970 Census, among divorced women aged thirty-five to forty-four, only 43 percent of those without children had remarried while 83 percent of those with children had married again. These statistics reflect the relative ease with which a woman who has a career or an occupation can support herself and the lack of options other than marriage for a woman without a job or job skills—especially if she has children at home (Glick, 1980).

Adjustment to Remarriage

The demographics give some sense of the differences between first and subsequent marriages, but statistics tell only a small part of the story. There are qualitative differences between first and subsequent marriages which may say much about the effects of divorce on remarriage.

Weingarten (1980) has examined the adjustment to remarriage of 184 adults chosen from a national sample of 2264 persons over twenty-one living in private households. She compared their adjustment to that of 1068 first-married adults from the same sample. Her principal goal was to examine the influence of remarriage after divorce on the well-being of remarrieds as compared to the well-being of first-marrieds. She discovered that the two groups were equally optimistic about the future and content with the present. Both groups had similarly high levels of self-esteem and self-acceptance, and the remarrieds had no higher levels of worry or anxiety than the first-marrieds. But while the two groups were similar in many ways, there were subtle differences. The stress of the divorce process seemed to have a permanent effect on the way the remarried saw life. They were more likely than the never-divorced to regard the way they were spending their life as unsatisfying, although it is not clear why.

The effects of divorce are most clearly revealed by the way in which the remarried viewed their lives over a long period of time. The remarried were significantly more likely to see themselves as vulnerable to the disasters of life. They were likely at some point in their lives to have felt as if they were about to have a nervous breakdown or that their problems were simply too much to endure. The remarried were also more likely to have sought help from a mental-health professional during their lifetime than the never-divorced. In short, Weingarten found evidence that the remarried were more likely to be subject to chronic stress.

When Weingarten examined the influence of prior marriage and divorce on the current adjustment of marital partners to each other she found similar patterns for first-marrieds and remarrieds. Both groups felt that the changes marriage caused in their lives were positive, and neither group was more likely than the other to report marital distress more fequently. This particular comparison may hide an important distinction between the two groups. The first-marrieds were describing their current married life and were making their comparisons to what they had experienced in that marriage or to an abstract standard, while the remarried were likely to be comparing their current condition with their previous marriage. Weingarten also found that the remarried were more likely to report anxiety over their performance of marital roles. This may be a result both of feelings of inadequacy arising out of their first marriage and of the ambiguities and difficulties of the remarried's role, especially if children are involved. Weingarten, however, concluded that the remarried do not have greater difficulty than first-marrieds in getting along with their spouses, perhaps because they enter their new marriages with a more realistic attitude and more modest objectives than do their first-married counterparts.

Another difference between the adjustment of first-marrieds and remarrieds is in the area of role divisions. In Weingarten's study, as well as in an ongoing study of remarried couples in central Pennsylvania (Furstenberg, 1980), remarrieds reported more sharing of household tasks and decision making and more emotional interaction between husband and wife than was true in their first marriages. Furstenberg believes that the greater gender equality of remarried couples may be influenced by changing cultural expectations about the nature of marriage. Whereas first-married couples probably feel more bound by traditional ideas of marriage, remarried individuals are free to "modernize" their conception of marriage in line with the changing times and their particular needs.

One crucial factor in the adjustment to remarriage is the presence of children by the previous marriage. Children can affect the happiness of the remarrieds more directly than almost any other factor.

 BLENDED FAMILIES

Remarriage generally results in the formation of **blended** or **reconstituted** families in which at least one of the spouses has a child or children by a previous marriage (Weingarten, 1980). Visher and Visher (1979) have concluded that first-married households and reconstituted households are fundamentally different both in structure and complexity. They identified five characteristics of the blended household which make it different from the original. First, virtually all of the members have suffered a loss of a primary relationship. Second, when the previous marriage ended in divorce, one biological parent resides outside the household. Third, the relationship between the biological parent and his or her children antedates the relationship with the new spouse. Fourth, the role definitions of the stepparent are poorly defined. And, fifth, because one biological parent lives outside the household, most children in blended families are members of more than one family.

Adjustment in Blended Families

Research on adjustment in blended families suggests that in addition to the financial difficulties of supporting children from the former marriage and the adjustments the marital partners must make to each other, perhaps the most difficult area of adjustment is in parent-child relationships.

PARENTAL ROLE ADJUSTMENT   For the wife's children, gaining a stepfather means they will no longer have their mother to themselves as they did when she was a single parent. But their acceptance of the stepfather is crucial to the happiness of their mother's remarriage (Weiss, 1975). In addition to redefining her relationship to her own children as she did when she was divorced, the mother may have to work out an acceptable way to relate to her new husband's children. She may want to be a friend, advisor, comforter, and supporter to them, but if she overplays these roles, their biological mother may resent her interference. And both stepparents are likely to have problems disciplining and establishing authority over their stepchildren. Stepmothers in particular have this problem because they typically spend more time with the children than their father does. This fact increases the likelihood of at least some disharmony since it will place the burden of discipline on the stepmother (Duberman, 1973).

Duberman (1973) found several possible explanations for the difficulties stepparents have in establishing good relationships with their stepchildren. One is the myth that stepparents are evil, a myth children are likely to believe. But according to surveys, stepparents are likely to be confused rather than malevolent, uncertain just what their role requires. Another problem is that many American children learn that their entire security depends on their parents and are not taught that other adults can be loved and trusted, too. As a result they are unprepared to learn to trust a stepparent. A third difficulty is that our society has no norms for the role of stepparent. It may be inappropriate for a stepfather, for instance, to try to be a replacement father to his stepchildren when they still have a real father. Stepparents need a role of their own, as special additional parents, not as replacement ones. Many stepparents do manage to fill their roles as supplementary parents well. Stepfathers are more often successful at this than stepmothers, and younger stepmothers are more likely to get along well with their stepchildren than older stepmothers.

Kompara (1980) notes that a major problem in the mutual adjustment of stepparents and stepchildren is that the children have been socialized by a different parent and that parent is still in evidence. This may contribute to the feelings of inadequacy reported by the remarried with respect to their parental

The marriage of Ringo Starr and Barbara Bach resulted in the formation of a blended family. The couple have five children between them from their previous marriages.

roles. However, despite their doubts about their parenting, stepparents do not appear to have any greater difficulties with their family role performance than do first-married parents. Their feelings of dissatisfaction may well grow out of the divided allegiance of their children more than anything else. There appears to be some evidence that adjustment is improved if the new couple has a child of their own; otherwise, children belonging to one or the other but not both may drive the couple apart (Weingarten, 1980).

STEPSIBLINGS   Children of blended families must share with each other their parents, their rooms, and their possessions, as well as their daily lives. They may experience the same jealousy and disruption of normal patterns children do when siblings are born. Friendship, or at least accommodation, between stepsiblings may develop only slowly.

In Duberman's study of stepsibling relationships, less than a fourth were rated "excellent," with the rest evenly divided between "good" and "poor." She pointed out, however, that siblings don't always get along well, either. Relationships between stepsiblings were more likely to be rated excellent if the children lived in the same house than if they didn't. At any rate, the better the relationships between stepsiblings, the better the integration of the new family as a close-knit group (Duberman, 1973).

While it is clear that blended families face many challenges, Weingarten and others regard remarriage as an opportunity not only for the adults to achieve what they want from marriage, but also for the children to learn how to cope successfully with life and how to adapt to the changing circumstances, later in their lives, of marriage (Kulka and Weingarten, 1979; Weingarten, 1980).

SUMMARY

1. This chapter explores the ways marriages end and examines the experience of divorce and remarriage. Until recently, most marriages ended with the death of one spouse. However, it is increasingly common for marriages to end voluntarily. A large majority of divorced people enter marriage for a second time.

2. Desertion is an informal means of ending a marriage in which one partner simply abandons the other. It is primarily a phenomenon of lower-class men and recently of middle- and upper-middle-class women. It has severe effects on all those involved.

3. Annulment is a legal termination of an invalid marriage. The marriage has to have been invalid at the time it was entered into for reasons of fraud, including bigamy. Annulment is usually chosen by persons who are forbidden by moral or religious beliefs to divorce.

4. Separation is a voluntary means of ending aspects of the marital relationship. It can take two forms. Informal separation simply amounts to the partners' deciding to go their separate ways and making all financial and custodial arrangements between themselves. Legal separation involves the termination of certain marital rights—such as living together and sexual relations—but essentially leaves other marital obligations intact. This method is used primarily by those for whom divorce or annulment are not viable options.

5. Divorce is by far the most common method for the voluntary termination of marriage. It involves obtaining a legal decree ending a valid marriage. In most states, a divorce can be obtained without establishing fault; under older systems, one partner had to be blamed. The no-fault system does not appear to have had any significant effect, positive or negative, on the divorce rate or on postdivorce adjustment.

6. In divorce, there may be six processes occurring simultaneously to which the individual must adjust. (a) Emotional divorce: repression or rejection of emotional ties. (b) Legal divorce: establishing the right of the partners to marry someone else. (c) Economic divorce: dividing money and joint possessions. (d) Coparental divorce: deciding custody of the children, visitation rights, and financial support. (e) Community divorce: alteration of relationships with kin, friends, and social activities. (f) Psychic divorce: becoming a single, independent individual.

7. When divorced persons remarry, they face some marital stresses not found in first marriages, especially when children are involved. Relationships between stepparents, stepchildren, and stepsiblings may take time to work out, particularly because our society has no norms for these relationships.

REVIEW AND DISCUSSION

1. One view of the high divorce rate is that it reflects the decline of the family; another view is that it reflects the greater willingness of people to terminate unsatisfactory relationships and try again. Which of these views is closest to your own? Do you have an alternative view?

2. Identify the six processes of divorce and explain briefly what is involved in each of them.

3. What are the benefits and/or drawbacks to no-fault divorce as compared to divorce that requires establishing fault?

4. What are some differences in the adjustment of first-marrieds and remarrieds?

5. In what ways may divorce and remarriage be regarded as opportunities for personal growth?

SUGGESTED READINGS

Duberman, L. (1975). *The Reconstituted Family.* Chicago: Nelson-Hall.

Presents results of a study of eighty-eight "step-families." Examines factors related to the varying levels of marital and parental adjustment to remarriage when children from a previous marriage are involved.

Epstein, J. (1974). *Divorced in America: Marriage in an Age of Possibility.* New York: E. P. Dutton.

Uses a combination of autobiography, novels, and social science literature to analyze why the divorce rate has increased. Reports on divorce from the male viewpoint and gives a picture of the author's life as a divorced man with custody of his children.

Hetherington, E. M., M. Cox, and R. Cox (1977). "Divorced Fathers." *Psychology Today* **10**:13:42–46.

Focuses on problems of new divorced fathers and how they handled them. Three basic kinds of problems are those involved with the matters of day-to-day living; those associated with emotional stress and changes in self-concept; and those involving new definitions of relationships with ex-wives, children, and others.

Maddox, B. (1975). *The Half-Parent: Living with Other People's Children.* New York: Evans.

Discusses the emotional problems and rewards of being a second parent. Considers myths, legal questions, etiquette, discipline, and communication between stepparents and stepchildren.

Wallerstein, J. S., and J. B. Kelly (1980). *Surviving the Breakup: How Children Actually Cope with Divorce.* New York: Basic.

A nontechnical presentation of a study of sixty families of divorce. Includes a five-year followup of the immediate and long-range effects of divorce on children ages three to eighteen.

Alternatives to Traditional Marriage

14

"How glorious it is—and also how painful—to be an exception."

ALFRED DE MUSSET

The family, as we defined it in Chapter 1, is a social group having specified roles and statuses, who usually share a common residence and cooperate economically. It is usually based on the marriage of one or more sexually cohabiting couples. This definition includes the possibility of having children for whom the adults accept responsibility. It is also broad enough to include the variety of family forms found the world over. In the United States, the "traditional" family consists of one husband, one wife, and their children. The ideal "traditional" marriage is legal, lifelong, and monogamous. The husband has traditionally been the ultimate authority and the primary provider (Macklin, 1980).

If the nuclear family is the traditional form, it is clear that there are numerous nontraditional forms of marriage and family life in this country. In preceding chapters, we looked at single-parent families, voluntarily childless couples, and dual-worker families, and we pointed out that marriages are becoming increasingly egalitarian rather than husband-dominant. In this chapter, we will consider several other nontraditional life-styles, including singlehood, cohabitation, open marriages and open families, "swinging," the homosexual life-style, multilateral or group marriages, and communal living arrangements.

As shown in Table 14.1, in recent years the percentage of traditional nuclear families has been declining and the percentage of nontraditional family forms has been rising. Why is this so? According to Macklin (1980), the emergence of nontraditional forms is a consequence of the concurrent decline of emphasis on family life and growth of individu-

475

Table 14.1 **Composition of U.S. Households in the 1970s (In Percent)**

TYPE OF HOUSEHOLD	1970	1975	1978	1979
Family households				
Married couple—no children under 18	30.3	30.6	29.9	29.9
Married couple—children under 18	40.3	35.4	32.4	31.7[a]
One parent with children under 18	5.3	6.7	7.3	7.4
Other (e.g., extended)	5.6	5.4	5.3	5.4
Total	81.5	78.1	74.9	74.4
Nonfamily households[b]				
Persons living alone	17.1	19.6	22.0	22.2
Other	1.7	2.3	3.1	3.4
Total	18.8	21.9	25.1	25.6

Note. Percentages are derived from the U.S. Bureau of Census, 1980a: Table A.

[a] Slightly over half of all children under 18 living in two-parent families in March, 1979 had mothers who were in the labor force, as compared to 38 percent of such children in 1970 (U.S. Department of Labor, 1979).

[b] Maintained by a person or persons who do not share their quarters with any relatives.

alism which accompanied industrialization and the spread of universal education. Individuals today have gained more control over their lives and have less dependence on their families than in earlier generations. Technological developments in our postindustrial society have had a tremendous impact on family life. For example, advances in the technology of reproduction have separated sexual behavior from procreation, reduced the risks of sex outside marriage, and made family planning considerably easier. These technological achievements have meant that an increasingly affluent people could direct energy other generations spent on meeting fundamental needs, like food and shelter, to developing themselves as individuals and accomplishing philosophical goals. The variety and range of alternative life-styles seem to be a direct product of these forces.

 SINGLEHOOD

At no other time in our history have so many people been unmarried as in recent years. Nonfamily households (most of which consist of one person) are only about one-third as numerous as family households. Yet between 1970 and 1979, the number of nonfamily households increased by 66 percent, while family households increased only 12 percent (U.S. Department of Commerce, 1980). In 1976, 15 percent of women and 21 percent of men aged eighteen and over had never married. When the individuals who are single because of separation, divorce, and widowhood are added to the figures for never-married singles, 30 percent of adult males and 37 percent of adult females were unmarried in 1976 (U.S. Bureau of the Census, 1977). Who are these single people? The research indicates that women who remain single are likely to be better educated, have a better job, and be in better mental health than single men (Bernard, 1972; Gove, 1972a). A study of persons who were applying for Social Security benefits found that men with higher intelligence and job status were least likely to be single; women in those categories were most likely to be single. At the same time, individuals of both sexes who had had an unhappy family life as children were two or three times more likely to be single. This was particularly true of men (Spreitzer and Riley, 1974).

Changing Views of Singlehood

Remaining single by choice is a surprising trend in a society where marriage not only has been associated with normality but also has been considered nearly synonymous with "the good life" (Stein, 1975). Traditionally, single adults in the United States have been viewed as being somehow deviant: it has been assumed that a well-adjusted individual would not choose to remain single. In his analysis of the never-married in the 1950s, for example, Manfred Kuhn suggested that single people were likely to have personal and social problems. Some of the reasons proposed for why they had not married were: hostility toward marriage or people of the opposite sex, homosexuality, attachment to a parent, ill health or other physical problems, physical unattractiveness, refusal to accept responsibility, being too hard to please, ineptness in the dating-mating process, inability to finance a marriage, and extreme geographical or occupational isolation from potential mates (Stein, 1975).

While some single people may have problems that prevent them from marrying, sociologists now recognize that singlehood may be a choice of healthy, well-adjusted people. Macklin (1980), for instance, indicates that changing mores have created a situation where previous generalizations about singlehood may not apply to current cohorts. She believes singles today are better adjusted and have more fulfilling lives than was the case in earlier generations.

Stein (1975) interviewed ten single men and ten single women, all middle-class urban professionals, to determine why they had chosen to remain single. The men ranged in age from twenty-seven to forty-five and the women from twenty-two to thirty-three. Some of them had been married previously or had lived in an exclusive heterosexual relationship. None was currently involved in an exclusive relationship. Stein found little evidence among this sample of the negative reasons for singlehood suggested in earlier studies. None of the respondents was unattractive, homosexual, overly romantic, or isolated from the dating market. None was inept at dating, although some had rejected it as being old-fashioned, competitive, and exploitative.

What Stein found was an entirely different list of motivations for single-hood. As shown in Table 14.2, he called some of these "pushes" away from unsatisfactory experiences with marriage or exclusive cohabitation; others he called "pulls" toward the values perceived in being single. The strongest of the "pushes" was the feeling that marriage or an exclusive relationship restricted personal growth. The second major push was a sense of isolation and loneliness in monogamous relationships, a feeling of being cut off from other people and unable to share all one's feelings with one's mate. A third push was the feeling that marriage would restrict friendships to people who were acceptable to one's mate as well as oneself. The majority of the single people interviewed felt that marriage represented restraint and compromise, limiting opportunities for enjoying a variety of experiences, independence, and learning.

The "pulls" toward singlehood included the desire for freedom, the opportunity to develop multiple friendships, financial independence, sexual availability, and personal growth. Men were especially attracted by the possibility of trying out a variety of roles, instead of being restricted to those of breadwinner, husband, and father. In general, those interviewed felt that in singlehood they could find fulfillment and personal growth, and that marriage was no longer the only avenue to emotional support, sexual satisfaction, and social activity (Stein, 1975).

OTHER MOTIVATIONS FOR SINGLEHOOD As noted, Stein's study focused on a small group of people who were committed to singlehood as their life-style. But in fact, the single population is highly diverse. Those never married, those formerly married with children, and those formerly married without children may show significant differences both in their motivations for remaining single and in their life-styles. As with any way of life, singlehood has as many subtle variations as there are individual personalities, and each variation is affected by social and economic realities.

Certainly, uppermost among the attractions of singlehood is the element of free choice, whether of job, home, friends, or sexual partner. When married or living in an exclusive relationship, one's choices are determined in part by the partner. Where one lives, for example, will probably be a matter of compromise. The choice of a job—which involves location, income level, and time available for domestic life—may be as much a family matter as an individual decision. Once married, the couple tends to become a social unit, so even personal friends are often determined by one's marriage. Several of the singles in Stein's sample mentioned that while married, they had had to associate only with mutually satisfying friends; individual friendships, partic-ularly with members of the opposite sex, were often seen as threatening by their mates (Stein, 1975).

Singlehood, by contrast, offers the possibility of autonomy. Writer Judith Thurman, in an article discussing her desire to remain single, remarks that, "Choice . . . for people who live in twos and threes and fours, is a process. Agreement is a process—a necessary self-limitation. But alone, one is the

Table 14.2 **Choosing Marriage or Singlehood**

	PUSHES TOWARD MARRIAGE	PULLS TOWARD MARRIAGE

The table may be read either vertically or horizontally. The pushes in the left-hand column represent felt needs not being met in one's present condition. That is, pushes toward marriage might be thought of as deficits felt by single people, while pushes toward singlehood might be thought of as deficits felt by married people. Pulls, in the right-hand column, represent positive values associated with the state of being married or the state of being single. Reading across the top two boxes, one becomes aware of the combination of pushes and pulls experienced by single people in U.S. society which may eventually result in marriage if a suitable partner can be found. Reading across the bottom two boxes provides a feeling for the combined pushes and pulls toward becoming or remaining single.	Economic security
	Influence from mass media
	Pressure from parents
	Need to leave home
	Interpersonal and personal reasons
	   Fear of independence
	   Loneliness
	   Alternatives did not seem feasible
	Cultural expectations, Socialization
	Regular sex
	Guilt over singlehood
		Influence of parents
		Desire for family
		Example of peers
		Romanticization of marriage
		Love
		   Physical attraction
		   Emotional attachment
		Security, social status, Prestige

	PUSHES TOWARD SINGLEHOOD	PULLS TOWARD SINGLEHOOD

	Restrictions
	   Suffocating one-to-one relationships, feeling trapped
	   Obstacles to self-development
	   Boredom and unhappiness and anger
	   Role playing and conformity to expectations
	Poor communication with mate
	Sexual frustration
	Lack of friends, isolation, loneliness
	Limitations on mobility and available experience
	Influence of and participation in women's movement
		Career opportunities
		Variety of experiences
		Self-sufficiency
		Sexual availability
		Exciting life-style
		Freedom to change and experiment
		Mobility
		Sustaining friendships
		Supportive groups
		   Men's and women's groups
		   Group living arrangements
		Specialized groups

Adapted from Peter J. Stein, "Singlehood: An Alternative to Marriage," *The Family Coordinator* 24:4. Copyright 1975 by The National Council on Family Relations. Reprinted by permission.

author of every choice. One's choices are one's identity, even in petty things"
(Thurman, 1975, p. 64).

On the whole, single life seems more satisfying for the upper-middle class
than for any other group. To a great extent, the reason for this is economic.
If singleness is attractive for the freedom it offers, it is often affluence that
makes this freedom possible to achieve. An unemployed parent of three
children has little freedom, single or not. The substantial income of the upper-
middle-class person permits a choice in such basic aspects of life as housing;
it also makes possible entertainment, vacations, and other outside activities
which are a source of social contacts. Moreover, members of the upper-middle
class are more likely to have satisfying careers which, in addition to offering
a purposeful focus for their interests, provide another source of social contacts.

Establishing Interpersonal Relationships

The desire of many single people to remain free of an exclusive relationship
does not usually imply an avoidance of relationships in general; on the
contrary, the possibility of exploring a variety of relationships is often cited
as one of the major attractions of singlehood. However, forming meaningful
heterosexual friendships can be very difficult.

In many areas, singles bars have sprung up in response to the perceived
needs of single people. Unfortunately, these establishments focus almost
entirely on the sexual aspects of singlehood and going to one of them can be
a depressing experience. Starr and Carns (1972) found that men who frequented
singles bars tended to be sexually oriented, whereas women were more often
seeking friendship and lasting relationships. As a result of this disparity,
women in singles bars often felt degraded and exploited.

Studies suggest that many single people eventually become disillusioned
with singles bars as a setting where relationships can begin. Starr and Carns,
for example, found that the longer the subjects in their study lived in the
urban singles environment, the less frequently they attended singles bars.

Another source of personal contacts are the singles clubs and housing
complexes. Like the singles bars, these commercial enterprises tend to exploit
the single population. In one housing complex, described by an observer as a
"sexual Disneyland," the men seemed to be interested primarily in developing
sexual liaisons and, as a result, women who were seeking more lasting
friendships felt degraded. Thus, the singles housing complex does not seem to
provide the type of environment where lasting friendships are likely to be
formed (Proulx, 1973).

Single college graduates in urban areas find that the work world offers a
more satisfactory setting for making friends and meeting people of the opposite

Forming lasting interpersonal relationships is one of the more difficult challenges of singlehood. Singles bars seem more conducive to casual encounters than to deeper friendships.

sex. The process of meeting people usually occurs in two stages: the single person becomes friends with others at work and then through these friends is introduced to potential dates (Proulx, 1973).

In contrast to college-educated singles, blue-collar and low-level white-collar workers may find that the working environment affords fewer opportunities to meet dating partners. Jobs at these levels tend to be sex segregated; as a result, many low-income singles are denied the social aspects of the work world and are forced to look elsewhere to meet others (Jacoby, 1974).

Stein (1975) believes that more formal structures are emerging that may help meet the needs of single people for friendship and intimacy. Social support may come from men's and women's groups, therapy and encounter groups, and organizations centered around special interests. While these groups are not specifically oriented toward single people, says Stein, they do offer an environment more conducive to developing friendships and more supportive of the unique concerns of single people. People involved in such groups expressed their relief at finding that other people shared feelings and experiences similar to their own and reported that their association with these types of groups helped them to grow as individuals.

 COHABITATION

For some singles, cohabitation provides a solution—sometimes permanent, but usually temporary—to the problem of establishing personal relationships. But cohabitation can take a variety of forms. Perhaps the best general definition of **cohabitation** is that of Newcomb and McDonald (1981): "an intimate heterosexual relationship involving an unmarried couple who share a common abode."

In recent years, there has been a huge increase in the number of couples who cohabit. This is in many respects a more surprising development than the emergence of singlehood as an option because of the traditionally strong societal disapproval of cohabitation. While cohabitation, or "living together," is popularly associated primarily with college students, young adults, intellectuals, and entertainers, it is not restricted to those groups. It occurs among all age groups and among different social classes. For example, many elderly people have discovered that living together allows them to share pension and Social Security payments that would be reduced if they married.

Recent Trends

The number of people who cohabit is considerably smaller than the number of people who are either single or married. Still, as shown in Fig. 14.1, the number of cohabitants is increasing rapidly: in 1970, 1.1 million adults cohabited, but by 1979, that number had risen to 2.7 million. Between 1977 and 1978 alone, the number of cohabitants increased by 19 percent. In 1979, nearly 3 percent of all couple households consisted of cohabitants, and nearly 4 percent of all unmarried adults lived in this type of relationship (U.S. Bureau of the Census, 1980; Newcomb and McDonald, 1981).

DOONESBURY   **by Garry Trudeau**

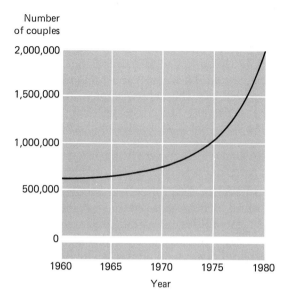

Number
of couples

Fig. 14.1
Rates of unmarried cohabitation from 1960 to 1980. (Source: Data from Paul Glick and Graham Spanier, 1980, "Married and Unmarried Cohabitation in the United States," Journal of Marriage and the Family 42:19–30.)

The trend, as these numbers show, is toward considerably more cohabitation, especially if young adults are any guide. One nationally representative study of 2,510 young men showed that 18 percent had lived with a woman for more than six months (Clayton and Voss, 1977). Another study has noted that those results greatly understate the likelihood of cohabitation because of the substantial probability of relationships lasting less than six months and the great likelihood of individuals engaging in cohabitation in the future (Newcomb, 1979). Bower and Christopherson (1977) confirmed that as many as 25 percent of college students of both sexes have cohabited. And the results of attitudinal surveys indicate that, if anything, the number of cohabitants will increase in the years to come. In one study, 71 percent of males and 43 percent of females indicated they would cohabit (Henze and Hudson, 1974). Another survey showed that 79.2 percent of its respondents would cohabit under the right circumstances (Arafat and Yorburg, 1973). These same studies also show an increasing acceptance of couples living together, at least among the young (see also, Macklin, 1972, 1976, 1980).

Who Cohabits?

As to the people living in these arrangements, about half of them in 1979 had never been married; 35 percent of the women and 42 percent of the men were separated or divorced. About 8 percent of all divorced men under thirty-five were cohabitants. While 75 percent of cohabitants' households consisted of only two adults, in approximately 25 percent there was at least one child under fourteen. As might be inferred from the studies noted above, most cohabiting relationships appear to be brief. U.S. Census statistics indicate that 63 percent of cohabiting couples lived in the same residence for two years or less before they married or separated (Newcomb and McDonald, 1981). Also, although cohabitation is perceived as a characteristic of youth, one out of ten cohabiting couples included a partner sixty-five or over (Macklin, 1980; Newcomb and McDonald, 1981).

Characteristics of Cohabitants

Most studies of cohabitation have focused on college students. Keeping that possibly distorting factor in mind, it is possible to make some generalizations about people who cohabit. Many studies have indicated that cohabitants do not differ significantly from those who have not cohabited. No study has yet established consistent differences between cohabitants and noncohabitants as to social class, urban or rural background, or any of a number of family background variables (Newcomb and McDonald, 1981). In short, people who cohabit are not deviant.

Cohabitants do seem to have different attitudinal and behavioral patterns from persons who have not cohabited. Cohabitants are, and regard themselves as being, more liberal about life-styles—including sex and drugs. They are considerably less religious than noncohabitants (Bayer and McDonald, 1981), and they plan to have fewer children (Macklin, 1980; Newcomb and McDonald, 1981). These attitudes, one study concluded, are simply part of a larger pattern associated with an orientation toward nontraditional values and life-styles (Newcomb and McDonald, 1981).

Although the evidence is inconclusive, some studies have found that cohabitants are actually better adjusted on the average than noncohabitants, and their heterosexual relationships are of a higher quality. Even when couples have broken up, they usually feel that they have gained in self-understanding, personal growth, and understanding of the opposite sex as a result of cohabiting. There are couples, however, who are not ready for living together, and for them it may be a wholly bad experience. The desire for intimacy is not enough: living together requires skill in communication, decision making, and conflict management, and these skills in turn require healthy, positive self-concepts (Peterman, Ridley, and Anderson, 1974; Cole, 1977).

Why People Cohabit

There has been considerable debate about whether cohabitation should most appropriately be viewed as an alternative to marriage, a trial marriage, or an emerging stage of the courtship process. Peterman, Ridley, and Anderson

(1974) compared cohabiting students on several campuses and found that living together is neither trial marriage nor an alternative to marriage. Rather, it is a stage of courtship, and is usually an extension of strong, affectionate

HIGHLIGHT 14.1 *Living Together: A Personal View*

Paul and I wear matching white-gold bands, I respond to "Mrs. Liang" although it is not my name, my seven-year-old daughter Jenni calls him Daddy, and we live together. But Paul and I are not married.

Evolving from a decade of young friendship that grew into an adult loveship, our relationship roots not on the dotted line of a marriage license but in the very minds of our hearts. Our commitment to each other and the viability of our relationship thrive on the deep sense of personal honor and integrity that makes us us. We are—lovingly, mindfully, heartfully, and physically—bonded with our own intimate handshake of trust. And because our boundaries are self-defined and self-applied—and not hinged to the societal definition of marriage— we are that much more intense in maintaining our level of love. Any disloyalty to our trust, in thought or action, would be that much more magnified and intolerable.

We seem to flex, depending on circumstance, between living-together and married. Because we have Jenni (who was born during my former brief marriage), we have the semblance of the typical nuclear family, and people who want to see us as "stable and married"— our neighbors, parents of Jenni's friends, even our car dealer—do. People who want to think of us as "living-together"—acquaintances at cocktail parties, college friends, even our colleagues—do, too. We've come to realize that "marriage" and "living together" are exterior labels for the sake of others; they provide others with convenient cues for how to relate to us.

There is, for us, such an indistinct line between living together and married that sometimes we seem more "married" than some of our married friends and more living-together than our "roommate" friends. We are, through and through, faithful, and guarded and possessive about our time together. We mirror a marriage in practical terms, too: our lease is in both our names; we cosigned our car loan as "best friends"; we share one checking and savings account. On holidays, we make the trip home to our families—together. Unlike some living-togethers, we do not consider living together a temporary means to some distant end, but an entity in itself growing in the present. The spirit, energy, and emotions we invest in our relationship bring us generous returns today and many tomorrows. Like those who are warmed by the "forever" clause in marriage, we fantasize about the time when we'll be sixty-four.

We are not stridently trying to change the tradition of marriage, not abrasive in trying to declare a personal statement. We are convinced that we ourselves define our labels, and that two people can, in their quiet private world, be ultimately loving and committed without marriage. And if indeed we were to be married tomorrow, we would still be living together.

involvement. At Penn State, 83 percent of the cohabiting men and 86 percent of the cohabiting women surveyed considered theirs an intimate or love relationship, rather than something like friendship.

Despite their often exclusive sexual involvement with each other, most cohabiting students in this study were pragmatic about their relationships and were unlikely to consider them permanent. For a large majority, cohabiting lasted less than six months; half had cohabited with someone else before. Only 6 percent were committed to marrying their partner, and only 7 percent were committed to working toward a lasting relationship. Instead, most were planning to staying together only as long as the relationship was mutually satisfying and personally enjoyable. Many kept their old dorm rooms in case living together didn't work, or to provide retreat from too much togetherness. This orientation was especially noticeable among males and younger students. Cohabiting relationships of the later undergraduate years seemed to be more durable (Peterman, Ridley, and Anderson, 1974).

Cohabitation does not serve the same function in all cases; sometimes it does not serve the same function for both partners. Couples often come to their arrangement with different expectations—just as married couples do. While women may express a desire for marriage and thus view cohabitation as a stage in courtship or trial marriage, men tend to see the arrangement as an alternative to marriage, or as a way of obtaining sexual gratification. Whether marriage actually takes place apparently depends on which partner's position prevails (Lyness, Lipetz, and Davis, 1972; Newcomb and McDonald, 1981).

Although student cohabitation is not usually regarded as trial marriage, it may nonetheless prevent mismatched pairs from marrying. Couples who live together can discover conflicts and work them out in a marriagelike setting, with the option of breaking up if the costs of adjustment seem to outweigh the rewards of the relationship (Cole, 1977).

Despite increasing cohabitation, interest in eventual marriage is still strong, though not necessarily to the person one is cohabiting with. When a sample of undergraduates—including both cohabitants and noncohabitants—was asked what living arrangement they would prefer after they finished college, marriage was the most popular option. Cohabitation took second place. However, when the responses of cohabitants were tabulated separately, it was found that males who had experienced cohabitation thought they would prefer it to marriage, and females who had cohabited ranked cohabitation after college almost as high as marriage (Peterman, Ridley, and Anderson, 1974).

Perhaps this ambivalence toward their style of relationship is a function of the way most cohabiting arrangements develop. According to Newcomb and McDonald (1981), cohabitants usually know each other for more than six months when they begin to live together, usually in the male's apartment or house. But the critical difference between couples who marry and those who

There is evidence that living together may be regarded somewhat differently by men and women. Women may view cohabitation as a stage of courtship, whereas men are more likely to see it as an alternative to marriage.

cohabit is that most cohabitants never really make a decision to live together. They just begin to cohabit, usually as a result of staying in one partner's place more and more often.

Interpersonal Dynamics in Cohabitation

Certain problems are unique to couples who pursue alternative life-styles, and cohabiting couples are no exception. In particular, cohabiting may create difficulties with landlords, employers, neighbors, and parents. Parental disapproval can be especially worrisome. Parents often feel that the female in the cohabitant relationship is being exploited sexually. For this reason, some cohabiting couples—even those in their twenties and thirties—do not tell their parents they are living together. In one extreme case, a young woman in her late twenties had her partner move out whenever her parents were expected.

CASE STUDY   *Cohabiting: A Question of Commitment*

David and Sally had known each other for ten months before deciding that they were in love with each other and wanted to live together. Although Sally would have preferred to get married, David said he felt marriage wasn't necessary to prove that two people were ready to make a serious commitment.

The couple got along well together, and in general Sally was satisfied with her decision to live with David. Nevertheless, she experienced a nagging discomfort because of her parents' reaction to the arrangement. She had been raised in a devoutly religious, middle-class home where she had been taught that sexual relations were appropriate only within the context of marriage. When her parents learned that Sally planned to live with David they objected strenuously. Sally's mother told her that David was immature and not ready to commit himself to a lifetime relationship. Otherwise, why didn't David want to get married? In her parents' eyes, Sally was being used. When Sally responded by insisting that she had made the right decision, her mother stopped her weekly telephone calls and wrote her daughter that she would resume their relationship only when Sally either stopped living with David or married him.

Sally felt hurt and cut off by her parents' reaction. She was not completely confident about her decision anyway, and although she believed there was nothing immoral about her relationship with David, she could not shake her guilty feelings.

Sally and David were both working at full-time jobs, but as time went by Sally found herself doing more and more of the household chores and cooking. For a while this didn't bother her, since she liked doing things for David, but as she began to take on more responsibility at work she came to resent what she regarded as having to carry more than her share of the load at home. When she tried to talk to David about it, his response was, "One of the main reasons I wanted to live together rather than get married was that we wouldn't have to hassle over mundane things like who does the chores."

Sally decided to drop the issue, at least for the time being. She hoped that as David's commitment to her grew, he would become more willing to share responsibilities and discuss problems when they arose. This incident, however, marked the beginning of a pattern in their relationship. An easy-going, good natured young man, David was fun to be with but he liked things to go smoothly and wanted to avoid "hassles." He criticized Sally for trying to be too "structured" and implied that if she couldn't come to terms with her dissatisfactions, he might end the relationship.

Eventually Sally felt herself drawing away from David. She realized that their views of what living together meant were very different. While she had hoped that they would grow closer and eventually marry, David seemed very content having companionship and affection without the responsibilities that a deeper commitment implied. In addition, Sally became more and more disturbed over her parents' rejection of her. She became aware that their approval mattered a great deal to her after all. Finally she decided to break off her relationship with David. While this proved to be a difficult adjustment for them both, Sally felt she was

(continued)

CASE STUDY   *(continued)*

making the right decision. She believed she would be happier if she could find a man who wanted the same things she did, and she was much more comfortable knowing that she would have the emotional support of her parents.

FOR CLASS DISCUSSION

1. If Sally and David had decided to marry instead of living together, do you think there would have been more incentive for them to come to terms with their problems instead of ending their relationship? Why or why not?

2. Do you think it is appropriate for parents to try to influence young adults in their choice of life-styles?

While this meant locking certain rooms and putting away his possessions, the couple felt it was preferable to creating a serious family disruption.

DECISION MAKING   Cole (1977) interviewed forty long-term cohabiting couples and found that within a year of living together primary responsibility for making decisions in particular areas fell to one partner rather than both. Frequently the person most involved in a particular area had responsibility for it. For example, if one partner had owned a car prior to cohabitation, that partner would continue to be responsible for it. All of the couples in Cole's sample indicated that some decisions were made jointly, but he observed that women were responsible for more areas than men.

GENDER ROLES   A number of studies have found that there is a tendency for cohabiting couples to assume traditional gender roles. Cohabiting women tend to do the same housekeeping tasks as married women, such as dishes and laundry (Stafford, Backman, and diBono, 1977). And, as in legal marriages, men take out the garbage. The men in Cole's study believed they were sharing housekeeping tasks, while the women perceived themselves to be doing most of the housework (Cole, 1977).

MAINTAINING THE RELATIONSHIP   The factors that help to maintain a cohabiting relationship seem to be the same ones that make for lasting marriages: mutual trust, willingness to share personal feelings, the sense of needing one's partner, and satisfactory sexual adjustment (Lyness, Lipetz, and Davis, 1972).

Cole cites research indicating that effective communication is vital to keeping a cohabiting relationship viable, just as it is in legal marriages. While most long-term cohabiting couples say they believe in the idea of individual sexual freedom, the majority practice monogamy. Otherwise, jealousy is likely to be a problem. Also, some nonmonogamous individuals report that they find themselves feeling guilty about their sexual activities (Lobsenz, 1974b).

ENDING THE RELATIONSHIP   Dissolution of cohabiting relationships seems to follow much the same pattern as dissolution of a legal marriage. The divorce process may be seen as a series of stages in which the persons involved suffer loss, depression, and anger, then begin to reorient their lives and finally come to accept a new life-style. Cole believes these stages apply equally to ending cohabitation. In addition, the legal aspects of marriage are increasingly being reflected in cohabitation, as evidenced by the development of "palimony" lawsuits in a number of states.

Possible Effects on Marriage

Some people think cohabitation, when coupled with the high divorce rate, indicates an erosion of marriage and the family and, by extension, an erosion of the fabric of society. By contrast, many social scientists view living together as functional and beneficial. Trost (1975) suggests that cohabitation, operating as a trial marriage, may in time become a social institution. Partners who discover they should not form a permanent relationship will be able to end the arrangement more easily than legal marriages, and those marriages that do form will be more likely to last. As yet, it is not clear to what degree cohabitation will serve as a prelude to marriage and to what degree it will be a true alternative to marriage.

What should be clear from the studies discussed above is that cohabitation does not threaten the institution of marriage, if for no other reason than that the vast majority of cohabitants—as well as noncohabitants—wish to get married eventually. For young people at least, cohabitation may be only a short-term alternative to marriage. They clearly regard living together as a part of the process of finding a mate rather than as an end in itself. The fact that young people regard cohabitation as a stage in courtship has caused a number of scholars to speculate that its principal effect may be to delay the age at which people enter first marriage.

EFFECTS ON THE PREVIOUSLY MARRIED AND THE ELDERLY   Where cohabitation may have a real effect on marriage is among the previously married and older persons. There is evidence, for example, that people who have been married make up a large percentage of those who cohabit. One study of males indicated that 14 percent of those married once and 35 percent of those married more than once had cohabited, as compared to 21 percent of those who had never married (Clayton and Voss, 1977). According to another study (Glick and Norton, 1977), divorced men made up the largest single category of unmarried persons participating in these relationships (5.4 percent of all divorced men were cohabiting in 1976). Of divorced men under thirty-five, 8.3 percent were living with a woman they weren't married to. Newcomb (1979) suggests that men who have experienced several failed marriages may look more favorably on cohabitation as a viable alternative to marriage.

The trends relating to cohabitation among the elderly are harder to assess. As is true of many aspects of sexuality and life-style, the old seem less willing than the young to answer researchers' questions candidly. Nonetheless, one researcher (Yllo, 1978) found that in a national sample .3 percent of those between fifty-one and sixty cohabit, but that percentage climbs to .9 for those over sixty. This rise, Yllo believes, was the result of Social Security laws which reduce benefits to widowed people who remarry.

In speculative articles, two researchers have noted that the elderly may be restrained from entering into cohabiting relationships for fear of disrupting their relationships with their families (Rosenburg, 1970; Cavan, 1973). Cavan argued that the benefits of cohabitation for older persons included companionship, financial gain, and sexual satisfaction. Thus, the principal inhibiting factor and the main positive features of cohabitation are quite similar for college students and the elderly. Still, much research needs to be done in this area (Newcomb, 1979).

In sum, cohabitation may be a long-range alternative to marriage for the previously married and the elderly; but for the young, it remains a short-term option, and usually one of short duration.

COHABITATION AND CHILDREN Two studies have noted a tendency among present and former cohabitants to want fewer children (Bower and Christopherson, 1977; Weitzman et al., 1978), and Weitzman et al. indicated that former cohabitants are less likely to have children than noncohabitants. However, Newcomb (1979), in an analysis of these studies, pointed out that there was no necessary connection between cohabitation and family size. People inclined to cohabit may also be likely to want fewer children, but while family size and cohabitation may be linked to each other in a complex pattern of attitudes, there is no support for a causal connection between the two.

Although few cohabiting college couples have children living with them (Bower and Christopherson, 1977), nearly 20 percent of all cohabiting couples did in 1977 (Glick and Norton, 1977). While many divorced people establish joint living arrangements with friends of the opposite sex, those with children must give very serious thought to the consequences of doing so. Lack of clarity about the roles each partner is to play can cause problems. If, for example, a man moves in with a woman who has children, his relationship with them is something between what it was when he was only going with her and what it would be if he married her. He is not the children's stepfather, and may have only the authority of an adult guest. He has no legal parental rights or responsibilities. Weiss (1975) suggests that adjustment will be facilitated if the children are informed ahead of time that the parent plans to have the friend move in and their acceptance is obtained before the actual move takes place.

OPEN MARRIAGES AND OPEN FAMILIES

The publication of the book *Open Marriage* (O'Neill and O'Neill, 1972) caused much fanfare. Its authors called upon couples to alter traditional approaches to roles in marriage fundamentally and across the board. One of the roles they dealt with was the sexual role, and most of the attention the book generated concentrated on its approach to "open" extramarital activity. "Open marriage" came to be regarded as a synonym for mutually approved extramarital sexuality, and this tended to obscure the much broader approach advocated by the book. The O'Neills, according to Macklin (1980):

> . . . concluded that the major problem facing the modern marriage is the inability of the majority to find in their marriage both intimacy and opportunity for personal development. Their solution is open marriage, a relationship characterized by: functioning in the "here-and-now" with realistic expectations, respect for personal privacy, role flexibility, open and honest communication, open companionship, equality of power and responsibility, pursuit of identity, and mutual trust. (p. 910)

The open-marriage approach is not an aberration. It is a logical outgrowth of the trend we have noted several times before toward more androgynous family roles. In these relationships, there is considerably less stereotyping of roles by gender, and there is more sharing of household chores and childraising than in traditional American marriages (Macklin, 1980). Relations between husband and wife are more egalitarian and are characterized by negotiation rather than the acceptance of societal norms for particular roles.

One might expect to find open marriage to be characteristic of "commuter" marriages, for example, where spouses live in different cities or even areas of the country because of their jobs. These couples only see each other on weekends or intermittently, and might be expected to have evolved a marriage style that enables each partner to pursue personal goals and at the same time have the emotional support of a spouse. One might also expect to find open marriages among many dual-career couples.

The O'Neills' hypotheses have not been widely tested. However, Wachowiak and Bragg (1980), surveyed twenty-seven married, college-educated employees of a southern university. Their subjects responded to a series of questions about their marriages designed to allow the researchers to place responses on a continuum which had the O'Neills' hypotheses at one end and traditional marital values at the other.

Only 21 percent of Wachowiak and Bragg's respondents subscribed to the O'Neills' idea of living for the here and now. Instead, they considered their marriages to be permanent. As for privacy, when asked whether there were places in their home that were the exclusive province of one partner or the other, 96 percent indicated all areas of the house were open to both partners. Ninety-six percent also agreed that: "Extramarital sex could never be tolerated in our marriage"; only 4 percent thought, "If handled properly, extramarital sex could be acceptable." As to the ability of the spouses to pursue their individual "identity," most of the subjects believed they and their spouse had compromised on their choice of life-style, that in fact it was a joint life-style. Only 15 percent indicated that each partner had developed a unique life-style.

The one area in which the subjects Wachowiak and Bragg studied did lean toward the open-marriage characteristics was with respect to equality of freedom and responsibility in the relationship. In particular, 90 percent of the respondents agreed that both parents should share the childcare responsibilities. The responses to questions relating to open and honest communication, role flexibility, and trust did not reveal any leaning toward either the open or the traditional end of the scale. The results of this study, then, would seem to suggest that the "open-marriage" concept has not caught on to any great degree, but certainly more research is needed.

A recent concept related to open marriage is that of "the open family." Some writers (McGinnis and Finnegan, 1976; Constantine, 1977) have proposed a family form that emphasizes flexible role responsibilities for all family members, regardless of sex or age, clear communication involving intensive negotiation, decisions arrived at by consensus, free expression of feelings, and mutual respect. Thus far this concept has received little attention from researchers, perhaps because it lacks the controversial aspects of open marriage (Macklin, 1980).

Sexually Open Marriages

As noted earlier, the aspect of open marriage that has received the most publicity is its apparent endorsement of mutually approved extramarital sexual relationships. But it is important to keep in mind what many commentators forgot in examining the O'Neills' work: having an open marriage does not compel the partners to have a *sexually* open marriage. That is something the partners must decide for themselves. In fact, Nena O'Neill has subsequently concluded that sexually open marriage is almost always destructive and she no longer advocates it. Our discussion here, then, does not refer to "open marriage" in the O'Neill's sense but rather to sexually open marriage in contrast to sexually exclusive marriage. Outside sexual relationships take one of two forms in sexually open marriages: swinging, often referred to as mate-swapping, and sexual openness.

SWINGING **Swinging** has been defined by Gilmartin (1977) as "legally married spouses sharing coitus with other legally married couples in a social context defined by all participants as a form of recreational convivial play" (p. 161). Swinging, then, is a jointly shared activity, though it seems to be initiated more often by the male partner than by the female. The sexual activity usually occurs in the presence of both spouses at one of the couple's homes. Sexual activity may occur in separate rooms or together in one room. Many swingers do not regard their activities as extramarital sex, and in fact, one of the general rules of swinging is that the partners are not to become emotionally involved with the outside sexual partners and are not to arrange liaisons outside of the swinging "party."

Gilmartin (1977, 1978) has discerned differences between the backgrounds of swingers and nonswingers. Swingers tend to be individuals who have less interaction with their families because of a background of less happy relationships with their parents. They are also more likely to have frequent interactions with friends. Typically, they began sexual activity earlier, married younger, and are more likely to have been divorced than nonswingers. They appear to have intercourse with their spouses more frequently than nonswingers do. Generally, swingers tend to be a highly permissive and sexually experienced group. They often rate their own marriages as happier than do couples who do not swing or couples in which one partner is having a secretive extramarital relationship. However, in considering these findings, one should take into account the fact that studies of swingers generally include only people who are actively involved in swinging and not those who have dropped out.

According to Gagnon and Simon (1974) most women engage in swinging to meet their husband's, not their own, sexual needs. They suggest that the wife becomes a token which can be used by the husband in sexual trading with other men. Sex with another man may also enhance the erotic image of the wife for the husband and perhaps increases her desirability.

Studies by Gilmartin (1978) and Bartell (1971) both conclude, however, that, despite their initial reluctance, women eventually seem to enjoy swinging more than men. One reason for this is that whereas wives often are pleased to discover that they are capable of having multiple orgasms at a swinging party, husbands find that they may only be capable of a limited number. Often, after a period of months, husbands, who had initially insisted on trying swinging, insist on quitting.

Swinging does not appear to be particularly widespread. Only about 2 percent of all couples have tried mate-swapping, and Murstein (1978) has estimated that about three-fourths of those who try swinging drop out within a year. One swinger admitted to Masters and Johnson (1974) that it was hard to find enough emotional energy to cope with the numerous relationships involved in swinging. And many men find that swinging creates performance fears as well as jealousy toward other men whom their wives might find more virile and sexually satisfying.

SEXUAL OPENNESS IN MARRIAGE **Sexual openness** in marriage is characterized "by a mutual decision of the couple to allow one or both partners to have openly acknowledged, independent sexual relationships with satellite partners" (Macklin, 1980, p. 912). What distinguishes sexual openness from swinging is that dating is done individually and the involvement is both sexual and emotional. Another contrast is that sexual openness is usually initiated by the wife. According to participants, the advantages of sexual openness include enhanced self-esteem, an increased capacity to give and receive love, a better ability to communicate, and an increased awareness of self and others. Among the problems experienced by couples experimenting with this concept are the need for continual negotiations about it, jealousy and possessiveness, loneliness, conflicts over the allocation of time between partners, and difficulties in adapting other aspects of the couple's social life to include this behavior (Macklin, 1980).

Studies have indicated that sexual openness in marriage can work only if there is a high degree of mutual affection, respect, and understanding between husband and wife; if the couple is able to cope with extremely complex and stressful emotional relationships; and if the outsiders have neither the need nor the desire to compete with the nonparticipating spouse for the primary affections of the participating spouse (Knapp, 1976; Knapp and Whitehurst, 1977; Macklin, 1980). In short, sexual openness in marriage is not a role to adopt casually. Ramey (1975, 1976) has identified a variant of the sexual-openness phenomenon which he calls "intimate friendship." This relationship is defined as a friendship which permits intimacy on a number of levels including the sexual level. Ramey focused particularly on what he termed intimate friendship "networks" which sometimes grew out of this life-style. In some cases, these networks were open-ended; that is, additional persons could be asked to participate. In others, they were closed. The characteristics of the relationships between the primary couple were very similar to those engaging in a sexually open life-style (Macklin, 1980). Table 14.3 contrasts intimate friendships with swinging.

Table 14.3 **Differences between Intimate Friendships and Swinging**

	INTIMATE FRIENDSHIP	SWINGING
Ramey compares the characteristics of intimate friendships as he has observed them with characteristics of swinging relationships in a way that clarifies the nature of each of these types of comarital involvement.	Individual activity	Couple-front activity
	Emotional and personal involvement	Emotional and personal involvement taboo
	Personal commitments	No personal commitments
	Long-term relationships	Usually one-night stand or very short-term
	Interpersonal-interaction emphasis	Sexual-activity emphasis
	Much discussion/intellectual sharing	Talk limited, generally shallow
	Intimate friendship philosophy permeates life-style	Usually male-dominant traditional marriage
	Considerable family interaction	Family interaction avoided
	Many kinship-type roles	No concerns except sexual activity
	Considerable business involvement	No business involvement
	Career ties and help	Avoid revealing professional information
	May invest money in joint projects	Discussing money matters taboo
	Tend to be politically liberal	Tend to be more conservative
	Lean toward peer marriage and gender-role equality	Swinging "compartmentalized"
	Below-average sexual frequency	Above-average sexual frequency
	Includes singles, divorcées, etc.	Almost exclusively a married-couple activity, but may include singles to make a couple
	Includes male and female homosexuals	Avoids homosexuals
	One out of three males bisexual	Extremely few male bisexuals
	Wide age range	Usually compressed to approximate age peers
	No youth cult	Heavy emphasis on youth and physical attractiveness

Source: James W. Ramey, "Intimate Groups and Networks: Frequent Consequence of Sexually Open Marriage," *The Family Coordinator* 24:4. Copyrighted 1975 by the National Council on Family Relations. Reprinted by permission.

THE HOMOSEXUAL LIFE-STYLE

The very idea of the homosexual life-style as an alternative to traditional forms of intimacy is highly controversial. For many generations, our society has regarded homosexuality as deviant; many people still regard it as such today. But any discussion of alternative life-styles would be incomplete without some mention of it, and for that reason, as well as because most Americans know very little about the homosexual life-style, we have included it here. Statistics on homosexuality are hard to gather, but contemporary sources estimate that 2 to 3 percent of all adult men and women are exclusively homosexual. Far more admit to some interest in people of the same sex. About half of the people in one survey agreed with the statement, "There is some homosexuality in all of us" (Hunt, 1974).

An Historical and Cross-Cultural Perspective

Until quite recently, homosexuality was viewed by American society as an abnormality. Classified as sex offenders by the law and viewed by the majority of Americans as dangerous, sinful, or at least deviant, homosexuals were forced to lead secret lives.

This attitude toward homosexuality is by no means universal. According to a survey of research data on seventy-six cultures by Ford and Beach (1951), forty-nine cultural groups approved of some form of homosexual activity. Among the Siwans of Africa, for instance, all men and boys were expected to engage in anal intercourse; those who did not were considered peculiar. Women and girls of many cultures stimulated each other's clitorises.

The idea that homosexuality is unnatural stems from the Judeo-Christian religious tradition which encouraged forms of sexuality that led to large, intact families and discouraged those that did not (Weinberg and Williams, 1974). Recent scholarship supports the idea that until the thirteenth century, the Catholic church did not view homosexuality as deviant.

In the United States, homosexuals have been persecuted and even imprisoned. This was true from the colonial period throughout much of the nineteenth century. Even during most of the twentieth century, homosexuals have faced harassment, if not outright persecution. With the advent of psychoanalysis homosexuality was categorized as a mental illness traceable to family dynamics in childhood. A dominating mother and a weak father were the usual explanation. Later theories introduced the idea of hormonal imbalance or negative sexual socialization—seduction by an older homosexual, for example.

It was only during the late 1960s and early 1970s that the belief that homosexuals were "sick" underwent serious challenge. Much of the impetus

In some societies, such as that of ancient Greece, homosexuality was regarded as life-enriching. The female poet Sappho, depicted here, wrote lyric poetry celebrating love between women.

for the change came from homosexuals themselves. Members of the "gay liberation" movement, which arose in the wake of the Civil Rights movement, argued that homosexuals are as diverse as heterosexuals and that homosexuality is not a "problem," but an alternative life-style. Pressure from the gay rights movement contributed to the decision by the American Psychiatric Association (APA) in 1973 to remove homosexuality from its list of mental disorders. The APA announced that psychiatrists would no longer try to "cure" homosexuals unless these individuals wanted to change their sexual orientation (Lyons, 1973).

Recent Research Findings

Research has tended to support the argument that homosexuality is not an illness. Weinberg and Williams (1974) found that homosexuality is a sexual pattern which is within the normal range psychologically. Homosexuals, like heterosexuals, vary widely in personality traits and psychological problems, and these features are not necessarily related to their homosexuality either as a symptom or a cause.

The increasing acceptance of the idea of homosexuality as an alternative life-style is suggested by the fact that studies done during the mid-to-late 1970s have stopped focusing on the causes and cures of homosexuality and have begun to focus on the life strategies of homosexuals (Macklin, 1980). For instance, there has been a great deal of recent research on the way homosexual couples live and interact together (e.g., Tuller, 1978; Harry and Lovely, 1979), which has established the variety and range of homosexual life-styles, the many similarities between homosexual and heterosexual couples, and the stability of homosexual couple relationships (Bell and Weinberg, 1978). Many of these studies revealed adjustment patterns in homosexual relationships similar to adjustment in marriages.

Masters and Johnson (1979) examined sexual response among homosexuals and found no differences between their responses and those of heterosexuals. They also reported a success rate for their treatment of sexual dysfunction among homosexuals that was about the same as that for heterosexuals (Macklin, 1980).

An area of research that was largely ignored until the 1970s was the lesbian and her community. Most earlier research on homosexuality focused on the male and largely ignored the female except to repeat the "butch/femme" stereotype (Macklin, 1980). Much of the research of the past decade has centered on the processes that lead women to identify themselves as lesbians and the implications of that self-identification (e.g., Moses, 1978; Tanner, 1978; and Lewis, 1979).

While little has been written on children raised by homosexual couples, there have been court cases over the custody of children by a homosexual parent. The press and television have featured stories on children and gay parents. In many of these presentations, homosexual parents have been shown in a favorable light. According to Nass et al. (1981), the two major fears have been that the children will become homosexuals and that bigoted heterosexuals will hurt them because of their parent's homosexual orientation. However, neither of these fears seem to have materialized for the majority of cases.

MULTILATERAL OR GROUP MARRIAGE

Another alternative to traditional marriage is called **multilateral** or **group marriage.** Group marriage involves a marriagelike arrangement among three or more adults in which each adult considers himself or herself married to at least two other partners (Constantine and Constantine, 1973). Although it is not legally recognized by the state, the marital relationship includes not only sexual privileges but also economic cooperation and public acknowledgment of the status and responsibilities of being married persons in the society. Thus group marriage contrasts strongly with the more transitory arrangements between swingers which are based solely on sexual relationships.

Characteristics of Participants

According to research by Joan and Larry Constantine (Constantine and Constantine, 1973; Constantine, 1978), the typical group marriage includes four adults and their children from the couples' existing conventional marriages. Most report their conventional marriages to have been happy. The adults are most often relatively young, liberal in their attitudes, and well educated. There is no particular distinguishing characteristic in their backgrounds. Participants exhibit a strong need for change, autonomy, and heterosexual relationships, low requirements for deference and order, and low levels of guilt. Sexual interaction among the participants is usually heterosexual, although they tend to have liberal attitudes toward homosexuality. At least half of the Constantines' sample had engaged in extramarital sex, and many had tried swinging and not found it satisfying.

Motivations for Forming Group Marriages

Among reasons given by participants for forming a group marriage, the most common is the desire to participate in a larger number of intimate relationships than monogamy permits. Group marriage has the potential to provide a sense of community or extended family not found in the nuclear unit. Moreover, by permitting an extension of the intimate relationship usually limited to one husband and one wife, group marriage can seem to provide more opportunity for personal growth. Other reasons given for the formation of group marriages include more sexual freedom, economic efficiency, and approval of the idea of group marriage. The participants view sexual intimacy as a necessary and central feature of group marriage (Constantine and Constantine 1973; Constantine, 1978).

Problems in Group Marriages

Once a group marriage has been established, certain problems may arise that may lead to the group's dissolution. Cooperative living demands more compromise than most individuals in our society are accustomed to making. In addition, there may be financial problems, personality conflicts, and the pressure of social disapproval. Another common source of friction is conflicting attitudes toward disciplining children. Jealousy can also be a problem, given the widespread cultural association between love and exclusive possession. This may be attributable to the fact that the original marriage partners retain strong ties to their original mates. These bonds seem to survive the breakup of the multilateral group (Constantine and Constantine, 1973).

The effects of the dissolution of group marriages on the participants seem to contrast with the effects of the dissolution of a two-person marriage. Constantine and Constantine (1972) studied sixty persons ranging in age from twenty-three to sixty who had been involved in group marriages that dissolved. The marriages included from three to six partners; some lasted as long as five years, but the median duration was sixteen months. The Constantines found that the main cause of breakups was incompatibility in basic personality traits. Without exception, these group marriages dissolved without creating serious disruptions. Financial issues and property settlements—matters that are frequently disruptive in ordinary divorce—were handled efficiently and satisfactorily by the members themselves.

While typically the original marital couples remained together after the group dissolved, in some instances it was difficult for them to return to their previous relationship. Group marriage tends to expose the interpersonal strategies on which particular relationships are based. Such strategies, once exposed, are not easily resumed. The couple may be faced with the need to develop an entirely new relationship, based on new definitions of their roles. The Constantines reported that despite the failure of the group, the participants were often better off for having participated in the experiment. "The vast majority evaluate the experience as beneficial even if difficult, and most state that they would try again, given the right people" (Constantine and Constantine, 1972, pp. 93–94).

It does not seem likely that group marriage will become a widespread alternative to traditional marriage. The difficulties in establishing it, the demands of maintaining it, and the well-established pattern of monogamy into which most Americans have been socialized make it likely that group marriage will continue to attract only a small group of people (Ellis, 1970; Constantine and Constantine, 1973).

COMMUNAL LIVING

The idea of communal living has a relatively long history in America. During the nineteenth century a variety of communal experiments were tried, with varying degrees of success. Among the best known was Brook Farm, which was founded in 1841 to provide a center for the application of transcendentalist views. The Oneida community, an unusually successful experiment in communal living and group marriage, was established in 1848 and endured for over thirty years. The early Mormons also practiced communal living, although they are better known for their practice of polygyny.

The late 1960s and early 1970s witnessed a new flowering of communal experiments in the United States. Many communes were organized to avoid, challenge, or replace the living patterns of urban-industrial society. Others sought to establish family systems and marital forms that would foster individual growth. Whatever the goals, communes tended to be formed by groups of people who believed they could create an ideal society in which their particular goals could be attained. One researcher estimated that at their height in the early 1970s there were 45,000 communes with some 755,000 residents (Conover, 1975). Most of these experiments—like their predecessors throughout history—did not succeed (Ruth, 1978). Nevertheless, communes are an important, recurring alternative to traditional marriage and family structures.

Forms of Communal Organization

By definition, communal living requires members to cooperate with each other and coordinate their activities in building a common life. Caplow (1964) has said that in order to survive as social organizations, communes have to maintain stability, social integration, and voluntary participation. Contemporary communes make decisions on how to achieve these goals in a variety of ways, so they resist being put into any neat classification system. However, based on an extensive analysis of data on contemporary communes which she compared with successful nineteenth-century communal groups, Kanter identified four ways in which communes approach decision making: she calls these anarchism, organized democracy, charisma, and managed democracy (Kanter, 1973). Kanter's assessment of the factors contributing to communes that have endured is shown in Table 14.4.

ANARCHISM Anarchism tends to be associated with communes that are in the early stages of development, with a membership that shares rejection of the larger society more than they share any affirmative philosophy. The desire to be free—of rules and of commitments—provides little basis for order or productivity. Less stable than other types, anarchistic communes are often transient. When the commune survives, it is usually because anarchy has given way to some other form of decision making, such as organized democracy or charisma (Kanter, 1973).

The story of Morningstar Ranch, a hippie commune established in California in 1966, is an example of the problems that accompany anarchism. When Lou Gottlieb, the founder of Morningstar, first declared his thirty acres to be open land and began permitting anyone who wished to build there, he intended the area be a sanctuary. He also felt that he was making a statement against private ownership of land. Gottlieb and his cofounders made no rules and set up no structure. It was their hope that at Morningstar people could live in freedom and in harmony with the land.

Since Morningstar was established at the same time that Haight-Ashbury, the original hippie district in San Francisco, was on the decline, the commune was immediately deluged by hundreds of people. The results were disastrous. The land was ravaged, buildings were wrecked, and, since it lacked sufficient sanitary facilities, the water became polluted. Local authorities closed the commune as a health hazard.

Table 14.4 **Comparison of Successful and Unsuccessful Nineteenth-Century Communities**

	SUCCESSFUL	UNSUCCESSFUL
NUMBER	9	21
	PERCENTAGE THAT ADHERED TO THE PRACTICE	

Kanter's study of characteristics of successful and unsuccessful nineteenth-century communities may provide some clues as to ways modern communes can ensure their survival. The nine communities designated as successful by Kanter had all lasted more than one generation. The shortest duration of any of this group was thirty-three years. The twenty-one communities designated as unsuccessful had a much shorter existence. The longest any of these lasted was sixteen years, never for more than one generation.

	SUCCESSFUL	UNSUCCESSFUL
GROUP RELATIONS		
Communal family structure:		
Free love or celibacy	100	29
Parent-child separation	48	15
Biological families not living together	33	5
Ritual:		
Songs about the community	63	14
Group singing	100	73
Special community occasions celebrated	83	50
Mutual criticism:		
Regular confession	44	0
Mutual-criticism sessions	44	26
Daily group meetings	56	6
PROPERTY AND WORK		
Communistic sharing:		
Property signed over to community at admission	100	45
Community-as-whole-owned land	89	76
Community-owned buildings	89	71
Community-owned furniture, tools	100	79
Community-owned clothing, personal effects	67	28
Communal labor:		
No compensation for labor	100	41
No charge for community services	100	47
Job rotation	50	44
Communal work efforts	100	50
Fixed daily routine	100	54

Source: Reprinted from Psychology Today magazine. Copyright © 1970 Ziff-Davis Publishing Company.

A description of Morningstar is essentially a description of its problems. It is impossible to speak of the commune's systems of marriage, childrearing, or decision making, since the commune was based on its lack of system (Roberts, 1971). The question raised by any anarchist experiment is whether it can exist without organizational structure and, if so, for how long. Lack of rules within Morningstar concerning work, interpersonal relationships, and economic cooperation led to such internal disorder that the commune could not withstand external pressure.

ORGANIZED DEMOCRACY   In communes that operate on a system of organized democracy, authority and responsibility are delegated to members in a well-defined, orderly manner. Organized democracy is characteristic of more complex communes (Kanter, 1973).

Twin Oaks, an example of this type, was started in 1967 by eight individuals who wanted to test the theories and principles of B.F. Skinner, the behavioral psychologist. Twin Oaks was designed after the commune described in Skinner's utopian novel *Walden Two*. According to Skinner's theories, all human behavior is externally conditioned; that is, it is determined by the environment. Behavior that is positively reinforced or rewarded will continue, while behavior that is not positively reinforced will be eliminated. Thus reward, not punishment, is the most effective tool for influencing behavior.

Twin Oaks began as an anarchistic commune but over time evolved into an organized democracy, reluctantly adopting rules and requirements in order to ensure its survival. By the early 1970s it was a highly organized community. There was an elected board of planners and a manager for each work area. No prestige was accorded the role of manager. Work was distributed on a credit for labor system and jobs were rotated. The reward system was based on personal preferences: a person who found a particular job undesirable received more credit for doing that job than someone who found it desirable. All work was considered equally worthy and individual accomplishments were deemphasized (Kanter, 1972).

Gender equality was one of the basic ideals of the community. Members even replaced the personal pronouns "he" and "she" with a neutral pronoun, "co," in speaking and writing (Kanter, 1973). What kind of relationships to form and whether or not to marry were decisions left to the individual. Children were cared for communally by the "child-raising manager" according to the principles of behaviorism. A goal of the communards was eventually to phase out the biological family, believing it to be an outmoded social institution (Roberts, 1971).

CHARISMA   In communes directed by charismatic leaders, authority is vested in a leader considered to be in some way extraordinary—possibly having divine authority—and whose teachings guide the basic beliefs of the group. Histori-

A Successful Nineteenth-Century Commune

Many people interested in understanding why some communes survive over long periods while others quickly fail have looked closely at the Oneida Community.

The Oneida Community was founded by John Humphrey Noyes, a minister whose doctrine of Perfectionism challenged the traditional Protestant view of man as a sinner. Noyes's teachings that Christ had already returned to earth and that humans were therefore capable of living a sinless life were considered to be heretical and his license to preach was revoked. Nevertheless, the doctrine of Perfectionism attracted followers, and by 1846 a community was established in Putney, Vermont, where Noyes's theories were put into practice.

The central teaching of Perfectionism was spiritual equality, and this idea was implemented in all aspects of community life. The economy of the group was collectivist; there was no private ownership; and monogamy—viewed by the Perfectionists as selfish—was replaced by sexual communism, whereby all adult females had marital privileges with all adult males in the community (Kephart, 1963).

Although the practices of the Putney Community were based on religious ideals, they shocked the outside world, and Noyes, charged with adultery, was forced to flee to New York State where he established a new community along Oneida Creek. The Oneida Community barely survived until one of its members, Sewell Newhouse, invented a steel trap. Production and sales of this trap, the best of its kind, became for many years the economic mainstay of the Oneida Community. The Oneidans also produced fine silverware, and the company they founded, Oneida, Ltd., is still in operation today.

What was life like at Oneida? All members of the community lived in one house. Although each adult had his or her own room, large areas, such as the dinning hall and recreation rooms, were communal. Work was shared and all were expected to participate. Jobs were rotated, so that everyone would have a turn at the more desirable tasks. This system proved to be an effective way of promoting harmony and satisfaction. Differences in natural ability were neither rewarded nor penalized, and no one type of work was awarded higher status than any other.

The Oneidans dealt with interpersonal conflicts and deviations from accepted behavior by a system called mutual criticism. Members who were considered to be deviating from group norms were required to meet with a committee to undergo criticism. The process, although painful, was regarded as cleansing. Mutual criticism eventually came to be used as a method of self-improvement, with those who had committed no offense volunteering for group criticism.

In order to achieve a perfect society, Noyes believed, only those who were superior both mentally and physically should bear children. He therefore instituted a system called stirpiculture whereby couples wishing to have children would be evaluated by a committee before receiving permission to do so. Couples not selected for stirpiculture were expected to practice birth control, which was accomplished by the difficult technique known as *coitus reservatus* (copulation without ejaculation). Because

(continued)

HIGHLIGHT 14.2   *(continued)*

this technique required considerable practice to perfect, younger men were often permitted to have intercourse only with women past the age of childbearing.

During the ten years in which stirpiculture was practiced, fifty-eight children were born. Infants remained with their mothers until the age of fifteen months. Thereafter they were cared for communally. A special relationship between the natural parents and child was considered to be out of keeping with the principles of universal love. Evidence indicates that the children born in the Oneida Community fared uncommonly well. As adults they reported that they had had a remarkably happy childhood (Robertson, 1970).

In 1879, the Oneida Community disbanded. As Noyes grew older, his behavior became increasingly erratic and he eventually fled to Canada. Leadership fell to his sons, but they lacked the charismatic quality of their father. Weakened by jealousies between factions, the community was unable to withstand the pressures from the outside, which by this time had become extreme.

Despite its eventual end, the Oneida Community remains an example of an alternative marital and family experiment that had exceptional success because of strong leadership, organization, and the commitment of its members.

cally, communes led by charismatic persons have been fairly common: Oneida was founded on the teachings of John Noyes, a Perfectionist; the Shaker community was founded by Ann Lee, considered to be divine. This form of organization is, of course, efficient, for one person can make decisions more swiftly and easily than many, but it carries with it the danger of authoritarian rule. However, charismatic leaders are not necessarily dictatorial, and historically they usually have not been.

MANAGED DEMOCRACY In a managed democracy, officials or managers exercise a degree of centralized authority, and the commune members do not participate in every decision. Thus, in this regard, managed democracies share some traits with communes centered on charismatic leaders (Kanter, 1973). An example of managed democracy is the Bruderhof.

A Protestant sect with Hutterite origins, the Bruderhof was established in Germany in the 1920s. Settlements are also found in Great Britain and North and South America. The three in the United States have about 800 members. Their religion and their commitment to living by its teachings form the backbone of the Bruderhof community. Members view themselves as a separate people and as one family. Their unity is emphasized in every feature of their organization.

Unlike many successful communes, the Bruderhof strongly supports monogamous marriage and the nuclear family. Families are large, and they form the unit around which many community activities center. Being single is difficult since both marriage and childbearing improve one's status. Despite its significant role, however, the nuclear family is not a self-contained unit. Childrearing is communal, and children are considered to be the children of all adults in the community. The relationship of the married couple is based on the spiritual brotherhood of the entire community and subordinate to the unity of the church. The marital relationship is thus regarded as more than a bond between two individuals; founded in the eternal, it cannot be broken. Married couples spend a good deal of time together, either alone or with their children, as well as in the work areas. One observer found that marriages in the Bruderhof seemed unusually happy (Zablocki, 1971).

Work and labor are shared in the Bruderhof. Although not all jobs are rotated, the emphasis is on work as service, an attitude which minimizes the importance of individual achievement and emphasizes cooperation. Property is shared, including personal property (members refer to "our cup," "our chair"), and money is not used (Zablocki, 1971).

Children and Communes

In general, one of the difficulties facing parents entering a commune is the reduction of their control over the child's rearing. Instead of one set of adult relationships, the child has many. This can also mean that instead of one set of rule makers and enforcers, there are many (Weisberg, 1975, 1977; Macklin, 1980). The effects on children raised in contemporary communes are hard to judge. For one thing, since most communes do not survive long, it is difficult to obtain a representative sample to study. The Family Life Styles Project at the University of California at Los Angeles is attempting to study children raised in a variety of alternative life-styles, including communes. While the project has had difficulties with its sample because of the shifts of individuals from life-style to life-style, the researchers have concluded tentatively that a child's motor and mental development do not vary appreciably according to family life-style. Nor, remarkably, does the interaction between parent and child (Eiduson, 1979; Weisner and Martin, 1979).

Urban Communes

Urban communes can be described using Kanter's categories. They, too, are voluntary, value-based, communal social orders (Kanter, 1972). However, most investigators have noted that the physical and social boundaries of urban communes are less clearly defined than when a group seeks a rural area to establish a new life-style. Urban communards are more limited in the extent to which they can reject the surrounding culture. For instance, the nudity found in many anarchistic rural communes would not be tolerated by city neighbors.

Berger, Hackett, and Millar (1974) indicate that urban communes are easier to start since all that is necessary is a rented house and a group of willing people. As a result, membership tends to be more fluid and participation often represents a less serious commitment to the communal ideal. Rothschild and Wolf (1976) noted the greater involvement of urban communards in the surrounding culture. Three of the six adult members of the commune they studied worked at competitive professional jobs, returning to communal living nights and weekends. Although several of the children had elected not to attend the local public school for that year, they were bored at home and looking forward to reentering school in the fall.

The Voluntary-Simplicity Movement

Alternative life-styles are developed to meet the needs of particular times. As we have seen, the social rebels of the 1960s tried a number of different forms, and their efforts are going forward even today. One interesting recent alternative is the voluntary-simplicity movement, which arose in response to the energy crisis and economic problems of the 1970s.

The voluntary-simplicity movement has its roots in the tradition of cooperation among the settlers on the American frontier: "cooperative individualism" one article called it (Cornille, Oransky, and Pestle, 1979). The movement calls for a return to the type of community spirit that would bring out whole communities to help a farmer put up a barn. Obviously, returning to rural conditions is not practical or desirable for most people today, nor do

The voluntary-simplicity movement has roots in the American past, when cooperation among families in such activities as barn-raising was widespread.

many of the alternative life-styles hold much appeal for the majority of Americans. So, the voluntary-simplicity movement focuses on cooperation among traditional nuclear families in contemporary urban or suburban environments.

As a life-style, voluntary simplicity emphasizes self-determination, practical living and work places, material simplicity, and ecological sensitivity. It emphasizes conservation and sharing of resources with other families. In some instances, people adopting this life-style may share a multi-family home, though not in communal fashion. The movement has a broader dimension than a simple sharing of resources; it also calls upon its followers to adopt a simpler way of life, one that, for instance, emphasizes reading and walking as recreation (Cornille, Oransky, and Pestle, 1979).

The voluntary-simplicity movement differs from some of the other alternative life-styles we have discussed in this chapter in that it does not require a real break with the concept of the nuclear family. In fact, it seeks to reinstate traditions central to the American past. But even though many of the other alternatives focus on deliberate breaks with tradition, they all share a common thread: the desire to improve one's life both individually and in relation to others.

SUMMARY

1. The purpose of this chapter is to explore some alternatives to traditional marriage and family relationships: singlehood, cohabitation, open marriage, group marriage, the homosexual life-style, and communal arrangements.

2. Remaining single is increasingly popular, although permanent singlehood is still chosen by relatively few people. Singlehood offers the possibility of greater freedom in many areas of living. Establishing satisfactory intimate relationships is perhaps the greatest need felt by singles.

3. Cohabitation is regarded by most sociologists as a stage of courtship, at least for never-married young people. For divorced people and the elderly, it may emerge as a long-lasting alternative to marriage. A primary attraction of cohabitation is the sense of intimate involvement without formal legal commitment. Cohabiting couples are similar to married couples in the dynamics of their relationships.

4. Homosexuality is coming to be regarded not as a social problem but as an alternative life-style. Homosexuals are as varied in their adjustment and personalities as heterosexuals. Recent research on homosexuality has been focusing on patterns of living and coping.

5. An alternative life-style that attracts a very small number of people is group marriage. People give as reasons for forming group marriages the

desire to participate in a larger number of intimate relationships, to gain a sense of extended family, and to gain more opportunity for personal growth.

6. Open marriage refers to a marital relationship characterized by functioning in the here and now, realistic expectations, respect for privacy, role flexibility, open communication and companionship, egalitarianism, pursuit of individual identity, and mutual trust. At present, the open-marriage concept does not appear to characterize large numbers of marriages.

7. Communes are formed by people who seek to create an ideal society in which their particular economic, religious, social, or political goals can be attained. Although most communes are short-lived, communal experiments have a long history and will undoubtedly continue. A recent variation on the communal idea is the voluntary-simplicity movement.

REVIEW AND DISCUSSION

1. What advantages might there be to living as a single person for at least some period of one's adult life?

2. If you have cohabited, describe the adjustments you had to make. For example, what arrangements did you work out concerning household tasks, telling your parents, sexual exclusiveness or nonexclusiveness, and the like? Do you think the experience helped make you aware of what marriage might be like?

3. Have you ever considered living in a communal setting? Why? If you would not like to be part of a commune, explain why not.

4. Do you think the concept of open marriage is one you would like to strive for in your own marriage? What aspects would appeal to you most? least?

5. Not much is known about the effects on children of being reared in alternative family settings such as cohabitation or communes. Can you suggest some possible outcomes for children in these settings—either positive or negative?

SUGGESTED READINGS

Bell, A.P., and M.S. Weinberg (1978). *Homosexualities: A Study of Diversity Among Men and Women.* New York: Simon and Schuster.

   Presents the results of a ten-year study of the sexual, psychological, social, and political dimensions of the homosexual experience as represented by the San Francisco Bay Area gay scene.

Gilmartin, B. C. (1977). "Swinging: Who Gets Involved and How?" In R. W. Libby and R. N. Whitehurst (eds.) *Marriage and Alternatives: Exploring Intimate Relationships.* Glenview, Ill.: Scott, Foresman, 1977.

Analysis and appraisal of spouse-swapping in a collection of essays arguing for some of the various alternatives to traditional sexuality and commitment in marriage.

O'Neill, N., and G. O'Neill (1972). *Open Marriage, A New Life Style for Couples.* New York: M. Evans and Company, Inc.

Based on the idea that partners in a marriage cannot be expected to totally fulfill each other's needs. Explains how two people, accepting one another as equals, can make their differences in interest and temperament work for them. Illustrates through examples how the average couple can develop an open marriage.

Stein, P. (1976). *Single.* Englewood Cliffs, N.J.: Prentice-Hall.

Through interviews and and statistical data, the author analyzes life-styles of single adults in America today and their experiences at work, in interpersonal relationships, and in society.

Weisberg, D. K. (1977). "The Cinderella Children." *Psychology Today* **10**:11:84–87.

Discusses the problems and benefits of children raised in urban communal households—problems such as too many rules and too many people ordering them to do things; and benefits such as learning responsibility, more bedtime stories, and more companionship.

Marriages and Families: Changing Values and Perspectives

Postscript

The preceding chapters in this book have demonstrated that marriage and family relationships in the contemporary United States are in a process of transition and that couples and families are confronting very different challenges from those that faced previous generations. The question arises, then, of what the future holds for intimate male-female relationships for the remainder of this century and into the next. In order to address this question, this postscript summarizes a number of important changes occurring in American marriages and families today. We believe that identifying and characterizing existing trends is the best means of determining what we are moving toward in the future. It should be noted that our discussion encompasses only a limited number of trends related to marital and family relationships or alternative forms of intimate relationships. The list of trends that we will discuss is not exhaustive by any means, but we believe that it represents the major ones affecting intimate male-female relationships today.

First, it should be restated that, although there is an increasing concern in our society about the stability of marriage, marriage is far from becoming extinct. Those who believe that the institutions of marriage and the family have been weakened point to the rising divorce rate, the development of alternative living arrangements to traditional marriage, and the increasing number of people who remain single. However, to look at marriage in a more positive light, one need only recognize that almost everyone in America gets married at some time or other. Among men and women born during the nineteenth and twentieth centuries, between

513

90 and 95 percent married at least once. In fact, the proportion is somewhat higher among women born in the twentieth century than among those born in the nineteenth century. Instead of focusing on the "decline" of marriage, then, it is perhaps more appropriate to ask, What is so attractive about the institution of marriage that over 90 percent of our population enter into it?

Most Americans think of marriage as a permanent, life-long commitment between two adults that involves maintaining a household and usually raising children. It is very different from the more temporary, changing relationships of dating and friendship. The stability and permanency offered by marriage have profound appeal for most men and women.

The attractiveness of the institution of marriage is also reflected in men's and women's evaluations of their general well-being. Married men and women are much more likely to report that they are, in general, "very happy" than men and women who are single, widowed, or divorced. Although, as discussed earlier in the text, men seem to be somewhat better off than women in marriage, marriage seems to make both men and women happier than other ways of living.

But while marriage continues to be the choice of the vast majority of people, there is no doubt that the nature of marriage and family relationships has changed significantly over the last several decades and is continuing to change in the 1980s. Among the major changes that have been mentioned in the text and that will help us in assessing both the present and future status of marriage in America, are the following: (1) the increasing length of marriage and smaller family size; (2) the larger proportion of married women working at paid jobs; (3) the increasingly egalitarian, or democratic, power and decision-making structure in the marital unit; (4) the increasingly prevalent trend toward cohabitation, or living together without a formal marriage contract; and, (5) the rising divorce rate.

INCREASING LENGTH OF MARRIAGE AND SMALLER FAMILY SIZE

Marriage as an anticipated lifetime commitment has been dramatically influenced by the increasing life expectancy of men and women in modern America. Though this is not an altogether recent phenomenon, the medical advances of this century which have contributed to increased life expectancy have clearly influenced the character of American marriage and family patterns. In contrast to a century ago when the average American could expect to live only perhaps fifty years, modern Americans can expect to live well into their seventies. This increased life expectancy means that those couples who marry and remain married will stay married considerably longer than the married couples of several decades ago. This increased life expectancy has prompted sociologists to add new stages to their models of the family life cycle.

Also, the modern American marriage can be expected to produce a significantly smaller family than past generations. Whereas a century ago the average couple had about six children, the average modern American couple has only about two children.

Given the longer life expectancy and increased "time in marriage" for most individuals and the smaller number of children in families, the marital experience of the next few decades can be expected to be quite different from that of previous decades. Marriages that last can be expected to last upwards of fifty years or more in many cases. One consequence will be that couples will spend a much smaller proportion of their married lives raising children. Couples marrying in the 1980s are likely to spend almost half of their married lives with no children at home (assuming, of course, that they remain married). The majority of this time will be when the children have grown and left home. Some of this time will be when neither partner is employed full-time due to retirement, although experts believe that employment until the age of seventy may soon become the new norm. The couple's ability to adjust to this lengthened "empty nest" stage will be a major factor contributing to their marital satisfaction and happiness in their middle and later years. Though research is not conclusive, several research efforts have indicated that marital satisfaction tends to be higher during this stage of the family life cycle. Much depends on the couple's continued intimacy and closeness during the earlier family life-cycle stages, the degree to which the wife in particular centered her life on childrearing and the homemaker role, and the ability to find new shared interests and activities in the postretirement years.

INCREASING NUMBER OF MARRIED WOMEN IN THE LABOR FORCE

As indicated throughout the book, a major change in American marriages during the last several decades is the increasing proportion of married women working outside the home. The data show that well over half of wives are now employed outside the home.

We are also witnessing the related phenomenon of women going back to college or seeking employment for the first time after their children are in school. This can be explained in part by the factors of longer life expectancy and smaller family size. For many women, the last child has started school by the time the woman is thirty years of age, leaving a period of thirty-five years of possible outside employment before age sixty-five. Even women who stay home until their children are launched still have fifteen to twenty years before the age of sixty-five that they are likely to spend in paid work.

The ability of the husband and wife to develop a compatible marital relationship while both are employed outside the home is very important to their marital satisfaction and stability. The redistribution of resources in the marriage and the movement away from traditional expectations of husband-wife roles are becoming inherent consequences of working and/or career-oriented wives. Researchers seem to have obtained consistent indications that working outside the home is good for women; wives who hold paying jobs apparently have fewer physical and psychological problems than wives who remain at home. However, the research remains somewhat inconclusive as to whether wives' employment is good for their marriages. Some studies have found that such marriages may be less stable and that the couple may have lower marital satisfaction. This may depend in part on whether the wife works solely out of economic necessity or whether she works for her own satisfaction as well as for economic reasons. In addition, the overload currently experienced by working wives—sharing the provider role while still having the major responsibility for housework and child care—may generate increased pressure and tension both for the wife and for the marital relationship. It may also cause conflict over who performs household and childrearing tasks. Alternatively, one could argue that the increased economic resources of the wife created by her working provide her with more bargaining power and more options. Research has shown that wives who have their own economic resources are less likely to feel that remaining married is their only choice.

To the extent that marital conflict does occur as a result of wives' employment, it could be debated whether this conflict is a permanent aspect of marital relationships in which wives work for pay, or whether it is only a temporary problem which will be resolved as society adjusts to wives partic-

As growing numbers of married women with children join the paid labor force, traditional notions of men's and women's roles in marriage are being readjusted.

ipating full-scale in employment outside the home. We believe that marital-adjustment problems related to wives' employment are of only a temporary nature. Our reasons for thinking so will be developed in discussing the next major change in modern American marriages: the move toward more egalitarian power and decision-making structures.

 FROM PATRIARCHAL TO EGALITARIAN MARRIAGES

Our culture's conception of how power and decision making are distributed in marriages has developed out of the basic tenets of patriarchal society. We have traditionally assumed that marriages and families should be male-dominant. Governmental, legal, religious, educational, and economic systems in the United States have historically reinforced the idea that it is the husband who should have primary authority and power in the family. The husband has traditionally been the marital partner supplying such necessary resources as money, occupational and educational status, and social-class status. The wife has traditionally been expected to assume the nurturing role, taking care of the home, the children, and the family's emotional needs.

As late as 1955, two sociologists—Talcott Parsons and Robert Bales—lent support to the traditional arrangement through their theory of role differentiation, or division of labor in American families. This theory specified two types of roles: first, the instrumental role which included those tasks necessary, or instrumental, for the family in maintaining contact with the broader society. Instrumental tasks include establishing an occupation, and thus an economic base for the family, involvement in political activities, social participation, and the like. This could be generally regarded as the breadwinner role, and it was characterized by Parsons and Bales as being the domain of the husband. The second role specified was the expressive role. The expressive role is that set of behaviors internal to the family and focusing upon maintaining smooth operation of the family unit. This could be generally considered the nurturant, caring role, and it was characterized as the domain of the wife. Although this theory has been challenged since its inception, it nevertheless operates as an indication of the pervasive nature of the traditional, patriarchal, male-dominant marital relationship.

However, our discussion of the increasing proportion of wives working demonstrates how this role division has increasingly broken down in modern American marriages. In fact, we are now seeing instances in which those role relationships have been reversed. There are marriages today in which the wife performs the breadwinner, or instrumental, role while the husband is employed outside the home only part-time or not at all and instead performs the child-care function and other aspects of the expressive role in the marriage.

As these role relationships have become less rigid, the distribution of power in the marriage has shifted dramatically. We are experiencing more and more marriages moving toward a democratic, egalitarian power structure in which the husband and wife participate equally in bringing in the resources and in all areas of decision making.

One result of this more egalitarian relationship, however, is the redefinition of who does what in the family. A division of labor has to exist in order for both marital partners to contribute equally to the relationship. In the past, that division of labor was generally predefined with certain tasks being "man's work" and certain tasks being "woman's work."

We have generally been socialized into these predefined patterns and have had few problems in adapting to them. However, as women become increasingly involved in paid jobs, traditionally "man's work," it becomes necessary to rethink this division of labor. Otherwise, what generally happens is that the division of labor in the marriage becomes stacked in favor of the husband, with the wife working at her outside job and still carrying the full responsibility for the household. This certainly leads to marital tension and possibly marital instability as the woman feels the need for a more equitable division of labor. In extreme cases, the woman perhaps feels that she cannot achieve and enjoy her more independent, instrumental activities of career seeking unless freed from the traditional role of wife with its necessarily expressive functions.

From the husband's perspective, the expectations of "wearing the pants in the family," as he has been socialized to believe is his role, may die hard,

The requirements of egalitarian marriage are likely to have profound implications for the socialization of children. Many parents will seek to foster both instrumental and expressive skills in their children regardless of the child's sex.

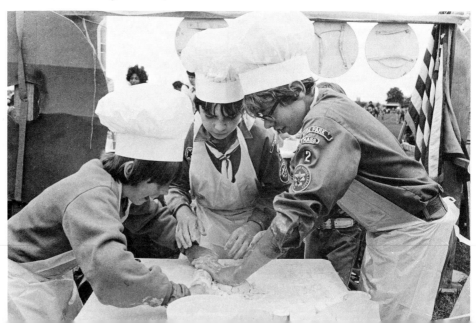

causing continued marital friction. Or, the husband may feel some resentment if his wife views her own career goals as being equally important or more important than his career goals. Or, the husband may be willing to redivide the labor in the family, but because of his socialization may feel that he is incapable of preparing nutritious meals, adequately caring for children, and performing other "expressive" tasks. Such changes in the marital power structure and division of labor certainly can generate marital tension and marital dissatisfaction.

This type of marital tension, however, may be viewed as temporary rather than permanent in nature because modern American society is still in the process of legitimizing this more democratic marital structure and accepting, if not encouraging, a redivision of labor, based on the needs of specific couples. This is only the first generation of marriages in which it is generally expected that both husband and wife will work and participate actively in the broader society. As men and women enter marriage in the next generation with the expectation that both will work, more couples can be expected to think through their marital roles ahead of time and tailor their marriages to their individual needs. When this happens, the personal satisfactions or dissatisfactions that each derives from work are likely to be crucial in the marriage, rather than the simple fact of there being outside work or no outside work. Since paid work brings more money, financial satisfaction should rise. When the wife likes her work, her increased satisfaction is likely to contribute still more to the happiness of the marriage.

INCREASING TREND TOWARD COHABITATION

A fourth significant change in modern male-female relationships—one that may have profound effects on marriage in the future—is the increasing popularity of unmarried cohabitation. Though there have probably always been instances of cohabitation in America, the number of couples living together without a formal marriage contract has increased greatly within the past two decades. The census data indicate that there was an eightfold increase in the number of cohabiting couples in the United States during the 1960s and that the number of cohabiting couples has continued to rise dramatically since then. The popularity of cohabitation on college campuses is well known, but the practice now encompasses all segments of the population. In fact, census data from the 1970s demonstrated that one of the largest increases in cohabitation by age group was in the sixty-five-year-old and older category. This, of course, was largely a result of the structure of the Social Security system, which drastically reduces payments to widowed persons who remarry. So, many elderly couples choose to cohabit rather than marry and face losing much of their Social Security income. For the other age groups, however, cohabitation is chosen more for personal than for economic reasons.

For our purposes, the most relevant question is, What impact does the increasing prevalence of cohabitation have on marriage in the United States? A major issue concerns whether cohabitation functions as a new stage in the courtship process, potentially replacing the engagement stage and functioning as a type of trial marriage, or whether it functions as an alternative to marriage. If cohabitation is a stage of courtship, its primary impact would be to delay the age at first marriage for the cohabitants. However, if it is an alternative to marriage, it could be expected to have the consequence of decreasing the proportion of the population entering into marital relationships. Though the answer is not clear, we can speculate from present research that cohabitation will increasingly emerge as a stage in the mate-selection process, with the major impact on marriage being the delay of onset of first marriage. The vast majority of cohabitants indicate that they plan to marry at some time, though not necessarily to their cohabitating partner.

The concept of commitment is especially important in viewing cohabiting and marital relationships. Unfortunately, the data at this time do not tell us if commitment works differentially in these relationships. It is clear that for many couples cohabitation goes far beyond a convenient sexual arrangement and demands a great deal more interpersonal involvement and commitment than its detractors would imply. It may be that the similarities between cohabitation and marriage are more numerous than the differences between them. Research has shown, for example, that the division of labor is similar for married and cohabiting couples. A major difference between the two arrangements, however, aside from the legal status of the relationship, is that males and females who cohabit seem to emphasize their interest in personal growth, rather than in interpersonal growth. Couples who marry seem more committed to the idea of interpersonal growth. However, the emphasis of cohabiting couples on personal growth could be a consequence of cohabitation relationships rather than a cause.

Another difference between marriage and cohabitation concerns the place of children. A primary function of marriage in any society is reproduction. Cohabitation, by contrast, does not have reproduction as a legitimate function. It will be interesting to see how this situation is resolved in the future. It could well be that marriage will become a two-step process, with society legitimizing cohabitation as the first step and parenting becoming a contractual option as the second step. We are already seeing cohabitation becoming legally accepted as evidenced by recent court decisions providing property settlements in terminated cohabitation relationships and the coining of the term "palimony."

In any case, cohabitation is more than just a passing fad, and it will, in all probability, continue to become increasingly prevalent in American society.

Cohabitation may, at some point in the distant future, become almost universal in the United States. If this happens, it will require a redefinition of marriage as we know it today. That time will be long in coming, however, and it is impossible to make an educated guess at what restructuring will be necessary.

INCREASING DIVORCE RATES

The last and most obvious major change affecting intimate relationships that we will consider is rising divorce rates. Certainly, the divorce rate is increasing over the past. Among women born from 1900 to 1904, about 12 percent of their marriages ended in divorce, and it has been calculated that about 40 percent or more of all marriages entered into in the early 1980s will end in divorce.

Ma ' people view the rising divorce rate with alarm. Indeed, divorce rates are the most frequently cited evidence of the decline of marriage and the family in the United States. However, mere numbers or percentages can tell us little about the reasons for and effects of rising divorce rates. Some things are fairly clear: first, the majority of marriages do not end in divorce; second, the vast majority of divorced people remarry; and third, only a small proportion of people marry more than twice. We are a long way from being a society of people who have rejected marriage or replaced it with a series of short-term relationships.

In Chapter 13, we discussed several factors as possibly contributing to the rise in divorce rates, but two other possible reasons for the increase in divorce should be considered. First, it may be that in our society people's expectations of marriage are too high. Some have argued that in our society the family has become less functional, and thus less important, because other social institutions—educational, religious, economic, and political—have taken over some of the primary tasks, or functions, of marriages and families. However, a major function of marital and family relationships includes providing a nurturant socialization environment for offspring, allowing personality expression, and relieving adult personality tensions in a nonthreatening atmosphere. This "caring function" has not been taken over by other institutions and, in fact, may have become more necessary in modern society as we have become more mobile, both socially and geographically. The data indicate that the average American family moves every four and a half years. These moves separate us from our kin and friends and make it more difficult to develop and maintain long-term friendships. When no other support systems are available, married couples have to turn to each other almost exclusively for love and support. Perhaps such a responsibility is beyond the capabilities of most marital units.

A second factor related to high divorce rates may be that as Americans have achieved a higher standard of living and relative affluence, their basic needs of food, shelter, and safety have been satisfied. This allows individuals to concentrate on trying to fulfill more personal needs. The recent emphasis on individual fulfillment is demonstrated by the large number of courses offered and books written on techniques of personal growth. This emphasis on personal fulfillment will cause some individuals to leave unhappy marriages and search for happiness in other marriages or in alternative living arrangements, such as cohabitation, communes, remaining single, and others.

It is especially important to note that individuals seem to be dissatisfied not with marriage per se, but with specific marital partners. This is evidenced by the fact that, within five years, most divorced people marry again. At least half of those who remarry manage to remain married, and their marriages are long-term.

The basic reasons for divorce are significant indicators of the future of marriage. If more people are getting divorced because more liberal divorce laws and more alternatives for women have made divorce easier, but not because intolerable marriages are increasing, that is one matter. But if the rising divorce rates occur because more marriages are intolerable or because less serious tensions are being resolved by divorce, that is something else. In other words, divorce, like marriage, can be a growth experience if it frees people to seek greater satisfaction and happiness, or it can be a damaging experience if it is a means of escape from tensions that are inherent in all interpersonal relationships. It seems unlikely that the number of intolerable marriages has increased. Rather, constraints against divorce clearly are loosening. Also, opportunities for a happy and productive life after divorce have improved as divorce has become more common. Thus, increased work opportunities for women and increased social acceptance of divorce have made divorce a reasonable alternative to a bad marriage.

IMPROVING MARITAL QUALITY AND STABILITY

What does all of this tell us about improving the quality and stability of marriage relationships? First, we need to recognize that the institution of marriage is changing and that change is not synonymous with decline. Second, we have to understand that traditional notions of husband-wife roles may not be appropriate for the time we live in. Marriages are more likely to succeed if individual couples are permitted to tailor their relationships to their specific needs. This includes a consideration of their desired life-style and work habits. It may also entail the verbal negotiation of the marital-role relationship before they marry. Third, parents need to encourage their children to take their time in selecting a marital partner. Many young people are coerced into marriage rather than making the personal "choice" to marry. We know that the best predictor of divorce is age at marriage: the younger the age, the higher the chance of divorce. Young people should be encouraged to maintain a degree of personal independence before entering into the responsibility of marriage. Fourth, parents, in long-term preparation of their children for marriage, should try to teach a wide range of skills to both male and female children. Fifth, parents should attempt to keep an open mind toward cohabitation and similar alternative forms of intimate relationships, recognizing that these nontraditional alternatives are also ways of seeking intimacy.

Marriage certainly is not a dying institution. However, it is changing. In the future, we will witness not only a change in marital structure and process, but also an increase in alternatives to marriage. If our primary concern is marital satisfaction and interpersonal happiness, we may find that different people seek and achieve these needs in varying ways. If marriage is a healthy and viable institution, as the authors think it is, it will continue to flourish.

The Family as an Economic Unit

Appendix

"Always have a plan. Leave nothing to chance."

NAPOLEON BONAPARTE

Since colonial times, the American family has changed from a unit of production to a unit of consumption. No longer are we growing it, making it, or doing without it. No longer is the whole family involved in serving the needs of a single enterprise. In fact, the majority of urban/suburban children have little idea of the production processes that provide for them, let alone have a hand in their success or failure.

To be a successful unit of production, yesterday's family had to work together. When a family's resources were not great enough to complete a project, often their community would provide the necessary manpower and special skills (Kramer, 1976). Today's family is part of a different social structure. The role of family provider requires earning money which is then used to purchase the things the family needs and wants. Instead of being indebted to our neighbors for their help in providing goods and services, we owe various financial institutions and businesses. And despite hard times, our financial obligations must be met. Yet, just as the producing family had to work together to survive, so must today's consuming family. Just as the successful producing unit had control of the means of production, so must the consuming unit have control over the means of consumption—money.

 MONEY IN MARRIAGE

The change in the family from a producing to a consuming unit has had profound effects upon the way people

525

view money, and, equally important, on the way they view themselves and others. Many people equate money with status and use it as a measure of intelligence, character, and worthiness. Those who are unable to "measure up" in the world of work are likely to be less well regarded by others and by themselves as well. Similarly, those who are very successful at making money tend to be judged as worthy, whether or not their personal qualities warrant this belief.

In the political and economic spheres, money has long been a symbol of power. It is also a source of power in marriage. Traditionally, the husband earned the money and for the most part decided how it would be spent. Even in marriages in which the wife worked, her income tended to be used for "extras." While her earnings helped the family, they were not regarded as essential. As a result, it was the husband who had more power in the relationship, for it was he who controlled the more valuable resources. Today this is considerably less true than it was even twenty years ago. As the number of households with two wage earners increases, this imbalance is gradually disappearing. Sociologists who have examined the issue of family power have found that wives who are employed outside the home tend to have more influence in family financial decision making and expect to take part in all other decisions that affect the family (McDonald, 1977).

Factors Affecting Attitudes toward Money

Perceptions about money are influenced by a number of factors. Perhaps one of the most compelling is the very nature of our society. Americans place a great deal of emphasis on the accumulation of material things. Our economy produces an abundance of goods, and its very existence depends on creating a market for these goods. Advertising assaults our senses daily, urging us to spend. Very often the implied message is that buying a particular product—a mouthwash, a breakfast cereal, a car—will ensure that others will love us. This is a powerful incentive, since it touches our most profound psychological needs.

Attitudes about money are formed first in the family. A family's particular financial situation deeply affects the way individual members come to think about money. For example, the person raised in a family of limited economic means is likely to have different perceptions of what is a necessity and what is a luxury than the person raised in a wealthy family (Donnelly, 1976). Often these ideas carry over into later life. Thus the person who came from a poor family but who later earns a high income might still be frugal about his or her spending.

Even within the same income levels, families may spend their money differently because they value different things. For example, one family will buy the best on the theory that it will last longer. Another will buy the least expensive because it has a low replacement cost. Yet both believe they are getting the most for their money. Personality differences can also affect attitudes toward money. Within a marriage one person may be a spender and one a saver. Or, the spouses may have different attitudes toward spending **discretionary income** (money available after necessities have been purchased). For one, spending this money on an experience (a trip, a cultural event, a gourmet dinner) is the most satisfying way of improving the quality of life. For the other, buying something that can be enjoyed every day (an antique, a couch, a piece of jewelry) is the best use of discretionary income. The conflict may start when they marry, but it is likely to be evident during courtship as well.

Ignorance about Money

Even though Americans feel that money is very important, a surprisingly large number of them have very little control over their finances. Many otherwise intelligent people cannot balance a checkbook, fill out a tax form, or tell which item at the supermarket is a better value than a competing item. Few couples enter marriage with a clean economic slate. Both spouses are likely to have outstanding debts, such as department-store charges, educational loans, and the expenses related to the wedding or honeymoon. In addition, many couples start their families when they are least able to afford it. The wife who has worked for only a few years delays and sometimes gives up her chances for advancement if she decides to take several years off to care for her children. The loss of her income can put stress on the family at a time when child-related expenses are especially high. Even if the wife does return to work soon after having a child, she is likely to find that a large portion of her income is now going toward child care.

Many couples lack an understanding of the kinds of financial management they will need over the course of their lives. Even spouses who are earning a substantial income may be ill informed about how to save and invest it. Should they invest in money market funds? Are stocks and bonds a good choice? What about investing in real estate? The choices are many and the right choices require that spouses examine their own needs and desires as well as becoming informed about money matters.

Of course, no family can have total control over its financial future even with the most careful planning. Changes in the national economy such as a recession or an energy-price increase that affects a particular industry can cost any individual his or her job. But even though the future is an unknown, families that evaluate their own economic circumstances and cooperatively plan for the future will be better equipped to deal with unforeseen events and chart a new course.

Money and Marital Conflict

Planning requires communication, and it is here that many couples have the greatest difficulty. Studies indicate that couples quarrel over money more than over most other issues and that economic stress is a major cause of marital instability. One national survey found that of the families surveyed, 54 percent argued frequently about money; of families that were hard pressed by money problems, the number that quarreled about money a great deal rose to 64 percent (Yankelovich, Skelly, and White, 1975). As shown in Table A.1, families' arguments about money covered a variety of topics. Being economically hard pressed is not necessarily synonymous with lower income, although those who are less well off are more likely to experience conflict. Even affluent families argue about money because they have not negotiated sound agreements about their finances. No one is immune from the emotional consequences of bad financial management.

Fights over money can also be part of a struggle for supremacy. As noted previously, until recently, in most families the husband earned the money and controlled its expenditure. Today, as a result of the increasing numbers of working wives, many women expect to have an equal voice in all aspects of the marriage relationship, including financial matters. Although decision-making authority may vary with income, age, and situation, across all categories the power of the husband in family purchasing decisions has declined (Green and Cunningham, 1975).

Holmstrom (1972) notes that some couples use a double standard in evaluating income contributions. If the husband's career is seen as primary and the wife's career as secondary, a double standard of cost accounting may develop. For example, one professional woman reported:

Table A.1 **Arguments about Money***

SUBJECT	PERCENTAGE
Money in general	59
Need for family to economize	47
Wasting money	42
Unpaid bills	38
Keeping track of where money goes	33
Saving for future	25
Borrowing money	17
Bad investment	10
Lending money	8

Source: Yankelovich et al., 1975, p. 45. Courtesy of General Mills, Inc.
* Based on those who say they argue about money.

CASE STUDY   *Money: His, Hers, or Ours?*

Her mother always told her that she needed to have some money of her own. "Traveling money," she'd called it. The only working woman on the block, her mother, a fourth-grade teacher, had always had a private bank account which she kept secret from her father. Never more than a thousand dollars, not very much twenty years ago and even less today, the money gave her the illusion of freedom, the sense that she could, if she had to, strike out with some independence. Or so she convinced her daughter, Nancy.

The thirty-five-year-old woman recalled that she set up her own private bank account almost immediately after she married Jack, who'd just graduated from law school, in 1964. She was working as a secretary in a publishing firm at the time.

They arranged their finances so that his salary paid the rent for their one-bedroom apartment, took care of the weekly household expenses and the bills and went into the savings account that would become the foundation of their future long-term financial planning. Her salary, meager in comparison, was banked toward a down payment for a house, vacations, and any unexpected expenditures.

She did the food shopping, took his suits to the cleaners, his shirts to the laundry, and paid the cleaning woman out of the money he gave her every Friday. Still she managed to shave off $5 to $10 a week which she slipped into her account on payday.

Ten years and two kids later, she had close to $5000 in the secret account and a guilty conscience as well as a better job as a technical editor and increasing resentment that her salary was being used for the family's extras.

Jack's salary was still paying for the mortgage, taxes, child care, the two second-hand cars, household expenses, insurance, and medical bills. They banked half of her wages and used the other half to pay for their vacation/investment home.

"Psychologically, the effect was devastating. Despite my firm career commitment, I felt like my weekly paycheck merely helped out the family. Like what I did wasn't as crucial. All of this was complicated, of course, by my slush fund," she explained. "Finally I realized we had to talk about it. That's when it hit me. We hadn't ever sat down and talked about money frankly."

For Class Discussion

1. When both spouses are working, do you think it really makes any difference how each partner's earnings are allocated? Could Jack and Nancy have avoided conflict if they had pooled their earnings rather than regarding them as "his" and "hers"?

2. What evidence is there in this case study

that financial arrangements can reflect the power structure of a marriage? How does Nancy's reaction to how her paycheck was spent relate to her increasing commitment to her job?

Source: *Boston Globe*, July 11, 1977. Reprinted courtesy of The Boston Globe.

> [My husband] sat down and figured out one day ... that when you consider household help, second car, professional clothes, a higher income bracket, the whole bit—and I was earning in the $10,000 a year category at that time—that I was making about 10 cents an hour. So that you can't say that it's a matter of bringing home a good second salary. (Holmstrom, 1972, p. 100)

This is actually a faulty system of accounting. For one thing, the items mentioned in the quote—household help, a car, clothing—have an independent desirability. That is, while they may be necessary for the wife to work, they are also desirable in themselves. Despite this, these items are subtracted from her income. By contrast, things that the husband's job requires which also have independent desirability—his car, for example—are not included in an argument that it is not profitable for him to work (Holmstrom, 1972).

In some cases where both partners work, the pendulum has swung to the other side. Some working wives tend to regard their husbands' earnings as "our" money and their own income as "my" money (Donnelly, 1976). Like yesterday's male breadwinner, today's female breadwinner sees the earning of money as conferring the right to decide how it should be used.

Changing economic and social conditions can also create stresses that lead to conflict over money. In a period of high inflation and unemployment, where people are losing jobs or the purchasing power of income is dropping, families feel great pressure about not being able to maintain a desired standard of living. This pressure often translates into arguments. For many couples in their later years, inflation has meant that money saved for travel and recreation is being spent on living expenses. Frustration over this situation may erupt in arguments between the spouses. The prevalence of blended families creates many economic pressures, including the possibility that each partner may resent the money being spent on the other partner's children.

What sets apart the married people who don't argue about money? The major factor seems to be that these couples talk to each other and don't have secrets about money. The Yankelovich, Skelly, and White survey (1975) showed that of families that fight a lot, half are unable to communicate freely with each other about money matters. Failures in communication may be rooted in both different spending patterns and personal anxieties. People attach subjective meanings to spending. They are buying security or status, love or authority. These intangibles are even harder to discuss than money because they are part of each partner's personality. Couples who can remember that attitudes about money are the result of previous cultural and social experiences will have an easier time discussing and resolving money problems.

 THE FINANCIAL LIFE CYCLE

At appropriate points throughout this book, we have used the family life cycle as a convenient tool for analyzing phenomena. The life cycle concept is particularly useful when examining how a family should plan for its financial obligations because it reveals the needs at each stage and the flow of financial resources the family can expect to have at these stages. Families or couples who take the time to analyze their plans using the family life cycle model may decide to alter the timing of some key events, such as childbearing, in order to avoid unnecessary pressures (Gross, et al. 1980). Table A.2 provides two ways of looking at the financial life cycle.

Major Financial Events

Virtually overnight, the newly married couple is thrown into the position of making important financial decisions that will affect the long-term pattern of their lives. The early years of the family life cycle, when both partners are working and childless, are financially the most carefree. However, during this

Table A.2 **Stages in the Family Financial Life Span**

FAMILY LIFE COURSE	FAMILY OR HOUSEHOLD LIFE SPAN[3]
Period of establishment[1] Childbearing and preschool: from birth of first child until that child enters school	Foundation years: 0–4 years of marriage or of establishing one's own household
Elementary school: oldest child in elementary school	Developmental years: 5–19 years of marriage
High school: oldest child in high school	
College (optional stage): oldest child in college	
Launching period[2]: from time oldest child leaves home for a job, for marriage, or to establish his or her own household until last child leaves home.	Assessment, achievement, and readjustment years: 20–39 years of marriage
Period of financial recovery[1]: between departure of last child and retirement	
Retirement to death of both spouses	Retirement years: 40+ years of marriage or of maintaining one's own household

Source: D. Gross, E. Crandall, and M. Knoll, *Management for Modern Families*, 4th edition, © 1980, p. 67. Reprinted by permission of Prentice-Hall, Inc., Englewood Cliffs, New Jersey.
[1] Term from Howard F. Bigelow, *Family Finance*, rev. ed. (Philadelphia: J. B. Lippincott, 1953).
[2] Term from Evelyn Duvall, *Family Development*, 4th ed. (Philadelphia: J. B. Lippincott, 1971).
[3] Adapted from Cleo Fitzsimmons, Dorothy Larery, and Edward Metzen, *Major Financial Decisions and Crises in the Life Span*, North Central Regional Research Publication No. 208 (Lafayette, Ind.: Purdue University Agricultural Experiment Station, 1971). Reprinted courtesy of North Central Agricultural Experiment Stations (Purdue University).

period decisions about buying or renting a home, choosing a car, and buying furniture and clothing are sometimes made without much thought for the future. As a result, some couples enter the next stage, the addition of children, already in debt. With the coming of children, the wife either stops working or provides for child care out of the income she earns. Food, medical care, clothing, toys, and baby-sitters all contribute to a list of expenses that grows along with the baby.

As we noted in Chapter 10, the total dollar cost of raising a child of a moderate-income family to age eighteen was about $73,000 in 1980. These costs include food, clothing, medical care, housing, and many miscellaneous expenses. When the cost of four years at a public university is added, the total rises to over $85,000. Private education at any level increases these costs substantially. With these figures in mind, it is obvious that college poses a financial crisis for many families. As a result of inflation and increased energy costs, these expenses are unlikely to lessen in the foreseeable future.

The next major change in the family financial life cycle occurs when all of the children have finished their education and are no longer living at home. Depending on the size of the family's outstanding debts for the children's education, this may be a period of relative affluence. Assuming that both spouses are working, and have worked throughout their marriage, they will be reaching their peak earning years. Also, their home, furniture, and appliances will soon be paid off. At this point, the couple should use any surplus income to build up money for retirement. One in four retired persons have no income other than their Social Security checks. In recent years, because of inflation it has been virtually impossible for a retired person to live above the subsistance level on Social Security alone.

The effects of inflation and increased energy costs have altered much that has been written about the financial life cycle in the past. For instance, ownership of a single-family home may well be permanently out of the price range of many couples. Elderly people who do own a home may find themselves hard pressed because they cannot keep up with high energy costs on a fixed income. Inflation and high-cost energy were not things the average family could have foreseen in, say, 1965. But that family could have laid the groundwork for effectively coping with these pressures in the 1970s and 1980s by the planning and communication they started then.

MEETING FAMILY ECONOMIC NEEDS

In order to remain a stable unit, every family must meet certain needs. All families need food, clothing, shelter, certain household goods, and transportation. (Financial security is also an economic need; it will be discussed in the next section.) Many families also have a long list of things they want. For example, most Americans seem to regard a television set as an essential item even though it is not a real necessity. Similarly, parents regard toys for their children as a necessity rather than as a luxury. But whether or not a family can have more than its basic needs will depend in large part on how well the family is able to handle its finances. Here we will consider the basic economic needs of families today.

Housing

Housing is the single largest expense for most families. Although there are variations on each type, housing basically falls into two categories: rented and owned.

Despite today's high rents, the average middle-income family pays less for housing when they rent than when they own a home. On the average, renters paid about 23 percent of their annual income for gross rent in 1975 (U.S. Department of Commerce, CB77-64). The cost of rental housing covers not only the rooms but also certain utilities (usually water), upkeep and repairs to buildings and grounds, the property taxes, and some depreciation of the value of the property. Renters have no **equity** (the money value of a property

In the past, couples usually bought a modest first home; then, as their income increased, they "traded up." Current economic conditions, however, have led many homeowners to remodel their home. They believe they will probably not be able to afford a different home later on.

or of an interest in a property) in the housing unit. Their capital is kept fluid, and they have no obligation for upkeep, maintenance, or property improvement.

Some people feel they are more secure financially because they own. While taxes and mortgage rates rise, increasing land values tend to offset these costs. In addition, a home is a type of forced savings program, and in twenty years the home owner will have built up considerable equity. Home owners also have certain income-tax advantages over renters, since they may deduct real-estate taxes and interest on the mortgage loan.

A **mortgage** is a contract between the borrower and the lender in which the borrower agrees to repay the lender the money lent plus interest over a period which usually ranges between twenty and thirty years. When the borrower takes out a mortgage, he or she is using the house as **collateral** or security for the mortgage. The value of the property guarantees the lender's money. The amount a buyer can afford to put into a house is the amount he or she can borrow, plus the cash available for a down payment, minus all settlement costs. The U.S. Department of Housing and Urban Development says that the value of owner-occupied homes in 1975 was about twice the income of their owners, though the ratio varies considerably according to income level (U.S. Department of Commerce CB77-64).

Banks use a rule of thumb to determine what they will lend: a debt-free person who has money for a 20–30 percent down payment on a home can

---

HIGHLIGHT A.1   *Home Buying Trends*

National surveys conducted by Investors Mortgage Co., a national mortgage insurance organization, sampled at random 2500 mortgage applications from across the United States for the years 1970, 1979, and 1980. Some of the findings from these surveys suggest that major changes in home-buying trends have occurred:

☐ In 1970, home buyers without children numbered slightly less than 6 percent. In 1980, the number had jumped to 78 percent.

☐ In 1970, people thirty-five or younger accounted for less than 10 percent of home buyers. In 1980 they accounted for 68 percent.

☐ Dual-worker families bought 59 percent of the homes in 1979 and 57 percent in 1980. The drop apparently reflects the economic problems facing the country. Although no comparable figures are available for 1970, conservative estimates range from 10 to 15 percent.

☐ Single persons accounted for less than half of 1 percent of home purchases in 1970. By 1980, 24 percent of home purchases were by singles, with women buyers outnumbering men.

Source: *Boston Globe*, April 27, 1981.

afford to spend between 25 and 30 percent of his or her monthly income on the property including the mortgage costs, real-estate taxes, and fire insurance. On an income of $36,000 a year, a buyer could safely allocate $750 a month for these items, $250 of which might go for taxes and insurance and $500 for interest and repayment of the principal. It is this payback rate which determines how much money the mortgage company or bank will loan. By shopping around individuals can save money. Even a difference of half of one percent in the interest rate can mount up over a twenty-year period.

It used to be that home owners had a real advantage when they took out a mortage at a fixed rate. In effect, they gambled that the inflation rate would drive interest rates up and devalue the dollar so that they paid a relatively lower rate of interest and repaid the bank with dollars that were worth less than the ones they borrowed. Because of inflation in recent years, banks were not getting the maximum return on their money from this arrangement so they instituted the **variable rate mortgage** which allows them periodically to adjust the rate of interest on the mortgage. This arrangement benefits the bank by enabling it to keep pace with rising interest rates. It offers no real benefit to the home buyer.

In terms of cash outlays for a house in addition to the down payment, a buyer must cover settlement charges and lawyer's fees. These costs vary by locality and can be high. Knowing these figures, as well as the amount of mortgage money they are eligible to borrow, a couple can go house hunting.

Food

Shopping for food, like deciding what kind of housing to select, involves personal choices about life-style and individual needs. For example, buying convenience foods and items from the bakery or the delicatessen adds considerably to a family's food budget, but the extra cost may be worth it to a couple who are pressed for time. The important thing is to be aware of the trade-offs being made rather than spending money and later wondering where it went.

Psychologists tell us that food purchases, like purchases of all consumer goods, are not simple matters. Some people view food buying as simply the purchase of nutrition, while others are in effect buying status, love, or perceived convenience. Many people buy food on an emotional basis, making purchases according to whim rather than planning them. The foods a family buys tend to reflect both its level of income and its life-style. For example, poor families do not generally buy steak because they cannot afford it. But a well-off family might also decide not to buy steak because its life-style precludes eating animal protein. In economic terms, purchasers should try to become aware of their food patterns and to maximize the value they are purchasing as they would any other product.

In an affluent society like our own, people purchase food and clothing to satisfy psychological needs as well as physical needs.

Clothing

Like food, clothing is often bought not simply for practical reasons but for the psychological benefits it brings to the purchaser. For example, many families invest heavily in new clothes for a wedding or other major family event despite the fact that they may not need new clothing of that type. The same family may otherwise have no interest in stylish apparel. Likewise, teenagers (and adults!) may insist on buying designer-label jeans which offer no greater value than nondesigner jeans, but which are regarded as more stylish or prestigious.

If practical considerations of longer wear and easier care weigh greater than matters of style, there are a number of shopping strategies that can extend the clothing dollar. Clothing expenses can be reduced substantially by taking advantage of after-season sales. However, the shopper must beware of phony markdowns and close-outs, and the substitution of lower quality sale merchandise for the store's regular line. The wise consumer buys only what he or she would buy anyway, even if it were not on sale. Buying something that won't be used is certainly no bargain.

Some excellent values are featured in surplus shops and manufacturers' outlets. It is important to know something about fabrics and construction and to read labels for material content and laundering instructions. Even when the initial expense of a washable dress or suit is more, the upkeep may be so much less that it pays in the end.

"Big-Ticket" Household Purchases

Choices of "big-ticket" household items depend a great deal on a family's sense of its own stability of taste and on its life-style. One family may look upon its purchase of an oriental rug as an investment it will use for a lifetime. Another family may see rugs as simply floor coverings and look for something that is less expensive but serviceable and that can be replaced without another major investment.

Furniture is one category where buying good quality is the most economical choice. Poor quality goods quickly break or wear out. Good quality furniture can last a lifetime and may even grow in value. Because there is generally no urgency in selecting furniture, householders should take time to plan.

Of course, furniture of some kind is a necessity. For "make-do" pieces, to use until a couple can afford what they really want, it is wise to investigate sources of supply other than furniture stores. Warehouse sales may offer bargains, especially on damaged items. The classified section in the newspaper lists furniture for sale, and some flea markets sell used furniture.

One merchandising swindle to be aware of is what is called a "bait and switch." Stores using it often specialize in selling furniture by the room. An ad reads something like "three rooms of furniture for $498." The person who responds is shown the advertised furniture stacked in a dark corner. The salesperson then leads the prospect to a different area with better lighting— and higher prices. Store operators count on the fact that many customers are unable to resist showing the salesperson that they can afford and have the taste to appreciate the "better" merchandise (often outrageously overpriced). Appliance and carpeting dealers also have their share of swindles. Carpeting seems to lend itself particularly well to shady dealing.

Buying appliances can be confusing unless the customer is aware of the differences in various brands and models. Like cars, major appliances (refrigerators, dishwashers, dryers) can be the basic model, or they can be loaded with options. The more options, the more expensive the appliance. A family needs to decide if the convenience of a clothes dryer with ten cycles warrants the added cost. A recent consideration in buying appliances is the amount of energy they consume. Many appliances now feature devices that help the user save on energy use. Appliances often can be purchased on sale, at considerable savings. The magazine *Consumer Reports*, which features independent test results on a great many products, is a useful guide when buying household appliances. *Consumer Reports* also publishes a yearly *Buyer's Guide* to consumer items.

Transportation

With the exception of a place to live, an automobile is usually the most expensive item any family buys. The actual cost of a car includes the purchase price, financing costs, gas, oil, maintenance, license, registration, taxes, and insurance. Thus, buying the car is just the beginning of a series of purchases of automotive products and services. Some of these purchases vary markedly in cost in different areas. A car owner living in a metropolitan area may pay more than $1000 for insurance coverage while the same person in a rural area would pay a few hundred dollars for the same coverage. Insurance costs also vary with the value of the car being insured and with other factors such as the age of the owner and the owner's driving record.

Many people, of course, never own a car and depend instead on public transportation. For city dwellers, the cost of parking the car and the difficulties of city driving may make car ownership a burden rather than a convenience. In this case, it is often more economical to rent a car for occasional trips than to own one. But for people living in suburban and rural areas, a car may be a necessity.

In the past, many people bought cars for the psychological satisfaction they provided as much as for transportation. But with the cost of gasoline more than tripling since 1973, Americans have become more sensitive to the costs of their romance with the automobile. Car owners are driving less, and car buyers are looking more at high gas mileage, serviceability, and durability than at comfort and style.

BUYING A CAR   A new car is generally not a very good investment. Its value declines 25 to 30 percent the first year, another 18 percent the second year, and another 14 percent the third year. At the end of three years, it is worth, at most, 40 percent of what it cost new. The depreciation of a used car is less, but the maintenance costs may be more. With any older car the question must be asked, at what point is the saving in a car's depreciation balanced by the increasing costs of maintaining the aging car? Statistically, annual maintenance costs become greater than the annual depreciation half way through the fourth year. Buying a two-year-old car to drive for two years and trade in on another two-year-old car avoids the enormous initial depreciation of the first two years as well as the rise in repair costs.

These days compact cars are more expensive than they were a few years ago, especially when compared to the big "gas guzzlers." The smaller, more economical cars are also holding their value longer than larger cars, and people are tending to keep them longer than they used to.

Before looking at cars, the shopper should determine the most he or she can afford to pay. To do this, deduct from expected income for the next 12 months one's obligations for taxes, debt payments, and the necessities of living. The remainder is the amount of cash available for monthly payments on a car. The total can be found by multiplying the monthly amount by the number of months one is prepared to be paying on the car, and adding this to the total trade-in expected on the present car—if there is one. If this total is not sufficient to buy the car selected, the shopper may then decide to use other resources such as savings to help pay for it (DeCamp, 1972).

The general rule is that cash in hand plus the trade-in should equal at least one-third the cost of the car, with the other two-thirds to be paid off in monthly installments. Conservative buyers finance no more than half of the total cost and plan to pay off the debt within two years, but with the high costs of new cars, according to the Federal Reserve Board, one out of five automobile loans is for more than three years (*Christian Science Monitor*, March 18, 1976).

 PLANNING FOR FINANCIAL SECURITY

If you asked twenty people at random whether planning for the economic security of their families was important, they would all agree it was, but almost all of them would then admit that in practice it was far down their lists of things to take care of. Fixing a rattle in the car; buying a new refrigerator to replace the one that's on its last legs—things like this frequently demand the dollars that might have gone into some form of investment to provide for the future. You can see a new refrigerator and you may notice the rattle is gone from the car, but except for periodic statements, you can't see or appreciate investments and savings programs. Also, many people think that dying young or developing a disability that keeps them out of work is something that only happens to others.

Until very recently, life insurance has been the most popular approach to providing family security, and it remains a good way for many to force themselves to save money and build an estate. However, many people work for companies that offer pension plans and life insurance as part of their employee-compensation package. These fringe benefits have caused many families, especially those with two incomes, to reappraise basing their financial-security strategy on life insurance alone. A general consensus has developed that a family's strategy should include a variety of programs.

The government has taken an interest in encouraging citizens to plan for the future and has authorized the establishment of a variety of investment accounts that allow people, in essence, to set up their own supplementary pension funds and defer the tax on the money invested in them until they are retired and in much lower tax brackets. These devices are called Individual Retirement Accounts (IRA's) and Keogh Plans.

The reason the government wants people to save for their retirement is that, as we've seen, the income of retirees relying primarily on Social Security barely reaches the poverty line. Also, many company and union pension plans offer less protection to retirees than they may seem to on the surface.

In short, whether one looks at financial security as something that will take care of the retirement years or as a means to ensure the smooth functioning of the family after the death or disability of one or both wage earners, it is important to begin planning life insurance, pension, savings, and investment strategies early in the family's financial life cycle.

Savings

Savings as a concept emphasizes preparing to spend in the future. It is a very different means of putting aside money from **investment** which emphasizes purchasing an asset (an article like an antique or an intangible like stock) and watching its value grow.

There is no single answer to the question of how much money to save. However, having some cash reserve should be a high priority for every individual and certainly every family. How much to save or what to save for are goals that are likely to change as the family life cycle progresses. Partners should decide jointly on these goals and work together to achieve them (DeCamp, 1972). As a minimum, however, a family should have cash available to cover living expenses for three months should an emergency, such as unemployment or illness of the wage earner, arise. Savings accounts are both a safe and a convenient place to accumulate this cash reserve.

The kind of institution—commercial bank, savings bank, savings and loan association, or credit union—chosen for saving is not nearly so critical as the interest rate offered. In choosing the place to put savings, depositors should consider their overall financial situation and what services might be needed in the future. An established relationship with a bank or a credit union can result in more favorable loan terms, for example. Depositors should also consider what other services the bank makes available. Some banks offer checking accounts completely free of service charges; some impose a monthly charge unless a minimum balance is maintained. Other banks may offer what are often called "Now" accounts which are a hybrid between checking and savings accounts. These checking accounts pay interest on the amounts deposited in them, but they usually require the depositor to maintain a minimum balance.

"Now" accounts are not a good place to put savings because they typically pay the lowest interest of any of the accounts offering interest. Regular savings accounts offer somewhat better rates, but the best rates are paid on accounts that restrict the depositor's ability to withdraw funds for a certain period without a substantial interest penalty. These accounts are often called **certificates of deposit.**

Most financial counselors recommend that a specified amount for savings be deposited regularly. One painless way to save is through a payroll-deduction plan at work. Or arrangements can be made for a bank to transfer a set amount from a checking account to a savings account automatically each month (Blodgett, 1971).

Investment

Once a family has accumulated sufficient cash to weather an emergency and has arranged for life insurance, it should look into other forms of investment. While savings accounts do pay interest, the amount the dollar earns in interest is less than the amount lost through inflation. The major emphasis with investing, such as the purchase of bonds, stocks, real estate, commodities, or collectibles, is on the distant future and upon long-term growth of capital. None of these investments should be made by the uninformed. Unlike savings accounts, which are insured by the federal government, investments are by definition risks taken by the investor. There is always the possibility the investment will be bad and the money lost. The most important things for the investor to do are to get the advice of trustworthy people in the field while at the same time educating himself or herself in the particular area.

SECURITIES   The term **securities** usually means bonds or stocks. A **bond** is evidence of the issuer's debt. All levels of government and a variety of corporations issue bonds in return for money. Each bond has a date of maturity when it is scheduled to be repaid. Each bond bears an interest rate fixed when the bond is sold, with interest payable twice a year. Bonds vary in risk from the extremely safe to the highly speculative. The riskier ones usually carry higher interest rates to persuade investors to buy them. Investors can make money in two ways: through the interest paid and through selling the bond for more than they paid for it.

A **stock** certificate is evidence of ownership of a share in the business issuing the stock. If a company has 1000 shares of stock and an investor holds 10, that person owns 1 percent of the company. If the company doubles in value, the share's value doubles. If the company's value declines, the share's value declines. Two other factors enter into the value of the stock as an investment: (1) Many stocks pay dividends. These are paid at management's discretion and can be raised or lowered depending on company profits. (2) There is also the possibility of a gain or loss through a change in the price of the shares. The company does not control the price. Instead, the price is determined by what people are willing to pay at a given moment in a public trading market such as the New York Stock Exchange. However, this price is generally a function of the value of the company in terms of what the company is earning and is anticipated to earn.

COMMODITIES, PRECIOUS METALS, AND COLLECTIBLES   Commodities, precious metals, and collectibles are not for the faint-hearted or for those who cannot afford to lose much, if not all, of their investment. **Commodities**, which are things like grain and meat, require a high degree of sophistication on the part of the investor. Prices can fluctuate dramatically, and large paper profits can turn into real losses in a matter of hours. The same is true of gold and silver.

"Sure-fire" collectibles like figurines and commemorative medals are far from certain to increase in value, especially if they are not truly limited editions. Even if they are, someone else is going to have to want them—something the investor should always be sure of. This is an area that has had more than its share of fraudulent activity. Salvador Dali, the famous artist, made a very substantial profit by signing thousands of blank sheets of paper which were then sold to printers to produce "limited edition" prints and lithographs. When this was discovered, it was thought to have had the effect of diminishing the market for all Dali works in those media.

 BORROWING AND CREDIT

Until very recently, Americans did not approve of buying on credit except when the purchase was of some item—a house or a car—for which they simply did not have sufficient cash on hand. Now people analyze the credit markets to make advantageous use of money to buy assets. Usually people try to borrow money at a fixed rate of interest, preferably a low one, and repay the loan later with dollars whose real value has declined because of inflation, and if the speculator has been very lucky, at a time when the cost of borrowing money is significantly less than the current rate. Again, this is not a game for the uninformed. For most of us, borrowing will remain something we do only when we must. But credit and its abuse are another matter. Credit has become almost an American vice with virtually everyone having his or her own plastic money to make purchases regardless of the immediate availability of cash.

Borrowing

Borrowing refers to the use of someone else's money for which there is a charge—**interest**. It can be combined with overhead costs and called a service charge, a fee, a carrying charge, or a finance charge. Today, there are few places where credit may not be obtained. Some credit is, in a sense, free. Often, plumbers, carpenters, doctors, dentists, and others provide a service, do not bill until the end of the month, and allow the individual several more weeks to pay the bill. Stores sometimes offer free charge accounts so long as the bill is paid in full within thirty days after it is sent out. The costs of deferred payments are included in the prices charged for the service or item, so this credit is paid for whether or not it is used. If the buyer does not pay the bill within the time set by the store, the store usually adds a hefty interest charge—often 1.5 percent per month—to the balance.

The danger of charge accounts is that they make buying seem very easy. The buy-now-pay-later approach has trapped many inexperienced or undisciplined consumers. When the bills come in they cannot pay them within the allotted thirty days, and the credit charges begin to pile up.

Credit costs vary a great deal from place to place. Under the Federal Truth in Lending Law, every credit agreement must clearly state both the annual percentage rate of interest plus any other costs of borrowing and the total dollar finance charge. An interest rate of 1.5 percent per month may sound easy to pay, but when the account runs on for a year, the annual rate is 12 times 1.5, or 18 percent. In other words, it costs $18 to use $100 worth of credit for a year. Shopping for low credit rates is important both for revolving credit accounts and for borrowing cash. The type of loan sought has a direct bearing on the cost. A mortgage may cost from 13 to 17 percent annual interest. A debt-consolidation loan from a finance company operating under state small-loan laws may cost from 24 to 48 percent. In other words, to borrow $400 for a year, the borrower may agree to pay back $500 or more (DeCamp, 1972).

OBTAINING CREDIT   Another factor in obtaining credit is the lender's assessment of the individual's ability to repay. If the lender thinks the person is a good credit risk, the interest rate is more likely to be favorable. Job, family situation, and credit rating are all examined. Ironically, a totally clean financial record (no previous loans) is a negative factor. Lenders would prefer to see that a person has repaid a previous debt on schedule. So there is reason to take out a bank loan early in a career, repay it on schedule, and thus establish a good credit rating for future borrowing (Garrison, 1976).

WOMEN AND CREDIT   Factors that affect one's credit rating include how long one has been employed at one's current job, how long one has lived at a particular address or in a particular community, one's marital status, and, despite laws to the contrary, one's gender. Women often have a more difficult time obtaining credit than men, particularly newly divorced or widowed women whose previous financial transactions have all been in the husband's name. If credit or a loan is refused, individuals now have a right to know the contents of their credit-information file. By supplying additional information or correcting misinformation, they may be able to get the unfavorable decision reversed.

While the credit situation for women has improved considerably in the last ten years, it can still be a difficult process. One way a woman can avoid problems is to retain credit cards in her maiden name, thus keeping a separate credit identity. To some, this may seem an unpleasant reflection of their view of the stability of their marriages, but it is a wise precaution in the event of an unexpected death. However, some states require a woman to choose which surname she will use at the time the marriage license is issued. These states may not allow her to use both names. In any event, however they choose to do it, women should retain an independent credit identity after marriage.

Types of Consumer Loans

INSTALLMENT BUYING **Installment buying** is one of the most widespread types of consumer credit. Repayment is made in regular monthly installments usually over a period of one to three years. Once the buyer's signature is on paper, he or she is obligated to pay periodic installments on the purchase price plus high financing costs. An article bought on time remains the property of the creditor until the final payment is made. If a payment is late, the creditor may ask for immediate payment of all outstanding principal and interest. If the buyer does not pay, the creditor may repossess the article and keep a portion of the money already paid on the account. The revolving charge account is similar to installment buying in that regularly scheduled repayments must be made. It may be used like a monthly charge account as free credit, but when the bill comes due it changes to a long-term credit account at a fairly high interest rate (Blodgett, 1971).

BANK ACCOUNT LOANS Many banks offer "overdraft" checking accounts. When a check is written for more than the account's balance, the difference is charged as a loan. Passbook loans are available from savings and loan associations and savings banks. Only customers who have money on deposit can borrow and only up to the amount on deposit.

PERSONAL LOANS Money for a vacation, education, medical expenses, or bill consolidation may be obtained in several places. A person who belongs to a credit union would be wise to start there. A **credit union** is a cooperative association, frequently of company employees or trade-union members, which makes loans to members at low interest rates. Other lenders to investigate are commerical banks. They can be relatively flexible about structuring the size and payments to the customer's needs. They are the biggest lenders of all, 40 percent of all installment credit in America. A final, last-resort, source of money is a finance company. They will take more risks and are more lenient in their requirements for granting loans, but the interest rates they charge are correspondingly high (Blodgett, 1971).

FINANCIAL PLANNING AND MANAGEMENT

In one way or another, we all plan our finances. The style may vary; the time we spend on it may differ; and the amount of involvement of persons outside the family may not be the same, but it's something we can't escape.

When one is just starting out and, say, living in a studio apartment, it is easy to plan. But with marriage and, perhaps, a second income, a house, and children, matters become more complicated. To keep detailed inventories and to maintain the kind of precise control that is possible as a single is very difficult. This is especially true of single-parent households where the family finances may depend in some part on the ex-spouse. Still, it is worth the effort to develop limited inventories of assets and liabilities and spending plans—regardless of the complexity of the living arrangements. Experts in all areas of personal and family finance are readily available, and every family should consult with a trusted expert, particularly when tax and investment decisions have to be made.

We have not dealt with taxes here because it is such a complicated area and is so dependent upon individual circumstances that generalizations may not be useful. However, potential tax liability is an important factor in any financial plan. It is also an area where expert help can save a family a good deal of time and often can save them money. The person a family chooses to help with tax preparation should be someone who is available year round for advice and not someone who disappears on April 15. Even if a family has someone to help with taxes, spouses should attempt to fill out the forms themselves to see what the Internal Revenue Service is interested in. It also provides a good opportunity for couples to examine their financial position and to develop intelligent questions for the tax adviser.

Finally, one vital part of any financial planning—whether it is for a single or a couple or a family—is a will. No adult should be without one, and it should be reviewed annually and when there is a major change in family circumstances. The problems caused for their survivors by persons who die without a current will can be enormous and can cost the estate a great deal of money. Worse, it can deprive the surviving spouse and children of money that should go to them. Tax time is a good time to review the will because of the tax implications of financial transactions for the estate. In the sections below, we will look at some basic devices which can make the financial-planning process a little easier.

Inventory of Assets and Liabilities

The first step in financial planning is to find out what you have and what you owe. That is done by drawing up a list of **assets** and **liabilities**, and netting them against each other. Assets would include the cash you have in your wallet or in bank accounts, the value of your life-insurance policies if you can cash them in, and the money you have lent to others, as well as other items of the same nature. Other assets would be equity in your house, stocks, bonds, other investments, and personal property. Weighed against those are liabilities. These include outstanding loans, charge accounts, and the like. A current statement of personal assets and liabilities is useful not only in planning one's own finances. It might be useful in filing insurance claims in case of fire or theft. It can help in establishing whether or not you would be eligible for a loan.

In estimating the value of assets, it should be remembered that they are worth not what was paid for them but what the owner can reasonably expect to get if they are offered for sale. If assets exceed liabilities, the financial planner is on solid footing. If the balance sheet shows as many or more debts than assets, then it is time to curtail spending and reorganize spending habits. Assets and liabilities should be reviewed each year to see how the picture has changed. This check will show whether a person or a family is accumulating equity or slipping further into debt. Small variations are not important; rather, the focus is on the long-term increase of assets over liabilities. No family should expect an increase in real net worth every year. Extraordinary expenses, like money that suddenly has to be invested in a family business or the arrival of college tuition bills, can halt the steady progress of the family's net worth. These fluctuations emphasize the importance of planning with the family financial life cycle in mind, as well as the economic picture for the area the family lives in. It also shows how important it is to plan expenditures carefully.

The Spending Plan

Financial planning involves directing the flow of cash in and out. Each person must direct income where he or she most wants it to go. This involves setting priorities. In matters of economics, everything a person does involves choosing between alternatives, and choosing one eliminates the possibility of the other. In money management, the technique for defining the choices and setting priorities is called a **budget**. A budget does not tell what to do with money; it merely sets forth the alternatives. If the decision is made to buy a car, what will that mean in terms of saving for a vacation or buying a dishwasher? A budget also is indispensable in providing a record of where the money is going. When actual expenditures are compared to planned expenditures, the budget

Table A.3 **Plan for Family Spending**

	INCOME, SET-ASIDES, AND EXPENSES	AMOUNT PER MONTH	
Sample budget forms may be changed by adding or deleting categories to suit your family's needs.	TOTAL INCOME		$_____
	Set-asides:		
	Emergencies and future goals		$_____
	Seasonal expenses		_____
	Debt payments		_____
	Regular monthly expenses:		
	Rent or mortgage payment	$_____	
	Utilities	_____	
	Installment payments	_____	
	Other	_____	
	Total		_____
	Day-to-day expenses:		
	Food and beverages	$_____	
	Household operation and maintenance	_____	
	Furnishings and equipment	_____	
	Clothing	_____	
	Personal	_____	
	Transportation	_____	
	Medical care	_____	
	Recreation and education	_____	
	Gifts and contributions	_____	
	Total		_____
	Total set-asides and expenses		$_____

becomes both a record and a plan (DeCamp, 1972). A sample plan for family spending is shown in Table A.3.

STEPS IN BUDGETING   Budgeting involves four basic steps.

1. List annual or monthly income from all sources.
2. List all fixed expenses, the expenses a family or individual must meet. These include taxes, rent or mortgage payments, premiums on insurance, and debt payments.
3. List semifixed or variable expenses. These expenses are absolutely necessary but their cost can vary. They include food, clothing, transportation, and medical expenses.

4. List optional expenses over which the individual or family should have complete control. These items include recreation, entertainment, and luxury goods and services.

The fixed and variable expenses represent the family's major living expenses. If the estimated basic cost of living, plus debts, taxes, and other fixed expenses equal or exceed projected income, there is nothing left over for optional purchases and nothing to put aside for reserves and investments. There may even be too little to cover various unexpected expenses not itemized in the plan. At this point, it is necessary to reexamine the tentative spending plan. Are there heavy debts because too many things are being bought on installment? Perhaps the problem is much less serious. Overly large sums for food or clothing may be included because the consumer has no real idea what these things cost. Anyone not sure how much to allow for variable expenses may want to begin the budgeting process by keeping a detailed record of current spending for two or three months. Monthly totals for the various categories can be compared and used as a basis for determining where to cut, if necessary (Mork, 1972).

Allocating available funds to optional expenses in a family budget should take into account all members of the family. If the family discusses money and financial planning in a spirit of openness, children will develop an awareness of and competence in economic matters.

A spending plan is basically a yearly plan. Many of the largest expenses, like taxes or insurance payments, are due only once or twice a year. Others, like doctors' bills, occur at random. Still others, like food, are substantially the same month in and month out. There are also peak spending periods like Christmastime or vacations. In well-managed financial plans, there are periods when income can be accumulated for the next round of heavy spending. Therefore, in building a sound spending plan, it may be necessary first to consider total expenses on an annual basis. Later this plan may be refigured to fit a monthly or weekly paycheck (DeCamp, 1972).

Since living costs have been rising every year, and income also varies, no budget can remain an exact guide. Furthermore, family needs change as the family moves through the life cycle. Therefore, a budget must be revised yearly to fit the particular family pattern. Using the old budget and the records of family spending for that period to compare amounts planned with amounts actually spent will indicate ways the next year's plan can be drawn to better serve the needs of the individual budgeter or the family unit.

An important part of financial management is keeping accurate, complete records of money coming in and going out. They are invaluable for timing new purchases, for using credit successfully, for preparing income-tax returns, and for making health-insurance claims, as well as for planning the next year's budget.

Evaluating the Family's Life-Style

Financial planning is not done in a vacuum. Decisions have to be made about what kind of life-style the family really wants. Over time, these ideas may change, and the family's financial planning should reflect the new concept. These are not the kinds of decisions that are made in an annual review of the family finances, but are ones that evolve. A decision to alter the family's way of living may become final in the process of planning, but it is not usually a product of the process.

Often, a decision to alter the family's pattern involves short-term costs, but these may well be offset by the satisfaction gained from the new way of living. In any change a family contemplates, the highest priority has to go to the degree of personal satisfaction the new can provide over the old. Financial considerations, particularly if they have little relation to emotional needs, should not play a major role.

There is an old Scottish adage that one's marriage is not something to be examined but accepted. The truth behind this bit of folklore is that the more one looks at his or her marriage, the more may appear dissatisfying about it. The same thing is true of one's life-style. There are choices to be made and values to be considered, but it is fruitless and emotionally taxing to persistently question a family's way of life. Instead, these choices need to be made a part of the family's growth together.

Impact of Crises

Even with the most careful planning, no family can entirely avoid the impact of an unforeseeable crisis. One wage earner may lose a job, thus placing all the burden on the other. One may lose pension benefits because of a poorly written employment contract. A child may fall ill and require hosptial care.

Vulnerability to crisis is somewhat variable according to class. The affluent are usually better able to weather an economic disruption, assuming they are not overextended before it occurs. But for the working class and the poor a crisis can wipe out resources and destroy a family. These are the groups that are most vulnerable to changing economic conditions.

Often family financial crises are not rooted in the economy but in the health of one of the family members. When illness or accident strikes, the effects can be far more devastating to the fabric of the family than unemployment or underemployment, and the impact can seriously damage the physical and mental health of other family members.

In any crisis, most families can turn to kin or to outside agencies for help. But no matter how much assistance others can provide, the ability of the family to survive depends on its own strength. The systems of mutual support—emotional and financial—have to be in place before the onset of the crisis. They must have been built up through communication, understanding, and planning. Family members accustomed to dealing openly with routine emotional and financial matters—the kinds of things that come up every day in every family—will be as well prepared as is possible for crises.

SUMMARY

1. The main purposes of this appendix are to show why financial matters are important in marriage, to illustrate how financial choices can be made intelligently, and to outline the steps involved in financial planning.

2. Couples quarrel more over money than almost anything else. Attitudes about money and how to use it are a combination of cultural, social, and economic influences. Our culture influences us by its emphasis on accumulation of material things. Ethnic, religious, and geographical backgrounds and differences in personality influence our feelings about money. In addition, conflicts over money may be the result of power struggles, inability to communicate effectively, or lack of knowledge needed to make sound spending and saving decisions.

3. When making either long-term or short-term purchases, consumers can make intelligent decisions if they follow three basic steps. (a) Study the pros and cons of various aspects of the situation or product, such as owning a home compared with renting, or whole-life compared with term insurance. (b) Become familiar with the product—its value or usefulness as well as comparative prices and the relation of price to quality. (c) Plan ahead in order to take advantage of sales or special opportunities.

4. If ready cash isn't available at the time a family wants to make a purchase, they can borrow money by taking out a loan or they can use other forms of credit. However, credit also costs money, and easy credit can be a trap. Consumers should limit credit purchases so they won't get buried under bills they can't pay.

5. Individuals and families can gain and keep control of their resources and maximize the value of their income by financial planning. The first step in financial planning is to take an inventory of assets (what you own) and liabilities (what you owe). The difference between the two is net worth. The next step is to direct and control the flow of cash by making a budget which sets priorities and defines the choices the family wishes to make. The third step is to keep accurate and complete records of money coming in and money going out. This information is an aid to making a realistic budget or spending plan for the following months or years.

6. A family needs to keep itself informed about economic trends in the country and its own community so that it can plan intelligently. This

information, as well as the family's individual financial situation, should be updated regularly.

REVIEW AND DISCUSSION

1. Were you or are you actively involved in your family's financial planning? Do you think this is a beneficial experience for children and young adults? Why or why not?

2. Consider your attitudes toward spending and saving money and those of a friend. In what ways are they similar? different? What do you think accounts for the differences?

3. Do you think married couples should have individual checking accounts or joint checking accounts? What are some of the considerations in deciding how to handle this phase of money management?

4. In what ways is money linked with power in our society? How is this link manifested in marriage?

5. What are the major stages in the financial life cycle? How can families help prepare themselves for the expenses that occur at each of these stages?

SUGGESTED READINGS

Consumer Reports.

Magazine published monthly by the Consumer's Union, a nonprofit organization. Presents independent test results evaluating packaged food, clothing, automobiles, appliances, and many other products for quality, durability, safety, effectiveness, and price value. Excellent resource when making any major purchase.

Donnelly, C. (1976). "How to Stop Arguing about Money." *Money* **5**:1, pp. 24–27.

Explores the problems of arguing about money in a relationship. Includes opinions of marriage counselors and techniques for handling money conflicts.

Garrison, M. L. (1976). "Credit-Ability for Women." *The Family Coordinator* **25**:3, pp. 241–248.

Explores the area of credit for women and problems of discrimination that women encounter when applying for credit. Also offers some procedures for women to follow to establish credit.

How to Prepare Your Personal Income Tax Return. Englewood Cliffs, N.J.: Prentice-Hall.

An annual publication intended to help individuals and families prepare their tax returns. Keeps up-to-date on changes in tax regulations.

Porter, S. (1980). *Sylvia Porter's New Money Book for the 80's.* New York: Avon (paper).

Expanded and updated edition of the author's popular book on personal finance and consumer economics. Well organized and readable.

# Glossary

Abortion. The termination of a pregnancy by removing the embryo or fetus from the woman before it is capable of independent existence. An abortion may be surgically or chemically induced or it may occur naturally (a miscarriage).

Adoption. Voluntary assumption of legal custody of a child who is not biologically one's own.

Aggression. Hostile or injurious behavior toward another, including verbal attacks, gestures, bodily responses, and failure to respond, as well as actual physical attempts to harm another.

AIDS (artificial insemination with donor sperm). Artificial insemination with sperm from an anonymous donor; frequently used when a husband's sperm production is inadequate.

Alcoholism. A psychobiological disease characterized by physical addiction to alcoholic drinks, the compulsion to which is extensive enough to adversely affect behavior.

Alienation. Withdrawal or separation of an individual from the values of the society. A sense of powerlessness and inability to control one's destiny.

Alternative attractions. Other persons, relationships, or commitments outside a relationship that compete with its attractions.

Amnesics. Drugs used medically that erase the memory of pain.

Amniocentesis. A fetal chromosome analysis performed between the fourteenth and sixteenth weeks of pregnancy; used to determine if certain chromosomal abnormalities are evident in the fetus.

Analgesics. Drugs used medically to decrease the sensation of pain.

Androgens. Hormones produced by the testicles in males and by the adrenal glands in both sexes, influencing the development of secondary sexual characteristics in males (deep voice, hair on face and chest, etc.) and essential to experiencing sexual desire in both sexes.

Androgyny. Behavior in which traditional characteristics of men and women are merged and there is no gender-role differentiation.

553

Anesthetics. Drugs that block all pain sensations, either by producing unconsciousness or by blocking the neural transmission of pain sensations to the brain.

Annulment. Legal pronouncement that a marriage is void and does not exist.

Anus. An opening at the rear of the body through which wastes are excreted from the large intestine. Also an erogenous zone.

Aphrodisiacs. Foods or chemicals that are thought to increase sexual desire and the enjoyment of sexual activity.

Artificial insemination. A procedure by which sperm obtained under medical supervision by masturbation are introduced into the vagina with a syringe so that fertilization might take place; impregnation of a woman through artificial rather than natural procedures.

Assets. Things of value owned by a business or individual, such as cash or real property.

Attractions. The forces that impel people toward a relationship.

Banns. A public announcement, especially in church, of a proposed marriage, to give those who may object to the marriage an opportunity to make their objections known.

Barriers. The restraining forces that keep a relationship intact when one partner wishes it ended.

Bartholin's glands. Two small mucus-producing glands located on each side of the vaginal opening; they contribute a small amount of lubricating fluid late in sexual arousal.

Basal body temperature. Body temperature at the resting stage upon waking in the morning; prior to ovulation there is a slight drop in temperature, with a slight increase following ovulation. Helpful for more precise and effective use of rhythm method.

Betrothal. A mutual promise or contract between a woman and a man for their future marriage; an engagement.

Bilineal. Traced through both the female and male lines instead of just one of them.

Birthrate. The number of births per year per 1000 population. Used in making comparisons of the rates at which populations are reproducing at different points in time or in different societies.

Blaming. Indicating a pattern of ineffective communication in which any effective exchange is blocked by one partner excessively criticizing or interrupting the other.

Blended family. A family group resulting from the remarriage of divorced persons, so that stepparent relationships are established and children from two families may be blended into one. Also known as a reconstituted family.

Bloody show. The discharge from the cervix of the protective mucus plug, and thus an indication of the onset of labor.

Bonds. Certificates representing a loan of money by the purchaser to the issuer (as when a citizen purchases a government bond). The issuer repays the principal amount within a given period of time, paying interest on the principal periodically.

Breech presentation. A baby's position at birth when it is delivered buttocks down or feet first, rather than the usual headfirst position.

Bride price. A gift of money, goods, or property from a man or his family to the family of the bride at the time of the marriage.

Budget. A written plan for coordination of resources and expenditures, showing amounts of money available for, required for, or assigned to a particular purpose.

Bundling. A courting custom in colonial America, by which an engaged couple would spend the evening or the whole night lying together, fully dressed and physically separated by a board or feather bolster.

Caesarian section. An incision made through the abdominal wall into the uterus to deliver an infant in cases when some condition prevents delivery through the birth canal.

Career. The sequence of a family's progressive fulfillment of social roles as family members grow older, from family formation to dissolution; history.

Certificate of deposit. A savings account that restricts the depositor's ability to withdraw funds; pays a higher interest rate than some other savings accounts.

Cervical cap. A rubber contraceptive device, smaller and deeper than the diaphragm, which fits securely over the cervix and may be left in the vagina from one menstrual period to the next.

Cervix. The narrow, slightly protruding lower end (neck) of the uterus with a narrow opening which connects uterus and vagina.

Child abuse. Intentional behavior of a parent or a custodian which causes lasting physical and psychological injury to a child; an active form of mistreatment of children.

Circumcision. The surgical removal of the foreskin of the penis, generally for hygienic reasons, performed in our society shortly after birth. In other societies and cultures, this may take place later in the boy's life, for ritualistic or religious reasons as well.

Clitoral hood. The fold of skin partially covering the clitoris.

Clitoris. A small, very sensitive erectile organ in the female, consisting of a glans and shaft, which lies under the upper portion of the labia minora. Of similar embryonic origin to the male penis, it is the prime organ for sexual arousal in the female.

Cognitive orientation. In the context of social exchange theory, a person's beliefs, values, and attitudes; determined largely by socialization experiences and personal expectations prior to marriage.

Cohabitation. Two adults of different sex sharing a house while unmarried, with or without children in the household.

Cohort. A group of individuals having a statistical factor, such as age or class membership, in common in a demographic study.

Coitus. Sexual intercourse; the insertion of a male's penis into a female's vagina.

Collateral. Security for a mortgage or any contractual loan; anything of value against which money can be borrowed to which the lender is entitled if the borrower fails to pay the debt.

Comarital sex. Sexual relationships outside of marriage which are approved and expected by both marital partners.

Combination pill. A variety of oral contraceptive containing various mixtures of synthetic progesterone and estrogen.

Commodities. Economic goods, such as agricultural or mining products, often purchased as an investment for later resale.

Communication apprehensive. Indicating the severe anxiety experienced by some people about communicating with others.

Computing. Indicating a pattern of ineffective communication in which any exchange is logical, analytical, entirely reasonable, but lacking any spontaneity or emotional content.

Conception. The fertilization of a ripe egg (ovum) by a sperm cell.

Condom. A disposable sheath of rubber, latex, or animal membrane, which is placed over the erect penis before intercourse; used both as a contraceptive device and a protection against STDs. Also known as a rubber, prophylactic, safe, or skin.

Confirmation. A pattern of feedback response indicating one partner's acceptance of the other's self-definition and view of their relationship.

Conflict-habituated marriage. A form of utilitarian marriage in which tension and argument are the primary modes of interaction, the expression and endless resolution of which apparently proves satisfactory to each partner.

Conflict theory. A theoretical framework that places emphasis on conflicting forces within social units (such as a society or a family) in explaining the behavior of individuals and groups.

Conjugal. Pertaining to the married state, particularly to the bond of intimacy between married persons.

Conjugal love. The enduring and constantly developing love of husband and wife for one another, growing through the course of the marriage due to increasing intimacy and familiarity.

Consanguinal. Of the same blood or origin.

Contactful. A style of self-disclosing communication that fully and explicitly deals with an emotionally charged situation, offering and seeking input on the situation.

Controlling. A style of self-disclosing communication that acknowledges an emotionally charged situation but declines efforts or overtures to explore it.

Conventional. A style of self-disclosing communication that avoids an emotionally charged situation by pretending nothing unusual has happened.

Corona. A crownlike ridge of the tissue that encircles the penis where shaft and glans join. Laced with nerve endings, it is particularly sensitive to erotic arousal.

Cowper's glands. In the male, two glands embedded in the muscle of the urethra at the base of the penis. It is believed these glands excrete a few drops of alkaline fluid into the urethra prior to ejaculation to provide a more hospitable chemical environment in the urethra to the sperm.

Credit union. A cooperative association that makes small loans to its members at low interest rates, usually composed of members of a particular trade union, neighborhood, or members of a particular business.

Crisis. A state of disorganization during which family members experience disruption of their life pattern or their methods of coping with stress.

Culdoscopy. A medical procedure for the sterlization of females in which the fallopian tubes are sealed or clipped and then tied off to prevent contact of ovum and sperm. The incision is made through the back of the vaginal wall.

Cunnilingus. Oral stimulation of the female genitals.

Depressant. A medicine, drug, or other substance that reduces activity of the higher brain centers; a sedative.

Desertion. The sudden withdrawal of one spouse from the family without the agreement of the other spouse and no provision made for financial support. Not a legal termination of marriage.

Developmental crises. Normative and predictable crises which occur in the course of most families' life cycles—such as a child entering school, a move to a new location, or retirement. When coped with successfully, these crises move the family on to the next stage in its development.

Developmental tasks. Steps to be accomplished at various stages of the life cycle in accord with physical condition, age, and social expectations so that the individual can move on to the next stage of development.

Devitalized marriage. A form of utilitarian marriage that, though originally established in intimate and genuine affection, is marked by a progressive divergence of interests and mutual feeling and maintained largely out of habit or hope for some improvement.

Diaphragm. A contraceptive device consisting of a fitted dome of thin rubber stretched over a flexible, covered wire rim; it blocks the entry of sperm into the uterus by covering and thus blocking the cervix. Inserted into the vagina before intercourse, it is used in conjunction with spermicidal jelly or cream.

Direct costs. The out-of-pocket expenses for such articles as food, clothing, and education. Used in addition to opportunity costs to calculate the total economic cost of children.

Disconfirmation. A pattern of feedback response indicating one partner's refusal to recognize the other's self-definition and/or view of their relationship.

Discretionary income. Money available after necessities have been paid for, generally used to improve the quality of life.

Disengagement theory. A theory related to aging wherein successful adjustment to retirement depends on the ability of an individual to withdraw from the role of worker when society requires it.

Disorganized family. A family that is not well integrated and adaptable, often headed by spouses with poor marital adjustment and conflict with their children. Such families are often socially isolated and more likely to be crisis-prone.

Distracting. Indicating a pattern of ineffective communication in which, when one partner in an exchange speaks, the other responds with something unrelated to the topic, effectively ending the communication.

Divorce. The legal termination of a marriage.

Double bind. A mixed messsage of such extreme contradiction that its conflict of context and content results in an unresolvable, no-win situation for the message's recipient.

Douching. A hygienic measure in which a liquid is injected into the vagina. Not effective as a form of contraception.

Dowry. A gift of money, property, or goods transferred by the family of the bride to the new husband at the time of the marriage.

Dual-career marriage. A marriage in which both partners work at jobs requiring continuous and extensive planning and commitment.

Dual-worker marriage. Any marriage in which both partners work outside the home.

Dyspareunia. A sexual dysfunction in women in which intercourse causes intense pain in the clitoris, vaginal barrel, or soft tissue of the pelvis.

Dystocia. Any difficult labor situation, from weak contractions to a baby too big to be delivered vaginally.

Early pregnancy tests (EPTs). Nonprescription test kits to determine the presence of HCG in a woman shortly after a missed period. Presently, such home tests are not as reliable as those done by doctors or medical labs.

Egalitarian. Characterized by equal rights and opportunities among the participants.

Ejaculation. The forcible, rhythmic discharge of seminal fluid from the penis during male orgasm.

Embryo. The developing human organism from the time of implantation to the end of the eighth week after conception.

Empirical method. An approach to systematic investigation based on observation and experience.

Empty-nest syndrome. The depression experienced by some parents when their children have left home.

Endogamy. Marriage exclusively within one's specific group, especially as required by custom or law.

Epididymis. A small organ attached to the upper surface of each testicle, composed of a long, tightly coiled mass of tubes and serving as a storage chamber for maturing sperm. It also adds an essential secretion to the seminal fluid.

Episiotomy. A small incision in the perineum made during childbirth just before the baby's head appears; performed to enlarge the vaginal opening to prevent tearing of the perineum during delivery.

Equity. The changing money value of a property; effectively, a buyer's initial and progressively increasing ownership rights in a house as the mortgage is paid off.

Erectile inhibition. Impotence.

Erogenous zones. Erotically sensitive areas of the body which respond to touch with sexual arousal, such as the genitalia, mouth, breasts, and neck.

Estrogen replacement therapy. A controversial treatment of menopause through restoration of the premenopausal hormone balance.

Estrogens. Hormones produced by the ovaries which influence the development of female secondary characteristics (breasts, skin texture, etc.) and stimulate the changes of the menstrual cycle.

Exchange relationship. In the context of social exchange theory, the general dynamics and patterns of social transactions between spouses, and the costs, benefits, and expectations of these exchanges.

Excitement. The first phase of the human sexual response cycle.

Exogamy. Marriage exclusively outside of one's specific group, especially as required by custom or law.

Expressive. Revealing thoughts and feelings; emphasizing personal qualities and the emotional contents of interpersonal relationships over their effectiveness in accomplishing specific tasks.

Extended family. A family structure more complex than the nuclear family. May be based on a household shared by three or more generations, including a number of married couples and related adults or children, or on plural marriages in which one individual has several spouses.

Extramarital sex. Sexual relationships outside of marriage which have not been previously negotiated with one's spouse.

Failure rate. A measurement of the effectiveness of various birth control methods. The ratio is expressed as the likelihood of pregnancy occurring during one year in 100 sexually active women using a particular method of contraception.

Fallopian tubes. The two tubes in the female that link the ovaries to the uterus. Eggs released periodically from the ovaries are carried down these tubes toward the uterus.

Family. Two or more persons related to each other by blood, marriage, or adoption, sharing a common residence, and cooperating economically.

Family adaptability. The ability of a family to change to meet new circumstances. An influential factor in determining a family's reaction to a crisis.

Family integration. Having common interests, affections, and a sense of economic interdependence that binds a family's members together. An influential factor in determining a family's reaction to a crisis.

Family of orientation. The family into which one is born and in which one is reared.

Family of procreation. The family established when one marries; implies that a married couple will procreate, or produce offspring.

Feedback. In communication, giving an individual evaluative or correlative information about that individual's behavior, both verbal and nonverbal. People in a communication set are continually providing feedback to each other.

Fellatio. Oral stimulation of the male genitals.

Fertility rate. The number of births per year per 1000 population; a more highly refined indication of trends in childbearing than the birthrate.

Fetus. A developing human organism from eight weeks after conception to birth.

Foreplay. Development of sexual responsiveness as a preparation or substitute for sexual intercourse through kissing, caressing, licking, and nibbling of sensitive body areas.

Frenum. A thin ridge of erotically sensitive tissue on the underside of the penis where the corona is joined to the shaft.

Gender identity. An individual's self-awareness as male or female, generally the result of early childhood socialization by parents or other primary care givers.

Glans. The smooth, conical structure at the tip of the penis or clitoris, and a chief source of erotic response. In the male, it is covered at birth by a retractable foreskin sometimes removed by circumcision.

Gonorrhea. A highly contagious STD caused by the bacteria *gonococcus* and characterized by painful discharge and inflammation of the mucous membranes of the genitals.

Group marriage. Marriage of two or more persons of each sex, including sharing of sexual privileges and economic responsibilities.

Herpes. An extremely contagious form of STD caused by a virus known as Herpes simplex, type 2; characterized by painful, blisterlike sores in the genital area and sometimes elsewhere on the body.

Heterogamy. The tendency to pick a mate with personal or group characteristics different from one's own.

History. The sequence of a family's progressive fulfillment of social roles as family members grow older, from family formation to dissolution; career.

Homogamy. The tendency to pick a mate with personal or group characteristics similar to one's own.

Human chorionic gonadotropin (HCG). A hormone secreted by the developing embryo; thus the test determining its presence in the mother's urine or blood is a test to determine pregnancy.

Hymen. A membrane of varying thickness and shape which stretches across the vaginal opening. The breaking of this membrane at a woman's first experience of sexual intercourse sometimes causes mild bleeding.

Hysterectomy. A medical procedure in which the uterus is removed, usually as a treatment for severe medical problems.

Hysterotomy. An abortion technique in which the fetus is removed from the uterus through a surgical incision in the abdomen.

Impotence. The inability of some men to achieve and maintain an erection of the penis as a means to copulation.

Infertility. Inability to conceive after a year or more of sexual relations without contraception.

Installment buying. A type of consumer credit by which goods or services are paid for by fixed-interval partial payments and for which interest must be paid as well.

Instrumental. Task-oriented; concerned with rational and efficient behavior directed toward achievement of specific goals.

Interest. The cost, or charge paid, for borrowing money; usually figured as a percentage of the amount borrowed and calculated daily, monthly, or yearly.

Intrauterine device (IUD). One of the various small devices, usually made of plastic or metal, inserted by a doctor into the uterus and worn continuously as a contraceptive.

Intrinsic marriages. Those marriages established and maintained due to the paramount importance both partners place on their relationship.

Investment. An outlay, usually of money, made in expectation of gaining income or profit.

In vitro fertilization. "Test-tube" conception; fertilization of ovum outside the mother's body and subsequent implantation (upon ovum's initial cell division) into the mother's uterus through the cervix.

Joint family. A family unit, common in India, consisting of a number of brothers and their respective wives and children living in the same household and sharing mutual resources and obligations.

Kibbutz. A collective farm in Israel.

Kibbutzim. Plural of kibbutz.

Kinship system. The way in which a society defines the relationships of persons interrelated by blood, marriage, or adoption; a key element in the social structure, especially with respect to social rights and obligations.

Labia majora. An erotically sensitive outer fold of skin running downward and backward on each side of the vaginal opening.

Labia minora. The erotically sensitive inner folds of skin located on either side between the labia majora and the vaginal opening.

Laparoscopy. A medical procedure for the sterilization of females in which the fallopian tubes are seared or clipped and then tied off. The incision is very small and frequently made in the navel.

Leveling. Indicating communications in which content and context are expressed equally, in contrast to various ineffective modes of communication.

Liabilities. Obligations, generally financial; corporate or individual debts.

Lifetime family. The family seen in terms of progressive stages as members age and pass from one set of social roles to another; the family in terms of its career.

Lightening. The process by which the fetus's head moves into position in the pelvis four to two weeks before delivery. Also known as engagement.

Lineage family. The family seen as a continuing structure, including the activities of successive generations of the same line.

Marital adjustment. The process by which marriage partners adapt to each other's and their own conflicting needs; a process of accommodation between marriage partners.

Marital cohesiveness. The various incentives, attractions, and restraints that act on married partners to remain in their marriage.

Marital quality. A subjective evaluation of a married couple's relationship, encompassing all aspects and components of marital success or failure.

Marital stability. The aspects of a marriage relating to its continuance or dissolution.

Marriage. The set of laws and customs specifying the ways in which the family relationship should be established, conducted, or terminated.

Masturbation. Erotic self-stimulation of the genitalia.

Matching hypothesis. The assumption that people are likely to choose dates and marriage partners who are like themselves in terms of social desirability.

Matriarchal. Characterized by the supremacy of the mother, or elder woman, in family affairs.

Matrilineal. Traced through the female family lines only.

Matrilocal. Pertaining to the custom by which the place of residence of a married couple is with or near the woman's family.

Meatus. The urethral opening, in the male, at the tip of the penis.

Menopause. The time in a woman's life, usually between 45 and 55, when the menstrual cycle ceases, due to the cessation of ovulation and accompanying hormonal changes.

Menstrual aspiration. An abortion technique in which the monthly menstrual lining of the uterus is suctioned out by means of a slender tube inserted through the cervix.

Menstruation. The final stage of the menstrual cycle when the menstrual fluid, consisting of blood, dead tissue, and glandular secretions, is discharged.

Metacommunication. The relational aspect of communication, distinguished from and informing the content level (the speaker's words), frequently in a nonverbal manner; communication about communication.

Mini-pill. A variety of oral contraceptive containing only synthetic progesterone; somewhat less effective than combination pills.

Mixed message. Contradictory or distorting form of metacommunication, saying one thing with words and another with actions, attitude, etc.

Modified extended family. A variant of the extended family, in which married offspring and their older parents keep kinship ties through residential proximity, visits, and mutual aid, rather than sharing the same household.

Morning-after pill. A variety of oral contraception that is a series of massive doses of synthetic estrogen taken as pills in order to prevent implantation of a fertilized ovum.

Mortgage. A contract between borrower and lender, acting as conveyance of property, such as for security on a loan on condition that the conveyance becomes void on payment or performance of the terms of the loan.

Motility. Ability of the sperm to swim, and thus to fertilize an ovum.

Multilateral marriage. Group marriage.

Neolocal. Pertaining to the custom by which a married couple sets up a new household separate from that of either spouse's family.

Normative orientations. In the context of social exchange theory, a couple's expectations of the benefits and behaviors pertinent to marriage, based on similarities in socialization, motivation, values, etc.

Norms. Cultural standards that define correct and incorrect behavior; principles of right action binding upon members of a group and serving to guide, control, or regulate behavior.

Opportunity costs. In raising children, the income that a woman (primarily) forgoes when she decides to stay home. Used in addition to direct costs to calculate the total economic cost of children.

Organized family. A family that is well integrated and adaptable; the spouses tend to have good marital adjustment and companionable relations with their children. Such families are less likely to be crisis-prone.

Orgasm. The release of peak sexual tensions; it is characterized by involuntary, rhythmic, muscular contractions, a loss of self-awareness, and varying degrees of intense sensory pleasure. The next-to-last phase of the human sexual response cycle.

Orgasmic platform. The engorged state of the vagina and nearby sexual organs in the female during the plateau phase of sexual intercourse, which provides pleasurable friction for both partners and leads to the orgasmic phase.

Os. The opening of the cervix, which connects the upper end of the vagina to the uterus.

Ova. Eggs; female reproductive cells. (Singular: "ovum.")

Ovarectomy. A medical technique in which the ovaries are removed as treatment for severe medical problems.

Ovaries. Two almond-sized organs in the female which store and release the egg cells (ova) and the female sex hormones, estrogen and progesterone.

Ovulation. The process in the fertile female whereby the ovary releases a mature egg (ovum) at regular intervals, usually once every 28 days.

Passive-congenial marriage. A form of utilitarian marriage effectively lacking emotional depth or exchange, maintained largely as a convenience and necessity for each partner's individual outside vocational and/or avocational interests and commitments.

Patriarchal. Characterized by the supremacy of the father, or other elder male, in family affairs, and the legal dependency of wives and children.

Patrilineal. Traced through the male family lines only.

Patrilocal. Pertaining to the custom by which the place of residence of a married couple is with or near the man's family.

Penis. The male organ of copulation, consisting of a root, shaft, and glans. Erect when sexually stimulated, it is the most erotically sensitive area of the male body.

Perineum. The erotically sensitive area between the anus and the genitalia.

Petting. Erotic stimulation and arousal of another's body by sensual caresses without actual copulation.

Pill. Collective term ("The Pill") for oral contraceptives that prevent pregnancy by somehow preventing ovulation.

Placating. Indicating a pattern of ineffective communication in which one partner, avoiding an argument at any cost, always agrees aloud with whatever the other says, regardless of the placater's own feelings.

Placenta. A mass of soft tissue formed during pregnancy and attached to the inner surface of the uterus. It serves as a medium of exchange between maternal and fetal blood, nourishing the fetus and discharging its wastes.

Plateau. The second phase of the human sexual response cycle, following preliminary excitement and prior to orgasm.

Plural marriage. Forms of marriage involving more than two spouses; polygamy.

Polyandry. A type of plural marriage in which a woman has two or more husbands.

Polygamy. Plural marriage.

Polygyny. A type of plural marriage in which a man has two or more wives; the most widespread form of plural marriage.

Population. A group of individuals.

Premature ejaculation. A difficulty or inability of some men in controlling their ejaculatory reflexes.

Primogeniture. The exclusive right of the eldest son to inherit his father's money, property, etc.

Propinquity. The tendency to pick a mate from among those with whom one has frequent contact.

Prostaglandins. Hormonelike substances present in seminal, menstrual, and amniotic fluids and various mammalian tissues. Since prostaglandins stimulate contractions of the uterus, they may be used to induce labor, bring on delayed menstruation, or terminate unwanted pregnancies.

Prostate gland. A gland that passes alkaline secretions through its ducts into the urethra; these secretions mix with the seminal fluid and activate the sperm.

Refractory period. The rest period following a man's orgasm, during which he cannot produce another erection.

Rejection. A pattern of feedback response involving one partner's acknowledgment of, but disagreement with, the other's self-definition and/or view of their relationship.

Resolution. The fourth and final phase of the human sexual response cycle, following orgasm.

Resources. In the context of social exchange theory, an individual's possessions, tangible and intangible, considered by others to be rewarding; anything that people can give to or take away from another.

Retarded ejaculation. A difficulty or inability of some men to ejaculate during coitus.

Rhythm. A contraceptive method in which the couple abstains from intercourse during the female's monthly fertile period (three to four days before ovulation and one day after); also known as the rhythm method.

Role-flexibility theory. A theory related to aging wherein successful adjustment to retirement depends on an individual's ability to take up new roles as older ones are dropped.

Role identity. A term used to indicate the combination of one's role, or expected behavior pattern, as defined both by the society and an individual's personal conception of how the role should be fulfilled.

Sample. A representative fraction of a larger population chosen to participate in a survey of that population.

Savings. Money deposited in a bank, on which interest is paid at regular intervals.

Scrotum. The pouch of loose, elastic skin that contains the testicles.

Securities. Evidence of debt or ownership, such as stocks or bonds.

Self-disclosure. The act of revealing personal information to others.

Self-esteem. One's sense of one's own worth or value.

Semen. The thick, whitish fluid produced by the male reproductive organs and ejaculated during orgasm; it consists of sperm, their nutrient plasma, and various glandular secretions.

Seminal vesicle. A small pouch between the vas deferens and the urethra where sperm collect and are mixed with a secretion to form the semen and ejaculate.

Separation. The ending of cohabitation of a married couple without the legal right to marry again. Separations can be informal, without the intervention of lawyers, or formal, with legal sanction.

Serial monogamy. A succession of marriages such that one may have several spouses in the course of a lifetime, but only one at a time.

Sex flush. A transitory skin rash accompanying the acceleration of the pulse and blood pressure rise during the excitement phase of the sexual response cycle.

Sexual anesthesia. The inability of some women to experience erotic pleasure from sexual contact.

Sexual openness. A married life-style distinguished by a mutual decision allowing one or both partners sexual relationships outside the marriage; the practice and pursuit of comarital sex.

Sexually transmitted diseases (STDs). Bacterial or viral infections that attack the genital areas, with possibly severe complications resulting in other parts of the body. Until recently, referred to also as venereal diseases.

Shaft. The length-wise component of the clitoris or penis.

Situational adaptability. A couple's ability to relate to each other in a manner most appropriate to a given situation.

Situational crises. Nonnormative crises that occur only in some families and are almost always regarded as serious problems, such as alcoholism, marital violence, child abuse. These crises can be long lasting and require resolution by therapists or other professionals. Also known as event crises.

Smegma. A thick, cheesy, glandular secretion which may accumulate under the foreskin of the penis.

Social exchange theory. Sociological framework based on the idea that social interaction involves a give-and-take similar to that of the economic marketplace; that is, people offer their own desirable traits and behaviors to bargain for social status and to bring about desired behaviors in another person.

Socialization. The process by which an individual acquires the skills, norms, and values of a group or society; the process by which culture is transmitted to the individual.

Speculative. A style of self-disclosing communication that deals with an emotionally charged situation by seeking to explain one's thoughts about it without revealing one's feelings.

Spermicides. Chemical substances, used as contraceptives, which immobilize or destroy sperm.

STD. Sexually transmitted disease.

Stem family. A family system, common in agricultural societies, in which one child, usually the eldest son, inherits all the family property.

Sterilization. Rendering a person sterile—unable to produce offspring—through medical procedures such as vasectomy in males or tubal ligation in females.

Stimulant. A medicine, drug, or other substance that helps activate the central nervous system.

Stocks. Certificates representing the acquisition of ownership of a portion or share of a business enterprise.

Structure-functional. Referring to a theoretical framework for human behavior which holds that people act in certain ways to fulfill social needs or functions and that the patterns of interaction best suited to fulfilling those needs form a society's structure; implies a close interrelationship between structure—the patterns of social interaction—and function—the purposes accomplished by the interaction.

Survey research. Investigation involving data gathered through interviews questioning people about their opinions, attitudes, beliefs, and behaviors.

Swinging. Indicating a life-style in which two or more married couples engage in sexual activity with each other, generally as a form of play, or social recreation.

Syphilis. A form of STD caused by a spirochete bacterium and passed from person to person, transmitted from open lesions, by direct physical contact. Primarily a disease of the blood vessels, it thus may affect any part of the body if untreated.

Testes. Testicles; oval-shaped glands in the male, suspended in the scrotum by spermatic cords, which produce sperm cells and the male sex hormone, testosterone. (Singular: "testis.")

Theoretical framework. A system of concepts used in the analysis of scientific data, which helps to give order and meaning to observations and research findings.

Throwaways. Teenagers who are expelled from the house by their parents. This is often the result of stress created by a divorce or remarriage.

Total marriage. A form of intrinsic marriage marked by a virtually complete meshing of all important aspects of both partner's lives, often working together in their professional pursuits.

Transaction management. A couple's ability to regulate their communication by establishing and maintaining realistic and workable rules for interaction.

Trimester. A three-month period; one of three equal periods into which the nine months of pregnancy are divided.

Tubal ligation. A method of sterilization of women in which a portion of the fallopian tubes is cut, tied, or removed so that eggs are blocked from moving down the fallopian tube and sperm are blocked from moving up, thus preventing conception.

Urethra. The duct in male and female mammals through which urine passes from the bladder to the outside; in the male, it also functions as a passage for sperm.

Uterus. The hollow, pear-shaped, muscular organ in the female that nurtures the fetus. Its cavity opens into the fallopian tubes on either side above and into the vagina below.

Utilitarian marriages. Those marriages established upon mutually satisfactory grounds and goals generally other than those for intimate expression or satisfaction; effectively, a marriage of convenience.

Vagina. The elastic organ of the female which extends between the external genitalia and the cervix.

Vaginismus. Involuntary muscular spasms of the vagina, caused by the woman's anxiety, which may tighten the vagina to the point of preventing intercourse.

Variable rate mortgage. A mortgage with a variable interest rate attached to the amount of the mortgage, allowing the lender (generally a bank) to keep pace with variable interest rates in the general economy.

Vas deferens. A continuation of the duct of the epididymis, which carries sperm on toward the seminal vesicles.

Vasectomy. A method of sterilization of men in which a small piece of each vas deferens is removed and the ends tied off to prevent movement of the sperm into the seminal vescicles, so that the ejaculate of the male orgasm will not contain any sperm.

Violence. An act carried out with the intention of, or perceived as having the intention of, physically hurting another person.

Vital marriage. A form of intrinsic marriage marked by the prime satisfaction each partner finds in their life together.

Vulva. The external female genitalia, including labia majora, labia minora, clitoris, and vaginal opening.

Withdrawal. A contraceptive method in which the penis is withdrawn from the vagina just before ejaculation. Also called coitus interruptus.

Bibliography

Abernathy, V. (1974). "Dominance and sexual behavior: an hypothesis." *American Journal of Psychiatry* 131(7):813–817.

Abramson, E., H. Cutler, R. Kautz, and M. Mendelson (1958). "Social power and commitment: a theoretical statement." *American Sociological Review* 23 (February):15–22.

Adams, B.N. (1980). *The Family: A Sociological Interpretation.* Chicago: Rand McNally.

Adams, R.N. (1960). "An inquiry into the nature of the family." In G. Dole and R.L. Carneiro (eds.), *Essays in the Science of Culture: In Honor of Leslie A. White.* New York: Thomas Y. Crowell, pp. 30–49.

Albrecht, S.L. (1980). "Reactions and adjustments to divorce: differences in the experiences of males and females." *Family Relations* 29(1):59–69.

Aldous, J. (1978). *Family Careers: Developmental Change in Families.* New York: Wiley.

Aldridge, D.P. (1974). "Problems and approaches to black adoptions." *The Family Coordinator* 23(4):407–410.

Aleksandrowicz, M.K., and D.R. Aleksandrowicz (1974). "Obstetrical pain-relieving drugs as predictors of infant behavior variability." *Child Development* 45:935–945.

American Association of University Women, News Conference (1978). *New York Times,* April 8, 1978.

Anderson, L.S. (1976). "When a child begins school." *Children Today* (August):16–19.

Anspach, D.F. (1976). "Kinship and divorce." *Journal of Marriage and the Family* 38:323–330.

Antunes, C., P. Stolley, N. Rosenshein, J. Davies, J. Tonascia, C. Brown, L. Burnett, A. Rutledge, M. Pokempner, and R. Garcia (1979). "Endometrial cancer and estrogen use." *New England Journal of Medicine* 300:9–13.

Arafat, I., and G. Yorburg (1973). "On living together without marriage." *Journal of Sex Research* 9 (May):97–106.

Araji, S.K. (1977). "Husbands' and wives' attitude-behavior congruence on family roles." *Journal of Marriage and the Family* 39:309–320.

569

Ard, B. (1974). "Premarital sexual experience: a longitudinal study." *Journal of Sex Research* 10(1):32–39.

Arling, G. (1976a). "Resistance to isolation among elderly widows." *International Journal of Aging and Human Development* 7:67–86.

——— (1976b). "The elderly widow and her family, neighbors, and friends." *Journal of Marriage and the Family* 38:757–768.

Askham, J. (1976). "Identity and stability within the marriage relationship." *Journal of Marriage and the Family* 38:535–547.

Atchley, R.C. (1971). "Retirement and leisure participation: continuity or crisis." *The Gerontologist* 11(1):13–17.

——— (1976). *The Sociology of Retirement.* New York: Halsted Press.

——— (1977). *The Social Forces in Later Life.* Belmont, Calif.: Wadsworth.

Athanasious, R., P. Shaver, and C. Tavris (1970). "Sex." *Psychology Today* 4 (July):37–52.

Atwater, L. (1979). "Getting involved: women's transition to first extramarital sex." *Alternative Lifestyles* 2(1):33–68.

Babbie, E. (1980). *Sociology: An Introduction.* Belmont, Calif.: Wadsworth.

Bahr, H.M., and F.I. Nye (1974). "The kinship role in a contemporary community: perceptions of obligations and sanctions." *Journal of Comparative Family Studies* 5(1):17–25.

Balkwell, C. (1981). "Transition to widowhood: a review of the literature." *Family Relations* 30:117–127.

Ball, J.F. (1976–1977). "Widow's grief: the impact of age and mode of death." *Omega* 7:307–333.

Balswick, J.O., and C.W. Peek (1971). "The inexpressive male: a tragedy of American society." *The Family Coordinator* 20(4):363–368.

Barbach, L.G. (1976). *For Yourself: The Fulfillment of Female Sexuality.* New York: Anchor Press.

Bardis, P.D. (1964). "Family forms and variations historically considered." In H.T. Christensen (ed.), *Handbook of Marriage and the Family.* Chicago: Rand McNally.

Bardwick, J. (1971). *Psychology of Women.* New York: Harper & Row.

Bardwick, J.M., and E. Douvan (1971). "Ambivalence: the socialization of women." In V. Gornick and B.K. Moran (eds.), *Woman in Sexist Society: Studies in Power and Powerlessness.* New York: Basic Books, pp. 225–241.

Barfield, A. (1976). "Biological influences on sex differences in behavior." In M. Teitelbaum, (ed.), *Sex Differences: Social and Biological Perspectives.* Garden City, N.Y.: Anchor Books, pp. 62–121.

Barnes, G.M. (1977). "The development of adolescent drinking behaviors: an evaluative review of the impact of the socialization process within the family." *Adolescence* 12:571–588.

Barry, H. III, M.K. Bacon, and I.L. Child (1957). "A cross-cultural survey of some sex differences in socialization." *Journal of Abnormal and Social Psychology* 55 (November):327–332.

Bartell, G. (1971). *Group Sex.* New York: Wyden Books.

Bateson, G. (1956). "Toward a theory of schizophrenia." *Behavioral Science* 1:251–273.

——— (1972). *Steps to an Ecology of Mind.* New York: Ballantine.

Baumrind, D. (1971). "Current patterns of parental authority." *Developmental Psychology Monographs* 4(1)1:102.

——— (1972). "From each according to her ability." *School Review* (February):161–195.

Baumrind, D., and A.E. Black (1967). "Socialization practices associated with dimensions of competence in preschool boys and girls." *Child Development* 38(2): 291–327.

Bayer, A.E. (1975). "Sexist students in American colleges: a descriptive note." *Journal of Marriage and the Family* 37:391–397.

Bayer, A.E., and G.W. McDonald (1981). "Cohabitation among youth: correlates of support for a new American ethic." *Youth and Society* 12 (4):387–402.

Beck, D.F., and M.A. Jones (1973). *Progress on Family Problems, A Nationwide Study of Clients' and Counselors' Views on Family Agency Services.* New York: Family Service Association of America.

Bell, A.P., and M.S. Weinberg (1978). *Homosexualities: A Study of Diversity Among Men and Women.* New York: Simon and Schuster.

Bell, R.Q., and L.V. Harper (1977). *Child Effects on Adults.* New York: Wiley.

Bell, R.R. (1979). *Marriage and Family Interaction,* 5th ed. Homewood, Ill.: Dorsey Press, pp. 404–412.

Bell, R.R., and J.B. Chaskes (1970). "Premarital sexual experience among coeds, 1958 and 1968." *Journal of Marriage and the Family* 32:81–84.

Bell, R.R., S. Turner, and L. Rosen (1975). "A multi-variate analysis of female extramarital coitus." *Journal of Marriage and the Family* 37:375–384.

Belliveau, F., and L. Richter (1970). *Understanding Human Sexual Inadequacy.* Boston: Bantam Books, pp. 46–57.

Bennet, E.M., and L.R. Cohen (1959). "Men and women: personality patterns and contrasts." *Genetic Psychology Monographs* 59:101–155.

Berardo, F.M. (1968). "Widowhood status in the United States: perspective on a neglected aspect of the family life-cycle." *The Family Coordinator* 17:191–203.

Berger, B.M., B.M. Hackett, and R.M. Millar (1974). "Child-rearing practices in the communal family." In A. Skolnick and J.H. Skolnick, *Intimacy, Family, and Society.* Boston, Mass.: Little, Brown, pp. 441–463.

Berger, D., and M. Wenger (1973). "The ideology of virginity." *Journal of Marriage and the Family* 35:666–676.

Berheide, C., S. Berk, and R. Berk (1976). "Household work in the suburbs: the job and its participants." *Pacific Sociological Review* 19(4)491–518.

Bernard, J. (1972). *The Future of Marriage.* New York: World Publishing Company.

——— (1977). "Jealousy and marriage." In G. Clanton and L.G. Smith (eds.), *Jealousy.* Englewood Cliffs, N.J.: Prentice-Hall, pp. 141–150.

Berscheid, E., K. Dion, E. Walster, and G.W. Walster (1971). "Physical attractiveness and dating choice: a test of the matching hypothesis." *Journal of Experimental Social Psychology* 7:173–189.

Berscheid, E., and E. Walster (1969). *Interpersonal Attraction.* Reading, Mass.: Addison-Wesley.

———(1974). "Physical attractiveness." In L. Berkowitz (ed.), *Advances in Experimental Social Psychology,* Vol. 7. New York: Academic Press, pp. 158–216.

Berscheid, E., E. Walster, and G. Bohrnstedt (1973). "Body image—the happy American body: a survey report." *Psychology Today* 7(6):119–131.

Biddle, B., and E. Thomas (1966). *Role Theory: Concepts and Research.* New York: Wiley.

Bienvenu, M.J., Sr. (1970). "Measurement of marital communication." *The Family Coordinator* 19(1):26–31.

Bierstedt, R. (1974). *The Social Order.* New York: McGraw-Hill.

Biller, H.B. (1971). "The mother-child relationship and the father-absent boy's personality development." *Merrill Palmer Quarterly* 17(3):227–241.

Biller, H.B., and R.M. Baum (1971). "Father absence, perceived maternal behavior, and masculinity of self-control among junior high school boys." *Developmental Psychology* 4(2):178–181.

Blake, J. (1974). "The changing status of women in developed countries." *Scientific American* 231:137–147.

Blau, P. (1964). *Exchange and Power in Social Life.* New York: Wiley.

Block, J.H. (1976). "Issues, problems, and pitfalls in assessing sex differences: a critical review of *The Psychology of Sex Differences.*" *Merrill-Palmer Quarterly* 22 (Spring):283–308.

Blodgett, R.E. (1971). *The New York Times Book of Money.* New York: New York Times Book Co.

Blood, R.O., and D.M. Wolfe (1960). *Husbands and Wives.* New York: Free Press.

Blough, H.A., and R.L. Giuntoli (1979). "Successful treatment of human genital herpes infections with 2-deoxy-D-glucose." *Journal of the American Medical Association* 241:2798–2801.

Blumberg, P.M., and P.W. Paul (1975). "Continuities and discontinuities in upperclass marriages." *Journal of Marriage and the Family* 37:63–77.

Blumstein, P.W. (1975). "Identity bargaining and self-conception." *Social Forces* 53(3):476–485.

Bock, E.W., and I.L. Webber (1972). "Suicide among the elderly: isolating widowhood and mitigating alternatives." *Journal of Marriage and the Family* 34:24–31.

Bohannon, P. (1971). *Divorce and After.* New York: Anchor Books.

Bolte, G.L. (1970). "A communications approach to marital counseling." *The Family Coordinator* 19(1):34–40.

The Book of Common Prayer (1979). Philadelphia: The Church Hymnal Corp. and the Seabury Press.

Bonham, G.S. (1977). "Who adopts: the relationship of adoption and social-demographic characteristics of women." *Journal of Marriage and the Family* 39:295–306.

Booth, A. (1977). "Wife's employment and husband's stress: a replication and refutation." *Journal of Marriage and the Family:* 39:645–650.

Booth, A., and L. White (1980). "Thinking about divorce." *Journal of Marriage and the Family* 42:605–615.

Borland, D.M. (1975). "An alternative model of the wheel theory." *The Family Coordinator* 24:289–292.

Bornstein, P.E., P.J. Clayton, J.A., Halikas, W.L. Maurice, and E. Robbins (1973). "The depression of widowhood after thirteen months." *British Journal of Psychiatry* 122:561–566.

Boss, P.G. (1980). "Normative family stress: family boundary changes across the life-span." *Family Relations* 29:445–452.

Boston Women's Health Book Collective (1978). *Ourselves and Our Children.* New York: Random.

———— (1979). *Our Bodies, Ourselves,* Revised expanded edition. New York: Simon and Schuster.

Bower, D.W., and V.A. Christopherson (1977). "University student cohabitation: a regional comparison of selected attitudes and behavior." *Journal of Marriage and the Family* 39:447–452.

Brammer, L.M. (1979). *The Helping Relationship.* Englewood Cliffs, N.J.: Prentice-Hall.

Brandwein, R.A., C.A. Brown, and E.M. Fox (1974). "Women and children last: the social situation of divorced mothers and their families." *Journal of Marriage and the Family* 36:498–514.

Bremer, J. (1959). *Asexualization.* New York: Macmillan.

Brickman, P. (1974). *Social Conflict.* Lexington, Mass.: D.C. Heath.

Brody, E. (1978). "The aging of the family." *The Annals of Political and Social Science* 438 (July):13–27.

Bruce, J.A. (1974). "The role of mothers in the social placement of daughters: marriage or work?" *Journal of Marriage and the Family* 36:392–397.

———— (1976). "Intergenerational solidarity versus progress for women?" *Journal of Marriage and the Family* 38:519–524.

Bullock, S.C., and E.H. Mudd, (1959). "The interrelatedness of alcoholism and marital conflict." *American Journal of Orthopsychiatry* 29:519–527.

Bumpass, L.L., and R. Rindfuss (1978). "Children's experience of marital disruption," Discussion Paper. Madison: Institute for Research on Poverty, University of Wisconsin, pp. 512–578.

Bumpass, L.L., and J.L. Sweet (1972). "Differentials in marital instability: 1970." *American Sociological Review* 37 (December): 754–766.

Burchell, R.C., G.V. Laury, and B. Sochet (1975). "Self-esteem and sexuality." *Medical Aspects of Human Sexuality* (Jan.): 74–90.

Burgess, E.W. (1926). "The family as a unity of interacting personalities." *Family* 7:3–9.

Burgess, E.W., H.J. Locke, and M.M. Thomes (1963). *The Family: From Institution to Companionship*, 3d ed. New York: American Book.

Burgess, E., and P. Wallin (1953). *Engagement and Marriage*. Philadelphia: Lippincott.

Burke, D.J., and T. Weir (1976). "Relationship of wives' employment status to husband, wife and pair satisfaction and performance." *Journal of Marriage and the Family* 38:287–297.

Burns, J. (1973). "A structural theory of social exchange." *Acta Sociologia* 16 (3):188–208.

Campbell, A. (1975). "The American way of mating: marriage *si*, children only maybe." *Psychology Today* 8:12, 37–43.

Caplow, T. (1964). *Principles of Organization*. New York: Harcourt, Brace.

Carey, R.G. (1977). "The widowed: a year later." *Journal of Consulting Psychology* 24:125–131.

Carlson, J. (1976). "The sexual role." In F.I. Nye (ed.), *Role Structure and Analysis of the Family*. Beverly Hills: Sage Publications, pp. 101–110.

Carter, H., and P.C. Glick (1976). *Marriage and Divorce: A Social and Economic Study*, Rev. ed. Cambridge: Harvard University Press.

Cassady, M. (1975). "Runaway wives." *Psychology Today* 8 (May):42.

Cavan, R. (1973). "Speculations on innovations to conventional marriage in old age." *The Gerontologist* 13 (Winter):409–410.

Chambliss, W.J., ed. (1973). *Sociological Readings in the Conflict Perspective*. Reading, Mass.: Addison-Wesley.

Chatfield, W.F. (1977). "Economic and sociological factors influencing life satisfaction of the aged." *Journal of Gerontology* 32 (5):593–599.

Cherlin, A. (1978). "Remarriage as an incomplete institution." *American Journal of Sociology* 84 (November):634–650.

Chiriboga, D.A., and L. Cutler (1978). "Stress responses among divorcing men and women." *Journal of Divorce* 1 (Winter):95–106.

Christensen, H.T. (1964). *Handbook of Marriage and the Family*. Chicago: Rand McNally, Chapter 1.

Christensen, H.T., and C.F. Gregg (1970). "Changing sex norms in America and Scandinavia." *Journal of Marriage and the Family* 32:616–627.

Christensen, H.T., and L.B. Johnson (1978). "Premarital coitus and the Southern black: a comparative view." *Journal of Marriage and the Family* 40:721–732.

Christian Science Monitor (1976). "4-year car loans increasing in U.S." Boston, Mass. *Christian Science Monitor*, March 18, 1976.

Cissna, K., and E. Sieburg (1979). *Interactional Foundations of Interpersonal Confirmation*. Paper presented at the Communication Association, and San Francisco State University Postdoctoral Conference in Honor of Gregory Bateson, Asilomar, Calif.

Clanton, G., and L.G. Smith (1977). *Jealousy*. Englewood Cliffs, N.J.: Prentice-Hall.

Clark, M. (1969). "Cultural values and dependency in later life." In R. Kalish (ed.), *The Dependencies of Old People*. Ann Arbor: Institute for Gerontology.

Clarke, F. (1973). *Interpersonal Communication Variables as Predictors of Marital Satisfaction-Attraction.* Unpublished doctoral dissertation, University of Denver.

Clarke-Stewart, K.A. (1978). "And daddy makes three: the father's impact on mother and young child." *Child Development* 49(2):466–478.

Clavan, S., and E. Vatter (1972). "The affiliated family: a continued analysis." *The Family Coordinator* 21:499–504.

Clayton, P.J., J.A. Halikas, W.L. Maurice, and E. Robbins (1973). "Anticipatory grief and widowhood." *British Journal of Psychiatry* 122:47–51.

Clayton, R.R., and J.L. Bokemeier (1980). "Premarital sex in the Seventies." *Journal of Marriage and the Family* 42:759–776.

Clayton, R.R., and N.L. Voss (1977). "Shacking up: cohabitation in the 1970s." *Journal of Marriage and the Family* 39:273–283.

Clinton, C. (1980). "Women's graves of academe." *New York Times*, November 5, 1980.

Cole, C.L. (1977). "Cohabitation in social context." In R.W. Libby and R.N. Whitehurst (eds.), *Marriage and Alternatives: Exploring Intimate Relationships.* Glenview, Ill.: Scott, Foresman, pp. 62–79.

Cole, C.L., A.L. Cole, and D.G. Dean (1980). "Emotional maturity and marital adjustment: a decade replication." *Journal of Marriage and the Family* 42:533–539.

Colletta, N.D. (1979). "Support systems after divorce: incidence and impact." *Journal of Marriage and the Family* 41:837–846.

Collins, J.K., J.R. Kennedy, and R.D. Francis (1976). "Insights into a dating partner's expectations of how behavior should ensue during the courtship process." *Journal of Marriage and the Family* 38:373–378.

Connell, E. B. (1975). "The pill revisited." *Family Planning Perspectives* 7(2):62–71.

Conover, P.W. (1975). "An analysis of communes and intentional communities with particular attention to sexual and gender relations." *The Family Coordinator* 24 (October):453–464.

Constantine, L.L. (1977). "Open family: a lifestyle for kids and other people." *The Family Coordinator* 26 (April):113–121.

———(1978). "Multilateral relations revisited: group marriage in extended perspective." In B.I. Murstein (ed.), *Exploring Intimate Life Styles.* New York: Springer, pp. 131–147.

Constantine, L.L., and J.M. Constantine (1972). "Dissolution of marriage in a non-conventional context." In M.B. Sussman (ed.), *Non-Traditional Family Forms in the 1970's.* Minneapolis: National Council on Family Relations, pp. 89–94.

——— (1973). *Group Marriage: A Study of Contemporary Multilateral Marriage.* New York: Macmillan.

Consumer Reports (1979). "Condoms." (October), pp. 583–588.

Cook, K. (1975). "Expectations, evaluations and equity." *American Sociological Review* 40 (June):372–388.

Cooper, P.E., B. Cumber, and R. Hartner (1978). "Decision-making patterns and postdecision adjustment of childfree husbands and wives." *Alternative Lifestyles* 1(1):71–94.

Coopersmith, S. (1967). *The Antecedents of Self-Esteem.* San Franciso: W.H. Freeman.

Cordell, A., R.D. Parker, and D.B. Sawin (1980). "Fathers' views on fatherhood with special reference to infancy." *Family Relations* 29(3):331–338.

Cornille, T.A., K.S. Oransky, and R. Pestle (1979). "Changing family lifestyles: adapting to the energy crisis." *Journal of Home Economics* (Winter): 36–37.

Cozby, P.C. (1973). "Self-disclosure: a literature review." *Psychological Bulletin* 79(2):73–91.

Crawford, M.P. (1972). "Retirement as a psycho-social crisis." *Journal of Psychosomatic Research* 16:375–380.

Crooks, R., and C. Baur (1980). *Our Sexuality.* Menlo Park, Calif.: Benjamin-Cummings.

Crosby, J.F. (1980). "A critique of divorce statistics and their interpretation." *Family Relations* 29(1):51–58.

Cuber, J. (1969). "Adultery: reality versus stereotype." In G. Neubeck, (ed.), *Extramarital Relations.* Englewood Cliffs, N.J.: Prentice-Hall.

Cuber, J.F., and P.B. Harroff (1965). *The Significant Americans: A Study of Sexual Behavior Among the Affluent.* New York: Appleton-Century-Crofts.

Cumming, E., and W. Henry (1961). *Growing Old.* New York: Basic Books.

Cushman, D., and R. Craig (1976). "Communication systems: interpersonal implications." In G.R. Miller (ed.), *Explorations in Interpersonal Communication.* Beverly Hills, Calif.: Sage.

Cutright, P. (1971). "Income and family events: marital stability." *Journal of Marriage and the Family* 33:291–306.

Darnley, F. (1975). "Adjustment to retirement: integrity or despair." *The Family Coordinator* 24:217–226.

Davidson, E.S., A. Yasuna, and A. Tower (1979). "The effects of television cartoons on sex-role stereotyping in young girls." *Child Development* 50:597–600.

Davidson, L., and L.K. Gordon (1979). *The Sociology of Gender.* Chicago: Rand McNally.

Davis, J.E. (1972). "The reversibility of male sterilization." In L. Lader, (ed.), *Foolproof Birth Control.* Boston: Beacon Press, pp. 191–197.

Davis, K. (1936). "Jealousy and sexual property." *Social Forces* 14(3):395–405.

——— (1972). "The American family in relation to demographic change." In C.F. Westoff and R. Parke, Jr. (eds.), *Commission on Population Growth and the American Future, Research Reports,* Vol. 1, *Demographic and Social Aspects of Population Growth,* pp. 235–265. Washington, D.C.; Government Printing Office.

Dean, D.G. (1966). "Emotional maturity and marital adjustment." *Journal of Marriage and the Family* 28:454–457.

DeCamp, C.C. (1972). *The Money Tree.* New York: Signet Books.

DeLamater, J.D., and P. MacCorquodale (1979). *Premarital Sexuality: Attitudes, Relationships, Behavior.* Madison: University of Wisconsin Press.

Delissovoy, V. (1973). "High school marriages: a longitudinal study." *Journal of Marriage and the Family* 35:245–255.

Demos, J. (1975). "America in past time." In H. Grunebaum and J. Christ (eds.), *Contemporary Marriage: Structure, Dynamics, and Therapy*. Boston: Little, Brown.

Desimone, L.J., K. O'Mahoney, and D. Hunt (1979). "Children of separation and divorce: factors influencing adjustment." *Journal of Divorce* 3(1):37–42.

Deutscher, I. (1962). "Socialization for postparental life." In A.M. Rose (ed.), *Human Behavior and Social Processes*. Boston: Houghton Mifflin.

Dickinson, G.E. (1975). "Dating behavior of black and white adolescents before and after desegregation." *Journal of Marriage and the Family* 37:602–608.

Dies, D.R., and L. Cohen (1973). *Content Consideration in Group Therapist Self-disclosure*. Paper presented at the American Psychological Association Convention.

Dixon, R.R., and L.T. Weitzman (1980). "Evaluating the impact of no-fault divorce in California." *Family Relations* 29(3):297–307.

Donnelly, C. (1976). "How to stop arguing about money." *Money* 5(1):24–27.

Douglas, J.H., and J.A. Miller (1977). "Record breaking women." *Science News* 112 (September 10):172–174.

Douvan, E. (1980). "The family is undergoing stress, strain, time pains." *Lawrence Eagle Tribune*, Lawrence, Mass., Sept. 15, 1980.

Duberman, L. (1973). "Step-kin relationships." *Journal of Marriage and the Family* 35:283–292.

Duvall, E.M. (1965). "Marriage makes in-laws." In R. S. Cavan (ed.), *Marriage and Family in the Modern World*. New York: Thomas Y. Crowell, pp. 383–387.

Duvall, E.M., and R. Hill (1960). *Being Married*. New York: Association Press.

Edwards, J.N. (1969). "Familial behavior as social exchange." *Journal of Marriage and the Family* 31:518–526.

———(1973). "Extramarital involvement: fact and theory." *The Journal of Sex Research* 9(3):210–224.

Edwards, J.N., and A. Booth (1976). "Sexual behavior in and out of marriage." *Journal of Marriage and the Family* 38:73–81.

Eiduson, B.T. (1979). "Emergent families of the 1970s: values, practices, and impact on children." In D. Reiss and H. Hoffman (eds.), *The American Family: Dying or Developing*. New York: Plenum Publishing, pp. 157–201.

El-Guebaly, M., and D. Offord (1977). "The offspring of alcoholics: a critical review." *American Journal of Psychiatry* 134:357–365.

Ellinwood, E.H., Jr., W.J.K. Rockwell, R.D. Chessick, G.G. Nahas, and P. Cushman (1975). "Effect of drug use on sexual behavior." *Medical Aspects of Human Sexuality* (March 1975):10–32.

Ellis, A. (1970). "Group marriage: a possible alternative?" In H.A. Otto (ed.), *The Family in Search of a Future, Alternate Models for Moderns*. New York: Appleton-Century-Crofts, pp. 56–97.

Emerson, W.A., Jr. (1975). "Traditional wife: adoring husband." *Woman's Day* (Nov):75, 170–172.

Epstein, J. (1974). *Divorced in America.* New York: Penquin.

Espenshade, T.J. (1977). "The value and cost of children." *Population Bulletin* 32 (1). Washington, D.C.: Population Reference Bureau.

——— (1979). "The economic consequences of divorce." *Journal of Marriage and the Family* 41:615–625.

——— (1980). "Raising a child can now cost $85,000." *Intercom* 8(9). Washington, D.C.: Population Reference Bureau, pp. 1, 10–12.

Etaugh, C. (1974). "Effects of maternal employment on children: a review of recent research." *Merrill-Palmer Quarterly* 20(2):71–98.

Fabe, M., and N. Wikler (1979). *Up Against the Clock: Career Women Speak on the Choice to Have Children.* New York: Random.

Fagot, B.I., and G.R. Patterson (1969). "An in vivo analysis of reinforcing contingencies for sex role behaviors in the preschool child." *Developmental Psychology* 1:563–568.

Farber, B. (1981). *Conceptions of Kinship.* New York: Elsevier.

Fein, G, D. Johnson, N. Kosson, L. Stork, and L. Wassermann (1975). "Sex stereotypes and preferences in the toy choices of 20-month-old boys and girls." *Developmental Psychology* (July):527–528.

Feldman, H. (1964). "Development of the Husband-Wife Relationship." Preliminary report, Cornell Studies of Marital Development: Study in the Transition to Parenthood. Department of Child Development and Family Relationships, New York State College of Home Economics, Cornell University.

Fengler, A.P. (1975). "Attitudinal orientations of wives toward their husbands' retirement." *International Journal of Aging and Human Development* 6(2):139–152.

Ferrell, M.Z., W.L. Tolone, and R.H. Walsh (1977). "Maturational and societal changes in the sexual double-standard: a panel analysis (1967–1971; 1970–1974)." *Journal of Marriage and the Family* 39:255–271.

Feshback, S., and N. Feshback (1973). "The young aggressors." *Psychology Today* (April): 90–95.

Fisher, B., and D. Sprenkle (1978). "Therapists' perceptions of healthy family functioning." *International Journal of Family Counseling* 6:9–17.

Fisher, S. (1973). *The Female Orgasm.* New York: Basic Books.

Foa, E.B., and U.G. Foa (1980). "Resource theory: interpersonal behavior as exchange." In K.L. Gergen, M.S. Greenberg, and R.H. Willis (eds.), *Social Exchange: Advances in Theory and Research.* New York: Plenum Press, pp. 77–94.

Ford, C.S., and F.A. Beach (1951). *Patterns of Sexual Behavior.* New York: Harper.

Fox. J.F. (1977). "Effects of retirement and former work life on women's adaptation in old age." *Journal of Gerontology* 32(2):196–202.

Fox, R. (1967). *Kinship and Marriage.* Baltimore: Penguin Books.

Freilich, L. (1975). "December song." *New York Sunday News*, November 16, 1975, pp. 12–14, 21.

Friedl, E. (1975). *Women and Men: An Anthropologist's View*. New York: Holt, Rinehart and Winston.

Furstenberg, F.K., Jr. (1980). "Reflections on remarriage." *Journal of Family Issues* 1(4):443–453.

Gagnon, H., and W. Simon (1974). *Sexual Conduct*. London: Hutchinson.

Gallup, G. (1979). "Eighty percent of Americans believe abortion should be legal." *Family Planning Perspectives* 11:189–190.

Garrison, M.L. (1976). "Credit-ability for women." *The Family Coordinator* 25(3):241–248.

Gecas, V., and R. Libby (1976). "Sexual behavior as symbolic interaction." *Journal of Sex Research* 12(1):33–49.

Gelles, R.J. (1973). "Child abuse as psychopathology: a sociological critique and reformulation." *American Journal of Orthopsychiatry* 43:611–621.

—— (1974). *The Violent Home*. Beverly Hills, Calif.: Sage Publications.

Gelles, R.J., and M.A. Straus (1979). "Determinants of violence in the family: toward a theoretical integration." In W. Burr et al. (eds.), *Contemporary Theories About the Family*. New York: Free Press.

Gerber, G., and L. Gross (1976). "The scary world of TV's heavy viewer." *Psychology Today* (April):41–45.

Gerber, I., R. Rusalem, N. Hannon, D. Battin, and A. Arkin (1975). "Anticipatory grief and aged widows and widowers." *Journal of Gerontology* 30:225–229.

Gerstel, N. (1979). "Marital alternatives and the regulation of sex." *Alternative Lifestyles* 2(2):145–176.

Gil, D.G. (1970). *Violence Against Children*. Cambridge, Mass.: Harvard University Press.

Gilbert, S.J. (1976). "Self-disclosure, intimacy and communication in families." *The Family Coordinator* 25(3):221–231.

Gilmartin, B.G. (1977). "Swinging: who gets involved and how?" In R.W. Libby and R.N. Whitehurst (eds.), *Marriage and Alternatives: Exploring Intimate Relationships*. Glenview, Ill.: Scott, Foresman, pp. 161–185.

—— (1978). *The Gilmartin Report*. Secaucus, N.J.: The Citadel Press.

Glenn, N.D., A.A. Ross, and J.C. Tully (1974). "Patterns of intergenerational mobility of females through marriage." *American Sociological Review* 39:683–699.

Glick, I.O., R. Weiss, and C.M. Parkes (1974). *The First Year of Bereavement*. New York: Wiley.

Glick, P.C. (1980). "Remarriage: some recent changes and variations." *Journal of Family Issues* 1(4):455–478.

Glick, P.C., and A.J. Norton (1971). "Frequency, duration, and probability of marriage and divorce." *Journal of Marriage and the Family* 33:307–317.

—— (1977). "Marrying, divorcing, and living together in the U.S. today." *Population Bulletin* 32 (October). Washington, D.C.: Population Reference Bureau.

—— (1979). "Marrying, divorcing, and living together in the U.S. today." *Population Bulletin* 32 (5). Washington, D.C.: Population Reference Bureau.

Goldberg, P. (1968). "Are women prejudiced against women?" *Trans-Action* 5:28–30.

Goode, W.J. (1959). "The theoretical importance of love." *American Sociological Review* 24:38–47.

—— (1964). *The Family*. Englewood Cliffs, N.J.: Prentice-Hall.

Gorad, S.L. (1971). "Communicational styles and interaction of alcoholics and their wives." *Family Process* 10(4):475–489.

Gordon, H.L. (1974). "Daily production of sperm." *Medical Aspects of Human Sexuality* (August):119–120.

Gough, K.E. (1971). "The origins of the family." *Journal of Marriage and the Family* 33:760–771.

Gove, W.R. (1972a). "The relationship between sex roles, marital status, and mental illness." *Social Forces* 51 (September):34–44.

—— (1972b). "Sex, marital status, and suicide." *Journal of Health and Social Behavior* 13:204–213.

Green, R.T., and I.C.M. Cunningham (1975). "Feminine role perception and family purchasing decisions." *Journal of Marketing Research* 12:325–332.

Green, R.T., and J. Money (1969). *Transsexualism and Sex Reassignment*. Baltimore: Johns Hopkins Press.

Greenberg, M., I. Rosenberg, and J. Lind (1973). "First mothers rooming-in with their newborns: its impact upon the mother." *American Journal of Orthopsychiatry* 43:783–788.

Greenfield, S.M. (1965). "Love and marriage in modern America: a functional analysis." *The Sociological Quarterly* 6:361–377.

Gross, I.H., E.W. Crandall, and M.M. Knoll (1980). *Management for Modern Families*, 4th ed. Englewood Cliffs, N.J.: Prentice-Hall.

Greenson, R.R. (1970). "On sexual apathy in the male." In J. Robbins and J. Robbins (eds.), *An Analysis of Human Sexual Inadequacy*. New York: The New American Library, pp. 261–270.

Grover, J.W. (1971). *VD: The ABC's*. Englewood Cliffs, N.J.: Prentice-Hall.

Gruver, R. (1981). *An American History*. Reading, Mass.: Addison-Wesley.

Gullotta, T.P. (1979). "Leaving home: family relationships of the runaway child." *Social Casework* 60:111–114.

Alan Guttmacher Institute (1979). *Abortions and the Poor: Private Morality, Public Responsibility*. New York: Planned Parenthood Federation of America.

Guttmacher, A.F. (1970). *Understanding Sex: A Young Person's Guide*. New York: Signet Books.

—— (1973). *Pregnancy, Birth, and Family Planning*. New York: Viking Press.

Hansen, S.L. (1977). "Dating choices of high school students." *The Family Coordinator* 26:133–138.

Hanson, I. (1980). "Sex education for young children." Lecture Care Institute, Detroit, Mich. (February).

Harris, C.S. (1978). *Fact Book on Aging: A Profile of America's Older Population.* Washington, D.C.: National Council on the Aging.

Harry, J., and R. Lovely (1979). "Gay marriages and communities of sexual orientation." *Alternative Lifestyles* 2 (May):177–200.

Harris, L., and Associates (1975). *The Myth and Reality of Aging in in America.* New York: National Council on Aging.

Hartley, R.E. (1959). "Sex role pressures and socialization of the male child." *Psychological Reports* 5 (April):457–468.

Hatcher, R., G. Stewart, F. Steward, F. Guest, P. Stratton, and A. Right (1980). *Contraceptive Technology, 1978–1979,* 10th Rev. Ed. New York: Irvington Publishers.

Havemann, E. (1967). *Birth Control.* New York: Time-Life Books.

Havighurst, R.J. (1954). "Flexibility and the social roles of the retired." *American Journal of Sociology* 59:309.

Hawkins, J.L., C. Weisberg, and D.L. Ray (1977). "Marital communication style and social class." *Journal of Marriage and the Family* 39:479–490.

—— (1980). "Spouse differences in communication style: preference, perception, behavior." *Journal of Marriage and the Family* 42:585–593.

Heer, D.M. (1974). "The prevalence of black-white marriage in the United States, 1960 and 1970." *Journal of Marriage and the Family* 36:246–259.

Heiman, J.R. (1975). "The physiology of erotica: women's sexual arousal." *Psychology Today* 8(11):90–94.

Henze, L.F., and J.W. Hudson (1974). "Personal and family characteristics of cohabiting and non-cohabiting college students." *Journal of Marriage and the Family* 36:722–726.

Herold, E.S. (1973). "A dating adjustment scale for college students." *Adolescence* 8:29, 51–61.

Hetherington, E.M., M. Cox, and R. Cox (1976). "Divorced fathers." *The Family Coordinator* 25:417–428.

—— (1978). "The aftermath of divorce." In J.H. Stevens, Jr., and M. Mathews (eds.), *Mother-Child, Father-Child Relations.* Washington, D.C.: National Association for the Education of Young Children, pp. 149–176.

Hicks, M.W., and M. Platt (1970). "Marital happiness and stability: a review of the research in the sixties." *Journal of Marriage and the Family* 32:553–574.

Hill, C.T., Z. Rubin, and L.A. Peplau (1976). "Breakups before marriage: the end of 103 affairs." *Journal of Social Issues* 32:147–168.

Hill, R. (1958). "Generic features of families under stress." *Social Casework* 39:32–52.

———— (1971). *The Strengths of Black Families.* New York: Emerson Hall.

———— (1974). "Modern systems theory in the family: a confrontation." In M.B. Sussman (ed.), *Sourcebook in Marriage and the Family,* 4th ed. Boston: Houghton Mifflin.

Hite, S. (1976). *The Hite Report, A Nationwide Study of Female Sexuality.* New York: Dell.

Hobart, C.W. (1958). "The incidence of romanticism during courtship." *Social Forces* 36:364.

Hobbs, D.F., Jr., and S.P. Cole (1976). "Transition to parenthood: a decade replication." *Journal of Marriage and the Family* 38:723–731.

Hochschild, A.R. (1973a). *The Unexpected Community.* Englewood Cliffs, N.J.: Prentice-Hall.

———— (1973b). "Communal life styles for the old." *Society* 10(5):50–57.

Hock, E., P.C. McKenry, M.D. Hock, S. Triolo, and L. Stewart (1980). "Child's school entry: a stressful event in the lives of fathers." *Family Relations* 29:467–472.

Hoffman, L.W. (1972). "Early childhood experiences and women's achievement motives." *Journal of Social Issues* 28:129–152.

———— (1975). "The value of children to parents and the decrease in family size." *Proceedings of the American Philosophical Society* 119(6):430–438.

———— (1979). "Maternal employment, 1979." *American Psychologist* 34 (October): 859–865.

Hoffman, L.W., and J.D. Manis (1979). "The value of children in the United States: a new approach to the study of fertility." *Journal of Marriage and the Family* 41:583–596.

Hoffman, S. (1977). "Marital instability and the economic status of women." *Demography* 14 (February):67–76.

Holman, T.B., and W.R. Burr (1980). "Beyond the beyond: the growth of family theories in the 1970s." *Journal of Marriage and the Family* 42:729–740.

Holmstrom, L.L. (1972). *The Two-Career Family.* Cambridge, Mass.: Schenkman Publishing Co.

Homans, G.C. (1961). *Social Behavior: Its Elementary Forms.* New York: Harcourt, Brace and World.

Hoover, R., L. Gray, and P. Cole (1976). "Menopausal estrogens and breast cancer." *New England Journal of Medicine* 295:401–405.

Horner, M.S. (1972). "Toward an understanding of achievement-related conflicts in women." *Journal of Social Issues* 28 (Summer):175–176.

Hoult, T.F., L.F. Henze, and J.W. Hudson (1978). *Courtship and Marriage in America.* Boston: Little, Brown.

Houseknecht, S.K. (1979). "Childlessness and marital adjustment." *Journal of Marriage and the Family* 41:259–265.

Houseknecht, S.K., and G.B. Spanier (1976). "Marital disruption and higher education among women in the United States." Paper presented at the Conference on Women in Midlife Crisis, Ithaca, New York (October).

Hunt, M. (1966). *The World of the Formerly Married.* New York: McGraw-Hill.

—— (1973). "Sexual behavior in the 1970's." *Playboy* (December):90–91.

—— (1974). *Sexual Behavior in the 1970's.* New York: Dell.

Hunt, M., and B. Hunt (1977).*The Divorce Experience.* New York: McGraw-Hill.

Hutchison, I.W. (1975). "The significance of marital status for morale and life satisfaction among lower income elderly." *Journal of Marriage and the Family* 37:287–293.

Jackson, D. (1977). "Family rules: marital quid pro quo." In P. Watzlawick and J. Weakland (eds.), *The Interactional View.* New York: Norton.

Jackson, J.K. (1956). "The adjustment of the family to alcoholism." *Marriage and Family Living* 18:361–369.

Jacoby, S. (1973). "What do I do for the next twenty years?" *New York Times Magazine*, June 17, 1973.

—— (1974). "49 million singles can't all be right." *The New York Times Magazine*, February 17, 1974.

Jaffee, B. (1974). "Adoption outcome: a two-generation view." *Child Welfare* 53:211–224.

Jaffee, B., and D. Fanshel (1970). *How They Fared in Adoption: A Follow-Up Study.* New York: Columbia University Press.

James, W.H. (1974). "Marital coital rates, spouses' ages, family size, and social class." *Journal of Sex Research* 10(3):205–218.

Jaslow, P. (1976). "Employment, retirement, and morale among older women." *Journal of Gerontology* 31(2):212–218.

Jessor, S.L., and R. Jessor (1975). "Transition from virginity to nonvirginity among youth: a social-psychological study over time." *Developmental Psychology* 11(4):473–484.

Johnson, E.S., and B.I. Bursk (1977). "Relationships between the elderly and their adult children." *The Gerontologist* 17 (February):90–96.

Johnson, R.E. (1970). "Some correlates of extramarital coitus." *Journal of Marriage and the Family* 32:449–456.

Johnson, S.K. (1975). "The business in babies." *New York Times Magazine*, Aug. 17, 1975.

Jorgensen, S.R., and J.C. Gaudy (1980). "Self-disclosure and satisfaction in marriage: the relation examined." *Family Relations* 29:3:281–287.

Jorgenson, S.R., and A.C. Johnson (1980). "Correlates of divorce liberality." *Journal of Marriage and the Family* 42:617–626.

Jourard, S. (1971). *The Transparent Self.* New York: Van Nostrand.

Kagan, Jerome (1979). "Family experience and the child's development." *American Psychologist* 34 (October):886–891.

Kagan, Julia (1975). "The new doubts about abortion." *McCall's* 102(9):121–123.

Kanin, E.J., K.R. Davidson, and S.R. Scheck (1970). "A research note on male-female differentials in the experience of heterosexual love." *Journal of Sex Research* 6:64–72.

Kanoy, K., and B.C. Miller (1980). "Children's impact on the parental decision to divorce." *Family Relations* 29(3):309–315.

Kanter, R.M. (1972). *Commitment and Community.* Cambridge, Mass.: Harvard University Press.

———— (1973). *Communes: Creating and Managing the Collective Life.* New York: Harper & Row.

Kaplan, H.S. (1974a). *The New Sex Therapy.* New York: Brunner/Mazel.

———— (1974b). "Friction and fantasy: no-nonsense therapy for sexual malfunctions." *Psychology Today* 8 (October):76–80.

Katchadourian, H.A., and D.T. Lunde (1980). *Fundamentals of Human Sexuality.* New York: Holt, Rhinehart and Winston.

Katcher, A. (1955). "The discrimination of sex differences by young children." *Journal of Genetic Psychology* 87:131–143.

Katz, A., and R. Hill (1958). "Residential propinquity and marital selection: a review of theory, method and fact." *Marriage and Family Living* 20 (February):27–36.

Katz, J. M. (1976). "How do you love me? Let me count the ways (The Phenomenology of Being Loved)." *Sociological Inquiry* 46:17–22.

Kaufman, D., et al. (1980). "Decreased risk of endometrial cancer among oral contraceptive users." *The New England Journal of Medicine* 303(18):1045–1047.

Kaufman, R.H., and W.E. Rawls (1974). "Herpes genitalis and its relationship to cervical cancer." *Cancer Journal for Clinicians* 24(5):258–265.

Kaufman, S.A. (1978). *You Can Have a Baby.* Nashville, Tenn.: Thomas Nelson.

Kelly, J.B., and J.S. Wallerstein (1976). "The effects of parental divorce." *American Journal of Orthopsychiatry* 46(1):20–32.

Kempler, H.L. (1976). "Extended kinship ties and some modern alternatives." *The Family Coordinator* 25:143–147.

Kenkel, W. F. (1973). *Family in Perspective,* 3d ed. New York: Appleton-Century-Crofts.

Kent, S. (1975). "Being aware of a patient's sexual problems should be the concern of every physician." *Geriatrics* (January):140–142.

Kephart, W. M. (1963). "Experimental family organization." *Marriage and Family Living* 25(3):261–271.

———— (1972). *The Family, Society, and the Individual,* 3d ed. Boston: Houghton Mifflin.

Kerchoff, A.C., and K.E. Davis (1962). "Value consensus and need complementarity in mate selection." *American Sociological Review* 27:295–303.

Kessin, K. (1971). "Social and psychological consequences of intergenerational occupational mobility." *American Journal of Sociology* 77:2–9.

King, K., J.C. Balswick, and I.E. Robinson (1977). "The continuing premarital sexual revolution among college females." *Journal of Marriage and the Family* 39:455–459.

Kinsey, A.C., W.B. Pomeroy, and C.E. Martin (1948). *Sexual Behavior in the Human Male.* Philadelphia: Saunders.

Kinsey, A.C., W.B. Pomeroy, C.E. Martin, and P.H. Gebhard (1953). *Sexual Behavior in the Human Female.* Philadelphia: Saunders.

Kirkpatrick, C. (1963). *The Family as Process and Institution.* New York: Ronald Press.

Kline-Graber, G., and B. Graber (1976). *A Guide to Sexual Satisfaction: Woman's Orgasm.* New York: Popular Library.

Knapp, J.J. (1976). "An exploratory study of seventeen open marriages." *Journal of Sex Research* 12 (August):206–219.

Knapp, J.J., and R.N. Whitehurst (1977). "Sexually open marriage and relationships: issues and prospects." In R.W. Libby and R.N. Whitehurst (eds.), *Marriage and Alternatives: Exploring Intimate Relationships,* Glenview, Ill.: Scott, Foresman, pp. 147–160.

Knox, D.H., Jr., and M.J. Sporakowski (1968). "Attitudes of college students toward love." *Journal of Marriage and the Family* 30:638–642.

Kohen, J.A., C.A. Brown, and R. Feldberg (1979). "Divorced mothers: the costs and benefits of female family control." In G. Levinger and O.C. Moles (eds.), *Divorce and Separation.* New York: Basic Books.

Kohlberg, L. (1966). "A cognitive-developmental analysis of children's sex role concepts and attitudes." In E.E. Maccoby (ed.), *The Development of Sex Differences.* Stanford, Calif.: Stanford University Press.

——— (1969). "Stage and sequence: the cognitive-developmental approach to socialization." In D.A. Goslin (ed.), *Handbook of Socialization Theory and Research.* Chicago: Rand McNally.

Komarovsky, M. (1964). *Blue-Collar Marriage.* New York: Random House.

——— (1976). *Dilemmas of Masculinity.* New York: Norton.

Kompara, D.R. (1980). "Difficulties in the socialization process of stepparenting," *Family Relations* 29(1):69–73.

Korner, A.F. (1971). "Individual differences at birth: implications for early experience and later development." *American Journal of Orthopsychiatry* 41(4):608–619.

Kuchera, L.K. (1972). "Stilbestrol as a 'morning-after' pill." *Medical Aspects of Human Sexuality* 6(10):168–177.

Kulka, R.A., and H. Weingarten (1979). "The long-term effects of parental divorce in childhood on adult adjustment." *Journal of Social Issues* 35(4):50–78.

Lamb, M.E. (1979). "Paternal influences and the father's role." *American Psychologist* 34 (October): 938–943.

Lamb, M.E., M.T. Owen, and L. Chase-Lansdale (1979). "The father-daughter relationship: past, present, and future." In C.B. Kopp and M. Kirkpatrick (eds.), *Becoming Female.* New York: Plenum Publishing, pp. 113–140.

Lambert, B.G., B.F. Rotschild, R. Altland, and L.B. Green (1972). *Adolescence.* Monterey, Calif.: Brooks/Cole.

Landis, J.T., and M.G. Landis (1977). *Building a Successful Marriage,* 7th ed. Englewood Cliffs, N.J.: Prentice-Hall.

Lasch, C. (1977). *Haven in a Heartless World: The Family Besieged.* New York: Basic.

Lee, G.R. (1977). *Family Structure and Interaction: A Comparative Analysis.* Philadelphia: Lippincott.

——— (1978). "Marriage and morale in later life." *Journal of Marriage and the Family* 40:131–139.

Lee, J.A. (1973). *The Colours of Love.* Toronto, Canada: New Press.

Lee, P.C., and A.L. Wolinsky (1973). "Male teachers of young children: a preliminary empirical study." *Young Children* 28:342–352.

LeMasters, E.E. (1957). *Modern Courtship and Marriage.* New York: Macmillan.

——— (1977). *Parents in Modern America,* 3d ed. Homewood, Ill.: Dorsey Press.

Lerner, R.M., and G.B. Spanier (1980). *Adolescent Development: A Life-Span Perspective.* New York: McGraw-Hill.

Levin, R.J., and A. Levin (1975a). "Sexual pleasure: the surprising preferences of 100,000 women." *Redbook,* September, pp. 51–58.

——— (1975b). "The Redbook report on premarital and extramarital sex—the end of the double standard?" *Redbook,* October, pp. 38–44, 190–192.

Levinger, G. (1965). "Marital cohesiveness and dissolution: an integrative review." *Journal of Marriage and the Family* 27:19–28.

——— (1979). "A social psychological perspective on marital dissolution." In G. Levinger and O.C. Moles (eds.), *Divorce and Separation: Context, Causes and Consequences.* New York: Basic Books.

Lewis, A.A., and B. Berns (1975). *Three Out of Four Wives: Widowhood in America.* New York: Macmillan.

Lewis, R.A. (1973). "Social reaction and the formation of dyads: an interactionist approach to mate selection." *Sociometry* 36:409–418.

Lewis, R.A., and G.B. Spanier (1979). "Theorizing about the quality and stability of marriage." In W.R. Burr, R. Hill, F.I. Nye, and I.L. Reiss (eds.), *Contemporary Theories About the Family: Research-Based Theories,* Vol. 1, New York: The Free Press, pp. 268–294.

Lewis, S.G. (1979). *Sunday's Women, A Report on Lesbian Life Today.* Boston: Beacon Press.

Libby, R.W. (1977). "Creative singlehood as a sexual life-style: beyond marriage as a rite of passage." In R.W. Libby, and R.N. Whitehurst (eds.), *Marriage and Alternatives: Exploring Intimate Relationships.* Glenview, Ill.: Scott, Foresman.

Libby, R.W., and J.E. Carlson (1973). "Exchange as concept, conceptual framework or theory? The case of Goode's application of exchange to the family." *Journal of Comparative Family Studies* 12:159–170.

Libby, R.W., and R.N. Whitehurst (1973). *Renovating Marriage.* Danville, Calif.: Consensus Publishers.

Lidz, T. (1976). *The Person.* New York: Basic Books.

Lifton, B.J. (1976). "The search." *New York Times Magazine,* Jan. 25, 1976.

Lobsenz, N.M. (1974). "Living together: a newfangled tango—or an oldfashioned waltz?" *Redbook* 143(2):86–87.

Locksley, A. (1980). "On the effects of wives' employment on marital adjustment and companionship." *Journal of Marriage and the Family* 42:337–346.

Lopata, H.A. (1971). *Occupation: Housewife.* New York: Oxford University Press.

—— (1973). *Widowhood in an American City.* Cambridge, Mass.: Schenkman.

Lo Piccolo, J., and L. LoPiccolo (1978). *Handbook of Sex Therapy.* New York: Plenum Press.

Lowenthal, M.F., and D. Chiriboda (1972). "Transition to the empty nest." *Archives of General Psychiatry* 26:8–14.

Lyness, J.L., M.E. Lipetz, and K.E. Davis (1972). "Living together: an alternative to marriage." *Journal of Marriage and the Family* 34:305–311.

Lynn, D. (1969). *Parental and Sex Role Identification: A Theoretical Formulation.* Berkeley, Calif.: McCutchan.

Lyons, R.D. (1973). "Psychiatrists, in a shift, declare homosexuality no mental illness." *New York Times,* Dec. 16, 1973, pp. 1, 25.

McCary, J.L. (1971). *Sexual Myths and Fallacies.* New York: Schocken Books.

—— (1973). *Human Sexuality: A Brief Edition.* New York: D. Van Nostrand.

McCleary, E.H. (1974). *New Miracles of Childbirth.* New York: David McKay.

Maccoby, E.E., and C.N. Jacklin (1974). *Psychology of Sex Differences.* Stanford, Calif.: Stanford University Press.

McDaniel, C.O., Jr. (1969). "Dating roles and reasons for dating." *Journal of Marriage and the Family* 31:97–107.

McDonald, G.W. (1977). "Parental identification by the adolescent: a social power approach." *Journal of Marriage and the Family* 34:705–719.

—— (1980). "Parental power and adolescents' parental identification: a reexamination. *Journal of Marriage and the Family* 42:289–296.

—— (1981). "Structural Exchange and Marital Interaction." Unpublished manuscript.

McDonald, G.W., and M.O. Osmond (1980). "Jealousy and trust: unexplored dimensions of social exchange dynamics." Paper presented at the National Council on Family Relations Annual Pre-Conference Workshop on Theory Construction and Research Methodology, Portland, Ore., October, 1980.

McGinnis, R. (1958). "Campus values in mate selection: a repeat study." *Social Forces*: 368–373.

McGinnis, T.C., and D.G. Finnegan (1976). *Open Family and Marriage: A Guide to Personal Growth.* St. Louis: C.V. Mosby.

McGuiness, D., and K.H. Pribram (1979). "The origins of sensory bias in the development of gender differences in perception and cognition." In M. Bortner (ed.), *Cognitive Growth and Development—Essays in Honor of Herbert C. Birch.* New York: Brunner/Mazel.

McIntire, W.G., G.D. Nass, and D.L. Battistone (1974)."Female misperception of male parenting attitudes and expectancies." *Youth and Society* 6(1):104–112.

McIntyre, J. (1981). "The structure—functional approach to family study." In I.F. Nye and F.M. Berardo (eds.), *Emerging Conceptual Frameworks in Family Analysis.* New York: Praeger.

McKee, J.P., and A.C. Sherriffs (1956). "The differential evaluation of males and females." *Journal of Personality* 25:256–371.

McKenry, P.C., and C.L. Tishler (1979). "Adolescent suicide: an overview of the problem with implications for practitioners." *Family Perspective* 13:189–196.

McKenry, P.C., L.H. Walters, and C. Johnson (1979). "Adolescent pregnancy: a review of the literature." *The Family Coordinator* (January): 17–28.

Mackey, W.C., and R.O. Day (1979). "Some indicators of fathering behaviors in the United States: a cross-cultural examination of adult male-child interaction." *Journal of Marriage and the Family* 41:287–298.

Macklin, E.D. (1972). "Heterosexual cohabitation among unmarried college students." *The Family Coordinator* 21:463–472.

——— (1976). "Unmarried heterosexual cohabitation on the university campus." In J.P. Wiseman (ed.), *The Social Psychology of Sex.* New York: Harper & Row.

——— (1980). "Nontraditional family forms: a decade of research." *Journal of Marriage and the Family* 42:905–921.

McQuarrie, H.G., and A.D. Flanagan (1979). "Accuracy of early pregnancy testing at home." *Family Planning Perspectives* 11:190–191.

Maddison, D. (1968). "The relevance of conjugal bereavement for preventive psychiatry." *British Journal of Medical Psychology* 41:223–233.

Madigan, F.C. (1957). "Are sex mortality differentials biologically caused?" *Milbank Memorial Fund Quarterly* 35:202–223.

Maddox, G.L., and D.C. Delinger (1978). "Assessment of functional status in a program evaluation and resource allocation model." *Annals of the American Academy of Political and Social Science* 438 (July):59–70.

Mancini, J.A. (1978). "Leisure satisfaction and psychological well-being in old age: effects of health and income." *Journal of the American Geriatrics Society* 26:550–552.

Mancini, J.A., and D.K. Orthner (1978). "Recreational sexuality preferences among middle-class husbands and wives." *Journal of Sex Research* 14:96–106.

Manis, J.G., and B.N. Meltzer (1978). *Symbolic Interaction: A Reader in Social Psychology.* Boston: Allyn & Bacon.

Masters, W.H., and V.E. Johnson (1966). *Human Sexual Response.* Boston: Little, Brown.

———— (1974). *The Pleasure Bond.* Boston: Little, Brown.

———— (1979). *Homosexuality in Perspective.* Boston: Little, Brown.

Matchan, L. (1981). "Tubal ligation no longer a finality." *The Boston Globe,* May 6, 1981.

Mathes, E.W. (1975). "The effects of physical attractiveness and anxiety on heterosexual attraction over a series of five encounters." *Journal of Marriage and the Family* 37:769–773.

Mazur, R. (1977). "Beyond jealousy and possessiveness." In G. Clanton and L.G. Smith (eds.), *Jealousy.* Englewood Cliffs, N.J.: Prentice-Hall, pp. 181–187.

Mead, M. (1935). *Sex and Temperament in Three Primitive Societies.* New York: Mentor Books.

Meehan, T. (1973). "Letting the rest of the world go by at Heritage Village." *Horizon* 15:16–25.

Mehrabian, A. (1972). *Nonverbal Communication.* Chicago: Aldine-Atherton.

Meyer, M.B., and J.A. Tonascia (1977). "Maternal smoking, pregnancy complications and perinatal mortality." *American Journal of Obstetrics and Gynecology* 128:494–502.

Miller, B.C., and D.L. Sollie (1980). "Normal stresses during the transition to parenthood." *Family Relations* 29:459–466.

Miller, P.Y., and W. Simon (1974). "Adolescent sexual behavior: context and change." *Social Problems* 22(1):58–76.

Miller, S.J. (1965). "The social dilemma of the aging leisure participant." In A.M. Rose and W. Peterson (eds.), *Older People and Their Social Worlds.* Philadelphia: F.A. Davis, pp. 77–92.

Mishell, D.R., Jr. (1975). "Assessing the intrauterine device." *Family Planning Perspectives* 7(3):103–111.

Mitchell, E. (1973). "The learning of sex roles through toys and books: a woman's view." *Young Children* 28:226–231.

Mitchell, J.J. (1976). "Adolescent intimacy." *Adolescence* 42:275–280.

Mnookin, R. H. (1973). "Foster care: in whose best interest?" *Harvard Educational Review* 43(4):599–638.

Modern Maturity (1976). February–March, pp. 5–7, 17–19.

Moller, A.S. (1975). "Jewish-Gentile divorce in California." *Jewish Social Studies* 37 (Summer–Fall):279–290.

Monahan, T.P. (1970). "Are interracial marriages really less stable?" *Social Forces* 48:461–473.

Monahan, T.P. (1976). "An overview of statistics on interracial marriage in the United States, with data on its extent from 1963–1970." *Journal of Marriage and the Family* 38:223–231.

Money, J., and A.A. Ehrhardt (1972). *Man and Woman, Boy and Girl: Differentiation and Dimorphism of Gender Identity.* Baltimore: Johns Hopkins University Press.

Montgomery, B.M. (1981). "The form and function of quality communication in marriage." *Family Relations* 30(1):21–30.

Montreal Health Press (1974). *Birth Control Handbook.* Montreal: Montreal Health Press.

Morgan, E.S. (1973). "The Puritans and sex." In M. Gordon (ed.), *The American Family in Social-Historical Perspective.* New York: St. Martin's Press, pp. 282–295.

Morgan, L.A. (1976). "A re-examination of widowhood and morale." *Journal of Gerontology* 31:687–695.

Mork, L.F. (1972). *A Guide to Budgeting for the Family,* Home and Garden Bulletin No. 108. Washington, D.C.: U.S. Dept. of Agriculture.

Morris, N.M. (1975). "The frequency of sexual intercourse during pregnancy." *Archives of Sexual Behavior* 4(5):501–507.

Moses, A. (1978). *Identity Management in Lesbian Women.* New York: Praeger.

Moss, H.A. (1967). "Sex, age, and status as determinants of mother-infant interaction." *Merrill Palmer Quarterly* 13:19–36.

Movius, M. (1976). "Voluntary childlessness—the ultimate liberation." *The Family Coordinator* 25(1):57–63.

Murdock, G.P. (1937). "Comparative data on the division of labor by sex." *Social Forces* 15:551–553.

——— (1949). *Social Structure.* New York: Macmillan.

Murstein, B.I. (1970). "Stimulus-value-role: a theory of marital choice." *Journal of Marriage and the Family* 32:465–481.

——— (1974). *Love, Sex, and Marriage Through the Ages.* New York: Springer.

——— (1978). "Swinging, or comarital sex." In B.I. Murstein (ed.), *Exploring Intimate Life Styles.* New York: Springer, pp. 109–130.

——— (1980). "Mate selection in the 1970s." *Journal of Marriage and the Family* 42:777–792.

Murstein, B.I., M. Cerreto, and M. MacDonald (1977). "A theory and investigation of the effect of exchange-orientation on marriage and friendship." *Journal of Marriage and the Family* 39:543–548.

Myricks, N., and R.H. Robin (1977). "Sex laws and alternative life styles." *Family Coordinator* 26 (October):357–360.

Nadelman, L. (1974). "Sex identity in American children: memory, knowledge and preference tests." *Developmental Psychology* 10:413–417.

Naeye, R.L. (1979). "Coitus and associated amniotic-fluid infections." *New England Journal of Medicine* 301(22):1986–2000.

Nass, G.D., R.W. Libby, and M.P. Fisher (1981). *Sexual Choices: An Introduction to Human Sexuality.* Belmont, Calif.: Wadsworth.

Neubeck, G. (1972). "The myriad motives for sex." *Sexual Behavior* 2(7):50–56.

Neugarten, B.L. (1971). "Grow old along with me! The best is yet to be." *Psychology Today* 5(7):45.

——— (1975). "The future and the young-old." *Gerontologist* 15:4–9.

Neugarten, B., and C. Weinstein (1964). "The changing American grandparent." *Journal of Marriage and the Family* 26:199–204.

Neugarten, B., V. Wood, R. Kraines, and B. Loomis (1963). "Women's attitudes toward the menopause." *Vita Humana* 6:110–151.

Newcomb, P.R. (1979). "Cohabitation in America: an assessment of consequences." *Journal of Marriage and the Family* 41:597–603.

Newcomb, P.R., and G.W. McDonald (1981). "Cohabitation of young couples: answers to some questions." An invited paper to the *Medical Aspects of Human Sexuality*. Submitted Dec. 9, 1979.

Newsweek (February 1980). "The children of divorce." p. 58.

——— (October 1980). "Too many caesareans?" p. 105.

Norton, A.J. (1974). "The family-life cycle updated." In R.F. Winch and G.B. Spanier (eds.), *Selected Studies in Marriage and the Family*. New York: Holt, Rinehart and Winston.

Novak, E.R., et al. (1970). *Novak's Textbook of Gynecology*, 8th ed. Baltimore: The Williams and Wilkins Co.

Nydegger, C. (1974). "The older father: late is great." *Psychology Today* 7(11):26–27.

Nye, F.I. (1976). *Role Structure and Analysis of the Family*. Beverly Hills, Calif.: Sage Publications.

Nye, F.I., and F.M. Berardo (1973). *The Family: Its Structure and Interaction*. New York: Macmillan.

——— (1981). *Emerging Conceptual Frameworks in Family Analysis*. New York: Praeger.

Oakley, A. (1974). *The Sociology of Housework*. New York: Pantheon.

O'Leary, V.E. (1977). *Toward Understanding Women*. Monterey, Calif.: Brooks/Cole.

Ollison, L. (1977). Study referred to in C. Tavris and C. Offir, *The Longest War*. New York: Harcourt Brace Jovanovich.

O'Neill, N., and G. O'Neill (1972). *Open Marriage*. New York: Avon Books.

Orford, J., S. Guthrie, P. Nicholls, E.S. Oppenheimer, and C. Hensman (1975). "Self-reported coping behavior of wives of alcoholics and its association with drinking outcome." *Quarterly Journal of Studies of Alcohol* 36:1254–1267.

Orthner, D.K. (1975). "Leisure activity patterns and marital satisfaction over the marital career." *Journal of Marriage and the Family* 37:91–102.

Parke, R.D., and S. O'Leary (1975). "Father-mother-infant interaction in the newborn period: some findings, some observations and some unresolved issues. In K.F. Riegel and J.A. Meacham (eds.), *The Developing Individual in a Changing World*, (Vol. 2), *Social and Environmental Issues*. Chicago: Aldine.

Parke, R.D., and D.B. Sawin (1976). "The father's role in infancy: a re-evaluation." *The Family Coordinator* 25(4):365–371.

Parkes, C.M. (1975). "Determinants of outcome following bereavement." *Omega* 6:303–323.

Parkes, C.M., B. Benjamin, and R.G. Fitzgerald (1969). "Broken heart: a statistical study of increased mortality among widowers." *British Medical Journal* 1:740–743.

Parsons, T., and R.F. Bales (1955). *Family, Socialization and Interaction Process.* Glencoe, Ill.: Free Press of Glencoe.

Patton, C.V. (1977). "Early retirement in academia: making the decision." *The Gerontologist* 17(4):347–354.

Pearlin, L.I., and J.S. Johnson (1977). "Marital status, life strains and depression." *American Sociological Review* 42 (October): 704–715.

Pearlman, J., J. Cohen, and K. Coburn (1981). *Hitting Our Stride.* New York: Delacorte Press.

Pengelley, E.T. (1974). *Sex and Human Life.* Reading, Mass.: Addison-Wesley.

Peterman, D.J., C.A. Ridley, and S.M. Anderson (1974). "A comparison of cohabiting and noncohabiting college students." *Journal of Marriage and the Family* 36:344–354.

Pfeiffer, E. (1974). "Sexuality in the aging individual." *Journal of the American Geriatrics Society* 22(11):481–484.

Pilpel H.F., and T. Zavin (1964). *Your Marriage and the Law.* New York: Macmillan.

Planned Parenthood of New York City, Inc. (1973). *Abortion: A Woman's Guide.* New York: Abelard-Schuman.

Pollis, C.A. (1969). "Dating involvement and patterns of idealization: a test of Waller's hypothesis." *Journal of Marriage and the Family* 31:765–771.

Pollman, A.W. (1971). "Early retirement: a comparison of poor health to other retirement factors." *Journal of Gerontology* 26(1):41–45.

Porter, C.W., Jr., and J.F. Hulka (1974). "Female sterilization in current clinical practice." *Family Planning Perspectives* 6(1):30–37.

Powers, W.G., and K. Hutchinson (1979). "The measurement of communication apprehension in the marriage relationship." *Journal of Marriage and the Family* 41:89–95.

Price-Bonham, S., and J.O. Balswick (1980). "The noninstitutions: divorce, desertion, and remarriage." *Journal of Marriage and the Family* 42:959–972.

Proctor, F., N. Wagner, and J. Butler (1974). "The differentiation of male and female orgasm: an experimental study." In N. Wagner (ed.), *Perspectives on Human Sexuality.* New York: Behavioral Publications.

Proulx, C. (1973). "Sex as athletics in the singles complex." *Saturday Review of the Society* 1:61–66.

Ramey, J.W. (1975). "Intimate groups and networks: frequent consequence of sexually open marriage." *The Family Coordinator* 24 (October):515–530.

——— (1976). *Intimate Friendships.* Englewood Cliffs, N.J.: Prentice-Hall.

Rapoport, R. (1963). "Normal crises, family structure, and mental health." *Family Process* 2:75–87.

——— (1973). "The transition from engagement to marriage." In M.E. Lasswell and T.E. Laswell (eds.), *Love-Marriage-Family, A Developmental Approach*. Glenview, Ill.: Scott, Foresman.

Rapoport, R., and R.N. Rapoport (1980). "Three generations of dual-career family research." In F. Pepitone-Rockwell (ed.), *Dual-Career Couples*. Beverly Hills, Calif.: Sage Publications, pp. 23–48.

Raschke, H.J. (1977). "The role of social participation in post-separation and post-divorce adjustment." *Journal of Divorce* 1:129–140.

Reiss, I.L. (1960). "Toward a sociology of the heterosexual love relationship." *Marriage and Family Living* 22:139–145.

Reiss, I.L., R.E. Anderson, and G.C. Sponaugle (1980). "A multivariate model of the determinants of extramarital sexual permissiveness." *Journal of Marriage and the Family* 42:395–411.

Rheinstein, M. (1972). *Marriage Stability, Divorce and the Law*. Chicago: University of Chicago Press.

Ridley, C.A. (1973). "Exploring the impact of work satisfaction and involvement on marital interaction when both partners are employed." *Journal of Marriage and the Family* 35:229–237.

Roberts, R.E. (1971). *The New Communes: Coming Together in America*. Englewood Cliffs, N.J.: Prentice-Hall.

Robertson, C.N., ed. (1970). *Oneida Community, An Autobiography, 1851–1876*. Syracuse, N.Y.: Syracuse University Press.

Robertson, J.F. (1976). "Significance of grandparents: perceptions of young adult grandchildren." *The Gerontologist* 16 (April):137–140.

——— (1977). "Grandmotherhood: a study of role conceptions." *Journal of Marriage and the Family* 39:165–174.

Robinson, I.E., K. King, and J.O. Balswick (1972). "The premarital sexual revolution among college females." *The Family Coordinator* 21:189–194.

Rogers, C. (1961). *On Becoming a Person*. Boston: Houghton Mifflin.

Rodgers, R.H. (1973). *Family Interaction and Transaction: The Developmental Approach*. Englewood Cliffs, N.J.: Prentice-Hall.

Rollins, B.C., and K.L. Cannon (1974). "Marital satisfaction over the family life cycle: a re-evaluation." *Journal of Marriage and the Family* 36:271–282.

Rollins, B.C., and H. Feldman (1970). "Marital satisfaction over the family life cycle." *Journal of Marriage and the Family* 32:20–27.

Rollins, B.C., and D.L. Thomas (1975). "A theory of parental power and child compliance." In R.E. Cromwell and D.H. Olson (eds.), *Power in Families*. New York: Halsted Press, pp. 38–60.

Rose, V.L., and S. Price-Bonham (1973). "Divorce adjustment: a woman's problem?" *The Family Coordinator* 22(3):292–297.

Rosenberg, H.S. (1970). "Implications of new models and the family for the aging population." In H. Otto (ed.), *Family in Search of a Future*. New York: Meredith Corporation.

Ross, D.M., and S.A. Ross (1972). "Resistance by pre-school boys to sex-inappropriate behavior." *Journal of Educational Psychology* 63:342–346.

Rossi, A.S. (1968). "Transition to parenthood." *Journal of Marriage and the Family* 30:26–39.

Roth, N. (1975). "Neurotic fears that sex is debilitating." *Medical Aspects of Human Sexuality* (September):91–92.

Rothschild, J., and S.B. Wolf (1976). *The Children of the Counterculture*. Garden City, N.Y.: Doubleday.

Rowe, G.P. (1981). "The development conceptual framework to the study of the family." In F.I. Nye and F.M. Berardo (eds.), *Emerging Conceptual Frameworks in Family Analysis*. New York: Praeger.

Rubin, L.B. (1976). *Worlds of Pain: Life in the Working-Class Family*. New York: Basic.

Rubin, Z., C.T. Hill, L.A. Peplau, and C. Denkel-Schetter (1980). "Self-disclosure in dating couples: sex roles and the ethic of openness." *Journal of Marriage and the Family* 42:305–317.

Rubin., Z., F.J. Provenzano, and Z. Luria (1974). "The eye of the beholder: parents' views on sex of newborns." *American Journal of Orthopsychiatry* 44:512–519.

Rugh, R., and L.B. Shettles (1971). *From Conception to Birth*. New York: Harper & Row.

Russell, C. (1974). "Transition to parenthood: problems and gratifications." *Journal of Marriage and the Family* 36:294–301.

Ruth, D.J. (1978). "The commune movement in the middle 1970s." In B.I. Murstein (ed.), *Exploring Intimate Life Styles*. New York: Springer, pp. 69–82.

Ryder, R.G. (1973). "Longitudinal data relating marriage satisfaction and having a child." *Journal of Marriage and the Family* 35:604–606.

Safilios-Rothschild, C. (1976). "A macro- and micro-examination of family power and love: an exchange model." *Journal of Marriage and the Family* 38:355–362.

Sarrel, P., and L. Sarrel (1980). "The *Redbook* report on sexual relationships." *Redbook*, (October):73–80.

Satir, V. (1972). *Peoplemaking*. Palo Alto, Calif.: Science and Behavior.

Scales, P. (1977). "Males and morals: teenage contraceptive behavior amid the double standard." *The Family Coordinator* 26 (July):211–220.

Scanzoni, J. (1972). *Sexual Bargaining: Power Politics in American Marriage*. Englewood Cliffs, N.J.: Prentice-Hall.

———— (1975). *Sex Roles, Life Styles, and Childbearing: Changing Patterns in Marriage and the Family*. New York: Free Press.

———— (1979). "Social processes and power in families." In W.R. Burr, R. Hill, F.I. Nye, and I.L. Reiss (eds.), *Contemporary Theories About the Family: Research-Based Theories*, Vol. 1. New York: The Free Press, pp. 295–316.

Scanzoni, J., and G.L. Fox (1980). "Sex roles, family and society: the seventies and beyond." *Journal of Marriage and the Family* 42:743–756.

Scanzoni, J., and P. Polonko (1980). "A conceptual approach to explicit marital negotiation." *Journal of Marriage and the Family* 42:31–44.

Scanzoni, L., and J. Scanzoni (1976). *Men, Women and Change: A Sociology of Marriage and the Family.* New York: McGraw-Hill.

Schaie, K. W., and K. Gribbin (1975). "Adult development and aging." *Annual Review of Psychology* 26:65–96.

Scheck, D.C., and R. Emerick (1976). "The young male adolescent's perception of early child-rearing behavior: the differential effects of socioeconomic status and family size." *Sociometry* 39(1):39–52.

Schnucker, R.V. (1975). "Birth control and Puritan attitudes." *Journal of Interdisciplinary History* 4:655–667.

Seaman, B., and G. Seaman (1977). *Women and the Crisis in Sex Hormones.* New York: Rawson.

Seligson, M. (1973). *The Eternal Bliss Machine: America's Way of Wedding.* New York: Morrow.

Serbin, L.A., and K.D. O'Leary (1975). "How nursery schools teach girls to shut up." *Psychology Today* (December):56–58ff.

Serbin, L.A., K.D. O'Leary, R.N. Kent, and I.J. Tonick (1973). "A comparison of teacher response to the pre-academic and problem behavior of boys and girls." *Child Development* 44:796–804.

Sexton, L.G. (1979). *Between Two Worlds: Young Women in Crisis.* New York: Morrow.

Sgroi, S.M. (1974). *VD: A Doctor's Answers.* New York: Harcourt Brace.

Shanas, E. (1968). "A note on restriction of life space: attitudes of age cohorts." *Journal of Health and Social Behavior* 9:86–90.

——— (1973). "Family-kin networks and aging in cross-cultural perspective." *Journal of Marriage and the Family* 35:505–511.

——— (1979). *National Survey of the Elderly,* Report to Administration on Aging. Washington, D.C.: Department of Health and Human Services.

Shanas, E., P. Townsend, D. Wedderburn, H. Friis, P. Milhhoj, and J. Stehouwer (1968). *Older People in Three Industrial Societies.* New York: Atherton Press.

Sherman, J.A. (1971). *On the Psychology of Women: A Survey of Empirical Studies.* Springfield, Ill.: Charles C. Thomas.

Sheskin, A., and S.E. Wallace (1976–1977). "Differing bereavements: suicide, natural, and accidental death." *Omega* 7:229–242.

Shulman, N. (1975). "Life cycle variations in patterns of close relationships." *Journal of Marriage and the Family* 37:813–821.

Shyne, A.W., and A.G. Schroeder (1978). "National study of social services to children and their families." Washington, D.C.: National Center for Child Advocacy.

Silber, S.J., and R. Cohen (1978). "Normal intrauterine pregnancy after reversal of tubal sterilization in the wife and vasectomy in the husband." *Fertility and Sterility* 30:606–608.

Simon, W., A.S. Berger, and J.H. Gagnon (1972). "Beyond anxiety and fantasy: the coital experiences of college youth." *Journal of Youth and Adolescence* 1:203–222.

Simon, W., and J.H. Gagnon (1968). "Sex talk—public and private. Etc." A Review of General Semantics 25:173–191.

Simpson, R. (1972). *Theories of Social Exchange.* Morristown, N.J.: General Learning Press.

Singer, J.E., M. Westphal, and K. Niswander (1968). "Sex differences in the incidence of neonatal abnormalities and abnormal performance in early childhood." *Child Development* 39:103–112.

Skarsten, S. (1974). "Family desertion in Canada." *The Family Coordinator* (January):23.

Skipper, J.K., Jr., and G. Nass (1966). "Dating behavior: a framework for analysis and an illustration." *Journal of Marriage and the Family* 28:412–420.

Slater, P. (1963). "Social limitations on libidinal withdrawal." *The American Sociological Review* 28:339–364.

Smith, B.K. (1973). *Aging in America.* Boston: Beacon Press.

Snyder, L.M. (1979). "The deserting, nonsupporting father: scapegoat of family non-policy." *The Family Coordinator* 28(4):595–598.

Somerville, J.K. (1974). "The Salem (Mass.) woman in the home, 1660–1770." *Eighteenth-Century Life* 1(1):11–14.

Sosa, R., J. Kennell, M. Klaus, S. Robertson, and J. Urrutia (1980). "The effect of a supportive companion on perinatal problems, length of labor, and mother-infant interaction." *New England Journal of Medicine* 303(11):597–600.

Spanier, G.B. (1972). "Romanticism and marital adjustment." *Journal of Marriage and the Family* 34:481–487.

——— (1976). "Measuring dyadic adjustment: new scales for assessing the quality of marriage and similar dyads." *Journal of Marriage and the Family* 38(1):15–28.

Spanier, G.B., and E.A. Anderson (1979). "The impact of the legal system on adjustment to marital separation." *Journal of Marriage and the Family* 41:605–613.

Spanier, G.B., and P.C. Glick (1980). "Paths to remarriage." *Journal of Divorce* 3 (Spring):283–298.

Spanier, G.B., and R. Casto (1979a). "Adjustment to separation and divorce: an analysis of 50 case studies." *Journal of Divorce* 2 (Spring):241–253.

——— (1979b). "Adjustment to separation and divorce: a qualitative analysis." In G. Levinger and O.C. Moles (eds.), *Divorce and Separation.* New York: Basic Books.

Spanier, G.B., and S. Hanson (1978). "The role of extended kin in the adjustment to marital separation." Paper presented at the annual meeting of the Southern Sociological Society, New Orleans (April).

Spanier, G.B., R.A. Lewis, and C.L. Cole (1975). "Marital adjustment over the family life cycle: the issue of curvilinearity." *Journal of Marriage and the Family* 37:263–275.

Spence, J.T., and R.L. Helmreich (1978). *The Psychological Dimensions of Masculinity and Femininity: Their Correlates and Antecedents.* Austin: University of Texas Press.

Spencer, S. (1979). "Childhood's end." *Harper's* (May):16–19.

Spicer, J.W., and G.D. Hampe (1975). "Kinship interaction after divorce." *Journal of Marriage and the Family* 38:113–119.

Spinetta, J.J., and D. Rigler (1972). "The child-abusing parent: a psychological review." *Psychological Bulletin* 77:296–304.

Spreitzer, R., and L.E. Riley (1974). "Factors associated with singlehood." *Journal of Marriage and the Family* 36:533–542.

Sprenkle, D., and D. Olson (1978). "Circumplex model of marital systems: an empirical study of clinic and non-clinic couples." *Journal of Marriage and Family Counseling* 4:59–74.

Sprey, J. (1972). "Family power structure: a critical comment." *Journal of Marriage and the Family* 34:235–238.

———— (1979). "Conflict theory and the study of marriage and the family." In W.R. Burr, R. Hill, F.I. Nye, and I.L. Reiss (eds.), *Contemporary Theories About the Family*, Vol. 2. New York: The Free Press.

Stafford, R., E. Backman, and P. diBono (1977). "The division of labor among cohabiting and married couples." *Journal of Marriage and the Family* 39:43–45.

Stanton, M.D. (1979). "Drugs and the family." *Marriage and Family Review* 2(1):3–10.

Starr, J.R., and D.E. Carns (1972). "Singles in the city." *Society* 9(4):43–48.

Stein, P.J. (1975). "Singlehood: an alternative to marriage." *The Family Coordinator* 24(4):489–503.

Steinglass, P. (1979). "Alcoholism and the family: a review." *Marriage and Family Review* 2(1):12–19.

Steinmetz, S.K. (1977). *The Cycle of Violence.* New York: Praeger.

———— (1978). "Violence between family members." *Marriage and Family Review* 1(1):3–16.

Stember, C.H. (1975). "Interest in breasts vs. buttocks." *Medical Aspects of Human Sexuality* February: 88–89.

Stephens, W.N. (1963). *The Family in Cross-Cultural Perspective.* New York: Holt, Rinehart and Winston.

Sternglanz, S.H., and L.A. Serbin (1974). "Sex role stereotyping in children's television programs." *Developmental Psychology* 10:710–715.

Stinnett, N., L.M. Carter, and J.E. Montgomery (1972). "Older persons' perceptions of their marriages." *Journal of Marriage and the Family* 34:665–670.

Stinnett, N., J. Collins, and J.E. Montgomery (1970). "Marital need satisfaction of older husbands and wives." *Journal of Marriage and the Family* 32:428–434.

Stockard, J., and M.M. Johnson (1980). *Sex Roles: Sex Inequality and Sex Role Development.* Englewood Cliffs, N.J.:Prentice-Hall.

BIBLIOGRAPHY

Stoll, C.S. (1974). *Female and Male: Socialization, Social Roles, and Social Structure.* Dubuque. Iowa: William C. Brown.

Streib, G.F. (1978). "An alternative family form for older persons: need and social context." *The Family Coordinator* 27 (October):413–420.

Streib, G.F., and R.W. Beck (1980). "Older families: a decade review." *Journal of Marriage and the Family* 42:937–956.

Streib, G.F., and M.A. Hilker (1980). "The cooperative family: an alternative lifestyle for the elderly." *Alternative Lifestyles* 3 (May):167–184.

Sviland, M.A.P. (1975). "Helping elderly couples become sexually liberated: psycho-social issues." *Counseling Psychologist* 5(1):67–72.

Sweet, J.A., and L.L. Bumpass (1974). "Differentials in marital instability of the black population: 1970." *Phylon* 35 (Winter):323–331.

Tanner, D.M. (1978). *The Lesbian Couple.* Lexington, Mass.: Lexington Books.

Tanner, J.M., and G.R. Taylor (1968). *Growth.* New York: Time-Life Books.

Tauber, M. (1979). "Sex differences in parent-child interaction styles in a free-play session." *Child Development* 50:981–988.

Tavris, C., and S. Sadd (1977). *The Redbook Report on Female Sexuality.* New York: Redbook Publishing Co.

Tedesco, N. (1974). "Patterns in prime time." *Journal of Communication* 24:119–124.

Teicher, J.D., and J. Jacobs (1966). "Adolescents who attempt suicide: preliminary findings." *American Journal of Psychiatry* 122:1248–1257.

The Harvard Medical School Health Letter (March, 1981). "Incest." Vol. VI, No. 5. Cambridge, Mass.: Harvard Medical School.

Thibaut, J., and H. Kelley (1959). *The Social Psychology of Groups.* New York: Wiley.

Thompson, B., and D. Baird (1972). "Follow-up of 186 sterilized women." In L. Lader (ed.), *Foolproof Birth Control.* Boston: Beacon Press, pp. 142–159.

Thornton, A. (1978). "Marital instability differentials and interactions: insights from multivariate contingency table analysis." *Sociology and Social Research* 62 (July):572–595.

Thornton, A., D. Freedman, and R. Freedman (1980). *Study of American Families. 1980 Report to Respondents.* Ongoing study conducted by the University of Michigan Survey Research Center and Population Studies Center.

Thurman, J. (1975). "Living alone—by choice." *Ms.* IV(1):64–67.

Todres, R. (1978). "Runaway wives: an increasing North-American phenomenon." *The Family Coordinator* 27 (January):17–21.

Tolor, A., and P.V. DiGrazia (1976). "Sexual attitudes and behavior patterns during and following pregnancy." *Archives of Sexual Behavior* 5(6):539–551.

Tortora, G.A., and N.P. Anagnostakos (1975). *Principles of Anatomy and Physiology.* San Francisco: Canfield Press.

Treas, J. (1977). "Family support systems for the aged: some social and demographic considerations." *The Gerontologist* 17(6):486–491.

Troll, L.E. (1971). "The family of later life: a decade review." *Journal of Marriage and the Family* 33:263–290.

Troll, L.E., and J. Smith (1976). "Attachment through the life span: some questions about dyadic relationships in later life." *Human Development* 19:156–171.

Trost, J. (1975). "Married and unmarried cohabitation: the case of Sweden, with some comparisons." *Journal of Marriage and the Family* 37:677–682.

Tuller, N.R. (1978). "Couples: the hidden segment of the gay world." *Journal of Homosexuality* 3 (Summer):331–343.

Turner, J.H. (1978). *The Structure of Sociological Theory.* Homewood, Il.: Dorsey Press.

T.V. Guide (1980). December 8.

Udry, J.R. (1968). "Sex and family life." *The Annals of the American Academy of Political and Social Science* 376(2):25–35.

—— (1974). *The Social Context of Marriage.* Philadelphia: Lippincott.

U'Ren, M.B. (1971). "The image of women in textbooks." In V. Gornick and B.K. Moran (eds.), *Women in Sexist Society.* New York: Basic Books.

U.S. Bureau of the Census (1977). *Current Population Reports,* Series P-20, No. 306. "Marital status and living arrangements: March 1976." Washington, D.C.: U.S. Government Printing Office.

—— (1978). *Statistical Abstract of the United States.* Washington, D.C.: U.S. Government Printing Office.

—— (1979). *Statistical Abstract of the United States.* Washington, D.C.: U.S. Government Printing Office.

—— (1979). *Household and Family Characteristics. Current Population Reports,* 20:352. Washington, D.C.: U.S. Government Printing Office.

—— (1980). *Statistical Abstract of the United States* (101st ed.). Washington, D.C.: U.S. Government Printing Office, pp. 404–405, Tables 668 and 671.

—— (1980). *Current Population Reports, Special Studies,* P-23:104. "American families and living arrangements." Washington, D.C.: U.S. Government Printing Office.

—— (1980). *Current Population Reports,* P-23:106. "Child support and alimony: 1978." Washington, D.C.: U.S. Government Printing Office.

—— (1980). *Current Population Reports, Special Studies,* P-23:107. "Families maintained by female householders, 1970–79." Washington, D.C.: U.S. Government Printing Office.

U.S. Bureau of Labor Statistics (1979). *Special Labor Force Report.* Washington, D.C.: U.S. Government Printing Office.

U.S. Department of Commerce (1977). "Increase in housing costs outstripping income gains, census-HUD report shows," News Release CB77-64. Washington, D.C.: U.S. Department of Commerce.

—— (1980). *Household and Family Characteristics, March 1979,* P-20:352 (July), p. 1.

U.S. Department of Labor (October, 1980). "Perspective on working women: a data-book." Bulletin 2080. Washington, D.C.: Bureau of Labor Statistics.

U.S. National Center for Health Statistics (1979). *Monthly Vital Statistics Report*, Vol. 27, No. 3, June 1978, and DHEW Publication No. (PHS) 78-1120. Washington, D.C.: U.S. Government Printing Office.

U.S. National Commission for UNESCO (1977). *Report on Women in America*. Washington, D.C.: Department of State.

U.S. News and World Report (1980). "Special report: battle of the sexes: men fight back." December 8:50–54.

Vaillant, G.E., and C.C. McArthur (1972). "Natural history of male psychologic health. I. The adult life cycle from 18–50." *Seminars in Psychiatry* 4(4): (November).

Veevers, J.E. (1973). "Voluntarily childless wives: an exploratory study." *Sociology and Social Research* 57(3):356–366.

Verbrugge, L.M. (1979). "Marital status and health." *Journal of Marriage and the Family* 41:267–285.

Vener, A.M., and C.S. Stewart (1974). "Adolescent sexual behavior in middle America revisited: 1970–1973." *Journal of Marriage and the Family* 36:728–735.

Victor, J.B., and C.F. Halverson, Jr. (1976). "Behavior problems in elementary school children. A follow-up study." *Journal of Abnormal Child Psychology* 4(1):17–29.

Visher, E.B., and J. Visher (1979). *Stepfamilies: A Guide to Working with Stepparents and Stepchildren*. New York: Brunner/Mazel.

Wachowiak, D., and H. Bragg (1980). "Open marriage and marital adjustment." *Journal of Marriage and the Family* 42:57–62.

Wade, M.E. (1979). "A randomized perspective study of the use-effectiveness of two methods of natural family planning: an interim report." *American Journal of Obstetrics and Gynecology* 134:628–631.

Wake, S.B., and M.J. Sporakowski (1972). "An intergenerational comparison of attitudes toward supporting aged parents." *Journal of Marriage and the Family* 34:42–48.

Wakil, S.P. (1973). "Campus mate selection preferences: a cross-national comparison." *Social Forces* 57:271–276.

Waldron, I., and S. Johnston (1976). "Why do women live longer than men?" *Journal of Human Stress* 2(2):19–30.

Waller, W., and R. Hill (1951). *The Family: A Dynamic Interpretation*. New York: Dryden Press.

Wallerstein, J.S., and J.B. Kelly (1975). "The effects of parental divorce: experience of the pre-school child." *Journal of Child Psychiatry* 14:600–616.

——— (1976). "The effects of parental divorce: experience of the child in later latency." *American Journal of Orthopsychiatry* 46:256–269.

Walnut Creek Drug Study (1980). *Journal of Reproductive Medicine* 25(6): supplement, December.

Walster, E., E. Aronson, D. Abrahams, and L. Rottman (1966). "Importance of physical attractiveness in dating behavior." *Journal of Personality and Social Psychology* 4:508–516.

Walster, E., and G.W. Walster (1978). *A New Look at Love.* Reading, Mass.: Addison-Wesley.

Walters, J., and L.H. Walters (1980). "Parent-child relationships: a review, 1970–1979." *Journal of Marriage and the Family* 42:807–822.

Wassenberg, R. (1980). "Breakups before marriage: an attributional and exchange analysis." Unpublished notes for doctoral research, University of Connecticut.

Wasow, M., and M.B. Loeb (1978). "Sexuality in nursing homes." In R.L. Solnick (ed.), *Sexuality and Aging* (revised). Los Angeles: The University of Southern California Press, pp. 154–163.

Watson, J.A., and V.R. Kivett (1976). "Influences on the life satisfaction of older fathers." *The Family Coordinator* 25(4):482–488.

Watzlawick, P., J.H. Beavin, and D.D. Jackson (1967). *Pragmatics of Human Communication.* New York: Norton.

Waxenberg, S., M., Drellich, and A. Sutherland (1959). "Changes in female sexuality after adrenalectomy." *Journal of Clinical Endocrinology* 19:193–202.

Wear, J., and K. Holmes (1976). *How to Have Intercourse without Getting Screwed.* Seattle: Madrona

Wecht, C.H. (1975). "A comparison of two abortion-related legal inquiries." *The Journal of Legal Medicine* 3(8):26–34.

Weinberg, M.S., and C.J. Williams (1974). *Male Homosexuals.* New York: Oxford University Press.

Weingarten, H. (1980). "Remarriage and well-being: national survey evidence of social and psychological effects." *Journal of Family Issues* 1(4):533–559.

Weinstock, E., C. Tietze, F.S. Jaffe, and J.G. Dryfoos (1975). "Legal abortions in the U.S. since the 1973 Supreme Court decisions." *Family Planning Perspectives* 7(1):23–31.

Weisberg, D.K. (1975). "Children and communal life." Unpublished doctoral dissertation, Brandeis University.

———(1977). "The Cinderella children: growing up in an urban commune." *Psychology Today* 10 (April):84–86, 103.

Weisner, T.S., and J.C. Martin (1979). "Learning environments for infants: communes and conventionally married families in California." *Alternative Lifestyles* 2 (May):201–242.

Weiss, R.S. (1975). *Marital Separation.* New York: Basic Books.

———(1976). "The emotional impact of marital separation." *Journal of Social Issues* 32(1):135–145.

Weitzman, L.J. (1975). "To love, honor, and obey? Traditional legal marriage and alternative family forms." *The Family Coordinator* (October): 531–548.

Weitzman, L.J., C.M. Dixon, J.A. Bird, N. McGinn, and D.M. Robertson (1978). "Contracts for intimate relationships: a study of contracts before, within, and in lieu of legal marriage." *Alternative Lifestyles* 1 (August):303–378.

Weitzman, L., D. Eifler, E. Hokada, and C. Ross (1972). "Sex role socialization in picture books for pre-school children." *American Journal of Sociology* 77:1125–1150.

Wells, J.G. (1976). "A critical look at personal marriage contracts." *The Family Coordinator* 25:33–37.

Westoff, C.F. (1976). "Trends in Contraceptive Practice: 1965–1973." *Family Planning Perspectives* 8:54.

Westoff, C.F., and J. McCarthy (1979). "Sterilization in the United States." *Family Planning Perspectives* 11:145–149.

Wheeler, M. (1974). *No-Fault Divorce.* Boston: Beacon Press.

Wiemann, J. (1977). "Explication and a test of a model of communication competence." *Human Communication Research* 3:195–213.

Will, J.A., P.A. Self, and N. Datan (1976). "Maternal behavior and preceived sex of infant." *American Journal of Orthopsychiatry* 46:135–139.

Williams, R.M. (1970). "Kinship and the family in the U.S." *In American Society,* 3d ed. New York: Knopf.

Wilson, C.W. (1975). "The distribution of selected sexual attitudes and behaviors among the adult population of the United States." *Journal of Sex Research* 11(1):46–64.

Winch, R.F. (1958). *Mate-Selection: A Study of Complementary Needs.* New York: Harper & Brothers.

———— (1971). *The Modern Family.* New York: Holt, Rinehart and Winston.

Yancy, W.S., P.R. Nader, and K.L. Burnham (1972). "Drug use and attitudes of high school students." *Pediatrics* 50:739–745.

Yankelovich, Skelly, and White, Inc. (1975). *The General Mills American Family Report,* 1974–75. Minneapolis, Minn.: General Mills.

———— (1977). *The General Mills American Family Report,* 1976–1977. Minneapolis, Minn.: General Mills.

Yllo, K.A. (1978). "Nonmarital cohabitation: beyond the college campus." *Alternative Lifestyles* 1 (February):37–54.

Young, T.R. (1976). "Some theoretical foundations for conflict methodolgy." *Sociological Inquiry* 46(I):23–29.

Yorburg, B. (1975). "The nuclear and extended family: an area of conceptual confusion." *Journal of Comparative Family Studies* 6:5–14.

Zablocki, B.D. (1971). *The Joyful Community.* Baltimore: Penguin Books.

Zelnick, M., and J.F. Kantner (1977). "Sexual and contraceptive experience of young unmarried women in the United States, 1976 and 1971." *Family Planning Perspectives* 9:55–71.

Zelnick, M., K. Young, and J.F. Kantner (1979). "Probabilities of intercourse and conception among U.S. teenage women, 1971 and 1976." *Family Planning Perspectives* 11:177–183.

Photograph Acknowledgments

frontispiece, Gregg Mancuso, Jeroboam, Inc.
2, Reprinted from *The Saturday Evening Post* © 1959, The Curtis Publishing Co.
11, Bernard Pierre Wolff/Magnum
13, Alain Keler/Black Star
18, The Bettmann Archive
28, The Library of Congress
36, Owen Franken/Stock, Boston
41, The Library of Congress
51, Rick Smolan
62, © Metro-Goldwyn-Mayer, courtesy The Bettmann Archive
68, Wide World
74, Ruth Silverman/Stock, Boston
75, Leonard Freed/Magnum
80, U.P.I.
90, Culver Pictures
96, *The Love Scene*, Collection Haags Gementemuseum The Hague
99, Frank Siteman/Stock, Boston
109, Stephen Shames, Woodfin Camp & Associates
121, U.P.I.
128, Elizabeth Hamlin/Stock, Boston
138, Peter Simon/Stock, Boston
174, © Twentieth-Century Fox, courtesy Culver
176, Maureen Fennelli/Photo Researchers
177, John Vincent Veltri/Photo Researchers
183, Erika/Photo Researchers
187, Rick Smolan
199, Michael Malyszko/Stock, Boston
208, Dale Wittner, *People Weekly* © 1978 Time Inc.
211, Thomas Hopker, Woodfin Camp & Associates
223, © Vitagraph, courtesy The Bettmann Archive

603

233,   Steve Schapiro/Sygma

239,   Robert B. Goodman, Black Star

248,   Richard Frieman/Photo Researchers

251,   Ed Lettau/Photo Researchers

262,   Frank Siteman/Stock, Boston

266,   Harry Wilks/Stock, Boston

270,   © Rose Skytta/Jeroboam, Inc.

272,   © Paramount Pictures, courtesy Culver

282,   Jim Harrison/Stock, Boston

300,   Patricia Hollander Gross/Stock, Boston

317,   The Bettmann Archive

322,   Abigail Heyman/Magnum

328,   The Bettmann Archive

340,   Michael Hardy, Woodfin Camp & Associates

341,   Linda Ferrer, Woodfin Camp & Associates

344,   Jack Prelutsky/Stock, Boston

353,   Wide World

358,   U.P.I.

364,   George Bellerose/Stock, Boston

377,   Eric A. Roth, The Picture Cube

384,   Boston Globe Photo

393,   Sylvia Johnson/Woodfin Camp & Associates

395,   Jean Boughton

402,   Culver Pictures

405,   Jeff Albertson/Stock, Boston

412,   Jean Boughton

422,   Culver Pictures

429,   Creative Media Group, Inc., Charlottesville, Va.

436,   Boston Globe Photo

455,   Bruce Roberts/Photo Researchers

461,   Jim Ritscher/Stock, Boston

466,   Mike Mazzaschi/Stock, Boston

470,   Keith Butler/Spooner, Gamma/Liaison

474,   Cary Wolinsky/Stock, Boston

481,   David Krathwohl/Stock, Boston

487,   Anestis Diakopoulos/Stock, Boston

497,   Courtesy of the Spencer Collection, the New York Public Library

508,   The Massillon Museum

512,   Erika Stone

516,   Erika Stone

518,   Elizabeth Hamlin/Stock, Boston

524,   Fred Bodin/Stock, Boston

533,   Sybil Shelton, Monkmeyer Press

536,   Jean Boughton

Author Index

☙ Subject Index